MODERN HUMANITIES RESEARCH ASSOCIATION
TUDOR AND STUART TRANSLATIONS
VOLUME 19

General Editors
ANDREW HADFIELD
NEIL RHODES

THE PSALMS IN ENGLISH
1530–1633

MODERN HUMANITIES RESEARCH ASSOCIATION
TUDOR AND STUART TRANSLATIONS

General Editors
Andrew Hadfield (University of Sussex)
Neil Rhodes (University of St Andrews)

Associate Editors
Guyda Armstrong (University of Manchester)
Fred Schurink (University of Manchester)
Louise Wilson (Liverpool Hope University)

Advisory Board
Warren Boutcher (Queen Mary, University of London)
Colin Burrow (All Souls College, Oxford)
A. E. B. Coldiron (Florida State University)
Patricia Demers (University of Alberta)
José María Pérez Fernández (University of Granada)
Robert S. Miola (Loyola College, Maryland)
Alessandra Petrina (University of Padua)
Anne Lake Prescott (Barnard College, Columbia University)
Quentin Skinner (Queen Mary, University of London)
Alan Stewart (Columbia University)

For details of published and forthcoming volumes please visit our website:

www.tudor.mhra.org.uk

The Psalms in English
1530–1633

Edited by
Hannibal Hamlin

Modern Humanities Research Association
Tudor and Stuart Translations 19
2024

Published by

The Modern Humanities Research Association
Salisbury House
Station Road
Cambridge CB1 2LA
United Kingdom

© Modern Humanities Research Association, 2024

Hannibal Hamlin has asserted his right under the Copyright, Designs and Patents Act 1988 to be identified as the author of this work. Parts of this work may be reproduced as permitted under legal provisions for fair dealing (or fair use) for the purposes of research, private study, criticism, or review, or when a relevant collective licensing agreement is in place. All other reproduction requires the written permission of the copyright holder who may be contacted at rights@mhra.org.uk.

First published 2024

ISBN 978-1-78188-096-8 (hardback)
ISBN 978-1-78188-097-5 (paperback)

Typeset in Minion Pro by Allset Journals & Books, Scarborough, UK

CONTENTS

General Editors' Foreword	x
Acknowledgements	xi
Abbreviations	xiv
Introduction	1
Further Reading	56

The Psalms in English

1. George Joye, *The Psalter of David in English* (1530)	61
2. George Joye, *Ortulus Animae* (1530)	62
3. George Joye, *David's Psalter* (1534)	63
4. George Joye, *A Primer in English* (1534)	64
5. Miles Coverdale, *A Paraphrasis upon All the Psalms* (1534)	69
6. Miles Coverdale, *Biblia. The Bible* [The Coverdale Bible] (1535)	71
7. Miles Coverdale, *Ghostly Psalms* (1535)	72
8. Anon., *Stories and Prophesies out of the Holy Scripture* (1536)	74
9. John Rogers, *The Bible* [The Matthew Bible] (1537)	75
10. Miles Coverdale, *The Bible in English* [The Great Bible] (1539)	77
11. Richard Taverner, *The Most Sacred Bible* [The Taverner Bible] (1539)	85
12 Richard Taverner, *An Epitome of the Psalms* (1539)	87
13. Miles Coverdale, *The Psalter or Book of Psalms* (1540)	88
14. John Croke, *A Book of Certain Chosen Psalms* (1540s?)	89
15. Anon., *Prayers of Holy Fathers* (1544?)	92
16. Queen Katherine (Parr), *Psalms or Prayers Taken out of Holy Scripture* (1544)	95
17. Anne Askew, *The First Examination of Anne Askew* (1546)	101
18. Henry Howard, Earl of Surrey (c. 1546–1547)	102
19. Thomas Sternhold, *Certain Psalms* (1547?)	111
20. John Bale, *A Godly Meditation* (1548)	114
21. John Bale, *A Dialogue or Communication* (1549)	115

CONTENTS

22. John Hopkins, *All Such Psalms of David as Thomas Sternhold, Late Groom of the King's Majesty's Robes, Did in his Life Draw into English Metre* (1549) — 116
23. Sir Thomas Wyatt, *Certain Psalms* (1549) — 118
24. Robert Crowley, *The Psalter of David* (1549) — 145
25. Sir Thomas Smith, *Certain Psalms or Songs of David* (1549) — 148
26. John Hall, *Certain Chapters Taken out of the Proverbs of Solomon, with Other Chapters of the Holy Scripture, and Certain Psalms of David* (1550) — 154
27. William Hunnis, *Certain Psalms* (1550) — 159
28. William Forrest, *Certain Psalms* (1551) — 160
29. Francis Seager, *Certain Psalms* (1553) — 164
30. Thomas Bownell, *A Godly Psalm of Mary Queen* (1553) — 166
31. Thomas Becon, *A Comfortable Epistle to God's Faithful People in England* (1554) — 168
32. John Dudley, Earl of Warwick (1554) — 171
33. Robert Dudley, Earl of Leicester (1554) — 173
34. William Kethe, in *The Appellation of John Knox* (1558) — 175
35. Various Translators, *The Bible and Holy Scriptures* [The Geneva Bible] (1560) — 179
36. Anne Vaughan Lock?, *Sermons of John Calvin* (1560) — 185
37. William Kethe, in *Four Score and Seven Psalms* (1561) — 197
38. William Whittingham, in *The Whole Book of Psalms* (1562) — 200
39. John Hopkins, in *The Whole Book of Psalms* (1562) — 204
40. Thomas Norton, in *The Whole Book of Psalms* (1562) — 207
41. John Craig, in *The Form of Prayers* (1564) — 211
42. Robert Pont, in *The Form of Prayers* (1564) — 215
43. John Wedderburn?, *Godly and Spiritual Songs* (1565) — 220
44. John Hall, *The Court of Virtue* (1565) — 228
45. John Pits, *A Poore Man's Benevolence* (1566) — 230
46. Matthew Parker, *The Whole Psalter* (1567) — 232
47. Thomas Bickley, *The Holy Bible* [The Bishops' Bible] (1568) — 243
48. Roger Edwardes, *A Book of Very Godly Psalms and Prayers* (1570) — 247
49. Arthur Golding, *The Psalms of David and Others* (1571) — 250
50. Elizabeth Tyrwhit, *Morning and Evening Prayers* (1574) — 259

51. George Gascoigne, *The Posies* (1575)	264
52. Robert Fills, *Godly Prayers and Meditations* (1577)	268
53. Anthony Gilby, *The Psalms of David* (1580)	268
54. John Stubbs (1580?)	272
55. Sir Philip Sidney (c. 1580–1586)	274
56. Richard Stanihurst, *The First Four Books of Virgil* (1582)	280
57. Thomas Bentley, T*he Fifth Lamp of Virginity* (1582)	284
58. William Hunnis, *Seven Sobs of a Sorrowful Soul for Sin* (1583)	287
59. William Patten, *1583. An: Foelicissimi Regni Reginae Elizabeth: XXVI* (1583)	305
60. George Flinton, *A Manual of Prayers* (1583)	307
61. King James VI of Scotland, *The Essays of a Prentice in the Divine Art of Poesy* (1584)	309
62. King James VI of Scotland (late 1580s)	313
63. William Byrd, *Psalms, Sonnets, and Songs* (1588)	314
64. William Byrd, *Songs of Sundry Natures* (1589)	318
65. Richard Robinson, *A Golden Mirror* (1589)	319
66. Michael Cosworth, *Psalms* (c. 1590?)	321
67. Abraham Fraunce, *The Countess of Pembroke's Emmanuel* (1591)	325
68. Barnabe Barnes, *A Divine Century of Spiritual Sonnets* (1595)	331
69. Francis Sabie, *Adam's Complaint* (1596)	332
70. Henry Lok, *Ecclesiastes* (1597)	337
71. James Melville, *Ane Fruitful and Comfortable Exhortation Anent Death* (1597)	338
72. William Patten, *Anno foelicissimi regni augustae reginae nostrae Elizabeth* (1598)	340
73. Mary Sidney Herbert, Countess of Pembroke (by 1599)	342
74. Richard Verstegan?, *The Primer, or Office of the Blessed Virgin Mary* (1599)	356
75. Sir John Harington (c. 1600)	358
76. Richard Verstegan, *Odes in Imitation of the Seven Penitential Psalms* (1601)	360
77. Henry Dod, *Certain Psalms of David* (1603)	365
78. Simon Forman (1604)	366
79. Alexander Montgomerie, in *The Mind's Melody* (1605)	380

80. Anon., in *The Mind's Melody* (1605) — 382
81. Sir William Temple, *A Logical Analysis of Twenty Select Psalms* (1605) — 386
82. Joseph Hall, *Holy Observations* (1607) — 387
83. Gregory Martin, *The Holy Bible* [Rheims-Douay Bible] (1609–1610) — 389
84. William Byrd, *Psalms, Songs, and Sonnets* (1611) — 393
85. Various Translators, *The Holy Bible* [King James Bible] (1611) — 394
86. Edmond Scory, *Two Psalms of David* (after 1611?) — 399
87. John Davies of Hereford, in *The Muses Sacrifice* (1612) — 403
88. Francis Davison, in *Certain Selected Psalms of David* (c. 1612?) — 405
89. Christopher Davison, in *Certain Selected Psalms of David* (c. 1612?) — 409
90. Joseph Bryan, in *Certain Selected Psalms of David* (c. 1612?) — 409
91. Henry Ainsworth, *The Book of Psalms* (1612) — 414
92. Sir John Harington (c. 1612?) — 418
93. Sir William Leighton, *The Tears or Lamentations of a Sorrowful Soul* (1613) — 424
94. Thomas Campion, *Two Books of Ayres* (1613) — 428
95. Sir Edwin Sandys, *Sacred Hymns* (1615) — 430
96. Sir David Murray, *A Paraphrase of the CIV Psalm* (1615) — 436
97. Henry Dod, *All the Psalms of David* (1620) — 440
98. William Loe, *Songs of Sion* (1620) — 441
99. Thomas Carew (1620s?) — 443
100. John Milton, *Poems of Mr. John Milton* (1645, composed 1623) — 448
101. Sir John Davies, *The Psalms* (1624) — 452
102. Sir Robert Ker, *Psalms in English Verses* (1624) — 458
103. Sir Francis Bacon, *Certain Psalms* (1625) — 465
104. Anon., *One and Forty Divine Odes Englished* (1627) — 467
105. Alexander Top, *The Book of Praises, Called the Psalms* (1629) — 472
106. Francis Quarles (1620s–1630s?) — 475
107. John Vicars, *England's Hallelujah* (1631) — 477
108. William Slatyer, *Psalms, or Songs of Sion* (1631) — 483
109. Sir John Glanville, The Younger, *A Paraphrase upon the Psalms of David* (1615–1631) — 486

110. King James I and William Alexander, Earl of Stirling, *The Psalms of King David* (1631) — 488

111. John Standish, in *All the French Psalm Tunes with English Words* (1632) — 497

112. Joshua Sylvester, in *All the French Psalm Tunes with English Words* (1632) — 498

113. Thomas Salisbury, in *All the French Psalm Tunes with English Words* (1632) — 502

114. George Wither, *The Psalms of David* (1632) — 507

115. Richard Crashaw, *Steps to the Temple* (1646, composed 1633?) — 511

116. Phineas Fletcher, *The Purple Island* (1633) — 515

117. John Donne, *Poems* (1633) — 521

118. George Herbert, *The Temple* (1633) — 525

119. Lady Anne Blount (c. 1620s?) — 527

120. Henry Clifford, Fifth Earl of Cumberland, *Poetical Translations of Some Psalms* (early 1630s?) — 529

121. George Sandys (c. 1633?) — 535

122. Sir Henry Wotton, *Reliquiae Wottonianae* (1651; composed post-1627) — 541

Glossary — 545

Textual Notes — 566

Psalms by Translator — 636

Psalms in Numerical Order — 639

Index of Translators and Translations — 644

Bibliography — 649

GENERAL EDITORS' FOREWORD

The aim of the *MHRA Tudor & Stuart Translations* is to create a representative library of works translated into English during the early modern period for the use of scholars, students and the wider public. The series will include both substantial single works and selections of texts from major authors, with the emphasis being on the works that were most familiar to early modern readers. The texts themselves will be newly edited with substantial introductions, notes, and glossaries, and will be published both in print and online.

The series aims to restore to view a major part of English Renaissance literature which has become relatively inaccessible and to present these texts as literary works in their own right. For that reason it will follow the same principle of modernisation adopted by other scholarly editions of canonical literature from the period. The series will have a similar scope to that of the original *Tudor Translations* published early in the last century, and while the great majority of the works presented will be from the sixteenth century, like the original series it will not be rigidly bound by the end-date of 1603. There will, however, be a very different range of texts with new and substantial scholarly apparatus.

The *MHRA Tudor & Stuart Translations* will extend our understanding of the English Renaissance through its representation of the process of cultural transmission from the classical to the early modern world and the process of cultural exchange within the early modern world.

Andrew Hadfield
Neil Rhodes

ACKNOWLEDGEMENTS

This volume has been many years in the making, and I thank first Andrew Hadfield and Neil Rhodes for inviting me to edit a collection of early modern English Psalms and for recognizing the need to include Bible translations in the Tudor and Stuart Translations series. Having now spent a quarter century researching and writing on various aspects of the Psalms, I thank those who first helped pique my interest, the many choir directors in churches I sang in from the age of 9 (in Toronto, St Simon's, St Thomas's, St Paul's, the Church of the Holy Family; in New Haven, Christ Church; in New York, St Mary the Virgin, St Thomas's Fifth Avenue, St Luke in the Fields), as well as professional and semi-professional ensembles in Toronto, New Haven, and New York. Over the decades the Coverdale Psalms were lodged firmly in my memory along with various verses in other translations set to Anglican and Gregorian chant, introits, antiphons, motets, anthems, hymns, and larger works like Bach's chorales and Bernstein's *Chichester Psalms*. I first heard of metrical Psalms in conversation with Ian Sloan in Toronto in undergraduate days, and John Hollander led me into their serious study in graduate school, advising the dissertation that developed into my first book. Valuable advice at many stages was also provided from Larry Manley, Annabel Patterson, David Quint, Tom Greene, and Leslie Brisman. The late Stephen Parks facilitated research at the Beinecke Library on the Sternhold and Hopkins Psalms and encouraged my first publication in the field in the *Yale Library Gazette*. I learned a great deal about Wyatt's and Aretino's Psalms during a 2004 RSA panel with Bill Sessions and Raymond Waddington. My friend and Ohio State colleague Chris Highley organized a conference on exile and the Reformation that led to an article on Psalms and exile, and from my first arrival at Ohio State, the late John King was a supportive mentor, always interested in my Psalms work. Alec Ryrie invited me to join the Early Modern Worship Network, which sponsored a valuable roundtable discussion on Reformation Psalms at the SCSC in 2008 with Margaret Hannay, Beth Quitslund, and others, and a paper session with Alec and Micheline White. The Network also sponsored a session on Forms of Devotion at the 2014 Chicago MLA that I chaired, and the discussion spilled over into an invitation from Susannah Monta to guest edit an issue of *Religion & Literature* on Poetry and Prayer. The contributors I gathered — John Felstiner, Roger Ferlo, Peter Hawkins, Andrew Hudgins, Gary Kuchar, Erica Longfellow, Manijeh Mannani, Alicia Ostriker, Catherine Philips, Carl Philips, and Alison Shell (Alison and Erica part of the original MLA discussion) — wrote articles that illuminated many aspects of this fascinating topic, so essential to the Psalms. Margaret Hannay invited me to join a panel on voice in lyric at the MLA with Roland

Greene and Clare Kinney, from whom I learned a great deal. I thank Ruth Ahnert and Tamara Atkin for inviting me to participate in a conference on medieval and Renaissance Psalms at Queen Mary London in 2015 that was terrifically stimulating, reconnecting me with scholarly friends and introducing many new ones, out of which came an article on the matter of voice in the Psalms, further developing ideas begun at the MLA. Tom Fulton, another old friend, invited me to join sessions on Psalm culture at the RSA in 2018, where I explored John Harington's Psalms more than I previously had, and where I heard terrific papers by Clare Costley King'oo, Hilary Bogert-Winkler, and Jeremy Specland. I have been in conversations with Clare about Psalms since we met at a Barnard conference on David in 2002, where I think I may also have met Anne Lake Prescott, Heather Dubrow, and Roger Kuin, who have been among my most supportive mentors, colleagues, and friends, as well as constant sources of insight. I was enormously fortunate to have the opportunity to edit the World's Classics edition of the Sidney Psalms with three brilliant, more experienced editors, Michael Brennan, and the late Noel Kinnamon and Margaret Hannay, Margaret especially being another of my longest-term supporters and influences.

There will inevitably be some friends and colleagues whose support and influence over the years I fail to acknowledge, and I hope they will forgive what is not ingratitude but a fault of memory. Lawrence Venuti and Robert Alter offered their wisdom on matters of translation and voice when I was thinking about these some years ago. Jason Powell has been remarkably generous in sharing his considerable editorial expertise, especially on Wyatt's Psalms. Cynthia Herrup and Lauren Kassell were kind enough to take time to answer questions about the Southwell-Sibthorpe manuscript and Simon Forman, respectively, and I was also grateful to draw on Jeremy Smith's expertise on William Byrd. Jim Doelman shared with me his notes on William Drummond's identification of the authors of Psalms in Standish's *All the French Psalm Tunes*. Christopher Burlinson not only informed me of the existence of John Stubbs's metrical Psalms but shared his transcription of them. I have benefitted from discussions with James Simpson about the Bible generally as well as about the metrical Psalms of Tudor prisoners. Aaron Pratt has always been a stimulating interlocutor about matters biblical, but he was especially helpful in sorting out the murky textual history of Coverdale's Bibles. As I was finishing the book, I came across a reference to the unpublished dissertation of Amy Bowles, a chapter of which she very graciously shared with me, along with some research notes on the Davison Psalms. Among librarians and archivists whose names hang in my personal Hall of Fame are the indefatigable Eric Johnson at Ohio State, Clare French at the Albert Sloman Library, University of Essex, who astonishingly just emailed me a scan of the only copy of William Patten's *Ann: foelicissimi regni Reginae Elizabeth: XXVI*, Anette Hagen at the National Library of Scotland for helping me fill in some holes in the EEBO scan of *One and Forty*

Divine Odes, and the many expert and helpful librarians at the Edinburgh University Library, the Bodleian, and the British Library. A former Renaissance colleague and department chair, Richard Dutton, provided support of all kinds, including (as chair) help with grants and fellowships. Robyn Warhol, a later chair, also lent her time (and authoritative signature) to help me get additional days at libraries in the UK, and my most recent chair, Susan Williams, has been supportive and encouraging, especially through a time of personal difficulty. The ultimate source of many small but significant grants was The Ohio State University, for which I am enormously grateful. Two of my OSU graduate students have also been terrific help, Daniel Knapper and Elise Robbins. Research funds allowed me to employ Dan to do some initial formatting of the text, and Elise did more extensive work on formatting, editing, and the glossary over a summer, funded by the Division of Arts and Humanities at OSU. Both are also exceptional junior colleagues and have shared ideas with me as well as their technical skills. I have also been very fortunate in having so fine and so patient a copy editor in Simon Davies, and a skilful and equally patient typesetter in John Beck.

My wife Cori Martin, always my closest partner in all things, did more rounds of copy editing than I can count, prepared the initial glosses, consulted on various textual matters, advised on the introduction, and talked with me about Psalms, the Bible, poetry, and most everything else for almost forty years. To my immense sorrow, she did not live to see this book to completion. The fruits of her labours are everywhere in this volume, as in the rest of my work, even if I can no longer point to them all precisely.

ABBREVIATIONS

Alter	Robert Alter, *The Book of Psalms: A Translation with Commentary* (New York: W. W. Norton, 2007)
BCP	The Book of Common Prayer. Unless otherwise indicated, quotations are from *The Book of Common of Prayer: The Texts of 1549, 1559, and 1662*, ed. by Brian Cummings (Oxford and New York: Oxford University Press, 2011)
Bishops'	The Bishops' Bible (*The Holy Bible*, London, 1568)
EEBO	Early English Books Online
Geneva	The Geneva Bible (*The Bible and Holy Scriptures*, Geneva, 1560). Unless otherwise indicated, quotations are from *The Geneva Bible: A Facsimile of the 1560 Edition* (Peabody: Hendrickson Bibles, 2007)
KJV	The King James Version, also known as the King James Bible, the Authorized Version (*The Holy Bible*, London, 1611). Unless otherwise indicated, quotations are taken from *The Bible*, ed. by David Norton (London: Penguin Classics, 2006)
NT	New Testament
ODNB	*The Oxford Dictionary of National Biography*
OED	*The Oxford English Dictionary*, online edition
OT	Old Testament
Quitslund and Temperley	Beth Quitslund and Nicholas Temperley, *The Whole Book of Psalms Collected into English Metre by Thomas Sternhold, John Hopkins and Others: A Critical Edition of the Texts and Tunes*, 2 vols (Tempe: Arizona Center for Medieval and Renaissance Studies, 2018)
STC	*The Short-Title Catalogue of Books Printed in England, Scotland and Ireland and English Books Printed Abroad, 1475–1640*, ed. by A. W. Pollard and G. R. Redgrave
Whole Book	*The Whole Book of Psalms*, also known as Sternhold and Hopkins (London, 1562)

Wing	*The Short-Title Catalogue of Books Printed in England, Scotland and Ireland and English Books Printed Abroad, 1641–1700*, ed. by Donald G. Wing
Zim	Rivkah Zim, *English Metrical Psalms: Poetry as Praise and Prayer, 1535–1601* (Cambridge: Cambridge University Press, 1987)

INTRODUCTION

This introduction begins with the Bible, since the history of the Psalms is inextricable from that of Jewish and Christian Scripture as a whole. This is not to say that these histories are entirely identical, however. During the centuries before Christianity, Jewish Scripture (the Tanakh or Hebrew Bible, to use the modern labels) did not exist as a material object. Jews wrote on scrolls, and only so much could be included on a single scroll (hence the divisions of I and II Kings and Samuel). The Jewish 'Bible' thus consisted of many separate scrolls, which could be stored together or read and circulated separately. It was only with the Christian preference for the codex that the various biblical books were bound together as a single 'book'.[1] Yet before printing, it was still easy to produce manuscripts of parts of the Bible, and the Book of Psalms was often copied separately. On its own, it even took on a different name, the psalter, from the post-classical Latin, *psalterium*, which was then adopted into all the Christian vernaculars, including Old and Middle English. In its contents, a psalter is identical with the Book of Psalms, but a psalter is a separate volume designed for devotional or liturgical use. This was especially useful given the prominence of the Psalms in the liturgy. Psalms were clearly sung in ancient Israel, though any reconstruction of the precise contexts remains speculative. It is intriguing that not all surviving ancient Psalms scrolls include all 150 in the canonical order, suggesting that they were selected and arranged for various purposes, public and private, just as they were for later Christians.[2]

Throughout the Middle Ages, the psalter was an essential volume for worship. The *Rule of St Benedict* required the complete psalter to be recited in monasteries each week. The key elements of the Mass — introit, gradual, alleluia, offertory, and communion — all developed out of Psalm texts, and in the secular (non-monastic) celebration of the Office, Psalm 94 was recited at Matins, Psalms 66 and 148 to 150 at Lauds, Psalms 4, 90, and 133 at Compline, and further Psalms

---

[1] Peter Stallybrass, 'Books and Scrolls: Navigating the Bible', in *Books and Readers in Early Modern England: Material Studies*, ed. by Jennifer Andersen and Elizabeth Sauer (Philadelphia: University of Pennsylvania Press, 2002), pp. 42–79.

[2] Nancy L. deClaissé-Walford notes the variety of Psalms 'editions' discovered among the Dead Sea scrolls. 'The Meta-Narrative of the Psalter', in *The Oxford Handbook of The Psalms*, ed. by William Brown (Oxford: Oxford University Press, 2014), pp. 363–76. In the Christian era, the most common alternative selection was the seven Penitential Psalms, paraphrased by Richard Maidstone (late fourteenth century) and Richard Rolle (1530s). The Gradual Psalms (120–134) were also recited and copied as a unit, and other selections were also made, including the Old English translations of Psalms 1 to 50 by Alfred the Great.

at other Offices as well as on Feast Days.³ Some of the most luxurious psalters of the Middle Ages were not liturgical books, however, but prized possessions of the rich and powerful: the Utrecht Psalter, for instance, or the Stuttgart Psalter, the Paris Psalter, the Luttrell Psalter, and the Macclesfield Psalter. By the twelfth century, psalters had developed into the breviary, which included the Psalms arranged according to the liturgy for the convenience of monastics. Breviaries developed further into the books of hours that were used for secular personal devotion, and some of these, like the *Très Riches Heures* of the Duc de Berry or the *Visconti Hours*, were also magnificent illuminated books. Nonetheless, though the Psalms have a history of their own, they remain one of the most read and cherished books of the Bible.

The Bible

The translator Ross Benjamin describes translation as a handshake between translator and original author: 'With the handshake you are reaching out to them, and you are always asking for their trust'.⁴ In translating the Bible, however, at least for believers, the hand you are reaching for is God's, as in Michelangelo's famous painting of the creation of Adam on the Sistine Chapel ceiling. No work was more important to translate, and translate accurately, than the Bible, for the simple reason that it was essential to the eternal salvation of every man, woman, and child. The same could not quite be said for Homer, Virgil, Ovid, Cicero, Plutarch, Boccaccio, Petrarch, Ariosto, Machiavelli, or Montaigne, however revered their writings.

The authority of the Bible varied among different kinds of Christians, of course. It was Protestants who believed in *sola scriptura*, 'Scripture alone', while Catholics held that the Church (governed by the pope) was an equal, and in some cases superior, authority. This is not to say that Catholics did not revere the Bible, however, which was the foundation of the liturgy and central to doctrine. In fact, it was the Bible that confirmed the authority of the Roman Catholic Church, in its account of Jesus's words to Peter, 'upon this rock will I build my church; and the gates of hell shall not prevail against it. And I will give unto thee the keys of the kingdom of heaven' (Matthew 16. 18–19). By the

---

³ James W. McKinnon, 'The Book of Psalms, Monasticism, and the Western Liturgy', in *The Place of the Psalms in the Intellectual Culture of the Middle Ages*, ed. by Nancy Van Deusen (Albany: State University of New York Press, 1999), pp. 43–58; John Harper, *The Forms and Orders of Western Liturgy from the Tenth to the Eighteenth Century* (Oxford: Clarendon Press, 1991), pp. 67–72. As in monasteries, so too in the office of secular churches the complete psalter was recited or sung through each week, even if particular Psalms came to be prominent in particular offices.

⁴ Ross Benjamin, 'The Translator Relay', *Words without Borders* (29 Jan 2013) <https://www.wordswithoutborders.org/dispatches/article/the-translator-relay-ross-benjamin> [accessed 24 May 2022].

sixteenth century, the Bible was largely inaccessible to most English Christians, since, apart from a few passages (including Psalms) translated for private devotion, it was available only in Latin, the universal (European) language of the Church and scholarship, but known only by the educated.[5] The vast majority of English people could not read Latin (or indeed any language), and they were not expected to understand the Latin read, recited, or sung in church services.[6]

Ironically, the Latin Bible used by European Christians in 1500 was originally designed to make the Bible accessible to the common people, hence its name, *Biblia sacra vulgata*, or the Vulgate, from the Latin verb *vulgare*, to make public or common.[7] The books of the Bible were originally written in Hebrew (with a little Aramaic) and Greek: the Old Testament (or Hebrew Scripture) in Hebrew, because that was the common language of ancient Israel, and the New Testament in Greek, because that was the common language of the first-century Mediterranean, especially Palestine and Northern Egypt. Greek was spoken in that part of the world because of the conquests of Alexander the Great in the fourth century BCE and the subsequent Hellenizing of his empire. For that reason too the Hebrew Scriptures were themselves translated into Greek, at that time the language of Jews in Alexandria and Palestine, in the text known as the Septuagint. In the first centuries CE, however, a new empire dominated the Mediterranean, and Rome imposed Latin on its many subjects. Latin

---

[5] There were still manuscripts of the Wycliffite translation in clandestine circulation, but these were obviously not widely available. See below.

[6] Defining the rate of literacy in the sixteenth and seventeenth centuries (or many others) is exceptionally difficult, not least because 'literacy' itself is a complex term. Not all who could read could write, for instance, and being able to sign one's name did not necessarily imply a more general ability. It is safe to say, nevertheless, that the majority of the European population in this period were not literate by any standard, and that the rate was significantly lower among the lower class than the upper, and among women than men, for the obvious reason that they had less access to formal education. Literacy rates rose significantly in the post-Reformation period, but the reasons for this are, again, complex. Earlier historians, partly following the views of the reformers themselves, linked increased literacy to Protestantism and the vernacular Bible. More recent scholars have pointed out the reliance of Protestant propaganda on visual and oral media, the anxiety of the authorities of church and state about the potential dangers of unauthorized reading, and the rise of literacy among early modern Catholics as well as Protestants. See Alexandra Walsham, '"Domme Preachers"? Post-Reformation English Catholicism and the Culture of Print', *Past & Present*, 168 (2000), 72–123; 'Literacies and Early Modern England', special issue of *Critical Survey*, 14.2, ed. by Eve Rachelle Sanders and Margaret W. Ferguson (2008); Andrew Cambers, 'Demonic Possession, Literacy, and Superstition in Early Modern England', *Past & Present*, 202 (2009), 3–35.

[7] On the pre-Reformation history of the Bible, see *The New Cambridge History of the Bible*, vol. I, *From the Beginnings to 600*, ed. by James Carleton Paget and Joachim Schaper (Cambridge: Cambridge University Press, 2013), and vol. II, *From 600–1450*, ed. by Richard Marsden and E. Ann Matter (Cambridge: Cambridge University Press, 2012).

translations of the New Testament (known as the *Vetus Latina*, 'old Latin') were already circulating, but these were based on the Greek Septuagint and highly inconsistent. In 382, Jerome was commissioned by Pope Damasus I to revise the existing Latin translations of the gospels, but Jerome instead took on the larger task of producing a complete new Bible translation from both Hebrew and Greek. Jerome's Vulgate was the Bible used throughout Catholic Christendom for the next thousand years. It was officially and exclusively approved as authoritative by the Council of Trent in 1546. The Clementine Vulgate (the edition promulgated by Pope Clement VIII in 1592) was the official Bible of the Catholic Church until 1979.

Despite the official status of the Vulgate, there were translations into European vernacular languages before the Reformation, including into French (1297), Italian (1471), Castilian (1280), Catalan (1478), German (1466), Czech (1360), and Hungarian (1456), to name only the most important.[8] Most of these were translated without any reformist intent, and most were uncontroversial. Local authorities sometimes suppressed translations but without any consistency, and there was no official ban issued from Rome. In England, portions of the Bible were translated into Old English in the first millennium, in various dialects, and this continued after the Norman Conquest. The first complete English Bible was translated in the fourteenth century (in at least two different versions) by followers of John Wycliffe, called Lollards, and this resulted in the very peculiar history of Bible translation in English. Wycliffe was a reformer with radical ideas about both Church and state, and because of his association with Bible translation (he felt strongly that the Bible should be accessible to everyone), the practice itself became tainted with radicalism. The Constitutions of Oxford, decreed by a council of the English Church convened in 1408 by the Archbishop of Canterbury, Thomas of Arundel, banned Wycliffe's writings and teaching and declared any unauthorized Bible translation to be heretical. Wycliffe himself was declared a heretic by the Council of Constance in 1415, but since he was already dead, his corpse was exhumed and burned, and his ashes dispersed into the River Swift. Thus, the translation of the Bible into English became, uniquely in Europe, not only a crime but heresy, punishable by burning at the stake.

The most famous translator to suffer this punishment was William Tyndale. Influenced by the reformed teaching of Martin Luther, especially Luther's translation of the Bible into German, Tyndale was moved to produce a Bible in his own language. Wycliffite manuscripts were still in circulation, but those translations were made second-hand from the Latin Vulgate, and Tyndale

---

[8] For much of the following material, I rely on *The New Cambridge History of the Bible*, vol. III, *The Bible from 1450 to 1750*, ed. by Euan Cameron (Cambridge: Cambridge University Press, 2016), and David Daniel, *The Bible in English: Its History and Influence* (New Haven: Yale University Press, 2003).

(following Luther) wanted a more accurate vernacular Bible translated from the original Hebrew and Greek. After failing to gain approval in England, Tyndale moved to the Continent in 1524, where he completed an English New Testament, printed in 1526 in Worms and Antwerp.[9] Tyndale's translation of the Pentateuch (Genesis to Deuteronomy) was printed in 1530, and his Jonah perhaps in 1531, both at Antwerp. In 1535 he was betrayed and captured, declared a heretic, and condemned to death by burning. As a mercy he was strangled before his body was burned. Further translations by Tyndale, from Joshua through Chronicles, somehow survived his death and found their way into the hands of John Rogers, who incorporated them into the Matthew Bible of 1537.

For all the controversy surrounding Bible translation, at least in England, it is one of the peculiarities of Christianity that it has depended upon translation since its beginnings in the first century. Not only did the authors of the gospels, Paul, and other early Christians read Jewish Scripture in Greek translation, they recorded the words of Jesus in Greek, although he spoke them in Aramaic. Jesus's teachings, the heart of Christianity, are only available in translation, no original record of them having survived. So the Latin gospels and Bibles are not the first translations but rather retranslations, just as were those of Wycliffe, Tyndale, and later translators. This makes Christianity distinct among the Abrahamic 'religions of the book', since despite the Septuagint, Jews have continued to read their holy books in Hebrew, wherever the diaspora has taken them. Islam is even more attached to the original language of the Qur'an, the spread of the religion across the world always necessitating the spread of Arabic, even if only in madrasa and mosque.

In the sixteenth century, the translation of the Bible into vernacular languages was one of the fundamental commitments of Protestant reformers. Luther's first publications were Bible translations, the New Testament in 1522 and the complete Bible in 1534 (in England too New Testaments were often published first, the Old Testament following later in a complete Bible). Luther's followers translated Bibles into Italian (1530), French (1530), Dutch (1526), Swedish (1541), Danish (1550), and Spanish (1569). When the French Protestant John Calvin, exiled from France, established himself in Geneva, that city became a dynamo of Bible translation and publication, produced by reformed scholars in exile from other Catholic countries. In the 1540s and 50s, Bibles were printed in Geneva in French (1540, 1546, 1553, NTs in 1546, 1552), Italian (1562, NTs in 1555, 1556), Spanish (NT 1556, Psalms 1557), and Latin (NT 1556, 1565). Since Geneva in the 1550s attracted Protestant exiles from England as well as other countries, they too produced a new translation of the Bible, and an

---

[9] An earlier translation of the New Testament was begun at Cologne but not completed. On Tyndale, see David Daniell, *William Tyndale: A Biography* (New Haven: Yale University Press, 1994).

important one. The Geneva Bible was the first complete English Bible translated from original languages. While Tyndale was a competent Hebraist, Miles Coverdale was not, and it was Coverdale who first translated the entire Bible into English in 1535, relying on intermediary translations in German and Latin. The Coverdale Bible was supplanted by the Matthew Bible in 1537, the work of John Rogers (under the pseudonym 'Thomas Matthew'), supplementing all of Tyndale's surviving translations with parts of Coverdale, and revising the whole himself. Then in 1539, Coverdale's Great Bible was published, a further revision by Coverdale of the Matthew Bible, and the first to be approved by Henry VIII, who appeared prominently on its elaborate title page. The Great Bible was ordered to be placed and used in churches, and it remained the standard for the next twenty years, though in fact revisions continued to be made in its early editions, perhaps by Coverdale (these have never been thoroughly researched).[10]

The Geneva Bible was the first English Bible to include verse as well as chapter numbers,[11] and it came with an impressive apparatus to aid the ordinary reader: tables, introductions, maps, and thousands of marginal notes providing information on translation, cross-references, and historical and interpretive comments. First printed in Geneva in 1560, it quickly became popular with readers of all sorts (not just those who shared the strong Calvinism of its translators), even if it was not approved for use in churches. There were at least 140 editions, in whole or in part, up to 1644, and there were two substantial revisions: in 1576 Laurence Tomson revised and annotated the Geneva New Testament based on the Latin edition of Calvin's successor, Theodore Beza, and in 1599 a new set of notes was added to Revelation, translated from those of Franciscus Junius. (The Psalms, of course, were unaffected by these revisions.) A second edition of the Geneva Bible was printed in Geneva in 1562 and a third in 1570, but the first English printing (an NT) was not until 1575. Editions of the Great Bible also continued to be printed in the 1560s, but in 1568 a new translation appeared, the Bishops' Bible, supervised by Archbishop Matthew

---

[10] There were some other revised English Bibles published, most notably by Richard Taverner (1539) and Edmund Becke (1549, 1551), but they had little impact. Taverner was a serious Greek scholar and made significant revisions to the text, but the Becke Bibles changed only notes and prologues. See Vivienne Westbrook, *Long Travails and Great Paynes: A Politics of Reformation Revision* (Dordrecht: Kluwer Academic Publishers, 2001). A revision of Tyndale's New Testament by (probably) Sir John Cheke reached a larger readership, printed by Richard Jugge from about 1553 to 1568, but as a New Testament it has no bearing on the history of the Psalms. See Aaron Pratt, 'The Trouble with Translation: Paratexts and England's Bestselling New Testament', in *The Bible on the Shakespearean Stage: Cultures of Interpretation in Reformation England*, ed. by Thomas Fulton and Kristen Poole (Cambridge: Cambridge University Press, 2018), pp. 33–48.

[11] Verse numbers appeared in the 1557 Geneva psalter, *The Psalms of David* (Geneva: M. Blanchier) and the Geneva New Testament printed in the same year (Geneva: Conrad Badius), the numbers based on those of the printer Robert Estienne.

Parker, and designed to be the official English Bible of the Elizabethan Church. Although it was used in worship, it never approached the popularity of the Geneva Bible, which continued to be the Bible of choice for reading at home.[12] In 1611, the most famous English Bible was printed, the King James, the product of years of scholarly labour by teams of translators commissioned by the king. Also known as the Authorised Version,[13] it was, like the Great Bible and Bishops' before it, ordered to be placed and used in churches across the country. It supplanted the Bishops' Bible fairly quickly, and eventually it replaced even the Geneva Bible, the last editions of which were printed in the 1640s.

The history of the English Bible, as David Norton has pointed out, is really a long history of revision rather than a sequence of entirely separate projects.[14] Tyndale and Coverdale were revised by Rogers, then again by Coverdale himself. The Geneva Bible translators went back to the Hebrew and Greek, but they also worked from the English Bibles they already had to hand. The Bishops' Bible translators revised further, and the King James Bible teams, instructed to work from the Bishops' text, subsumed all previous translations into their version, also returning to the Hebrew and Greek, and consulting other translations in Latin and German. The one English Bible that was a genuine outlier was translated by Gregory Martin and printed at the English Catholic press at Rheims (NT 1582) and later Douay (1609–10). As an English Bible for Catholics, the Rheims-Douay Bible was based on the Latin Vulgate rather than Hebrew and Greek texts, but even Martin obviously consulted previous English translations, since some of the language is clearly similar. This translation may also have had a different purpose than the other English Bibles. It couldn't be used in worship, since the Catholic Mass was banned in England, and even those clandestine services that took place would still have been in Latin. The principal purpose of this translation may have been to supply English Catholic priests

---

[12] It seems likely that the Geneva Bible was used for worship in some parishes, but no specific record survives. However, a Geneva Bible was printed by Christopher Barker in 1578 in a large folio format seemingly designed for use in churches. Parker also complained to Queen Elizabeth in 1568 that the Geneva Bible was being 'publicly used', which may suggest use in public worship. See Jeremy Specland, 'Competing Prose Psalters and Their Elizabethan Readers', *Renaissance Quarterly*, 74.3 (2021), 829–75. See also Pratt, 'The Trouble with Translation', on the popularity of the 'Cheke New Testament' (including, from 1568, the Bishops' translation).

[13] As David Norton in particular has emphasized, the notion of 'authorisation' is more problematic than is usually acknowledged, since the so-called 'Authorised' Version never actually was, and it is not clear in any case what might constitute 'authorisation'. The title page of the Great Bible claimed that it was authorised, which referred to Edward IV's proclamation 'the Bible of the largest and greatest volume to be had in every church', though of course later translations in a large format would also have satisfied this requirement. *The King James Bible: A Short History from Tyndale to Today* (Cambridge: Cambridge University Press, 2011), pp. 17–18.

[14] Norton, *The King James Bible*, p. 7.

with a reliable text they could use for pastoral and polemical purposes, ministering to the remaining Catholic community or debating Protestant adversaries. To this end it was also supplied, like the Geneva Bible, with a substantial critical-interpretive apparatus, some of its notes directly challenging those in the Geneva, correcting Protestant readings with Catholic ones.

In the sixteenth and seventeenth centuries, thousands of copies of the Bible were in circulation, perhaps as many as a million by 1640, and in at least half a dozen different versions, since Bibles were sturdy books and took a long time to wear out. Many passages in the Great, Geneva, Bishops', and King James Bibles were similar or even identical, but others were not. What the general public thought of all this is difficult to say, since there isn't much evidence, but Norton has argued convincingly that the King James Bible was met with an almost total lack of interest, despite its later acclaim. For most readers, the various translations were simply the latest edition of the Bible in English. Even the immense popularity of the Geneva Bible was probably due to its critical apparatus rather than its translation, as a few editions of the King James Bible with the Geneva notes attest. In the services of the English Church, worshippers might experience several different translations: extensive readings in the lessons and gospel were presumably from the large-format lectern Bibles 'authorized' for that purpose, but the liturgy incorporated words, phrases, and verses from the Bible in all its services, and since the Book of Common Prayer (BCP) was not significantly revised between 1559 and 1660, these passages were in Coverdale's Great Bible translation, as were the Psalms that were regularly printed with the BCP (and which remained there into the twentieth century, even though the rest of the Bible readings were updated to the KJV after the Restoration).[15] If the Psalms were chanted by a trained choir (as in cathedrals and college chapels) the Coverdale translations were used, but from at least 1562 congregations in many parish churches sang the Psalms together in the metrical translations (and using the tunes) of *The Whole Book of Psalms*, known as Sternhold and Hopkins.[16] Some of this complexity is reflected in two folio editions of the Bible that printed two different translations of the Psalms, in parallel columns. The first, in 1572, was a Bishops' Bible; the second, in 1578, was a Geneva. In both, Coverdale's BCP Psalms were printed alongside those of the other translation, with a note describing it as the 'translation used in common prayer' (the other, both for the Bishops' and the Geneva, was described as being the translation 'after' or 'according to' the Hebrew).[17]

---

[15] It was actually a 1541 edition of the Great Bible Psalms that came to be attached to the BCP. See Nicholas Pocock, '"The Great Bible", A.D. 1539', *Book-Lore*, 7 (1885), 1–5, and 'Cranmer's Bible', *Book-Lore*, 13 (1885), 22.

[16] See Nicholas Temperley, *The Music of the English Parish Church*, 2 vols (Cambridge and New York: Cambridge University Press, 1979); Christopher Marsh, *Music and Society in Early Modern England* (Cambridge and New York: Cambridge University Press, 2013).

[17] See Specland, 'Competing Prose Psalters', pp. 855–59. Specland argues convincingly that

Furthermore, many preachers, whether John Prime before Queen Elizabeth at Oxford (1588) or Richard Bancroft to the London crowd gathered at Paul's Cross (1589), continued to quote the Latin Vulgate (as well as the Church Fathers) from the pulpit, though they generally (if not always) translated it for the less learned. These translations did not always correspond to the English Bibles, however, as when Bancroft quotes Colossians 2. 6, *Sicut accepistis Iesum Christum Dominum, ita in eo incedite*, translating it, 'As you have received Christ Jesus the Lord, so walk in him'.[18] The Bishops' Bible, which one would expect Bancroft to promote, is close but not exactly the same: 'As ye have therefore received Christ Jesus the Lord, so walk ye in him'. The Geneva Bible is equally but differently close: 'As ye have therefore received Christ Jesus the Lord, so walk in him'. It seems that either Bancroft just translated the Vulgate for himself, or he remembered a combination of the Bishops' and Geneva, preferring the latter's terse, 'so walk in him', but omitting the adverb 'therefore'. Earlier, Bancroft quotes 1 John 2. 19 in English: 'They went out from us, because they were not of us: for if they had been of us, they should have continued with us'.[19] This is also not the Bishops' Bible translation, but in fact that of the Great Bible. Bancroft then quotes Matthew 3. 12 in Latin, *Triticum non rapit ventus, nec arborem solida radice fundatam: sedinanes duntaxat paleas jactat tempestas*, which in the Bishops' Bible is '[God will] gather his wheat into his garner: but will burn up the chaff with unquenchable fire'. But the Latin here is not the Vulgate. Nor is it the Latin Bible of Immanuel Tremellius and Franciscus Junius, sometimes called the Protestant Vulgate (an edition of which was printed in London in 1580). It is instead a version found in St Cyprian's *On the Unity of the Church* (*De Unitate Ecclesiae*), which Bancroft then translates:

> The wind (saith saint Cyprian) carrieth not away the wheat, nor overthroweth the tree that is deeply rooted, but the light chaff only is tossed and carried away with the tempest.[20]

---

the inclusion of the two versions reflects a conflict between the Geneva exiles and translators, who opposed common prayer and the organization of Bible reading according to the lectionary (as opposed to the more spontaneous and occasional approach advocated by the Sternhold and Hopkins psalter and the table of Athanasius, on which see below), and more conservative members of the Church of England.

[18] Richard Bancroft, *A Sermon Preached at Paul's Cross the 9. of February Being the First Sunday in the Parliament, Anno. 1588* [i.e. 1589] (London, 1588 [i.e. 1589]), p. 104.

[19] Bancroft, *Sermon*, p. 13.

[20] Bancroft, *Sermon*, pp. 14–15. There is instability even in the quotation from Cyprian, since Bancroft's text differs from that in the *Patrologia Latina* (*triticum non rapit ventus, nec arborem solida radice fundatam procella subvertit; inanes paleae tempestate jactantur*). Cyprianus Carthaginensis, *Liber de Unitate Ecclesiae*, in *Patrologiae cursus completes*, Series Latina, vol. 4, ed. by J. P. Migne (Paris: Sirou, 1844), col. 0507A. It accords instead with that found in *D. Caecilii Cypriani Episcopi Carthaginiensis De unitate Ecclesiæ libellus singularis, cum vet. mss. diligenter à Theologis Oxoniensibus collates* (London, 1632), p. 22.

Cyprian (*c.* 210–258 CE) used a text of the *Vetus Latina*, a Latin translation prior to Jerome's Vulgate.[21] Bancroft thus quotes from two different Latin translations and the English of the Great Bible and a combination of the Bishops' and Geneva. The verse on the title page of the sermon, from II Timothy, is straight out of the Geneva Bible: 'Stay prophane and vain babblings, for they will increase unto more ungodliness' (II Timothy 2. 16). Of course, the congregation wouldn't have heard this verse, which is a feature of the printed text, but I John 4. 1, which Bancroft quotes at the opening of the sermon, is also in the Geneva Bible translation. Did the simultaneous experience of so many different versions of the Bible undermine its truth? Seemingly not. The ordinary parishioner may not even have considered the problem, and even the most highly educated seem not to have been troubled.

Matthew Parker, for instance, in his preface to the Bishops' Bible, praises Thomas Cranmer's preface to the Great Bible (1540 edition), and modestly explains the justification for the new translation, in that

> the copies thereof [the Great Bible] be so wasted, that very many churches do want their convenient Bibles, it was thought good to some well disposed men, to recognize the same Bible again into this form as it is now come out, with some further diligence in the printing, and with some more light added, partly in the translation, and partly in the order of the text, not as condemning the former translation, which was followed mostly of any other translation, excepting the original text from which as little variance was made as was thought meet to such as took pains therein.[22]

And if anyone still finds errors that have crept in, either in the process of translation or of printing, they should simply 'correct the same in the spirit of charity, calling to remembrance what diversity hath been seen in men's judgements in the translation of these books before these days, though all directed their labours to the glory of God, to the edification of the Church, to the comfort of their Christian brethren'.[23] But Parker goes further than simply asking charity of potential critics; he seems to believe that not only is a diversity of different translations unproblematic, it somehow conduces to a better knowledge of God, on which he cites Augustine:

> by God's providence it is brought about, that the holy Scriptures which be the salves for every man's sore, though at the first they came from one language, and thereby might have been spread to the whole world: now by

---

[21] H. A. G. Houghton, *The Latin New Testament: A Guide to Its Early History, Texts, and Manuscripts* (Oxford: Oxford University Press, 2016), pp. 9, 17.

[22] Matthew Parker, 'A Preface to the Bible Following', *The Holy Bible* [Bishops' Bible] (London: Richard Jugge, 1568), sig. *2ᵛ. Many contemporary documents on Bible translation (and translation of other materials) are included in Neil Rhodes's MHRA anthology, edited with Gordon Kendal and Louise Wilson, *English Renaissance Translation Theory* (London: Modern Humanities Research Association, 2013).

[23] Parker, 'Preface to the Bible', sig. *2ᵛ.

diversity of many languages, the translators should spread the salvation (that is contained in them) to all nations, by such words of utterance, as the reader might perceive the mind of the translator, and so consequently to come to the knowledge of God his will and pleasure.[24]

Lurking beyond this is probably the Pentecost scene early in Acts, where the Holy Spirit descends upon the disciples in tongues of fire, and they speak in tongues, so that everyone listening hears them speak in their own language. That this is not the thought of a moment, attempting to justify a flawed translation, is indicated by Parker's return to the argument in the preface to Psalms:

> Now let the gentle reader have this Christian consideration within himself, that though he findeth the Psalms of this translation following, not so to sound agreeably to his ears in his wonted words and phrases, as he is accustomed with: yet let him not be too much offended with the work, which was wrought for his own commodity and comfort. And if he be learned, let him correct the word or sentence (which may dislike him) with the better, and whether his note riseth either of good will and charity, either of envy and contention not purely, yet his reprehension, if it may turn to the finding out of the truth, shall not be repelled with grief, but applauded to in gladness, that Christ may ever have the praise.[25]

The concern about potential critics (which is also reflected in Miles Smith's preface to the King James Bible) does imply that such criticism existed, but Parker himself seems to feel that the truth of the Bible is somehow independent of and unaffected by the language of any particular translation. As Norton concludes, for most Tudor and Stuart Bible readers, even priests and scholars, 'biblical truth did not lie in any particular form of English words', or indeed of Latin.[26] This explains the otherwise puzzling fact that in the preface to the King James Bible, Smith sometimes quotes from the earlier Bibles the translation was produced to replace, including the Geneva Bible that so irritated James himself.[27]

---

[24] Parker, 'Preface to the Bible', sig. *3ʳ. Parker cites Augustine, *De doctrina christiana* (*On Christian Doctrine*), book II, chap. 5.

[25] This preface, untitled, appears below a paragraph entitled 'Saint Austen [Augustine]', beneath a longer 'Prologue of Saint Basil the Great, Upon the Psalms'. David Norton describes it as Parker's in *A History of the English Bible as Literature* (Cambridge: Cambridge University Press, 2000), p. 38.

[26] Norton, *A History of the English Bible as Literature*, p. 38

[27] Smith quotes Ecclesiastes 1. 9, for instance, in a version closest to the Geneva: 'What is that that hath been done? that which shall be done: and there is nothing new under the sun' (sig. A4ʳ). The Geneva has 'what is it that hath been done? that which shall be done: and there is no new thing under the sun'. Bishops' has 'the thing that hath been done, shall be done again: There is no new thing under the sun'; the King James, 'that which is done is that which shall be done: and there is no new thing under the sun'. None of the English Bibles have 'there is nothing new under the sun', though Hugh Broughton does in his *A Comment Upon Qoheleth or Ecclesiastes* (Amsterdam, 1605), and the phrase appears in several other publications as well.

There is, therefore, a peculiar contradiction in the practice of Bible translation in early modern England. On the one hand, all of the translators from Tyndale on aimed for what today (after Eugene Nida) is known as 'formal equivalence', an accuracy that was word-for-word rather than sense-for-sense.[28] Thus, as Gerald Hammond has shown, the King James Bible translators followed the repetitive parataxis of the Hebrew rather than introducing the subordinating conjunctions more familiar from contemporary English prose. 'And the earth was without form, and void; and darkness was upon the face of the deep. And the Spirit of God moved upon the face of the waters' (Genesis 1. 2), rather than, say, the New English Translation's 'Now the earth was without shape and empty, and darkness was over the surface of the watery deep, but the Spirit of God was moving over the surface of the water'. Hebrew idioms were also carried over into English, even when they made no sense, as in Job's remark, 'I am escaped with the skin of my teeth' (Job 19. 20). The Geneva Bible was the first English Bible to include this expression, since Coverdale did not know Hebrew and the Vulgate is distinctly different: *et derelicta sunt tantummodo labia circa dentes meos* ('only there is left me the skin about my teeth' in the Great Bible). The idiom has lodged itself in the English language, such that most modern Bible translations (including the New English Translation) include it, and it has slipped into ordinary usage, as the titles of many recent books demonstrate.[29] The Tudor-Stuart translators understood the idiom no better than English speakers or indeed Hebrew scholars today, but it was part of the Hebrew text so it became part of the English one.

The contradiction lies in the translators' tolerance of multiple translations. Even as they devoted their energies to newly translating from 'the original tongues' and diligently comparing and revising former translations, as the King James Bible title page announced (earlier ones had too), the appearance of a new translation did not render others obsolete, nor was there any sense that having dozens of different translations in various languages in simultaneous circulation posed any threat to the understanding of scriptural truth. Quite the contrary, as Coverdale put it most explicitly:

> Whereas some men think now that many translations make division in the faith and in the people of God, that is not so. For it was never better with the congregation of God than when every Church almost had the Bible of a sundry translation. [...] Seeing then that this diligent exercise of translating

---

[28] On translation practice, see Gerald Hammond, *The Making of the English Bible* (Manchester: Carcanet New Press, 1982). On Nida's distinction between dynamic and formal equivalence, see Eugene A. Nida and Charles R. Tabor, *The Theory and Practice of Translation, With Special Reference to Bible Translating* (Leiden: Brill, 1969).

[29] Ann Walsh, *By the Skin of His Teeth: A Barkerville Mystery*, Bill Robinet, *By the Skin of My Teeth: A Cropduster's Story*, Colin Walker Downes, *By the Skin of My Teeth: Flying RAF Spitfires and Mustangs*, G. O. Nickalls, *By the Skin of Their Teeth: Great Sporting Finishes*.

doth so much good and edifieth in other languages, why should it do evil in ours? Doubtless like as all nations in the diversity of speeches may know one God in the unity of faith, and be one in love, even so many diverse translations understand one another, and that in the head, articles and ground of our most blessed faith, though they use sundry words.[30]

Two further qualifications need to be made, however. First, as Coverdale himself indicates, not everyone was so positive as he was about diverse translations. Sir Thomas More famously took offense at a number of decisions William Tyndale made in his Bible translations, and Tyndale defended himself just as vehemently as More attacked him, generating one of the most interesting exchanges in the history of Bible translation. A similar disagreement occurred later in the sixteenth century between Gregory Martin, translator of the Rheims-Douay Bible, and William Fulke, who condemned it as corrupt and heretical. Ironically, the Rheims-Douay would likely have had little impact except that Fulke included large portions of it in his massive *A Defense of the Sincere and True Translations of the Holy Scriptures into the English Tongue, against the Manifold Cavils, Frivolous Quarrels, and Impudent Slanders of Gregory Martin* (1583). Nevertheless, the polemical skirmishes were exceptional. Perhaps more telling is the evidence that, despite the polemics, Martin drew on the earlier Protestant English Bibles while translating the Rheims-Douay, just as Martin's translation was one of those consulted by the King James Bible teams.

The second qualification is that the English Bible translators were perfectly comfortable abandoning formal equivalence when they felt the situation warranted it. Smith states openly in the preface, for instance, that the King James Bible translators have not 'tied ourselves to a uniformity of phrasing or to an identity of words', by which he means that the same Hebrew or Greek word has not been rendered into English the same way in every instance. If the word had the same sense, they 'were especially careful, and made a conscience, according to our duty', to use the same English word. But they thought it 'more curiosity than wisdom', 'to translate the Hebrew or Greek word once by "purpose", never to call it "intent"; if one where "journeying", never "traveling"; if one where "think", never "suppose"', and so forth.[31] And yet one might wonder about the translation of one of the words at the heart of the Tyndale-More conflict: Greek *agape*, translated by Tyndale as 'love' and by More (in his critique, following the Vulgate's *caritas*) as 'charity'.[32] Among the other controversial words were those having implications for the institution of the church, like *ekklesia*, and

---

[30] Miles Coverdale, 'Unto the Christian Reader', *Biblia, the Bible* [The Coverdale Bible] (London: J. Nicholson, 1537), sig. +5ᵛ.
[31] [Miles Smith], 'The Translators to the Reader', *The Holy Bible* [King James Bible] (London: Robert Barker, 1611), sig. A8ᵛ.
[32] See Brian Cummings, *The Literary Culture of the Reformation: Grammar and Grace* (Oxford: Oxford University Press, 2002), pp. 190–96.

Bancroft's instructions to the translators were quite explicit about these: 'The old ecclesiastical words to be kept, as the word "Church" not to be translated "congregation" etc.'[33] Tyndale had used 'congregation', which not only was more accurate for designating the groups of early followers of Jesus but undercut the arguments of the Roman Catholic Church that it had been established by Jesus and the disciples. Bancroft said nothing specific about 'love' versus 'charity', but the King James Bible does have 'charity' in one of the key verses, 1 Corinthians 13. 13, 'And now abideth faith, hope, charity, but the greatest of these is charity'. Yet the word *agape* occurs many times throughout the New Testament, and the King James translators more often rendered it as 'love', following Tyndale rather than More. In Ephesians, for instance, Paul writes of 'God, who is rich in mercy, for his great love wherewith he loved us' (2. 4). Of course, as Tyndale noted, it would be absurd to use 'charity' as a verb, since no one says in English, 'charity God' or 'charity your neighbour',[34] but this covers only a few cases. Galatians 5. 22 has 'But the fruit of the Spirit is love, joy, peace, longsuffering, gentleness, goodness, faith'; Romans 13. 10, 'Love worketh no ill to his neighbour: therefore love is the fulfilling of the law'; John 13. 35, 'By this shall all men know ye are my disciples, if ye have love one to another'. Why 'love' in these passages, but 'charity' in 1 Corinthians?

Turning from the controversial to the more mundane, the translators did not always subordinate their own social and cultural prejudices to those of the Hebrew and Greek authors. The most obvious examples of this are the European mythical creatures that inhabit ancient Palestine in the King James Bible: unicorns (Deuteronomy 33. 17, Psalm 22. 21), satyrs (Isaiah 13. 21, 34. 14), cockatrices (Isaiah 11. 8, Jeremiah 8. 17), and many dragons (Job 30. 29, Psalm 148. 7, Micah 1. 8).[35] None of these accurately reflects the Hebrew, but instead they substitute what were thought to be European equivalents for mythological creatures unknown to the translators. But even real creatures were sometimes treated the same way. The badgers in Exodus (25. 5, 36. 19) and Numbers (4. 6), for instance, were likely dugongs, a marine mammal once much more widespread but still common in the Persian Gulf, Australia, and elsewhere. Deuteronomy 14. 5 in the King James Bible lists 'The hart, and the roebuck, and the fallow deer, and the wild goat, and the pygarg, and the wild ox, and the chamois'. Chamois were never in Palestine, so the word probably designates an antelope or some other kind of deer, mountain sheep, or goat. Roe deer and fallow deer are common in Great Britain but not the Middle East, and hart was

---

[33] Cited in Norton, *The King James Bible*, p. 87.

[34] William Tyndale, *An Answer Unto Sir Thomas More's Dialogue* (Antwerp: S. Cock, 1531), fol. 11.

[35] Gregory Martin also adds basilisks to the Rheims-Douay Bible in Psalm 90. 13, Proverbs 23. 32, and several places in Isaiah. The Vulgate has *basiliscus* in the Psalm, *regulus* (some kind of serpent) in Proverbs.

an English name for a male deer, especially the red deer, another species indigenous to England and Scotland. The Hebrew words for all these may refer to some kind of deer, or perhaps goats, gazelles, or antelopes, though the originals may now be extinct. The same is true of the 'wild ox' and the 'wild goat', which may not be an ox or goat at all. The 'pygarg' is simply a scholarly shot in the dark, the Hebrew word *dison* appearing only this once in the Bible. Pliny and Herodotus mention the pygarg, some kind of antelope, and Jerome inserts the *pyrargon* into this verse in the Vulgate, though no English person can have had any idea what such a creature might be.[36] Naomi Tadmor points out that five different birds are called 'owl' in the King James Bible, and at least eight different insects are lumped together as 'locusts'.[37]

More important, perhaps, is the layer of sixteenth-century English mores covering the King James Bible translation and absorbed into centuries of interpretation of the Bible. Tadmor notes that the Hebrew word *'ishah*, to take a striking example, makes no distinction between 'wife' and 'woman' and can mean either or both. The English translators always choose 'wife', however, when they want to have the biblical text support the institution of monogamous marriage, as in the seminal moment in Genesis 2. 24, when Adam pronounces that 'a man shall leave his father and mother, and shall cleave unto his wife'. The patriarchal bias is evident in the translation of *'ish* as 'man', rather than 'husband', but *'ishah* as 'wife', though it might easily mean 'woman'. English translators also converted Jewish family practices into marriages along more or less early modern Christian lines. Thus in the strange episode of Tamar, whose first husband Er is killed by God for some unnamed wickedness, Judah tells his second son, Onan, 'Go in unto thy brother's wife, and marry her, and raise up seed to thy brother' (Genesis 38. 8). The Hebrew makes no mention of marriage, and the verse in the Jewish Study Bible reads, 'Join with your brother's wife and do your duty by her as a brother-in-law, and provide offspring for your brother'.[38] No marriage, just obligatory sex and procreation. Yet the English Bibles reflected not only the early modern English family structure but its political system. At least fourteen different Hebrew words (designating rulers, leaders, the anointed, the exalted, judges, local governors, nobles, chiefs, kings) are all translated 'prince', which no doubt comforted King James and his sons. As Tadmor demonstrates, this consolidation of vocabulary intensified over the

---

[36] The Vulgate for Deuteronomy 14. 5 also has a camelopardus, the word combining 'camel' and 'leopard' but designating the giraffe, a creature the ancient Israelites were unlikely to have encountered.

[37] Naomi Tadmor, 'The Social and Cultural Translation of the Hebrew Bible in Early Modern England: Reflections, Working Principles, and Examples', in *Early Modern Cultures of Translation*, ed. by Karen Newman and Jane Tylus (Philadelphia: University of Pennsylvania Press, 2015), pp. 175–88 (p. 181).

[38] *The Jewish Study Bible, Featuring the Jewish Publication Society Tanakh Translation*, ed. by Adele Berlin and Marc Zvi Brettler (Oxford: Oxford University Press, 2004).

sixteenth century, the Great Bible using 'prince' 251 times while the King James Bible increased the number to 423 (Rheims-Douay had 766).³⁹

The essential point here is that even in the major, 'official' Tudor-Stuart Bibles, translation was a complex practice. In his King James Bible preface, Smith famously described translation as that which 'openeth the window, to let in the light', but there is a Platonism lurking behind this metaphor, and with the *Republic*'s image of the cave in mind, we might say that translation just opens onto another window. There may be more light (certainly than a text in a language we don't understand), but we are not seeing the thing itself, and sometimes a translation doesn't so much open a window as substitute one for another, even one with a bit of stained glass that lets in the light but tints it in the process. There are sound arguments for the success of the King James Bible in accurately translating the original Hebrew and Greek, and perhaps Tyndale was right in claiming that there was a particular affinity between English and Hebrew which didn't exist between Hebrew and Latin.⁴⁰ No translation can be perfect, however, and all translation is to some degree interpretation and adaptation, since no two languages are identical, and the verbal artefacts of a culture thousands of years in the past and thousands of miles across the planet are never going to be wholly comprehensible. The peculiarity of Bible translation, however, at least in Tudor-Stuart England, was that for both translators and readers God was somehow involved in it, and with God all things are possible. Smith writes, 'the very meanest translation of the Bible in English set forth by men of our profession [i.e. Protestants] [...] containeth the word of God, nay, is the word of God', and later that 'we desire that the Scripture may speak like itself, as in the language of Canaan, that it may be understood of the very vulgar'.⁴¹ How the word of God 'in the language of Canaan' can speak to the common people of England using different actual words is a mystery, but Smith clearly believed it possible. The miracle of the disciples speaking in tongues at Pentecost may again be relevant, but so too is the opening of the Gospel according to John, in which Jesus is described as God's 'only begotten son', 'the true Light, which lighteth every man that cometh into the world', and the 'Word' (John 1. 18, 9, 14). Jesus is surely the light that Smith wanted the

---

³⁹ Tadmor, 'Social and Cultural Translation', pp. 183–84.

⁴⁰ Hebrew and English, unlike Latin, are uninflected and depend more upon word order. Tyndale wrote: 'the Greek tongue agreeth more with the English than with the Latin. And the properties of the Hebrew tongue agreeth a thousand times more with the English than with the Latin. The manner of speaking is both one, so that in a thousand places thou needest not but to translate it into the English word for word, when thou must seek a compass in the Latin, and yet shalt have much work to translate it well-favouredly, so that it shall have the same grace and sweetness, sense, and pure understanding with it in the Latin as it hath in the Hebrew'. *The Obedience of A Christian Man* (Antwerp: Hans Luft [i.e. J. Hoochstraten], 1528), fol. 15ᵛ.

⁴¹ Smith, 'Translators to the Reader', sigs A6ᵛ, A8ᵛ.

new translation to let in, and Jesus is the Word that ultimately lies behind, speaks through, and sanctions all the words in the English Bible, just as he had sanctioned all those in the Latin, the Greek, and the Hebrew. This is why Parker (and, according to Smith, Augustine) can see the diversity of translations as positively advantageous, because the truth lies beyond all of them, accessible to the faithful by means of the grace of God.

Psalms

Most simply, the Psalms are the collection of Hebrew texts included in the Book of Psalms, part of the Hebrew Scriptures and the Christian Old Testament. For Jews and most Christians, there are 150 of them, though they are numbered differently in two distinct textual traditions, and Orthodox Christians include one more to make up 151.[42] The Psalms are divided into five sections, marked by doxologies (a formulaic, liturgical praise of God) after Psalms 41, 72, 89, and 106. Psalm 1 is generally considered a prologue to the whole book. The Greek word *psalmos*, imported into Latin via the Septuagint and then into European vernaculars, means a song sung to a plucked instrument, like a harp. Hebrew uses other words: *tehilla* (from which comes the title of the book, *Tehillim*),[43] 'praise', and *mizmor*, or 'song'. None of these terms are of much help in clarifying the genre of the Psalms, though one may safely say they are analogous to the Greek 'lyric' as texts written to be sung. They vary in length from the two verses of Psalm 117 to the 176 of Psalm 119 (though this huge Psalm is made up of a series of shorter sections). Most are in the range of ten to twenty, some shorter, some longer.

The subject matter of the Psalms is famously diverse; even though the Hebrew title lumps them together as 'praises', not all are exclusively devoted to praise. Hermann Gunkel arranged the Psalms into different genres in the early twentieth century, and his taxonomy has proved relatively durable: communal and individual complaints, royal Psalms (connected with rites and ceremonies), Psalms of thanksgiving, blessings and curses.[44] Some of Gunkel's genres (like 'Victory Song', 'legends', and 'Torah') amount only to components of some

---

[42] Psalms 9 and 10 and 114 and 115 (according to the Protestant numbering) are joined together in the Latin Psalms of the Vulgate Bible and translations deriving from it, and Psalms 116 and 147 are each divided into two. This means that for Psalms 10 to 148, Protestant and Catholic numbering differ by one.

[43] The Hebrew Bible, or *Tanakh*, is arranged in three parts: the five books of Moses or the Torah (in Greek, Pentateuch), the Prophets or *Nevi'im*, and the Writings or *Ketuvim* (hence Ta-Na-Kh). The Psalms fall into the third section.

[44] Other seminal studies of the genre of the Psalms include Sigmund Mowinckel, *The Psalms in Israel's Worship*, 2 vols, trans. by D. R. Ap-Thomas (Oxford: Blackwell, 1962), and Claus Westermann, *Praise and Blame in the Psalms*, trans. by Keith R. Crim and Richard N. Soulen (Atlanta: John Knox Press, 1981).

Psalms, and his putative genre of pilgrimage Psalm fits only Psalm 122. His categories are based on his reading of the subject matter and what he called 'form criticism', positing that each genre grew out of a specific social-historical context, but these are largely speculative. Many of the Psalms have superscriptions that might seem to suggest contexts of the kind that interests Gunkel, naming authors, genres, or performers, or providing instructions for performance. Psalm 74, for instance, is labelled 'Maschil of Asaph', Psalm 16 'Michtam of David', Psalm 42 'To the chief Musician, Maschil, for the sons of Korah', Psalm 51 'To the chief Musician. A Psalm of David, when Nathan the Prophet came unto him, after he had gone in to Bathsheba', Psalm 72 'A Psalm for Solomon', Psalm 120 'A song of Degrees'. These superscriptions are not original, however, but were added later in the history of the Book of Psalms. Moreover, their meaning is often ambiguous or obscure. The terms 'maschil' and 'michtam', for instance, as well as 'shiggaion' (Psalm 7), seem to be generic labels, but their meaning has been lost. Psalm 5 is superscribed, 'To the chief Musician upon Nehiloth', but a Nehiloth might be an instrument (flute?), a melody, or something else entirely (the word appears nowhere else). The meaning of Psalm 30's 'A Psalm or song at the dedication of the House of David' is clear, but whether it is true cannot be determined. Similarly obscure is the word 'selah', which appears seventy-one times in the Psalms, and is included (untranslated) by some translators. The consensus among scholars is that it is an instruction related to recitation or singing, but its precise meaning is unknown. Attributions of authorship are similarly open to question, especially since the Hebrew for 'of David' or 'of Solomon' might mean several things: written by, written for, associated with, in the tradition of, and so forth.[45]

In his Latin paraphrases and commentary on the Psalms, Theodore Beza listed the genre of each Psalm, in Greek, beside its number.[46] In the English translation by Anthony Gilby, the genres were described in a table at the beginning of the book, listing Psalms concerned with Doctrine, Prophecy, Prayer, Consolation, Thanksgiving, Victories or Triumphs, and combinations of these (Doctrine and Prophecy, Prophecy and Prayer, Prayer and Consolation, etc.).[47] Richard Bernard made his own generic taxonomy in the early seventeenth century, listing Psalms in twelve categories: doctrinal, prophetical, praises, eucharistical, glorying, contesting, annunciative, admonitory/exhortatory/instructive, confessing of sins, complaining and reprehension, precatory, and

---

[45] Nancy L. deClaissé-Walford, Rolf A. Jacobsen, and Beth LaNeel Tanner, *The Book of Psalms* (Grand Rapids and Cambridge: William B. Eerdmans, 2014), pp. 11–13.

[46] *Psalmorum Dauidis et aliorum prophetarum, libri quinque* (London: Thomas Vautrollier, 1580). The genres include *didaktikos* (didactic), *prophetikos* (prophetic), *euktikos* (petitionary), etc.

[47] *The Psalms of David Truly Opened and Explained by Paraphrasis* (London: John Harrison and Henry Middleton, 1580), sig. ¶8ʳ. Beza's genres, especially in Gilby's English, sound rather like Polonius's description of theatrical genre in *Hamlet*, 'tragedy, comedy, history, pastoral, pastoral-comical, historical-pastoral, tragical-comical-historical-pastoral' (II. 2. 421–23).

consolatory. The 'eucharistical' is obviously not a genre that would have been recognized in ancient Israel (though the Greek εὐχαριστία, eucharistia, actually means 'thanksgiving', one of Beza's categories), and there might also be some disagreement about the 'prophetical' (the Christian reading of Psalm 22 as about the suffering Christ, most notably), but otherwise Bernard's list seems as reasonable as Gunkel's or Beza's, though a few more genres might be added: historical (recounting events in the history of Israel as told in the Bible) and wisdom (imparting traditional teachings of the sort found also in Proverbs, Job, and Ecclesiastes), for instance. Many Psalms also mix genres, as Beza recognized. Psalm 137, for instance, begins by lamenting the condition of Jews exiled in Babylon, but then calls down ferocious curses on Israel's enemies. Psalm 22 begins in despair, complaining of suffering and God's neglect, then prays for deliverance, promising to praise God thereafter, and finally closing with such praise. Psalm 73 begins with praise for God's goodness, but then turns to a combination of confession and blame, the Psalmist having succumbed to envy and despair, but because of the pride of the wicked and prosperity of the ungodly; he recognizes his foolishness, however, prophesies the downfall of the wicked, and closes with praise. Psalm 114 retells the story of the Exodus and calls on the earth to recognize God's power. Psalm 73 opens with the Psalmist saying he will tell a parable, but he then recaps the history of Israel from Jacob through the Exodus (in more detail than Psalm 114) to the building of the Temple. Whatever the generic categories we use to describe the Psalms, it is evident that there are many of them, and that their tone and subject matter are diverse.

Since at least the time of the Christian Church Fathers, the Psalms have stood out for their variety, as St Basil preached in one of his homilies:

> All Scripture is inspired by God and is useful, composed by the Spirit for this reason, namely, that we men, each and all of us, as if in a general hospital for souls, may select the remedy for his own condition. For, it says, 'care will make the greatest sin to cease'. Now, the prophets teach one thing, historians another, the law something else, and the form of advice found in the proverbs something different still. But, the Book of Psalms has taken over what is profitable from all. It foretells coming events; it recalls history; it frames laws for life; it suggests what must be done; and, in general, it is the common treasury of good doctrine, carefully finding what is suitable for each one. The old wounds of souls it cures completely, and to the recently wounded it brings speedy improvement; the diseased it treats, and the unharmed it preserves. On the whole, it effaces, as far as is possible, the passions, which subtly exercise dominion over souls during the lifetime of man, and it does this with a certain orderly persuasion and sweetness which produces sound thoughts.[48]

---

[48] St Basil, Homily 10 'A Psalm of the Lot of the Just Man (Psalm 1)', in *Saint Basil, Exegetic Homilies*, trans. by Sister Agnes Clare Way, The Fathers of the Church: A New Translation, vol. XLVI (Washington, DC: Catholic University of America Press, 1963), pp. 151–52.

Basil's conception of the Psalms as an epitome of the Bible, containing the essence of the whole in miniature, became commonplace. The English theologian Richard Hooker asked, 'What is there for man to know that the Psalms are not able to teach?'[49] John Calvin called the Psalms 'an anatomy of all the parts of the soul',

> in as much as a man shall not find any affection in himself, whereof the image appeareth not in this glass. Yea, rather, the Holy Ghost hath here lively set out before our eyes, all the griefs, sorrows, fears, doubts, hopes, cares, anguishes, and finally all the troublesome motions wherewith men's minds are wont to be turmoiled. The rest of Scripture containeth what commandments God hath enjoined to his servants to be brought unto us. But in this book, the prophets themselves talking with God, because they discover all the inner thoughts, do call or draw every one of us to the peculiar examination of himself, so as no whit of all the infirmities to which we are subject, and of so many vices wherewith we are freighted, may abide hidden. It is a rare and singular profit when by searching out all the lurking holes, the heart is cleansed from the most noisome infection of hypocrisy and laid open to the light.[50]

Anthony Gilby, who translated Beza's Psalms commentary as well as (likely) the Psalms in the Geneva Bible, had obviously read Calvin, when he wrote that 'whereas all other Scriptures do teach us what God saith unto us, these prayers of the saints do teach us, what we shall say unto God, and how we must prepare ourselves to appear before his majesty, both in prosperity and adversity'.[51] This too was an important part of the special appeal of the Psalms: their diversity was especially valuable given their mode of first-person address, since they thus provided models for people to follow in their own lives. Athanasius in the fourth century wrote that 'each one sings the Psalms as though they had been written for his special benefit, and takes them and recites them, not as though someone else were speaking or another person's feelings being described, but as himself speaking of himself, offering the words to God as his own heart's utterance, just as though he himself had made them up'.[52] To further facilitate this practice, Athanasius provided a table of various situations in which Christians might find themselves, along with the appropriate Psalms for the occasion. Many editions

---

[49] Richard Hooker, *Of the Laws of Ecclesiastical Polity. The Fifth Book* (London: John Windet, 1597), p. 75.
[50] John Calvin, *The Psalms of David and Others. With M. John Calvin's Commentaries*, trans. by Arthur Golding (London: Thomas East and Henry Middleton for Lucas Harrison and George Bishop, 1571), sig. 6ᵛ.
[51] Anthony Gilby, 'Epistle Dedicatory' to Theodore Beza, in *The Psalmes of David, truely opened and explaned by Paraphrasis*, trans. by Gilby (London: Henry Denham, 1581), sig. ¶4ʳ.
[52] Athanasius, 'Letter to Marcelinus', in *On the Incarnation: The Treatise De Incarnatione Verbo Dei*, trans. by a religious of C.S.M.V., intro. by C. S. Lewis, new rev. edn (New York: St Vladimir's Seminary Press, 1996), p. 105.

of the immensely popular Sternhold and Hopkins psalter included versions of this table. Psalm 18 was recommended, for instance, for those who were 'escaped from enemies, and delivered from them which persecute them', or 'If thou seest any man troubled, comfort them, and praying for them, say the words of the Psalm 20'. There are Psalms for if you see the wicked prosper (73), if God seems angry with you (74), if your enemies curse you (46), if you marvel at Creation (19, 26, 27), if you have suffered a false allegation before an evil king (52), or if 'because of the imbecility of our nature, thou art, after the manner of a physician, irked and weary of the manifold mischiefs of life, and wouldest comfort thy self' (102). And countless people did turn to the Psalms, in these situations and many others, as they still do.[53]

Composition

The Hebrew Psalms were composed over a long period. Some may date back as far as the ninth or tenth century BCE. It is possible that some were written by King David or his son and successor Solomon, though there is no clear evidence outside of the Bible, and indeed the actual history of these figures is itself murky. Psalm 137, on the other hand, about the Babylonian Exile, cannot predate that event, which lasted from 597 to 539 BCE, so the Psalms were created over five centuries, as long a period as between Tyndale's New Testament and the present. During the fifth century BCE the Psalms were redacted into their canonical form and arrangement, along with the rest of the Hebrew Scriptures composed by that date. As mentioned above, these were translated into Greek in the third and second centuries BCE, and the Septuagint (as it was known) was in wide use by Jews in the Eastern Mediterranean during the Second Temple period (560 BCE–70 CE) and by early Christians. When Jerome translated the Bible into Latin, however, he used not the Greek Septuagint but the Hebrew Old Testament, albeit alongside a variety of secondary literature in Greek. Jerome's decision to base his translation on the Hebrew was criticized by other Christian leaders, including Augustine, but his claim was that this took him back closer to the original texts. Jerome actually produced several different versions of the Psalms in Latin: the Roman Psalter (a revision of the *Vetus Latina*, now lost, the version formerly called the 'Roman Psalter' being actually the *Vetus Latina* itself), the Gallican Psalter (so called because it became popular in Gaul, translated from Origen's Hexapla, containing the Septuagint, three other Greek versions, a Hebrew text, and a transliteration of the Hebrew), and the Hebrew Psalter (translated from the Hebrew). The Gallican Psalter stays close to the Septuagint, and since it was the version that became part of the Vulgate Bible,

---

[53] *The Whole Book of Psalms* (London: John Day, 1562), sigs +7ʳ–A2ᵛ. Then continues a section of additional Psalms and situations not covered by Athanasius.

the result was that even though the rest of the Vulgate was translated from the Hebrew, the Psalms were not, or only partly.[54]

The Hebrew text of the Psalms, meanwhile, had its own complex history, as part of the general history of Hebrew Bible manuscripts. By the first century of the Common Era, the Hebrew Scriptures were in circulation in a wide variety of forms: there were a number of traditions of the Hebrew text, but there were also texts in Aramaic, a related but separate language, though they cross-pollinated, and post-Exilic Hebrew was (and still is) actually written in the Aramaic script. The Hebrew texts were consonantal, however; that is, following the custom of written Hebrew, consonants required a set of diacritical marks above and below to indicate the vowels, and thus essentially to distinguish one word from another, since the same set of consonants, pronounced with different vowels, could have an entirely different meaning. A standard pointing of the Hebrew text was established by the Masoretes, groups of scholar-scribes in Tiberias, Jerusalem, and Babylonia, between the fifth and tenth centuries CE, notably long after Jerome's Vulgate, but this is the Hebrew textual tradition upon which Tudor and Stuart translators depended, whether they could read Hebrew or accessed it through intermediary translations and commentaries.

Given the antiquity of the Psalms and other Hebrew Scriptures, nothing like original manuscripts survive (though determining just what might constitute an 'original' would be a challenge). Furthermore, many of the earliest biblical manuscripts available today were unknown in the Middle Ages and early modern periods. The knowledge of Greek was rediscovered by Western European Renaissance scholars with the help of Greek-speaking exiles fleeing the Byzantine Empire after the fall of Constantinople to the Turks in 1453. Hebrew came more slowly, partly because of Christian distrust of the Jews whose knowledge was essential, but who were suspected of corrupting or lying about the text of the Hebrew Scriptures. Eventually, however, Christian scholars did learn Hebrew and translated the books of the Hebrew Bible into Latin. With the development of sophisticated printing, editions of the Hebrew texts themselves were published, and grammars and dictionaries were produced to aid in the learning of the language. Universities established Chairs of Greek and Hebrew, including the Regius Professorships at Cambridge and Oxford, and new institutions were founded to promote scholarship in biblical languages, as at Louvain (encouraged by Erasmus), and the Collège Royal (later the Collège de France) in Paris.

By the time Tyndale set to work on his Pentateuch (1530), he could rely on the Hebrew grammars of Konrad Pellikan and Johannes Reuchlin, the dictionary and grammar of Sante Pagnini (based on the work of Rabbi David Kimchi), and the even better grammars and dictionaries of Sebastian Münster.

---

[54] Scott Goins, 'Jerome's Psalters', in *The Oxford Handbook of the Psalms*, ed. by William P. Brown (Oxford: Oxford University Press, 2014), pp. 185–200.

Jewish printers produced editions of the Hebrew Scriptures in Italy and Portugal (beginning with the Psalms in Bologna in 1477), and Daniel Bomberg printed his massive Rabbinic Bible (Mikraot Gdolet) in Venice from 1517 to 1519. The four volumes, edited by the Jewish convert Felice da Prato, included not only the biblical texts of the Pentateuch, the five scrolls, and selections from the Prophets, but the Aramaic translation of the Targum Onkelot and commentaries by Rashi and other Jewish scholars. In 1522 the Complutensian Polyglot was published at Alcalá de Henares, containing the Old Testament in Hebrew, the Latin Vulgate, and the Greek Septuagint, with the Aramaic Targum for the Pentateuch and a Latin translation of the Aramaic (the New Testament was printed in Greek and Latin, and the six-volume set also included dictionaries, commentary, and study guides). Of course, some of these volumes were too expensive and out of reach for Tyndale, translating in hiding at Antwerp, but there was a steady proliferation of Hebrew Bibles, grammars, and dictionaries, as well as translations of and commentaries on the Hebrew in Latin. David Norton describes the library of Edward Lively, head of the first Cambridge team of translators of the King James Bible (responsible for 1 Chronicles to the Song of Solomon), which included more than thirty-five Hebrew and Aramaic (then called Chaldee) grammars, commentaries, and concordances, as well as four Hebrew Bibles. Laurence Chaderton, a member of the same Cambridge team, had a two-volume third edition of the Bomberg Hebrew Bible, and his college library (Emmanuel) had eight Hebrew Bibles and over a dozen commentaries and dictionaries. Norton suggests that the King James Bible translators may have been more familiar with Hebrew and Greek, curiously, and certainly with Latin, than they were with previous English Bibles, copies of which are scarce in the booklists of college libraries and their personal collections.[55]

Few of the translators in this volume knew Hebrew, however. Even Coverdale, as stated earlier, worked from translations of the Hebrew: for the Coverdale Bible, the Vulgate and the Latin Bible of Pagnini, and the Luther and the 1524–29 Zurich Bibles in German, and for the Great Bible, Münster's 1535 Old Testament and the Complutensian Polyglot. Those who only translated or paraphrased the Psalms worked from these and other translations and paraphrases, like Johannes Campensis's Latin paraphrase (1532), Martin Bucer's Latin with commentary (1529), the French metrical psalter of Clément Marot and Théodore de Bèze (1562), or other metrical Psalms in French, Italian, Spanish, German, Dutch, or the classical Latin of George Buchanan. Yet many simply 'translated' from other English translations, most often rewriting the prose translations in the English Bibles into different metres and stanza forms.

---

[55] Norton, *The King James Bible*, pp. 62–69.

Categories and Kinds

Poems or Prose. The Psalms are poems. So said Philo and Josephus, Eusebius and Jerome. So say Benjamin Harshav, Adele Berlin, Robert Alter, and F. W. Dobbs-Allsopp.[56] And yet the ancient and modern scholars understand this claim entirely differently. In describing the community of Jews near Alexandria known as 'Therapeutae', Philo writes that they 'compose hymns and psalms to God in all sorts of metres and melodies which they write down with the rhythms necessarily made more solemn', and then describes their rites:

> Then the President rises and sings a hymn composed as an address to God, either a new one of his own composition or an old one by poets of an earlier day who have left behind them hymns in many measures and melodies, hexameters and iambics, lyrics suitable for processions or in libations and at the altars, or for the chorus whilst standing or dancing, with careful metrical arrangements to fit the various evolutions.[57]

Josephus describes the practice of those 'poets of an earlier day', specifically David, who 'composed songs and hymns to God in varied meters — some he made in trimeters, and others in pentameters'.[58] Eusebius writes several centuries later of the instruction of the Jews 'even from the age of infancy', teachers delivering 'to them recitations of holy words, and tales from sacred histories, and metrical compositions of psalms and canticles, problems also and riddles, and certain wise and allegorical theories, combined with beauty of language, and eloquent recitation in their own tongue'.[59] Finally, Jerome writes to his follower and close collaborator Paula (St Paula of Rome) about biblical poems written in alphabetical acrostics, noting other of their formal features as well:

> But before I speak about the single letters, you should know that four psalms begin according to the order of the Hebrew alphabet: the 110th [111], the 111th [112], the one of which we are now writing [118th, i.e. 119], and the 144th [145], single verses connected by the preceding single letters, which are in iambic trimeter, the later in iambic tetrameter, as the canticle of

---

[56] Benjamin Hrushovski [Harshav], 'Prosody (Hebrew)', in *Encyclopedia Judaica*, ed. by Cecil Roth and Geoffrey Wigoder, 16 vols (Jerusalem: Keter, 1972), XIII, 1195–1240; Adele Berlin, *The Dynamics of Biblical Parallelism* (Bloomington: Indiana University Press, 1985); Robert Alter, *The Art of Biblical Poetry* (New York: W. W. Norton, 1985); F. W. Dobbs-Allsopp, *On Biblical Poetry* (Oxford: Oxford University Press, 2015).

[57] Philo, *On the Contemplative Life or Suppliants*, in Philo, vol. XIX, *Every Good Man is Free. On the Contemplative Life.* [etc.], trans. by F. H. Coulson, Loeb Classical Library 363 (Cambridge, MA: Harvard University Press, 1941), pp. 112–71, 129–31, 163.

[58] Josephus, *Jewish Antiquities*, vol. III: Books 7–8, trans. by Ralph Marcus, Loeb Classical Library 281 (Cambridge, MA: Harvard University Press, 1934), p. 167.

[59] Eusebius of Caesarea, *Praeparatio Evangelica* (Preparation for the Gospel), book XI, chap. 5, *Eusebii Pamphili Evangelicae Praeparationes*, ed. and trans. by E. H. Gifford (Oxford: Oxford University Press, 1903), III, part 2, 550.

Deuteronomy is written. [...] You have in the Lamentations of Jeremiah four alphabets, of which the first two are as if in Sapphic meter, since three little lines which are connected begin from only one letter, and conclude with a pause/punctuation in heroic style; the third alphabet is written in trimeter and three verses begin from three letters, but the same letter; the fourth alphabet is similar to the first two. A final alphabet closes the Proverbs of Solomon, which is considered tetrameter.[60]

In the preface to his translation of Eusebius's *Chronicle* (addressed to his friends Vincentius and Gallienus), Jerome again addresses the metres of biblical poetry, citing the authority of Josephus and Origen:

> In fact, what can be more musical than the Psalter? Like the writings of our own Flaccus [i.e. Horace] and the Grecian Pindar it now trips along in iambics, now flows in sonorous alcaics, now swells into sapphics, now marches in half-foot metre. What can be more lovely than the strains of Deuteronomy and Isaiah? What more grave than Solomon's words? What more finished than Job? All these, as Josephus and Origen tell us, were composed in hexameters and pentameters, and so circulated amongst their own people.[61]

Lamentations and some Psalms do use alphabetical acrostics, but biblical poetry, including the Psalms, is non-metrical, and, if pressed, none of these ancient writers could possibly have shown how the Hebrew includes iambics, alcaics, sapphics, hexameters, pentameters, trimeters, or any other Greek metres. It doesn't.

When modern Hebrew scholars talk about biblical poetry, they mean something entirely different. As Robert Lowth argued in his lectures on Hebrew Poetry at Oxford between 1741 and 1751, the distinguishing formal feature of the Psalms is what he called parallelism, 'the correspondence of one Verse, or Line, with another'.[62] They are not metrical, they do not rhyme, and they are formally utterly different from ancient Greek and Latin poetry, or indeed Renaissance poetry in European vernaculars. The easiest way to explain parallelism is with an example, as Psalm 114:

---

[60] Jerome, 'Letter to Paula the Elder' (384), in *Epistolae: Medieval Women's Letters*, trans. by Joan Ferrante and colleagues <https://epistolae.ctl.columbia.edu/letter/280.html> [accessed 24 May 2022]. Latin text from *Sancti Eusebii Hieronymi Epistulae*, ed. by Isidor Hilberg, for the Corpus Scriptorum Ecclesiastocorum Latinorum, 3 vols (Vienna: F. Tempsky; Leipzig: G. Freitag, 1910), I, 243–49, esp. pp. 244–45.
[61] Jerome, 'Preface to the Chronicle of Eusebius', *A Select Library of Nicene and Post-Nicene Fathers of the Christian Church*, second series, trans. by Philip Schaff and Henry Wace, vol. VI, *St. Jerome: Letters and Selected Works* (New York: The Christian Literature Company; Oxford and London: Parker and Company, 1893), p. 484.
[62] Robert Lowth, *Isaiah. A New Translation; with a Preliminary Dissertation, and Notes Critical, Philological, and Explanatory* (London: J. Nichols for J. Dodsley and T. Cadell, 1778), p. x.

> When Israel came out of Egypt: and the house of Jacob from among the strange people,
> Juda was his sanctuary: and Israel his dominion.
> The sea saw that and fled: Jordan was driven back.
> The mountains skipped like rams: and the little hills like young sheep.
> (Psalm 114. 1–4, BCP)

The relationship between the two corresponding parts (and it is occasionally three) is clear. The 'house of Jacob' is simply another name for Israel, and the Egyptians were 'strange people' to the Israelites, so the two halves of the first verse say essentially the same thing in different words. The same is true in the next verse, with 'Juda/Israel' and 'sanctuary/dominion', though the implications of the words in the second part are different enough to generate some interest. Verse three follows the same pattern, though in verse four the parallel terms are not synonyms but larger and smaller versions of the same thing. There are, in fact, a variety of relationships that can exist between the verse halves, including the synonymous, expansion or contraction, qualification, contradiction, climactic intensification, the sequential, and so forth. In some verses, there seems to be no relationship at all, though the regular pattern encourages the reader to infer one. Hebrew poets do employ more than parallelism, including various tropes and schemes, especially punning and wordplay (for which Hebrew is extremely convenient), as well as various aural effects. But in English, all of these features are found in prose as well as poetry (or verse). At least one major Hebrew scholar has actually questioned the validity of the term 'poetry' for Hebrew writing like Psalms, Lamentations, the Song of Solomon, and elsewhere, arguing that the difference between these texts and 'prose' ones is simply a matter of degrees of rhetorical density or self-consciousness.[63]

Nevertheless, the consensus view is, and certainly was in the early modern period, that there are poems in the Hebrew Bible, and that the Psalms are preeminent among them. As Dobbs-Allsopp observes, any definition of 'poetry' is inevitably historically and culturally determined. Though in the English Renaissance a non-metrical poem was inconceivable, sub-Saharan African poetry is not composed in metre, and ancient Sumerian poetry may not have been either.[64] Certainly since the nineteenth century, poetry in English has often

---

[63] James L. Kugel, *The Idea of Biblical Poetry: Parallelism and Its History* (New Haven: Yale University Press, 1981). Kugel is a lone voice in questioning the existence of biblical poetry, but his argument is clearly powerful enough that every subsequent scholar has felt the need to address it. It is also telling that Kugel himself is comfortable enough with idea of biblical poetry in more informal contexts to compile a collection of *The Greatest Poems of the Bible: A Reader's Companion with New Translations* (New York: Free Press, 1998) that includes many Psalms.

[64] Walter Pitts, 'West African Poetics in the Black Preaching Style', *American Speech*, 64.2 (1989), 137–49; Benjamin Foster, 'Sumerian Poetry', in *The New Princeton Encyclopedia of Poetry and Poetics*, 4th edn, ed. by Roland Greene (Princeton: Princeton University Press, 2012), pp. 1376–77.

eschewed metre. Walt Whitman's *Leaves of Grass* and Allen Ginsberg's *Howl* actually adopt the style of Old Testament prophecy, but modern free verse may take any number of shapes, and the 'prose poem' blurs the distinction between poetry and prose entirely. Modern readers are thus likely to be untroubled calling Psalm 114, quoted above, a poem, even though it has little formal similarity to, say, a broadside ballad or a Spenserian stanza. One further implication of Hebrew poetry's focus on parallel rhetorical structures rather than metre or rhyme is that it is easily translatable. As C. S. Lewis put it, 'It is (according to one's point of view) either a wonderful piece of luck or a wise provision of God's that poetry which was to be turned into all languages should have as its chief formal characteristic one that does not disappear (as mere metre does) in translation'.[65]

Before the nineteenth century, however, the form of the Psalms produced more confusion than wonder. Jerome and the early commentators, for instance, had a fixed conception of poetry that required metre, following the practice of the great poetry of Greece and Rome. Moreover, a perhaps forgivable or at least natural chauvinism persuaded them to think that the best poetry required the same metres used by Homer, Virgil, Pindar, and Horace. At the same time, at least for the Christian Church Fathers, their reverence for the Bible led them to believe that the poetry of ancient Israel must in fact be superior to that of Greece and Rome, and was even the original source from which classical poetry flowed. Even John Milton, who esteemed classical literature as much as anyone ever has, wrote that the 'frequent songs throughout the law and prophets [...], not in their divine argument alone, but in the very critical art of composition may be easily made appear over all the kinds of lyric poesy, to be incomparable'. Among those less worthy, he specifically included the 'magnific odes and hymns' of Pindar and Callimachus.[66] And yet if one translated these songs scrupulously, aiming at a word-for-word accuracy, the results were inevitably English Psalms like those of Coverdale, who, though without knowing Hebrew himself, consulted the best Hebraists he could find and had an innate gift for the syntactic and semantic rhythms of parallelism. Brilliant as they are, they look like no poem Milton ever wrote, and even less like those of Pindar and Callimachus.

This dilemma, the disjunct between received and approved knowledge and empirical evidence, was the greatest engine of creative energy for early modern European Psalm translation. Coverdale and his fellow Bible translators followed their principles to produce versions of the Psalms in English prose, at least prose as they would have described it. Hundreds of other translators, however, converted the Psalms into metre, rhyme, and stanza forms that made them recognizable as poems for contemporary readers. A few went further still, trying

---

[65] C. S. Lewis, *Reflections on the Psalms* (San Diego, New York, London: A Harvest Book/Harcourt, Inc., 1958), pp. 4–5.
[66] John Milton, *The Reason of Church Government Urged Against the Prelaty* (London: E. G. for John Rothwell, 1641), p. 39.

to turn them into poems that even Pindar and Horace, or Philo and Jerome would have recognized as such, using versions of classical quantitative metres like hexameters, alcaics, and sapphics. As a result, even though one might expect Psalm translation to be a fairly monotonous business, producing and reproducing the same 150 texts in nearly identical English versions, in fact any two versions of Psalms 23, 42, 51, 104, or 137 can look as if they had quite different originals. For the reader, this is especially exciting, and for the poet, the drive to produce a version of a Psalm measuring up to King David's was inspiring. And the sense that it was the Holy Spirit doing the inspiring, and that the divine Word was both accessible through and yet independent of any English version of it, kept early modern Christians from feeling overwhelmed and confused by the babble of so many Psalms in so many voices.

Music. The distinction between prose and poetry is one obvious way to categorize the many Psalms in this collection. The Psalms of Coverdale (in his Bibles and the BCP), the other English Bibles, as well as those of George Joye, Katherine Parr, Arthur Golding, and Anthony Gilby are in prose. The Psalms of Robert Crowley, Sir Thomas Wyatt, Henry Howard, Earl of Surrey, George Gascoigne, Sternhold and Hopkins, Philip and Mary Sidney, John Donne, and George Herbert are in poetry.[67] Modern readers might happily call them all poems, but early modern readers certainly would not have.

Another seemingly uncomplicated distinction can be made according to the intended use for which the translations were made, and the context in which they would have been used. The prose Bibles were designed primarily for use in churches, either read in services or by parishioners who might not be able to afford their own copy.[68] As they were printed in smaller, cheaper editions, Bibles

---

[67] I am taking the terms 'poetry' and 'verse' to be synonymous, though in both early modern and modern poetics they are not always so. Sidney, for instance, in his *Defence of Poesy*, uses 'poesy' (or poetry) as a term for both verse and prose, which is logical, since as he stresses the word comes from the Greek ποεῖν, 'to make', which has nothing to do with metre. John Hollander, on the other hand, distinguishes 'verse' and 'poetry' in terms of quality, which allows him to make such claims as that 'the ability to write good or even extremely well-turned verse was in the past not the province of poets, but of good writers generally'. But then he also claims that even though not all verse is poetry, 'all poetry is framed in some kind of verse'. Yet if the defining feature of poetry is not formal but qualitative (as it appears), it is not clear why a work of prose (like a novel) cannot be a poem, which Hollander does not allow (though Sidney would). The popular distinction between poetry and prose seems clear enough for my purposes in writing about the sixteenth and seventeenth centuries and earlier (before the 'prose poem'). See Hollander, 'My Poetic Generation', in *The Work of Poetry* (New York: Columbia University Press, 1997), pp. 143–51.

[68] As with almost any attempt at a neat distinction among kinds of Psalms, this one too is imperfect, since it is possible the prose Psalms of Coverdale or later English Bibles were chanted by professional choirs in institutions that employed them, like cathedrals, the Chapels Royal, and college chapels. John Marbeck, who had been a chorister at St George's Chapel,

were also read in private homes, either individually or as a family, and pocket-sized Bibles allowed for reading virtually anywhere. Golding's and Gilby's prose versions accompanied their translations of commentaries by Calvin and Beza, to be read by those interested in a deeper study of the Psalms. The Psalms of the Sternhold and Hopkins psalter, as well as those of Coverdale (*Ghostly Psalms*), Robert Crowley, William Hunnis, Henry Dod, George Wither, and King James I were intended to be sung, some as part of domestic devotions or godly entertainment, others in church services as well. Hunnis's Psalms were sung at home, as were those of Thomas Campion (as well as at the royal court). The Sternhold and Hopkins Psalms were sung in every context one might imagine, including apparently in battle,[69] and (in later sophisticated musical settings by William Byrd, John Dowland, Richard Allison, and others) at home or at court. Crowley, Matthew Parker, Henry Ainsworth, Dod, Wither, and King James intended their Psalms for worship, but they were probably never actually sung in churches.

Yet wherever and however these Psalms were sung, one can generally distinguish them from Psalms that were intended only to be read. There is no evidence that Wyatt and Surrey's Psalms were written for singing, for instance, and the same seems true of Gascoigne, the Sidneys, Abraham Fraunce, Donne, Herbert, and Henry Clifford, Earl of Cumberland. The border between these two categories is somewhat permeable, since one could of course still read singing Psalms such as Sternhold and Hopkins, and it is clear that many did (and many editions were printed without music, though people might have remembered the tunes from church). On the other side, any text can be set to music, even if it was not originally intended to be sung, and song manuscripts do survive for a few of the Sidney Psalms. Others, like Phineas Fletcher's, were written in complex stanzas like the Sidney Psalms, and were not printed with music, but did have instructions to sing them to particular tunes. Whether they were actually sung is impossible to know. The only Psalms that seem unquestionably 'reading' Psalms are those written in classical quantitative metres, like those of Richard Stanihurst, Abraham Fraunce, and the Countess of Pembroke (Psalms 120–27). Thomas Campion did set one of his quantitative (non-biblical) poems to music, but the result is a very strange song by early

---

Windsor, published *The Book of Common Prayer Noted* in 1550, showing how the English Psalms might be chanted to versions of the traditional Latin Psalm tones. No evidence has been discovered, however, of whether and how often these were actually sung.

[69] Most famously, Oliver Cromwell led his troops in a Psalm, pausing as they pursued the fleeing Scots after the Battle of Dunbar. Appropriately, he chose Psalm 117, which has only two verses, so they could continue with the pursuit. In 1642, during a siege of Leeds, a minister apparently led Parliamentarian troops in singing Psalm 68. The translation is not mentioned, but it would surely have been Sternhold and Hopkins. David Starkey and Katie Greening, *Music & Monarchy* (London: BBC Books, 2013), p. 159.

seventeenth-century standards and an experiment that does not seem to have been repeated.⁷⁰

A further complication to this categorical distinction has to do with the kinds of musical setting composed for the Psalms. The singing Psalms of the Sternhold and Hopkins type were written in a narrow range of simple metres designed to be easily singable to the tunes popularized in Germany, France, and (later) England, all of them having melodic arcs that correspond to and reinforce the lines of verse, whether the single line (as in the eight syllables of common metre) or in pairs (stretching across two lines). The most famous melody associated with the psalter, the 'Old Hundredth', sung to William Kethe's 'All people that on earth do dwell', is a good example.⁷¹

The melody for the first line begins at a comfortable medium pitch (for both men and women) and descends a fourth stepwise along the scale, then leaps back to the original pitch and ascends three notes higher, creating a sense of incompleteness that needs to be resolved in the second line, which begins on that same higher note, descends to the original pitch, then leaps up a fourth for a second descending half-line. This also ends on a pitch that is unresolved, leaving the singer or listener with a desire for one further descending step, which the melody satisfies on the first note of the third line. The phrase descends only to reascend to the pitch where it began. The final melodic phrase begins with a large leap up to the highest pitch in the whole tune, which descends by an arpeggio and a closing figure that resolves the tune decisively. The full range of the tune is only an octave, and most of the time it ranges just a few notes above and below the opening and closing pitch. These Psalms were all strophic, the same melody repeated for each stanza (or sometimes pairs of stanzas), verse after verse.⁷² Most parishioners had limited musical knowledge and ability, and

---

⁷⁰ The song is 'Come let us sound with melody', no. 21 from *A Book of Ayres* (London: Peter Short, 1601), a collection co-written with Philip Rosseter.

⁷¹ The tune first appeared with an English Psalm (100) in the fourth edition of the Anglo-Genevan *Form of Prayers and Ministration of the Sacraments* (1560), but it was printed earlier in a French Geneva psalter of 1551, *Pseaumes octantetrois de David*, for use with Theodore Beza's Psalm 134. See Quitslund and Temperley, II, 723–25. All musical transcriptions are mine.

⁷² This does not necessarily reflect Sternhold's original intention and practice, however, since his Psalms were written to be sung at court to Edward VI. A manuscript of Sternhold's

the demands made upon them were minimal (though editions of Sternhold and Hopkins were printed with instructions on music and singing, and some, like many modern hymnals, included four parts). This was in fact part of the logic behind Luther's use of Psalm paraphrases and hymns, that if you could convey them upon singable, memorable tunes, even borrowing already popular tunes from secular songs, you could spread reformed teachings quickly and effectively.

If the Psalms of the Sidneys and those like them were sung, on the other hand, it was not in church, nor would the popular congregational Psalm tunes have been suitable to the complex forms of their verse. A different style of music would have been required, more like that of secular lute songs, still strophic but composed individually according to the specific, often more complex, stanza form.[73] Anonymous settings in just this style do survive, in fact, for Mary Sidney's Psalms 51 and 130.[74] Campion's two Psalm paraphrases provide good examples. His Psalm 137, 'As by the streams of Babylon', has a simple melody that a congregation might manage:

Psalm 4 survives in a lutebook from the Edwardian period with a musical setting described by Nicholas Temperley as 'in a style influenced by the contemporary pavan, suited to dancing as well as singing', but in either case inappropriate for use in church. See Quitslund and Temperley, II, 514–20; Temperley, '"All skillful praises sing": How Congregations Sang the Psalms in Early Modern England', *Renaissance Studies*, 29.4 (2015), 531–53.

[73] Quitslund, 'Teaching Us How to Sing?: The Peculiarity of the Sidney Psalter', *Sidney Journal*, 23.1–2 (2005), 83–110.

[74] See Katherine R. Larson, *The Matter of Song in Early Modern England: Texts in and of the Air* (Oxford: Oxford University Press, 2019), pp. 53–63. Larson includes photographs of the manuscript and, in a companion recording accessible online, performs both settings with a lutenist accompanying. These are successful settings and beautiful lute songs, Larson demonstrating how a sensitive singer can accommodate many of the poetic effects in performance. The Sidneys might well have delighted in this music, if they had heard the songs performed, but this does not mean that they intended their Psalms for singing, and this is a very different kind of music than that to which Sternhold and Hopkins' Psalms were sung. As Quitslund points out, moreover (as Larson acknowledges), many of the Sidney Psalms would prove more challenging to composers than 51 and 130. Quitslund, 'Teaching Us How to Sing?', p. 103.

The accompaniment, however, or the other three parts (if sung in harmony), contains more chromaticism (occasional accidentals for harmonic colour) than is usual in church settings, as well as a rather complex cadential figure in the alto. Campion's Psalm 130, 'Out of my soul's depth to thee', is much more complex harmonically and melodically, well beyond the skills of ordinary churchgoers:

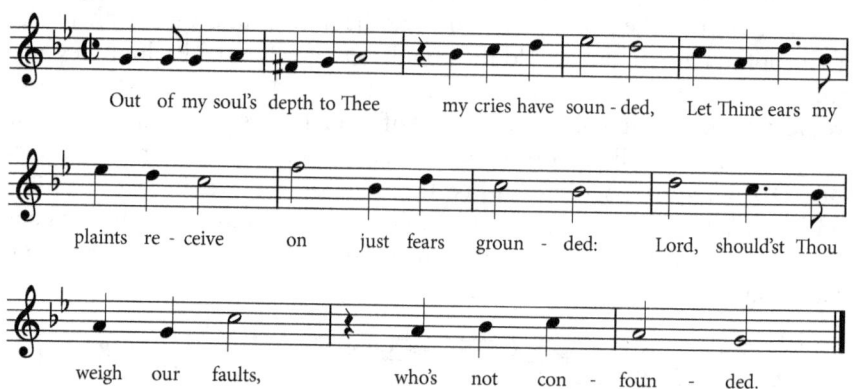

The development of music publishing in the later sixteenth century allowed composers and printers (William Byrd had a monopoly from 1587) to cater to the interests of those who could both afford the books and perform this music, accompanying themselves on the lute or orpharion.

Literature. In an earlier study, I attempted a further distinction among English metrical Psalms between those written primarily for church worship or devotion and those written with a 'literary' purpose. I confessed at the time (in a footnote) to some reservations about the category of the 'literary', since, as I wrote then, 'the Psalms produced by many translators writing for primarily liturgical or devotional purposes are clearly works of "literature" in some senses of the term'.[75] In fact, this is true in almost every sense of the 'term', a term which is of dubious application to early modern writing in any case. According to the *OED*, 'literature' in the sense of 'written works considered collectively; a body of literary works' dates from the early eighteenth century, while the qualitative sense of 'written works valued for superior or lasting artistic merit' is a mid-nineteenth-century development. Etymologically, 'literature' means simply letters, writing, or scholarship, and the latter was also the prevailing sixteenth-century usage, as when Sir Francis Bacon praises James I for being 'so learned in all literature and erudition, divine and human'.[76]

---

[75] Hannibal Hamlin, *Psalm Culture and Early Modern English Literature* (Cambridge: Cambridge University Press, 2004), p. 10, note 35.
[76] Sir Francis Bacon, *The Two Books of Francis Bacon. Of the Proficience and Advancement of Learning, Divine and Human* (London: [Thomas Purfoot and Thomas Creede], for Henry Tomes, 1605), sig. A3ᵛ.

What I was trying to articulate was not that the Sidney Psalms are better poems than Henry Dod's, though I suspect most readers would agree that they are. Such an evaluation misses a fundamental point, I think, that the Sidneys and Dod had different goals, whatever their differing abilities. Dod had no intention of producing 'poems', but was simply trying to remedy a problem in the Sternhold and Hopkins psalter: some of the tunes provided for the Psalms were too difficult, he felt, but the Psalms texts that fit them didn't fit the other popular tunes. So Dod took it in hand to provide texts that fit the easier tunes, most in double common metre.[77] He confesses no 'presumption or rashness', and defers to anyone 'better learned' who might do a superior job. There is no evidence, on the other hand, that Philip and Mary Sidney intended their Psalms to be used in worship, and despite the few surviving musical settings, it seems unlikely they intended them for singing either, since their formal variety would require a different tune for almost every Psalm (including the twenty-two sections of Psalm 119), and most would have to be newly composed. Furthermore, the formal complexity of the Sidney Psalms, often making subtle use of enjambment and medial caesuras, parenthesis, internal rhyme, chiasmus, acrostics, and other devices, would be largely bulldozed by any musical setting, especially strophic ones that effaced variations among stanzas. These were Psalms to be read, as poems, just as were the secular poems of Philip Sidney's *Astrophil and Stella*, Donne's love poems, or Shakespeare's sonnets.[78] The goal of the Sidneys, which they achieved, was to 'translate' the Psalms into the most sophisticated English poems conceivable in Elizabethan England, such that they realized the 'highest matter in the noblest form' (as Donne put it) of the original Psalms of David, inspired by the Holy Spirit.

As so often, however, such distinctions tend to blur at their borders, or perhaps even at their centres. The Sidneys, for instance, surely also had religious motives in translating the Psalms.[79] Donne was not simply praising the Sidney Psalms for their excellence as poems, but because, as he put it,

---

[77] Quitslund and Temperley, II, 572–73.

[78] There was an enormous number of poems written for singing at this time, and as acknowledged above one could set to music even poems not intended for singing, whatever the results. There has recently been a renewed appreciation of the relationship between lyric poetry and music in the period, which has advanced our understanding of the culture in many ways, but I remain sceptical of claims that most lyric poems, whether Psalms or secular verse, were written or printed to be sung. The poems we know were written for singing (like Henrician courtly songs, lute ayres, madrigals, singing Psalms) seem generally well suited to musical setting in terms of rhythm, metre, and the treatment of line ends. Others, like many poems by Wyatt, Gascoigne, Sidney, Donne, or Herbert, do not. For a different yet still balanced view, see Scott Trudell, *Unwritten Poetry: Song, Performance, and Media in Early Modern England* (Oxford: Oxford University Press, 2019), pp. 54–58.

[79] Furthermore, it seems the Sidney Psalms were also sometimes used for the private devotional reading of the Psalms, since two manuscripts (I BL MS Add. 12047 and K BL MS Add. 46372) were annotated according to the Psalms designated for reading at Morning and Evening Prayer in the BCP. Such annotations do not imply use in worship, since one of the

> these Psalms are become
> So well attired abroad, so ill at home,
> So well in chambers, in thy church so ill,
> As I can scarce call that reformed, until
> This be reformed.[80]

The target of his criticism is clearly Sternhold and Hopkins, the metrical Psalms sung in English churches, as opposed to those (like the Marot-Beza psalter) sung in foreign churches, or those (like the Sidneys) confined to English chambers. This doesn't necessarily mean the Sidney Psalms are being sung in chambers, nor does it mean that Donne wishes they were sung in church, and when he says 'they teach us how to sing', anticipating that day when in the heavenly choir we shall all 'sing our part', he uses singing in a broad, figurative sense, including writing poetry, praying, and participating in the divine harmony (perhaps imagining something like the Pythagorean proportional 'music' of the spheres). But Donne's praise is thoroughly focused on the Psalms as biblical, sacred poems, and the reform he has in mind is not just an aesthetic movement but the Protestant Reformation. Mary Sidney's dedication of the Sidney Psalms to Queen Elizabeth also focused on the religious, justifying her presumption in presenting them, since 'A king should only to a queen be sent', and 'God's loved choice [given] unto his chosen love, | Devotion to devotion's president'.[81] For a queen, only the poems of a king like David are worthy, the Psalms of one divinely appointed monarch for another, a work of devotion for devotion's 'president', probably meaning both governor and patron (as head of the Church) and model or exemplar (i.e. 'precedent', since the two words could be spelled identically). Psalm translation had a devotional purpose for the Sidneys, just as it surely did for Dod, Sternhold and Hopkins, and everyone else included in this volume, and reading their Psalms could equally be an act of devotion, with which any appreciation of the poetry as poetry was probably inextricably intertwined.

Blurring the border from the opposite side, Sternhold's motives may well have been 'literary' as well as devotional, since to write a poem in common, or what came to be called 'Sternhold's' metre does not make it any less a poem, and he was writing for king and court (even if King Edward was only 10 or 12 years old). Like so many of those who wrote metrical Psalms, Sternhold was responding to the popularity of secular, even scandalously erotic, poems and

---

ways the regular devotional reading of the Psalms was organized was according to these listings. On this practice, see Specland, 'Competing Prose Psalters and Their Elizabethan Readers'.

[80] John Donne, *Poems, by J. D.* (London: M. F. for John Marriot, 1635), p. 367.

[81] Mary Sidney Herbert, Countess of Pembroke, 'Even now that care', in *The Collected Works of Mary Sidney Herbert, Countess of Pembroke*, ed. by Margaret P. Hannay, Noel J. Kinnamon, and Michael G. Brennan, 2 vols (Oxford: Clarendon, 1998), I, 103.

songs, aiming to supplant them with a more godly alternative. As he writes to King Edward in his preface, 'your tender and godly zeal doth more delight in holy songs of verity than in any feigned rhymes of vanity'.[82] John Hall seems to have Sternhold's preface in mind as he writes his own dedication to John Bricket of Eltham, 'I thought you had more delight and pleasure to read or hear, or sing the word of God in metre than any other rhymes of vanity and song of bawdry the which of long heretofore hath been used rather than any other thing profitable for the body or soul'.[83] Hall's later *Court of Virtue* was specifically designed to replace *The Court of Venus*, containing love poems by Wyatt and others, and Hall's 'My lute awake and praise the Lord' was included as a sacred parody of Wyatt's popular 'My lute awake'. Many readers will probably feel that Wyatt's is still the better poem, but it's not clear that Wyatt had 'literary' ambitions and Hall did not. Hall's prologue to *The Court of Virtue* is a dream vision in (tetrameter) rhyme royal in which he sees 'fair ladies three': Faith, who heals the wound in his heart made by justice, Love, who embraces him, and Virtue (called Arete, Christianizing the classical ideal of excellence), who takes him by the hand and teaches him about human vice, urging him to write his book. They all kiss him and then depart for heaven, at which point he wakes with his purpose. The model is obviously Chaucer, probably his *Parliament of Fowls*, a dream vision in which the narrator is led through the temple of Venus, while Hall's Arete condemns 'Venus court' (the symbolic dwelling as well as the book).[84] The poem demonstrates both Hall's knowledge of English poetry and his ambition to steer it in a different direction with his own contribution, even if his talents were modest.[85]

Even in terms of literary influence it may be difficult to distinguish Sternhold (if not Hall) from the Sidneys. Though the Sidney Psalms were not printed until the nineteenth century, they circulated widely in manuscript, had a powerful and formative influence on George Herbert and were admired by Donne and Milton. The Sternhold and Hopkins Psalms possibly had a much greater influence, however, given how many millions of English men and women sang them in the sixteenth and seventeenth centuries, as well as the number of other

---

[82] Thomas Sternhold, 'Preface', *Certain Psalms Chosen Out of the Psalter of David* (London: Edward Whitchurch, 1549), sig. A3ʳ.

[83] John Hall, *Certain Chapters Taken Out of the Proverbs of Solomon* (London: Thomas Raynald, 1550?), sig. [A4ʳ].

[84] For more on Hall's evident learning, see Russell A. Fraser's introduction to his edition, *The Court of Vertue by John Hall (1565)* (New Brunswick: Rutgers University Press, 1961).

[85] Robert Southwell, a far greater poet than Hall but with the same ambition, wrote a sacred parody of Edward Dyer's love poem 'A Fancy' entitled 'Dyer's Fancy Turned to a Sinner's Complaint', and also lamented that 'finest are 'stilling Venus' rose: | In paynim toys the sweetest veins are spent; | To Christian works few have their talents lent'. Southwell, 'The Author to the Reader', in *Collected Poems*, ed. by Peter Davidson and Anne Sweeney (Manchester: Caracanet, 2007), p. 63.

singing Psalms they spawned, in Scotland and North America as well as England. Out of Sternhold and Hopkins came also the Protestant hymn in the same metres, popularized throughout the English-speaking world by Isaac Watts, Charles and John Wesley, Christopher Smart, William Cowper, and so many more. The common metre, whose commonness may owe far more to Sternhold than to the English ballad, shaped the later poetry of Emily Dickinson, A. E. Houseman, James Fenton, and countless others.[86] Nonetheless, aware of many possible objections and qualifications, I persist in making a distinction, however tentative, between those with a particularly strong motive to write Psalms that might be considered great poems according to the standards of early modern English prosody, and those whose primary motives were religious and devotional, whatever else they included.

One further comment on the Psalms and literature or poetry has more to do with modern prejudices than early modern intentions. It is a commonplace of literary history that the dominant form of poetry in the Renaissance was the Petrarchan love lyric. Thousands of such poems, especially sonnets, were written across Europe between 1400 and 1700, and in England the so-called Golden Age of poetry was marked by the sonnets of Sidney, Spenser, and Shakespeare, along with lesser lights like Samuel Daniel, Michael Drayton, Fulke Greville, and Lady Mary Wroth. As should be evident from this anthology, at least as many Renaissance men and women wrote metrical Psalms as Petrarchan sonnets, including a large sample of the great poets of the age. Shakespeare wrote no Psalms, it seems, but Sidney did, as did Spenser, though his do not survive.[87] If we must also exclude Daniel, Drayton, and Greville, the list of Psalms poets does include Sir Thomas Wyatt and Henry Howard, Earl of Surrey, George Gascoigne, Mary Sidney Herbert, Countess of Pembroke, Sir Philip Sidney, John Donne, George Herbert, Alexander Montgomerie, Phineas Fletcher, Thomas Carew, Richard Crashaw, George Sandys, and John Milton, as well as (later) Henry Vaughan, John Oldham, and Sir John Denham. Continental Psalms poets include Marot and Beza, but also Philippe Desportes, Christine de Pizan, Jacques Davy du Perron, Guillaume du Vair, Pietro Aretino, Laura Battiferri, Luigi Alamanni, Luis de León, Jorge de Montemayor, Luís de Camões, Jan Utenhove, Martin Luther, Martin Opitz, Simeon Polotskii, Jan Kochanowski,

---

[86] William Wordsworth's Lucy Poems, for instance, or Edna St. Vincent Millay's 'The Betrothal', Henry Wadsworth Longfellow's 'The Children's Hour', Thomas Hardy's 'The Darkling Thrush', W. H. Auden's, 'As I Walked Out One Evening', to name just a few.

[87] On Shakespeare, see Alison Shell, 'Why Didn't Shakespeare Write Religious Verse?', in *Shakespeare, Marlowe, Jonson: New Directions in Biography*, ed. by Takashi Kozuka and J. R. Mulryne (Burlington: Ashgate, 2006), pp. 84–112. According to William Ponsonby, he was trying get hold of and publish some works of Spenser that have not survived, including 'The Seven Psalms', presumably a version of the Penitential Psalms. See Jack B. Oruch, 'works, lost', in *The Spenser Encyclopedia*, ed. by A. C. Hamilton (Toronto: University of Toronto Press, 1990, repr. 1997), pp. 737–38.

Jiří Strejc, and Albert Szenczi Molnár. The writers of literary histories have considered love sonnets literature and metrical Psalms as something other, but this distinction is outdated and simply wrong, and it should be recognized that the Psalm dominated and shaped Renaissance poetry just as much as the Petrarchan lyric.[88]

Voice. For the past two centuries, much of the writing on lyric poetry has focused on voice, and the Psalms offer an unusual though also perhaps useful testing ground for such debates. John Stuart Mill wrote that 'eloquence is heard, poetry overheard', poetry being also 'feeling expressing itself to itself, in moments of solitude'.[89] Over a century later, T. S. Eliot distinguished three voices of poetry: the first (corresponding to Mill's) is 'the poet talking to himself — or nobody', the second 'the voice of the poet addressing an audience' (what Mill called 'eloquence'), and the third 'the voice of the poet when he attempts to create a dramatic character speaking in verse'.[90] Eliot admitted that in any actual poem these voices tend to overlap. At roughly the same time, Reuben Brower argued that all poems are dramatic, 'someone speaking to someone else', but that both speaker and audience are fictional constructs, the voice we hear never actually that of the author, 'however piercingly real'.[91] Helen Vendler rejects the idea that poems are overheard, stating that 'the act of the lyric is to offer its reader a script to say'. 'One is to utter them as one's own words, not as the words of another', she continues, in reference to what she terms the 'private literary genres', including 'Psalms, or prayers printed in prayer books, or secular lyrics'.[92] Heather Dubrow hears a polyphony comprised of many voices in the Renaissance lyrics she studies.[93] Proponents of the New Lyric Theory, on the

---

[88] Also worth noting are the Psalm translations that incorporate and perhaps seek to subsume the conventions of secular Petrarchan lyric, such as (among Psalms in this anthology) Wyatt's Penitential Psalms, Surrey's Psalm 88 and headnote to Psalm 73, Mary Sidney's Psalm 73, and John Davies of Hereford's Psalm 32. See Danielle Clarke, '"Lover's Songs Shall Turne to Holy Psalmes": Mary Sidney and the Transformation of Petrarch', *Modern Language Review*, 92.2 (1997), 282–94.
[89] John Stuart Mill, 'Thoughts on Poetry and Its Varieties', *Dissertations and Discussions*, 2 vols (London: John W. Parkers and Sons, 1859), I, 63–94 (p. 71).
[90] T. S. Eliot, 'The Three Voices of Poetry [1953]', in *On Poetry and Poets* (New York: Octagon Books, 1975), pp. 96–112 (p. 96).
[91] Reuben Brower, 'The Speaking Voice', in *The Lyric Theory Reader: A Critical Anthology*, ed. by Virginia Jackson and Yopie Prins (Baltimore: Johns Hopkins University Press, 2014), pp. 211–18 (p. 211).
[92] Helen Vendler, *The Art of Shakespeare's Sonnets* (Cambridge, MA: The Belknap Press of Harvard University Press, 1997), p. 18.
[93] Heather Dubrow, *The Challenges of Orpheus: Lyric Poetry and Early Modern England* (Baltimore: Johns Hopkins University Press, 2008), pp. 32–33.

other hand, stress that 'there is no literal voice in the poem: voice is an oral metaphor employed in the description and analysis of the written word'.[94]

When poems are read or sung out loud, we obviously hear a voice reading or singing them, and in the period when all of these Psalm translations were written it was still common to read aloud, even when alone.[95] Even when we read poems silently, however, we can hear a voice in our heads. It may be that poems have no literal voice, in the limited sense that a volume of poems alone in the woods makes no sound. As soon as a poem is read, however, there is a voice. The voice in my head as I read is not audible to others, and I don't hear it with my ears, but it is not a metaphor. Even audible voices are not, strictly speaking, heard with the ears; the ears receive sound waves and these are passed on through the eardrum, tiny bones, the fluid in the cochlea, the basilar membrane, and still tinier hair cells, where eventually electrical signals are produced that are carried along the auditory nerve to the brain, which processes them as sounds I can understand. Since the ultimate producer of sound, or at least the phenomena I experience as sound, is the brain, the sounds I 'hear' in my mind are not perhaps very different from those I hear in the world. Unless we suffer from certain kinds of mental illness, we can distinguish between real and imagined sounds, but presumably the brain produces the imagined ones on the basis of the real, on what we have actually heard before. So the voice I hear in my mind as I read is real, not metaphorical, even if it is 'real' in a different way from my actual speaking voice.[96]

This voice may be my own, an internalized version of my speaking voice, but it is also an imaginative construction of the voices of the poet or the speaker of the poem. Brower may be right to caution that we should distinguish poet from speaker, since the voice of the speaker is always to some extent a fictional creation of the actual poet. On the other hand, the same could be said of any words uttered in our presence by the actual poet (or anyone else). We can never know whether the words we read or hear perfectly reflect the true inner self of the writer or speaker (assuming we believe in such a self). But we can perceive

---

[94] Virginia Jackson, 'Voice', in *The New Princeton Encyclopedia of Poetry and Poetics*. Yopie Prins concurs, asking 'Why do we insist on reading literally what the Victorians understood to be a metaphor?', though she offers no evidence for this Victorian understanding, nor does she explain why it is so urgent, as she claims it is, to 'reverse our tendency to read these poems as the utterance of a speaker, the representation of speech, the performance of song'. Prins, 'Voice Inverse', *Victorian Poetry*, 42.1 (2004), 43–59.

[95] Paul Saenger, *Space Between Words: The Origins of Silent Reading* (Stanford: Stanford University Press, 1997).

[96] As anyone who has listened to themselves on a recording knows, moreover, my voice as I hear it myself is startlingly different from my voice as others do. Is my own voice then, as I myself hear it, at least to some extent an imagined sound? From a religious perspective, moreover, one might say with John Trapp, 'The voice which is made in the mouth is nothing so sweet as that which comes from the depth of the breast' (*A Clavis to the Bible, or, A New Comment Upon the Pentateuch: or Five Books of Moses* (London, 1650), p. 117).

degrees. We assume that Robert Browning is not the speaker of 'Porphyria's Lover', since that speaker describes strangling his lover with her own hair, something we hope Browning never did. When we read Henry King's 'Exequy', however, mourning his dead wife, we feel sure that the speaker of the poem is indeed King, however carefully he has crafted his expression of loss. Most poems lie in between the two poles represented by these examples. Shakespeare's sonnets have tempted many readers to try to identify the young man and so-called 'Dark Lady' who are the objects of the poet's tangled affections, but there is no evidence these were real people, nor that the speaker of the sonnets should be identified with Shakespeare himself. That the speaker of the sonnets is a poet, rather than a pirate or a bishop, encourages the reader to suppose that Shakespeare may have fashioned him to some degree out of his own external and internal experience, but reading the sonnets is not the same experience as reading someone's private correspondence with their lovers, and countless readers have surely read them as if they were to some extent their 'own words', as Vendler puts it, though this is surely only partly true. In Evelyn Waugh's satirical novel *The Loved One*, the protagonist Dennis Barlow seduces the young mortuary cosmetician Aimée Thanatogenos by selecting poems out the *Oxford Anthology of English Verse* and passing them off as his own original expressions of love in verse. We recognize this as ridiculous, not only because of Aimée's naïveté but because the idea of any twentieth-century lover pretending that Shakespeare's 'Shall I compare thee to a summer's day', Tennyson's 'Now sleeps the crimson petal', and Housman's 'On your midnight pallet lying' are their own actual words is absurd. This doesn't mean, however, that Dennis could not have read them to Aimée as poems not his own but expressing what he felt, or that he could not have read them (to himself or to her) hearing them in his own voice.

When Athanasius advised Christians to turn to the Psalms in various circumstances, he understood that his readers might make the words of the Psalm their own, expressing their own personal emotions and needs. That these words were also those written by the Psalmists hundreds of years earlier presented no difficulty. In times of crisis or heightened emotion, human beings often resort to conventional language. When offering condolences to the bereaved, for instance, few of us have the imagination and conviction to say something original, so we turn to the comfortably tried and true: 'I'm so sorry for your loss', 'she's in a better place', 'at least his suffering is over'. In times of joy we do the same: 'congratulations', 'you seem so happy together', 'you must be so proud'. Such conventional phrases can seem insincere, but they need not be. Sometimes the conventional is just what we want to hear.[97] The Psalms are

---

[97] There may also be an element of the phatic about such phrases, the term linguists use for expressions without meaning in themselves but that are important in social interactions. Thus, saying to someone 'How are you?' does not necessarily mean we really want to hear at length; it can simply serve as a warm greeting.

far more complex than such phrases, of course, but they can work in a similar way. Psalm 23, 'The Lord is my shepherd, I shall not want', has been read, spoken, and sung by millions over the millennia, and its power to comfort and console does not diminish.[98] Psalm 137 has also been popular as an expression of loss, alienation, resentment, and anger, and the very specific circumstances of the Jews in exile in Babylon, with harps hung on trees, has not impeded those in exile in other countries at other times, or those who have felt alienated in their own country, or even those for whom earthly life was itself a condition of exile from eternal life in heaven.[99] Jesus said on the cross, according to Matthew and Mark, 'My God, my god, why hast thou forsaken me?' This is the first verse of Psalm 22, so was Jesus asking this anguished question himself, or just quoting the Psalm? As mentioned above, Christians have traditionally interpreted Psalm 22 as a prophecy of Christ, so Jesus could also be confirming or fulfilling the prophecy. But he could be doing all of these, and since Jesus is God (for Christians), all-knowing, all-inspiring, and ever-present, we could say that his utterance on Golgotha was actually the original, the Psalm imitating it prophetically (even in the past). Despite the theological complexity, however, the synoptic gospel writers (Matthew, Mark, and Luke) presumably thought it important that Jesus should have a human moment of agony and despair in his suffering, just he does in the garden of Gethsemane (Matthew 26. 36), and this is compatible with the fulfilment of prophecy. In the Gospel of Luke, Jesus cries at the end, 'Father, into thy hands I commend my spirit' (Luke 23. 46). In Acts, written by the same author, Stephen, the first Christian martyr, cries 'Lord Jesus, receive my spirit' (Acts 7. 59), in obvious imitation of Jesus himself. Countless subsequent Christians have used the same last words, including apparently St Basil (379), Charlemagne (814), Jan Hus (1415), Martin Luther (1546), Bishop Nicholas Ridley (1555), Philip Melanchthon (1560), John Knox (1572),

---

[98] In 2021, Sarah Eberle received a Gold Award at the Chelsea Flower Show for 'The Psalm 23 Garden' (Stephanie Mahon, 'Chelsea Flower Show 2021 Sanctuary Garden Profile', *Country Living*, 29 August 2021 <https://www.countryliving.com/uk/homes-interiors/gardens/a37317967/chelsea-flower-show-the-psalm-23-garden-the-bible-society/> [accessed 24 May 2022]). US Poet-Laureate Jo Harjo, a member of the Muscokee/Creek Nation, writes in her memoir, *Poet Warrior*, that she cherishes Psalm 23 as a 'prayer poem of protection' (New York: W. W. Norton, 2021), p. 57.

[99] In 2015, Will Butler of the band Arcade Fire wrote a song based on Psalm 137 for *The Guardian* based on its coverage of Isis's ransacking of the Mosel Museum (<https://www.theguardian.com/music/2015/feb/27/will-butler-final-song-for-the-guardian-by-the-waters-of-babylon> [accessed 24 May 2022]). The *Denver Catholic Register* reported on the local impact of the global flu pandemic, quoting a parishioner who lamented 'We feel like the Children of Israel in exile, as they watched by the waters of Babylon and wept when they remembered Sion' (Aaron Lambert, 'Looking Back at the 1918 Flu Epidemic in the Archdiocese of Denver', 29 July 2020 <https://denvercatholic.org/looking-back-at-the-1918-flu-epidemic-in-the-archdiocese-of-denver/> [accessed 24 May 2022]).

Torquato Tasso (1595), the Jesuit Father St John Francis Regis (1640), the Scottish Covenanter Donald Cargill (1681), and Lady Jane Grey (1553/54), sister-in-law to the Dudley brothers whose Psalms are included here. These men and women were surely aware that the words they were speaking had been spoken by Jesus, but they were also their own personal expressions at the hour of death. And Jesus was himself, again, quoting the Psalms: 'Into thine hand I commit my spirit' (Psalm 31. 5, KJV); 'Into thy hands I commend my spirit' (Psalm 31. 5, BCP).

Another of the many peculiarities of the Psalms involves the relationship between singular and plural. Although most of them are written in the first person, they have also been said and sung collectively, which undermines Mill's distinction between poetry and eloquence. When 'I will lift up mine eyes unto the hills' is sung by five hundred people together is it still a personal utterance? Or should the text be changed to 'we lift'? Ramie Targoff has noted that just these kinds of changes were made in some Psalms quoted in the Book of Common Prayer in order to adapt them for group worship.[100] Thus, 'O Lord open thou my lips' from Psalm 51 becomes 'O Lord open thou our lips' in the opening of the versicles and responses for Morning and Evening Prayer. Yet in Sternhold and Hopkins, William Whittingham's Psalm 51 remains in the first person throughout, though it too was sung collectively by whole congregations. Psalm 51 is also among the most intensely personal of the Psalms, traditionally understood (as described in the superscription) to be the Psalm composed and sung by David in remorse for his adultery with Bathsheba and murder of her husband Uriah. 'Have mercy upon me, O Lord', he prays, and begs forgiveness for his 'bloodguiltiness' in Coverdale's powerful coinage. David then acknowledges that God desires not animal sacrifices but a 'broken and contrite heart', although when the walls of Jerusalem are built, God will indeed be pleased 'with burnt offering and whole burnt offering' (Psalm 51. 1, 14, 17–19). Even if one subscribes to the view that all humans became corrupt after the Fall, few actually commit murder, and not everyone commits adultery as David did. One would think, then, that the specific details in this Psalm would stand in the way of most readers or singers making the words their own, reading or singing them in their own voices. Curiously, however, just the opposite seems true. The close, detailed association with David, his sins, and his penitence draws people to Psalm 51 all the more powerfully, as if the more clearly they hear David's own voice, the more encouraged they are to join their voice to his.

Moreover, as I've argued before, those translating and paraphrasing the Psalms emphasised and reinforced the Davidic details rather than suppressing them.[101] Wyatt's paraphrase is perhaps a special case, his interpolated linking

---

[100] Ramie Targoff, *Common Prayer: The Language of Public Devotion in Early Modern England* (Chicago: University of Chicago Press, 2001), pp. 28–35.
[101] Hamlin, *Psalm Culture*, pp. 191–92.

narratives (adapted from Aretino) elaborating the story. But Francis Sabie adds a similar framing stanza to his 'David's Ode', reminding his readers that 'thus did the psalmist warble out his plaints'. Anne Vaughan Lock's 'David' (or Thomas Norton's, if he was the author) cries for absolution from 'guilt of guiltless blood', and prays, 'strike me not with thy revenging sword'. In his immensely popular *Seven Sobs of a Sorrowful Soul for Sin*, William Hunnis adds penitential precedents beyond David, including Jonah, Naman, Adam, Moses, Peter, Hezekiah, and Mary Magdalene. Penitence seems, like misery, to love company. On Ash Wednesday, to mark the beginning of the penitential season of Lent, the whole company of English Christians gathered in their churches for the service of the Commination of Sinners, at the centre of which was the collective recitation of Psalm 51, in Coverdale's translation, 'Have mercy upon me, O God after thy great goodness'. And though millions of men and women across the country were saying these words at the same time, the pronouns remained singular: me, my, I.

Some Psalms also include more than one voice. Psalm 2, for instance, begins with the voice of the Psalmist (in this case unspecified) asking 'Why do the heathen so furiously rage together?', but then describes kings and rulers conspiring against God. Verse 3, 'Let us break their bonds asunder', seems to be the voice of the conspirators, and then we are told that the Lord shall 'have them in derision', saying, 'I have set my king upon my holy hill in Zion'. Verse 7, 'I will declare the decree: the Lord hath said unto me, Thou art my son, this day have I begotten thee', takes some parsing. The last sentence is clearly spoken by God, introduced by the Psalmist, who may also be the one saying 'I will declare', the 'decree' being God's statement about his son. God continues to speak in verses 8 and 9, but at some point it seems the Psalmist takes over, perhaps in verse 10, certainly by 11 and through to the end. There are no quotation marks or other indicators of indirect speech in the Hebrew or Greek, nor in the Latin Vulgate, nor in early modern English translations. There is sometimes, as a result, uncertainty as to just who is speaking, further blurring, or perhaps blending, voices.

In both reading aloud and reading to myself, however, I can adjust for other voices, those quoted in a poem, as are God's and the kings' in Psalm 2. To some degree the voice is still mine, but it is also not mine, or at least differentiated from my normal voice, as it would be if I were doing a vocal impression. This is the polyphony or heteroglossia Dubrow describes (borrowing the latter term from Mikhail Bakhtin). In any case, these voices are all still real, not metaphorical, though of course this is not the same as saying that I am actually listening to the voices of the ancient kings. The voice of God, however, may be more complicated. Much of the theoretical writing on lyric poetry written over the past century has failed to consider the peculiar properties of religious poetry from the perspective of the religious believer. The Bible, for many believers, is the Word of God. If this is so, is it not possible that when such believers read words said to be actually spoken by God, in Psalms or elsewhere, they might, in some special sense, hear God's actual voice? God's voice can do peculiar things, as when Adam and Eve 'heard the voice of the Lord God walking in the garden' (Genesis 3. 8). One Jewish exegetical tradition, including the work of David Kimchi, Maimonides, Ibn Ezra, and Sa'adia Gaon, holds that this verse should be taken literally and that what is walking is not God, but God's voice itself, however mysterious this seems.[102] Christian readers have generally preferred a more rational explanation, with the 'voice' being the sound made by God's walking, or God simply talking as he walks through Eden.

Yet even if for Christians God's voice is not ambulatory, it is understood to be able to do things human voices cannot. Thomas Bilson, for instance, paraphrasing Augustine's commentary on Psalm 86, explains the Psalmist's statement, 'thou hast delivered my soul from utmost hell' (86. 13).[103] These are David's words, Bilson begins, but they are also Christ's, since it is Christ who delivers believers' souls from hell by his own descent there after his death. But 'those are Christ's words in the psalm, not by man's conjecture, but by the Apostle's exposition, where he saith; thou hast not left my soul in hell'. (Peter preaches in Acts 2. 27 that David was speaking of Christ when he said, 'Because thou wilt not leave my soul in hell, neither wilt thou suffer thine Holy One to see corruption'.) Bilson continues, 'So that this verse, Thou hast delivered my soul from the nethermost hell, is either the voice of Christ in this psalm, or it is our voice in the person of Christ our Lord, because he therefore went to hell, least we should abide (forever) in hell'. The words are David's, but they are really Christ's, as Peter points out when he says them, but they are also our own, since the whole point is that Christ (the logical antecedent of 'thou') delivers our souls from hell.

Another instance of divine ventriloquism appears in John Bale's account of *The Latter Examination of Anne Askew*, when at the end he directs an apostrophe to Bishop Nicholas Shaxton, once a reformer but who had recanted and was sent to examine Askew as a test of his orthodoxy: 'O Shaxton, I speak now unto thee and (I think) in the voice of God. What devil bewitched thee to play this most blasphemous part as to become of a faithful teacher, a tempting spirit?'[104] God's voice is channelled through Bale's, or at least so he believes. God's voice is more regularly heard speaking through 'Moses, the Psalms, and the Prophets, and so forth in the whole evangelical, and apostolical Scripture', as the Danish theologian Niels Hemmingsen writes, but Thomas Vincent

---

[102] Marc Shell, *Talking the Talk & Walking the Walk* (New York: Fordham University Press, 2015), pp. 41–49.
[103] Thomas Bilson, *The Effect of Certain Sermons Touching the Full Redemption of Mankind by the Death and Blood of Christ Jesus* (London: Peter Short for Walter Burre, 1599), p. 187.
[104] John Bale, *The Latter Examination of Anne Askew* (Marburg [i.e. Wesel by D. van der Straten], 1547), fols 39^{r-v}.

discusses the voice of God at greater length, noting that while he can if he wishes 'speak with man's voice' (though he 'hath no mouth nor tongue as man doth'), he can also speak in 'extraordinary ways', as when he gave the law to Moses on Mount Sinai, or in the destruction of Jerusalem, or in 'the cry of the stones and walls, of timber and beams in their fall and flame', during the Great Fire of London'.[105] If God can speak through stones and timber, speaking through Psalms should be no problem.

Even if one sets aside (while not discounting) phenomena of voice dependent upon faith, the experience of the Psalms blends together many voices, none of them metaphorical.[106] In addition to the reader's voice, projected or internalized, the voice of the Psalmist as represented in the Psalm, along with the voices represented by indirect speech, there is also the voice of the translator. Just as the author's voice seems more present in some poems than others, so too the translator's voice may be louder or softer depending on whether we are particularly conscious of the Psalm as a translation. I suspect most singers of Sternhold and Hopkins thought little of the translators as they sang, though this may have been less true of those reading from copies of the printed text. In many of these, the initials of the translators were printed with the Psalm texts, so the title of Psalm 2, for instance, read 'Quare fremuerunt. Psal. ii. T.S.'.[107] There was no key to these initials, so readers might not have known who 'W. K.' or 'N.' were, but 'T. S.' and 'I. H.' should have been obvious. In many churches, however, especially smaller parishes, congregations practiced lining out, in which each line of the Psalm would be sung (or perhaps read, if the tune were well known) by a leader, the congregation then repeating it in call-and-response fashion.[108] If only the leader was reading from a printed psalter, then obviously the congregation would have no way of knowing the translator, though it is possible that since the collection was popularly known as 'Sternhold and Hopkins', many might have thought of those two as the translators of the whole. Congregations may have been even less aware of Coverdale as the translator of the Psalms in the Book of Common Prayer, since he is not named anywhere. Anyone reading a manuscript of the celebrated Sidney Psalms, however, would surely be very much aware of the translators, so that their voices (either or both) blended with David's and the others. This is in fact exactly what Donne describes in his poem on these Psalms, playing on various vocal doublings. The first

---

[105] Niels Hemmingsen, *The Way of Life*, trans. by Nicholas Denham (London: [W. Howe] for Richard Jones, 1578), p. 25; Thomas Vincent, *God's Terrible Voice in the City* ([London?], 1667), pp. 2-3.

[106] For another critique of the argument that lyric voice is metaphorical, see David Nowell Smith, *On Voice in Poetry: The Work of Animation* (Houndmills and New York: Palgrave Macmillan, 2015), pp. 1-14.

[107] *The Whole Book of Psalms* (London: John Day, 1569) STC 2439.5.

[108] Temperley, *Music of the English Parish Church*, I, 81, and throughout.

doubling is in David himself, described by Donne as combining with the 'cloven tongue' of the Holy Spirit, inspiring him to sing the 'highest matter in the noblest form', and the Sidneys as another pair made one by the Spirit, Philip and Mary together the organ and God the harmony. Donne goes on to imagine further harmonies: heaven, earth, and the heavenly spheres; God and man (Jesus, 'tuned' by God); and the heavenly choir to which everyone, including Donne, aspires. Whether Donne is expressing sacred mysteries or indulging in extended metaphors is a matter of personal belief. The blend of David's voice with those of the Sidneys, however, requires no leap of faith.

Allusion and Fiction. In an influential article, Roland Greene proposed that sixteenth-century English poets were exploring 'the boundaries between what we might call the ritual and the fictional dimensions of lyric', and that metrical Psalms were at the forefront of this exploration (even if critics had not recognized it).[109] The ritual dimension is the lyric poem as script for performance, not in Vendler's universal sense that we read all lyric in our own voice, but in the narrower sense involved in actual ritual, as when prayers like the Book of Common Prayer's General Confession are recited together, as instructed by the priest ('make your humble confession to almighty God, before the congregation here gathered together in his holy name, meekly kneeling upon your knees'), and as scripted in 'The Order for the Administration of the Lord's Supper, or Holy Communion'. The General Confession is not a poem, but the Psalms of Sternhold and Hopkins are, and when they are sung congregationally as part of the worship service, they exemplify lyric as ritual (according to this argument). The fictional dimension is lyric as 'represented speech', as described by Barbara Herrnstein Smith: 'what is central to the concept of the poem as fictive utterance is not that the "character" or "persona" is distinct from the poet, or that the audience purportedly addressed, the emotions expressed, and the events alluded to are fictional, but that the speaking, addressing, expressing, and alluding are themselves fictive verbal acts'.[110] Fictional lyrics resist assimilation by the reader, the voice of the poem remaining distinctly other (according to this view).

The complexities of voice in the Psalms have been discussed earlier, but one aspect of the 'fictive' deserves its own space: allusion. Greene points out, for instance, that verse 15 of Philip Sidney's Psalm 7 is a possible allusion to his earlier secular sonnet sequence, *Astrophil and Stella*. The Psalmist states,

---

[109] Roland Greene, 'Sir Philips Sidney's "Psalms", the Sixteenth-Century Psalter, and the Nature of Lyric', *SEL*, 30.1 (1990), 19–40.
[110] Barbara Herrnstein Smith, *On the Margins of Discourse: The Relation of Literature to Language* (Chicago: University of Chicago Press, 1978), p. 28, cited in Greene, 'Sir Philip Sidney's "Psalms"', p. 21.

> Lo, he that first conceived a wretched thought,
>   And great with child of mischief travailed long,
>   Now brought abed, hath brought naught forth, but naught.[111]

In the first sonnet of *Astrophil and Stella*, Astrophil struggles to find a way to begin writing, describing himself as 'great with child to speak, and helpless in my throes'.[112] There is no equivalent for Sidney's Psalm stanza in the translations of Psalm 7 by Coverdale or Sternhold, though it is a reasonable version of the statement that the wicked man 'hath conceived sorrow, and brought forth ungodliness' (Psalm 7. 15, BCP). Greene suggests that Sidney is here presenting the Psalm's generic wicked man as Astrophil, 'Sidney's other powerful and notorious lyric character — or someone like him'.[113]

This seems all the more persuasive given Mary Sidney's allusion in her own Psalm 73 to the fifth sonnet of Philip's *Astrophil and Stella*, in which Astrophil opens with the pious acknowledgement, 'It is most true that eyes are formed to serve | The inward light', only to cast it aside in the conclusion, 'and yet true that I must Stella love'.[114] Mary's Psalm begins,

> It is most true that God to Israel,
>   I mean to men of undefilèd hearts,
>   Is only good, and naught but good imparts.
> Most true, I see, albe I almost fell
>   From right conceit into a crooked mind
> And from this truth with straying steps declined.[115]

As I argue in the note to these lines (note 565), Mary's allusion constitutes a gentle rebuke to her late brother, at least in his Astrophil persona, the Psalm acknowledging the danger of falling even while knowing better, but going beyond the secular poem in not succumbing to the temptation. Implicit is also a comment on the relative superiority of sacred over secular lyric, Psalms over sonnets. All the more intriguing, then, that Philip seems to be making exactly the same move in his Psalm 7, as Greene argues, anticipating Mary's rejection of both Astrophil and Petrarchan sonnets.

Does this make the Sidneys' Psalms more fictive, though, at least in terms of the fictive mode as Herrnstein Smith describes it? Or does it rather make the Sidney Psalms all the more personal for them, following Athanasius's advice to Christians to adapt the Psalms to their own situations, making David's voice

---

[111] Sir Philip Sidney, trans., Psalm 7, *The Sidney Psalter: Psalms of Sir Philip and Mary Sidney*, ed. by Hannibal Hamlin, Michael G. Brennan, Margaret P. Hannay, and Noel J. Kinnamon (Oxford: Oxford University Press, 2009), p. 19.

[112] Sidney, *Astrophil and Stella*, in *The Countess of Pembroke's Arcadia* (London: William Ponsonby, 1598), p. 519. This is the edition upon which modern editions are based.

[113] Greene, 'Sir Philip Sidney's "Psalms"', p .34.

[114] Ibid.

[115] See below (73), p. 348.

their own? Sidney's Psalm 7 is not written in the voice of Astrophil, after all, but as one (like Sidney?) who recognizes Astrophil as just the sort of man the Psalmist condemns and from whom he prays for protection. 'Astrophil' is certainly a fiction, despite Sidney's self-referential gameplaying with 'Phil' and his Stella, but he is not given voice in the Psalm, just referenced as a character, and covertly at that, by means of the implications of allusion. If the allusion leads a discerning reader to hear Sidney's own voice more distinctly, it doesn't silence David's, or even the reader's own, and all of these voices remain not metaphorical, but real.[116]

The Sidneys are not the only translators to employ allusion. Wyatt's Penitential Psalms, for example, allude many times to conventions of both epic and Petrarchan love poems (see notes 116, 117, 129, 140, 143, and 156 to main text), and Surrey also alludes to Petrarchan conceits in his Psalms (see notes 91, 107). A number of the more educated Psalm translators allude to classical gods and goddesses, surprising as it seems to find these in biblical poetry: Stanihurst and Fraunce both have God dwelling on Olympus (Psalms 2 and 50, respectively), and Sir David Murray inserts Aeolus, Phoebus, and Thetis into his Psalm 104. Lock (or perhaps Norton) alludes to Wyatt's Psalm 51 in her own paraphrase of that Psalm (see notes 130 and 242), and the allusion is all the more appropriate since her paraphrase is a sonnet sequence, and Wyatt was largely responsible for importing the sonnet into England. Carew's Psalm 51 alludes to Mary Sidney's, taking her unusual phrasing of verse 15, 'Unlock my lips', shifting it to the first verse and elaborating it into a military metaphor: 'Good lord, unlock thy magazines | Of mercy'. Another allusion to Wyatt's Psalms may be Matthew Parker's use of the singular word 'sparpled' (scattered) in his Psalm 44: 'Thou letst us all: as sparpled sheep' (and in his Psalm 106, God is described as vowing to cast out the seed of the sinful Israelites and to 'sparple them as runagates'). Wyatt's Penitential Psalms opens with a description of David smitten with Bathsheba, 'With creeping fire sparpled for the nonce'. The word is uncommon and appears in no other Psalm translations.

Allusion is a common figure in the Bible, of course, as in the striking instance of Christ alluding to Psalm 22 on the cross, though what for one reader is an allusion to another is the fulfilment of prophecy, as in the other elements of Psalm 22 that feature in the Crucifixion narrative: the piercing of hands and

---

[116] There are other allusions to *Astrophil and Stella* in the Sidney Psalms. Zim (200–01) notes that Mary Sidney's Psalm 73, line 73, 'O what is he will teach me climb the skies?' alludes to Philip's sonnet 31, which begins, 'With how sad steps, O moon, thou climbst the skies'. In Mary's Psalm 51, the Psalmist confesses, 'My truant soul in thy hid school hath learned'. Since Astrophil, in the opening sonnet, is biting his 'truant pen' in frustration at his inability to write, Mary is again both acknowledging a debt to her brother and moving beyond him, or perhaps thinking that they have both moved beyond *Astrophil and Stella* in writing Psalms rather than secular love poems.

feet, the casting lots over the vesture. But many intra-biblical allusions do not involve the theological and temporal complexities of typology. Psalm 11. 6 alludes to the destruction of Sodom and Gomorrah, Psalm 33. 7 alludes to the division of the waters in both Genesis and Moses's Song of the Sea in Exodus (15. 8), and the Song of the Sea is also alluded to in Psalms 48. 6–7 and 76. 7. As Alter (who notes the preceding allusions) points out, there may even be an allusion in Psalm 104. 24, 'The lions roar for prey, seeking from God their food', to a fourteenth-century BCE Egyptian hymn to the sun connected to Pharoah Akhenaten.[117] In fact, for at least the past forty years the study of intra-(or inner) biblical allusions has been a scholarly growth industry.[118] When Job says to his interlocutors, 'What is man, that thou shouldest magnify him? and that thou shouldest set thine heart upon him?' (Job 7. 17), he is not just expressing traditional wisdom but alluding to Psalm 8, 'What is man, that thou art mindful of him? and the son of man, that thou visitest him?' (Psalm 8. 4), which is interpreted by some scholars as bitterly ironic, and by at least one other as a mocking rebuttal of his friend Eliphaz.[119] The description of the plagues visited upon Egypt in Psalm 78. 43–51 not only references the description of the event in Exodus 12 but alludes to its specific language.[120] Isaiah (or really Deutero-Isaiah) alludes to Psalm 37. 26–29 when he writes,

> The sun shall be no more thy light by day; neither for brightness shall the moon give light unto thee: but the LORD shall be unto thee an everlasting light, and thy God thy glory.
> Thy sun shall no more go down; neither shall thy moon withdraw itself: for the LORD shall be thine everlasting light, and the days of thy mourning shall be ended.
> Thy people also shall be all righteous: they shall inherit the land for ever, the branch of my planting, the work of my hands, that I may be glorified. (60. 19–21)

---

[117] Robert Alter, *The Book of Psalms: A Translation with Commentary* (New York and London: W. W. Norton and Co., 2009), p. 66.

[118] The seminal study was Michael Fishbane, *Biblical Interpretation in Ancient Israel* (Oxford: Clarendon Press, 1985), though of course readers of the Bible have been aware of allusions, borrowings, and intertextual relations within and between books (and Testaments) throughout its history.

[119] Charles Yu, 'A Ridiculous God: Job Uses Psalm 8.5 [4] to Respond to Eliphaz', in *Inner Biblical Allusion in the Poetry of Wisdom and the Psalms*, ed. by Mark J. Boda, Kevin Chau, and Beth LaNeel Tanner (London and New York: T&T Clark, 2018), pp. 83–101.

[120] Jeffrey M. Leonard, 'Identifying Inner-Biblical Allusions: Psalm 78 as a Test Case', *Journal of Biblical Literature*, 127.2 (2008), 241–65. Leonard points out that the Psalmist also adapts the narrative to eliminate the inconsistency in Exodus when hail is described as wiping out all of Egypt's crops and then locusts are sent to consume the same crops that have already been destroyed. In the Psalm, the hail destroys just vines (and frost kills sycamores), but the locusts are also shifted to before the hail, so they have plenty to consume.

One interpreter suggests that the Isaiah author is using this and other allusions to Psalm 37 as well as Jeremiah in order to revisit and counter the arguments of the earlier prophet.[121] The use of the metaphor of washing away sin, used by both Isaiah ('Wash you, make you clean', 1. 16) and Jeremiah ('For though thou wash thee with nitre, and take thee much soap, yet thine iniquity is marked before me, saith the Lord God', 2. 22), is alluded to in Psalm 51. 2 and 7 ('Wash me thoroughly from mine iniquity'; 'wash me, and I shall be whiter than snow').[122]

These allusions are all complex, and there is much more to say about them, but the salient point here is simply that the Bible, like any complex secular literary work, is a dense web of allusions. Thus, when translators add their own allusions to English Psalms translations or paraphrases, this does not introduce a foreign trope to the biblical texts, even when Philip and Mary Sidney allude to Philip's secular love poetry, since the Bible itself alludes to extra-biblical, non-Jewish and non-Christian texts as well as to itself, as in the example from Psalm 104 mentioned above, or when Paul alludes to the Greek playwright Menander and the Cilician poet Aratus in 1 Corinthians 15. 33 and Acts 17. 28.[123] The Bible is a work of fiction, not that it is 'made up' but that it is a work full of self-conscious literary craft. Yet parts of the Bible have also always been used in ritual, especially the Psalms, but also the other Old and New Testament songs, and passages like the Passover rite, the scapegoat ritual in Leviticus 15, or the Lord's Prayer. Greene is surely right that there are ritual and fictional aspects of lyric, but as he admits, no lyric is either purely one or the other, and the distinction seems to have more to do with conditions of use and the attitude of the reader or singer than with any intrinsic features.[124] Moreover, it is not clear that the identification of the reader with the speaker of the poem depends upon the ritual element, nor that the fictional element makes this identification more difficult. What Gary Kuchar concludes about the poems of George Herbert is all the more true of the Psalms that so influenced Herbert's poetry: 'the lyric as medium places us in a concrete situation with an implied backstory, an evolving present, and a particular speaker, one whose potential exemplarity does not efface the force of the particular'.[125]

---

[121] Benjamin D. Sommer, *A Prophet Reads Scripture: Allusion in Isaiah 40-66* (Stanford: Stanford University Press, 1998), pp. 111-12.
[122] Lesley DiFrancisco, 'Identifying Inner-Biblical Allusion through Metaphor: Washing Away Sin in Psalm 51', *Vetus Testamentum*, 65.4 (2015), 542-57.
[123] James Clackson, *Language and Society in the Greek and Roman Worlds* (Cambridge: Cambridge University Press, 2015), p. 150.
[124] 'All poems, I think, hold the ritual and fictional modes in some relation to each other', he writes ('Sir Philip Sidney's "Psalms"', p. 22).
[125] Kuchar continues, 'the ritual element of lyric as an event in the participating consciousness of the reader combines with the fictive element as exegetical process in order to encourage spiritual neatness rather than distraction', 'neatness' being a spiritual as well as

Obviously, this is only true if readers and singers understand the language of the Psalms they are reading and singing, and Eamon Duffy has recently raised some remarkable questions about the Psalms before the Reformation. The usual cliché in Protestant descriptions of medieval religion is that because the Bible and liturgy were in Latin, the laity were alienated from worship, reduced to watching the rites performed without being able to understand the 'hocus pocus' of the Mass (the word for the babble of magic spells derived from the liturgy's *hoc est corpus meum*, 'this is my body'). As one of the proponents of the revisionist history of the Reformation, strongly contesting the view that medieval Catholicism was corrupt and in decline, the people desperate for reform, Duffy would have no patience with the progressivist view. Yet he is willing to confront the peculiarity of a lay devotional practice that involved the reading of Latin by those who could not understand it. For most medieval Christians, the Psalms were experienced either as chanted in church or chapel by the clergy or as selected and arranged in books of hours, which were designed for private devotion.[126] Focusing on the latter, Duffy concludes that the vast majority of users of these books 'will have prayed the psalms rapidly, without close comprehension of the precise meaning of the Latin'.[127] This, surely, is the true ritual extreme, the Psalms scarcely experienced as language, let alone as 'lyric', and this practice has surprising and intriguing implications. First, devotional reading did not involve understanding but performance, the assumption being that the spiritual effect depended on the act of recitation purely as an act, without any sense that the words became one's own. Second, the effect depends upon the recitation being done in the sacred language of Latin, regardless of whether one understands it. Duffy cites *De Laude Psalmorum* ('In Praise of the Psalms'), attributed to Augustine and included in many medieval psalters, which makes clear that it 'was the *ipsissima verba* of the psalmist — as it were, his original Latin — which worked these transformations and purifications [washing away sin, driving out demons, etc.], *ex opera operatum*'.[128] Any translation of the Psalms would thus have an entirely different status than those read by later English Protestants, and even perhaps by later Catholics — as a potentially useful crib bringing one closer to the original, but useless in its own right and not in any sense a substitute for the Latin.

---

aesthetic state toward which Herbert strove, amidst the increasing spiritual and political 'distraction' of seventeenth-century England; 'Introduction: Distraction and the Ethics of Poetic Form in *The Temple*', *Christianity & Literature*, 66.1 (2016), 4–23 (p. 15).

[126] Duffy does the math and concludes that in the Sarum Office of the Blessed Virgin used in English books of hours, only about fifty-five Psalms were included, in standard groupings like the Penitential Psalms, the Gradual Psalms, the Office of the Dead, etc.

[127] Duffy, 'The Psalms and Lay Piety', p. 67.

[128] Meaning 'from the work performed' (as opposed to from the person performing it). Duffy, 'The Psalms and Lay Piety', p. 62.

Selection

I have cast as wide a net as possible for this anthology, in order to represent the remarkable diversity of what I have called 'Psalm culture'. The chronological scope was determined by the Tudor and Stuart focus of the MHRA series, though I have played somewhat fast and loose with the terminal date. Any Psalms printed up to 1633 were fair game, but when there was uncertainty about the dating of manuscripts, I favoured the earlier end of a range and allowed myself the benefit of any doubt. In order to yoke in a few more interesting Psalms and Psalm translators, I have also felt justified in including examples known to have been written before 1633, even if (like Milton's and Crashaw's) they were printed later. The Tudor and Stuart Translations series is also admirably inclusive of Scots as well as English translations, reflecting what one might call the un-Englishing of or the archipelagic turn in the history of the British Isles in recent decades.[129] Scotland was a separate kingdom until 1707, but it was under the same monarch as England from the accession of James VI and I in 1603, and there was considerable cultural interaction before that. Including Psalms in Welsh, Irish, or Cornish might have even better reflected the diversity of peoples inhabiting the archipelago, but these (unlike Scots) are not comprehensible to English speakers. The history of these translations is not accommodating either: a Welsh translation of the Bible was printed in 1588 and there were several versions of the Psalms in metre (1595, 1603, 1621), as well as a 1567 Book of Common Prayer, but no Old Testament in Irish was printed until 1690 (though a New Testament was published in 1602). Portions of Matthew were translated into Cornish in the later seventeenth century, and a few Psalm fragments in the eighteenth, but no complete Bible (or psalter) until the twentieth. A metrical psalter was printed in Scots Gaelic (as opposed to Scots) in 1694, but the complete Bible was not available until 1801 (apart from earlier translations in manuscript). The Bible was even translated into Manx (spoken on the Isle of Man), but not until 1767 (NT) and 1772 (OT), though a Manx Book of Common Prayer, including the Psalms, was translated by Bishop John Philips, completed by 1610.[130] A nod at least is given to these Celtic peoples and languages by including Psalms by Welshmen who wrote in English (Roger Edwardes, Thomas Salisbury) as well as two by Michael Cosworth, who lived in Cornwall even if he was born in London. The Irish are represented by Richard Stanihurst, appropriately enough given his contribution to the history of Ireland in Holinshed's *Chronicles*.

Some of the Psalms included here (like Coverdale's) are so familiar as scarcely

---

[129] See, for instance, John Kerrigan, *Archipelagic English: Literature, History, and Politics, 1603–1707* (Oxford: Oxford University Press, 2008).

[130] *The Book of Common Prayer in Manx Gaelic Being Translations Made by Bishop Phillips in 1610, and by the Manx Clergy in 1765*, ed. by A. W. Moore assisted John Rhys, vol. I (London: Henry Frowde, 1895), pp. ix–xxii.

to need reprinting, but to omit them would seriously skew the overall picture. Some are well known among the various works of their translators, others known only to specialists but still available in print. Still others are either scarce (William Patten's exceptionally rare broadsides) or entirely obscure, printed here for the first time (the Psalms of William Forrest, John Stubbs, Edmond Scory, Sir John Glanville, and Henry Clifford, fifth Earl of Cumberland, for instance). There are Psalms by kings and queens (James VI and I, Katherine Parr), the nobility (the Earls of Surrey, Warwick, Leicester, and Cumberland, and the Countess of Pembroke), as well as a humble silkman (Dod). Many of the translators were clergymen (John Donne, Henry Ainsworth, Phineas Fletcher, George Herbert), some even bishops (Coverdale, John Bale, Thomas Bickley, Joseph Hall) or archbishops (Matthew Parker). It seems safe to say that all the translators were Christian, even the magician Simon Forman, though they were of very different sorts, from pillars of the Church of England to recusant or exiled Catholics like Forrest, Richard Stanihurst, William Byrd, Gregory Martin, George Flinton, Richard Verstegan, and Alexander Montgomerie. Among the Protestants, some were martyrs (Anne Askew, John Rogers), though some Psalm translators were also executed or mutilated for 'secular' reasons (Surrey, Stubbs). Some were among the Puritan component of the English Church, like the contributors to the Geneva Bible (Anthony Gilby) and the Sternhold and Hopkins psalter (William Whittingham, William Kethe, Thomas Norton). Some, like Ainsworth, were more radical separatists. A number of women Psalmists are also featured, including Askew, Parr, and Mary Sidney, as well as Anne Vaughan Lock (perhaps), Elizabeth Tyrwhit, and Lady Anne Blount or Anne Brydges (another case of uncertain attribution). Some of these translators are known best as poets (Wyatt, Surrey, Gascoigne, the Sidneys, Barnabe Barnes, Campion, Donne, Herbert, George Wither, Thomas Carew, Crashaw, Milton), others as major translators (Norton, Arthur Golding, Sir John Harington, Joshua Sylvester, George Sandys). Some are known as writers, but not poets, let alone Psalm poets (Stubbs, Forman, Sir Thomas Smith, Sir Edwin Sandys, Sir Francis Bacon). About some we know little to nothing at all (Thomas Bentley, John Pits, Thomas Bownell, Joseph Bryan, Robert Fills, and the ever-mysterious Anon.). Together these Psalm translators make up a surprisingly wide cross-section of Tudor and Stuart English society, something that is not true for the English translators of any other works.

   A further word should be said about my definition of both 'Psalm' and 'translation'. I favour a very broad use of the latter, since no attempt to offer a precise taxonomy of different approaches to an original text works well for this period. Some would distinguish translation from paraphrase, the latter often looser, more expansive, less strictly faithful to the text. Still broader, we might say, are adaptations or (as they might be called in devotional contexts) meditations. Late in the seventeenth century, John Dryden offered a range stretching from metaphrase (the most literal, translation proper) to imitation, with paraphrase in between.[131] Dryden's 'metaphrase' was idiosyncratic, however, few others even using the term, and many might have reversed imitation and paraphrase, since paraphrases can be very broad and imitations fairly close. Imitation, moreover, seems a different category of practice, not primarily intended to convey an original into a different language but to demonstrate the ability of the imitator. Many also used the term 'Englishing', which would seem to cover any act of translation, though as mentioned above some Psalm translators were really turning one or more existing English versions into another, as when prose was converted to poetry. Etymologically, translation is a matter of transportation, carrying something from one language into another. No translation can ever be perfectly literal, and even those that claim to be faithful usually involve at least some measure of interpretation and adaptation. Languages are simply not perfectly equivalent. Since critics usually run into trouble when they try to force their neat categories onto an unruly body of materials, and it is obvious enough that there is a different approach to the original Psalms reflected in, say, Gilby's careful rendering of the Hebrew for the Geneva Bible, Wyatt's English verse paraphrase of an Italian prose paraphrase of the Penitential Psalms, or the Sidneys' ingenious but relatively compact metrical Psalms versus the almost unending expansion of William Hunnis's *Seven Sobs*, calling all of these translations is unlikely to cause great confusion, provided attention is paid to the kinds of translation being exercised.

Questions might also be raised about my inclusion of 'Psalms' that do not correspond to any of the Psalms in the Hebrew Bible, what I have called (following Susan Felch) collage Psalms.[132] At a certain point in the Tudor-Stuart, post-Reformation history of psalmody in English, people began not only applying various individual Psalms according to their particular needs (as Athanasius recommended), but extracting verses from several different Psalms and rearranging them in new compositions that, presumably, more precisely suited their situation. A further development along these lines was the composition of entirely original 'Psalms', perhaps using biblical language and idioms, or just a psalmic style, but not identifiable as any of the biblical 150, in whole or part. Petrarch wrote a set of Penitential Psalms, for instance, that were entirely original, and George Chapman translated these into English in 1612, and Ralph Buckland's *Seven Sparks of the Enkindled Soul* (1604–05) contains powerful original Psalms, thoroughly in the biblical style (perhaps via

---

[131] John Dryden, preface to *Ovid's Epistles, Translated by Several Hands* (London: Jacob Tonson, 1680), sigs R8^{r-v}.

[132] Susan M. Felch, '"Halff a Scrypture Woman": Heteroglossia and Female Authorial Agency in Prayers by Lady Elizabeth Tyrwhit, Anne Lock, and Anne Wheathill', in *English Women, Religion, and Textual Production, 1500–1625*, ed. by Micheline White (Aldershot: Ashgate, 2011), pp. 147–66 (pp. 150–51).

Coverdale) and idiom. Interesting as the compositions are, they do not belong in this anthology, but including several collage Psalms allowed me to bring in some extremely interesting writers (Parr, Bownell, Tyrwhit, Forman) as well as to show another way in which the Psalms were translated or carried over into the lives of the British and Scottish people.

This technique might also be said to have its roots in ancient practice, since Psalm 19, for instance, is generally agreed to be an amalgamation of two different Psalms, one singing the praises of Creation, the other celebrating the Torah. Psalm 21 may also be a composite Psalm, since the first half addresses God, refers to the king in the third person, and a victory seems to have taken place, whereas in the second half it is the king who is addressed, God is referenced in the third person, and victory is hoped for in the future.[133] Psalms 14 and 53, moreover, are virtually identical, the standard explanation being that they derive from different traditions (North and South). Early modern readers had little sense of the textual history of the Hebrew Bible, but they could see for themselves the abrupt thematic and grammatic shifts and the repetitions, which may have had some influence on the practice of collage. The practice of extracting and recombining biblical verses in the Book of Common Prayer may also have contributed, though this practice derived from earlier medieval liturgies. Moreover, late medieval Books of Hours, at the centre of lay devotional practice and continuing in print long after the Reformation, include two catena of Psalm verses, the so-called 'Psalter of St Jerome' and 'St Bernard's Verses', a 'catena' (a string or series of writings) being essentially another name for the collage Psalm.[134]

Conclusions

Never before have so many different early modern English translations and paraphrases of the Psalms been collected together in one volume. This abundance alone should help readers realize the immense influence of these biblical poems on virtually every aspect of early modern English life and culture, not least its literature. But the sheer diversity of these dozens of versions of the Psalms (representing hundreds of others), which surely surpasses that of any other translated work, is also important for thinking about just what translation meant to early readers, what it did, and how it worked. There will no doubt be many surprises here for those coming to the volume with twenty-first-century presuppositions about translation. I hope these surprises will be productive. Some of these surprises may challenge expectations about attitudes toward and the treatment of the Bible as Scripture. I also hope that readers will appreciate these Psalms in as many ways as early modern readers did. Among much that

---

[133] Alter, *Book of Psalms*, p. 69.
[134] Duffy, 'The Psalms and Lay Piety', p. 63.

is mediocre and downright incompetent, there is great poetry here as well as great prose, which can be enjoyed aesthetically, though students and scholars of literature, the Bible, and religious, social, and political history may find them of intellectual interest as well, not that the aesthetic and intellectual are easily extricable from each other. I would hope too, however, that some readers will find these Psalms of spiritual value, just as (I am certain) every one of the writers in this volume did. I am not myself a person of faith, but I have powerful memories of the experience of the Psalms in the liturgies (primarily) of the Anglican Church of Canada and the Episcopal Church, and my deep interest in the Bible, religious literature, and the history of religion includes a genuine respect for faith and those who have it. This volume has been put together with the firm conviction that religious belief and aesthetic appreciation are not mutually incompatible but potentially reinforcing, just as were the devotion and literary craft of early modern writers.

It seems appropriate to close with a Psalm, so I turn to Coverdale's Psalm 148, expressing the united voices of all Creation in a great, universal song of praise:

> Praise the Lord upon earth: ye dragons and all deeps;
> Fire and hail, snow and vapours: wind and storm fulfilling his word;
> Mountains and hills: fruitful trees and all cedars;
> Beasts and all cattle: worms and feathered fowls;
> Kings of the earth and all people: princes and all judges of the world;
> Young men and maidens, old men and children, praise the name of the Lord.

* * *

This edition presented some challenges to the standard format of the series. As in other volumes, words that may be unfamiliar to a modern reader, either in themselves or in their context here, are glossed: in verse texts, these glosses appear in italics in the right-hand margin; in prose Psalms, glossed words have the symbol ° indicating they are to be found in the Glossary. Some more complicated matters are addressed in the footnotes.

Many Psalms feature both verse numbering and line numbering (some feature stanza numbering in roman numerals). Line numbering is given in the left-hand margin; this is for ease of this edition only. Verse numbering follows the practice of the original copy-text, thus practice varies throughout. Notable quirks of usage are discussed in the commentary.

FURTHER READING

The Bible

The bibliography on the Bible is vast and continually growing, but a good place to start is *The New Cambridge History of the Bible*, especially vol. III, *From 1450 to 1640*, edited by Euan Cameron (Cambridge: Cambridge University Press, 2016). The earlier *Cambridge History of the Bible* is also still useful.

FULTON, THOMAS, *The Book of Books: Biblical Interpretation, Literary Culture, and the Political Imagination from Erasmus to Milton* (Philadelphia: University of Pennsylvania Press, 2021)

Bible Translation

CAMPBELL, GORDON, *Bible: The Story of the King James Version, 1611–2011* (Oxford and New York: Oxford University Press, 2010)
HAMMOND, GERALD, *The Making of the English Bible* (Manchester: Carcanet Press, 1982)
NORTON, DAVID, *A History of the English Bible as Literature*, 2 vols (Cambridge: Cambridge University Press, 1993; rev. and repr. in one vol., 2000)
—— *The King James Bible: A Short History from Tyndale to Today* (Cambridge: Cambridge University Press, 2011)

Hebrew Poetry

ALTER, ROBERT, *The Art of Biblical Poetry* (New York: Basic Books, 1985)
BERLIN, ADELE, *The Dynamics of Biblical Parallelism* (Bloomington: Indiana University Press, 1985)
DOBBS-ALLSOPP, F. W., *On Biblical Poetry* (New York: Oxford University Press, 2015)
KUGEL, JAMES, *The Idea of Biblical Poetry: Parallelism and its History* (New Haven and London: Yale University Press, 1981)

Psalms

ALTER, ROBERT, *The Book of Psalms: A Translation with Commentary* (New York: W. W. Norton, 2007)
AUSTERN, LINDA PHYLLIS, KARI BOYD MCBRIDE, and DAVID ORVIS, eds, *Psalms in the Early Modern World* (Farnham: Ashgate, 2014)
DAHOOD, MITCHELL, ed., *Psalms I, II, and III*, The Anchor Bible, 3 vols (New York, 1965, 1968, and 1970)
DUGUID, TIMOTHY, *Metrical Psalmody in Print and Practice: English 'Singing Psalms' and Scottish 'Psalm Buiks', c. 1547–1640* (Farnham: Ashgate, 2014)

GREENE, ROLAND, 'Sir Philip Sidney's Psalms, the Sixteenth Century Psalter, and the Nature of Lyric', *Studies in English Literature*, 30.1 (1990), 19–40

GUNKEL, HERMANN, *The Psalms: A Form-Critical Introduction*, trans. by T. M. Horner (Philadelphia: Fortress Press, 1967)

HAMLIN, HANNIBAL, *Psalm Culture and Early Modern English Literature* (Cambridge: Cambridge University Press, 2004)

—— 'My tongue shall speak: the Voices of the Psalms', *Renaissance Studies*, 29.4 (2015), 509–30

HANNAY, MARGARET P., '"House-Confinéd Maids": The Presentation of Woman's Role in the *Psalmes* of the Countess of Pembroke', *English Literary Renaissance*, 24 (1994), 44–71

—— '"So May I With the *Psalmist* Truly Say": Early Modern English Women's Psalm Discourse', in *Write or Be Written: Early Modern Women Poets and Cultural Constraints*, ed. by Barbara Smith and Ursula Appelt (Aldershot and Burlington: Routledge, 2001), pp. 105–34

KING'OO, CLARE COSTLEY, *Miserere Mei: The Penitential Psalms in Late Medieval and Early Modern Literature* (Notre Dame: University of Notre Dame Press, 2012)

LEAVER, ROBIN, *Goostly Psalmes and Spirituall Songes: English and Dutch Metrical Psalms from Coverdale to Utenhove 1535–1566* (Oxford: Clarendon Press, 1991)

MOWINCKEL, SIGMUND, *The Psalms in Israel's Worship*, trans. by D. R. Ap-Thomas (Oxford: Blackwell, 1962)

QUITSLUND, BETH, *The Reformation in Rhyme: Sternhold, Hopkins and the English Metrical Psalter, 1547–1603* (Aldershot and Burlington: Ashgate, 1991)

ZIM, RIVKA, *English Metrical Psalms: Poetry as Praise and Prayer, 1535–1601* (Cambridge: Cambridge University Press, 1987)

Psalms and Music

MARSH, CHRISTOPHER, *Music and Society in Early Modern England* (Cambridge and New York: Cambridge University Press, 2013)

TEMPERLEY, NICHOLAS, *Music of the English Parish Church*, 2 vols (Cambridge: Cambridge University Press, 1979)

The Psalms in English

1. George Joye, *The Psalter of David in English Purely and Faithfully Translated after the Text of Feline* (1530)

[George Joye (1490/95–1553) was educated at Cambridge and elected fellow of Peterhouse. In the late 1520s Joye became the subject of ongoing investigations for heretical opinions and possessing heretical books. Fleeing to Antwerp, Joye announced his rejection of papal power in letters he printed in 1531. Joye's 1530 translation of the Psalms was the first complete psalter in English in the Reformation period. The Psalms were rendered into prose, and no music was included. Joye translated from the Latin translation of 'Feline' or Martin Bucer (his 1529 Psalms commentary, *Sacrorum Psalmorum Libri Quinque*, was published under the pseudonym Aretius Felinus). Although printed in Strasbourg ('Argentine' on the title page), these Psalms achieved wide dissemination, since not only was the psalter reprinted, but some of the Psalms were included in Joye's primer, the *Ortulus animae*, and in other Tudor primers like William Marshall's. His later 1534 psalter (see 3) was a translation from the Latin of Huldrych Zwingli. Joye was a prolific writer and translator. Both volumes were printed in Antwerp by Martin de Keyser, who printed Bible translations by Jacques Lefèvre d'Étaples, William Tyndale, and others. Joye published translations of Isaiah (1531) and Jeremiah (1534) and a massive study of Daniel (1545), incorporating much Reformation commentary, as well as works on the Lord's Supper, priestly marriage, and other controversial religious matters. In 1534 Joye published a revision of Tyndale's 1526 New Testament that caused a rift between the two reformers, Tyndale in his own 1534 revised New Testament charging Joye with rewriting rather than simply revising. Tyndale objected, for instance, to Joye's revision of 'resurrection' to 'the life after this'. A copy of the [1542?] edition of Joye's psalter belonging to Henry VIII contains the king's own annotations, often on verses on kingship, in red ink. See Charles C. Butterworth and A. Chester, *George Joye, 1495?–1553: A Chapter in the History of the English Bible and the English Reformation* (Philadelphia: University of Pennsylvania Press, 1962); Gerald Hobbs, 'Martin Bucer and the Englishing of the Psalms: Pseudonymity in the Service of Early English Protestant Piety', in *Martin Bucer: Reforming Church and Community*, ed. by D. F. Wright (Cambridge and New York: Cambridge University Press, 1994); Ian Christie-Miller, 'Henry VIII and British Library, Royal MS. 2 A. XVI: Marginalia in King Henry's Psalter', *Electronic British Library Journal*, 8 (2015), 1–19; H. L. Parish (Joye) and Alec Ryrie (Marshall) in *ODNB*.]

Psalm 1

Blessed is that man which walketh not in the counsel of the ungodly: and standeth not in the way of sinners, and sitteth not in the seat° of the pestilent scorners.
But hath all his pleasure in the law of the Lord: and upon it his mind is occupied,
5 both day and night.
Such a man shall be like a tree planted by the riverside: which will give forth her fruits in due time, and her leaves shall not wither: for whatsoever he shall do shall prosper.
But so shall not the ungodly: for they shall be like dust which is dispersed with
10 the wind.
Wherefore these ungodly shall not stand in the judgment: neither these sinners may abide in the company of the rightwise.°
For the Lord approveth the way of the rightwise: but the way of sinners shall perish.

2. George Joye, *Ortulus Animae: The Garden of the Soul: or, The English Primers* (1530)

[Joye had composed an earlier primer (1529?) of which no copy survives. Joye's revised primer (attributed to him by Butterworth and Chester), the single surviving copy of which was discovered in the British Library in 1949, drew heavily on Continental reformers and revised the calendar of saints' days, replacing traditional saints with Protestant martyrs. It was printed in Strasbourg ('Argentine') and condemned along with Joye's psalter in 1531. The *Ortulus* was the first known primer in English, though Latin devotional books of this kind were popular in the late Middle Ages. The collection contains liturgies, an account of the Passion, a catechism, various prayers, and excerpts from the Bible in translation, including Psalms. The Psalms, including the Penitential seven and thirty-nine others sprinkled throughout, were taken from Joye's 1530 psalter (complete with woodcut initials), translated from Martin Bucer's 1529 *Sacrorum Psalmorum Libri Quinque* (see 1). The *Ortulus* spawned a tradition of what Susan Felch terms 'Godly Garden' prayer books and primers, including William Marshall's *Primer in English* (see 4), Elizabeth Tyrwhit's *Morning and Evening Prayers* (see 50), and two versions of *A Godly Garden* published by Henry Middleton (1574, 1581), among many others. See Charles C. Butterworth, *The English Primers (1529–1545)* (Philadelphia: University of Pennsylvania Press, 1953); Butterworth and Chester, *George Joye*; Hobbs, 'Martin Bucer and the Englishing of the Psalms'; *Elizabeth Tyrwhit's 'Morning and Evening Prayers'*, ed. by Susan M. Felch (London: Routledge, 2008).]

Psalm 131

Domine non. [O Lord, I am not]

Lord, my heart is not proud, neither look I aloft: I take not stoutly° upon me in great matters, neither presume I in marvellous things above my estate.

But verily I repressed and put my soul to silence, like a weanling° from his mother's teat: even like a weanling was my soul in very deed.

5 Let Israel wait and trust upon the Lord: from this time into everlasting. Glory be to the Father.

3. George Joye, *David's Psalter, Diligently and Faithfully Translated by George Joye* (1534)

[Joye's second English psalter, printed in Antwerp, was translated from the Latin of Huldrych Zwingli, whose *Enchiridion Psalmorum* was printed in 1532.]

Psalm 19

The Title of the Psalm 19.
The song of David adhortatory.°
The Argument.
He compareth the brightness of the word of God unto the light of the sun, expressing the wholesome virtue thereof.

The heavens declare the almighty majesty of God: and the firmament showeth forth the work of his hands.

Every day preacheth the same: and every night layeth forth the same also unto our knowledge.

5 There is neither speech nor tongue: but among them are the voices of these all heard.

Into all the world goeth forth the speech of them: and their word is unto the world's end.

He hath set in them a tabernacle° for the sun: whence he proceedeth like a
10 bridegroom out of his chamber, and like a giant he dresseth himself to pursue his course.

From the one side of the heavens he goeth forth mightily to the other: and there is no man that may hide him[1] from his heat.

And even so is the law of the Lord perfect, restoring the mind: the testimony of
15 the Lord is true, teaching children wisdom.

The chastisings of the Lord are right, making glad the heart: the precept° of the Lord is pure, illumining the eyes.

The fear of the Lord is clean and firm forever: the judgements of the Lord are egall° and just.

---

[1] him] himself.

20   More pleasant than gold or any precious stone: and sweeter than either honey or the honeycomb.
   Which, whoso is thy servant, he keepeth° them: for in keeping them there followeth great reward.
   Who taketh heed unto his faults: absolve me from those sins which I know not.
25   And also from them which I have boldly committed that they have no dominion over me: for so shall I be purged and absolved from full great sin.
   Let the words of my mouth please thee: let the meditation of my heart be accepted unto thee, O Lord my rock and my Redeemer.

4. George Joye, *A Primer in English with Certain Prayers and Godly Meditations, Very Necessary for All People that Understand Not the Latin Tongue* (1534)

[The compiler of this primer, William Marshall (d. 1540?), was a translator and printer, beginning his career with a translation of Marsilio of Padua's political tract *Defensor pacis* (1533), which argued for limitations on the power of the pope. His translation of Martin Bucer's treatise against images caused considerable controversy, but his most influential work was his English primer, the first such to have official approval. Marshall also translated Girolamo Savonarola's popular meditation on Psalm 51 and Lorenzo Valla's refutation of the Donation of Constantine. Much of the material for Marshall's primer came from Joye's *Ortulus animae*, the Psalms in which were taken from Joye's earlier psalter translated from Bucer. See Butterworth, *The English Primers*; Parish (Joye) and Ryrie (Marshall) in *ODNB*.]

Psalm 119[2]

The argument into the C.xix. Psalm.
This Psalm declareth in how great price and reverence the saints or holy men have the laws of God: how earnestly they are occupied in them, how they sorrow to see them broken and said against of the ungodly: how they pray to be taught them of God, and to be acquainted and accustomed with them and, to be short, how they desire those men to be destroyed (whatsoever they be) which break and say against them.

Beati immaculati.   [Blessed are the pure]

Blessed are they which live pure and innocently, even them, I mean, which live after the law of the Lord. Blessed are they which observe his testimonies: and search them with all their heart. For they shall do no wickedness: that thus tread

---

[2] More than any other of the Psalms, Psalm 119, by far the longest in the book, reads very differently before the text was broken up into verses, as it first was with the Geneva Bible of 1560.

his ways. Thou hast commanded: that thy commandments should be kept with earnest diligence. Would God that my life were so instructed: that I might observe thy ordinances.° Then should I not be disappointed: when I shall have all thy commandments before mine eyes. I shall magnify thee with a pure heart: when I shall learn thy righteous judgements. I shall observe thy ordinances: forsake me not at any time. How should the young man amend his living? He shall well amend it in observing thy pleasures. With all my heart have I sought thee: suffer° me not to swerve from thy commandments. In my heart have I hid thy words: to th'intent I would not offend thee. Lord thou art praiseworthy: teach me thy ordinances. With my lips shall I show forth all the pleasures of thy mouth. I shall rejoice of the way which thy testimonies teach: as upon all manner of richesse.° Upon thy commandments shall I set all my mind: and shall set thy paths before my eyes. In thy ordinances shall I delight: and I shall not forget thy words. Reward thy servant, that I may live and observe thy pleasures. Uncover my eyes: that I may perfectly see the marvellous things in thy law. I am but a stranger in the earth: yet hide not thy commandments from me. My soul is broken with desire: to know at all times thy pleasures. Thou shalt sharply rebuke the ungodly: cursed are they that err from thy commandments. Take away from me opprobry° and ignominy, for I shall observe thy testimonies. Even the chief° rulers sit and speak against me: but yet thy servant is occupied ever in thy ordinances. Also thy testimonies are my delight and my counsellors. My soul cleaved to th'earth: restore me according to thy promises. My life I have showed unto thee: and thou hast granted me, teach me thy ordinances. Make me to understand the ways of thy commandments: and then shall I think upon thy marvels. My soul was melted away with sorrowful thoughts: make me stiff again according to thy promises. Turn thou away from me the deceitful way: and make thy law pleasant unto me. The true way have I chosen: and thy pleasures I set before my eyes. I cleaved to thy testimonies (O Lord) let me not be shamed. I shall run in the way of thy commandments: for thou wilt ease my heart. Teach me (Lord) the way of thy ordinances: and I shall mark it forever. Give me understanding and I shall keep thy law: I shall keep it with all my heart. Lead me by the path of thy precepts°: for in it is my pleasure. Bend my heart unto thy testimonies: and not unto lucre.

Turn away my eyes lest they behold vain things: in thy way quicken° me. Make fast° thy promises to thy servant: which is addict° unto thy worship. Turn away my shame which I feared: for thy judgements are favourable. Lo, I desired thy commandments: restore me for thy righteousness. Be present with me (O Lord) with thy mercy: come to me with thy help according to thy promises. That I might have to answer my revilers: for I stick to thy promises. Suffer not at any time the word of truth to be taken from my mouth: for I have respect unto thy ordinances. And I shall observe thy law studiously, ever world without end. I shall begin to be at large restrained with nothing: for I have sought thy commandments. I shall preach thy testimonies before kings: and shall not be confounded.° But shall delight in thy precepts, which I have loved. I shall lift up my hands to do thy precepts, which I have loved: and shall think busily upon thy ordinances. Remember thy promise to thy servant: unto the which thou hast caused me to trust. Thy promise is my comfort in my affliction: for it is it that restoreth me. These proud ungodly have scorned me sore: but yet I swerved not from thy law. I remember thy judgements which thou hast done from the beginning (Lord) and I was well comforted. It kindled my heart and fretted° me sore: to see these proud ungodly thus to forsake the law. Thy ordinances were my songs whiles I here wayfared a stranger. In the night shall I think upon thy name (O Lord) and I shall observe thy law. This grace hast thou given me: that I might observe thy commandments. Thou art my lot, Lord: I am full purposed to observe thy commandments. I long for thy presence with all my heart: have mercy upon me according to thy promises. I called to mind my ways and I turned my feet unto thy testimonies. I hasted myself and deferred not: to th'intent I would observe thy precepts. The ungodly congregation° hindered me sore: yet did I not forget thy law. At midnight shall I rise up to praise thee: for thy righteous judgements. I associate myself with all that worship thee, and with them that observe thy commandments. The earth is full of thy goodness Lord, nurture me in thy ceremonies. Thou hast dealt favourably with thy servant (O Lord) according to thy promise. Learn° me rightly to savour and to know: for I believe thy commandments. Before I was tamed with affliction I erred: but now I mark thy sayings. Thou art good and gracious: instruct me in thy ordinances. These proud ungodly framed together their painted lies against me, but I shall observe thy commandments with all my heart. Their gross hearts are congealed like tallow: but I shall delight in thy law. I was happy that thou tamed me with affliction: that I might yet so be instructed in thy ordinances. Better is the law of thy mouth to me: than thousands of gold and silver. Thy hands have fashioned and ordained me: give me understanding to learn thy commandments. They that fear thee shall be glad: to see me so to cleave to thy promises. Now know I, Lord, that thy judgements are right good: and that thou hast scourged me of good intent. But I beseech thee, let thy mercy be my comfort: according to those words which thou promised to thy servant. Let me be in thy favour, and I shall live: for thy law is my delight. Let these proud ungodly be confounded, for they go about to destroy me faultless: but yet shall I in the meantime set all my mind upon thy commandments. Let them that worship thee and know thy testimonies turn unto me. My heart shall be perfect in thy ordinances: wherefore I shall not be shamed. My soul fainted, longing after thy saving help: but yet I lift up my eyes unto thy promises. My eyes dazzled with looking up after thy promise: and I said, when wilt thou comfort me? I was dried away like a bladder[3] hanged in the smoke: but yet forget I not thy ordinances. How long shall thy servant suffer

---

[3] bladder] According to the Hebrew, an animal bladder used as a container. Synonymous with Vulgate Latin, *uter*. KJV has 'bottle'.

these things: when wilt thou at last give sentence against my pursuers? These proud ungodly digged pitfalls for me: which have no respect unto thy law. All thy precepts are faithful and true: they persecute me unworthily, help thou me. They had almost made an end of me in th'earth: but yet in no manner wise[4] forsook I thy commandments. Restore me for thy mercy's sake: and then shall I keep the testimonies of thy mouth.

O Lord, thy word standeth forever: in the heavens. From generation to generation continueth thy truth: thou hast set the earth, and it standeth still. The time continueth still according to thine ordinance: for all things are at thy commandment. Except thy law had been my delight: I had perished in mine affliction. I shall never, therefore, forget thy commandments: for by them thou hast refreshed me. I am thine, save thou me: for I searched thy commandments. The ungodly wait to destroy me: but I in the meantime shall endeavour me[5] to understand thy testimonies. I perceive that everything comprehensible hath an end: but thy commandments are incomprehensible.

Oh, how exceedingly loved I thy law: continually do I think thereof. Thou hast made me wiser than my enemies through thy precepts: for they are ever in my mind. I exceeded all my teachers in right understanding: for I am ever speaking of thy testimonies. I passed even the seniors° in true understanding: for I observe and mark thy commandments. From every evil path I refrained my feet: to th'intent I would observe thy speeches. I have not swerved from thy pleasures: for thou shalt instruct me. Oh, how sweet are thy speeches in my taste: they are sweeter than any honey in my mouth. I fetch my understanding at thy commandments: wherefore I hate every deceitful path. I have sworn and shall perform it to keep thy just pleasures. I am feebled with affliction: Lord restore me after thy promises. O Lord, I beseech thee, let the willing sacrifices of my mouth be accepted: and teach me thy pleasures. I myself bring my life ever into peril: but yet thy law do I not forget. These proud ungodly have set snares for me: but yet I swerved not from thy commandments. I have challenged thy testimonies for my perpetual heritage: for they are my heart's joy. I have bowed down my heart to do thy ordinances: yea, and that forever without end. The frantic hard-necked do I hate: and thy law have I loved. Thou art my lurking place and my shield: I wait for thy promises. Avoid° from me ye hurtful men: and I shall keep the precepts of my God. Strengthen me according to thy promises, that I may live: let me not, shamed, be disappointed of my hope. Stay° thou me, and I shall be saved: and I shall delight busily in thy ordinances. Thou shalt tread down all that err from thy ordinances: for all these crafty men's study, is to deceive with lies. Like rust thou rubbedst away all those proud ungodly of the earth: wherefore I loved thy testimonies. My flesh trembled for fear of thee:

---

[4] no manner wise] no way.
[5] endeavour me] i.e. endeavour (obsolete ethical dative).

and I fear thy judgements. All my mind was to do equity and righteousness:[6] leave me not to mine unjust vexers. Delight thy servant with good things: lest these ungodly make me sorrowful with their injuries. My eyes dazzled looking up for thy saving help: and waiting for the promises of thy righteousness. Deal with thy servant mercifully: and instruct me with thy ordinances. I am thy servant: make me to understand and know thy testimonies. It is time (Lord) to do judgement: for they have scattered abroad thy law. And therefore I loved thy precepts: above gold and precious stones. And for this I acknowledge all thy commandments to be righteous and I hate every false path. Marvellous are thy testimonies: wherefore my soul observeth them. To come but to the door of thy Scripture lighteneth: and giveth understanding to the unlearned. I drew in my breath faintly: for that I laboured so sore to attain unto. Behold and have thy precepts mercy upon me, according to thy judgements: wherewith thou governest the lovers of thy name. Rule my steps after thy pleasures: and suffer no iniquity to have dominion over me. Redeem me from the injuries of men and I shall keep thy commandments. Make thy face to shine upon thy servant: and instruct me in thy ordinances. Streams of water gushed out of my eyes: because I see men not observing thy law. Righteous art thou (O Lord): and right are thy judgements. Thou hast commanded in thy testimonies righteousness and faithfulness most chiefly. My zeal to thy word killed me: because my pursuers forgot it. Thy words are purely tried,° like as with fire: and thy servant loveth them. I was a little one, and an abject°: but yet forgot I not thy commandments. Thy righteousness is everlasting: and thy law is the very truth. Then affliction and heaviness had taken me: then thy commandments refreshed me. The believing of thy promises is everlasting righteousness: give me understanding of this, and I shall live. I called upon thee with all my heart: grant me (Lord) and I shall observe thy ordinances. I called upon thee, save thou me: I shall keep thy testimonies. I prevent° the dawning of the day: and cry unto thee; I wait for thy promises. My eyes prevented the watches: that I might be occupied in thy pleasures. Hear me, Lord, for thy mercy's sake: quicken me after thy pleasures. My pursuers laid their own faults upon my neck: but they are gone far back from thy law. Thou art present, O Lord: and all thy precepts are the very self° truth. I knew this before of thy testimonies: for thou hast established them to abide forever. Behold my affliction and defend me, for I forget not thy law. Defend my cause and deliver me: quicken me after thy promises. Health is far from the ungodly: for they regard not thy ordinances. Bounteous is thy gentleness (O Lord) quicken me at thy pleasure. Many there

---

[6] The Psalmist claims to have done what is 'lawful and right' (BCP), but 'equity', in English law, referred to court decisions that set aside common or statute law to take account of special circumstances and maintain the principle of natural justice, recognizing that what was strictly legal was not always what was just. The system of equity was developed during the course of the sixteenth century, particularly in the Court of Chancery.

are that persecute me and are against me: and yet have I not swerved from thy testimonies. I see these malicious men, and it irked me: because they observed
165 not thy sayings. Thou seest that I love thy commandments: Lord, for thy mercy's sake quicken me. The beginning of thy words is truth: and the judgements of thy righteousness standeth forever. The overmost in authority persecuted me faultless: and my heart feared at thy words. I am as glad of thy pleasures as one that had found many preys. I hate and abhor lies: and I love thy law. Seven times
170 in the day I praise thee: for thy rightwise° judgements. The lovers of thy law shall have much felicity and quietness and no hurt at all. I trust upon thy help (Lord) and give diligence to thy precepts. My soul observeth thy testimonies: and loveth them greatly. I observe thy commandments and thy testimonies: for all my ways are open unto thee. Let my crying ascend unto thy presence (O Lord), make me
175 rightly to understand thy words. Let my deep desire come in to thy sight: deliver me according to thy promises. My lips shall pour forth thy praise: thou shalt instruct me in thy ordinances. My tongue shall speak of thy pleasures: for all thy precepts are righteousness. Let thy hand help me: for I have chosen thy commandments. I desired thy saving help (Lord): and thy law is my delight. My
180 soul shall live and praise thee: and thy judgements shall be my help. I am strayed like a lost sheep: seek thou thy servant, for thy commandments have I not forgotten.

5. Miles Coverdale, *A Paraphrasis upon All the Psalms of David, Made by Johannes Campensis* (1534)

[Miles Coverdale (1488–1569) was the most influential sixteenth-century translator of the Psalms in English, since, not only did he produce a variety of different translations, but his translation for the Great Bible (1539) came to be printed and sold along with the Book of Common Prayer and was eventually (after 1660) incorporated into it. The Coverdale Psalms were thus the best-known version in England for over four centuries. Apparently born in Yorkshire, Coverdale was ordained in Norwich, became an Augustinian friar (Luther's order), and moved to the Augustinian house at Cambridge, where he came under the influence of the reformer Robert Barnes. Coverdale moved to the Continent during the period 1528 to 1535, at some point becoming associated with William Tyndale and, like Tyndale, devoting himself to translating the Bible into English. Coverdale translated the Latin Psalm paraphrases of Jan van Campen or Johannes Campensis (*Psalmorum omnium iuxta Hebraisam*, Antwerp, 1532) into English in 1534. Like Campensis's book, Coverdale's was printed in Antwerp. No translator was acknowledged in the volume, but the attribution was made by John Bale. Campensis's paraphrases became popular among English readers, including many subsequent translators of the Psalms. Unlike many of his reforming colleagues, Coverdale had a long life. After producing a series of whole or partial Bible translations in the 1530s, some on the Continent and some on returning to England in 1535, he went into exile again in the 1540s and again during the reign of Queen Mary, though he returned to England from 1551 to 1553 to become royal chaplain and then Bishop of Exeter. Coverdale was involved in the translation of the Geneva Bible (1560) and returned to England again in 1559. He continued to preach until his death at the age of 81. See Peter G. Beitenholz, 'Jan van Campen', in *Contemporaries of Erasmus*, ed. by Beitenholz, vols I–III (Toronto: University of Toronto Press, 1985), I, 255–56; David Daniell (Coverdale), *ODNB*.]

Psalm 72

The lxxii Psalm for Solomon.
Deus judicium tuum regi da.
O God, give the king a rule to judge after thee, and give the king's son a lust° to do right.
2. That he may judge thy people according to right, and the poor (which are left thee to care for) with judgment.
3. And let the rulers (which seem to be like hills) bring peace among people, and let righteousness follow the little hills.
4. Let him defend the poor which are many among the people, let him deliver the needy from falsehood of the law, and destroy the wrong-doer.
5. Let them fear thee (O King) so long as the sun showeth light to men, and the moon forever.
6. Let him be as welcome as is the rain upon the new mown corn,° and as the showers that water the dry land.
7. Let the righteous prosper in his time, and let there be great peace which may continue longer than the moon.
8. And let him bear rule from one sea to another, yea, from the east ocean unto the furthest parts of the west sea.
9. Let the Morians fall down before him,[7] but let his enemies be cast down, and bite upon the earth.
10. Let the kings of Tarshish and such as dwell in the isles bring presents unto him, let the kings of the Arabies and Sabies render him tribute.[8]
11. And let all kings worship him, let all the world serve him.
12. For he shall be very righteous, and shall deliver from trouble, the needy calling for succour of him, and the poor that is destitute of man's help.
13. He shall be good to the poor and needy, and shall bring the souls of the needy unto felicity.

---

[7] Morians] Moors, following the Vulgate *Aethiopes*. KJV, following the Hebrew, has 'they that dwell in the wilderness'.
[8] Arabies and Sabies] Following the Vulgate *Arabiae et Saba*. KJV, following the Hebrew, has 'Sheba and Seba'.

14. He shall deliver their souls from usury and unrighteousness, and shall not suffer° their blood to be shed for nought.°

15. The poor shall live by this king, and he shall make him partaker of the gold of Arabia, and shall always make intercession for him, he shall be ever liberal unto him.

16. Of few seed corns cast into the ground (yea, though they were sown upon the top of hills) there shall come a great harvest, and the corn shall grow so high, that if it be moved of the wind, the full ears shall make as great a sound, as the high cedar trees use to make upon the hill of Lebanon; the citizens also shall flourish, and be multiplied in the city, like as the herb in the fields.

17. His name shall be had in honour for evermore: for before the sun was created,[9] he was called sun from everlasting: all nations shall acknowledge thee to be blessed through his goodness, and shall preach him to be blessed above all other.

18. The Lord God is worthy of all praise, the God (I say) of Israel, which by his own strength without any other help, doth things that pass understanding.

19. And that excellent name of his Son shall be worthy of all praise for evermore, wherefore all the earth shall be fulfilled with the majesty of his name.

    It shall be so.   It shall be so.

20. This was the sum of the desires of David the son of Jesse: namely, that these things might come to pass.

6. Miles Coverdale, *Biblia. The Bible: That Is, the Holy Scripture of the Old and New Testament, Faithfully and Truly Translated out of the Dutch and Latin into English* [The Coverdale Bible] (1535)

[In 1535 the 'Coverdale Bible' was printed, the first complete Bible in English since the clandestine Bibles of the Wycliffites. Printed first in Antwerp and shortly thereafter in Southwark, it was translated not from the original languages, Hebrew and Greek, which Coverdale did not know, but from the intermediary languages of Latin and German. Coverdale's sources were a Swiss-German translation by Zwingli and Leo Jud (1524–1529), the Latin Old Testament of Sancte Pagninus (1528), Luther's German Bible (1532), the Latin Vulgate, and Tyndale's English New Testament and parts of the Old. It was a fine book in large folio format, with illustrations, including an elaborate title page by Hans Holbein featuring Henry VIII, likely in the hope that the king would approve and authorize the translation. He did not. Although this Bible was many times reprinted, it was also soon superseded, first by the Matthew Bible of 1537, and then by the Great Bible of 1539, which Henry did finally

---

[9] sun] 'sonne' in original, which allows (anachronistic) play against the 'sonne' (Christ) in the final added prayer.

authorize. See David Daniell, *The Bible in English: Its History and Influence* (New Haven and London: Yale University Press, 2003) and *ODNB*.]

Psalm 23[10]

A Psalm of David.
The Lord is my shepherd, I can want nothing. He feedeth me in a green pasture, and leadeth me to a fresh water. He quickeneth° my soul, and bringeth me forth in the way of righteousness for his name's sake. Though I should walk now in the valley of the shadow of death, yet I fear no evil, for thou art with me: thy
5 staff and thy sheephook comfort me. Thou preparest a table before me against° mine enemies: thou anointest my head with oil, and fillest my cup full. Oh, let thy lovingkindness[11] and mercy follow me all the days of my life, that I may dwell in the house of the Lord forever.

Psalm 43[12]

Give sentence upon me, O God, and defend my cause against the unholy people: O deliver me from the deceitful and wicked man. For thou, O God, art my strength: why hast thou shut me from thee? Why go I then so heavily, while the enemy oppresseth me? Oh, send out thy light and thy truth, that they may lead
5 me and bring me unto thy holy hill and to thy dwelling. That I may go in to the altar of God, even unto the God which is my joy and pleasure, and upon the harp to give thanks unto thee, O God, my God. Why art thou so heavy, O my soul, and why art thou disquieted within me? Oh, put thy trust in God, for I will yet give him thanks for the help of his countenance and because he is my God.

7. Miles Coverdale, *Ghostly Psalms and Spiritual Songs Drawn out of the Holy Scripture* (1535)

[Later in the same year he published his complete English Bible, Coverdale published a small book containing metrical Psalms — the first in English — and translations of popular Lutheran hymns. The book was officially condemned and publicly burned. This has tended to be used to support the claim that *Ghostly Psalms* had virtually no influence, but more recently it has been suggested that the burning might be a sign of its popularity, alarming for Church authorities. Coverdale's English version of Psalm 46 is a translation of Luther's influential paraphrase, *Ein feste burg*. See Robin A. Leaver, *Goostly Psalmes and Spirituall Songes: English and Dutch Metrical Psalms from Coverdale to Utenhove, 1535–1566* (Oxford: Clarendon Press, 1991); Diarmaid MacCulloch,

---

[10] 22 in text (following the Vulgate).
[11] lovingkindness] Coverdale's influential coinage.
[12] 42 in text (following the Vulgate).

Psalm 46

Deus noster refugium. [God is our refuge]

Our God is a defence and tower,
A good armour and good weapon;
He hath been ever our help and succour
In all the troubles that we have been in.
5   Therefore will we never dread
    For any wondrous deed
    By water or by land,
    In hills or the sea sand,
Our God hath them all in his hand.
10 Though we be alway greatly vexed   *always*
With many a great temptation,
Yet thankèd be God we are refreshèd;
His sweet word comforteth our mansion.[13]
    It is God's holy place,
15 He dwelleth here by grace;
    Among us is he
    Both night and day truly.
He helpeth us all and that swiftly.
The wicked heathen besiege us straitly,
20 And many great kingdoms take their part;
They are gathered against us truly
And are sore moved in their heart.
    But God's word as clear as day
    Maketh them shrink away.
25 The Lord God of power
    Standeth by us every hour;
The God of Jacob is our strong tower
Come hither now, behold and see
The noble acts and deeds of the Lord,
30 What great things he doth for us daily
And comforteth us with his sweet word.
For when our enemies would fight,
Then break he their might,   *broke*
    Their bow and their spear
35 (So that we need not fear),

---

[13] mansion] The metre requires three syllables ('man-shi-ion').

And burnt their chariots in the fire.
Therefore saith God, take heed to me,
Let me alone and I shall help you;
Know me for your God I say only   *alone*
40   Among all heathen that reign now.
     Wherefore then should we dread,
     Seeing we have no need,
     For the Lord God of power
     Standeth by us every hour;
45 The God of Jacob is our strong tower.

8. Anon., *Stories and Prophesies out of the Holy Scripture, Garnished with Fair Images and with Devout Prayers and Thanksgivings unto God* (1536)

[The illustrated title page announces that this book, published in Antwerp, has been examined and approved by Master Nicholas Coppin de Montibus, Dean of Saint Peters and Chancellor of the University of Louvain, appointed papal inquisitor in 1523. The book consists of retellings of Bible stories with illustrative woodcuts. This Psalm 51, by an unknown translator, comes from the story of David and Bathsheba, which begins with a picture of Bathsheba bathing naked with David watching from above. The Psalm is presented as David's penitential prayer after being confronted by Nathan. See Herman J. Selderhuis and Peter Nissen, 'The Sixteenth Century', in *Handbook of Dutch Church History*, ed. by Selderhuis (Gottingen: Vandenhoeck & Ruprecht GMBH & Co. KH, 2015).]

Psalm 51[14]

To the end, David's praise song, when Nathan the prophet came unto him, when he was gone in with Bethsabe.

Have mercy upon me God, for thy favourable goodness: and for thy manifold mercies wipe away my sins.

    And yet again, wash me more from wickedness, and make me clean from my ungodliness, for my grievous sins do I knowledge,° and mine ungodliness is ever
5 before mine eyes.

    Against thee only° have I sinned, and ill° have I done in thy presence, wherefore very just shalt thou be known in thy words: when it shall be judged of thee when thou overcomes.

    Lo, I was fashioned in wickedness, and my mother conceived me polluted
10 with sin.

---

[14] Psalm 51 is the central Psalm of the seven Penitential Psalms, traditionally understood as David's prayer after being chastised by Nathan for his adultery with Bathsheba and effective murder of her husband Uriah, as the headnote indicates (the story is told in II Samuel 11).

But lo, thou wouldest truth to occupy and rule in my inward parts, thou showedst me wisdom, which thou wouldest to sit in the secrets of my heart.[15] Sprinkle me with hyssop,[16] and so shall I be clean, thou shalt wash me, and then shall I be whiter than snow. Unto my hearing shall you give joy and gladness, and make my bones rejoice, the which thou hast smitten. Turn thy face from sins, and weep away all my wickedness. A pure heart create in me (O Lord) and a right steadfast sprite° make anew within me.

Cast me not away from thy face, and thy Holy Ghost take not from me.

Give me again the rejoicing of thy health and the principal governing spirit strengthen in me.

I shall instruct the wicked thy way, and the ungodly shall be converted unto thee.

Deliver me from the blood, God, the God of my salvation, and my tongue shall highly make high thy righteousness.

Lord, open thou my lips, and then my mouth shall show forth thy praise.

For and you would have had sacrifices I would have given them you, and as for burnt sacrifice you regard them not.

Acceptable sacrifice to God is a broken spirit, a contrite and a dejected heart shalt thou not despise, O God.

Deal gently of thy favourable benevolence with Zion, let the walls of Jerusalem be edified and preserved.

Then shall you receive sacrifice, in the right burnt sacrifice, and in the oblation of righteousness, then shall they lay upon thine altar the very calves.

9. John Rogers, *The Bible, Which Is All the Holy Scripture: In Which Are Contained the Old and New Testament Truly and Purely Translated into English by Thomas Matthew* [The Matthew Bible] (1537)

[The so-called 'Matthew Bible' was actually the work of John Rogers (*c.* 1500–1555). Rogers graduated from Pembroke College, Oxford, and was appointed rector at Holy Trinity-the-Less in London. In 1534 he became chaplain at the English House at Antwerp, where he met Tyndale. After Tyndale's arrest and execution in 1536, Rogers somehow came into possession of the manuscripts of Tyndale's translation of the Old Testament from Joshua to Chronicles. Rogers took this, along with Tyndale's printed translations of the Pentateuch and the New Testament, and filled in the remaining Old Testament books from Coverdale's 1535 Bible, revised according to his own knowledge of Hebrew and consultation with Continental scholarship. Rogers also added substantial commentary in introductions and marginal notes. The Bible was

---

[15] secrets] private places; 'secrets of the heart' is a biblical idiom. The Vulgate has *absconditus*.
[16] hyssop] Herb used in ritual purification.

printed in Antwerp under the pseudonym Thomas Matthew, perhaps based on the names of the disciples. At the end of the Old Testament, two large, floridly elaborated initials, 'W.T.', are a discreet homage from Rogers or the printer to Tyndale. The London merchants Richard Grafton and Edward Whitchurch paid for another edition of 1500 copies to be sent to England. One of these copies was forwarded by Grafton to Thomas Cranmer, Archbishop of Canterbury, who contacted Thomas Cromwell, Henry VIII's principal secretary and vicegerent on matters ecclesiastical. Cromwell showed the Bible to the king, who approved and licensed it for distribution to churches. The demand for additional copies of the Matthew Bible led to the production of Coverdale's revision of it, the Great Bible of 1539. Daniell, *Bible in English*; Daniell (Rogers) and Howard Leithead (Cromwell), *ODNB*.]

Psalm 23

He describeth the wonderful sureties and great grace of a faithful and sure confidence in God.

A Psalm of David.

The Lord is my shepherd, I can want nothing.
He feedeth me in a green pasture, and leadeth me to a fresh water.
He quickeneth° my soul, and bringeth me forth in the way of righteousness for his name's sake.
5   Though I should walk now in the valley of the shadow of death, yet I fear no evil, for thou art with me: thy staff and thy sheephook comfort me.
Thou preparest a table before me against° mine enemies: thou anointest my head with oil, and fillest my cup full.
Oh, let thy loving kindness and mercy follow me all the days of my life, that I
10 may dwell in the house of the Lord forever.

Psalm 60

He showeth how God, being displeased, had in times past given the people of Israel into the hands of their enemies, but did yet mercifully help them again: he showeth also the power and dominion of the Israelites, unto whom now are subdued the Moabites and the Philistines: and hopeth by the power of God to have the victory of the Ammonites.

To the chanter upon the rose of witness, Michtam of David, for to teach when he fought against Syria of Mesopotamia, and Syria of Zoba: and when Joab turned back, and slew twelve thousand Edomites, in the valley of Salt.[17]

---

[17] The episode is described in II Samuel 8, where he is described as slaying eighteen thousand Syrians (Hebrew, 'Aramaeans'). Some commentators describe these as Edomites, since the valley is between Judah and Edom. The Psalm headnote has suggested to some commentators that David sent Joab to deal with the threat.

O God, thou that hast cast us out, and scattered us abroad, thou that hast been so sore displeased at us, comfort us again.

Thou that hast removed the land and divided it, heal the sores thereof, for it shaketh.

Thou hast showed thy people heavy things, thou hast given us a drink of wine, that we slumber withal.°

Yet hast thou given a token for such as fear thee, that they may cast it up in the truth.   Selah.

That thy beloved might be delivered, help them with thy right hand, and hear me.

God hath spoken in his sanctuary, which thing rejoiceth me, I will divide Sichem, and meet out the valley of Succoth.

Gilead is mine, Manasses is mine, Ephraim is the strength of mine head, Judah is my captain.

Moab is my washpot, over Edom will I stretch out my shoe,[18] Philistia shall be glad of me.

Who will lead me into the strong city?

Who will bring me into Edom?

Shalt not thou do it, O God, thou that hast cast us out: thou, God, that wentest not out with our hosts?

Oh, be thou our help in trouble, for vain is the help of man.

Through God we shall do great acts, for it is he that shall tread down our enemies.

10. Miles Coverdale, *The Bible in English, That Is To Say the Content of All the Holy Scripture, Both of the Old and New Testament, Truly Translated after the Verity of the Hebrew and Greek Texts* [The Great Bible] (1539)

[The so-called 'Great Bible', first printed in 1539, was the work of Miles Coverdale. Like most sixteenth-century English Bibles, it was not a new translation, but a revision, in this case of the Matthew Bible, the work of John Rogers. Rogers himself used earlier translations by Tyndale and Coverdale. The Great Bible was the first translation officially authorized by Henry VIII, and a royal injunction ordered copies to be acquired by and made available in all churches. What has not been sufficiently recognized is that even within the history of the 'Great' Bible the process of revision was ongoing, so there are considerable variants from edition to edition. Whether Coverdale or someone else was responsible for these revisions remains to be discovered. A full collation of sixteenth-century English Bibles has yet to be written. The 1540 third edition is sometimes called the 'Cranmer' Bible, since it included a preface by Thomas

---

[18] will I stretch out my shoe] Idiomatic for conquest, as in placing the foot on the neck of the subjugated.

Cranmer, but Cranmer was not involved in the translation. Coverdale's revised Psalms were also printed separately, and they were soon printed to be bound and sold together with the Book of Common Prayer, though it seems that the BCP version derived from a later edition, printed in 1541. Even after the printing of the Bishops' Bible (1568) and King James Bible (1611), the Book of Common Prayer Psalms remained Coverdale's, albeit with some further revision over the years. Though Coverdale did not know Hebrew, the authors of some of his source texts did, and he seems to have had a knack for the parallelistic structure of Hebrew poetry. See Nicholas Pocock, '"The Great Bible", A.D. 1539', *Book-Lore*, 7 (1885), 1–5, and 'Cranmer's Bible', *Book-Lore*, 13 (1885), 22; Daniell, *Bible in English* and *ODNB*.]

Psalm 2

Quare fremuerunt gentes. [Why do the nations roar?]
To the chanter, a Psalm of David.
Why do the heathen grudge° together? and why do the people imagine a vain thing? The kings of the earth stand up, and the rulers take counsel together, against the Lord and against his anointed. Let us break their bonds asunder, and cast away their cords from us. He that dwelleth in heaven shall laugh them to
5 scorn: the Lord shall have them in derision. Then shall he speak unto them in his wrath, and vex them in his sore displeasure. Yet have I set my king upon my holy hill of Zion. I will preach the law, whereof the Lord hath said unto me, Thou art my Son, this day have I begotten° thee. Desire of me, and I shall give thee the heathen for thine inheritance, and the utmost parts of the earth for thy
10 possession. Thou shalt bruise them with a rod of iron, and break them in pieces like a potter's vessel. Be wise now therefore, O ye kings, be warned, ye that are judges of the earth. Serve the Lord in fear, and rejoice unto him with reverence. Kiss the Son, lest he be angry, and so ye perish from the right way if his wrath be kindled but a little: blessed are all they that put their trust in him.

Psalm 22

Deus deus meus. [O God, my God]
To the chanter upon the hind° of the dawning. A Psalm of David.
My God, my God: look upon me, why hast thou forsaken me: and art so far from my health, and from the words of my complaint°? O my God, I cry in the daytime, but thou hearest not: and in the night season° also I take no rest. And thou continuest holy, O thou worship of Israel. Our fathers hoped in thee: they
5 trusted in thee, and thou didst deliver them.
  They called upon thee, and were helped: they put their trust in thee, and were not confounded.° But as for me, I am a worm and no man: a very scorn of men and the outcast of the people. All they that see me, laugh me to scorn: they shoot

out their lips, and shake the head. He trusted in God, let him deliver him: let him deliver him, if he will have him.[19] But thou art he that took me out of my mother's womb: thou wast my hope, when I hanged yet upon my mother's breasts.

I have been left unto thee ever since I was born: thou art my God, even from my mother's womb. Oh, go not from me, for trouble is hard at hand, and here is none to help me. Great oxen are come about me, fat bulls of Basan[20] close me in on every side.

They gape upon me with their mouths, as it were a ramping and roaring lion.

I am poured out like water, and all my bones are out of joint: my heart also in the midst of my body is even like melting wax. My strength is dried up like a potsherd, and my tongue cleaveth to my gums, and thou shalt bring me into the dust of death.

For many dogs are come about me, and the council of the wicked lay siege against me. They pierced my hands and my feet, I may tell all my bones:[21] they stand staring and looking upon me.

They part my garments among them, and cast lots upon my vesture. But be not thou far from me, O Lord: thou art my succour, haste thee to help me. Deliver my soul from the sword, my darling[22] from the power of the dog. Save me from the lion's mouth: thou hast heard me also from among the horns of the unicorns.[23] I will declare thy name unto my brethren: in the midst of the congregation will I praise thee.

O praise the Lord, ye that fear him: magnify him all ye of the seed° of Jacob, and fear him all ye seed of Israel. For he hath not despised nor abhorred the low estate of the poor: he hath not hid his face from him, but when he called unto him, he heard him. My praise is of thee in the great congregation, my vows will I perform in the sight of them that fear him.

The poor shall eat and be satisfied: they that seek after the Lord shall praise him: your heart shall live forever. All the ends of the world shall remember themselves, and be turned unto the Lord, and all the kindreds of the nations shall worship before him. For the kingdom is the Lord's, and he is the governor

---

[19] This sentence is in the voice of those mocking the Psalmist.

[20] Bashan was historically an enemy of Israel, most famously when ruled by Og, last of the giants (Numbers 21, Deuteronomy 3). Amos uses the phrase 'kine of Bashan' (KJV) figuratively, for those 'which oppress the poor, which crush the needy, which say to their masters, Bring, and let us drink' (Amos 4. 1).

[21] tell] count; i.e. because of his thinness.

[22] darling] beloved, favourite. Coverdale seems drawn to the alliteration with 'deliver' and 'dog'.

[23] unicorns] A famous example of the translator's insertion of a European mythological creature when the precise animal mentioned (*re'em*) is unknown. NRSV has 'wild oxen', but this is speculative, since the animal is now extinct. Some scholars suggest the aurochs, an ancestor of modern cattle.

40 among the people. All such as be fat upon earth have eaten and worshipped. All they that go down into the dust,[24] and live so hardly shall kneel before him. My seed shall serve him: they shall be counted unto the Lord for a generation. They shall come, and the heavens shall declare his righteousness: unto a people that shall be born, whom the Lord hath made.

Psalm 23

Dominus regit me. [The Lord rules me]
A Psalm of David.
The Lord is my shepherd, therefore can I lack nothing. He shall feed me in a green pasture, and lead me forth beside the waters of comfort.[25] He shall convert my soul, and bring me forth in the paths of righteousness for his name's sake. Yea, though I walk through the valley of the shadow of death, I will fear no evil,
5 for thou art with me: thy rod and thy staff comfort me.
Thou shalt prepare a table before me against them that trouble me: thou hast anointed my head with oil, and my cup shall be full.
But thy loving kindness and mercy shall follow me all the days of my life: and I will dwell in the house of the Lord forever.

Psalm 46

Deus noster refugium. [God is our refuge]
To the chanter, a song of the children of Korah upon Alamoth.[26]
God is our hope and strength: a very present help in trouble. Therefore will we not fear, though the earth be moved, and though the hills be carried in the midst of the sea. Though the waters thereof rage and swell, and though the mountains shake at the tempest of the same. Selah. The rivers of the flood thereof shall make
5 glad the city of God, the holy place of the tabernacles° of the most highest. God is in the midst of her, therefore shall she not be removed: God shall help her, and that right early. The heathen make much ado, and the kingdoms are moved: but God hath showed his voice, and the earth shall melt away. The Lord of hosts is with us, the God of Jacob is our refuge. Selah. O come hither, and behold the
10 works of the Lord, what destructions he hath brought upon the earth. He maketh wars to cease in all the world: he breaketh the bow and knappeth° the

---

[24] All they that go down into the dust] i.e. mortals who will die. God in Genesis 3. 19 curses Adam to return to the dust from which he was made.

[25] waters of comfort] From the Vulgate *aquas refectionis*.

[26] Even though the Psalms were often thought of as the compositions of King David, a number of them are attributed to others in the headnotes. Eleven Psalms, including this one, are 'of' the sons of Korah, presumably descendants of the rebel against Moses, although the story in Numbers describes the whole family being destroyed (Numbers 16). See Introduction, p. 18.

spear in sunder, and burneth the chariots in the fire. Be still then and know that I am God: I will be exalted among the heathen, and I will be exalted in the earth.

The Lord of hosts is with us, the God of Jacob is our defence. Selah.

Psalm 81

Exultate deo. [Rejoice in God]
To the chanter upon Gittith.°
A Psalm of Asaph[27] on the fifth day of the Sabbath.
Sing we merrily unto God our strength: make a cheerful noise unto the God of Jacob. Take the Psalm, bring hither the tabret,° the merry harp with the lute.

Blow up the trumpet in the new moon, even in the time appointed, and upon our solemn feast day. For this was made a statute for Israel, and a law of the God of Jacob. This he ordained in Joseph for a testimony, when he came out of the land of Egypt, and had heard a strange language.

I eased his shoulder from the burden, and his hands were delivered from making the pots. Thou calledst upon me in troubles, and I delivered thee, and heard thee, what time as the storm fell upon thee. I proved thee also at the waters of strife. Selah. Hear, O my people, and I will assure thee, O Israel, if thou wilt hearken unto me. There shall no strange God be in thee, neither shalt thou worship any other God. I am the Lord thy God, which brought thee out of the land of Egypt, open thy mouth wide, and I shall fill it. But my people would not hear my voice, and Israel would not obey me. So I gave them up unto their own heart's lust,° and let them follow their own imaginations.

Oh, that my people would have hearkened unto me, for if Israel had walked in my ways, I should soon have put down their enemies, and turned mine hand against their adversaries. The haters of the Lord should have been found liars, but their time should have endured forever. He should have fed them also with the finest wheat flour, and with honey out of the stony rock should I have satisfied thee.

Psalm 90

Domine refugium. [God our refuge]
A prayer of Moses the man of God.
Lord, thou hast been our refuge from one generation to another.

Before the mountains were brought forth, or ever the earth and the world were made, thou art God from everlasting and world without end.

Thou turnest man to destruction. Again, thou sayest: come again, ye children of men. For a thousand years in thy sight are but as yesterday, seeing that is past

---

[27] Twelve Psalms are said to be 'of' Asaph, a Levite whose family became involved in Temple worship (1 Chronicles 6. 39).

as a watch in the night.[28] As soon as thou scatterest them, they are even as a sleep, and fade away suddenly like the grass.

In the morning it is green and groweth up, but in the evening it is cut down, dried up, and withered. For we consume° away in thy displeasure, and are afraid at thy wrathful indignation. Thou hast set our misdeeds before thee, and our secret sins in the light of thy countenance. For when thou art angry, all our days are gone: we bring our years to an end, as it were a tale that is told.

The days of our age are three score years and ten: and though men be so strong that they come to four score years, yet is their strength then but labour and sorrow: so soon passeth it away, and we are gone.

But who regardeth the power of thy wrath, for even thereafter as a man feareth, so is thy displeasure. O teach us to number our days, that we may apply our hearts unto wisdom. Turn thee again (O Lord) at the last, and be gracious unto thy servants. O satisfy us with thy mercy, and that soon: so shall we rejoice and be glad all the days of our life.

Comfort us again, now, after the time that thou hast plagued us, and for the years wherein we have suffered adversity.

Show thy servants thy work, and their children thy glory. And the glorious majesty of the Lord our God be upon us: prosper thou the work of our hands upon us, O prosper thou our handywork.

Psalm 95

Venite exultemus. [O come, let us rejoice]

O come, let us sing unto the Lord, let us heartily rejoice in the strength of our salvation. Let us come before his presence with thanksgiving, and show our self glad in him with Psalms. For the Lord is a great God, and a great King above all gods. In his hand are all the corners of the earth, and the strength of the hills is his also.

The sea is his, and he made it, and his hands prepared the dry land. O come, let us worship and fall down, and kneel before the Lord our Maker. For he is the Lord our God: and we are the people of his pasture, and the sheep of his hands. Today if ye will hear his voice, harden not your hearts, as in the provocation, and as in the day of temptation in the wilderness. When your fathers tempted me, proved me, and saw my works.

Forty years long was I grieved with that generation, and said: it is a people that do err in their hearts: for they have not known my ways. Unto whom I sware in my wrath, that they should not enter into my rest.

---

[28] watch in the night] Both Jews and Romans divided the night up into three or four shorter periods or 'watches'.

Psalm 107

Confitemini domino. [Confess to the Lord]
O give thanks unto the Lord, for he is gracious, and his mercy endureth forever. Let them give thanks whom the Lord hath redeemed, and delivered from the hand of the enemy. And gathered them out of the lands, from the east, and from the west, from the north, and from the south. They went astray in the wilderness
5 out of the way, and found no city to dwell in. Hungry and thirsty: their soul fainted in them. So they cried unto the Lord in their trouble, and he delivered them from their distress.[29] He led them forth by the right way, that they might go to the city where they dwelt. Oh, that men would therefore praise the Lord for his goodness, and declare the wonders that he doth for the children of men.
10 For he satisfied the empty soul, and filled the hungry soul with goodness.

    Such as sit in darkness and in the shadow of death, being fast° bound in misery and iron.

    Because they rebelled against the words of the Lord, and lightly regarded the counsel of the most highest. He also brought down their heart through
15 heaviness: they fell down, and there was none to help them. So when they cried unto the Lord in their trouble, he delivered them out of their distress. For he brought them out of darkness and out of the shadow of death, and broke their bands° in sunder. Oh, that men would therefore praise the Lord for his goodness, and declare the wonders that he doth for the children of men. For he hath
20 broken the gates of brass, and smitten the bars of iron in sunder. Foolish men are plagued for their offense, and because of their wickedness.

    Their soul abhorred all manner of meat,° and they were even hard at death's door.

    So when they cried unto the Lord in their trouble, he delivered them out of
25 their distress. He sent his word, and healed them, and they were saved from their destruction.

    Oh, that men would therefore praise the Lord for his goodness, and declare the wonders that he doth for the children of men.

    That they would offer unto him the sacrifice of thanksgiving, and tell out his
30 works with gladness. They that go down to the sea in ships, and occupy their business in great waters. These men see the works of the Lord, and his wonders in the deep. For at his word, the stormy wind ariseth, which lifteth up the waves thereof.

    They are carried up to the heaven, and down again to the deep, their soul
35 melteth away because of the trouble. They reel to and fro, and stacker° like a drunken man, and are at their wit's end. So when they cry unto the Lord in their trouble, he delivereth them out of their distress. For he maketh the storm to

---

[29] Like the French villanelle, this Psalm employs two refrains, this sentence and that beginning, 'O that men would therefore praise'. Each occurs four times, in the same order, each time with a description of some great work of God between them.

cease, so that the waves thereof are still. Then are they glad because they be at rest, and so he bringeth them unto the haven where they would be. Oh, that men would therefore praise the Lord for his goodness, and declare the wonders that he doth for the children of men. That they would exalt him also in the congregation° of the people, and love° him in the seat° of the elders.

Which turneth the floods into a wilderness: and drieth up the water springs.

A fruitful land maketh he barren, for the wickedness of them that dwell therein.

Again, he maketh the wilderness a standing water, and water springs of a dry ground. And there he setteth the hungry, that they may build them a city to dwell in. That they may sow their land, and plant vineyards, to yield them fruits of increase. He blessed them, so that they multiply exceedingly, and suffereth° not their cattle° to decrease. And again: when they are minished° and brought low through oppression, through any plague or trouble. Though he suffer them to be evil entreated through tyrants, and let them wander out of the way in the wilderness. Yet helpeth he the poor out of misery, and maketh him households like a flock of sheep. The righteous will consider this, and rejoice, and the mouth of all wickedness shall be stopped. Whoso is wise, will ponder these things: and they shall understand the loving kindness of the Lord.

Psalm 121

Levavi oculos. [I lifted my eyes]
A song of the stairs.[30]
I will lift up mine eyes unto the hills, from whence cometh my help. My help cometh even from the Lord, which hath made heaven and earth. He will not suffer° thy foot to be moved, and he that keepeth° thee, will not sleep. Behold, he that keepeth Israel, shall neither slumber nor sleep. The Lord himself is thy keeper, the Lord is thy defense upon thy right hand. So that the sun shall not burn thee by day, neither the moon by night. The Lord shall preserve thee from all evil, yea, it is even he that shall keep thy soul. The Lord shall preserve thy going out and thy coming in, from this time forth for evermore.

Psalm 148

Laudate dominum de ce. [Praise the Lord from the heavens]
Praise the everlasting.
O praise the Lord of heaven, praise him in the height. Praise him all ye angels of his, praise him all his host. Praise him sun and moon, praise him all ye stars and light.

Praise him all ye heavens, and ye waters that be above the heavens. Let them praise the name of the Lord, for he spake the word and they were made, he

---

[30] song of the stairs] or 'of ascent'; one of the gradual Psalms, from Latin *gradus*, having some liturgical function now unknown.

commanded and they were created. He hath made them fast° for ever and ever, he hath given them a law, which shall not be broken. Praise the Lord upon earth, ye dragons,³¹ and all deeps. Fire and hail, snow and vapours, wind and storm, fulfilling his word.

Mountains and all hills, fruitful trees and all cedars. Beasts and all cattle, worms and feathered fowls. Kings of the earth and all people, princes and all judges of the world. Young men and maidens, old men and children: praise the name of the Lord, for his name only° is excellent, and his praise above heaven and earth. He shall exalt the horn of his people,³² all his saints shall praise him, even the children of Israel, even the people that serveth him.

11. Richard Taverner, *The Most Sacred Bible, Which Is the Holy Scripture, Containing the Old and New Testaments, Translated into English* (1539)

[Richard Taverner (1505?–1575), cousin of the composer John Taverner, was educated at Corpus Christi College, Cambridge, and Cardinal College, Oxford. He returned to Cambridge where he became a fellow, and he also studied law at the Inns of Court. After sending Thomas Cromwell his translation of Erasmus's attack on clerical celibacy, Taverner was engaged by Cromwell as a propagandist for Lutheran reform, despite his moderate position on many controversial issues. This motivated Taverner's revision of the Matthew Bible, as he worked to adjust its positions on clerical celibacy, purgatory, fasting, and even the papacy. Like Coverdale, Taverner worked not from Hebrew but Latin intermediaries, including the Latin translation of the Old Testament from the Hebrew by Sancte Pagninus (Lyons, 1528). He was a good Greek scholar, however, and his New Testament had some small influence on subsequent translations. Since Taverner's Bible appeared in the same year as the Great Bible, it was quickly eclipsed, even though it was reprinted a number of times over the next two years, including in a further revised version by Edmund Becke. See Vivienne Westbrook, *Long Travails and Great Paynes: A Politics of Reformation Revision* (Dordrecht: Kluwer Academic Publishers, 2001); Andrew W. Taylor, ODNB.]

Psalm 23

A Psalm of David.

The Lord is my shepherd: I can want nothing.

He feedeth me in a green pasture, and leadeth me to a fresh water.

He quickeneth° my soul, and bringeth me forth in the way of righteousness for his name's sake.

---

³¹ dragons] Following the Vulgate *draconis*, but the Hebrew designates some kind of sea monster.
³² horn] A symbol of power or strength (Hebrew idiom).

5   Though I should walk now in the valley of the shadow of death, yet I fear no evil, for thou art with me: thy staff and thy sheephook comfort me.
   Thou preparest a table before me against mine enemies: thou anointest my head with oil, and fillest my cup full.
   O let thy loving kindness and mercy follow me all the days of my life, that I
10   may dwell in the house of the Lord forever.

Psalm 77

To the chanter, for Iduthun a Psalm of Asaph.

I cried unto God with my voice, yea, unto God cried I with my voice, and he heard me.
In the time of my trouble I sought the Lord, I held up mine hands unto him in the night season,° for my soul refused all other comfort.
5   When I was in heaviness, I thought upon God: when my heart was vexed, then did I speak. Selah.
Thou heldest mine eyes waking, I was so feeble, that I could not speak.
Then remembered I the times of old, and the years that were past.
I called to remembrance my song in the night, I communed with mine own
10   heart, and sought out my spirit.
Will the Lord cast out for ever?
Will he be no more entreated?
Is his mercy clean° gone?
Is his promise come utterly to an end for evermore?
15   Hath the Lord forgotten to be gracious?
Or, hath he shut up his loving kindness in displeasure?
At the last, I came to this point, that I thought: O why art thou so foolish, the right hand of the most highest can change all?
Therefore will I remember the works of the Lord, and call to mind thy wonders
20   of old time.
I will speak of all thy works, and my talking shall be of thy doings.
Thy way, O God, is holy: who is so great and mighty as God?
Thou art the God that doeth wonders, thou hast declared thy power among the people.
25   Thou with thine arm hast delivered thy people, even the sons of Jacob and Joseph. Selah.
The waters saw thee, O God, the waters saw thee, and were afraid, the depths were moved.
The thick clouds poured out water, the clouds thundered, and thine arrows went
30   abroad.
Thy thunder was heard round about, the lightnings shone upon the ground, the earth was moved and shook withal.°

Thy way was in the sea, and thy paths in the great waters, yet could no man know thy footsteps.
35 Thou leddest thy people like a flock of sheep, by the hand of Moses and Aaron.

12. Richard Taverner, *An Epitome of the Psalms, or Brief Meditations upon the Same* (1539)

[Translated by Taverner from Wolfgang Capito, *Precationes Christinae as imitationem psalmorum co[m]positae* (Strasbourg: Rihel, 1536). The *Epitome* is the second edition, the first, *The Sum or Pith of the 150 Psalms of David*, having been printed earlier in the same year, with an explicit reference to Capito that was removed from the new edition. Capito was a Protestant pastor in Strasbourg. The translation was dedicated to Henry VIII, who had authorized the publication of the Great Bible in the same year. Given the degree of paraphrase by both Capito and Taverner, these 'Psalms' are at a considerable remove from the originals. Some of Taverner's translations of Capito's Psalms were included by Elizabeth Tyrwhit in her manuscript Prayer Book (see 50). See *Elizabeth Tyrwhit's Morning and Evening Prayers*, ed. by Felch; Taylor, *ODNB*.]

Psalm 4

For the lightening° of the Holy Ghost.

Hear me when I cry for succour to thee (O Christ[33] which art my righteousness and innocency) and in adversity solace me with the joy of thy Spirit. Pour upon me thy grace and grant me my petitions, lift up over me the light of thy countenance (O Lord) and thy favour, that through thy Spirit I may knowledge°
5 thee, and with the same be heartily cheerful forever. Grave° within me (O Lord almighty) peace, fast° hope, burning love, and faith unfeigned° evermore to endure. So be it.

Psalm 47

For sending the ministers of the word.

Turn, Lord, the paynims° unto thee, which know thee not, that together with us they may joy and sing praises, that together with us they may be thy heritage, chosen of favour. Give us that all we may record thy renown, furnished with knowledge and faith of thy word. Raise up many that may defend the land with
5 preaching thy word, and make sure the same against the biting and rage of the helly° wolf, and against the ordinances° of the lying prophets, for they only seek their own gains. Amen.

---

[33] Christ] A Christian interpolation; KJV, following the Hebrew, has 'God'.

13. Miles Coverdale, *The Psalter or Book of Psalms Both in Latin and English* (1540)

[The Latin Vulgate is printed in the central columns of each opening of the book (on the right of the left-hand page and the left of the right-hand page), with Coverdale's English translation of it on the outside (left and right respectively). It is not clear why Coverdale chose to undertake this retranslation of the Psalms from the Vulgate, especially after the Six Articles of 1539 seemed to put an end to Protestant Reform.]

Psalm 23

The Lord governeth me,[34] and I shall lack nothing: in a place of pasture even there hath he set me.
Upon the water of refection[35] hath he nourished me, my soul hath he converted.
He hath led me forth upon the paths of righteousness, even for his own name
5 sake.
For though I walk in the midst[36] of the shadow of death, I will fear no evil, for thou art with me.
Thy rod and thy staff, those have comforted me.
Thou hast prepared a table before me, against them that trouble me.
10 Thou hast suppled° my head in oil: my cup also is full and exceeding fair.
And thy mercy shall go with me all the days of my life.
That I also may dwell in the house of the Lord long and many days.

Psalm 129

Many a time have they fought against me from youth (may Israel now say).
Many a time have they fought against me from my youth, because they might not overcome me.
Sinners have builded their works upon my back, they have prolonged their
5 iniquity.
The righteous Lord shall cut down the hard necks of sinners: let them be confounded° and turned backward, all they that have hated Zion.
Let them be as the grass of the house tops, that withereth away afore it be plucked up.
10 Wherewith, he that shall mow it, shall not fill his hand: neither he his bosom, that shall gather up the sheaves.

---

[34] governeth] Following the Vulgate *regit*, which removes the key opening term in the pastoral conceit, 'shepherd'.

[35] refection] Like 'waters of comfort' from Coverdale's Great Bible version, this follows the Vulgate *aquas refectionis*.

[36] in the midst] English Bibles all have 'through', but Coverdale's prepositional phrase expands the Vulgate preposition *in*.

And they that went by said not: the blessing of the Lord be upon you, we have wished you good in the name of the Lord.

14. John Croke, *A Book of Certain Chosen Psalms Translated into English Metre* (MS 1540s?)

[John Croke (1489–1554) was educated at Eton and King's College, Cambridge, and at Inner Temple. He became a chancery clerk and, in 1549, a master in chancery. He lived in Buckinghamshire where he was a Justice of the Peace. Croke translated the seven Penitential Psalms as well as Psalms 10, 13, 43, 139, 91, and 31. A note on the manuscript states that the translations were done at the request of his wife and that he translated them from the Latin Vulgate. The first few words of each verse of the Vulgate text are inserted before each of Croke's English stanzas. The initial letters for each Psalm are missing, suggesting that decorative initials were planned but never completed. See J. H. Baker, *ODNB*.]

Psalm 6

Domine ne in furore   [Lord, do not in anger]

Lord, hold thy hand in thy great might,
Smite me not after my defect,
Nor in thy wrath lay to my charge
The faults found in my sinful heart.

Miserere mei   [Have mercy on me]

5 Have mercy, Lord, upon the weak,
   My body feeble and low brought;
   I tremble as my bones would break,
   When thy stroke cometh in my thought.

Et anima mea   [And my soul]

   And yet my soul is troubled more
10 With vanities, with thought and cure
   And with temptations too sore;
   O Lord, how long shall they endure?

Convertere   [Turn]

   Turn to me, Lord, and have respect
   Unto thine accustomed grace,
15 And save my soul so far abject;   wretched
   To mend my life, give me some space.

Quoniam non est   [For there is none]

    For I am sure, among the dead
    There is no calling on thy name;
    In hell, who can hold up his head
20 To give praise worthy to thy fame?

Laboravi in genitu   [I have laboured in my groaning]

    My sinful life I do lament;
    Every night when I should sleep,
    My bed with tears is over sprent;   *sprinkled*
    Mine heart doth bray the sighs deep.   *loudly cry*

Turbatus est   [It is troubled]

25 Mine eyes wax dim, my sight doth fail,   *grow*
    And yet my troubles do increase;
    For fear of foe, I may bewail
    My chance, for that they never cease.

Discedite a me   [Depart from me]

    Yet, boldly trusting in thine aid,
30 I say, go back you en'mies all,
    For God will hear what shall be said;
    My weeping voice doth on him call.

Exaudivit dominus   [The Lord hath heard]

    My suit is heard, there is no doubt,   *petition*
    And granted too, I dare well say;
35 Cause is, how that is brought about,
    God gave good ear when I did pray.

Erubescant   [Let them not be ashamed]

    Therefore, my foes may turn and fall,
    And not without reproach and blame,
    So let my mortal en'mies all
40 Quickly be gone and go with shame.

Psalm 32

Beati quorum   [Blessed are they]

    Blessèd be they that may obtain
    Of their iniquities release;
    Whose sins been hid, likewise again,
    May say is blessèd and in peace.

Beatus vir [Blessed is the man]

5 Blessèd is he that God will not
   Impute to him his sinfulness,   *ascribe*
   And in whose sprite there is no blot   *spirit*
   Of fraud, or of deceitfulness.

Quoniam tacui [Because I was silent]

   Though I do seem to hold my peace,
10 Speaking no word (as it is thought),
   I howl, I cry, and do not cease;
   At length my strength is brought to nought.   *nothing*

Quoniam die [For day]

   For day and night thy mighty hand
   Is laid on me full grievously,
15 So that my strength cannot withstand;
   Thy thorn doth prick so painfully.

Delictum meum [My sin]

   Therefore my sin I will declare
   To thee, O Lord, and show my grief,
   Mine injustice I will not spare
20 To tell, and trust in thy relief.

Dixi confitebor [I said, I will confess]

   I say, I will confess the truth
   Unto the Lord of mine offense,
   Upon me then thou wilt take ruth,   *pity*
   And with my faults clearly dispense.

Pro hac orabit [For this he shall pray]

25 And for like cause all faithful men
   Will pray to thee for thy behest
   In time of need for help, and then
   They shall obtain all their request.

Verumtamen [Nevertheless]

   To such the surges cannot rise
30 Of worldly waves to change their cheer;   *spirits*
   If care they had power so to devise,
   They should not dare to come so near.

Tu es refugium   [Thou art a refuge]

   For refuge, Lord, I run to thee
   And there I find it even at hand,
35 For thou dost both deliver me
   And loosest me out of my band.   bond

Intellectum   [Understanding]

   And he doth say, I will thee teach
   And give thee wit my way to cast;   determine
   Keep that way straight and make no breach,   undeviating
40 Mine eyes on thee I will set fast.   secure

Nolite fieri   [Do not become]

   Ye may not be like horse or mule,
   That hath no wit nor perfect sense,
   Nor live like beast that knows no rule,
   For that they lack intelligence.

In camo   [With bit]

45 Bind fast their jaws up to the rack,
   And bridle them that beast will be,
   Prick them forward that draw back,   drive
   And will not learn to draw to thee.

Multa flagella   [Many are the scourges]

   Great pains for such prepare he must,
50 The sum of them cannot be found,
   But those that in the Lord will trust,
   His mercy shall environed round.   surrounded

Letamini   [Be glad]

   Now joy in God that such grace sent
   To make you good and give you space,
55 And all that be of pure intent
   Rejoice again for his great grace.

15. Anon., *Prayers of Holy Fathers, Patriarchs, Prophets, Judges, Kings, and Renowned Men and Women of Either Testament* (1544?)

[Richard Grafton printed this anonymous English translation of Otto Brunfels's *Precationes Biblicae Sanctorum Patrum* in London; the original had been printed in Strasbourg in 1528, and it was also translated into German and Dutch. Brunfels (*c.* 1488–1534) was born in Mainz and became a Carthusian monk and humanist scholar before converting to Lutheranism. A friend of Ulrich von

Hutten, Brunfels was drawn into the heated controversy between Hutten and Erasmus, publishing a defence of Hutten in 1524. In that same year, he settled in Strasbourg and opened a school at the request of the leading reformers Wolfgang Capito and Martin Bucer. Brunfels wrote a Bible concordance, lives of biblical men and women, and other religious works, but he became best known as a one of the most important botanists of his day. He earned a doctorate in medicine at the University of Basel and was appointed city physician in Bern. *Prayers* contains a number of Psalms interspersed at several points among a variety of other prayers and excerpts from the Bible. Several indexes at the back of the book direct readers to Psalms appropriate to various particular circumstances, and the headnotes serve the same function, some of them obviously directed to Protestants. See Miriam U. Chrisman, 'Otto Brunfels', in *Contemporaries of Erasmus*, ed. by Beitenholz, I, 206–07; Helen C. White, *Tudor Books of Private Devotion* (Madison: University of Wisconsin Press, 1951).]

Psalm 20

For rulers and for common peace.

The Lord might hear thee in time of trouble, the name of the God of Jacob might defend thee, and send thee help from the sanctuary, and strengthen thee out of Zion. Remember will he all thy offerings and accept thy burnt sacrifice. He shall grant thee thy heart's desire, and fulfil all thy mind. We will rejoice in thy health:
5 and triumph in the name of the Lord our God, for the Lord will perform all thy petitions. Now know I that the Lord helpeth his anointed: and will hear him from his holy heaven, mighty is the help of his right hand. Some put their trust in chariots and some in horses, but we will remember the name of the Lord our God. They are brought down: and fallen: but we are risen and stand
10 upright. Save, Lord, and help us: O King, when we call upon thee.

Psalm 37

This Psalm, because it is altogether evangelical, and teacheth the contempt of this world, we have put it at the end to the intent that in all our tribulation and in the pride of the wicked we may comfort ourselves. Let no day pass thee, but thou read this.

Fret° not thyself at the ungodly, be not thou envious against the evil doers. For they shall soon be cut down like the grass, and be withered even as the green herb.[37] Put thou thy trust in the Lord, and be doing good, so shalt thou dwell in the land, and verily it shall feed thee. Delight thou in the Lord, and he shall

---

[37] herb] General low-growing vegetation, rather than 'herb' in the narrower modern sense.

5 give thee thy heart's desire. Commit thy way unto the Lord, set thy hope in him, and he shall bring it to pass. He shall make thy righteousness as clear as the light, and thy just dealing as the noonday. Hold thee still in the Lord, and abide patiently about him. But grieve not thyself at one that hath prosperity, and liveth in abomination. Leave off from wrath, let go displeasure, let not thy
10 jealousy move thee also to do evil. For wicked doers shall be rooted out, but they that patiently abide the Lord shall inherit the land. Suffer yet a little while, and the ungodly shall be clean° gone, thou shalt look after his place, and he shall be away. But the meek spirited shall possess the earth, and have pleasure in much rest. The ungodly layeth wait for the just, and gnasheth upon him
15 with his teeth. But the Lord laugheth him to scorn for he seeth that his day is coming. The ungodly draw out the sword, and bend their bow to cast down the simple and poor, and to slay such as go the right way. Nevertheless, their sword shall go through their own heart, and their bow shall be broken. A small thing that the righteous hath is better than great riches of the ungodly. For the
20 arm of the ungodly shall be broken, but the Lord upholdeth the righteous. The Lord knoweth the days of the godly, and their inheritance endureth for ever. They shall not be confounded° in the perilous time, and in the days of dearth they shall have enough. As for the ungodly they shall perish, and when the enemies of the Lord are in their flowers they shall consume.° Yea, even as
25 the smoke shall they consume away. The ungodly borroweth and payeth not again, but the righteous is merciful and liberal. Such as be blessed of him, shall possess the land, and they whom he curseth shall be rooted out. The Lord ordereth a good man's going, and hath pleasure in his way. Though he fall, he shall not be hurt, for the Lord upholdeth him with his hand. I have been young
30 and now am old, yet saw I never the righteous forsaken, nor his seed° to seek their bread. The righteous is ever merciful and lendeth gently, therefore shall his seed be blessed. Flee from evil, and do the thing that is good, so shalt thou dwell for ever. For the Lord loveth the thing that is right, he forsaketh not his saints, but they shall be preserved forever. As for the seed of the ungodly, it
35 shall be rooted out. Yea, the righteous shall possess the land, and dwell therein forever. The mouth of the righteous is exercised in wisdom, and his tongue talketh of judgement. The law of his God is in his heart, therefore shall not his footsteps slide. The ungodly seeth the righteous, and goeth about to flee him. But the Lord will not leave him in his hands, nor condemn him when he is
40 judged. Hope thou in the Lord, and keep his way, and he shall so promote thee, that thou shalt have the land by inheritance, and see when the ungodly shall perish. I myself have sent the ungodly in great power, and flourishing like a green bay tree, but when I went by, lo, he was gone. I sought him, but he could nowhere be found. Keep innocency: and take heed unto the thing
45 that is right, for that shall bring a man peace at the last. As for the transgressors, they shall perish together, and the ungodly shall be rooted out at the last. The help of the righteous cometh of the Lord; he is their strength

in the time of trouble. The Lord shall stand by them, and save them. He shall deliver them from the ungodly, and help them, because they put their trust in him.

16. Queen Katherine (Parr), *Psalms or Prayers Taken out of Holy Scripture* (1544)

[Katherine Parr (1512–1548) was well educated and learned in several languages. Her first two husbands were Edward Borough (d. 1533) and John Neville, third Baron Latimer (d. 1543). After Latimer's death, Katherine joined the household of Princess Mary, where she attracted the attention of Henry VIII, whom she married in July 1543. Katherine was an active patron of poets, playwrights, and scholars. She commissioned Nicholas Udall to oversee the important translation of Erasmus's *Paraphrases upon the New Testament*, and she worked with Thomas Cranmer on the publication of the *King's Primer* (1545). The English translation of John Fisher's Latin *Psalmi seu Precationes* (c. 1525) that was printed in 1544 has been attributed to Parr. Parr's translation, along with a reprint of Fisher's Latin, was part of an effort to stir up support for Henry VIII's military ambitions in Scotland and France. Parr's work may have been done in collaboration with Henry, who liked to see himself as another King David. A series of fifteen pastiche or collage 'Psalms' (new Psalms composed by recombining various verses of the biblical 150) was followed by paraphrases of the Vulgate version of Psalms 22 (21) and 100 (99). The fifteen became known as the 'King's Psalms', perhaps because Henry approved of them (he was given a presentation copy). John Fisher (c. 1469–1535) was one of the most important churchmen in early Tudor England. He was elected vice-chancellor of Cambridge in 1501, became professor of theology in 1502, and was made bishop of Rochester in 1504 by Henry VII. Fisher was a staunch opponent of Protestant heresy, much of his theological writing focusing on refuting the works of reformers like Luther and Oecolampadius. In the crisis caused by Henry VIII's desire to divorce Katherine of Aragon, Fisher supported Katherine and opposed the king. He resisted the recognition of Henry as supreme head of the church, and he was finally arrested for his outspoken dissent in 1533. Despite the attempt by the pope to save Fisher by making him a cardinal, he was executed for treason in 1535. European Catholics saw Fisher as a martyr, and he was eventually canonized in 1935. Fisher's early success was due to the favour of Henry VII's mother, Lady Margaret Beaufort, who took him on as her spiritual director and advanced his academic, political, and ecclesiastical career. Fisher wrote a series of sermons on the Penitential Psalms, which he dedicated to Lady Margaret (1508), and which was many times reprinted. That his work should be reprinted to defend the policies of the king who executed him, and translated by his sixth wife, is one of the many grim ironies of this turbulent period. A further peculiarity in the history of these collage Psalms is that Parr's translations are incorporated (with some small changes) into George Flinton's Catholic *Manual of Prayers*, first printed in Rouen in 1583 and many times thereafter. Flinton likely did not know the translation of Fisher was Parr's, but this is nevertheless a singular instance of a Catholic text translated by a Protestant queen and then reappropriated for a Catholic devotional text. See *Katherine Parr: Complete Works and Correspondence*, ed. by Janel Mueller (Chicago: University of Chicago Press, 2011); Micheline White, 'The Psalms, War and Royal Iconography: Katherine Parr's *Psalms or Prayers* (1544) and Henry VIII as David', *Renaissance Studies*, 29.4 (2015), 554–75; Susannah Brietz Monta, 'The King's Psalms — or the Pope's? Katherine Parr's *Psalms or Prayers*, Scriptural Collage, and English Catholic Devotion', *Reformation*, 26.1 (2021), 8–22; Richard Rex (Fisher), Susan E. James (Parr), *ODNB*.]

> The Thirteenth Psalm.[38] In which he giveth thanks to God
> that his enemies have not gotten the overhand° of him.

I will magnify and praise thee (O Lord God) for thou hast exalted me and set me up: and my enemies have not gotten the overhand of me.
O Lord of hosts, I have cried unto thee: and thou hast saved me.
Thou hast brought my soul out of hell: thou hast holden° me up from falling
5 into the deep lake, from whence no man returneth.[39]
Thou hast not closed me up in the hands of mine enemies: but thou hast set my feet in a place both wide and broad.[40]
I have sought thee, and thou hast heard me: thou hast brought me into liberty out of great distress.[41]
10 Thou hast turned my sorrow into gladness: thou hast ceased my mourning, and compassed° me round about with mirth.[42]
Thou hast declared thy great magnificence in helping thy servant.[43]
Thou hast done mercifully with me in my miseries.[44]
Thou hast regarded the pain of the poor: thou hast not turned away thy face
15 from me.[45]

---

[38] Thirteenth Psalm] i.e. Parr's (based on Fisher's) thirteenth, not the biblical Psalm 13. The text combines in excerpt and paraphrase various Psalm verses, listed here according to the BCP numbering. In her translation, Parr somewhat further paraphrases Fisher's own Latin paraphrase.

[39] Psalm 30. 1–3; 'gotten the overhand' following Fisher's *praevaluerunt*; 'lake' from the Vulgate (and Fisher's) *lacum*.

[40] Psalm 31. 9.

[41] Psalm 34. 4, changed from third person to second.

[42] Psalm 30. 12.

[43] Perhaps Psalms 35. 27, 119. 1, 28. 8, though this verse and the next are so general and commonplace (in terms of phrases in Psalms) that specific sources are hard to identify.

[44] Psalm 44. 4 (?), though many other verses are similar.

[45] Psalm 22. 24.

I will ever be singing and speaking of thy mercies: and I will publish to other thy fidelity and truth so long as I shall live.[46]

My mouth shall never cease to speak of thy righteousness, and of thy benefits: which be so many, that I cannot number them.[47]

But I will give thee thanks till death take me away: I will sing in the praise of thee, so long as I shall continue.[48]

I will triumph and rejoice in thy mercy, for that thou hast looked upon my necessities, and regarded my soul in my great distress.[49]

Thou hast been my sure refuge, and the strength of my trust and hope.[50]

I thank the Lord for thy goodness alway: and for thy exceeding mercy.[51]

Thou hast been my comfort in the time of my trouble, thou hast been merciful unto me (O Lord) and hast revenged the wrongs that mine enemies have done to me.[52]

According to the multitude of the heavy thoughts that I had in my mind, thy comforts have cheered and lightened my heart.[53]

Thou hast sent me now joy for the days wherein I was in sorrow: and for the years in whom I suffered many a painful storm.[54]

Thou hast called to remembrance the rebuke that thy servant hath been put to: and how furiously mine enemies have persecuted me.[55]

O Lord God of hosts, who may be compared unto thee? Thou art great and greatly to be praised.

Thou art high upon all the earth, thou art exalted far above all gods.[56]

Glory and honour before thy face: holiness and magnificence in thy sanctuary.[57]

With justice and judgment thy royal throne is stablished°: mercy and truth go before thy face.[58]

Blessed art thou (O Lord) which hast not holden° back thy mercy from thy servant.[59]

---

[46] Psalm 89. 1.
[47] Psalm 71. 13.
[48] Psalm 104. 33.
[49] Psalm 31. 8.
[50] Psalm 91. 2, shifted from promise to present statement.
[51] Psalm 106. 1, shifted from the imperative to indicative.
[52] Psalm 138. 7? or possibly 37. 40–41.
[53] Psalm 73. 25?
[54] Psalm 30. 5, in part.
[55] Psalm 89. 50–51 (first half), though the phrase 'call to remembrance' comes from Psalms 25. 5 and 77. 6.
[56] Psalm 89. 6–7.
[57] Psalm 96. 6.
[58] Psalm 89. 15. Fisher and Parr stay close to the Vulgate, *iustitia et iudicium firmamentum throni*.
[59] Psalm 35. 27 (second half).

After that I had long looked for thee (O Lord) at the last thou didst attend unto me, and heardest my cry.⁶⁰

45 Thou hast taken me out of the lake of misery: and set my feet upon a rock, and made my steps sure.⁶¹

Thou hast given me my desire: I have seen thy joyful countenance.⁶²

Thou hast stricken all my adversaries, and hast abated their strength.⁶³

Thou hast rebuked the rabblement of them that vexed me: and hast plucked me
50 forth of their hands.⁶⁴

Thou hast cast them headlong into their own pit: their feet be wrapped in the net, which they laid privily for me.⁶⁵

Mine enemies are recoiled back: they are fallen down and destroyed from thy sight.⁶⁶

55 Thou hast been the poor man's defence, and his helper in tribulation, when most need was.⁶⁷

Thou hast done judgment for me: thou hast defended my cause against my accusers.⁶⁸

And although thou were very angry with me a little while: yet now I live through
60 thy mercy and goodness.⁶⁹

Verily I supposed with myself, that I was clean° cast away out of they favour.⁷⁰

But thou hast heard my prayers: and according to thy great mercy hast taken me again into thy favour.⁷¹

O Lord, of thine own mind and will thou hast given strength unto my soul: but
65 when thou hidst thy face from me (O Lord) how greatly was I astonied°?⁷²

When I was in adversity, then I cried unto thee: and thou didst answer me: when my soul was in great anguish and trouble, then (O Lord) I did remember thee.⁷³

I have tasted and seen how sweet thou art: truly blessed is that man that trusteth in thee.⁷⁴

70 According to thy name, so is thy commendation and praise: but thy counsels touching us be without example, and greater than can with words be expressed.⁷⁵

⁶⁰ Psalms 119. 166 and 77. 1, adapted.
⁶¹ Psalm 40. 2, following the Vulgate, *lacu miseriae*.
⁶² Psalm 21. 6, shifted from third person to first, future to past.
⁶³ Psalm 18. 49.
⁶⁴ Psalms 6. 10 and 140. 4 (first half).
⁶⁵ Psalm 9. 15.
⁶⁶ Psalm 9. 3.
⁶⁷ Psalm 9. 9.
⁶⁸ Psalm 43. 1, shifted from plea to statement of fact.
⁶⁹ Psalms 2. 12 and 25. 6, adapted.
⁷⁰ Psalm 31. 14?
⁷¹ Psalm 86. 5–6, adapted.
⁷² Psalm 104. 29 or Psalm 44. 24–25, adapted.
⁷³ Psalm 31. 25 or 106. 43 (?) and Psalm 42. 8.
⁷⁴ Psalm 34. 8, shifted to first person indicative.
⁷⁵ Combination of Psalms 48. 9, 139. 17, 40. 7.

Dominion, power, and glory be thine: for thou hast made all things: and because thy will is so: they do still continue.⁷⁶

Thy name be blessed, praised, and magnified, both now and ever and world without end.⁷⁷

Amen.

Psalm 22

The complaint° of Christ on the cross.⁷⁸

My God, my God, why hast thou forsaken me? It seemeth that I shall not obtain deliverance, though I seek for it with loud cries.

My God, I will cry all the day long, but thou wilt not answer: and all the night long, without taking any rest.

The meantime, thou most holiest, seemest to sit still, not caring for the things that I suffer: which so oft hast helped me heretofore, and hast given to thy people, Israel, sufficient argument and matter to praise thee with songs, wherewith they have given thanks to thee for thy benefits.

Our forefathers were wont° to put their trust in thee: and as often as they did so, thou didst deliver them.

As oft as they cried for help to thee, they were delivered: and oft as they committed themself to thee, they were not put to any shame.

But as for me, I seem rather to be a worm than a man: the dunghill of Adam:⁷⁹ the outcast of the vulgar people.

As many as have seen me: have laughed me to scorn, and reviled me, as shaking their heads in derision at me: have cast me in the teeth, saying:

He is wont to boast and glory, that he is in great favour with God: wherefore let God now deliver him, if he love him so well.

By thy procurement (O Lord) I came out of my mother's womb: and thou gavest me good comfort: even when I sucked my mother's breasts.

Through thy means I came into this world: and as soon as I was born, I was left to thy tuition: yea, thou wast my God, when I was yet in my mother's womb.

Wherefore go not far away from me: for danger is even now at hand, and I see no man that will help me.

---

⁷⁶ Psalm 96. 6 or parts of Psalm 145. 10–13; Psalm 119. 90–91.

⁷⁷ Psalm 113. 2.

⁷⁸ No such headnote appears in the Hebrew Psalms, but this was a standard typological reading of this Psalm, based on Christ's quotation of Psalm 22. 1 on the cross in Mark and Matthew as well as other verses which seem in retrospect to have predicted actions, like the piercing of his hands and feet or the casting of lots for his clothes.

⁷⁹ The 'dunghill of Adam' is Parr's addition, combining the dunghill upon which the suffering Job sits (Job 2. 8 in the Vulgate, though not in English Bibles, since they are based not on the Septuagint but the Hebrew) with some sense of the Hebrew meaning of 'Adam', 'earth'. Job was traditionally understood to be a type of Christ, as was Adam, whose sin was undone by Christ's sacrifice (Romans 5. 12–15).

Many bulls have closed me in, both strong and fat, they have compassed° me round about.

They have opened their mouth against me, like unto a lion that gapeth upon his prey, and roareth for hunger.

I am poured out like water, and all my limbs loosed one from the other, and my heart is melted within me, as it were wax.

All my strength is gone and dried up like unto a tile stone, my tongue cleaveth to the roof of my mouth: and at the last I shall be buried in the earth as the dead be wont.

For dogs have compassed me round about: and the most wicked have conspired against me, they have made holes through my hands and my feet.

I was so ungently entreated of them, that I might easily number all my bones:[80] and after all the pain and torment that they did to me, with grievous countenance they stared and looked upon me.

They divided my clothes among them, and cast lots for my coat.

Wherefore, Lord, I beseech thee, go not far from me: but forasmuch as thou art my power and my strength, make haste to help me.

Deliver my soul from danger of the sword, and keep my life, destitute of all man's help, from the violence of the dog.

Save me from the mouth of the lion, and take me from the horns of the unicorns.[81]

I will show unto my brethren the majesty of thy name: and when the people is most assembled together, I will praise and set forth thy most worthy acts and deeds.

All that worship the Lord, praise him, all the posterity of Jacob magnify him, all ye that be of the stock of Israel, with reverence serve and honour him.

For he hath not despised and set at nought° the poor man, because of his misery: nor he hath not disdainfully turned away his face from him: but rather as soon as the poor man cried unto him for help, he heard him by and by.

I will praise thee with my songs openly in a multitude of people, and I will perform my vows in the sight of them that honour thee.

The poor shall eat and be satisfied: they shall praise the Lord, that study to please him: and as many of you as continue still such, your hearts shall live.

All the ends of the world shall consider these things and be turned to the Lord: and all heathen nations shall submit themself, and do homage unto thee.

For the Lord hath a power royal, and an imperial dominion over the heathen.

The most mighty and greatest of all them that dwell on the earth have eaten, and after that they have tasted the spiritual gifts of the Lord, they have submitted themself, and made humble suit° unto him: yea, and all the dead, which are

---

[80] number all my bones] He is so thin, his bones are apparent beneath his skin.
[81] unicorns] See note 23, p. 79.

buried in the earth, shall kneel and make reverence in his honour: because he hath not disdained to spend his own life for them.

They that shall come after us, shall honour and serve him:

These things shall be written of the Lord, that our posterity may know and understand them.

That they also may come and show these things to the people that shall be born of them, that the Lord hath done these things, which be so marvellous.

17. Anne Askew, *The First Examination of Anne Askew Lately Martyred in Smithfield* (1546)

[Anne Askew (c. 1521–1546) was the daughter of Sir William Askew, sheriff of Lincolnshire. Details of her life depend upon the accounts of her martyrdom published by John Bale. The first of these, *The First Examination* (1546), includes at the end Askew's translation of Psalm 54. *The Latter Examination* (1547) includes the non-biblical 'Ballad Which Anne Askew Made and Sang When She Was in Newgate'. Both were published in Wesel (though the title page claimed the place was Marburg), though the *First Examination* was reprinted a number of times, several in London. Sir William arranged the marriage of Askew to Thomas Kyme, by whom she had two children, but she converted to Protestantism and left him. By 1544 Askew had arrived in London, and was connected to a community of those who shared her Protestant beliefs. She came to the attention of Church authorities, and in 1545 was taken for examination. For whatever reason, Askew was released, but she was soon re-arrested. In 1546, Askew was examined and tortured, asked in particular about her connection to suspected Protestants at court, including Queen Katherine Parr. She was taken to Newgate and then burned at Smithfield. Askew's account of her own trials was taken from Bale's editions and included in John Foxe's *Acts and Monuments*. It is not clear, however, exactly how much is really Askew's composition and how much Bale's, put in her own voice; barring any new archival discovery, Askew's and Bale's voices must remain inextricably blended together. Psalm 54 is presented as Askew's, and has often been accepted as hers, but it is strikingly similar in style to the metrical version of Psalm 14 that Bale included in his edition of Elizabeth's translation of Marguerite of Angueleme (see **20**). This Psalm may actually be his as well. See Claire Costley King'oo, 'Authenticity and Excess in *The Examinations of Anne Askew*', *Reformation*, 19.1 (2014), 21–39; *The Examinations of Anne Askew*, ed. by Elaine V. Beilin (New York: Oxford University Press, 1996); Diane Watt, *ODNB*.]

Psalm 54

The voice of Anne Askew out of the 54th Psalm of David, called *Deus in nomine tuo*. [God, by thy name]

For thy name's sake, be my refuge,
    And, in thy truth, my quarrel judge.
Before thee (Lord) let me be heard.
    And with favour my tale regard.
5 Lo, faithless men against me rise,
    And, for thy sake, my death practise.[82]
My life they seek, with main and might,
    Which have not thee afore their sight.
Yet helpst thou me, in this distress,
10   Saving my soul, from cruelness.
I wot thou wilt revenge my wrong,   *know*
    And visit them, ere it be long.
I will therefore, my whole heart bend
    Thy gracious name (Lord) to commend.
15 From evil[83] thou hast delivered me,
    Declaring what mine en'mies be.
        Praise to God.

18. Henry Howard, Earl of Surrey (MS *c*. 1546–1547)

[Henry Howard, Earl of Surrey (1516/17–1547) had one of the most prestigious aristocratic pedigrees of his day, with claims to the throne at least as good as the reigning Tudors, descending from Edward I and (through his mother) Edward III. He was the son of Thomas Howard, third Duke of Norfolk. Surrey had a private humanist education, rooted in classical languages and literature. He became a companion to Henry VIII's illegitimate son, Henry Fitzroy, Earl of Richmond, and with him, accompanying the king and queen, travelled to France, where at the French court he met French and Italian Renaissance artists and poets. This stimulated Surrey's ambitions to bring the Renaissance to England, and to be an active part of such a cultural renewal. Like Sir Thomas Wyatt, for whom Surrey wrote powerful elegies, Surrey imported the Petrarchan sonnet into English verse, and Wyatt's and Surrey's lyrics formed the core of the influential verse collection *Songs and Sonnets by the Right Honourable Lord Henry Howard Late Earl of Surrey, and Others*, published by Richard Tottel in 1557. Surrey's translation of books II and IV of Virgil's *Aeneid* (the latter published in 1554) was the first use of blank verse in English. The magnificent Surrey House, which Surrey had constructed on Mount Surrey outside Norwich,

---

[82] practise] The metre requires a stress on the second syllable: 'prac-TISE'.

[83] evil] The metre demands pronunciation as a monosyllable, perhaps 'ill' or 'ev'l'.

was the architectural equivalent of his English *Aeneid*, and symbolized the young earl's intemperate ambitions. Surrey served as a commander in the king's army in France in 1545 and 46, but was recalled in disgrace after reports of defeat and mismanagement. Surrey was arrested in 1546 after Sir Richard Southwell reported him for treason, especially the inclusion of the royal arms and insignia in his own. After some weeks in the Tower, Surrey was beheaded on 19 January 1547, the last execution in the reign of Henry VIII, who died on January 28. Surrey's translation project, an effort to bring into English the magnificence of the Italian Renaissance and the glories of the ancient world, included biblical poems. Despite being the heir of England's most illustrious Catholic family, Surrey himself was converted to the evangelical or Protestant faith. His paraphrase of Ecclesiastes was read by the martyr Anne Askew, who alludes to it in the ballad she composed in Newgate prison. Surrey translated several Psalms into metre, including Psalms 73, 88, and 55, which he composed while in the Tower, and Psalm 8, which most scholars feel must have been done earlier. In *Certain Chapters of the Proverbs of Solomon* (1549–1550), John Case printed Surrey's Psalm 88 as Sternhold's, hoping to cash in on the growing popularity of the Sternhold and Hopkins Psalms. It has been argued that versions of Psalms 31 and 51 in this volume were also by Surrey, though this attribution has not been widely accepted. A few years later, Francis Seagar re-plagiarized and revised these Psalms in his *Certain Psalms* (1553), claiming them as his own. Seagar converted them from poulter's measure into the common metre used by Sternhold, and he included tunes by which to sing them. Like many other sixteenth-century Psalms translators, Surrey draws on the paraphrases by Johannes Campensis, in print in England by 1534, as well as the Vulgate, but Surrey's approach to the Psalms is both personal and political. Psalms 73 and 88 are prefaced and autobiographically contextualized by verses addressed to Sir Anthony Denny, member of the Privy Council and secretary of state, and Sir George Blage (or Blagge), a staunch Protestant courtier and friend of Wyatt's. Psalm 55, the last poem Surrey wrote, departs most strikingly from the original, and breaks down in a reference to 'the other psalm of David', closing with the final verse of Psalm 55 (54) in the Latin Vulgate, untranslated. This is Surrey's only poem in unrhymed hexameters and is the first English poem to use this metre, probably derived from the French alexandrine. The rhythm of Surrey's poulter's measure Psalms (a metre whose invention is credited to Wyatt) is easier to read with the original virgules marking the half-line, so these have been retained. See Elizabeth Heale, *Wyatt, Surrey & Early Tudor Poetry* (London and New York: Longman, 1998); Charles Huttar, 'Poems by Surrey and Others in a Printed Miscellany Circa 1550', *English Miscellany*, 16 (1965), 9–18; William A. Sessions, *Henry Howard, the Poet Earl of Surrey: A Life* (Oxford: Oxford University Press, 1999); Rivkah Zim, *English Metrical Psalms: Poetry as Praise and Prayer, 1535–1601* (Cambridge and New York: Cambridge University Press, 1987); Susan Brigden, *ODNB*.]

Psalm 8

Thy name, O Lord, how great / is found before our sight.
It fills the earth and spreads the air, / the great works of thy might.
For even unto thy power / the heavens have given a place,
And closèd it above their heads / a mighty large compace.   *compass*
5 Thy praise what cloud can hide, / but it will shine again,
Since young and tender sucking babes / have power to show it plain;
Which, in despight of those / that would this glory hide,   *defiance*
Hast put into such infants' mouths / for to confound their pride.   *put to shame*
Wherefore I shall behold / thy figured heaven so high,   *patterned*
10 Which shows such prints of diverse forms / within the cloudy sky
As hills and shapes of men, / eke beasts of sundry kind,   *also*
Monstrous to our outward sight / and fancies of our mind;
And eke the wanish moon / which shines by night also,   *pale*
And each one of the wand'ring stars / which after her doth go;
15 And how to keep their course, / and which are those that stands,
Because they be thy wondrous works / and labours of thy hands.
But yet among all these / I ask, What thing is man,
Whose turn to serve in his poor need / this work thou first began?
Or what is Adam's son[84] / that bears his father's mark,
20 For whose delight and comfort eke / thou has wrought all this wark?   *work*
I see thou mindest him much / that dost reward him so,
Being but earth, to rule the earth / where on himself doth go.
From angels' substance eke, / thou madest him differ small,
Save one doth change his life awhile, / the other not at all.
25 The sun and moon also, / thou madest to give him light,
And catch one of the wand'ring stars / to twinkle sparkles bright.
The air to give him breath, / the water for his health,
The earth to bring forth grain and fruit / for to increase his wealth.
And many metals too, / for pleasure of the eye,
30 Which, in the hollow sounded ground, / in privy veins do lie.   *hidden*
The sheep to give his wool, / to wrap his body in,
And for such other needful things / the ox to spare his skin.   *necessary*
The horse, even at his will, / to bear him to and fro,
And as him list catch other beast / to serve his turn also.   *pleases*
35 The fishes of the sea / likewise, to feed him oft,
And eke the birds, whose feathers serve / to make his sides lie soft.
On whose head thou hast set / a crown of glory too,
To whom also thou didst appoint / that honour should be do.
And thus thou madest him Lord / of all this work of thine:

---

[84] Adam's son] Cain, marked by God after murdering his brother Abel (Genesis 4).

40 Of man that goes; of beast that creeps, / whose looks doth down decline;
Of fish that swim below; / of fowls that flies on high;
Of sea that finds the air his reign; / and of the land so dry.
And underneath his feet / thou hast set all this same,
To make him know and plain confess / that marvellous is thy name.
45 And Lord, which art our Lord, / how marvellous is it found
The heavens doth show, the earth doth tell, / and eke the world so round.
Glory therefore be given / to thee first, which art three,
And yet but one almighty God, / in substance and degree.
As first it was when thou / the dark confusèd heap
50 Clotted in one, didst part in four, / which elements we cleap,[85]   *call*
And as the same is now, / even hear within our time,
And ever shall hereafter be, / when we be filth and slime.

Psalm 55

Exaudi Deus orationem meam.   [Hear my prayer, O God]

Give ear to my suit, Lord, fromward hide not thy face.   *petition, away from*
Behold, hearken — in grief, lamenting, how I pray.
My foes, they bray so loud, and eke threpe on so fast,   *cry out, also, scold*
Buckled to do me scathe, so is their malice bent.   *girded, harm*
5 Care pierceth my entrails, and travaileth my spirit;
The grisly fear of death environeth my breast;   *surrounds*
A trembling cold of dread clean overwhelm'th my heart.   *completely*
Oh, think I, had I wings like to the simple dove
This peril might I fly, and seek some place of rest
10 In wilder woods, where I might dwell far from these cares.
What speedy way of wing, my plaints should they lay on   *laments*
To scape the stormy blast, that threatened is to me.   *escape*
Reign those unbridled tongues, break that conjured league,[86]   *conspiring*
For I deciphered have, amid our town, the strife;
15 Guile and wrong keep walls, they ward both day and night,   *guard*
And mischief, join'd with care, doth keep the marketstead,   *guard, marketplace*
Whilst wickedness with craft in heaps swarm through the street.   *strength*
Not my declarèd foe wrought me all this reproach,
By harm so lookèd for, it weigheth half the less;

---

[85] elements] The ancient Greek elements of air, fire, earth, and water, thought to be the constituent components of all matter, a notion that persisted into the Renaissance.
[86] The 'conjured league' is Surrey's addition, referring to his former friends who betrayed him, including among others Sir Edward Warner, his cousin Edmund Knyvet, George Blage, and especially Richard Southwell, the likely referent of Surrey's 'old fere and dear friend'. See Susan Brigden, 'Henry Howard, Earl of Surrey, and the "Conjured League"', *The Historical Journal*, 37.3 (1994), 507–37.

20 For though mine en'mies hap had been for to prevail,	*fortune*
I could have hid my face from venom of his eye.	
It was a friendly foe, by shadow of good will,	
Mine old fere and dear friend, my guide that trappèd me,	*comrade*
Where I was wont to fetch the cure of all my care,	*accustomed*
25 And in his bosom hide my secret zeal to God.	
Such sudden surprise quick may himself devour,	*living*
Whilst I invoke the Lord, whose power shall me defend.	
My prayer shall not cease from that the sun descends	
Till he his alture win, and hide them in the sea.	*high altitude*
30 With words of hot effect, that moves from heart contrite,[87]	
Such humble suit, O Lord, doth pierce thy patient ear.	
It was the Lord that break the bloody compacts of those	
That prelooked on,[88] with ire to slaughter me and mine,	
The everlasting God, whose kingdom has no end.	
35 Whom by no tale to dread, he could divert from sin,	
The conscience unquiet he strikes with heavy hand,	
And proves their force in faith, whom he sware to defend.	
Butter falls not so soft as doth his patience long,	
And over passeth fine oil, running not half so smooth.	
40 But when his sufferance finds that bridled wrath provokes	
He threateneth wrath, he whets more sharp, than any tool can file.	*sharpen*
Friar, whose harm and tongue presents the wicked sort	
Of those false wolves with coats, which do their ravin hide,[89]	*predatory greed*
That sware to me by heaven, the foot stool of the Lord	
45 Who though force had hurt my fame, they did not touch my life.	
Such patching care I loathe, as feeds the wealth with lies,	*deceitful*
But in the other Psalm[90] of David find I ease:	
Iacta curam tuam super dominum et ipse te enutriet. id est	
Cast thy care upon the Lord, and he shall nourish thee.	

Psalm 73

The sudden storms that heave me to and fro
Had well-near piercèd faith my guiding sail,
For I that on the noble voyage go,

---

[87] heart contrite] From Psalm 51. 17.

[88] prelooked] looked beforehand, or in anticipation (this is the only instance of the word cited in the *OED*).

[89] The metaphor derives from the false prophets described as wolves in sheep's clothing of Matthew 7. 15. From line 42, Surrey departs freely from the original Psalm.

[90] the other Psalm] Unclear, but perhaps the reference is to the following verse (verse 23 of the Psalm) from the Vulgate.

To succour truth and falsehood to assail,
Constrainèd am to bear my sails full low
And never could attain some pleasant gail,   *goal*
For unto such the prosp'rous winds do blow
As run from port to port to seek avail.[91]   *aid*
This bred despair, whereof such doubts did grow
That I gan faint and all my courage fail.   *began (to)*
But now, my Blage,[92] mine error will I see;
Such goodly light King David giveth me.

Quam bonus Israel Deus.   [How good is God to Israel]

Though, Lord, to Israel / thy graces plenteous be,
I mean to such with pure intent / as fix their trust in thee;
Yet, whiles the faith did faint / that should have been my guide,
Like them that walk in slipper paths / my feet began to slide,[93]   *slippery*
Whiles I did grudge at those / that glory in their gold,   *grumble*
Whose loathsome pride rejoiceth wealth, / in quiet as they would.
To see by course of years / what nature doth appair,   *weaken*
The palaces of princely form / succeed from heir to heir;[94]
From all such travails free / as 'long to Adam's seed,   *belong, descendants*
Neither withdrawn from wicked works / by danger nor by dread,
Whereof their scornful pride; / and gloried with their eyes,
As garments clothe the naked man, / thus are they clad in vice.
Thus, as they wish succeeds / the mischief that they mean,
Whose glutted cheeks sloth feeds so fat / as scant their eyes be seen.
Unto whose cruel power / most men for dread are fain   *glad*
To bend and bow with lofty looks, / whiles they vaunt in their reign;   *boast*
And in their bloody hands, / whose cruelty that frame
The wailful works that scourge the poor / without regard of blame.
To tempt the living God / they think it no offence,
And pierce the simple with their tongues / that can make no defence.
Such proofs before the just / to cause their hearts to waver

---

[91] The sailing metaphor was conventional in Petrarchan love poetry, as in Edmund Spenser's 'Like as a ship, that through the ocean wide', but it was also repurposed to devotional uses, as in Thomas Campion's later poem 'Never weather-beaten sail'.
[92] Blage] Sir George Blage (c. 1512–1551), a successful courtier, MP, and strong Protestant, close to Surrey, Sir Thomas Wyatt, and others interested in poetry. Blage opposed Surrey's political ambitions and may have testified against him, but they were reconciled before Surrey's execution, as this statement suggests.
[93] Surrey's wording, while staying close to the sense of the Psalm verse, recalls Sir Thomas Wyatt's poem on the dangers of court, 'Stand whoso list upon the slipper top'.
[94] There is nothing about royal succession in the Psalm, but this was in fact exactly what Surrey did 'grudge at', and what resulted in his arrest and execution.

  Be set with cups mingled with gall, / of bitter taste and savour.   *bile*
35 Then say thy foes in scorn / that taste no other food
  But suck the flesh of thy elect⁹⁵ / and bathe them in their blood:
  Should we believe the Lord / doth know and suffer this?   *allow*
  Foolèd be he with fables vain / that so abusèd is.
  In terror of the just⁹⁶ / thus reigns iniquity,
40 Armèd with power, laden with gold, / and dread for cruelty.
  Then vain the war might seem / that I by faith maintain
  Against the flesh, whose false effects / my pure heart would disdain.
  For I am scourgèd still / that no offence have done,
  By wrath's children and from my birth / my chastising begun.
45 When I beheld their pride / and slackness of thy hand,
  I gan bewail the woeful state / wherein thy chosen stand.
  And when I sought whereof / thy suffrance Lord should grow,
  I found no wit could pierce so far / thy holy dooms to know,   *judgements*
  And that no mysteries / nor doubt could be distrust
50 Till I come to the holy place, / the mansion of the just,⁹⁷
  Where I shall see what end / thy justice shall prepare
  For such as build on worldly wealth, / and dye their colours fair.
  Oh, how their ground is false / and all their buildings vain,
  And they shall fall, their powers fail / that did their pride maintain.
55 As chargèd hearts with care, / that dreams some pleasant turn,
  After their sleep find their abuse, / and to their plaint return,   *lament*
  So shall their glory fade; / thy sword of vengeance shall
  Unto their drunken eyes, in blood, / disclose their errors all.
  And when their golden fleece⁹⁸ / is from their back yshorn,   *shorn*
60 The spots that underneath were hid / thy chosen sheep shall scorn;   *hidden*
  And till that happy day / my heart shall swell in care,
  My eyes yield tears, my years consume / between hope and despair.   *wear away*
  Lo, how my spirits are dull, / and all thy judgments dark;
  No mortal head may scale so high, / but wonder at thy wark.   *work*
65 Alas, how oft my foes / have framèd my decay;
  But when I stood in dread to drench, / thy hands still did me stay.   *drown, secure*

---

⁹⁵ See note 103, p. 110. Surrey takes the wicked sucking (BCP, the Hebrew can also mean 'drain') advantage from the people and turns it into a horrible image of predatory cannibalism. The verb 'suck' in the English Bible is almost always used for breastfeeding.

⁹⁶ terror of] i.e. terror to.

⁹⁷ Surrey's 'mansion' is perhaps more suited to a Renaissance nobleman than the 'sanctuary of God' (BCP). It is hard not to think of his own prodigious Mount Surrey, overlooking the city of Norwich.

⁹⁸ golden fleece] From classical myth, the gold wool of the ram of the King of Colchis, stolen by Jason with the help of Medea, a symbol of power and authority, though most likely used by Surrey to symbolize wealth or perhaps courtly success.

And in each voyage that / I took to conquer sin,
Thou wert my guide, and gave me grace / to comfort me therein.
And when my withered skin / unto my bones did cleave,
70 And flesh did waste, thy grace did then / my simple sprites relieve.   *spirits*
In others' succours then, / O Lord, why should I trust,
But only thine, whom I have found / in thy behight so just.   *promise*
And such for dread or gain, / as shall thy name refuse
Shall perish with their golden gods, / that did their hearts seduce.
75 Where I, that in thy word / have set my trust and joy,
The high reward that longs thereto / shall quietly enjoy.   *belongs*
And my unworthy lips, / inspired with thy grace,
Shall thus forespeak thy secret works / in sight of Adam's race.   *prophesy, posterity*

Finis

Psalm 88[99]

Where reckless youth in an unquiet breast,
Set on by wrath, revenge, and cruelty,
After long war, patience had oppressed,
And justice wrought by princely equity,[100]
5   My Denny,[101] then mine error deep impressed
Began to work despair of liberty,
Had not David the perfect warrior taught
That of my fault thus pardon should be sought.

Domine deus salutis.   [O Lord, God of my salvation]

O Lord, upon whose will / dependeth my welfare,
10 To call upon thy holy name, / since day nor night I spare,
Grant that the just request / of this repentant mind
So pierce thine ears, that in thy sight / some favour it may find.
My soul is fraughted full / with grief of follies past;   *laden*
My restless body doth consume, / and death approacheth fast: *waste away*
15 Like them whose fatal thread, / thy hand hath cut in twain;[102]   *two*

---

[99] This Psalm was described as usual for those in prison by Sir Thomas More, Johannes Campensis, and Miles Coverdale (Zim 91).

[100] On equity, see note 6, p. 68.

[101] Denny] Sir Anthony Denny (1501-1549), gentleman of the privy chamber to Henry VIII, client of Thomas Cromwell and strong Protestant, keeper of the privy purse, a humanist educated at St Paul's by John Colet, possessor in the last days of Henry VIII of the king's dry stamp, serving as the royal signature. Denny could thus conceivably have cancelled the order for Surrey's execution.

[102] Surrey converts what in the BCP is simply those 'cut away from thy hand' to a classical allusion to the Fates, specifically Atropos who cuts each thread of life.

	Of whom there is no further bruit, / which in their graves remain.	*noise*
	O Lord, thou hast me cast / headlong, to please my foe,	
	Into a pit all bottomless, / whereas I plain my woe.	*complain*
	The burden of thy wrath / it doth me sore oppress;	
20	And sundry storms thou hast me sent / of terror and distress.	
	The faithful friends are fled / and banished from my sight:	
	And such as I have held full dear, / have set my friendship light.	
	My durance doth persuade / of freedom such despair,	
	That by the tears that bain my breast, / mine eyesight doth appair.	*bathe, weaken*
25	Yet do I never cease / thine aid for to desire,	
	With humble heart and stretchèd hands, / for to appease thine ire.	*anger*
	Wherefore dost thou forbear / in the defence of thine,	
	To shew such tokens of thy power / in sight of Adam's line;	
	Whereby each feeble heart / with faith might so be fed,	
30	That in the mouth of thy elect[103] / thy mercies might be spread.	
	The flesh that feedeth worms / cannot thy love declare	
	Nor such set forth thy praise as dwell / in the land of despair.	
	In blind indurèd[104] hearts / light of thy lively name	*hardened, life-giving*
	Cannot appear, nor cannot judge / the brightness of the same.	
35	Nor blazèd may thy name / be by the mouths of those	
	Whom death hath shut in silence, so / as they may not disclose.	
	The lively voice of them / that in thy word delight,	
	Must be the trump that must resound / the glory of thy might.	*trumpet*
	Wherefore I shall not cease, / in chief of my distress	
40	To call on thee, till that the sleep / my wearied limbs oppress.[105]	
	And in the morning eke / when that the sleep is fled,	*also*
	With floods of salt repentant tears / to wash my restless bed.[106]	
	Within this careful mind, / burden'd with care and grief,	*troubled*
	Why dost thou not appear, O Lord, / that should'st be his relief.	
45	My wretchèd state behold, / whom death shall straight assail;	*immediately*
	Of one, from youth afflicted still, / that never did but wail.	
	The dread, lo, of thine ire / hath trod me under feet:	*anger*
	The scourges of thine angry hand / hath made death seem full sweet.	
	Like as the roaring waves / the sunken ship surround,	

---

[103] Surrey adds the idea of election, making the persecuted described, and perhaps personified, by the Psalmist seem distinctly Protestant; in Calvinist theology, the elect were those predestined for salvation by God.

[104] indured] A 'hard heart' is a common biblical idiom for lack of feeling or sympathy, and resistance to God.

[105] As Zim points out (96), lines 37–40 are Surrey's addition to the Psalm, perhaps a reference to the godly or Protestants.

[106] Surrey elaborates the weeping by importing the image of tears washing the bed from Psalm 6. 6.

50   Great heaps of care did swallow me, / and I no succour found:
   For they whom no mischance / could from my love divide,
   Are forcèd, to my greater grief, / from me their face to hide.[107]

19. Thomas Sternhold, *Certain Psalms Chosen out of the Psalter of David and Drawn into English Metre by Thomas Sternhold, Groom of the King's Majesty's Robes* (1547?)

[Thomas Sternhold (d. 1549) was a gentleman in waiting to Henry VIII and then to his son and heir, Edward VI. His Protestant views prevented him from subscribing to the Six Articles, the 1539 Act reasserting Catholic orthodoxy, for which he was imprisoned in the Fleet with several other men of the royal household. He was MP for Plymouth at the end of Henry's reign, during which time he also acquired land and position in Gloucestershire. Sternhold, along with other favoured servants, received 100 marks in Henry's will. Sternhold may have begun translating Psalms into singing metres while Henry was still alive, but his first collection, *Certain Psalms Chosen out of the Psalter of David*, likely appeared in 1547, at the beginning of Edward's assertively Protestant reign. According to Sternhold's dedication to the young king, Edward enjoyed hearing Sternhold sing them. Sternhold's Psalms were designed to be sung, and though they obviously served as godly entertainment or devotion for king and court, it has been argued that the translations also promote a strong Protestant agenda, in keeping with official Edwardian policies. They were not sung in the way they later were, however, in unison (or harmony) to Genevan-style tunes. A contemporary manuscript survives, for instance, with a setting of Sternhold's Psalm 4 for solo voice and lute in the style of a pavan, a slow dance tune. No evidence survives for congregational Psalm singing before 1559. Sternhold used more than one metre for his Psalms, but the one that became known as 'Sternhold's metre' is identical to ballad metre and may also be thought of as broken fourteeners, since only the first and third lines rhyme. John Hopkins used rhymes for the odd lines as well and the *abab* pattern became the most common for singing Psalms (hence 'common metre'), following the immensely popular *The Whole Book of Psalms*, or 'Sternhold and Hopkins', as it became known. See Hannibal Hamlin, *Psalm Culture and Early Modern English Literature* (Cambridge: Cambridge University Press, 2004); Beth Quitslund, *The Reformation in Rhyme: Sternhold, Hopkins and the English Metrical Psalter, 1547–1603* (Aldershot and Burlington: Ashgate, 2008); Nicholas Temperley, '"All skillful praises sing": How Congregations Sang the Psalms in Early Modern England', *Renaissance Studies*, 29.4 (2015), 531–53; Zim, *English Metrical Psalms*; Zim, *ODNB*.]

---

[107] This final nautical image is Surrey's addition, ending the Psalm with what seems almost a Petrarchan figure, though it also suggests the dangerous waters of Psalms 107 or 130.

Psalm 1

Beatus vir. [Blessed is the man]

How happy be the righteous men,
This Psalm declareth plain:
And how the ways of wicked men,
Be damnable and vain.

5   The man is blest that hath not gone
By wicked rede astray, *counsel*
Nor sat in chair of pestilence,
Nor walked in sinner's way.
     But in the law of God the Lord,
10 Doth set his whole delight,
And in that law doth exercise
Himself both day and night.
     And as the tree that planted is
Fast by the river side: *securely*
15 Even so shall he bring forth his fruit
In his due time and tide.
     His leaf shall never fall away
But flourish still and stand;
Each thing shall prosper wondrous well
20 That he doth take in hand.
     So shall the ungodly do,
They shall be nothing so,
But as the dust which, from the earth,
The winds drive to and fro.
25   Therefore shall not the wicked men
In judgement stand upright,
Nor yet in council of the just,
But shall be void of might.
     For why the way of godly men, *because*
30 Unto the Lord is known,
And eke the way of wicked men, *also*
Shall quite be overthrown.

Psalm 120[108]

Ad dominum cum tribularer.   [I called to the Lord in trouble]

The good men cry and much lament,
That they so long do dwell
In company of carnal men,   *worldly*
The sons of Ishmael.[109]
5   In trouble and in thrall,   *bondage*
Unto the Lord I call,
And he doth me comfort:
Deliver me I say,
From liars' lips alway,   *always*
10 And tongue of false report.
How hurtful is the thing,
Or else how doth it sting,
The tongue of such a liar?
I hurt'th no less, I wean,
15 Than arrows sharp and keen
Of hot consuming fire.
Alas, too long I dwell
With the son of Ishmael,
That Chedar is to name.[110]
20 By whom the folk elect,
And all of Isaac's sect,[111]
Are put to open shame.
With them that peace did hate
I came a peace to make,
25 And set a quiet life.
But when my word was told,[112]
Causeless I was controlled
By them that would have strife.

---

[108] Zim (85–88) suggests that this was a personal Psalm, like those of Surrey (see 18) and the Dudleys (see 32, 33), perhaps written during Sternhold's imprisonment in the Fleet in March 1543, charged with supporting the Protestant opinions of the priest Anthony Persons.

[109] Ishmael] First son of Abraham by his concubine Hagar, cast out but promised by God to be founder of a great (non-Israelite) nation (Genesis 16-17); interpreted allegorically by Paul as figuring Jews, children of the flesh, as opposed to Christians, children of the promise (Galatians 4).

[110] Chedar] The second son of Ishmael (Genesis 25. 13), 'Kedar' in KJV.

[111] Isaac] Second son of Abraham, by his wife Sarah, inheritor of blessing and birthright (Genesis 21). Sternhold adds the distinction between Ishmael and Isaac, the Psalmist originally (as in BCP) lamenting his sojourn with Mesech (a son of Japheth) and Kedar (a son of Ishmael). The 'folk elect' suggests English Protestants, using the term they favoured for being chosen by God.

[112] Not indented in original.

20. John Bale, *A Godly Meditation of the Christian Soul, Concerning a Love Towards God and his Christ, Compiled in French by Lady Marguerite, Queen of Navarre, and Aptly Translated into English by the Right Virtuous Lady Elizabeth, Daughter to our Late Sovereign Henry the VIII* (1548)

[John Bale (1495–1563) was one of the most diversely prolific and influential writers of the English Reformation. He studied at Jesus College, Cambridge, where despite the increasing influence of Protestant ideas, he remained a faithful Catholic. In 1530 he became prior of the white friars' convent at Maldon, in 1533 he was promoted to the Carmelite convent in Ipswich, and in 1534 he was prior at Doncaster. By 1536, Bale had renounced his vows, embraced Reform, and married. After the fall and execution of Thomas Cromwell and Henry VIII's late turn against Reform, Bale went into exile on the Continent, returning after the accession of Edward VI. He moved to Ireland in 1552, where he was made bishop of Ossory, and he joined the effort to convert the Irish to Protestantism. Fearing a Catholic plot against him after the accession of Mary I, Bale fled to the Netherlands in 1553, and then moved on to Frankfurt and Basel. Bale returned to England with the accession of Elizabeth I, who appointed him to a position at Canterbury. Bale wrote in an extraordinary number of genres and modes, from religious polemic to drama, literary history, martyrology, and biblical exegesis. Bale's plays include the first English history play, *King Johan*, as well as moralities and biblical mysteries. His *Illustrium majoris Britanniae scriptorium* ('Summary of the Illustrious Writers of Great Britain') was an invaluable collection of information on five centuries of British authors. *The Image of Both Churches*, Bale's extensive commentary on Revelation, shaped thinking and writing on history and the apocalypse for the next century. Bale's Psalm 14, which is appended to the then-Princess Elizabeth's translation of Marguerite of Angouleme's *A Godly Meditation of the Christian Soul*, was also thought to be Elizabeth's work, but a conclusive case has been made for reattribution. Bale was responsible for the printing of Elizabeth's work in Wesel, and the metrical translation of Psalm 14 is inserted after Bale's own conclusion, in which he cites Elizabeth's own renderings of the first verse of Psalm 14 into Latin, French, Italian, and Greek. See Peter Happé, *John Bale* (New York: Twayne Publishers, 1996); David Scott Kastan, 'An Early English Metrical Psalm: Elizabeth's or John Bale's?', *Notes and Queries* (November 1974), 404–05; Oliver Wort, *John Bale and Religious Conversion in Reformation England* (London: Pickering & Chatto, 2013); John N. King, *ODNB*.]

Psalm 14

Fools, that true faith yet never had,
Saith in their hearts, there is no God.
Filthy they are, in their practise,[113]

---

[113] The metre requires a stress on the second syllable, 'prac-TISE'.

Of them, not one is godly wise.
5 From heaven, the Lord on man did look,
To know what ways he undertook;
All they were vain, and went astray,
Not one, he found, in the right way.
In heart and tongue have they deceit,
10 Their lips throw forth a poisoned bait.
Their minds are mad, their mouths are wode,   *insane*
And swift they be, in shedding blood.
So blind they are, no truth they know,
No fear of God in them will grow.[114]
15 How can that cruel sort be good?
Of God's dear flock, which suck the blood?
On him, rightly, shall they not call,
Despair will so their hearts appal.
At all times God is with the just,
20 Because they put in him their trust.
Who shall, therefore, from Zion give
That health which hangeth in our believe,   *belief*
When God shall take from his the smart,   *pain*
Then will Jacob rejoice in heart.
25   Praise to God.

21. John Bale, *A Dialogue or Communication To Be Had at a Table Between Two Children* (1549)

[Bale (see 20) included metrical Psalms in several of his publications, this theological dialogue apparently written for his sons John and Paul among them. The Psalm appears first, before the dialogue, and below it is John Bale's name and the date, 1543.]

---

[114] Lines 11–14 are Bale's translation of what constitute verses 5–7 in Coverdale's BCP version. These verses survive in the Septuagint, as reflected in the Vulgate (though in both the Psalm is numbered 13), but are not in the Masoretic Hebrew text. Thus in the Geneva Bible, Bishops' Bible, and the KJV, which (unlike Coverdale) goes back to the Hebrew, Psalm 14 has only 8 verses as opposed to the 11 in BCP. A further complication, unique in the Psalms, is that Paul, who read the Septuagint not the Hebrew, quotes the contested passage in full in Romans 3. 13–18. No mention is made of this discrepancy in the 1560 Geneva Bible, but an unavoidable awkwardness arose when in 1578 a Geneva Bible was printed with two different translations of the Psalms, Geneva and BCP, in parallel columns. In the extra space at the end of the Geneva text of Psalm 14, the editors add a note that the extra verses that have been put in 'more fully express the manners of the wicked', and are in fact verses taken from Isaiah 59 (vv. 7–8) and Psalms 5 (v. 9), 10 (v. 7), 36 (v. 3), and 140 (v. 3). See Specland, 'Competing Prose Psalters'.

Psalm 130

Called *De profundis*. [Out of the depths]

From faith of soul, and heart's rejoice,
I call to thee, Lord hear my voice.
   Thine ears, good Lord, inclinèd be
Unto the poor complaint of me   *lament*
5   If thou should'st weigh our wickedness,
Who can abide thy righteousness?
   Because I find all health in thee,
I doubt no fierce extremity.
   In my Lord God is all my trust,
10 To walk as his word hath discussed.
   The church, for her continuance,
Trust in the Lord's good governance.
   For in the Lord great mercy is,
And full redemption after this.
15 He will redeem all Israel,
From devil and death, from sin and hell.

22. John Hopkins, *All Such Psalms of David as Thomas Sternhold, Late Groom of the King's Majesty's Robes, Did in his Life Draw into English Metre* (1549)

[John Hopkins (1520/21–1570) is the second name made virtually a household word by the immensely popular *Whole Book of Psalms*, known as 'Sternhold and Hopkins'. Little is known about Hopkins's early life, but he was born in Staffordshire and may have earned a BA at Oxford. He moved to London, where he met the printer Edward Whitchurch, responsible for both the BCP and Sternhold's *Certain Psalms*. He added a number of his own metrical Psalms to fill out the expanded collection of Sternhold's (*All Such Psalms*). Hopkins was a clergyman and perhaps also a schoolmaster. More of Hopkins's Psalms, somewhat revised by William Whittingham and the Geneva exiles, were eventually included in the 1562 *Whole Book*, whose title forever linked his name with Sternhold's. Sixty-one of the 150 Psalms in the *Whole Book* were attributed to Hopkins, and his skill as a poet was praised by John Bale and (later) Thomas Wharton. While Sternhold's Psalms were written in the *abcb* rhyme scheme known as ballad metre, which could also be described as broken fourteeners (long lines just printed in two short halves), Hopkins added the second rhyme typical of what came to be called common metre (*abab*). See Quitslund, *Reformation in Rhyme*; Zim, *English Metrical Psalms*; Zim, *ODNB*.]

Psalm 30

Exaltabo te domine.   [I will magnify thee, Lord]

    The Church that ghostly Israel,[115]
        Her Lord and God doth praise:
    Which from the dread of death and hell,
        Doth her defend always.
5   All laud and praise with heart and voice,   *praise*
        O Lord, I give to thee:
    Which wilt not see my foes rejoice
        Nor triumph over me.
    O Lord, my God, to thee I cried,
10   In all my pain and grief:
    Thou gav'st an ear and didst provide
        To ease me with relief.
    Of thy good will thou hast called back
        My soul from hell to save:
15 Thou dost relieve when strength doth lack
        To keep me from the grave.
    Sing praise, ye saints, that prove and see
        The goodness of the Lord:
    In memory of his majesty,
20   Rejoice with one accord.
    For why, his anger but a space   *because*
        Doth last and slake again: *diminish*
    But yet the favour of his grace
        Forever doth remain.
25 Though gripes of grief and pangs full sore   *clutches*
        Do chance us overnight:
    The Lord to joy shall us restore,
        Before the day be light.
    When I enjoyed the world at will,
30   Thus would I boast and say:
    Tush, I am sure to feel none ill,
        This wealth shall not decay.
    For thou, O Lord, of thy good grace,
        Hadst sent me strength and aid:
35 But when thou turn'dst away thy face,
        My mind was sore dismayed.

---

[115] ghostly Israel] spiritual Israel; i.e. the Christian church (anachronistically inserted here) represents Israel in the spiritual, if not the literal, sense.

Wherefore again yet did I cry
    To thee, O Lord of might:
My God, with plaints I did apply   *laments*
40   And prayed both day and night.
What gain is in my blood, said I,
    If death destroy my days:
Doth dust declare thy majesty,
    Or yet thy truth doth praise?
45 Wherefore, my God, some pity take,
    O Lord, I thee desire:
Do not this simple soul forsake,
    Of help I thee require.
Then didst thou turn my grief and woe,
50   Unto a cheerful voice:
The mourning weed thou took'st me from,   *clothing*
    And mad'st me to rejoice.
Wherefore my soul incessantly
    Shall sing unto thy praise:
55 My Lord, my God, to thee will I
    Give laud and thanks always.

23. Sir Thomas Wyatt, *Certain Psalms Chosen out of the Psalter of David, Commonly Called the VII Penitential Psalms* (1549)

[Sir Thomas Wyatt (c. 1503–1542) was a courtier and diplomat as well as one of the most important early Tudor poets. Wyatt's father, Henry, was a privy councillor to Henry VII. Thomas attended St John's College, Cambridge, and in 1524 became clerk of the king's jewels, rising thereafter to esquire of the king's body. He accompanied diplomatic missions to the courts of France and the pope in Rome. In 1528, Wyatt presented Queen Katherine with his translation of Plutarch's *Quiet of Mind*, which was also printed that year. Wyatt returned to the Continent in 1529 and 30 when he was appointed high marshal of Calais, while it was still under English rule. In 1532 he was appointed commissioner of the peace for Essex, and in 1533 sewer-extraordinary to the king. He was likely knighted in 1535. In 1536, however, Wyatt was imprisoned in the Tower, accused of adultery with the now-fallen Queen Anne. There were rumours that Wyatt and Anne Boleyn had been lovers before she met the king, but there is no conclusive evidence. Wyatt was released in 1536, after the Queen's execution, and he continued to gain royal favour. In 1537 he was sent as ambassador to Emperor Charles V in Spain. Wyatt's mission was ultimately unsuccessful; he returned to England in 1540, but with the fall of Thomas Cromwell, his chief patron, Wyatt's political career took a turn. Charged with treason, in 1541 Wyatt was for the second time committed to the Tower. Once again, he was released, apparently after the intercession of Queen Katherine (Howard), and he was again restored to royal favour, though he died of fever in 1542. Wyatt's *Penitential Psalms* were his first poems to appear in print, published by John Harington (likely Harington of Stepney, the father of Sir John Harington the Psalm translator), but many of his lyrics were included in Tottel's Miscellany (*Songs and Sonnets*) in 1557, and his influence on subsequent English poetry was immense. Like Henry Howard, Earl of Surrey, Wyatt imported Italian and French poetic forms, like the Petrarchan sonnet and terza rima, into English verse. Wyatt's *Penitential Psalms* are in terza rima, perhaps derived from the Penitential Psalms of Luigi Alemanni in the same metre; the connecting narrative verses are in *ottava rima* stanzas, the metre common for narrative verse in Italy. Wyatt's principal source, which provided him with the narrative connections between the Psalms (loosely based on II Samuel), was Pietro Aretino's prose paraphrase, *I Sette Salmi de la Penitentia di David* (1534). Aretino was best known as a satirist, a master of invective, and even a pornographer, yet the *Sette Salmi* was a sincere devotional work, reflecting the influence of the reformist ideas of the Italian *spirituali*. Wyatt's own *Penitential Psalms*, like so much of his poetry, is difficult to pin down. Scholars have argued for its Protestant theology, but one of the charges against Wyatt in 1541 was that he was a papist. His defence against this charge — 'I should have more ado with a great sort in England to purge myself of suspect of a Lutheran than of a Papist' — just adds to the ambiguity. The sequence has also been read topically, with David as a figure for Henry VIII, Bathsheba as Anne Boleyn, and Wyatt perhaps as the chastising prophet Nathan, but there is no evidence for this in the text, just as there is no concrete evidence for Wyatt's affair with Anne. Topical interpretations especially depend upon the dating of the Psalms, and many scholars like to think of them as written in the Tower in 1541, but on this too there is no certainty. He may well have begun them earlier, perhaps on his embassy to Spain. At this point, the doctrinal position of the Church of England was still unfixed, and the very distinction between Catholic and Protestant was not as clear as it would later become, even in 1549, when the *Penitential Psalms* were printed. Other sources for Wyatt include Campensis's Latin paraphrases, John Fisher's treatise on the Penitential Psalms, the Vulgate, Luther's *Ennaratio psalmorum*, Cardinal Cajetan's *Psalmi Davidici*, and the translations of Joye and Coverdale. See Susan Brigden, *Thomas Wyatt: The Heart's Forest* (London: Faber and Faber, 2012); Heale, *Wyatt, Surrey & Early Tudor Poetry*; Clare Costley King'oo, *Miserere Mei: The Penitential Psalms in Late Medieval and Early Modern England* (Notre Dame: University of Notre Dame Press, 2012); William Rossiter, 'What Wyatt Really Did to Aretino's *Sette Salmi*', *Renaissance Studies*, 29.4 (2015), 595–614; Christopher Stamatakis, *Sir Thomas Wyatt and the Rhetoric of Rewriting* (Oxford: Oxford University Press, 2012); Zim, *English Metrical Psalms*; Colin Burrow, *ODNB*.]

Psalms 6, 32, 38, 51, 102, 130, 143

    Love,[116] to give law unto his subject hearts,
    Stood in the eyes of Barsabe the bright,   *Bathsheba*
    And in a look anon himself converts,   *at once*
    Cruelly pleasant before King David's sight;
5 First dazed his eyes, and further forth he starts
    With venomed breath, as softly as he might
    Touch his senses, and overruns his bones
    With creeping fire sparpled for the nonce.   *scattered, for once*
    And when he saw that kindled was the flame,
10 The moist poison in his heart he lanced,
    So that the soul did tremble with the same.
    And in this brawl as he stood and tranced,   *confusion, swooned*
    Yielding unto the figure and the frame
    That those fair eyes had in his presence glanced,
15 The form that love had printed in his breast[117]
    He honoureth it, as thing of thingès best.[118]

    So that forgot the wisdom and forecast   *foresight*
    (Which woe to realms when that these kings doth lack)
    Forgetting eke God's majesty as fast,   *also*
20 Yea, and his own, forthwith he doth to make
    Urie to go into the field in haste,   *Uriah*
    Urie I say, that was his idol's make,   *spouse*
    Under pretence of certain victory,
    For enemies' swords a ready prey to die.
25 Whereby he may enjoy her out of doubt[119]
    Whom more than God or himself he mindeth,

---

[116] A Petrarchan personification, perhaps Cupid, as in Wyatt's Petrarchan translation, 'The long love that in my thought doth harbour'. In Christian terms, 'God is love' (1 John 4. 8), and Paul writes of the 'love of God, which is in Christ Jesus our Lord' (Romans 8. 39). Zim (275 n.23) notes that 'subject hearts' is added by Wyatt, reflecting the theme of love as cruel tyrant so familiar in secular poetry.

[117] Another Petrarchism, which often plays with images of the lover or beloved in either's eye or heart.

[118] Wyatt places great emphasis on the usually bland word 'thing', which comes up regularly in his poetry as a disturbingly elusive quality of mind or heart, as in 'What no perdie', where he asks 'shall still that thing | Unstable, unsure, and wavering | Be in my mind without recure?'. The phrase 'thing of thinges' is a secular parody of biblical idioms like 'King of Kings' or 'God of gods'.

[119] Perhaps recalling the line in Wyatt's 'Whoso list to hunt', 'Who list her hunt, I put him out of doubt'.

And after he had brought this thing about
And of that lust possessed himself, he findeth — *desire*
That hath and doth reverse, and clean turn out — *completely*
30 Kings from kingdoms, and cities undermindeth; — *undermine*
He, blinded, thinks this train so blind and close — *trickery, secret*
To blind all things, that naught may it disclose.[120]

But Nathan hath spied out this treachery
With rueful cheer and sets afore his face — *countenance*
35 The great offence, outrage, and injury
That he hath done to God, as in this case:
By murder for to cloak adultery;
He show'th him eke from heaven the threats, alas,
So sternly sore this prophet, this Nathan,
40 That all amazed this aged woeful man.

Like him that meets with horror and with fear
The heat doth straight forsake the limbs cold, — *immediately*
The colour eke droopeth down from his cheer,
So doth he feel his fire manifold,
45 His heat, his lust, and pleasure all in fear
Consume and waste, and straight his crown of gold, — *waste away*
His purple pall, his sceptre he lets fall — *robe*
And to the ground he throw'th himself withal. — *likewise*

The pompous pride of state and dignity
50 Forthwith rebates repentant humbleness. — *reduces*
Thinner vile cloth than clotheth poverty[121]
Doth scantly hide and clad his nakedness,
His fair hoar beard of reverent gravity — *grey*
With ruffled hair, knowing his wickedness.
55 More like was he the selfsame repentance
Than stately prince of worldly governance.

His harp he taketh in hand to be his guide,
Wherewith he offer'th his plaints his soul to save, — *laments*
That from his heart distils on every side,
60 Withdrawing him into a dark cave
Within the ground, wherein he might him hide,
Fleeing the light as in prison or grave,

---

[120] Wyatt favours figures of repetition such as polyptoton, repeating the same word in different forms ('kings', 'kingdom'; 'blinded', 'blind'), though here the verbal density is increased by internal rhyme ('undermindeth', 'blinded'; 'thinks' and 'thing').

[121] clotheth] 1549 'clothed'.

In which as soon as David entered had,
The dark horror did make his fault adrad.[122]   *dreadful*

65 But he, without prolonging or delay,
  Of that that might his Lord, his God appease,
  Fall'th on his knees and with his harp, I say,
  Afore his breast, fraughted with disease   *filled*
  Of stormy sighs, his cheer coloured like clay,
70 Dressed upright, seeking to counterpoise
  His song with sighs, and touching of the strings
  With tender heart,[123] lo, thus to God he sings.

Psalm 6. Domine ne in furore.   [Lord, do not in anger]

 O Lord, since in my mouth thy mighty name
  Suffer'th itself 'my Lord' to name and call,   *allows*
  Here hath my heart hope taken by the same
 That the repentance which I have, and shall,
5   May at thy hand, seek mercy as the thing,
  Only comfort of wretched sinners all;
 Whereby I dare with humble bemoaning,
  By thy goodness, of thee this thing require.
  Chastise me not for my deserving,
10 According to thy just conceivèd ire.   *anger*
  O Lord, I dread, and that I did not dread
  I me repent, and evermore desire
 Thee, thee to dread. I open here and spread
  My fault to thee; but thou for thy goodness
15 Measure it not in largeness nor in bread.   *breadth*
 Punish it not as asketh the greatness
  Of thy furor provoked by my offence.
  Temper, O Lord, the harm of my excess
 With mending will that I for recompense
20 Prepare again; and rather pity me
  For I am weak, and clean without defence.   *completely*
 More is the need I have of remedy
  For of the whole the leech taketh no cure.   *physician*

---

[122] This word may echo the Office of the Dead in the Sarum rite *Primer in English* (Rouen, 1538): 'For of my sins | I am full sore adrad' (First Nocturn, Matins, Third Lesson).

[123] English Renaissance poets enjoyed the pun between the Latin words *chorda* ('string') and *cor, cordis* ('heart'), which lies behind the English 'heartstrings', but also suggests how music can affect the heart ('chord' means harmony but has a different etymology — 'accord', from late Latin *accordare*, 'bring into agreement').

The sheep that stray'th the shepherd seeks to see;[124]
25 I, Lord, am strayed, I sick without recure,   *recourse*
    Feel all my limbs, that have rebelled, for fear
    Shake, in despair unless thou me assure.
  My flesh is troubled, my heart doth fear the spear,
    That dread of death, of death that ever lasts,[125]
30   Threateth of right, and draweth near and near.
  Much more my soul is troubled by the blasts
    Of these assaults, that come as thick as hail,
    Of worldly vanity, that temptation casts
  Against the weak bulwark of the flesh frail,
35   Wherein the soul in great perplexity
    Feeleth the senses with them that assail,
  Conspire, corrupt by use and vanity;
    Whereby the wretch doth to the shadow resort
    Of hope in thee in this extremity.
40 But thou, O Lord, how long after this sort
    Forbearest thou to see my misery?
    Suffer me yet, in hope of some comfort,
  Fear and not feel that thou forgettest me.
    Return, O Lord, O Lord I thee beseech,
45   Unto thine old wonted benignity.   *accustomed*
  Reduce, revive my soul; be thou the leech   *restore*
    And reconcile the great hatred and strife[126]
    That it hath ta'en against the flesh, the wretch
  That stirrèd hath thy wrath by filthy life.
50   See how my soul doth fret it to the bones;   *gnaw*
    Inward remorse so sharp'th it like a knife
  That, but thou help the caitiff that bemoans   *wretch*
    His great offence, it turns anon to dust.   *again*
    Here hath thy mercy matter for the nonce,   *for the purpose*
55 For if thy righteous hand that is so just
    Suffer no sin or strike with damnation,
    Thy infinite mercy want needs it must
  Subject matter for his operation.
    For that in death there is no memory

---

[124] Wyatt's addition, alluding to the parable of the lost sheep in Luke 15, which itself derives from Psalm 119. 176.

[125] Another figure of repetition, epizeuxis, repeating words with no others in between for emphasis or emotion.

[126] Within four lines, Wyatt includes four words with the same prefix (re-), each subsequent word acoustically reinforcing the initial plea for God to 'return'. Something similar is effected with 'beseech', 'benignity', and 'be'.

60	Among the damned, nor yet no mention	
	Of thy great name, ground of all glory,[127]	
	Then if I die and go whereas I fear	
	To think thereon, how shall thy great mercy	
	Sound in my mouth unto the world's ear?	
65	For there is none that can thee laud and love	*praise*
	For that thou nilt no love among them there.	*do not will*
	Suffer my cries thy mercy for to move	
	That wonted is a hundred years' offence	
	In moment of repentance to remove.	
70	How oft have I called up with diligence	
	This slothful flesh long afore the day,	
	For to confess his fault and negligence,	
	That to the down, for aught that I could say,	*its*
	Hath still returned to shroud itself from cold,	*featherbed*
		shelter
75	Whereby it suffers now for such delay.	
	By nightly plaints instead of pleasures old	*laments*
	I wash my bed with tears continual	
	To dull my sight, that it be never bold	
	To stir my heart again to such a fall.	
80	Thus dry I up among my foes in woe	
	That with my fall do rise and grow withal	*as well*
	And me beset even now where I am, so	
	With secret traps to trouble my penance.	
	Some do present to my weeping eyes, lo,	
85	The cheer, the manner, beauty, and countenance	*demeanour*
	Of her whose look, alas, did make me blind.[128]	
	Some other offer to my remembrance	
	Those pleasant words, now bitter to my mind.	
	And some show me the power of my armour,	
90	Triumph and conquest, and to my head assigned	
	Double diadem; some show the favour	
	Of people frail, palace, pomp, and riches.	
	To these mermaids[129] and their baits of error	*temptations*

[127] Wyatt expands on the Psalmist's manipulative argument, adding an emphasis on 'name' and 'glory' that seems more the aspiration of a Renaissance nobleman than the Christian God.

[128] Wyatt connects the weeping eyes of the Psalmist with the effect of Bathsheba's eyes in the added prologue that 'dazed' David's own for a very different reason.

[129] mermaids] Wyatt converts Aretino's serpent lurking beneath pleasant flowers into mermaids, like the sirens that threatened to lure Odysseus onto the rocks, against whose song his crew stopped up their ears. Odysseus had his crew bind him to the mast so he could listen without peril. No mermaids appear in the Bible, whether in English or the original. Wyatt's

	I stop mine ears with help of thy goodness.	
95	And, for I feel it com'th alone of thee	*only*
	That to my heart these foes have none access,	
	I dare them bid: avoid, wretches, and flee.	*go away*
	The Lord hath heard the voice of my complaint.	*lament*
	Your engines take no more effect in me.	*devices*
100	The Lord hath heard, I say, and seen me faint	
	Under your hand and pity'th my distress.	
	He shall do make my senses by constraint	*compulsion*
	Obey the rule that reason shall express,	
	Where the deceit of your glosing bait[130]	*flattering*
105	Made them usurp a power in all excess.	
	Shamèd be they all, that so lie in wait	
	To compass me, by missing of their prey.	*surround*
	Shame and rebuke redound to such deceit.	*contribute*
	Sudden confusion's stroke without delay	
110	Shall so deface their crafty suggestion	*erase*
	That they to hurt my health no more assay,	*attempt*
	Since I, O Lord, remain in thy protection.	

* * *

Whoso hath seen the sick in his fever,
After truce taken with the hot or cold
115 And that the fit is passed of his fervour,
Draw fainting sighs, let him, I say, behold
Sorrowful David after his languor,
That with the tears that from his eyes down rolled
Paused his plaint and laid adown his harp,
120 Faithful record of all his sorrows sharp. *witness*

It seemed now that of his fault the horror
Did make afeared no more his hope of grace,
The threats whereof in horrible error
Did hold his heart as in despair a space,

---

mermaids are metaphors for the temptations offered by those that 'work vanity' (as Coverdale puts it), but as a borrowing from classical literature, they mark Wyatt's Psalms as a kind of penitential epic. The Earl of Surrey may have had this in mind when he compared Wyatt's Penitential Psalms to 'Homer's rhymes' in 'The great Macedon that out of Persia chased', a poem that precedes Wyatt's Psalms in both the Egerton MS and Arundel-Harington.

[130] For Wyatt, the penitential struggle is a verbal one, and he often converts vocabulary and metaphors to this effect. Just as the mermaids' 'bait of error' required David (with God's help) to stop his ears, so here the bait is 'glosing', which means to flatter or verbally seduce, but it derives from the Latin *glossa*, meaning words of explanation or commentary added to a text.

125 Till he had willed to seek for his succour,
   Himself accusing, beknowing his case, — *acknowledging*
   Thinking so best his Lord to appease.
   Eased, not yet healed, he feeleth his disease.

   Seemeth horrible no more the dark cave[131]
130 That erst did make his fault for to tremble. — *formerly*
   A place devout or refuge for to save
   The succourless, it rather doth resemble.
   For who had seen so kneel within the grave
   The chief pastor of th'Hebrews' assemble[132] — *head, assembly*
135 Would judge it made, by tears of penitence,
   A sacred place worthy of reverence.

   With vapoured eyes he looketh here and there,
   And when he hath awhile himself bethought, — *considered*
   Gathering his sprites that were dismayed for fear, — *spirits*
140 His harp again unto his hand he rought. — *reached*
   Tuning accord by judgement of his ear,[133] — *harmony*
   His heart's bottom for a sigh he sought,[134]
   And therewithal upon the hollow tree[135] — *in addition*
   With strainèd voice again thus crieth he

Psalm 32. *Beati quorum remisse sunt.* [Blessed are they who have been forgiven]

   Oh, happy are they that have forgiveness got
      Of their offence, not by their penitence,
         As by merit, which recompenseth not,[136]
   Although that yet pardon hath none offence
5   Without the same, but by the goodness

---

[131] i.e. the dark cave no longer seems horrible.

[132] pastor] Playing on the Latin origin of the word in 'shepherd' and David's youthful role as shepherd; the term becomes popular among Lutherans and other Protestants, including Tyndale, though it is not exclusive to reformers.

[133] See note 123, p. 122.

[134] In his *Preparation for Death* (1538), Erasmus recommends that the penitent 'cry for the mercy of God, even from the bottom of his heart'.

[135] hollow tree] i.e. a metonymy for the harp, though being 'upon' the 'tree' suggests the suffering of Christ upon the cross, since Peter says to the priests of the Temple that 'The God of our fathers raised up Jesus whom ye slew and hanged upon a tree' (Acts 5. [30] in Tyndale's 1534 NT, though the same word is used in the Wycliffite Bibles).

[136] This assertion that forgiveness is awarded not for merit but simply by God's goodness has been noted by scholars arguing for Wyatt's reformed theological views, though Rossiter points out that the same view is clear in Aretino; 'What Wyatt Really Did to Aretino's *Sette Salmi*'.

  Of him that hath perfect intelligence
Of heart contrite,[137] and cover'th the greatness
  Of sin within a merciful discharge.[138]
  And happy are they that have the wilfulness
10 Of lust restrained, afore it went at large,
  Provoked by the dread of God's furor,
  Whereby they have not on their backs the charge
  Of other's fault to suffer the dolour,   *pain*
  For that their fault was never execute
15 In open sight, example of error.
  And happy is he to whom God doth impute[139]   *ascribe*
  No more his fault, by knowledging his sin,
  But cleansèd now the Lord doth him repute,
  As adder fresh new strippèd from his skin,
20 Nor in his sprite is aught undiscovered.   *spirit, anything*
  I, for because I hid it still within,
  Thinking by state in fault to be preferred,
  Do find by hiding of my fault my harm,
  As he that feels his health to be hindered
25 By secret wound, concealèd from the charm   *magic power*
  Of leech's cure, that else had had redress,   *physician's*
  And feel my bones consume and wax unfirm *waste away, grow*
  By daily rage, roaring in excess.
  Thy heavy hand on me was so increased
30 Both day and night, and held my heart in press,   *torture*
  With pricking thoughts bereaving me my rest,   *piercing*
  That withered is my lustiness away   *vigour*
  As summer heats, that hath the green oppressed.
  Wherefore I did another way assay   *attempt*
35 And sought forthwith to open in thy sight
  My fault, my fear, my filthiness, I say,
  And not to hide from thee my great unright.
  I shall, quod I, against myself confess   *said*
  Unto the Lord all my sinful plight.   *misfortune*

---

[137] Psalm 51. 17.
[138] Egerton originally had 'under the mantel of mercy', which Wyatt crossed out and replaced. The word 'discharge' is ambiguous, since it might mean a pardon or the document granting such a pardon, a relief from debt, or even the matter emitted from a wound, like the metaphorical 'secret wound' a few lines below. Such a usage might seem less implausible in the context of sixteenth-century medicine, which often involved the letting of bodily fluids (and which in the case of cleaning an infected wound might even be effective).
[139] impute] attribute to a person by vicarious substitution (*OED*); a theological usage originating with Coverdale's Great Bible (Romans 4. 6).

40 And thou forthwith didst wash the wickedness
        Of mine offence; of truth right thus it is.
        Wherefore they that have tasted thy goodness
     At me shall take example as of this
        And pray and seek in time for time of grace.
45   Then shall the storms and floods of harm him miss
     And him to reach shall never have the space.
        Thou art my refuge and only safeguard
        From the troubles that compass me the place.   *surround*
        Such joy as he that scapes his en'my's ward   *escapes, guard*
50   With loosèd bonds hath in his liberty,
        Such joy, my joy, thou hast to me prepared;
     That as the seaman in his jeopardy
        By sudden light perceivèd hath the port,
        So by thy great merciful property
55   Within thy look thus read I my comfort:
        I shall thee teach and give understanding
        And point to thee what way thou shalt resort
     For thy address, to keep thee from wand'ring.   *guidance*
        Mine eye shall take the charge to be thy guide.¹⁴⁰
60   I ask thereto of thee alone this thing:¹⁴¹   *only*
        Be not like horse or mule that man doth ride
        That not alone doth not his master know,
        But, for the good thou dost him, must be tied
     And bridled lest his guide he bite or throw.
65   Oh, diverse are the chastisings of sin,
        In meat, in drink, in breath that man doth blow,   *food*
     In sleep, in watch, in fretting still within¹⁴²   *worrying*
        That never suffer rest unto the mind
        Filled with offence, that new and new begin
70   With thousand fears the heart to strain and bind.
        But for all this he that in God doth trust
        With mercy shall himself defended find.

---

¹⁴⁰ The Psalmist prays for safety in the 'great waterfloods' (Coverdale), Aretino adds the metaphor of God's eyes as two stars leading the Psalmist over rough water, but Wyatt further shapes the simile according to the Petrarchan convention of the lover, guided to safe port by the light of his beloved's starry eyes. For Wyatt, seeing is also, characteristically, reading, and the danger of wandering, as the form of the epic simile itself, reinforces the sense of the poem as an *Odyssey*.

¹⁴¹ Another instance of what Donald Friedman has called 'The "Thing" in Wyatt's Mind' (*Essays in Criticism*, 16 (1966), 375–81).

¹⁴² Wyatt links the first two Psalms, the inward fretting here recalling the soul fretting the flesh 'to the bones' in Psalm 6.

Joy and rejoice, I say, ye that be just,
   In him that mak'th and holdeth you so still,
75 In him your glory alway set you must,   *always*
All ye that be of upright heart and will.

* * *

This song ended, David did stint his voice,   *stop*
And in that while, about he with his eye
Did seek the dark cave, with which withouten noise   *without*
80 His silence seemed to argue and reply
Upon this peace, this peace that did rejoice
The soul with mercy, that mercy so did cry
And found mercy at mercy's plentiful hand,
Never denied but where it was withstand.   *withstood*

85 As the servant that, in his master's face
Finding pardon of his passed offence,
Considering his great goodness, and his grace,
Glad tears distils, as gladsome recompense,
Right so David, that seemèd in that place
90 A marble image of singular reverence
Carved in the rock, with eyes and hands on high,
Made as by craft to plain, to sob, to sigh.[143]   *lament*

This while a beam that bright sun forth sends,
That sun the which was never cloud could hide,[144]
95 Pierceth the cave, and on the harp descends,
Whose glancing light the chords did overglide   *strings*
And such lustre upon the harp extends
As light of lamp upon the gold clean tried,[145]   *refined*
The turn whereof into his eyes did start
100 Surprised with joy, by penance of the heart.[146]

---

[143] Another extended simile of the kind conventional in epic. In this instance, the implications are ambiguous, since David only seems like the servant, and his penitential pose is suspiciously 'made as by craft'. From a Protestant perspective, marble images are also disturbingly like false idols. After two Psalms, how far has David progressed?

[144] Wyatt's original spelling ('sonne') emphasizes the pun on sun/son (i.e. Christ, the Son of God).

[145] Ecclesiasticus 2. 5; 1 Peter 1. 7; Revelation 3. 18.

[146] penance] A highly controversial word after the Reformation, often denoting the Catholic sacrament as opposed to the Protestant practice of penitence, which was not a sacrament and not a 'work' that contributed to one's salvation; whether Wyatt's use of the word is significant in terms of his own beliefs is open to debate. See also note 123 on 'chords' and 'heart'.

>   He then, inflamed with far more hot affect[147]   *feeling*
>   Of God than he was erst of Barsabe,   *formerly, Bathsheba*
>   His left foot did on the earth erect
>   And just thereby remain'th the t'other knee.
> 105 To his left side his weight he doth direct,
>   Sure hope of health, and harp again tak'th he.
>   His hand his tune, his mind sought his lay
>   Which to the Lord with sober voice did say.

Psalm 38. Domine ne in furore tuo.   [O Lord, do not in anger]

>   O Lord, as I thee have both prayed and pray
>   (Although in thee be no alteration
>   But that we men, like as ourselves we say,
>   Measuring thy justice by our mutation)[148]
>   5   Chastise me not, O Lord, in thy furor
>   Nor me correct in wrathful castigation.
>   For that thy arrows of fear, of terror,
>   Of sword, of sickness, of famine, and fire
>   Sticks deep in me. I, lo, from mine error
> 10 Am plungèd up, as horse out of the mire
>   With stroke of spur. Such is thy hand on me
>   That in my flesh for terror of thy ire   *anger*
>   Is not one point of firm stability,
>   Nor in my bones there is no steadfastness;
> 15   Such is my dread of mutability[149]
>   For that I know my frailful wickedness.
>   For why? My sins above my head are bound   *why*
>   Like heavy weight that doth my force oppress
>   Under the which I stop and bow to ground   *bend down*
> 20   As willow plant haled by violence,   *dragged down*
>   And of my flesh each not well curèd wound
>   That festered is by folly and negligence
>   By secret lust hath rankled under skin,   *festered*
>   Not duly curèd by my penitence.
> 25 Perceiving thus the tyranny of sin

---

[147] Wyatt originally wrote 'desire', then crossed it out and substituted 'affect', a more ambiguous word meaning 'mood', 'disposition', or 'feeling', as well as 'passion' and even 'lust'.

[148] One might describe polyptoton ('prayed' and 'pray') as itself a figure of 'alteration' and 'mutation'.

[149] The fear of mutability is Wyatt's addition to the Psalm verse, characteristically connecting his suffering with what in a secular context would be the inconstancy of fortune, or at court the unreliability of favour.

>   That with his weight hath humbled and depressed
>   My pride, by grudging of the worm within[150]   *without*
>   That never dieth, I live withouten rest.
>   So are mine entrails infect with fervent sore,
> 30   Feeding the harm that hath my wealth oppressed
>   That in my flesh is left no health therefore.
>   So wondrous great hath been my vexation
>   That it hath forced my heart to cry and roar.
>   O Lord, thou know'st the inward contemplation
> 35   Of my desire, thou know'st my sighs and plaints,   *laments*
>   Thou know'st the tears of my lamentation
>   Cannot express my heart's inward restraints.
>   My heart panteth, my force I feel it quail,
>   My sight, mine eyes, my look decays and faints.
> 40 And when mine en'mies did me most assail,
>   My friends most sure wherein I set most trust,
>   Mine own virtues soonest then did fail[151]
>   And stand apart.[152] Reason and wit unjust,
>   As kin unkind,[153] were farthest gone at need.
> 45   So had they place their venom out to thrust
>   That sought my death by naughty word and deed.[154]   *wicked*
>   Their tongues reproach, their wits did fraud apply.
>   And I like deaf and dumb forth my way yede   *proceed*
>   Like one that hears not, nor hath to reply
> 50   One word again. Knowing that from thy hand
>   These things proceed and thou, O Lord, shalt supply
>   My trust in thee wherein I stick and stand.
>   Yet have I had great cause to dread and fear
>   That thou wouldst give my foes the overhand   *upper hand*
> 55 For in my fall they showed such pleasant cheer.   *mood*
>   And therewithal I always in the lash   *with all that*

[150] Wyatt's addition of pride to the troubles felt by David may derive from Aretino. Wyatt's worm, a conventional symbol of conscience since at least Chaucer's *Physician's Tale*, may derive from Jesus's description of hell, 'where their worm dieth not, and their fire goeth not out' (Mark 9, Coverdale Bible, where it is stated three times).
[151] Wyatt allegorizes his virtues as 'friends', just as he did the temptations as enemies earlier.
[152] The emphasis on the false friend here seems closer to Psalm 55 (translated in the Tower by Surrey, Sir Thomas Smith, and John Dudley) than Psalm 38, in which the Psalmist simply complains of his enemies and the neglect of friends and neighbours.
[153] These words are related etymologically, and in the sixteenth century 'unkind' meant both cruel and unnatural, neither of which one would expect of one's 'kin'. Shakespeare's Hamlet plays similarly, when he calls Claudius 'a little more than kin, and less than kind'.
[154] naughty] A much stronger word in Wyatt's day.

Abide the stroke, and with me everywhere	
I bear my fault that greatly doth abash	
My doleful cheer; for I my fault confess,	
60 And my desert doth all my comfort dash.	*recompense*
In the meanwhile mine en'mies safe increase	
And my provokers hereby do augment,	
That without cause to hurt me do not cease.	
In evil for good against me they be bent	
65 And hinder shall my good pursuit of grace.	
Lo now, my God, that seest my whole intent,	
My Lord, I am, thou know'st well, in what case.	
Forsake me not. Be not far from me gone.	
Haste to my help, haste, Lord, and haste apace,	*quickly*
70 O Lord, the Lord of all my health alone.[155]	

* * *

Like as the pilgrim that in a long way	
Fainting for heat, provokèd by some wind	
In some fresh shade lieth down at mids of day,	*middle*
So doth of David the wearied voice and mind	
75 Take breath of sighs when he had sung this lay	
Under such shade as sorrow hath assigned,	
And as the t'one still minds his voyage end,	
So doth the t'other to mercy still pretend.[156]	

On sonour chords his fingers he extends	*sonorous, strings*
80 Without hearing or judgement of the sound.	
Down from his eyes a storm of tears descends,	
Without feeling, that trickle on the ground,	
As he that bleeds in bain right so intends	*bath*
Th'altered senses to that that they are bound.[157]	

---

[155] Wyatt adds the dense repetitions, aided by the internal rhyme of 'haste' and 'apace', creating an urgency like that of the Bible's final line: 'He which testifieth these things saith, so be it, I come quickly. Amen. Even so, come Lord Jesu' (Tyndale's 1534 NT).

[156] Another 'epic' simile, this one suggesting another epic convention, the *locus amoenus* ('pleasant place'), a pastoral hiatus in the hero's journey. Homer's *Odyssey* provides the model in the island of Calypso or the gardens of Alcinous, followed by Dante's earthly paradise on Mt Purgatory and similar spots in Ariosto and Tasso.

[157] As Rebholz notes (see textual notes), the point is that David is conscious of his weeping no more than someone in a warm bath is conscious of bleeding (an interesting blending of the two bodily fluids). But the implication is surely that such a person is committing suicide, a shocking comparison, since it not only points to David's despair but warns of his spiritual peril, since suicide was a mortal sin. The most famous suicide by this method was Seneca, who opened his veins in a warm bath, having been ordered to kill himself by Nero.

85 But sigh and weep he can none other thing
    And look up still unto the heaven's king.

    But who had been without the cave's mouth[158]   *sing*
    And heard the tears and sighs that he did strain,
    He would have sworn, there had out of the south
90 A lukewarm wind brought forth a smoky rain.[159]
    But that so close the cave was and uncouth   *enclosed, desolate*
    That none but God was record of his pain,   *witness*
    Else had the wind blown in all Israel's ears
    The woeful plaint and of their king the tears.

95 Of which some part when he up suppèd had,
    Like as he whom his own thought affrays,   *frightens*
    He turns his look. Him seemeth that the shade
    Of his offence again his force assays   *tests*
    By violence despair on him to lade.   *load*
100 Starting like him whom sudden fear dismays
    His voice he strains and from his heart outbrings
    This song that I not whether he cries or sings.[160]   *know not*

Psalm 51. Miserere mei deus.   [Have mercy on me, Lord]

    Rue on me, Lord, for thy goodness and grace,   *have pity*
        That of thy nature art so bountiful,
        For that goodness that in the world doth brace   *embrace*
    Repugnant natures in quiet wonderful.
5   And for thy mercies' number without end
        In heaven and earth perceived so plentiful
    That over all they do themselves extend,
        For those mercies much more than man can sin,
        Do way my sins that so thy grace offend.   *away*
10 Again wash me, but wash me well within,[161]

---

[158] cave's] The metre calls for this word to be pronounced as two syllables ('ca-ves').
[159] A beautiful image, but troubling from a biblical perspective, since the son of man tells John to write to the angel of the church of the Laodiceans, 'because thou art lukewarm, and neither hot nor cold, I shall begin to spew thee out of my mouth' (Revelation 3. 16). This is Coverdale's 1538 *New Testament both in Latin and English*. The word does not appear in his 1535 Bible or the 1539 Great Bible, but earlier Wycliffite translations have 'lew', a version of 'luke', and it becomes standard later in the Geneva Bible, Bishops' Bible, the Rheims New Testament, the King James Bible, translations of Calvin's commentaries, and elsewhere.
[160] The first-person pronoun is startling. It has been used earlier for emphasis ('Urie I say'), but here it draws greater attention to the character of the narrator, since he admits his perspective and understanding are limited.
[161] Wyatt adds the interior washing. Rebholz suggests this is to avoid any implication of baptism, though it seems more likely to be related to the emphasis on interiority throughout.

       And from my sin that thus mak'th me afraid
         Make thou me clean as ay thy wont hath been.   *always, custom*
       For unto thee no number can be laid
         For to prescribe remission of offence
15   In hearts returned, as thou thyself hath said.
       And I beknow my fault, my negligence,   *confess*
         And in my sight my sin is fixèd fast,   *secure*
         Thereof to have more perfect penitence.
       To thee alone, to thee have I trespassed,
20   For none can measure my fault but thou alone.
       For in thy sight I have not been aghast
       For to offend, judging thy sight as none,[162]
         So that my fault were hid from sight of man,   *hidden*
         Thy majesty so from my mind was gone.
25   This know I and repent. Pardon thou then,
         Whereby thou shalt keep still thy word stable,[163]
         Thy justice pure and clean, because that when
       I pardoned am, then forthwith justly able,
         Just I am judged by justice of thy grace.[164]
30   For I myself, lo, thing most unstable,
       Formed in offence, conceivèd in like case,
         Am naught but sin from my nativity.
         Be not this said for my excuse, alas,
       But of thy help to show necessity.
35   For lo, thou loves the truth of inward heart
         Which yet doth live in my fidelity,
       Though I have fallen, by frailty overthwart,
         For wilful malice led me not the way
       So much as hath the flesh drawn me apart.

[162] Another figure of repetition, anaphora, in which the same word or phrase is used to begin successive lines.

[163] The stability, or instability, of language is a continual preoccupation of Wyatt's, as in the sonnet 'Each man telleth I change most my device', which ends with the vow, 'My word nor I shall not be variable | But always one, your own both firm and stable'. Here Wyatt plays the instability of human language against the stability of the divine, especially in the embodiment of the Word, Jesus Christ (John 1. 1). Not just language but David himself is a 'thing most unstable', and there is perhaps a further implicit pun in David's reference to his nativity, since the Nativity of the Word occurs in a stable.

[164] Stamatakis notes that a passage in Luther's *Enarratio psalmorum LI* ('Lecture on Psalm 51') uses as much polyptoton as Wyatt's lines here: 'sum justus et justificatus per justum et justificantem Christum' ('I am just and justified by a just and justifying Christ'). One might go further and suggest that Luther might actually be the source for Wyatt's wordplay here, especially since these verses of Psalm 51 were critical for Luther in developing his theology of justification by faith alone. Luther's lecture was delivered in 1532 and printed in 1538.

40	Wherefore, O Lord, as thou hast done alway,	*always*
	Teach me the hidden wisdom of thy lore	*teachings*
	Since that my faith doth not yet decay.	
	And as the Jews to heal the leper sore	
	With hyssop cleanse,[165] cleanse me, and I am clean.	
45	Thou shalt me wash, and more than snow therefore	
	I shall be white, how foul my fault hath been.	
	Thou of my health shalt gladsome tidings bring	
	When from above remission shall be seen	
	Descend on earth.[166] Then shall for joy upspring	
50	The bones that were afore consumed to dust.[167]	
	Look not, O Lord, upon mine offending	
	But do away my deeds that are unjust.	
	Make a clean heart in the midst of my breast	
	With sprite upright voided from filthy lust.	*spirit*
55	From thine eyes' cure cast me not in unrest	
	Nor take from me thy sprite of holiness.	
	Render to me joy of thy help and rest,	
	My will confirm with sprite of steadfastness.	
	And by this shall these goodly things ensue:	
60	Sinners I shall into thy ways address,	
	They shall return to thee and thy grace sue;	
	My tongue shall praise thy justification,[168]	
	My mouth shall spread thy glorious praises true.	
	But of thyself, O God, this operation	
65	It must proceed by purging me from blood,	
	Among the just that I may have relation.	
	And of thy lauds for to let out the flood	*praise*
	Thou must, O Lord, my lips first unloose.	
	For if thou hadst esteemèd pleasant good	
70	The outward deeds that outward men disclose	
	I would have offered unto thee sacrifice.	

[165] The biblical Psalm refers to cleansing with hyssop, but Wyatt adds the Jewish practice of cleansing lepers with the herb, as prescribed in Leviticus 14. Of course, for King David to refer to 'the Jews' is odd and clearly an anachronistic Christian perspective.
[166] Wyatt's addition. Rebholz suggests an allusion to the incarnation (long in the future for David), but it may also incorporate the classical myth of the virgin goddess of justice, Astraea, last of the gods to leave the earth as men descend into the Iron Age (Ovid, *Metamorphoses*). It was thought Astraea's return would usher in a new Golden Age.
[167] Wyatt moves beyond the Psalmist, who prays that 'the bones, which thou hast broken, may rejoice' (v. 8, Coverdale), incorporating Ezekiel's vision of the valley of dry bones which God restores to flesh and life (Ezekiel 37. 1–11).
[168] The reintroduction of justification and the just (below) are Wyatt's additions.

>   But thou delights not in no such gloze   *pretence*
>   Of outward deed, as men dream and devise.
>   The sacrifice that the Lord liketh most
> 75 Is sprite contrite; low heart in humble wise
>   Thou dost accept, O God, for pleasant host.[169]   *sacrifice*
>   Make Zion, Lord, according to thy will,
>   Inward Zion, the Zion of the ghost.   *spirit*
>   Of heart's Jerusalem strength the walls still.[170]
> 80 Then shalt thou take for good these outward deeds
>   As sacrifice thy pleasure to fulfil.
>   Of thee alone thus all our good proceeds.

* * *

>   Of deep secrets that David here did sing,
>   Of mercy, or faith, of frailty, of grace,
> 85 Of God's goodness, and of justifying,
>   The greatness did so astone himself a space,   *astonish*
>   As who might say: who hath expressed this thing?
>   I, sinner, I. What have I said, alas?
>   That God's goodness would within my song entreat
> 90 Let me again consider and repeat.
>
>   And so he doth, but not expressed by word.[171]
>   But in his heart he turneth and paiseth   *ponders*
>   Each word that erst his lips might forth afford.   *formerly, put forth*
>   He points, he pauseth, he wonders, he praiseth
> 95 The mercy that hides of justice the sword,
>   The justice that so his promise complisheth   *accomplishes*
>   For his words' sake to worthiless desert   *deserving*
>   That gratis his graces to men doth depart.   *freely*
>
>   Here hath he comfort when he doth measure
> 100 Measureless mercies to measureless fault,
>   To prodigal sinners infinite treasure,
>   Treasure termless that never shall default.
>   Yea, when that sin shall fail and may not dure   *endure*

---

[169] host] From Latin *hostia*, 'host' is also the term for the bread used in the Eucharist, conceived of as the body of Christ, either literally (by Catholics, via transubstantiation) or symbolically (by Protestants, often with some sense of real presence).

[170] The biblical Psalm prays for the building of the walls of Jerusalem, but Wyatt converts this to a metaphor of internal renewal, continuing the emphasis on inwardness from the previous verse.

[171] Following on the Psalm's recognition that God favours inner sacrifices (without 'gloze' or gloss, i.e. verbal commentary).

Mercy shall reign, 'gainst whom shall no assault
105 Of hell prevail, by whom, lo, at this day
Of heaven's gates remission is the key.

And when David hath pondered well and tried
And seeth himself not utterly deprived
From light of grace that dark of sin did hide,
110 He finds his hope much therewith revived,
He dare importune the Lord on every side
(For he know'th well to mercy is ascribed   *impartial*
Respectless labour), importune, cry, and call;[172]   *with all that*
And thus beginneth his song therewithal.

Psalm 102. Domine exaudi orationem meam.   [Lord, hear my prayer]

    Lord, hear my prayer and let my cry pass
        Unto the Lord without impediment.
        Do not from me turn thy merciful face,
    Unto myself leaving my government.
5   In time of trouble and adversity
        Incline to me thine ear and thine intent.
    And when I call, help my necessity,
        Readily grant th'effect of my desire.
        These bold demands do please thy majesty
10   And eke my case such haste doth well require.   *also*
        For like as smoke my days been passed away,
        My bones dried up as furnace with the fire.[173]
    My heart, my mind is withered up like hay
        Because I have forgot to take my bread,
15   My bread of life, the word of truth,[174] I say.
    And for my plaintful sighs and my dread,   *sorrowful*
        My bones, my strength, my very force of mind
        Cleaved to the flesh,[175] and from thy Sprite were fled   *Spirit*

---

[172] The idea of mercy (God's mercy, and thus a metonymy for God) labouring is odd, but Wyatt may intend a strategic ambiguity here, it not being quite clear whose labour is involved, the one being merciful, or the one seeking mercy.

[173] Rebholz notes that this follows Campensis.

[174] word of truth] Aretino turns the Psalm's bread into 'true bread of life', but Wyatt adds the appositional 'word of truth', which reinforces the Christological sense of this bread as the Eucharist. As Stamatakis notes, Wyatt initially writes, 'I have forgot to take my food, | My food of life', but changes 'food' to 'bread' in both cases, following Aretino's eucharistic implication (with which the word/Word is also involved) but also allowing for the contrast with the bread of ashes below.

[175] Wyatt's preoccupation with the internal leads him to the peculiar figure of the mind itself (or 'force of mind') cleaving to the flesh.

	As desperate thy mercy for to find.	
20	So made I me the solein pelican[176]	*solitary*
	And like the owl that fleeth by proper kind	
	Light of the day and hath herself beta'en	*taken its way*
	To ruin life out of all company.[177]	
	With waker care[178] that with this woe began,	*watchful*
25	Like the sparrow was I solitary	
	That sits alone under the house's eaves.	
	This while my foes conspired continually	
	And did provoke the harm of my disease.	*distress*
	Wherefore like ashes my bread did me savour;	
30	Of thy just word the taste might not me please.	
	Wherfore my drink I tempered with liquor	*liquid*
	Of weeping tears that from mine eyes do rain	
	Because I know the wrath of thy furor,	
	Provoked by right, had of my pride disdain	
35	For thou didst lift me up to throw me down,	
	To teach me how to know myself again;	
	Whereby I know that helpless I should drown.	
	My days like shadow decline and I do dry,	
	And thee forever eternity doth crown;	
40	World without end doth last thy memory.	
	For this frailty that yoketh all mankind	
	Thou shalt awake and rue this misery,	*pity*
	Rue on Zion, Zion that, as I find,	
	Is the people that live under thy law.	
45	For now is time, the time at hand assigned,	
	The time so long that doth thy servants draw	
	In great desire to see that pleasant day,	
	Day of redeeming Zion from sin's awe.	
	For they have ruth to see in such decay,	*pity*
50	In dust and stones, this wretched Zion lower.[179]	
	Then the gentiles shall dread thy name alway;	*always*
	All earthly kings thy glory shall honour	
	Then when thy grace this Zion thus redeemeth,	

[176] solein] An antique word even by Wyatt's day, familiar from both Chaucer and the Wycliffite Bible.

[177] Wyatt wrote often of being alone, away from society, as in 'Mine own John Poyntz' and 'Such vain thoughts' (which 'maketh me from company to live alone').

[178] Another familiar Wyatt topic (and phrase), as in the sonnet 'If waker care'.

[179] Within eight lines, Wyatt repeats 'Zion' four times (and another below), 'time' three times, and 'day' twice. The repetition of a word at the end of one line or phrase and the beginning of the next ('Zion, Zion', 'day, | Day', or 'that term, that term' below) is the figure anadiplosis.

When thus thou hast declared thy mighty power.
55 The Lord his servants' wishes so esteemeth
    That he him turn'th unto the poor's request.
    To our descent this to be written seemeth,
Of all comforts, as consolation best;
    And they that then shall be regenerate
60   Shall praise the Lord therefore, both most and least.
For he hath looked from the height of his estate,
    The Lord from heaven in earth hath looked on us
    To hear the moan of them that are algate   *continually*
In foul bondage, to loose and to discuss[180]   *set free*
65   The sons of death out from their deadly bond,
    To give thereby occasion gracious
In this Zion his holy name to stond   *last*
    And in Jerusalem his lauds, lasting ay,   *praises, forever*
    When in one church the people of the land
70 And realms been gathered to serve, to laud, to pray
    The Lord that above so just and merciful.
    But to this sembly running in the way   *assembly*
My strength faileth to reach it at the full.
    He hath abridged my days; they may not dure   *endure*
75   To see that term, that term so wonderful,
Although I have with hearty will and cure
    Prayed to the Lord: take me not, Lord, away
    In mids of my years, though thine ever sure   *the midst*
Remain eterne, whom time cannot decay.   *eternal*
80   Thou wrought'st the earth, thy hands th'heavens did make;
    They shall perish and thou shalt last alway.
    And all things age shall wear and overtake
Like cloth, and thou shalt change them like apparel,
    Turn and translate,[181] and they in worth it take.
85 But thou thyself the self remainest well
    That thou wast erst, and shalt thy years extend.   *at first*
    Then, since to this there may nothing rebel,
The greatest comfort that I can pretend

---

[180] discuss] The *OED* gives this as the first citation for this sense of the word ('shake off'; 'set free'), but the word may have appealed to Wyatt's word-obsessed imagination because of its more familiar verbal sense.

[181] translate] A perfect word for Wyatt, since it combines the sense of converting (lit. 'turning') one language into another, something he did frequently both as a poet and a diplomat, conveying someone from one place to another, and conveying the soul into heaven. Furthermore, the root sense of Latin *translatio, transferre*, is to carry across, which is also exactly the root sense of the Greek word μεταφέρειν, the root of English 'metaphor'.

> Is that the children of thy servants dear,
> 90   That in the world are got, shall without end
> Before thy face be stablished all in fere.[182]   *established*

* * *

> When David had perceivèd in his breast
> The Sprite of God returned that was exiled,
> Because he knew he hath alone expressed
> 95   These great things that greater Sprite compiled,
> As shawm or pipe lets out the sound impressed,
> By music's art forgèd tofore and filed,   *before, polished*
> I say when David had perceivèd this
> The Sprite of comfort in him revivèd is.

> 100 For thereupon he maketh argument
> Of reconciling unto the Lord's grace,
> Although sometime to prophecy have lent
> Both brute beasts and wicked hearts a place.
> But our David judgeth in his intent
> 105 Himself by penance clean out of this case,
> Whereby he hath remission of offence,
> And ginneth to allow his pain and penitence.   *begins*

> But when he weigh'th the fault and recompense,
> He damn'th his deed, and findeth plain
> 110 Atween them two no whit equivalence;[183]   *between*
> Whereby he takes all outward deed in vain
> To bear the name of rightful penitence,
> Which is alone the heart returned again[184]
> And sore contrite that doth his fault bemoan,   *contrition*
> 115 And outward deed the sign or fruit alone.[185]   *only*

> With this he doth defend the sly assault
> Of vain allowance of his void desert,

[182] all in fere] altogether; Stamatakis observes that even though 'fere' means 'altogether' here (a 'fere' being a friend or companion), Wyatt spells 'fear' the same way ('fere') and that after many expressions of his fear, David now uses the word 'fere' for the last time in the poem, and in the very different, positive sense.
[183] no whit] not a bit.
[184] Another reference to the 'heart contrite' of the central Psalm 51.
[185] Wyatt departs from Aretino in this narrative interval, and Mason suggests the relevance here of Tyndale's *A Prologue Upon St Paul's Epistle to the Romans* (1526): 'even so are all other good works outward signs and outward fruits of faith and of the Spirit; which justify not a man but shew that a man is justified already before God, inwardly in the heart, through faith, and through the Spirit purchased by Christ's blood'.

And all the glory of his forgiven fault
To God alone he doth it whole convert.
120 His own merit he findeth in default.[186]
And whilst he pondered these things in his heart,
His knee, his arm, his hand sustained his chin[187]
When he his song again thus did begin.

Psalm 130. De profundis clamavi. [Out of the depths I cry]

From depth of sin and from a deep despair,
   From depth of death, from depth of heart's sorrow,
   From this deep cave of darkness' deep repair,[188]   *abode*
Thee have I called, O Lord, to be my borrow.[189]   *deliverer*
5   Thou in my voice, O Lord, perceive and hear
   My heart, my hope, my plaint, my overthrow,   *lament*
My will to rise, and let by grant appear
   That to my voice thine ears do well intend.
   No place so far that to thee is not near,
10 No depth so deep that thou ne mayst extend   *may not*
   Thine ear thereto. Hear then my woeful plaint.
   For, Lord, if thou do observe what men offend
And put thy native mercy in restraint,
   If just exaction demand recompense,
15   Who may endure, O Lord? Who shall not faint
At such account? Dread, and not reverence
   Should so reign large. But thou seekest rather love,
   For in thy hand is mercy's residence,
By hope whereof thou dost our hearts move.
20   I in thee, Lord, have set my confidence;
   My soul such trust doth evermore approve.
Thy holy word of eterne excellence,   *eternal*
   Thy mercy's promise that is alway just,
   Have been my stay, my pillar, and pretence.   *support*

[186] A striking line for those seeking Protestant leanings in Wyatt's Psalms, given reformers' rejection of the efficacy of merit in achieving forgiveness or salvation, but it is interesting that a reference to 'merit' three lines above was struck out and replaced by 'glory'.
[187] It is hard to know how literally to take this description, but it would seem to imply that David's mouth is shut, so that he may not just be 'pondering' but in fact uttering 'these things in his heart'.
[188] The repetition in the opening of Psalm 130, a combination of anaphora, polyptoton, alliteration, and internal and external rhyme, is dense even for Wyatt. Such figures were thought to convey heightened emotion.
[189] borrow] 'deliverer' is the sense, but the word has strong financial connotations, suggesting redeeming a debt.

25 My soul in God hath more desirous trust
        Than hath the watchman looking for the day
        By the relief to quench of sleep the thrust.
    Let Israel trust unto the Lord alway
        For grace and favour are his property
30   Plenteous ransom shall come with him, I say,
    And shall redeem all our iniquity.

* * *

This word, redeem,[190] that in his mouth did sound
Did put David, it seemeth unto me,
As in a trance to stare upon the ground
35 And with his thought the height of heaven to see,
Where he beholds the word[191] that should confound   *defeat*
The sword of death, by humble ear to be
In mortal maid, in mortal habit made,
Eternal life in mortal veil to shade.

40 He seeth that word, when full ripe time should come,[192]
Do way that veil, by fervent affection,   *do away with*
Torn off with death, for death should have her doom,   *judgment*
And leapeth lighter from such corruption,
The glint of light that in the air doth loom.
45 Man redeemed, death hath her destruction,
That mortal veil hath immortality,
David assurance of his iniquity.[193]

---

[190] The narrator repeats and picks up on the word 'redeem' in the Psalm's final line, almost in the mode of a marginal gloss.

[191] word] Capitalized in Rebholz to reinforce the application to Christ, the Word, as in John 1, but the lower case allows the ambiguity Wyatt always favours. David's prophetic vision derives from Aretino, though Wyatt treats the original very freely. The 'word' plays also on the 'sword' in the next line, Christ ultimately defeating death, as in Revelation 21. 4, though the wordplay probably also implicitly includes the image of Christ in Revelation 1. 16, out of whose 'mouth went a two-edged sword'. Thus the Word, in Paul's words 'the sword of the spirit, which is the word of God' (Ephesians 6. 17), defeats the 'sword of death', and all of this is generated by the word 'redeem' that closes the Psalm.

[192] The phrase 'ripe time' suggests the theological idea of *kairos*, the fullness of time, or appointed time in God's plan, the metaphor of ripeness also suggesting the image of the final harvest in Revelation 14. 15.

[193] Rebholz's gloss, 'sureness of his forgiveness', obscures Wyatt's ambiguity. The point may indeed be that David is confident of forgiveness, but the line actually means the exact opposite, which is also good theology, whether Protestant or Catholic. The 'assurance' of election or salvation later became an obsession with English Protestants, but it was not so loaded a word in Wyatt's time.

	Whereby he frames this reason in his heart:	
	That goodness which doth not forbear his son	
50	From death for me and can thereby convert	
	My death to life, my sin to salvation,	
	Both can and will a smaller grace depart	
	To him that sueth by humble supplication.	
	And since I have his larger grace assayed,	*tested*
55	To ask this thing why am I then afraid?	
	He granteth most to them that most do crave	
	And he delights in suit without respect.	*indiscriminately*
	Alas, my son pursues me to the grave,	
	Suffered by God my sin for to correct.[194]	*allowed*
60	But of my sin, since I my pardon have,	
	My son's pursuit shall shortly be reject.	
	Then will I crave with sured confidence.	*assured*
	And thus begins the suit of his pretence.	*false claim*

Psalm 143. Domine exaudi orationem meam.   [Lord, hear my prayer]

	Hear my prayer, O Lord, hear my request.	
	Complish my boon, answer to my desire	*accomplish, request*
	Not by desert, but for thine own behest	*deserving*
	In whose firm truth thou promised mine empire	
5	To stand stable. And after thy justice	
	Perform, O Lord, the thing that I require;	
	But not of law after the form and guise	
	To enter judgement, with thy thrall bondslave	*captive*
	To plead his right, for in such manner wise	
10	Before thy sight no man his right shall save	
	For of myself, lo, this my righteousness,	
	By scourge and whip and pricking spurs I have	
	Scant risen up, such is my beastliness.	
	For that my en'my hath pursued my life	
15	And in the dust hath foiled my lustiness	*vigour*

---

[194] David's son Absalom rebels against him in II Samuel, though David oughtn't to know this yet. Wyatt may be fiddling with chronology in order to emphasize the parallel of fathers and sons between David and Absalom, God and Jesus. Absalom's revolt has also been interpreted as a punishment on David for his earlier sin with Bathsheba. Muir/Thomson interpret this line as a reference to the son of David and Bathsheba, who dies, which would sort out the chronology. It doesn't explain the son pursuing David, however, and E. originally had 'pursues me with his host', which makes clear that Wyatt is thinking of Absalom. The idea may have come from Psalm 143's general statement, 'my en'my hath pursued my life'.

> For that in herns[195] to flee his rage so rife　　　　　　　　　*hiding-places*
> 　　He hath me forced as dead to hide my head,
> 　　And for because within myself at strife
> My heart and sprite with all my force were fled,　　　　　　　　*spirit*
> 20　　I had recourse to times that have been past
> 　　And did remember thy deeds in all my dread
> And did peruse thy works that ever last;
> 　　Whereby I knew above those wonders all
> 　　Thy mercies were. Then lift I up in haste
> 25　　My hands to thee. My soul to thee did call
> 　　Like barren soil for moisture of thy grace.
> Haste to my help, O Lord, afore I fall,
> 　　For sure I feel my sprite doth faint apace.　　　　　　　　　*quickly*
> 　　Turn not thy face from me, that I be laid
> 30　　In count of them that headlong down do pass
> Into the pit. Show me betimes thine aid　　　　　　　　　　　　*in good time*
> 　　For on thy grace I wholly do depend.
> 　　And in thy hand, since all my health is stayed,　　　　　　　*secured*
> Do me to know, what way thou wilt I bend,
> 35　　For unto thee I have raised up my mind.
> 　　Rid me, O Lord, from them that do intend
> My foes to be. For I have me assigned
> 　　Alway within thy secret protection.　　　　　　　　　　　　　*always*
> 　　Teach me thy will that I by thee may find
> 40　　The way to work the same in affection
> 　　For thou, my God, thy blessèd upright sprite
> 　　In land of truth shall be my direction.
> Thou for thy name, Lord, shalt revive my sprite
> 　　Within the right that I receive by thee,
> 45　　Whereby my life of danger shall be quit.
> Thou hast fordone their great iniquity
> 　　That vexed my soul. Thou shalt also confound　　　　　　　　*defeat*
> 　　My foes, O Lord, for thy benignity,
> For thine am I, thy servant ay most bound.　　　　　　　　　　*always*

[195] herns] An extremely obscure word ('heins' in E), not in the *OED*. Rebholz glosses 'corners, nooks, hiding place', Daalder 'enclosed places', citing Campensis, *locis obscurissimis*. *Pierce the Ploughman's Creed* (1553) defines 'Hyrnes' as 'caves', Camden's *Remains* (1605) defines 'hurn' or 'horn' as 'corner', citing the tenth-century Grammar of Alfricus of Eynsham, and Elisha Coles's *English Dictionary* (1677) defines 'hern' as 'corner'. There is also what seems a proverbial expression in Jacobus de Cessolis, *To the Right Noble, Right Excellent [and] Virtuous Prince George Duke of Clarence* (1474): 'truth seeketh none herns ne corners'.

24. Robert Crowley, *The Psalter of David Newly Translated into English Metre* (1549)

[Robert Crowley (1517/19–1588) was educated at Magdalen College, Oxford, where he became a friend of John Foxe. Crowley worked in London as a printer and author of religious polemic. He published editions of Wycliffe and Tyndale, as well as the first printed edition of Langland's *Piers Plowman*, seen by reformers as a proto-Protestant work. Ordained deacon in 1551, Crowley fled to Frankfurt with other Marian exiles. After returning to England in 1559, he continued to write on theology and ecclesiastical history, and worked as a minister in London for the rest of his life, despite occasional set-backs due to his reforming zeal. Crowley's Psalms seem to have been intended for use in worship, and were translated from the Latin Psalms of the Swiss reformer Leo Jud, who translated them from the Hebrew (for the Zurich *Biblia Sacrosancta*, 1543). They were eclipsed by the Sternhold and Hopkins Psalms that were appearing in print at the same time, even though Crowley's was the only complete singing psalter until *The Whole Book of Psalms* was published in 1562, and the first complete metrical psalter in English. Crowley included a single tune, in four parts, to which all the Psalms could be sung. The lines look like fourteeners, but they are really just what becomes known as short metre printed as long lines, rhymed *abcb*. He also published a collection of satirical epigrams and a number of longer polemical and satirical poems. John King has called Crowley 'the most significant poet between Surrey and Gascoyne', but he may have been more influential as a printer. See John N. King, *English Reformation Literature* (Princeton: Princeton University Press, 1982); Basil Morgan, *ODNB*.]

Psalm 23

The Lord is my shepherd, and I shall never stand in need:
For in pasture exceeding good, he leadeth me to feed.
He causeth me to lay me down in pasture full of grass:
And driveth me to calm waters, that be so clear as glass.
5 He calleth my soul back again, and causeth me to make:
My journey in the way of right, for his holy name's sake.
Though I should go through the valley of the shadow of death:
I will be without fear of ill, all the days of my breath. *evil*
For thou art aye present with me, thou dost me not forsake: *always*
10 Thy rod and staff do comfort me, and do me merry make.
Over against my foes thou wilt spread a table for me:
Anoint mine head with oil, and fill my cup with great plenty:
But let thy merciful goodness follow me all my life:
And then shall I dwell in thine house without debate or strife.

Psalm 49

All people hearken and give ear to that, that I shall tell:
Both high and low, both rich and poor, that in the world do dwell.
    For why, my mouth shall make discourse, of many things right wise: *because*
In understanding shall mine heart his study exercise.
5   I will incline mine ear to know things full darkly spoken: *secretly*
And eke upon mine harp I will make my dark speech open.   *also*
    In the time of adversity, why should I stand in doubt?
If the wickedness of my steps should compass me about.   *encircle*
    Among them that have great richesse, and do trust therein most: *wealth*
10 And in the multitude thereof, do aye glory and boast: *always*
    There is not one that any way can his brother redeem:
Nor pay to God the ransom that he doth for him esteem.
    For, to redeem their souls from death the price would be too high:[196]
To make them so perfect that they might live eternally.
15 And to make them that in themselves they should no such cause have:
But that they might live ever and never come to the grave.
    For it is plain that as well the wise as the foolish dye:
And leave their goods to other men, but fools die utterly.
    Their grave shall be their house for aye, and eke their dwelling place:
20 Though living here they studied vainglory for a space.   *unwarranted pride*
    But man doth never long abide in estimation:
But shall be like a beast falling into destruction.
    This their purpose and way they walk is their folly indeed:
And yet of their posterity, their words are allowed.
25 They are placed among the dead, as they were flocks of sheep.
And death is he that feedeth them, and hath them for to keep.
    And at the judgment day the just shall rule them as a king:
Their beauty shall decay, and the pit shall be their dwelling.
    But God shall deliver my soul out of the power of hell:
30 Because he hath receivèd me in his house for to dwell.
    When any man is enrichèd, be not afeared therefore:
Or when the glory of his house increaseth more and more.
    For when he dieth he shall not all these things with him take:
His glory shall not go with him, but shall him quite forsake.
35 Because they count themselves happy in this vain life only:
When a man is good to himself, then praise they him greatly.
    Unto their father's nation, let all these men go right:

---

[196] Crowley has altered the original just enough to turn this verse into an expression of the ransom theory of the atonement, articulated by Origen and other early Church Fathers. Original sin burdened humanity with an impossible debt, so Christ made payment instead (to Satan, as was commonly understood) by his sacrifice.

Let them not have fruition of comfortable light.
　　But man doth not expend and weigh his own nobility:
40　Wherefore he shall be like the beast that dieth utterly.

Psalm 74

　　O God, why art thou still absent from us? What displeasure
　　Hath made thy wrath so hot against the sheep of thy pasture?
　　Oh think upon the church that hath of ancient been thine,[197]
　　And that thou hast redeemèd (Lord) even before our eyen.　　　　*eyes*
5　Think on the kindred that is thine by right succession:
　　And on the place where thou hast dwelt, the holy mount Zion.
　　Lift up thy foot and destroy all the enemies for aye,　　　　　　*forever*
　　That have wrought wickedness within thine holy place this day.
　　Thine enemies have roarèd in thy congregations,[198]　　　　　　*assemblies*
10　And have erected their own signs, to be signs and tokens.
　　Their axes are seen glitter as when men hew wood on hills,
　　The ceiling of the holy place they break down with their bills.
　　They have broken thine holy things and set fire on the same,
　　They have broke down and polluted the dwelling of thy name.
15　Thus said they in their heart, let us all vex them in one band,　　*company*
　　So burned[199] they all God's synagogues that were found in the land.
　　Our signs and tokens we see not, no prophet doth remain;
　　There is none among us that can tell us ought for certain.
　　O God, how long shall thine en'my do thee dispight and shame?
20　Wilt thou suffer him ever to blaspheme thine holy name?
　　Lord, why withdrawest thou thy power? Why doth thy right hand bide
　　Still in thy bosom? Pull it out and let thy foes destroyed.
　　O God, thou art my King for aye, and hast been evermore:
　　There is none health in all the earth that is not of thy store.
25　In thy great power thou didst divide the seas and break'st[200] the head
　　Of Pharaoh that great dragon, who of that wound is dead.
　　The heads (Lord) of the whale that was of exceeding greatness[201]

---

[197] of ancient] i.e. from ancient times.
[198] The metre requires 'congregations' to be pronounced as five syllables.
[199] burned] 1549 'brent'.
[200] break'st] 1549 'breakest' (monosyllable required by metre).
[201] whale] Naturalizing the Psalm's reference to the mythical sea beast Leviathan, though Crowley's identification of the dragon (the Psalm has 'dragons') as Pharaoh is presumably based on traditional interpretations of Pharaoh as the 'great dragon, that lyest in the waters' (Ezekiel 29, Great Bible) and even as Leviathan. In his commentary on Psalm 74, Calvin argues that Leviathan is a metaphor for Pharaoh, but this is an ancient reading, perhaps even implied in the Psalm's juxtaposition of the parting of the sea (clearly alluding to Exodus 14), the destruction of the 'dragons', and the breaking of Leviathan.

Thou hast broken and made him meat to men of wilderness.　　　　*food*
A wellspring and a running stream, thou hast made in dry land:
30　And hast made the great rivers dry, by the power of thine hand.
The day and eke the night are thine, thou hast them in thy power;　　*also*
Thou hast parared light and sun, to serve us at their hour.
Thou hast set and appointed all the limits of the land;
The summer and winter also are the work of thine hand.
35　Remember this (O Lord) because thy foes do thee revile,
And the brainsick and foolish folk, thine holy name defile.
Give not the life of thy turtle into thine enemies' hand,[202]
Neither forget thy Church for aye, that of the poor doth stand.
Be mindful of thy covenant, for all the earth is hid
40　With the dwellings of men that are most cruel and wicked.
O suffer not the simple to return again with shame,
For the poor and the indigent are they that praise thy name.
Arise (O God) and judge thy cause, and let thy servants see
That thou art mindful of the checks that fools use to give thee.
45　Do not forget the words of them, that withstand thee so sore,
for their pride and presumption, increaseth more and more.

25. Sir Thomas Smith, *Certain Psalms or Songs of David: Translated into English Metre by Sir Thomas Smith, Knight, Then Prisoner in the Tower of London, with Other Prayers and Songs by Him Made to Pass the Time There* (MS composed 1549)

[Sir Thomas Smith (1513–1577) was a scholar and politician, educated at Queen's College, Cambridge, where he became an academic star. In 1547 he became attached to the household of Edward Seymour, Duke of Somerset and Lord Protector. Smith was appointed to the privy council, elected MP, and then made Secretary of State, as well as provost of Eton and dean of Carlisle. After Somerset's fall, Smith lost his position as secretary and was imprisoned for several months in the Tower. His career took some time to recover. During the reign of Elizabeth he was once again elected to parliament, and he served as ambassador to France, negotiating an important alliance against Spain. Smith was again appointed Secretary of State and, in 1573, Keeper of the Privy Seal. Smith was also deeply involved in the plans to colonize Ireland. His metrical Psalms were written while he was in the Tower, a tradition of Tower Psalms having developed after those written during imprisonment by the Earl of Surrey and, perhaps, Thomas Wyatt. Psalm 55 was a particular favourite of courtier prisoners, given its complaint about betrayal by a close friend. Surrey's Psalm 55 is the most personal of his paraphrases, and the same Psalm was translated

---

[202] turtle] i.e. turtledove, a biblical term of endearment, as in Song of Solomon 2. 14.

by John Dudley, Earl of Warwick. Smith was not a skilled poet, but his Psalms are ambitious in their use of a variety of metres. See Mary Dewar, *Sir Thomas Smith: A Tudor Intellectual in Office* (London: Athlone Press, 1964); James Simpson, 'The Psalms and Threat in Sixteenth-Century English Court Culture', *Renaissance Studies*, 29.4 (2015), 576–94; Zim, *English Metrical Psalms*; Ian W. Archer, *ODNB*.]

Psalm 55

Exaudi deus orationem meam.   [Hear my prayer, O God]

Do thou, O Lord,
My prayer hear,
Thine help I do abide;
To my petition
5 Incline thine ear,
Do not thee from me hide.[203]
Take heed to me,
My God, I say
And hear me in my pain,
10 How piteously
I mourn and pray
And lamentably complain;   *lament*
The enemy
Crieth on me so,
15 Th'ungodly cometh on me so fast;
They mind to me
Great mischief to do,
Which maketh me aghast.
My heart is heavy
20 Within my breast,
As heavy as ever was lead;
With fear of death
I am sore pressed,[204]   *oppressed*

[203] One might say that the metre of this Psalm is identical to Smith's Psalm 86, except that the latter is written in long lines and this in very short ones. Such choices are not arbitrary, however, and in the sixteenth century the fourteener was not considered simply an unbroken common metre, but was used especially for classical epic, as in Golding's translation of Ovid's *Metamorphoses* or George Chapman's Homer. The lines of Smith's Psalm 55 are in fact shorter even than common metre, almost suggesting Skeltonics, though if it were arranged in common metre the rhyme scheme would be the same as Sternhold's, *abcb*.
[204] pressed] Perhaps also with a suggestion of torture by *peine forte et dure* (being crushed with weights); in common law, this was the punishment for any defendant who refused to enter a plea.

I were as good be dead.
25 For fear I tremble
Now and quake
As a ship that hath lost her helm;
An horrible dread
Maketh my heart ache,
30 And doth me overwhelm.
Oh, that I had wings,
I said, like a dove,
That I might fly to some nest,
And convey myself
35 By the sky above
To a place where I might rest.
Then would I hence
Get me away far,
And for a time remain,
40 And wilderness
Would I make my bar[205]   *defence*
To save me from this pain.
T'avoid this blustering
Stormy wind
45 I would make right great haste,
And hide me where
They should not me find
'Til the tempest were overpast.
O Lord, my God,
50 Destroy those tongues
And divide them into parts;
I see injustice then
Them amongst,
In the city spiteful hearts.
55 Lies and slanders
Both day and night
All about the walls doth fill,
Mischief and murder
And bloodwite   *fine for murder*
60 And vice in the midst of it still.
Ungodly wickedness
Is therein,
Falsehood, craft, and deceit;

---

[205] bar] Given other legal references in this translation, this may also suggest the bar at which trials were conducted.

Treachery and guile
65 Is not thine,
But full in every strait.[206]
If it were mine enemy,
I would it bear,
Or one that I did know
70 To have borne me ill will,
I would not fear
T'avoid this overthrow.
But now it is
Even thou I see,
75 My companion, guide, and friend,
Mine old familiar
That hurts me,
That makes me doubt the end.
Sweet communications
80 Have we had together,
And secretly have we talked;
In the house of the Lord
Hither and thither
Full lovingly have we walked.
85 For my part I will
On the Lord call,
And my moan to him I will make;
Help me, I know,
Then my God shall
90 And pity upon me take.
In the even and morn
And at noon day
I will mourn and complain;
For he doth hear
95 My voice always
And ease me of my pain.
It is he that keepeth
My soul in peace
From them that lieth in wait;
100 They lay many snares,
But he will me release
And snatch away their bait.

---

[206] The common sense of 'constraint' or 'difficulty' is clear enough, but as an adjective 'strait' also had legal meanings, including 'stringency' (of laws or penalties) and 'strict' (of proceedings). These tie into the other instances of legal language in Smith's Psalm.

	Even God that sits	
	On high, I say,	
105	And of heaven holdeth the crown,	
	Will hear me, when	
	To him I pray,	
	And bring mine enemy down.	
	For they will not turn,	
110	And why, say you?	
	For God they do not fear.	
	To his great justice	
	They will not bow	
	Nor his commandments hear.	
115	Upon such as he loveth	
	They lay their hands;	
	And such as be at peace	
	With God, they cast	
	Straight into bands;	*immediately, bonds*
120	God's promise they do release.	
	Their mouths than butter	
	Be more soft,	
	Yet battle they bear in their mind;	
	Smoother than oil	
125	Their words be wrought,	
	Yet words ye shall them find.	
	Well, cast thy care	
	Upon the Lord,	
	He will thee nourish and keep.	*guard*
130	He will not long	
	Leave thee in this cord,	
	Nor suffer his righteous to weep.	*allow*
	But them, O God,	
	Thou shalt cast down,	
135	And thrust into the pit,	
	That thus do stand	
	Against thy crown;[207]	
	Their malice shall them hit.	
	They that thirst blood	
140	And deceitful be	
	Shall not live half their days;	

---

[207] As Zim (100) notes, Smith's reference to the 'crown' (here and in line 105) is his addition, perhaps reflecting the perspective of a royal servant favoured by one monarch and cast down by the next.

> But my trust, O Lord,
> Is fixed on thee,
> And so shall it be always.

Psalm 86

Inclina Domine. [Incline, O Lord]

    Bow down thine eare to me, O Lord, and harken to my cry,
    For destitute of all comfort, a poor man am I.[208]
    Keep thou my life both sure and fast, for holy be that I am;   *secure*
    Help me, thy servant, that I be not aghast, for in thee is my trust and no man.
5 O Lord, to me be merciful, for I call on thee each day;
    Comfort my soul now doleful, which I yield to thee always.
    For thou art easy to forgive blame; and most gracious of all,
    To every man that for the same, upon thee will earnestly call.
    Give ear, O Lord, to my prayers all, and ponder my request;
10 In the time of my trouble to thee I call, for thou dost hear me best.
    Of all gods, O Lord, thou art alone, there is none like unto thee;
    As thou dost, there can do none, thy works so wonderful be.
    All nations, O God, whom thou hast made, shall fall down thee before;
    Thy name with praises they shall laud and glorify it evermore.   *praise*
15 For thou, my Lord, art a great one, and wonders thou dost make;
    There is no god but thou alone, whom heaven and earth doth quake.
    Lead me, O Lord, in thy pathway, that in thy truth I may walk;
    Let my heart delight in thy name alway, that with fear of it I may talk.   *always*
    Great thanks, O Lord, I give to thee, always I will praise thy name;
20 Great is thy mercy thou hast showed me, I shall ever remember the same.
    Great mercy, Lord, thou hast me showed, and my soul thou hast fetched out;
    From the deep hell where it was towed, in the sorrowful pang of doubt.
    The company of the mighty seeketh my life, the proud against me do rise;
    Unjustly, O Lord, they seek this strife, thou art not before their eyes.
25 But thou full of compassion art, and merciful I know,
    Long suffering, and patient on thy part, and for to punish slow.
    Great is thy goodness, great, O Lord, great is thy truth and pure,[209]
    Let me always in them accord, and in thy faith be sure.
    Turn to me, O God, and mine enemies daunt, and on me let thy mercy run;
30 Strengthen me, O Lord, thine own servant, and help thy handmaid's son.
    Some token for good upon me show, O my Lord, my comfort and my trust,
    That mine haters may be ashamed, and know, that help and defend me thou dost.

[208] On metre, see note 203, p. 149.
[209] Smith shows some rhetorical flair in the multiple repetitions of 'great', first using anaphora (repetition at the beginning of lines), then more densely in a single line. Each set of repetitions has three instances of 'great', which might signal the Christian idea of God as Trinity.

26. John Hall, *Certain Chapters Taken out of the Proverbs of Solomon, with Other Chapters of the Holy Scripture, and Certain Psalms of David Translated into English Metre* (1549/50)

[John Hall (1529/30–1568/69) was a practicing physician, living and working in Maidstone, who also wrote devotional poetry. He supported the failed rebellion against Queen Mary by Thomas Wyatt the younger, son of the poet, which started at Maidstone. *Certain Chapters of the Proverbs of Solomon Drawn Forth into Metre by Thomas Sternhold* was printed in 1549 or 1550 with a dedication to Thomas Spek, gentleman of the Privy Chamber to Henry VIII, by the printer, John Case, in which he claimed to have been given the contents by a friend who was a former servant of Sternhold. Hall published a new edition that same year, with his name on the title page along with a statement that the contents 'of late were set forth, imprinted and untruly entitled, to be the doings of Master Thomas Sternhold'. It does not seem to have been noticed, however, that the contents of the two volumes are not identical. Both contain Hall's metrical Proverbs, but the authorized edition contains also metrical excerpts from Wisdom, Ecclesiasticus, and Thessalonians. Case's volume includes versions (unnumbered) of Psalms 88, 70, and 51, while Hall's has 25 (mistakenly numbered 21), 34, 54, 65, 112, 113, 114–15 (as one Psalm), and 145, all numbered according to Catholic practice. The status of the Psalms printed by Case is a mystery, but that Hall omitted them suggests they were not his, and they are also not Sternhold's. Hall then included the Psalms (with the addition of 130, 137, and 140) in his collection *The Court of Virtue* (1565), a volume designed to supplant for a godly readership the collection of secular love songs *The Court of Venus*. The texts of Psalms 25 and 34 follow Hall's first versions, which he significantly revised (he revised even from one edition of *Certain Chapters* to another). He obviously developed as a poet, since although in many cases the sense is retained (changing word order, for instance, or shifting lines), the metre is much more confident, some awkward irregularities eliminated. Hall's *A Most Excellent and Learned Woorke of Chirurgerie* (also 1565), a translation from Italian, was an important publication in the history of English medicine. See John Hall, *The Court of Virtue*, ed, by Russell A. Fraser (New Brunswick: Rutgers University Press, 1961); Rivkah Zim, *ODNB*.]

Psalm 25[210]

Ad te domine levavi animam.   [To thee, Lord, I lifted my soul]

The faithful man that feareth God
   Doth pray with heart and mind
For help against his enemies,
   The perfect way to find.

---

[210] Misnumbered 21.

5 To thee I lift my soul, O Lord,
      My God, I trust in thee.
   Oh, suffer not mine enemies   *allow*
      To triumph over me.
   For all they that in the hope
10   Ashamèd shall not be,
   And they that useth scorn and spite   *shamed*
      Shall be confounded of thee.
   My King, my God, I pray to thee;
      Show me now thy ways,
15 O Lord, and teach thy paths to me,
      And I will give thee the praise.
   Lead me, Lord, thy truth to speak,
      And learn me to be just.   *teach*
   Thou art my God and my Saviour eke;   *also*
20   All day in thee I trust.
   O call to thy remembrance[211]
      Thy tender mercy pure,
   And eke thy loving kindness, Lord,
      That ever hath been sure.
25 Remember not my sins, O God,
      And frailty of my youth;
   For thy goodness and mercy's sake,
      Think on me, Lord, with ruth.   *pity*
   How friendly and how righteous[212]
30   Is God the Lord of might.
   Therefore, he will the sinners teach
      To walk the way of right.
   The simple he doth lead aright,   *justly*
      And keepeth them night and day;   *guard*
35 Such as be meek, them learneth he
      To walk right in his way.
   The ways of God are merciful,
      And faithfulness is plight
   To all that keep his testament
40   And covenant aright.
   For thy name sake, O living Lord,
      Be merciful to me,
   And to my sins, for they be great,
      And mine iniquity.

---

[211] remembrance] The metre requires four syllables ('re-mem-be-rance').
[212] righteous] The metre requires three syllables ('right-e-ous').

45 What so ever he be
       That feareth the Lord, I say,
    He shall to him show his precepts,   *commands*
       And eke his chosen way.
    His soul shall ever dwell at ease,
50   Thereof I you insure,
    His seed shall still possess the land,   *descendants*
       Forever to endure.
    The secrets of the Lord are known,
       To them that fear him still;
55 He showeth to them his testament,
       His covenant and will.
    Mine eyes are looking to the Lord,
       On whom my trust is set;
    For by his might, he shall pluck out
60   My feet out of the net.
    Turn thee unto me, O God,
       Now for thy mercy's sake.
    Have mercy, Lord, on me,
       For I am desolate.
65 The sorrows of my heart be great,
       Full sore it doth me grieve;
    O bring me out of troubles, Lord,
       In thee I do believe.
    Look upon my misery
70   And mine adversity;
    Forgive me all my sins, O Lord,
       I have offended thee.
    Consider how mine enemies
       Be many, much and great,
75 And bear an heart malicious,
       For they would me defeat.
    O keep thou my soul, O God,
       And eke deliver me.
    Let me not be confounded, Lord,
80   I put my trust in thee.
    Righteous dealing and innocency
       Now with me let them dwell,
    And out of his adversity
       Deliver Israel.

Psalm 34

Benedicam domino in omni. [I will bless the Lord in all things]

How God doth keep the righteous men
    And he will them defend,
How for to lead a godly life,
    If you do so intend.
5 I will unto the Lord
    Be giving thanks always;
My mouth and tongue shall ever be
    Aspeaking to his praise.
My soul shall make her boast
10   In God, the Lord of might;
The poor oppressed shall hear thereof
    And gladly shall delight.
I do you now exhort,
    O praise the Lord with me,
15 Together with an humble heart
    His name to magnify.
For I myself besought the Lord,
    He heard me by and by,
And out of all my pain and woe
20   He did deliver me.
O come and be you lightenèd
    And to him draw you near;
And then withouten shamefastness   *without, ashamedness*
    Your faces shall appear.
25 This poor man cried to God,
    And he did hear his prayer,
And from his troubles, every one,
    Delivered him full fair.   *at once/directly*
The angel of the Lord
30   Doth pitch his tent full round
About all them that doth him fear
    To keep them safe and sound.
How friendly is the Lord,
    O taste and see, who lust;   *desire*
35 And blessèd is that man therefore
    That in him putteth his trust.
O fear the Lord, his holiness,
    See that ye do him please,
For they that fear him lack nothing
40   But ever shall have ease.

>   The rich shall suffer hunger great
>   And want that living food,
>   But they that seek the Lord shall lack
>   Nothing that which is good.
> 45 Come hither, O you children,
>   And hearken to my voice;
>   I shall you teach the fear of God
>   And therein to rejoice.
>   Whoso lusteth for to live
> 50   To see good days is fain,   *content*
>   Let him his tongue and lippes keep²¹³
>   All evil to refrain.
>   All evil things let them eschew,
>   Do good, and never cease,
> 55 And let him seek and eke ensue   *also*
>   To live in rest and peace.
>   For why the eyes of God are set   *because*
>   Upon the righteous men;
>   His ears are open to their prayers,
> 60   And he provideth for them.
>   The face of God is also bent
>   Thy wicked men to see,
>   Them to destroy out of the earth
>   And all their memory.
> 65 When righteous men do cry
>   The Lord doth hear their moan,
>   And from their troubles by and by
>   He will them help anon.   *at once*
>   The Lord is near unto all them
> 70   That are in heart contrite,
>   And he will help such as be meek
>   And of an humble sprite.   *spirit*
>   The troubles of the righteous,²¹⁴
>   Although that they be great,
> 75 The Lord shall help them out of all
>   And fair will them entreat.
>   He keepeth all their bones
>   Together safe and sound,
>   So that not one of them is broke

---

²¹³ lippes] The metre requires a disyllable ('lip-pes').

²¹⁴ righteous] TThe metre requires three syllables ('right-e-ous'), as also below, line 83.

80 With any stripe or wound.²¹⁵ *lash*
   But yet misfortune great
      The wicked men shall kill,
   And they that hate the righteous
      Shall be accused of ill. *evil*
85 The Lord will the soul save
      Of them that doth him serve
   And all that put their trust in him,
      That they shall never swerve.

27. William Hunnis, *Certain Psalms Chosen out of the Psalter of David and Drawn Forth into English Metre* (1550)

[William Hunnis (d. 1597) was a musician, poet, perhaps playwright, and conspirator. His *Certain Psalms* describe him as servant to William Herbert, Earl of Pembroke. In 1552 he was a gentleman of the Chapel Royal. During the reign of Queen Mary, Hunnis was imprisoned in the Tower for his involvement in a plot to assassinate the queen and put Princess Elizabeth in her place. Somehow he escaped execution and was restored to favour when Elizabeth came to the throne. By 1562 he was again gentleman of the Chapel Royal, and in 1566 he became Master of the Children, a position which involved directing the boys not only in singing but in staging royal entertainments. Hunnis may have written plays for the boys to perform at court (he certainly directed them), but none of them survive. Hunnis published many collections of devotional poetry, including metrical Psalms. The most popular was his 1583 *Seven Sobs* (see 58). The modesty topos was a commonplace of authorial prefaces, but Hunnis's disclaimer to the reader is particularly endearing: 'although that in some places they be not so eloquently turned as peradventure the matter of them requireth, yet for the exceeding profit that doth proceed of them, reject them not, but accept my good will, which wholly endeavoured myself and go about to satisfy, and to accomplish thy desire to profit every man and disprofit in no wise, which thing if I do obtain, I have that I look for, if not, yet I ought to be pardoned, forasmuch as my good will to please and profit failed not, but power only lacked'. See Andrew Ashbee, *ODNB*.]

Psalm 113

Laudate pueri.   [Praise the Lord, children]

O all ye servants, praise the Lord,
   Praise ye his holy name;
And everything that beareth life
   Likewise do ye the same.

---

²¹⁵ Hall the physician elaborates the Psalmist's injury.

5   Bless ye the name of God, the Lord,
       And praises in great store   *sufficient supply*
    Be unto God and Christ his Son,
       From henceforth, evermore.

    From the uprising of the sun
10   Until his going down,
    Praise ye the Lord in every place,
       Both in the field and town.

    The Lord is high above all lands,
       His glory pass the heavens;
15 Like as the sun doth pass all light
       With clearness of his beams.

    Who may be like unto our God,
       That hath his seat on high,   *habitation*
    Which will not let to see the things
20   That on the earth doth lie?

    The simple men he doth upraise
       And sets them up aloft,
    Even with the princes of his flock;
       These be his doings oft.

25 And eke the woman he hath made,   *also*
       That long before was barren,
    Now she remaineth in her house,
       A glad mother of children.

    Praise we the Father and the Son,
30   And eke the Holy Ghost,
    As hath been, is, and still shall be
       In every age and coast.

28. William Forrest, *Certain Psalms of David in Metre Added to Master Sternhold's and Others'* (MS 1551)

[William Forrest (fl. 1530–1576) studied at Cardinal College, Oxford, and was ordained priest. Forrest's religious views were seemingly moderate, though complicated, and, like those of so many in this tumultuous period, hard to determine precisely. His metrical translation of forty-nine Psalms, for instance, was dedicated to the Protestant Protector Somerset and was expressly modelled on the Psalms of Thomas Sternhold, which he apparently admired. Forrest had dedicated another work to Somerset in 1548, but by 1551 Somerset had fallen from power, and in October of that year he was imprisoned in the Tower for the second time, to be executed in January 1552. Dating the manuscript precisely is impossible, but it has been argued that Forrest's dedication was timed to Somerset's brief, partial return to favour before his second fall, when he rejoined the privy council. Forrest's Psalms may also have been intended to offer Somerset models of penitence and hopeful prayer, like the metrical Psalms written by other fallen courtiers in the Tower (see **18, 23, 25, 32,** and **33**). But whether Forrest's Psalms indicate an acceptance of the Reformation as a fait accompli during the reign of Edward VI, or an attempt to reappropriate the Psalms from Protestants for a renewed Catholic devotional practice is another mystery. It has been pointed out, however, that Forrest was a former Cistercian, for whom the Psalms were especially important, and that Psalm 94, the first in Forrest's manuscript, was chanted every night before nocturns. Forrest became a chaplain to Queen Mary in 1555. Later, despite the shift in official religion from Mary to Elizabeth, Forrest continued his career in the church unfazed, serving as parson in Buckinghamshire until his death. Forrest was a prolific author, though little of his work was printed. He wrote a biblical epic, *The History of Joseph the Chaste*, and a life of Katherine of Aragon, *The History of Grisild the Second*, among other poems. Forrest was also an accomplished musician, and was responsible for preserving eighteen masses by such early Tudor composers as John Taverner and Robert Fayrfax. See Oliver Wort, 'A Cuckoo in the Nest? William Forrest, the Duke of Somerset, and the *Certaigne Psalmes of Dauyd*', *Reformation*, 21.1 (2016), 25–46; Peter Holmes, ODNB.]

Psalm 6

Domine ne in furore. [Lord, do not in anger]

David, for his odious sin
Saw vengeance towards him bent.
On knees to fall, he did begin
As a most penitent.
5 Lord, in thy furious passion[216]
Let me not now be checked:
Nor in thy indignation,
Do thou not me correct,
Have mercy (Lord) on me, I pray,
10 My grief is more and more:
Heal me, as thou know'st best which way,[217]
For all my bones are sore,
And my poor soul is perplexèd

---

[216] passion] Here and for 'indignation' below the metre requires an extra syllable (-iòn).
[217] An especially awkward line, probably best pronounced, 'HEAL me, as THOU know'st BEST which WAY'.

With pangs most grievously:
15 But (Lord) how long this wise vexèd   *in this manner*
   Shall I hope remedy?
   Turn thee (O Lord) and my soul make
   Safe from all jeopardy;
   Save me now for thy mercy's sake,
20 For mercy (Lord) I cry.
   For in his death, there is no man
   Hath thee in remembrance:
   Or in hell pain, who is that can
   Thy honour there advance?
25 In sorrow I have labourèd,
   Washing my bed nightly:
   My couch, which on the ground is spread,
   With tears water shall I.
   For very inward grief and pain,
30 My eye is much troublèd:
   I am a thing consumed and vain,   *eaten away, empty*
   Among my foes cumbered.[218]   *overwhelmed*
   Away 'fore me, all ye that work
   Or haunt iniquity:
35 My tears (that from all doth lurk)
   In the Lord hearing be.
   The Lord hath heard in his high chair
   My deprecation:[219]   *intercessory prayer*
   And hath received my meek prayer
40 In thankful fashion.
   Let all mine enemies be abashed
   And vexèd grievously:
   Let their devices be clean dashed   *completely*
   And brought to shame shortly.

Psalm 11

In Domino confido.   [In the Lord I trust]

In God I trust why say th'unjust
My soul that doth disdain,
And at her thrust that needs thee must
Flee up to the mountain.[220]

---

[218] cumbered] For the rhyme, pronounced 'cumbrèd'.
[219] deprecation] The metre requires '-ion' to be two syllables (as also 'fashion' below).
[220] Note Forrest's use of internal rhyme, 'trust', 'unjust', 'thrust', 'must', and so forth, which is unlike anything in Sternhold or Hopkins.

5 For sinners low hath bent the bow
   And whereby doth mark
   The poor follow to shoot thorow,   *through*
   They lurking in the dark.

   For things that thou Lord dost
10 They have destroyèd clean   *entirely*
   The just what now come they alone
   That he doth wrong demean.

   The Lord he is alone in bliss
   In his holy temple;
15 His seat iwis the heaven it is   *habitation, certainly*
   We know by example.

   His eyen most clear on the poor here   *eyes*
   He causeth to respect;
   His eyelids clear on children dear
20 Whom he list to elect.[221]   *desires*

   The righteous and vicious[222]
   The Lord will examine,
   Who found as thus ungracious
   His soul's loss doth define.

25 Upon sinners plagues shall reverse
   Of fire, brimstone, and such;
   Stormy vapours, wind and waters
   Their portion so shall touch.

   The Lord as thus is righteous[223]
30 And righteousness loveth he;
   Aye bounteous and gracious
   Sustaining equity.[224]

---

[221] For a Catholic to mention election, so strongly associated with Calvinist predestination, may seem odd, but in fact Catholics also believed in election, since it was a biblical term and concept. How it worked and for whom, however, was a matter of sharp disagreement.
[222] righteous] The metre requires an extra syllable ('righ-te-ous'), as well as for 'vicious' ('vi-ci-ous') and 'ungracious' ('un-gra-ci-ous').
[223] righteous] The metre requires an extra syllable, as above, though not in the next line (which also requires 'lov'th'), although 'gracious' also needs to be pronounced 'gra-ci-ous'.
[224] The Psalmist (as in BCP) refers simply to God favouring the just. On equity, see note 6, p. 68.

29. Francis Seager, *Certain Psalms Select out of the Psalter of David and Drawn into English Metre* (1553)

[Francis Seager (fl. 1549–1563) was a translator and poet. In addition to his Psalms, several times reprinted, he wrote *The School of Virtue* (1557), a popular work of moral education for children, and a poem in rhyme royal stanzas on Richard of Gloucester's murder of the young princes for the *Mirrour for Magistrates* (1563). *Certain Psalms* includes versions of Psalms 31, 51, and 88, plagiarized and revised from versions in *Certain Chapters of the Proverbs* (1549–50), passed off there as Sternhold's. Psalm 88 has been attributed to the Earl of Surrey, and an argument has been made for attributing Psalms 31 and 51 to him as well, though this has not been widely accepted. There is no reason to assume the other Psalms in the volume are not by Seagar. Since Seager's title was close to that of Sternhold's *Certain Psalms* (1547), he, like many others, was probably trying to cash in on Sternhold's popularity. Many of Seagar's lines are rhythmically awkward, but as always with singing Psalms this would have been less obvious when sung to the tunes provided. See John N. King, *ODNB*.]

Psalm 112

Beatus vir qui timet.   [Blessed is the man who fears]

    The man is blest, that feareth God
        And walketh in his way:
    That in his law hath his delight,
        And doth his will obey.

5   His seed on earth shall prosper well   *descendants*
        And wondrously increase:
    The faithful flock shall be blessèd
        With everlasting peace.

    His house with riches shall abound,
10   With plenty and great store: *sufficient supply*
    His righteousness shall still endure,
        And last for evermore.

    Unto the man, that mercy showeth,
        And walketh here aright: *justly*
15 From darkness great shall then appear
        Unto his eyes plain light.

    O happy is the merciful
        That lendeth liberally:
    And in his words is circumspect,
20   And speaks advisedly.

Nothing shall move, nor him molest,   *cause trouble*
    Ne yet him grieve or pain:
The memory, of the righteous
    For ever shall remain.

25 No fear can make him faint at all,
    Nor no kind of mischance:
Whose heart doth firmly trust in God
    In whom he hath affiance.[225]   *faith*

His heart so sure, is stablishèd   *established*
30   He will not shrink at all:
Until he have his enemies made
    To him subject and thrall.   *enslave*

He hath his goods abroad dispersed
    And given to the poor:
35 His righteousness, remain it shall
    And dure for evermore.   *endure*

The wicked and the ungodly
    Shall it behold and see:
And will conceive displeasure then
40   And sore offended be.

They shall for it gnash with their teeth
    And vanish quite away:
And all their desire and their will
    Shall perish and decay.

Psalm 149

Cantate Domino.   [Sing to the Lord]

O sing to the Lord a new song,
    Thy voice to him direct;
Let the whole company praise him
    Of the saints and elect.[226]

5 Let Israel in his Maker
    Be glad with thankful voice;
Let all the children of Zion
    In their King much rejoice.

---

[225] affiance] Probably to be pronounced 'aff-YANCE', something like the French.
[226] See note 103 on 'elect', p. 110.

	His name to laud and magnify	*praise*
10	In all their dance and plays;	
	Upon the tabret and the harp	*small drum*
	Let them sing to him praise.	

Let the saints and all the elect[227]
    Rejoice with great glory;
15 Let them be joyful and right glad
    In their beds where they lie.

Let all the words they shall utter
    Sound to the praise of God;
And in their hands a two-edged sword,
20   For the wicked a rod.

To be avenged on the heathen,
    That perverse generation,
Putting the people to reproof,
    To shame and great vexation.

	To subdue their kings and rulers	
25	And nobles of their lands,	
	Calling them in captivity	
	Into strong iron bands.	*bonds*

That they on them may be avenged,
30   Even as it is written;
Such honour have all the elect
    From the Lord above given.

The sure hope, trust, and confidence
    That he had on the Lord
35 Is here expressed and manifest
    As this Psalm doth record.

30. Thomas Bownell, *A Godly Psalm of Mary Queen, Which Brought Us Comfort All, Through God, Whom We of Duty Praise, that Gives his Foes a Fall. By Richard Beard* (1553)

[Thomas Bownell's metrical Psalm verses are appended to the non-biblical 'Psalm' of Richard Beard (fl. 1533–1574), a London clergyman and author of polemical literature. Bownell's is an example of a pastiche Psalm, in which verses of different Psalms are recombined to make a Psalm which is both biblical, in

---

[227] See note 103 on 'elect', p. 110.

its language, and original, in its particular arrangement. Music in four parts is provided at the beginning of the volume. Bownell, about whom nothing but this contribution to Beard's volume is known, combined Psalms 146. 1–2, 7–9; 147. 6; and 148. 11–12 (labelled as such), but he numbers the stanzas as if it were a single Psalm.]

A godly Psalm in metre.

Psalm 146

1. O praise the Lord (my soul and sprite),   *spirit*
   So will I while I live;
Yes, sure as long as I remain,
   I will him praises give.

2. Which helpeth them unto their right,
   That bide and suffer wrong,
That feedeth eke the hungry men   *also*
   And those that thirsted long.

3. The Lord from prison looseth men,
   And gives the blind their sight;
The Lord doth help them up that fall,
   And loveth well the right.

4. He cares for strangers, widows he
   Defends, and fatherless;
And overturns the ways of all
   That work ungodliness.

Psalm 147

5. The Lord sets up and lifteth those
   That meek in heart are found,
And bringeth down ungodly men
   From high unto the ground.

6. The legs of men delight him not,
   Nor any horse's strength;
But those that fear him, and do trust
   To have his grace at length.

Psalm 148

7. O praise the Lord, ye kings and people,
   Dwelling on the earth;
Ye princes and ye judges all,
   Rejoice at once for mirth.

8. Young men and maids, you agèd men
      And children, being young,
Exalt his name, and also let
      His praises be your song.

31. Thomas Becon, *A Comfortable Epistle to God's Faithful People in England, Wherein is Declared the Cause of Taking Away the True Christian Religion from Them, and How It May Be Recovered and Obtained Again* (1554)

[Thomas Becon (1512/13–1567) was a clergyman and theologian, educated at Cambridge where, at St John's College, he taught all his life. In the 1540s Becon wrote many controversial works advocating reformed ideas, published under the pseudonym Theodore Basil. During the reign of King Edward, Becon served as chaplain to both Protector Somerset and Thomas Cranmer. Cranmer appointed Becon one of the six preachers at Canterbury. He continued to write works of theology as well as devotional collections like *The Pomander of Prayer* (1553, pub. 1558) and *The Flower of Godly Prayers* (c. 1550). On Queen Mary's accession, Becon was imprisoned in the Tower; he was released in 1554, at which point he joined other Protestant exiles on the Continent. Two Psalm paraphrases by Becon (127 and 134, described as to be sung before Morning and Evening Prayer, respectively) were included in the 1561 *Psalms of David in English Metre*, printed by John Day, though they were dropped for the 1562 *Whole Book*. Beth Quitslund proposes Becon as a possible source of manuscripts of additional texts for Day's 1560 *Psalms of David*. When Elizabeth came to the throne, Becon returned to England, resumed a successful clerical career, and continued to write. Becon's metrical version of Psalm 103, appended to his *Comfortable Epistle*, was written 'for a thanksgiving unto God' after his release from the Tower on 22 March 1554. The metre is iambic pentameter, the only precedents for which in the history of metrical Psalms are Wyatt's Penitential Psalms in terza rima and Surrey's Psalm 55 in blank verse. Becon's choice suggests a serious poetic ambition and makes his Psalm unsuitable for singing to popular Psalm tunes. See Seymour Baker House, *ODNB*.]

Psalm 103

Be thankful, O my soul, unto the Lord,
And all that within me have their being;
Laud, praise, and magnify with one accord[228]   *praise*
His holy and blessèd name above all thing.

---

[228] with one accord] all together.

  O my soul, once again to thee I say,
 Be thankful unto the Lord evermore,
 And look thou forget not night nor day
 All his benefits that thou hast in store.   *sufficient supply*

  For he it is, yea, he it is alone
10 Which pardoneth all thy sins, both more and less;
 He delivereth thee from all grief and moan,
 And sendeth thee health in time of sickness.

  He saveth thy life from destruction,
 Which otherwise should perish without doubt;
15 He, of mere grace and tender compassion,   *pure*
 Crowneth thee with loving kindness round about.

  He, with good things, thy mouth doth satisfy,
 To eat and drink giving thee abundance;
 He maketh thee joyful, young, and lusty,   *lively*
20 Even as an eagle that is full of pleasure.   *pleasure*

  The Lord doth minister justice and judgement
 To such as are oppressed with violence;
 He defendeth the good and innocent,
 But the wicked he casteth from his presence.

25 He showed his ways unto faithful Moses,[229]
 And his works to the sons of Israel;
 That all his people might know both more and less   *greater and lesser*
 In all kind of virtue for to excel.

  Oh, the Lord God, even of his own nature
30 Is bent unto gentleness and mercy;
 Yea, friendly is he above all measure,
 Long suffering and eke of great pity.   *also*

  For though our sins be both great and many,
 Yet will not the Lord be alway chiding;   *always*
35 Neither will he forever be angry,
 But show himself to us both gentle and loving.

  After our sins he dealeth not with us,
 Neither according to our wickedness;
 But like a father, both gentle and gracious,
40 He forgiveth all our sins, both more and less.

---

[229] Moses talks with God, both through the Burning Bush and later 'face to face' (as the narrator has it) on Mount Sinai, though God himself states that no one can see his face and live, privileging Moses with a view of his 'back parts' (Exodus 33. 11, 20–23).

> For look how high is the heaven supernal   *divine*
> In comparison of the earth full low;
> So great is his mercy toward them all
> That fear him and wickedness away throw.
>
> 45   And look how wide the East is from the West,
> So far hath he set all our sins from us,
> Because our conscience should be at rest,
> And no more troubled with works odious.
>
> Yea, like as a father, gentle and tender,
> 50   Pitieth his own children natural,
> Even so is the Lord merciful ever
> Unto them that fear him, both great and small.
>
> For he, being our Maker, knoweth certès   *certainly*
> Of what matter we be made and formed;
> 55   He remembreth, we are but dust and ashes,
> All of vile and slimy earth created.[230]
>
> A man in his life is like unto grass,
> His days are few, and but a while endure;
> Like the flower of the field, away he pass,
> 60   Flourishing for a time, but nothing sure.
>
> For as a flower with fierce wind assailèd
> Fadeth shortly away and cometh to nought,   *nothing*
> So doth man, of cruel death oppressèd,
> Depart hence, and unto nothing is brought.[231]
>
> 65   But the merciful goodness of the Lord
> Doth continue for ever and ever
> Upon them that fear him with one accord,
> And his justice upon their childers' childer.   *children's children*

---

[230] Becon adds the 'slimy earth' to the Psalmist's 'dust' (alluding to Adam's creation in Genesis 2). The emphasis on its vileness reflects a Calvinist view of human corruption, but the creation of man was often described as being out of slime, as in Erasmus's *In Praise of Marriage* ('he made man out of the slime of the earth'), translated by Richard Taverner (*A Right Fruitful Epistle*, 1536). See *Erasmus in English, 1523–1584, Volume 1: The Manual of the Christian Soldier and Other Writings*, ed by Alex Davis, Gordon Kendal, and Neil Rhodes (Cambridge: MHRA, 2022), p. 316.

[231] This and the previous two stanzas express perspectives on human life in metaphors familiar from Hebrew Wisdom literature, as in Job 4. 18–19, 14. 1–2, 21. 18–26; Ecclesiastes 3. 19–20; Isaiah 40. 6–8.

	I mean upon such as keep his covenant,	
70	And do themselves diligently apply	
	To keep his precepts, and likewise do grant	*commands*
	To frame their whole life accordingly.	
	In heaven hath the Lord a seat preparèd	*habitation*
	For himself, both glorious and royal,	
75	And his prince-like power is so outstretchèd	
	That it reigneth and ruleth over all.	

    O praise the Lord all ye angels of his,
Ye that excel both in strength and virtue,
Ye that do his will without any miss,
80 Ye that harken to his voice, and that ensue.[232]

    O praise the Lord our God omnipotent,
All ye his hosts and armies supernal,
Ye servants of his, which always are bent
To do his will, Oh praise the Lord above all.

85   Yea, all things that ever God created,
Praise ye the Lord that God of might and power;
But thou, O my soul, with heart unfeignèd,
Look that thou praise the Lord at every hour.

    Give the glory to God alone

32. John Dudley, Earl of Warwick (MS composed 1554)

[John Dudley (1527?–1554) was the third but first surviving son of John Dudley, Duke of Northumberland, one of the most powerful men in England, a military leader, close counsellor of Henry VIII, Lord Admiral, ally of Protector Somerset during the reign of Edward VI, and, after Somerset's fall, Lord President of the Privy Council. On Edward's death in 1553, Northumberland tried to ensure a Protestant succession and his own power by placing Lady Jane Grey on the throne, married to his fourth surviving son, Guildford. Jane was queen, famously, for only nine days, after which she was ousted by Edward's half-sister Mary. Northumberland was executed, as were Jane and Guildford Dudley the following year. The duke's other sons, John, Ambrose, Robert, and Henry, were imprisoned in the Tower. John Dudley, who became Earl of Warwick in 1551 when his father, the first earl, became duke, was a rather unaccomplished courtier with seeming scholarly aspirations. He had an impressive library that

---

[232] Expressions of praise in the Psalms often employ anaphora (repeating a word or phrase at the beginning of successive clauses or lines), as with 'Praise him' in verses 2 to 4 of Psalm 148 (BCP).

included classical texts. He was released in October 1554 but died shortly after. John and Robert Dudley each composed a metrical Psalm while in the Tower, likely following the precedent of the Earl of Surrey. John Dudley chose the same Psalm that Sir Thomas Smith composed in the Tower and that Surrey chose to paraphrase just before his execution, an appropriate choice for a courtier betrayed and brought low. Warwick's Psalm looks at first to be in the poulter's measure invented by Wyatt, but it may just be in Sternhold's or common metre, printed in long lines. The virgules in the manuscript have been retained for ease of reading. See Zim, *English Metrical Psalms*; Simpson, 'The Psalms and Threat'; David Loades, *ODNB*.]

Psalm 55

Give ear to me, my God, / and hear my mourning voice:
Break down the wicked swarming flocks[233] / that at my fall rejoice,
Whose cruel ravening minds / to work my bane are bent,   *death*
So that my troubled, quiv'ring heart / with mortal broils is spent.   *quarrels*
5 Wherefore, I wish me oft / the swiftful pigeon's gifts,
That scape I might by far flown flight, / from all their devilish drifts.   *escape*
But, Lord, root out their tongues, / that sow such poisoned strife
Throughout the land dispartedly / that thus pursue my life.[234]   *dividedly*
For if they had been foes, / that would display their ire,   *anger*
10 Then warn'd thereby I might have been, / as by the flame the fire.
But even my mates they were / that seemed to hold me dear,
When under face of friendly faith / they bred this doleful cheer.   *mood*
Since so: devour them, Lord, / consume them every one,
And throw them in the dreadful pit, / where they shall stintless moan.   *endless*
15 Beseeching thee, my God, / with humble heart and mind
To succour me, oh helpless wretch, / from torments they assigned.
To whom with restless note, / all thankful praise I sing,
Both day and night and every hour, / as to my God and King,
That hast me guarded, aye, / with thy triumphant shield,   *always*
20 From fearful force of furious foes, / and granted me the field.[235]

[233] Animals that flock are not normally 'ravening', but Dudley may be combining complaint and insult, casting his enemies as simultaneously hungry wolves (though their 'ravening' is only in their minds) and lowly, timid sheep. Jesus says, 'Beware of false prophets, which come to you in sheep's clothing, but inwardly they are ravening wolves' (Matthew 7. 15), but Dudley's are like fierce predators in their own minds, though really just sheep.

[234] Dudley follows the original Psalm here in cursing 'tongues', but slander was a particular concern at court, represented famously by the rampaging 'Blatant Beast' in book VI of Spenser's *Faerie Queene*, the allegorical embodiment of the detraction that can ruin reputations and careers and land one in the Tower.

[235] The Psalmist celebrates God's deliverance of him in battle, but the terms used by Dudley are more suited to an Elizabethan joust, knights charging each other bearing elaborate shields,

Such careful opened ears, / thou, Lord, had'st in my need,
That still I hope this cursèd sort shall / be razèd up with speed.   *demolished*
Who with fair cloaks of truce / and fawning lowly bows
Have trait'rously conspired my death, / and falsed their solemn vows,
25 All soothing sugared speech, / eke past their fleering lips,   *also, grinning*
When they had led their fraudful snares / to snarl me fast in trips.[236]
But I appeal to thee, / that will, when fit time is,
Discharge my fraughtful breast of woe, / and pour in heaps of bliss,   *burdened*
And send consuming plagues / for their deserts most due,   *rewards*
30 That thirst so sore my guiltless blood / their tyrants' hands t'imbrue.   *stain*

Finis.

33. Robert Dudley, Earl of Leicester (MS composed 1554)

[Robert Dudley (1532/33–1588) was the fifth son of John Dudley, Duke of Northumberland. Like the rest of his family, Robert was sent to the Tower in 1553, where, like his older brother John, and the Earl of Surrey and Sir Thomas Smith earlier, he expressed his personal complaint in a Psalm paraphrase. This is the only poem Dudley is known to have composed. Dudley was released in 1554, fought in campaigns in France, and became close to Princess Elizabeth some time before her accession in 1558. Dudley was the queen's favourite from 1559, although he was married. Dudley's wife died in somewhat suspicious circumstances in 1560, but his career continued to rise. He was made a member of the Privy Council in 1562 and was created Earl of Leicester in 1564. He was banished from court in 1578 when Elizabeth found out he had secretly married Lettice Knollys. Leicester was an important patron of scholarship and the arts and was a powerful and influential supporter of Protestant nonconformists, those proponents of further reform later labelled Puritans. He was made viceroy of the Netherlands in 1584. Like his brother's Psalm 55, Leicester's Psalm looks at first to be in the poulter's measure invented by Wyatt, but it may just be in Sternhold's or common metre, printed in long lines. The original virgules in the manuscript have been preserved for ease of reading. See Zim, *English Metrical Psalms*; Simpson, 'The Psalms and Threat'; Simon Adams, *ODNB*.]

---

hoping to win the field. An accident in such a joust in 1536 resulted in the leg wound that plagued Henry VIII for the rest of his life. Alternatively, Dudley may be borrowing the metaphor of the armour of God (including 'the shield of faith') from Ephesians 6.
[236] to snarl me fast in trips] to trap me securely in mis-steps.

Psalm 94

    O mighty Lord, to whom / all vengeance doth belong,[237]
    And just revenge for their deserts, / which do oppress by wrong,   *rewards*
    Thy prayed-for presence show, / thou judge and righteous guide,
    And pay them with a due reward / that swell in hateful pride.[238]
5 For, Lord, if thou forbear / and suffer such to reign,   *allow*
    How long shall then those haughty men / so lordly us disdain,
    Which do despise thy flock, / and use with threats the just
    And widows with the faultless men / they order as they lust?   *desire*
    And eke the helpless babes, / which fatherless remain,   *also*
10 They spare not in their guiltless blood / their cruel hands to stain.
    And thus, among themselves, / they hold the Lord is blind,
    And deem his power too far, too short / their cloakèd faults to find. *hidden sins*
    But yet in time beware, / you forward bloody band,   *company*
    What things against the Lord, your God, / you seek to take in hand.
15 For who can hide from him / one deed or secret thought,
    Since ears and eyes with each good gift / alone by him were wrought?
    Or who can him restrain / to punish at his will,
    Since that his rod doth rule both sorts, / as well the good as ill?
    And eke the Lord doth know / no thought in man doth reign
20 That framèd is by nature's work / but is both frail and vain.
    But blessèd is that man, / whom, Lord, thou dost correct,
    And by those paths thou dost appoint / his ways aye to direct,   *always*
    And in his troubled state / doth grant him patient mind,
    Till wasteful[239] graves shall swallow up / the vile and wicked kind.
25 For from the faithful flock, / the Lord will never swerve,
    But guard them with his mighty shield / and safely them preserve,
    And eke restore again / true judgments to his seat,
    Till righteousness may guide the just / and vanquish all deceit.
    Where, when the wicked ruled / and bear the sway by might, *have authority over*

---

[237] From the first line, Robert Dudley demonstrates less rhythmic facility than his brother, with the awkward pause in the middle of the syntax (after 'whom') that the structure of poulter's measure (and Sternhold's common metre) naturally requires. It would be possible to read through the line continuously as a hexameter, which would be a radical innovation, but this seems not what Dudley had in mind, since the subsequent lines just fall into the normal poulter's rhythm.

[238] Dudley actually avoids the religious emphasis of the Psalmist, who complains specifically about the 'ungodly', which in England in 1554 would clearly point to Catholics like Mary and her supporters, since 'Protestants' did not call themselves such (or 'Puritans') but rather 'saints' or the 'godly'. Perhaps Dudley thought such language would be too dangerous and so shifted to the more generic 'proud', although he then specifies that God allows such people 'to reign' (the original refers to rejoicing or triumph), which points unavoidably to the queen.

[239] wasteful] unused or destructive; both could apply here.

30 No one would press to take my part, / or once defend my right.
   So that for want of help / I had been sore oppressed,
   If that the Lord had not with speed / my woeful plight redressed,   *misfortune*
   Who, when he heard me cry, / and for his goodness call,
   With mercy straight he stayed my foot, / and saved me from the fall.[240]
35 And eke from careful thoughts, / that did consume my breast,   *troubled*
   His endless power hath clean discharged / and filled my soul with rest.   *fully*
   He hates the cruel kind, / that wresteth justice still,
   And makes their laws obey their lusts, / as good men do God's will,
   And shameless ways conspire / the wicked to preserve,
40 And search by power to shed the blood / of such as least deserve.
   But sure the Lord, my God, / mine aid and only strength,
   Will them reward and sharply scourge / with endless pain at length,
   And them destroy each one, / that wails not other's woe,   *bewails*
   That they should know the mighty Lord / hath power to plague them so.

   Finis.

34. William Kethe, in *The Appellation of John Knox from the Cruel and Most Unjust Sentence Pronounced against Him by the False Bishops and Clergy of Scotland* (1558)

[William Kethe (d. 1594) was a Scot who somehow ended up in England writing Protestant polemical poems during the reign of Edward VI. With other Protestants, he sought refuge on the Continent during the reign of Catholic Queen Mary, moving first to Frankfurt and later to Geneva, where he joined the congregation of fellow Scot John Knox. He was a contributor to the Sternhold and Hopkins collection, but his translation of Psalm 94 was not one of those included in that volume. It appeared instead at the end of Knox's *Appellation to the Scottish Nobility* (as it is popularly known), published in Geneva, defending himself against charges of heresy and urging the nobles to support the Protestant faith against the Catholic monarchy. Psalm 94, with its petition for aid (and indeed vengeance) against the ungodly is of obviously topical application to Knox's situation. Kethe adds elements like the 'little flock', emphasizing the early Protestant sense of themselves as a persecuted minority (Knox refers to the Scots people as a flock in need of protection seven times), and God's 'heritage', perhaps connected to the sense that Protestantism reconnected to the tradition of the early church, corrupted after centuries of what Luther called the church's Babylonian captivity. Kethe returned to England in 1559, perhaps after assisting with the production of the Geneva Bible, and remained active as a Puritan clergyman and preacher in Dorset. See Timothy

---

[240] With mercy straight he stayed my foot] With undeviating mercy he secured my foot.

Duguid, *Metrical Psalmody in Print and Practice: English 'Singing Psalms' and Scottish 'Psalm Buiks', c.1547–1640* (Farnham: Ashgate, 2014); C. H. Garrett, *The Marian Exiles: A Study in the Origins of Elizabethan Puritanism* (Cambridge: The University Press, 1938); Jane Dawson, *John Knox* (New Haven and London: Yale University Press, 2015); Quitslund, *Reformation in Rhyme*; J. Fielding, ODNB.]

Psalm 94

O Lord, sith vengeance doth to thee,   *since*
   and to none else belong:
Now show thyself (O Lord our God),
   with speed revenge our wrong.

5 Arise thou great Judge of the world,
   and have at length regard,
That as the proud deserve and do,
   thou wilt them so reward.

How long (O Lord) shall wicked men
10   triumph thy flock to slay?
Yea, Lord, how long? For they triumph
   as though he, who now but they.[241]

How long shall wicked doers speak?
   their great disdain we see,
15 Whose boasting proud doth seem to threat
   no speech but theirs to be.

O Lord, they smite thy people down,
   not sparing young or old:
Thine heritage they so torment,
20   as strange is to behold.

The widow and the stranger both
   they murder cruelly:
The fatherless they put to death
   and cause they know none why.

25 And yet say they: tush, tush, the Lord
   shall not behold this deed,
Ne yet will Jacob's God revolve   *consider*
   the things by us decreed.

---

[241] An awkward pair of lines, requiring emphasis on the final syllable of 'triumph', and with an extra syllable in the final line, combined with a nearly incomprehensible syntax. The Psalmist complains that the ungodly triumph; Kethe adds a further complaint seemingly about their attitude or presumption, but it is unclear.

But now take heed ye men unwise,
30   among the folk that dwell:
Ye fools (I say) when will ye weigh
    or understand this well?

He that the ear did plant and place,   *stalk of grain*
    shall he be slow to hear?²⁴²
35 Or he that made the eye to see,
    shall he not see most clear?

Or he that whipped the heathen folk,
    and knowledge teacheth men,
To nurture such as went astray,
40   shall he not punish then?

The Lord our God, who man did frame,
    his very thoughts doth know,
And that they are but vile and vain,
    to him is known also.

45 But blessèd is that man (O Lord)
    whom thou dost bring in awe,
And teachest him by this thy rod
    to love and fear thy law.

That patience²⁴³ thou may'st him give
50   in time of troubles great,
Until the pit be diggèd up
    th'ungodly for to eat.

For why, the Lord will never fail   *because*
    his people, which him love:
55 Ne yet forsake his heritance,   *inheritance*
    which he doth still approve,

Till righteousness to judgement turn,
    as it must be indeed,
And such as be full true in heart
60   to follow it with speed.

---

²⁴² There is a pun in English that does not exist in the Hebrew, since English 'ear' can mean both the organ of hearing and a head of corn or grain. The Hebrew verb can suggest both fastening and planting, but only in English can 'ear' apply to both. The second half of the sentence refers to God hearing, which reflexively reinforces the sense of 'ear' as organ, but the agricultural sense lingers.
²⁴³ patience] The metre requires three syllables ('pa-ti-ence').

> Who now will up and rise with me
>   against this wicked band?
> Or who against these workers ill   *evil*
>   on my part stout will stand?   *resolute*
>
> 65 If that the Lord had not me helped,
>   Doubtless it had been done,
> To wit, my soul in silence brought,
>   and so my foes had won.
>
> But though my foot did swiftly slide,
> 70   Yet when I did it tell,
> Thy mercy (Lord) so held me up,
>   that I therewith not fell.
>
> For in the heaps of sorrows sharp,
>   that did my heart oppress,
> 75 Thy comforts were to me so great,
>   they did my soul refresh.
>
> Wilt thou (vain man) have ought to do
>   with that most wicked chair,[244]
> That museth mischief as a law
> 80   without remorse or fear?
>
> Against the souls of righteous men
>   they all with speed convent,   *convene*
> And there the guiltless blood condemn,
>   with one most vile consent.
>
> 85 But my refuge is to the Lord
>   in all these dangers deep,
> And God the strength is of my trust,
>   who always doth me keep.
>
> He shall reward their wickedness,
> 90   and in their wrath them kill,
> Yea, them destroy shall God our Lord,
>   for he both can and will.
>
>   FINIS.

---

[244] wicked chair] BCP Coverdale translation 'stool of wickedness', KJV 'throne of iniquity'; the metaphor seems to be of tyranny.

35. Various Translators, *The Bible and Holy Scriptures Contained in the Old and New Testament* [The Geneva Bible] (1560)

[The Geneva Bible was the first complete English Bible translated from the original languages. (Tyndale worked from Hebrew and Greek, but Coverdale relied on intermediary translations in Latin and German.) It was also the first English Bible to include verse as well as chapter numbers, based on the numbering used by the printer Robert Estienne for his Bibles in Latin, Greek, and French. The principal translator and editor was William Whittingham, but he was assisted by other Protestant exiles in Geneva, including Coverdale, Christopher Goodman, Anthony Gilby, Thomas Sampson, and William Cole. Gilby was apparently the most accomplished Hebraist of the group, and it has been argued that the translation of the Psalms in the Geneva Bible is largely his. The New Testament was published in 1557 and the complete Bible in 1560, both in Geneva. It was not printed in England until 1575, perhaps (the claim has been disputed) because of opposition from Archbishop Matthew Parker, who was the editor of the official Bible of the Elizabethan Church, the Bishops' Bible of 1567. Parker died in 1575, and from then until the middle of the next century the Geneva Bible was by far the most popular English translation, even though it was not generally used in church. The Geneva Bible was printed in over 150 editions, in a variety of formats, including small, inexpensive Bibles for the desk or coat pocket. Most useful for the general reader was the editorial apparatus, including extensive marginal notes, chapter introductions, maps, diagrams, genealogies, and tables of names and keywords. There were two substantial revisions of the Geneva Bible: the first, the so-called Geneva-Tomson, was in 1576 when Laurence Tomson revised the New Testament (not incorporated in a complete Bible until 1587); the second, the 1599 Geneva-Tomson-Junius, had expanded notes to Revelation based on the commentary by Francis Junius. These revisions did not supplant previous editions, however, and all three versions continued to be printed into the seventeenth century. Following Calvin's interpretive practice, the marginal notes of the Geneva Bible Psalms often situate them in their supposed historical context in terms of the life of David, even if there is no evidence for this in the text. See Thomas Fulton, *The Book of Books: Biblical Interpretation, Literary Culture, and the Political Imagination from Erasmus to Milton* (Philadelphia: University of Pennsylvania Press, 2021); Femke Molekamp, 'Genevan Legacies: The Making of the English Geneva Bible', in *The Oxford Handbook of the Bible in Early Modern England, c.1530–1700*, ed. by Kevin Killeen, Helen Smith, and Rachel Willie (Oxford: Oxford University Press, 2015), pp. 38–53; Daniell, *Bible in English*.]

Psalm 7

Shigaion[245] of David, which he sang unto the Lord, concerning the words of Chush the son of Jemini.

1. O Lord my God, in thee I put my trust: save me from all that persecute me, and deliver me.
2. Lest he[246] devour my soul like a lion, and tear it in pieces, while there is none to help.
3. O Lord my God, if I have done this thing: if there be any wickedness in mine hands,
4. If I have rewarded evil unto him that had peace with me (yea, I have delivered him that vexed me without cause),
5. Then let the enemy persecute my soul and take it: yea, let him tread my life down upon the earth, and lay mine honour in the dust. Selah.
6. Arise, O Lord, in thy wrath, and lift up thyself against the rage of mine enemies, and awake for me, according to the judgement that thou hast appointed.
7. So shall the congregation of the people compass° thee about: for their sakes, therefore, return on high.[247]
8. The Lord shall judge the people: judge thou me, O Lord, according to my righteousness, and according to mine innocency that is in me.
9. O let the malice of the wicked come to an end: but guide thou the just: for the righteous God tryeth the hearts and reins.°
10. My defence is in God, who preserveth the upright in heart.
11. God judgeth the righteous, and him that condemneth God, every day.
12. Except he turn, he hath whet° his sword: he hath bent his bow and made it ready.
13. He hath also prepared him deadly weapons: he will ordain his arrows for them that persecute me.
14. Behold, he shall travail with wickedness: for he hath conceived mischief, but he shall bring forth a lie.
15. He hath made a pit and digged it, and is fallen into the pit that he made.
16. His mischief shall return upon his own head, and his cruelty shall fall upon his own pate.°
17. I will praise the Lord according to his righteousness, and will sing praise to the name of the Lord most high.

---

[245] Shigaion] Meaning unknown, but Alter suggests something like 'rhapsody', since the root connotes extreme emotion.

[246] The note (along with others) identifies the persecutor as Saul, pursuing David in the wilderness.

[247] The note clarifies, in this case anachronistically with reference to the Christian (and presumably true Protestant) Church, 'Not only for mine, but for thy Church sake declare thy power'.

Psalm 23

A Psalm of David.

1. The Lord is my shepherd, I shall not want.
2. He maketh me to rest in green pasture, and leadeth me by the still waters.
3. He restoreth my soul, and leadeth me in the paths of righteousness for his name's sake.
4. Yea, though I should walk through the valley of the shadow of death,[248] I will fear no evil: for thou art with me: thy rod and thy staff, they comfort me.
5. Thou dost prepare a table before me in the sight of mine adversaries: thou dost anoint mine head with oil,[249] and my cup runneth over.
6. Doubtless, kindness and mercy shall follow me all the days of my life, and I shall remain a long season°[250] in the house of the Lord.

Psalm 24

A Psalm of David.

1. The earth is the Lord's, and all that therein is: the world, and they that dwell therein.
2. For he hath founded it upon the seas: and established it upon the floods.
3. Who shall ascend into the mountain of the Lord? And who shall stand in his holy place?
4. Even he that hath innocent hands and a pure heart: which hath not lift up his mind unto vanity,° nor sworn deceitfully.
5. He shall receive a blessing from the Lord, and righteousness from the God of his salvation.
6. This is the generation of them that seek him,[251] of them that seek thy face, this is Jacob. Selah.
7. Lift up your heads, ye gates, and be ye lift up, ye everlasting doors, and the King of glory shall come in.
8. Who is this King of glory? The Lord, strong and mighty, even the Lord mighty in battle.

---

[248] The note emphasizes a literal reading, resisting the allegorical suggestion of the 'valley of the shadow of death': 'though he were in danger of death, as the sheep in the dark valley without his shepherd'.

[249] **Marg.** 'As was the manner at great feasts.'

[250] a long season] BCP Coverdale 'for ever'; the Hebrew means 'length' but is open to various interpretations.

[251] Following Paul's radical reinterpretation (Romans 2. 25–29), the note explains, 'Though circumcision separate the carnal seed of Jacob from the Gentiles, yet he that seeketh God, is the true Jacob and the very Israelite'.

9. Lift up your heads, ye gates, and lift up yourselves, ye everlasting doors, and the King of glory shall come in.
10. Who is this King of glory? The Lord of hosts, he is the King of glory. Selah.

Psalm 48

A song or Psalm committed to the sons of Korah.[252]

1. Great is the Lord, and greatly to be praised, in the city of our God, even upon his holy mountain.
2. Mount Zion, lying northward, is fair in situation: it is the joy of the whole earth, and the city of the great King.
3. In the palaces thereof God is known for a refuge.
4. For lo, the kings were gathered, and went together.
5. When they saw it, they marvelled: they were astonished, and suddenly driven back.
6. Fear came there upon them, and sorrow, as upon a woman in travail.°
7. As with an east wind thou breakest the ships of Tarshish,[253] so were they destroyed.
8. As we have heard, so have we seen in the city of the Lord of hosts, in the city of our God: God will stablish° it forever. Selah.
9. We wait for thy loving kindness, O God, in the midst of thy temple.
10. O God, according unto thy name, so is thy praise unto the world's end: thy right hand is full of righteousness.
11. Let mount Zion rejoice, and the daughters of Judah be glad, because of thy judgements.
12. Compass° about Zion, and go round about it, and tell the towers thereof.
13. Mark well the wall thereof: behold her towers, that ye may tell your posterity.
14. For this God is our God for ever and ever: he shall be our guide unto the death.

Psalm 98

A Psalm.

1. Sing unto the Lord a new song:[254] for he hath done marvellous things: his right hand and his holy arm have gotten him the victory.

---

[252] **Marg.** 'Some put this difference between a song and Psalm, saying that it is called a song, when there is no instrument, but the voice: and the Psalm, the contrary. The song of the Psalm is when the instruments begin, and the voice followeth. The Psalm of the song, the contrary.' On genre, see Introduction, pp. 17–21.

[253] **Marg.** 'That is, of Cilicia, or of the sea called Mediterranean.'

[254] The note is boldly anachronistic: 'That is, some song newly made in token of their wonderful deliverance by Christ'. The notes for the second half of this verse explain that the reference is to the Church.

2. The Lord declared his salvation: his righteousness hath he revealed in the sight of the nations.
3. He hath remembered his mercy and his truth toward the house of Israel: all the ends of the earth have seen the salvation of our God.
4. All the earth, sing ye loud unto the Lord: cry out and rejoice, and sing praises,
5. Sing praise to the Lord upon the harp, even upon the harp with a singing voice.
6. With shawms and sound of trumpets sing loud before the Lord the King.
7. Let the sea roar, and all that therein is, the world, and they that dwell therein.
8. Let the floods clap their hands, and let the mountains rejoice together
9. Before the Lord: for he is come to judge the earth; with righteousness shall he judge the world, and the people with equity.[255]

Psalm 106

Praise ye the Lord.

1. Praise ye the Lord because he is good, for his mercy endureth forever.
2. Who can express the noble acts of the Lord or show forth all his praise?
3. Blessed are they that keep judgement, and do righteousness at all times.
4. Remember me, O Lord, with the favour of thy people: visit me with thy salvation,
5. That I may see the felicity of thy chosen, and rejoice in the joy of thy people, and glory with thine inheritance.
6. We have sinned with our fathers: we have committed iniquity and done wickedly.
7. Our fathers understood not thy wonders in Egypt, neither remembered they the multitude of thy mercies, but rebelled at the sea, even at the Red Sea.[256]
8. Nevertheless he saved them for his name's sake, that he might make his power to be known,
9. And he rebuked the Red Sea, and it was dried up, and he led them in the deep as in the wilderness.
10. And he saved them from the adversary's hand, and delivered them from the hand of the enemy.
11. And the waters covered their oppressors; not one of them was left.
12. Then believed they his words and sang praise unto him.

---

[255] The Geneva follows Coverdale (BCP), as does the KJV, but the Hebrew means just evenness or uprightness. On equity, see note 6, p. 68.

[256] The subject of this Psalm is the Exodus out of Egypt, recounted in Exodus 12–34, and (for Phineas) Numbers 25. The note explains the parting of the Red Sea: 'The inestimable goodness of God appeareth in this, that he would change the order of nature, rather than his people should not be delivered, although they were wicked.'

13. But incontinently° they forgot his works; they waited not for his counsel,
14. But lusted with concupiscence° in the wilderness, and tempted God in the desert.
15. Then he gave them their desire: but he sent leanness into their soul.
16. They envied Moses also in the tents, and Aaron the holy one of the Lord.
17. Therefore the earth opened and swallowed up Dathan, and covered the company of Abiram.
18. And the fire was kindled in their assembly; the flame burnt up the wicked.
19. They made a calf in Horeb, and worshipped the molten image.
20. Thus they turned their glory into the similitude of a bullock, that eateth grass.[257]
21. They forgot God their Saviour, which had done great things in Egypt,
22. Wondrous works in the land of Ham, and fearful things by the Red Sea.
23. Therefore he minded to destroy them, had not Moses his chosen stood in the breach before him to turn away his wrath, lest he should destroy them.
24. Also they condemned that pleasant land and believed not his word.
25. But murmured in their tents and hearkened not unto the voice of the Lord.
26. Therefore he lifted up his hand against them to destroy them in the wilderness.
27. And to destroy their seed° among the nations: and to scatter them throughout the countries.
28. They joined themselves also unto Baal-peor, and did eat the off'rings of the dead.
29. Thus they provoked him unto anger with their own inventions, and the plague broke in upon them.
30. But Phineas stood up, and executed judgement, and the plague was stayed.°
31. And it was imputed° unto him for righteousness from generation to generation forever.
32. They angered him also at the waters of Meribah, so that Moses was punished for their sakes.[258]
33. Because they vexed his spirit, so that he spoke unadvisedly with his lips.
34. Neither destroyed they the people, as the Lord had commanded them.
35. But were mingled among the heathen, and learned their works,
36. And served their idols, which were their ruin.
37. Yea, they offered their sons, and their daughters unto devils.
38. And shed innocent blood, even the blood of their sons, and of their daughters, whom they offered unto the idols of Canaan, and the land was defiled with blood.

---

[257] The notes are particularly vehement in denouncing idolatry, the worship of 'wood, stone, metal or calves', and the editors are no doubt thinking as much of Catholic statues and images as of the Israelites' golden calf.
[258] Exodus 17.

39. Thus were they stained with their own works, and went a-whoring with their own inventions.
40. Therefore was the wrath of the Lord kindled against his people, and he abhorred his own inheritance.
41. And he gave them into the hand of the heathen, and they that hated them were lords over them.
42. Their enemies also oppressed them, and they were humbled under their hand.
43. Many a time did he deliver them, but they provoked him by their counsels: therefore they were brought down by their iniquity.
44. Yet he saw when they were in affliction, and he heard their cry.
45. And he remembered his covenant toward them, and repented according to the multitude of his mercies,
46. And gave them favour in the sight of all them, that led them captives.
47. Save us, O Lord our God, and gather us from among the heathen: that we may praise thine holy name, and glory in thy praise.
48. Blessed be the Lord God of Israel for ever and ever, and let all the people say, So be it, Praise ye the Lord.

36. Anne Vaughan Lock?, *Sermons of John Calvin, upon the Song of Hezekiah Made After He Had Been Sick and Afflicted by the Hand of God* (1560)

[Anne Vaughan Lock (also Lok, Locke) (*c.* 1530–post-1590) was the daughter of Stephen Vaughan, a prosperous merchant, diplomat, and agent of Henry VIII in the Netherlands. Committed to Protestantism, Vaughan tried, without success, to save Tyndale from execution in Antwerp. Anne married the well-educated mercer Henry Lock with whom she had at least two children, including Henry, who became a poet and metrical Psalmist (see 70). Anne Lock became a staunch Protestant and was a close friend of the Scottish reformer John Knox, who stayed with the Locks in London and with whom she corresponded. In 1557 Lock joined the community of Protestant exiles in Geneva, taking her children but leaving her husband behind (though this seems not to have impaired their marriage). In Geneva she translated Calvin's sermons on the song of Hezekiah in Isaiah 38. Appended to the end of Lock's translation was a metrical paraphrase of Psalm 51, titled *A Meditation of a Penitent Sinner*. No author is given, and Lock's prefatory note suggests it is the work of a 'friend': 'I have added this meditation following unto the end of this book, not as parcel of Master Calvin's work, but for that it well agreeth with the same argument, and was delivered me by my friend with whom I knew I might be so bold to use and publish it as pleased me'. Although Patrick Collinson thought the poem to be by Knox, most scholars since have agreed with Susan Felch's attribution of the poem to Lock herself, despite the disclaimer, though the argument rests largely on the assumption that to claim in print the authorship of sonnets, even devotional ones, was potentially scandalous for a woman. Some have argued that the prefatory note is not by Lock but John Day, the printer. An argument for reattribution has recently been made by Steven May, proposing Thomas Norton as the author. Among other arguments are the close parallels between Norton's Psalm 51 in *The Whole Book of Psalms* and the vocabulary and rhymes of *A Meditation of a Penitent Sinner*. Jake Arthur raises serious questions about much of May's evidence for Norton, but offers no stronger argument than Felch for the attribution to Lock. Whoever wrote it, *A Meditation* is the first sonnet sequence in English, predating Thomas Watson's Petrarchan *Hekatompathia* by over twenty years. After returning to London, Lock continued to work for greater reform, maintaining her correspondence with Knox and sending him books and money. After the death of her first husband in 1571, she married the popular preacher Edward Dering. He died of consumption in 1575, and she married Richard Prowse, a successful draper and several times mayor of and MP for Exeter. Her translation of Jean Taffin's *Of the Marks of the Children of God, and of their Comfort in Afflictions* was printed in 1590 and seven times thereafter. She presumably predeceased her third husband, who died in 1607. On Norton, see 40. Lock's sonnets follow the English rhyme scheme established by Surrey and later popularized by Shakespeare. See Kimberly Ann Coles, *Religion, Reform, and Women's Writing in Early Modern England* (Cambridge: Cambridge University Press, 2008); *The Collected Works of Anne Vaughan Lock*, ed. by Susan Felch (Tempe: Arizona Center for Medieval and Renaissance Studies, 1999); Deirdre Serjeantson, 'Anne Lock's Anonymous Friend: A Meditation of a Penitent Sinner and the Problem of Ascription', in *Enigma and Revelation in Renaissance English Literature: Essays Presented to Eiléan Ní Chuilleanáin*, ed. by Helen Cooney and Mark S. Sweetnam (Dublin: Four Courts, 2012), pp. 51–68; Steven W. May, 'Anne Lock and Thomas Norton's Meditation of a Penitent Sinner', *Modern Philology*, 114.4 (2017), 793–819; Jake Arthur, 'Anne Lock or Thomas Norton? A Response to the Reattribution of the First Sonnet Sequence in English', *Early Modern Women*, 16.2 (2022), 213–36; Patrick Collinson, *ODNB*.]

Psalm 51

A Meditation of a Penitent Sinner: Written in Manner of a Paraphrase upon the 51. Psalm of David.

The preface, expressing the passioned mind of the penitent sinner.

The heinous guilt of my forsaken ghost	*spirit*
So threats, alas, unto my feebled sprite	*threatens, spirit*
Deservèd death, and (that me grieveth most)	
Still stand so fixed before my dazzled sight	

5 The loathsome filth of my disdainèd life,
   The mighty wrath of mine offended Lord,
   My Lord whose wrath is sharper than the knife,
   And deeper wounds than double-edgèd sword,[259]
   That as the dimmèd and fordullèd eyen *clouded eyes*
10 Full fraught with tears and more and more oppressed *burdened*
   With growing streams of the distillèd brine
   Sent from the furnace of a grief-full breast,[260]
   Cannot enjoy the comfort of the light,
   Nor find the way wherein to walk aright: *rightly*

15   So I, blind wretch, whom God's inflamèd ire *anger*
   With piercing stroke hath thrown unto the ground,
   Amid my sins, still grovelling in the mire,[261]
   Find not the way that others oft have found,
   Whom cheerful glimpse of God's abounding grace
20 Hath oft relieved, and oft with shining light
   Hath brought to joy out of the ugly place,
   Where I in dark of everlasting night
   Bewail my woeful and unhappy case,
   And fret my dying soul with gnawing pain. *wear away*
25 Yet blind, alas, I grope about for grace.
   While, blind for grace, I grope about in vain;[262]
   My fainting breath I gather up and strain,
   Mercy, mercy to cry and cry again.[263]

---

[259] double-edged sword] A common biblical idiom, as in Psalm 149. 6, Proverbs 5. 4, Hebrews 4. 12.

[260] Felch compares these lines to Lock's allusions to contemporary medical practice in her epistle to the Duchess of Suffolk (prefacing her translation of Calvin), but the image of tears ('brine') distilled in a furnace is more likely alchemical, as in Southwell's later poem 'The Burning Babe' ('My faultless breast the furnace is', as the babe sheds 'floods of tears'). The language of alchemical distillation, referring to both physical and spiritual purification, was appropriated for both love poems and religious literature. Lock may also have found this imagery in contemporary love poems, like the anonymous, 'Ah love how wayward is his wit', in Tottel's popular *Miscellany*: 'Grant grace to him that grates therefore with sea of saltish brine | By extreme heat of boiling breast distillèd through his eyes' (*Songs and Sonnets Written by the Right Honorable Lord Henry Howard late Earl of Surrey and Other* (London, 1557)).

[261] Compare II Peter 2. 22, referring to the ungodly as 'the sow that is washed [returned] to the wallowing in the mire' (Felch).

[262] An example of the figure of chiasmus ('crossing'), 'grope' and 'grace' repeated in the subsequent lines, but in reverse order.

[263] The desire to 'cry again' is represented in the repetition of 'mercy' and 'cry'. The couplet rhyme repeats the second rhyme of the third quatrain. Lock does sometimes reuse rhymes within a sonnet.

	But mercy, while I sound with shrieking cry,	
30	For grant of grace and pardon while I pray,	
	Even then despair before my ruthful eye	*compassionate*
	Spreads forth my sin and shame, and seems to say	
	In vain thou brayest forth thy bootless noise	*cry out, helpless*
	To him for mercy, O refusèd wight,	*creature*
35	That hears not the forsaken sinner's voice.	
	Thy reprobate and foreordainèd sprite,[264]	*unredeemable*
	Foredamnèd vessel of his heavy wrath[265]	*damned beforehand*
	(As self-witness of thy beknowing heart.	*confessing*
	And secret guilt of thine own conscience saith),	
40	Of his sweet promises can claim no part:	
	But thee, caitiff, deservèd curse doth draw	*wretch*
	To hell, by justice, for offended law.	

    This horror, when my trembling soul doth hear,
When marks and tokens of the reprobate,
45 My growing sins, of grace my senseless cheer   *mood*
Enforce the proof of everlasting hate,
That I conceive the heaven's King to bear
Against my sinful and forsaken ghost:
As in the throat of hell,[266] I quake for fear,
50 And then in present peril to be lost
(Although my conscience wanteth to reply,
But with remorse enforcing mine offence,
Doth argue vain my not-availing cry)   *ineffectual*
With woeful sighs and bitter penitence
55 To him, from whom the endless mercy flows,
I cry for mercy to relieve my woes.

    And then, not daring with presuming eye
Once to behold the angry heaven's face,
From troubled sprite, I send confusèd cry,
60 To crave the crumbs of all-sufficing grace.[267]
With faltering knee, I, falling to the ground,
Bending my yielding hands to heaven's throne,

---

[264] A reference to the Calvinist doctrine of double predestination, in which before all time God not only chooses the elect for salvation but the reprobate for damnation.

[265] Compare Romans 9. 22, 'What and if God would, to show his wrath, and to make his power known, suffer with long patience the vessels of wrath, prepared to destruction' (Geneva) (Felch).

[266] throat of hell] An anatomical extension of the conventional medieval representation of the hell mouth, the entrance to hell as the open maw of a giant beast, common in the Dooms painted in many churches.

[267] Possibly a reference to Matthew 15. 21–27, in which the Canaanite woman begs Jesus to heal her daughter, noting that 'the whelps [i.e. gentiles] eat of the crumbs, which fall from their master's table' (Geneva) (Felch).

Pour forth my piteous plaint with woeful sound,		*lament*
With smoking sighs, and oft repeated groan,		*steaming*
65 Before the Lord, the Lord, whom sinner I,		
I, cursèd wretch, I have offended so,[268]		
That dreading, in his wreakful wrath to die,		*vengeful*
And damnèd down to depth of hell to go,		
Thus tossed with pangs and passions of despair,		
70 Thus crave I mercy with repentant cheer.		*frame of mind*

A Meditation of a Penitent Sinner, upon the 51. Psalm.

Have mercy	Have mercy, God, for thy great mercy's sake.	
upon	O God, my God, unto my shame I say,	
me (O God)	Being fled from thee, so as I dread to take	
after thy	Thy name in wretchèd mouth, and fear to pray	
5 *great mercy.*	Or ask the mercy that I have abused.	
	But, God of mercy, let me come to thee:	
	Not for justice, that justly am accused:	
	Which self word justice so amazeth me,	*same*
	That scarce I dare thy mercy sound again.[269]	*test*
10	But mercy, Lord, yet suffer me to crave.	*allow*
	Mercy is thine: let me not cry in vain,	
	Thy great mercy for my great fault to have.	
	Have mercy, God, pity my penitence	
	With greater mercy than my great offence.	
15 *And according*	My many sins in number are increased,	
unto the	With weight whereof in sea of deep despair	
multitude	My sinking soul is now so sore oppressed,	
of thy	That now in peril and in present fear,	
mercies do	I cry: sustain me, Lord,[270] and, Lord, I pray	
20 *away mine*	With endless number of thy mercies take	
offences.	The endless number of my sins away.	

[268] Anadiplosis, in which the last word of a line or phrase is repeated at the beginning of the next, for emphasis or emotional intensity.

[269] Like Wyatt (and Luther), Lock plays variations on the word 'just', using the figure of polyptoton (repeating a word in various forms) to emphasize the critical importance of justification. The word 'mercy' is repeated ten times in this sonnet, five times in the next, no doubt because of its importance in the opening petition.

[270] This extended metaphor, added by Lock, may allude to the story of Peter trying to follow Jesus in walking across the Sea of Galillee. Because Peter lacks faith, he begins to sink and cries out, 'Master, save me' (Matthew 14. 22-33). Like David, Peter is favoured by God but more than once falls into sin. Lock's initial caesura, breaking the line after 'I cry', is an old rhythmic device, effectively adding to the drama. She often handles the sonnet line with sophistication, as in the four cases of enjambment later in this sonnet, running the syntax across from one line to the next.

		So, by thy mercy, for thy mercy's sake,	
		Rue on me, Lord, relieve me with thy grace.	*have pity*
		My sin is cause that I so need to have	
25		Thy mercy's aid in my so woeful case:	
		My sin is cause that scarce I dare to crave	
		Thy mercy manifold, which only may	*alone*
		Relieve my soul, and take my sins away.	
	Wash me	So foul is sin and loathsome in thy sight,	
30	*yet more*	So foul with sin I see myself to be,	
	from my	That, till from sin I may be washèd white,	
	wickedness,	So foul, I dare not, Lord, approach to thee.	
	and cleanse	Oft hath thy mercy washèd me before,	
	me from	Thou mad'st me clean: but I am foul again.	
35	*my sin.*	Yet wash me, Lord, again, and wash me more.	
		Wash me, O Lord, and do away the stain	
		Of ugly sins that in my soul appear.	
		Let flow thy plenteous streams of cleansing grace.	
		Wash me again, yea, wash me everywhere,	
40		Both leprous body and defilèd face.²⁷¹	
		Yea, wash me all, for I am all unclean.	
		And from my sin, Lord, cleanse me once again.²⁷²	
	For I	Have mercy, Lord, have mercy: for I know	
	acknowledge my	How much I need thy mercy in this case.²⁷³	
45	*wickedness,*	The horror of my guilt doth daily grow,	
	and my	And, growing, wears my feeble hope of grace.	
	sin is	I feel and suffer in my thrallèd breast	*enslaved*
	ever before	Secret remorse and gnawing of my heart.	
	me.	I feel my sin, my sin that hath oppressed	
50		My soul with sorrow and surmounting smart.	*pain*
		Draw me to mercy: for so oft as I	
		Presume to mercy to direct my sight,	
		My chaos and my heap of sin doth lie	
		Between me and thy mercy's shining light.²⁷⁴	

---

[271] The Psalm does not mention leprosy, but the idea may derive from the prayer to 'purge me with hyssop' (BCP), since in Leviticus 14 hyssop is used for the cleansing of lepers.

[272] Another sonnet dense with repetition, this time of 'so foul' and variations of 'wash me', adding urgency to the petition. Lock also creates an unusual sestet/octave structure by repeating the word 'again', which might be called the keyword of Lock's technique, so many words being repeated again and again.

[273] A particular effective combination of caesura and enjambment, playing the syntax against the formal boundary of the line.

[274] Perhaps a reference to the 'great gulf' that Abraham says lies between the rich man and

55	Whatever way I gaze about for grace,	
	My filth and fault are ever in my face.	
Against thee only have I sinned,	Grant thou me mercy, Lord: thee, thee alone	
	I have offended, and offending thee,	
	For mercy, lo, how I do lie and groan.	
60 *and done evil in thy sight.*	Thou with all-piercing eye beheldest me,	
	Without regard, that sinnèd in thy sight.	
	Behold again, how now my sprite it rues,	*spirit, regrets*
	And wails the time, when I with foul delight	*bewails*
	Thy sweet forbearing mercy did abuse.	
65	My cruel conscience with sharpened knife	
	Doth splat my rippèd heart,[275] and lays abroad	*cut up*
	The loathsome secrets of my filthy life,	
	And spreads them forth before the face of God.	
	Whom shame from deed shameless could not restrain,	
70	Shame for my deed is added to my pain.	
That thou mightest be found just in thy	But mercy, Lord, O Lord, some pity take,	
	Withdraw my soul from the deservèd hell,	
	O Lord of glory, for thy glory's sake:	
	That I may, savèd, of thy mercy tell,	
75 *sayings, and mayest*	And show how thou, which mercy hast behight	*promised*
	To sighing sinners, that have broke thy laws,	
overcome when thou art judged.	Performest mercy: so as in the sight	
	Of them that judge the justice of thy cause	
	Thou only just be deemèd, and no moe,	*more*
80	The world's unjustice wholly to confound:	*defeat*
	That, damning me to depth of during woe,	
	Just in thy judgement shouldest thou be found:	
	And from deservèd flames relieving me	
	Just in thy mercy mayest thou also be.[276]	

Lazarus in Luke 16. 26 (Geneva). The word 'chaos' is a classical term, somewhat surprising in a biblical context (only the Rheims NT uses it, following the Vulgate). Lock uses the word in her Calvin translation, which adds to Felch's argument about the shared vocabulary with the *Meditation*. On the other hand, 'chaos' is used for the state of matter at the beginning of Genesis, 'without form and void', and, interestingly, often in conjunction with the noun 'heap'. Roger Hutchinson, for instance, writes that 'God made first a confused heap, called in Greek *Chaos*' (*The Image of God* (London, 1550), fol. 49^r).

[275] splat] Perhaps not a strong case for attribution, but it is interesting that all the citations for 'splat' in the *OED* are from recipes or cookbooks, suggesting that this is a word from kitchen work, something Lock was likely more familiar with than Norton.

[276] Even more than earlier, though again in the mode of Wyatt, Lock emphasizes the importance of justice and judgement through repetition.

85 *For lo, I was shapen in wickedness, and in sin my*	For lo, in sin, Lord, I begotten was,	*conceived*
	With seed and shape my sin I took also,	
	Sin is my nature and my kind, alas,	*disposition*
	In sin my mother me conceivèd: lo,	
90 *mother conceived me.*	I am but sin, and sinful ought to die,	
	Die in his wrath that hath forbidden sin.[277]	
	Such bloom and fruit, lo, sin doth multiply,	
	Such was my root, such is my juice within.	
	I plead not this as to excuse my blame,	
	On kind or parents mine own guilt to lay:	
95	But by disclosing of my sin, my shame,	
	And need of help, the plainer to display	
	Thy mighty mercy, if with plenteous grace	
	My plenteous sins it please thee to deface.	*blot out*
But lo, thou	Thou lovest simple sooth, not hidden face	*truth*
100 *hast loved*	With truthless visor of deceiving show.	*mask*
truth, the hidden and secret things of thy	Lo, simply, Lord, I do confess my case,	
	And simply crave thy mercy in my woe.	
	This secret wisdom hast thou granted me,	
	To see my sins, and whence my sins do grow:	
105 *wisdom*	This hidden knowledge have I learned of thee,	
thou hast opened unto me.	To feel my sins, and how my sins do flow	
	With such excess, that with unfeignèd heart,	*sincere*
	Dreading to drown, my Lord, lo, how I flee,	
	Simply with tears bewailing my desert,	*recompense*
110	Relievèd simply by thy hand to be.	
	Thou lovest truth, thou taughtest me the same.	
	Help, Lord of truth, for glory of thy name.	
Sprinkle me, Lord,	With sweet hyssop besprinkle thou my sprite:	
115 *with hyssop and I shall be clean: wash me and I shall*	Not such hyssop, nor so besprinkle me,	
	As law, unperfect shade of perfect light,	
	Did use as an appointed sign to be	
	Foreshowing figure of thy grace behight.	
	With death and bloodshed of thine only Son,	
	The sweet hyssop, cleanse me, defilèd wight.[278]	*creature*

---

[277] Another instance of breaking the iambic pentameter, almost creating the illusion of ordinary speech, with the sigh, 'alas', at line end, then the terminal caesura in the next line, with another interjection, 'lo', the sense running over to the next, with another break between the pair (combining polyptoton and anadiplosis) 'sin' and 'sinful'. Sin (and variants) is repeated nine times in this sonnet.

[278] In Exodus 12, Moses instructs the Hebrews to take hyssop and sprinkle the lintels of their doors with blood to protect them from the slaying of the Egyptian firstborn. Typologically,

120 *be whiter than snow.*	Sprinkle my soul. And when thou so hast done,
	Bedewed with drops of mercy and of grace
	I shall be clean as cleansèd of my sin.
	Ah, wash me, Lord: for I am foul, alas:
	That only canst, Lord, wash me well within,
125	Wash me, O Lord: when I am washèd so,
	I shall be whiter than the whitest snow.
Thou shalt make me hear joy	Long have I heard, and yet I hear the sounds
	Of dreadful threats and thunders of the law,[279]
	Which echo of my guilty mind resounds,
130 *and gladness, all the bones which thou hast broken*	And with redoubled horror doth so draw
	My listening soul from mercy's gentle voice,
	That louder, Lord, I am constrained to call:
	Lord, pierce mine ears, and make me to rejoice
	When I shall hear, and when thy mercy shall
135 *shall rejoice.*	Sound in my heart the gospel of thy grace.[280]
	Then shalt thou give my hearing joy again,
	The joy that only may relieve my case.
	And then my bruisèd bones, that thou with pain
	Hast made too weak my feebled corpse to bear,
140	Shall leap for joy, to show mine inward cheer. *mood*

Turn away thy face from my sins, and   Look on me, Lord: though trembling I beknow   *acknowledge*
               That sight of sin so sore offendeth thee,
               That seeing sin, how it doth overflow
               My whelmèd soul,[281] thou canst not look on me,   *overwhelmed*
145 *do away*   But with disdain, with horror and despite.   *scorn*
    all my misdeeds.   Look on me, Lord: but look not on my sin.
               Not that I hope to hide it from thy sight,
               Which seest me all without and eke within.   *also*
               But so remove it from thy wrathful eye,
150   And from the justice of thine angry face,

this prefigures and is superseded ('as law') by the use of hyssop to give Jesus a sponge of vinegar on the cross, since Jesus's blood saved mankind from sin. See also Hebrews 9. The association of hyssop with the law may derive from Leviticus 14, where it is used in the ritual cleansing of lepers (see note 271, p. 190).

[279] Thunder is frequently connected to the voice of God (Psalm 18. 13, etc.), but the association with the law is in Exodus when the Israelites hear thunder as God gives the Commandments to Moses on Mt Sinai (Exodus 20. 18).

[280] An obvious Christian interpolation.

[281] A particularly fine use of enjambment, as with so many poets who exploit the device to represent flowing or especially overflowing, as the syntax seems itself to burst the boundary of the line.

        That thou impute it not.[282] Look not how I   *ascribe*
        Am foul by sin: but make me by thy grace
        Pure in thy mercy's sight, and, Lord, I pray,
        That hatest sin, wipe all my sins away.

Create a clean heart within me, O God: and renew a steadfast spirit within my bowels.

155   Sin and despair have so possessed my heart,
        And hold my captive soul in such restraint,
        As of thy mercies I can feel no part,
        But still in languor do I lie and faint.
        Create a new pure heart within my breast:
160 Mine old can hold no liquor of thy grace.[283]   *liquid*
        My feeble faith with heavy load oppressed,
        Staggering, doth scarcely creep a reeling pace,
        And fallen it is, too faint to rise again.
        Renew, O Lord, in me a constant sprite,
165 That stayed with mercy may my soul sustain,   *secured*
        A sprite so settled and so firmly pight   *resolved*
        Within my bowels,[284] that it never move,
        But still uphold th'assurance of thy love.[285]

Cast me not away from thy face, and take not thy Holy Spirit from me.

        Lo, prostrate, Lord, before thy face I lie,
170 With sighs deep drawn deep sorrow to express,
        O Lord of mercy, mercy do I cry:
        Drive me not from thy face in my distress,
        Thy face of mercy and of sweet relief,
        The face that feeds angels with only sight,
175 The face of comfort in extremest grief.
        Take not away the succour of thy Sprite,   *support*
        Thy Holy Sprite, which is mine only stay,
        The stay that when despair assaileth me,
        In faintest hope yet moveth me to pray,
180 To pray for mercy, and to pray to thee.
        Lord, cast me not from presence of thy face,
        Nor take from me the Spirit of thy grace.

Restore to me the comfort of

        But render me my wonted joys again,   *accustomed*
        Which sin hath reft, and planted in their place   *taken away*
185 Doubt of thy mercy, ground of all my pain.

---

[282] impute] See note 139, p. 127.

[283] Probably a Eucharistic reference, in that the wine taken at Communion symbolized (for Protestants) the blood of Christ.

[284] bowels] Seat of emotions in early modern (especially biblical) usage.

[285] assurance] When Wyatt used this term in the 1530s, it may not yet have acquired the weight it later took on, but by 1560, and increasingly later, it was a source of considerable interest and even anxiety for Calvinist Protestants, who sought clear signs of their election.

	thy saving	The taste, that thy love whilom did embrace	*formerly*
	help, and	My cheerful soul, the signs that did assure	
	stablish° me	My feeling ghost of favour in thy sight,	*spirit*
	with thy	Are fled from me, and wretched I endure,	
190	*free Spirit.*	Senseless of grace, the absence of thy Sprite.	
		Restore my joys, and make me feel again	
		The sweet return of grace that I have lost,	
		That I may hope, I pray, not all in vain.	
		With thy free Sprite confirm my feeble ghost.	
195		To hold my faith from ruin and decay	
		With fast affiance and assurèd stay.	*secure, faith*

	I shall teach	Lord, of thy mercy if thou me withdraw	
	thy ways	From gaping throat of deep devouring hell,	
	unto the	Lo, I shall preach the justice of thy law:	
200	*wicked, and*	By mercy saved, thy mercy shall I tell.	
	sins shall	The wicked I will teach thine only way,	
	be turned	Thy ways to take, and man's device to flee,	
	unto thee.	And such as lewd delight hath led astray,	*wicked*
		To rue their error and return to thee.	
205		So shall the proof of mine example preach	
		The bitter fruit of lust and foul delight:	
		So shall my pardon by thy mercy teach	
		The way to find sweet mercy in thy sight.	
		Have mercy, Lord, in me example make	
210		Of law and mercy, for thy mercy's sake.	

	Deliver me	O God, God of my health, my saving God,	
	from blood	Have mercy, Lord, and show thy might to save,	
	O God, God	Assoil me, God, from guilt of guiltless blood,	*absolve*
	of my health,	And eke from sin that I ingrowing have	
215	*and my tongue*	By flesh and blood and by corrupted kind.	
	shall joyfully	Upon my blood and soul extend not, Lord,	
	talk of	Vengeance for blood, but mercy let me find,	
	thy justice.	And strike me not with thy revenging sword.	
		So, Lord, my joying tongue shall talk thy praise,	
220		Thy name my mouth shall utter in delight,	
		My voice shall sound thy justice, and thy ways,	
		Thy ways to justify thy sinful wight.	
		God of my health, from blood I savèd so	
		Shall spread thy praise for all the world to know.	

	Lord, open	Lo, straining cramp of cold despair again	
225	*thou my lips,*	In feeble breast doth pinch my pining heart,	
	and my	So, as in greatest need to cry and plain,	*lament*

	mouth shall show thy praise.	My speech doth fail to utter thee my smart.
		Refresh my yielding heart, with warming grace,
		And loose my speech, and make me call to thee.
230		Lord, open thou my lips to show my case,
		My Lord, for mercy, lo, to thee I flee.
		I cannot pray without thy moving aid, *causing motion or action*
		Ne can I rise, ne can I stand alone.
		Lord, make me pray, and grant when I have prayed.
235		Lord loose my lips, I may express my moan
		And finding grace with open mouth I may
		Thy mercies praise, and holy name display.
	If thou haddest	Thy mercy's praise, instead of sacrifice,
		With thankful mind so shall I yield to thee.
240	*desired sacrifice,*	For if it were delightful in thine eyes,
		Or hereby might thy wrath appeasèd be
	I would have given.	Of cattle slain and burnt with sacred flame
		Up to the heaven the vap'ry smoke to send:
	Thou delightest	Of guiltless beasts, to purge my guilt and blame,
245	*not in burnt offerings.*	On altars broiled the savour should ascend,
		To 'pease thy wrath. But thy sweet Son alone,
		With one sufficing sacrifice for all
		Appeaseth thee, and maketh thee at one
		With sinful man, and hath repaired our fall.
250		That sacred host[286] is ever in thine eyes.
		The praise of that I yield for sacrifice.
	The sacrifice to God is a troubled	I yield myself, I offer up my ghost,
		My slain delights, my dying heart to thee.
		To God a troubled sprite is pleasing host.
255	*spirit: a broken and an*	My troubled sprite doth dread like him to be,
		In whom tasteless languor with ling'ring pain
	humbled	Hath feebled so the starvèd appetite,
	heart, O God, thou wilt	That food too late is offered all in vain,
		To hold in fainting corpse the fleeing sprite.
260	*not despise.*	My pining soul for famine of thy grace
		So fears, alas, the faintness of my faith.
		I offer up my troubled sprite: alas,
		My troubled sprite refuse not in thy wrath.

[286] host] See note 169, p. 136. Lock's use of 'host' in the same punning way as Wyatt, in her translation of the same Psalm, may constitute an actual allusion, especially given that she casts the Psalm into a sequence of sonnets, a form Wyatt was largely responsible for importing into English poetry.

		Such off'ring likes thee, ne wilt thou despise	*pleases*
265		The broken humbled heart in angry wise.	*manner*
	Show favour,	Show mercy, Lord, not unto me alone:	
	O Lord,	But stretch thy favour and thy pleasèd will,	
	in thy good	To spread thy bounty and thy grace upon	
	will unto	Zion, for Zion is thy holy hill:	
270	*Sion, that*	That thy Jerusalem with mighty wall	
	the walls	May be enclosèd under thy defense,	
	of Jerusalem	And builded so that it may never fall	
	may be	By mining fraud or mighty violence.	*undermining*
	builded.	Defend thy church, Lord, and advance it so,	
275		So in despite of tyranny to stand,	
		That trembling at thy power the world may know	
		It is upholden by thy mighty hand:	*upheld*
		That Zion and Jerusalem may be	
		A safe abode for them that honour thee.	
280	*Then shalt*	Then on thy hill, and in thy wallèd town,	
	thou accept	Thou shalt receive the pleasing sacrifice.	
	the sacrifice	The bruit shall of thy praisèd name resoune	*report, resound*
	of righteousness,	In thankful mouths, and then with gentle eyes	
	burnt	Thou shalt behold upon thine altar lie	
285	*offerings, and*	Many a yielden host of humbled heart,	*surrendered*
	oblations.°	And round about then shall thy people cry:	
	Then shall	We praise thee, God our God: thou only art	
	they offer	The God of might, of mercy, and of grace.	
	young bullocks	That I then, Lord, may also honour thee.	
290	*upon thine*	Relieve my sorrow, and my sins deface:	*blot out*
	altar.	Be, Lord of mercy, merciful to me:	
		Restore my feeling of thy grace again:	
		Assure my soul,[287] I crave it not in vain.	

37. William Kethe, in *Four Score and Seven Psalms of David in English Metre* (1561)

[Kethe contributed twenty-five metrical Psalms to the fluid collection of Sternhold and Hopkins Psalms, including the most famous and long-lasting, Psalm 100 ('All people that on earth do dwell'), still popularly known as the 'Old Hundredth'. Kethe's version of this Psalm is unremarkable, and the reason for the hymn's longevity is surely the strong tune to which it was sung. Psalm 58 is

---

[287] Assure] Theological term for assurance of salvation, a particular preoccupation of Calvinists.

one of the most ferocious invectives in ancient literature, so violent that the 1962 Book of Common Prayer of the Anglican Church of Canada omitted it. Both of these Psalms by Kethe were replaced in the 1562 *Whole Book* with other versions by John Hopkins. Beth Quitslund suggests that the printer, John Day, wanted to present as English a volume as possible, and so changed out many Psalms produced in Geneva. All of Kethe's Psalms were retained in the 1564 Scottish Psalter, and his Psalm 100 was reinserted in the *Whole Book* as early as 1565, though without any identifying initials and alongside Hopkins's alternative. Tellingly, Kethe's version was printed with the Bourgeois tune, while Hopkins's (in common as opposed to Kethe's long metre, 8.6.8.6. vs 8.8.8.8.) appeared without music. See Quitslund, *Reformation in Rhyme*. For more on Kethe, see 34.]

Psalm 58

He describeth the malice of his enemies, the flatterers of Saul, who both secretly and openly sought his destruction, from whom he appealeth to God's judgement, showing that the just shall rejoice, when they see the punishment of the wicked to the glory of God.

But is it true? O forward folk,
    Do ye now justly talk?
O sons of men in judging thus,
    Do ye uprightly walk?
5   Nay, nay, ye rather mischief muse,
    Whereto your hearts be bent,
To execute your cruel rage:
    On earth your time is spent.

	3.	But what? The wicked strangers are,	
10		And from the womb they stray.	
		Yea, from their birth they lewdly err,	*wickedly*
		And none so lie as they.	
	4.	Their subtle malice doth surmount	
		The crafty serpent's spear,[288]	
15	5.	Who could th'enchanter's charms avoid	*magic powers*
		By stopping close his ear.[289]	*shut*

---

[288] serpent's spear] i.e. its tongue.

[289] The 'deaf adder' is a mythical creature, popularized by this Bible verse. According to Brewer's *Dictionary of Phrase and Fable* (1870), tradition has it that the asp stops its ears to the snake-charmer by putting one ear on the ground and twisting its tail into the other. Frank Gibson, however, in *Superstitions About Animals* (1904), feels certain that 'The Psalmist never meant it to be understood that such a creature as a "deaf adder" had a real existence' (p. 108).

	6.	Break thou, O Lord, the teeth of such	
		As do thy truth devour:[290]	
		The jaws of these young lions, Lord,	
20		Break down, and 'suage their power	*assuage*
	7.	And as the waters do decrease:	
		Away so let them pass:	
		When that thou dost thine arrows shoot	
		Then let them break as glass.	
25	8.	Let such consume as doth a snail	
		Whose nature is to melt,	
		Or like untimely fruit,[291] whose eyes	
		No sun hath seen nor felt.	
	9.	As flesh red raw, unmete for meat,	*unsuitable, food*
30		Till change be made by fire,	
		So let them, Lord, fade hence, as with	
		A whirlwind in thine ire.	*anger*
	10.	The righteous shall in heart rejoice	
		Thy vengeance thus to see,	
35		And bathe his feet in such men's blood	
		With pure affect shall he.	*intention*
	11.	And men shall say, now of a truth	
		The righteous fruit may have,[292]	
		By seeing God to judge the earth	
40		And yet his flock to save.	

Psalm 100

He exhorteth all to serve the Lord, who hath chosen us, and preserved us, and to enter into his assemblies to praise his name.

All people that on earth do dwell,
Sing to the Lord with cheerful voice:
Him serve with fear, his praise forth tell:
Come ye before him and rejoice.

---

[290] The Psalm's curse simply calls for the breaking of the teeth, but Kethe inserts an apt reason, since the enemy has 'devoured' God's truth. Kethe seems not quite in control of the metaphor, however, since normally one would think that consuming God's truth would be a good thing, speaking falsehood perhaps something deserving punishment.
[291] untimely fruit] i.e. a stillborn or prematurely born foetus ('fruit' meaning 'foetus' in early modern usage).
[292] Kethe adds the fruit metaphor in this verse, playing back against the 'untimely fruit' (in a very different sense) earlier. He may be thinking of Jesus's use of the metaphor to distinguish true and false prophets: 'Ye shall know them by their fruits […] Even so every good tree bringeth forth good fruit; but a corrupt tree bringeth forth evil fruit' (Matthew 7. 16-17).

5	3.	The Lord, ye know, is God indeed:	
		Without our aid, he did us make:	
		We are his folk: he doth us feed.	
		And for his sheep he doth us take.	
	4.	O enter then his gates with praise:	
10		Approach with joy his courts unto.	
		Praise, laud, and bless his name always	*praise*
		For it is seemly so to do.	
	5.	For why? The Lord our God is good:	
		His mercy is forever sure:	
15		His truth at all times firmly stood,	
		And shall from age to age endure.	

38. William Whittingham, in *The Whole Book of Psalms, Collected into English Metre by T. Sternhold, J. Hopkins, and Others* (1562)

[William Whittingham (d. 1579) was an Oxford BA and MA who had already travelled on the Continent during the reign of Edward VI. When Catholic Queen Mary succeeded, Whittingham, like other Protestant leaders, went into exile, first in Frankfurt, where he was involved in disputes among the English Protestant community, and then in Geneva, where he became one of the leading figures of the English congregation. He was a major figure in the production of both the Geneva Bible and *The Whole Book of Psalms*, in their various editions. Whittingham, one of the few Sternhold and Hopkins contributors expert in Hebrew, contributed a number of metrical Psalms to the collection. He was later chaplain to Ambrose Dudley, Earl of Warwick, when Dudley led an expeditionary force against the French at Le Havre. In 1563, with Warwick's influence, he was appointed dean of Durham, where he was often involved in controversy, including the issue of clerical vestments and ecclesiastical politics. Whittingham's Psalms 51 and 124 first appeared in the collections printed on the Continent, *Psalms of David in Metre* (Wesel) and *One and Fifty Psalms of David in English Metre* (Geneva). His Psalm 51 was joined in the 1562 *Whole Book* by another version by Thomas Norton, the only instance in that edition where two different texts are provided. Whittingham's version is printed with a tune (covering eight octosyllabic line stanzas), but Norton's, in a different metre, is not. (A marginal note states that it is to be sung to the same tune as the Lamentation, 129 pages away at the beginning of the book.) Whittingham's Psalm 51 was also set and republished by prominent composers like John Cosyn (*Music of Six, and Five Parts*, 1585), William Damon (*The Second Book of the Music of William Damon*, 1591), Richard Alison (*The Psalms of David*, 1599), and John Dowland (*Mr. Henry Noell his Funeral Psalms*, written 1587, not printed). Many other Psalms were set to music as part-songs or lute ayres, but

Whittingham's was obviously among the more popular. See Duguid, *Metrical Psalmody*; Garrett, *The Marian Exiles*; Quitslund, *Reformation in Rhyme*; David Marcombe, *ODNB*.]

Psalm 51

Miserere mei deus. [Have mercy upon me, O God]

When David was rebuked by the Prophet Nathan for his great offences,[293] he did not only acknowledge the same to God, with protestation of his natural corruption, and iniquity: but also left a memorial thereof to his posterity. Therefore first he desireth God to forgive his sins, and renew in him his Holy Spirit: with promise that he will not be unmindful of those great graces. Finally, fearing lest God would punish the whole church for his fault: he requireth that he would rather increase his graces towards the same.

    O Lord consider my distress,
        And now with speed some pity take.
    My sins deface, my faults redress,   *blot out*
        Good Lord, for thy great mercy's sake.
5   Wash me (O Lord) and make me clean
        From this unjust and sinful act:[294]
    And purify yet once again
        My heinous crime and bloody fact.   *deed*

  2. Remorse and sorrow do constrain
10   Me to acknowledge mine excess:[295]
  3. My sin, alas, doth still remain
      Before my face without release.
  4. For thee alone I have offended,
      Committing evil in thy sight:
15   And if I were therefore condemnèd,
      Yet were thy judgement just and right.

---

[293] II Samuel 12.
[294] The Psalmist prays for forgiveness for his sin, which might be taken in a general sense, even including the concept of original sin (encouraged by the later verse on being sinful from conception). By altering the verse to what seems a particular 'sinful act', Whittingham may encourage the biographical interpretation of the Psalm in conjunction with David's adultery with Bathsheba and murder of Uriah.
[295] One challenge in strophic song or Psalm settings is making all verses align with the tune as well as the first (perhaps one reason why four-part songbooks often include only the first). The enjambment over the first line of Whittingham's second stanza does not present a serious problem, however, since the melody has an arc that covers the two lines. Some congregations might simply pause at the line end, of course, regardless of the syntax (Kethe's Psalm 100 includes the phrase 'Him serve with fear', after all), but there is also the option to sing through the phrase, joining 'constrain me'.

> 5. It is too manifest, alas,
>   That first I was conceived in sin:
>   Yea, of my mother so born was,
>   And yet, vile wretch, remain therein.
> 6. Also, behold, Lord, thou dost love
>   The inward truth of a pure heart:
>   Therefore, thy wisdom from above
>   Thou hast revealed me to convert.[296]
> 7. If thou with hyssop purge this blot,
>   I shall be cleaner than the glass:
>   And if thou wash away my spot,[297]
>   The snow in whiteness shall I pass.
> 8. Therefore (O Lord) such joy me send,
>   That inwardly I may find grace:
>   And that my strength may now amend,
>   Which thou hast 'suaged for my trespass. *assuaged*
> 9. Turn back thy face and frowning ire, *anger*
>   For I have felt enough thy hand:
>   And purge my sins I thee desire,
>   Which do in number pass the sand.
> 10. Make new my heart within my breast,
>   And frame it to thy holy will:
>   Thy constant Sprite in me let rest, *spirit*
>   Which may these raging enemies kill.
>
> *The second part.*
>
> 11. Cast me not (Lord) out from thy face,
>   But speedily my torments end:
>   Take not from me thy Sprite and grace,
>   Which may from dangers me defend.
> 12. Restore me to those joys again,
>   Which I was wont in thee to find: *accustomed*
>   And let me thy free Sprite retain,
>   Which unto thee may stir my mind.
> 13. Thus, when I shall thy mercies know,
>   I shall instruct others therein:

---

[296] The topic of conversion is not in the original and may be understood generally (converting from bad to good) or in terms of sixteenth-century concerns (converting to Protestantism, for instance).

[297] Whittingham may have in mind the word 'immaculate' (often used in the context of sinlessness, as with the Virgin Mary), which derives from the Latin, 'without spot'.

             And men that are likewise brought low
                 By mine ensample shall flee sin.   *example*
         14. O God that of my health art Lord,
                 Forgive me this my bloody vice:
55   My heart and tongue shall then accord
                 To sing thy mercies and justice.

         15. Touch thou my lips,²⁹⁸ my tongue untie,
                 (O Lord) which art the only key:
             And then my mouth shall testify
60   Thy wondrous works and praise alway.   *always*
         16. And as for outward sacrifice,
                 I would have offered many one:
             But thou esteemest them of no price,
                 And therein pleasure tak'st thou none.

65   17. The heavy heart, the mind oppressed,
                 O Lord, thou never dost reject:
             And, to speak truth, it is the best,
                 And of all sacrifice the effect.
         18. Lord unto Zion turn thy face,
70   Pour out thy mercies on thy hill:
             And on Jerusalem thy grace;
                 Build up the walls, and love it still.

         19. Thou shalt accept then our offerings
                 Of peace and righteousness, I say:
75   Yea, calves and many other things,
                 Upon thine altar will we lay.

Psalm 124

Nisi quia dominus. [Except the Lord]

The people of God, being delivered out of a great danger, acknowledge not to have escaped by their own power, but through the favour of God, and show in how great peril they were.

             Now Israel may say, and that truly,
             If that the Lord had not our cause maintained,
             If that the Lord had not our right sustained,

---

²⁹⁸ The Psalmist prays for God to open his lips, but Whittingham may have in mind the scene of Isaiah's prophetic vocation, when a seraph touches his unclean lips with a live coal (Isaiah 6. 5–7).

       When all the world against us furiously
 5   Made their uproars, and said we should all die.²⁹⁹

   3. Now long ago they had devoured us all:
       And swallowed quick, for ought that we could deem; *alive*
       Such was their rage, as we might well esteem.
   4. And as the floods, with mighty force do fall,
10   So had they now our life even brought to thrall. *bondage*
   5. The raging streams most proud in roaring noice *vigorous, noise*
       Had long ago overwhelmed us in the deep,
   6. But, loved by God, which doth us safely keep *guard*
       From bloody teeth, and their most cruel voice,
15   Which as a prey to eat us would rejoice.
   7. Even as the bird out of the fowler's gren³⁰⁰ *bird-catcher's, snare*
       Escap'th away, right so it fareth us:
       Broke are their nets, and we have scapèd thus,
   8. God that made heaven and earth is our help then,
20   His name hath saved us from these wicked men.

39. John Hopkins, in *The Whole Book of Psalms, Collected into English Metre by T. Sternhold, J. Hopkins, and Others* (1562)

[Since Hopkins died in 1570, it is possible that he had some involvement with putting together the complete *Whole Book of Psalms*, but there is no evidence except the additional translations by him that were included, which may have been composed earlier. Beth Quitslund suggests that the publisher, John Day, wanted to make the psalter as English as possible, favouring translations done in London over Geneva ones. During the reign of Queen Mary, Hopkins's whereabouts are unknown. He may have been teaching school somewhere, since he is referenced in print in 1574 as 'that worthy schoolmaster'. In 1561 Hopkins was made pastor of Great Waldingfield, Suffolk. Metrically, Hopkins's Psalms are poised between fourteeners and common metre: though they are printed in short lines, even lines begin in the original with lower case letters, suggesting that the line breaks may just accommodate the width of the page, yet the *abab* rhyme scheme (as opposed to Sternhold's *abcb*) suggests he is not thinking in long lines. The English tune for Hopkins's Psalm 61 appears for the first time,

---

²⁹⁹ This is an unusual stanza for the *Whole Book* (five lines of iambic pentameter, rhymed *abbcc*), but it fits the tune well, originating with the French Genevan Psalter of 1551, where it is also used for Psalm 124, in Beza's translation.

³⁰⁰ gren] Whittingham obviously liked this rather obscure word, since he also used it in the argument to Galatians in the Geneva Bible: 'men ought now to embrace that liberty, which Christ hath purchased by his blood, and not to have their consciences snared into the grens of man's traditions'.

like the Psalm, in the 1562 volume. Psalm 99 is to be sung to the same tune, also new to 1562, as Psalm 95 (another Hopkins text). See Quitslund, *Reformation in Rhyme*. For more on Hopkins, see 22.]

Psalm 61

Whether that he were in danger of the Amonites, or being pursued of Absalon, here he crieth to be heard and delivered. And confirmed in his kingdom, he promiseth perpetual praises.

<table>
<tr><td></td><td></td><td></td><td></td></tr>
</table>

		Regard (O Lord) for I complain,	*petition*
		And make my suit to thee,	
		Let not my words return in vain,	
		But give an ear to me,	
5		From off the coasts and utmost parts	
		Of all the earth abroad,	
		In grief and anguish of my heart	
		I cry to thee, O God.	
	3.	Upon the rock of thy great power,	
10		My woeful mind repose:	
		Thou art my hope my fort and tower,	
		My fence against my foes.	
	4.	Within thy tent I lust to dwell,	*desire*
		Forever to endure:	
15		Under thy wings I know right well,	
		I shall be safe and sure:	
	5.	The Lord doth my desire regard,	
		And doth fulfil the same:	
		With goodly gifts will he reward	
20		All them that fear his name.	
	6.	The king shall he in health maintain,	
		And so prolong his days:	
		That he from age to age shall reign,	
		Forever more always.	
25	7.	That he may have a dwelling place,	*forever*
		Before the Lord for aye,	
		O let thy mercy, truth, and grace,	
		Defend him from decay.	
	8.	Then shall I sing forever still,	
30		With praise unto thy name:	
		That all my vows I may fulfil,	
		And daily pay the same.	

Psalm 99

He commendeth the power, equity,[301] and excellency of the kingdom of God by Christ, over the Jew and Gentiles, and provoketh them to magnify the same and to serve the Lord, following the example of the ancient fathers, Moses, Aaron, Samuel, who calling upon God were heard in their prayers.

  The Lord doth reign, although at it,
    The people rage full sore: *furiously*
  Yea, he on cherubin doth sit,
    Though all the world would roar.
5 2. The Lord that doth in Zion dwell,
    Is high and wonders great:
  Above all folk he doth excel,
    And he aloft is set.

  3. Let all men praise thy mighty name,
10   For it is fearful sure:
  And let them magnify the same,
    That holy is and pure.
  4. The princely power of our King,
    Doth love judgement and right:
15 Thou rightly rulest every thing,
    In Jacob through thy might.

  5. To praise the Lord our God devise,   *resolve*
    All honour to him do:
  His foot stool worship ye likewise,
20   For he is holy too.
  6. Moses, Aaron, and Samuel,
    As priests on him did call:[302]
  When they did pray he heard them well
    And gave them answer all.

25 7. Within the cloud to them he spake,
    Then did they labour still:
  To keep such laws as he did make,
    And 'pointed them until.

---

[301] On equity, see note 6, p. 68.
[302] In rearranging the words of the Psalm, Hopkins makes an error in lumping Samuel together with Moses and Aaron as priests; in the original only the latter are called priests, Samuel simply one that calls upon God's name. Samuel was a prophet, and became the authoritative spokesman for God after the corruption of the priesthood in Eli and especially his sons Hophni and Phineas (1 Samuel 1–4).

	8.	O Lord, our God thou didst them hear	
30		And answerd'st them again:	
		Thy mercy did on them appear,	
		Their deeds didst not maintain.	
	9.	O laud and praise our God and Lord,	*praise*
		Within this holy hill:	
35		For why our God throughout the world	*because*
		Is holy ever still.	

40. Thomas Norton, in *The Whole Book of Psalms, Collected into English Metre by T. Sternhold, J. Hopkins, and Others* (1562)

[Thomas Norton (*c*. 1532–1584) was educated at Cambridge and the Inner Temple. He married Margery Cranmer, daughter of Archbishop Thomas Cranmer, and, after her death, Alice Cranmer, daughter of Thomas's brother Edmund. The Protestant printer Edward Whitchurch, who with Richard Grafton printed the Great Bible, became Norton's stepfather-in-law, marrying Cranmer's widow. Norton served Edward Seymour, Duke of Somerset, after his fall from power, further evidence of his commitment to reformed religion. A practiced lawyer, Norton served as a Member of Parliament, remembrancer (archivist) to the Mayor of London, examiner of Catholic prisoners, and as counsel to the Stationers' Company. In addition to writing numerous political pamphlets, Norton was the author, with Thomas Sackville, of *Gorboduc*, 'the first Senecan tragedy in blank verse' (Axton). Norton translated a number of works from Latin, including Calvin's *The Institution of the Christian Religion* (1561). Whitchurch printed Erasmus's *Paraphrases upon the New Testament* (1551), for which Norton prepared the index. He was also a poet, some of whose lyrics were included in Tottel's *Songs and Sonnets* (1557). Norton contributed twenty-four metrical Psalms to the Sternhold and Hopkins collection. His Psalm 51 is the only duplicate Psalm in the book, added after the one by William Whittingham, which appeared alone in earlier collections. A number of scholars have noticed similarities between Norton's Psalm 51 and *A Meditation of a Penitent Sinner*, leading to an argument by Steven May that the latter was not written by Anne Vaughan Lock, as most modern scholars have assumed, but by Norton himself (see **36**). See Duguid, *Metrical Psalmody*; M. A. R. Graves, *Thomas Norton: the Parliament Man* (Oxford and Cambridge, MA: Blackwell's, 1994); Quitslund, *Reformation in Rhyme*; Marie Axton, *ODNB*.]

Psalm 51

Have mercy on me, God, after
    Thy great abounding grace:
After thy mercies multitude
    Do thou my sins deface.[303]   *blot out*
5 Yet wash me more from mine offence
    And cleanse me from my sin:
For I beknow my faults, and still   *know*
    My sin is in mine eyen.   *eyes*

Against thee, thee alone, I have   *only*
10   Offended in this case:
And evil have I done before
    The presence of thy face.
That in the things that thou dost say,
    Upright thou may'st be tried:
15 And eke in judging, that the doom   *also, judgement*
    May pass upon thy side.

Behold in wickedness my kind and   *nature*
    Shape I did receive,
And lo, my sinful mother eke
20   In sin did me conceive.
But lo, the truth in inward parts
    Is pleasant unto thee:
And secrets of thy wisdom thou
    Revealèd hast to me.

25 With hyssop, Lord, besprinkle me,[304]
    I shall be cleansèd so:

---

[303] The verb 'deface' is used in both Norton's Psalm 51 and Lock's *Meditation*, which might argue for either a borrowing from one to the other or the same author writing both, though Wyatt also uses the verb in his first penitential Psalm (6) and Whittingham in his Psalm 51 immediately preceding Norton's. Norton plays this verb for erasure against God's face in the next stanza, all the more poignant since God created humans in his own image (Genesis 1. 26–27), though one might say that this image was 'defaced' by the sin of the Fall.

[304] Coles (*Religion, Reform, and Women's Writing*) notes that 'besprinkle' is an unusual word, used both by Norton and Lock in their paraphrases of Psalm 51. 7, but this is not necessarily evidence that Norton borrowed from Lock, as she suggests, since Norton also uses the verb three times in his translation of Calvin's *Institutes*, published the same year (1561) as Lock's translation of *Sermons*. The evidence could thus just as easily support May's argument that Norton wrote the *Meditation*, as indeed might any verbal similarity between the two versions. In any case, the verb here evokes the ritual sprinkling of the congregation with holy water by an aspergillum, a practice based on the rite for healing lepers in Leviticus 14. 3–7, where the priest is to 'sprinkle' (Geneva) the leper with blood and hyssop.

Yea, wash thou me, and so I shall
    Be whiter than the snow.
Of joy and gladness make thou me
30   To hear the pleasing voice:
That so the bruisèd bones, which thou
    Hast broken, may rejoice.

From the beholding of my sins,
    Lord turn away thy face:
35 And all my deeds of wickedness
    Do utterly deface:
O God, create in me a heart
    Unspotted in thy sight:
And eke within my bowels,[305] Lord,
40   Renew a stable sprite.   *spirit*

Ne cast me from thy sight, nor take
    Thy Holy Sprite away:
The comfort of thy saving help,
    Give me again, I pray:
45 With thy free Sprite establish me.
    And I will teach, therefore,
Sinners thy ways, and wicked shall
    Be turned unto thy lore.   *teachings*

O God, that art God of my health,
50   From blood deliver me:
That praises of thy righteousness
    My tongue may sing to thee.
My lips that yet fast closèd be,   *securely*
    Do thou, O Lord, unlose: *unloose*
55 The praises of thy majesty
    My mouth shall so disclose:

I would have offered sacrifice,
    If that had pleasèd thee.
But pleasèd with burnt offerings,
60   I know thou wilt not be.
A troubled sprite is sacrifice
    Delightful in God's eyes:
A broken and an humbled heart,
    God, thou wilt not despise.

---

[305] bowels] See note 284, p. 194.

65 In thy good will deal gently, Lord,
        To Sion, and with all
    Grant that of thy Jerusalem,
        Upreared may be the wall.
    Burnt offerings, gifts and sacrifice,
70   Of justice in that day
    Thou shalt accept, and calves they shall
        Upon thine altar lay.

Psalm 75

Confitebimur tibi deus. [We will confess to you, God]

The faithful do praise the name of the Lord, which shall come to judge at the time appointed, when the wicked shall be put to confusion, and drink of the cup of his wrath, their prayer shall be abated, and the righteous shall be exalted to honour.

      Unto thee, God, we will give thanks,
         We will give thanks to thee:
      Sith thy name is so near, declare   *since*
         Thy wondrous works will we.
5 2. I will uprightly judge, when get
         Convenient time I may.
      The earth is weak and all therein:
         But I her pillars stay.   *secure*

   3. I did to thee, mad people, say,
10   Deal not furiously:[306]
      And unto the ungodly ones,
         Set not your horns so high.[307]
   4. I said unto them, set not up
         Your raisèd horns on high,
15   And see that you do with stiff neck
         Not speak presumptuously.

   5. For neither from the eastern part,
         Nor from the western side,
      Nor from forsaken wilderness,
20   Protection doth proceed.
   6. For why, the Lord our God, he is   *because*
         The righteous judge alone:

---

[306] furiously] The metre requires four syllables, seemingly (and awkwardly) with the stress on the second.
[307] horns] See note 32, p. 85.

>   He putteth down the one, and sets
>   Another in the throne.
> 25 For why? a cup of mighty wine   *why*
>   Is in the hand of God:
>   And all the mighty wine therein
>   Himself doth pour abroad.
>   8. As for the lees and filthy dregs,   *sediments*
> 30   That do remain of it,
>   The wicked of the earth shall drink,
>   And suck them every whit.[308]
>
>   9. But I will talk of God (I say)
>   Of Jacob's God therefore:
> 35 And will not cease to celebrate
>   His praise for evermore.
>   10. In sunder break the horns of all
>   Ungodly men will I:
>   But then the horns of righteous men
> 40   Shall be exalted high.
>
> *Gloria patri.*   [Glory to the father]
>
>   To Father, Son, and Holy Ghost,
>   All glory be therefore:
>   As in beginning was, is now,
>   and shall be evermore.[309]

41. John Craig, in *The Form of Prayers and Ministration of the Sacraments* […] *Approved and Received by the Church of Scotland* (1564)

[Although the 1564 Scottish Psalter has often been mistaken as just a version of the English *Whole Book of Psalms*, it has recently been recognized as a distinctly different project. The English and Scottish psalters have a shared history in the services and Psalms developed by English and Scottish exiles in Geneva during the reign of Queen Mary. The title of the 1564 volume reflects those of the several editions of *The Form of Prayers and Ministration of Sacraments, &c., Used in the English Congregation at Geneva* (1556 and after). Moreover, like *The Whole Book*, the 1564 Scottish Psalter is based on the Psalms translations of Sternhold and Hopkins, but it includes different tunes and many more of them. Both the tunes and the metres of the Scottish Psalter have been described as

---

[308] every whit] every last bit.
[309] 41–44] The *Gloria patri* or lesser doxology was regularly added to the end of a Psalm when it was sung or recited liturgically.

more various than those of its English counterpart. Not only were new translations added by Scottish authors, but English versions were retained that were omitted from the 1562 *Whole Book*. Along with Robert Pont (see **42**), John Craig was one of the two new Scottish contributors, writing fifteen Psalms for the collection. That all the Psalms, including those by Pont and Craig, were in English rather that Scots (apart from a few words), perhaps reflects a desire by Scottish reformers for some alliance with their English co-religionists, like the close friendship of John Knox and Christopher Goodman, formed along with others in exile in Frankfurt and Geneva. Craig (1512–1600) became a Dominican monk after studying at St Andrews and fled to Rome where he gained favour with Cardinal Reginald Pole. At the Dominican house in Bologna, Craig read Calvin's *Institutes*, whereupon he converted to Protestantism. He was caught and condemned by the Inquisition but escaped, returned to his home country, and became a minister in the Church of Scotland. Craig was appointed one of the king's ministers, and he officiated at the coronation of Queen Anne in 1590. Craig's version of Psalm 145 is one of the most enduring of the Sternhold and Hopkins era translations, used in many churches to this day. See Duguid, *Metrical Psalmody*; James Kirk, *ODNB*.]

Psalm 56

    O God, to me thy mercy show,
    Whom me would swallow and devour:
    Each day they strive to bring me low,
    Vexing me sore from hour to hour.

5 2. Mine enemies daily would me eat,
      For many do against me fight:
      O thou most high, yet in this strait
   3. In thee my hope is surely pight.   *resolved*

   4. I will rejoice in God for aye,   *forever*
10   Because his words are true and just,
      And fear no whit what flesh do may   *not at all*
      To me, sith I in God do trust.   *since*

   5. The words which I myself did speak
      Are turnèd to my smart and grief: *pain*
15   Their thoughts echone tend them to wreak *each one*
      On me causeless, to my mischief.

   6. In companies convene do they,
      Keeping them secret in their strait:[310]

---

[310] in their strait] The sense of the word in verse 2 is clear, but in this verse less so, perhaps suggesting either the closeness of the enemy cliques or some narrow place from which they

	They to my steps take heed alway,	
20	For why, to trap my soul they wait.	*because*

7. They think they shall escape at last,
   Because they work iniquity:
   But thou, O God, in wrath down cast
   These wicked folk and them destroy.

25 8. My wand'rings thou hast numbered all
   And in thy bottle put my tears:[311]
   Are they not written great and small
   As thy register witness bears?

9. What time to thee I call and cry,
30   Mine en'mies then aback shall flee:
   This know I most assuredly,
   For God, the Lord, he is with me.

10. For this will I in God rejoice,
    Because his promises are sure:
35 To him will I lift up my voice,
    Whose word forever doth endure.

11. And since my trust on God doth stand,
    I will man's power not fear at all.
12. O Lord, thy vows are in mine hand,
40   To thee, I praises render shall.

13. For thou from death my soul madest free,
    And kept my feet from slip or fall:
    That I may walk, Lord, before thee
    With such as light have over all.

Psalm 145

	O Lord, that art my God and King,	
	Undoubtedly, I will thee praise,	
	I will extoll and blessings sing,	
	Unto thine holy name always.	
5	From day to day I will thee bless,	
	And laud thy name world without end.	*praise*

might surprise the Psalmist, or both. In any case, Craig is clearly making a connection between the verses as well as the predicament of the Psalmist and the strategy of his persecutors.

[311] bottle] A common biblical metaphor for rain clouds, though the usage here is somewhat different; the Hebrew means 'wineskin'.

> For great is God, most worthy praise,
> Whose greatness none may comprehend.

4. Race shall thy works praise unto race:[312] *posterity*
   And so declare thy power, O Lord.
5. The glorious beauty of thy grace,
   And wondrous works, will I record.
6. And all men shall the power (O God)
   Of all thy fearful acts declare:
   And I, to publish all abroad
   Thy greatness, at no time will spare.

7. They shall break out, to mention[313]
   And specify thy great goodness:
   And with loud voice their songs echone *each one*
   Shall frame to show thy righteousness.
8. The Lord our God is gracious,
   Yea, merciful is he also:
   In mercy he is plenteous,
   But unto wrath, and anger, slow.

9. The Lord to all men is bening: *gracious*
   Whose mercies, all his works exceed.
10. Thy works echone thy praises sing
    And eke thy saints thee bless indeed. *also*
11. The glory of thy kingdom, they
    Do show: and of thy power do tell.
12. That so men's sons his might know may
    And kingdom great, that doth excell.

13. Thy kingdom hath no end at all:
    Thy lordship ever doth remain.
14. The Lord upholdeth all that fall
    And doth the feeble folk sustain.
15. The eyes of all things, Lord, attend
    And on thee wait, that here do live:
    And thou in season due dost send *time*
    Sufficient food them to relieve.

16. Yea, thou thine hand dost open wide,
    And every thing dost satisfy,
    That live (and on this earth abide)
    Of thy great liberality.

---

[312] BCP, 'One generation shall praise thy works to another'.
[313] mention] The metre requires three syllables ('men-ti-on'); likewise for 'gracious' below.

45 17. The Lord is just in his ways all:
    And holy in his works echone.
    18. At hand, to all that on him call:
    In truth, that call to him alone.

    19. The Lord will the desire fulfil,
50   Of such as do him fear and dread:
    And he also their cry hear will,
    And save them in the time of need.
    20. He doth preserve them more and less,
    That bear to him a loving heart.
55 But workers all of wickedness
    Destroy will he, and clean subvert.   *completely*

    21. My mouth therefore my speech shall frame
    To speak the praises of the Lord:
    All flesh to bless his holy name,
60 For evermore, eke shall accord.

42. Robert Pont, in *The Form of Prayers and Ministration of the Sacraments […] Approved and Received by the Church of Scotland* (1564)

[Robert Pont (1524–1606) was the other new contributor, along with John Craig, to the Scottish Psalter of 1564, writing six Psalms for the collection. Pont was born and schooled in Culross in Fife and studied at St Leonard's College at St Andrews University. Little is known of Pont's early career, but he had settled at St Andrews by 1559 and attended the reformers' general assembly at Edinburgh in 1560. He became a leading figure in the Scottish church, elected six times as moderator of the general assembly, serving as commissioner for visiting churches and placing ministers, and eventually nominated by the crown to the provostship of Trinity College in Edinburgh as well as other ecclesiastical appointments. Pont was a staunch Presbyterian, however, and in 1584 he protested the Black Acts which asserted royal supremacy over the church as well as an episcopal church governance. These were pushed through parliament by the very young James VI, smarting after his brief captivity during the Ruthven Raid by the zealously Protestant earls of Gowrie and Angus. With the support of the powerful Earl of Arran, James had Gowrie, Angus, and their supporters banished, and Pont and other ministers followed them to England. Arran fell from power in 1585, and the Presbyterians returned to Scotland. Pont led the general assembly of 1586, and welcomed the king's presence, with reservations, also refusing his offer of a bishopric. Pont continued to assert the church's independence of the monarch, though he celebrated James's accession to the throne of England in 1604. In 1601, Pont was proposed by the assembly to produce a revision of the Scottish Psalter, but this came to nothing. Of Pont's early Psalm translations, Psalm 83 is especially interesting. It follows the prose translation of the Geneva Bible, yet Pont's translation also includes many parallels with the Scots version of Psalm 83 in the *Good and Godly Ballads*, which, while printed in 1567, contained much material that had circulated earlier. Pont's resulting mélange can be read as a 'prayer for divine deliverance from utter destruction at the hands of hostile oppressors' (Reid-Baxter, p. 52). For Protestants in 1564, the oppressors were Catholics like the late regent Mary of Guise. When George Bannatyne included Pont's Psalm 83 in a manuscript collection he prepared between 1565 and 1568, seemingly intended for publication, he may have considered that it could be read in two ways: by Protestants delivered from another Mary, the Queen of Scots, in prison in England by 1568, or by Catholics, who for all anyone knew might be delivered from their Protestant oppressors if Elizabeth I chose to restore her cousin to her throne. See Duguid, *Metrical Psalmody*; Jamie Reid-Baxter, 'Metrical Psalmody and the Bannatyne Manuscript: Robert Pont's Psalm 83', *Renaissance and Reformation*, 30.4 (2006), 41–62; James Kirk, *ODNB*.]

Psalm 76

Here is set forth the power of God, and care for the defence of his people in Jerusalem, in the destruction of the armies of Sennacherib. And the faithful are exhorted to be thankful.

1. In Jewry land God is well known
   In Israel great is his name.[314]
   He chose out Salem for his own,
   His tabernacle of great fame,   tent
5 2. Therein to raise and mount Zion
   To make his habitation,[315]
   And residence within the same.

3. There did he break the bowmen's shafts,
   Their fiery darts so swift of flight,
10   Their shields, their swords, and all their crafts
   Of war, when they were bound to fight.

4. More excellent and more mighty
   Art thou therefore than mountains high,
   Of ravenous wolves without all right.[316]

15 5. The stout-hearted were made a prey,
   A sudden sleep did them confound,

---

[314] Israel] The metre (and tune) require three syllables.
[315] habitation] The metre requires five syllables ('ha-bi-ta-ti-on').
[316] The wolves seem to be Pont's invention, and it's not entirely clear what they are doing and to whom, except providing an additional line of verse.

        And all the strong men in that fray
        Their feeble hands they have not found.
6. At thy rebuke, O Jacob's God,
     Horses with chariots overtrod,
     As with dead sleep were cast to ground.
7. Fearful art thou (O Lord our guide)
     Yea, thou alone; and who is he
     That in thy presence may abide,
     If once thine anger kindled be?
8. Thou makest men from heaven to hear
     Thy judgements just; the earth for fear
     Stillèd with silence then we see.
9. When thou, O Lord, begin'st to rise,
     Sentence to give, as judge of all,
     And in the earth dost enterprise
     To rid the humble out of thrall,   *bondage*
10. Certès, the rage of moral men   *certainly*
     Shall be thy praise; the remnant then
     Of their fury thou bind'st withal.   *likewise*
11. Vow, and perform your vows therefore
     Unto the Lord your God, all ye
     That round about him dwell; adore
     This fearful one with off'rings free.[317]
12. Which may cut off at his vintage
     The breath of princes in their rage;
     To earthly kings fearful is he.

Psalm 83

A prayer for the Church, being assaulted on all side by the unfaithful, confedered together to bring it to ruin: with rehearsal of certain examples how God hath supported his own in time past, to encourage the faithful with good hope.

1. God, for thy grace,
        thou keep no more silence,[318]

---

[317] In the preceding lines as well as earlier, Pont plays the syntax against the structure of the verse line in interesting ways unusual in Psalms in the Sternhold and Hopkins style. The combination of late caesura and enjambment in the second and third lines of this stanza would likely be obliterated in singing, but they add welcome variety to the reading experience of the Psalm.

[318] The short lines of the 1564 printing may just be due to the constraints of a very small page, since half lines do not begin with capitals, and the rhyme scheme suggests pentameters, but the original format has nevertheless been retained.

Cease not, O God,
  nor hold thy peace no more:
2. For lo, thy foes
  with cruel violence
Confedered are,   *confederate*
  and with an hideous roar.
In this their rage,
  these rebels brag and shore.   *threaten*
And they that hate
  thee, most maliciously,
Against thy might
  their heads have raised on high.

3. For to oppress
  thy people, they pretend
with subtle slight: *cunning*
  and move conspiracy.
For such as on
  thy secret help depend.
4. Go to, say they,
  and let us utterly
This nation[319]
  root out from memory:
And of the name
  of Israelites, let never
Further be made
  no mention forever.

5. Conspirèd are
  with cruel hearts and fell,   *savage*
Thus against thee
  together in a band.   *company*
6. The Edomites
  that in their tents do dwell,
And Ishmaelites
  joined with them do stand:
The Moabites,
  upon the other hand,
With the proud race
  of Hagarenes together:[320]

---

[319] nation] The metre requires three syllables.
[320] Less familiar than the Edomites and Moabites, the Hagarenes are another hostile neighbour of Israel, an Arab tribe living in the east, sometimes equated with the Ishmaelites (descendants of Ishmael, who eventually became the Muslims).

		Assembled are	
45		and wickedly confeder.	*gather*
	7.	Gebal, Ammon,	
		and Amalek all three:	
		March forth,	
50		each one with his garrison:	
		The Philistines	
		foremost they think to be;	
		The indwellers	*inhabitants*
		of Tyre with them are boun.³²¹	*bound*
55	8.	Asshur also	
		is their companion:	
		With the children	
		of Lot, to be arrayed	
		In their support	
60		his banner is displayed.	
	9.	Do thou to them	
		as thou didst to the host	
		Of Midian:	
		Jabin and Sisera	
65		At Kison flood.	
	10.	In Endor lives they lost	
		To dung the land	*fertilize*
		where as their bodies lay.	
	11.	Like Oreb, Zeb,	
70		Zeba, and Salmana	
		So make thou them:	
		even their most mighty princes,	
		And all the chief	*head*
		rulers of their provinces.³²²	
75	12.	Which said, let us	
		inherit as our own	
		God's mansions.	
	13.	My God, make them to be	

---

[321] Gebal is another enemy of Israel (Ezekiel 27. 9); the Ammonites are descended from Ammon, son of Lot and his younger daughter (Genesis 19. 36–38), the Amalekites from Amalek, grandson of Esau (Genesis 36. 12). Asshur, in the next line, was a son of Shem (Genesis 10. 22), founder of the Assyrians.

[322] The Midianites descended from Midian, son of Abraham by Keturah (Genesis 25. 2), Jabin was King of Hazor and Sisera his general (Judges 4). Oreb and Zeeb were Midianite princes (Judges 7. 25), Zeba and Salmana Midianite kings (Judges 7).

	Like rolling wheels,	
80	or as the stubble blown	
	Before the wind.	
	14. As fire the woods, we see,	
	Doth burn: and flame	
	devour on mountains high	
85	The heather crop.[323]	
	15. So let thy tempest chase them,	
	And thy whirlwind	
	with terror so deface them.	*erase*
	16. Their faces, Lord,	
90	with shamefulness fulfil:	
	That they may seek	
	thy name in mind to print.	
	17. Confounded let	*shamed*
	them be, and ever still	
95	Vexèd with woe:	
	yea, make them shamed and shent.	*disgraced*
	18. And let them know	
	that thou art permanent:	
	That, Jehovah,	
100	thy name alone pertaineth	
	To thee, o'er all	
	the earth whose glory reigneth.	

43. John Wedderburn?, *Here Follows a Compendious Book of Godly and Spiritual Songs, Newly Translated out of Latin into English, Gathered out of Many and Diverse Scriptures, with Many Pleasant Ballads, and Changed out of Vain Songs into Godly Songs For To Avoid Sin and Harlotry* (1565)

[Tradition has often credited three brothers with responsibility for the book known as 'Good and Godly Ballads': James Wedderburn (*c.* 1495–1533) and his brothers, John (*c.* 1505–1556) and Robert (*c.* 1510–1555x1560), all of whom studied at St Andrews. Alasdair A. MacDonald has recently noted, however, that James and Robert are unlikely to have been involved, since Robert died a Catholic priest and James, who may or may not have been sympathetic to reform, wrote only plays and then moved to France where he gave up literature for trade, dying over twenty years before the book was first printed. Only John was certainly a Protestant, though his conversion came after his ordination as a priest. To avoid arrest for heresy, he fled to the Continent in 1538/39. At Wittenberg he may have met both Martin Luther and Philip Melanchthon, and

---

[323] Pont has added this characteristically Scottish feature to the Psalm's landscape.

he is said to have followed Luther's practice of translating Psalms and converting secular songs into sacred hymns. He returned to Dundee in 1553, after the death of James V. Scotland failed to embrace reform, as he had hoped, and he spent his last years in exile in England. John Wedderburn may have had some role in the production of *A Compendious Book of Godly and Spiritual Songs*, later known as *The Good and Godly Ballads*, the most important early Scots book of Protestant verse. What this role was is unclear, and some of the contents may have been in circulation decades earlier than the 1565 edition. The theology of the volume is Lutheran rather than Calvinist, so in some ways the book became increasingly anachronistic with each edition. It contained religious poems, anti-Catholic satires, adaptations of Lutheran hymns, and biblical paraphrases, including Psalms. There were editions in 1565, 1567, 1578, 1600, and 1621. See Duguid, *Metrical Psalmody*; *The Gude and Godlie Ballatis*, ed. by Alasdair A. MacDonald (Woodbridge: Boydell Press for The Scottish Text Society, 2015); *A Compendious Book of Godly and Spiritual Songs, Commonly Known as 'The Gude and Godlie Ballatis,' Reprinted from the Edition of 1567*, ed. By A. F. Mitchell, Scottish Text Society (New York and London: Johnson Reprint Company Ltd., 1897); J. K. McGinley, *ODNB*.]

Psalm 31[324]

In te Domine speravi.   [In you, Lord, I trust]

Lord lat me never be confoundit	*put to shame*
That fermly dois confide in thee,	
Bot lat thy justice aye be groundit	*always*
With mercy to deliver me.	
5 Incline thy ruthful earis, in time,	*compassionate, ears*
To me, that am in misery,	
And from all sort of sin and crime,	
Thou, blessit Lord, deliver me.	
Be my defendand, God of grace,	*defender*
10 My guide, my governor, all three;	
And in thy heavenly dwelling place,	
Of all refuge thou succour me.	
For sen thou art my strength and force,	*since*
My hope, support, and hail supplie;	*perfect, aid*
15 Be thy sweit name, and deid on croce,[325]	*sweet, death, cross*
Thou sall upbring, and nourish me.	*shall*

---

[324] Only the first six verses are translated. As MacDonald notes, the final line in the first edition ends with a comma, suggesting it was unfinished.
[325] A Christian interpolation.

	Thou sall me guide from gyrne, and snair,	trap
	They hide in secret, quhair nane may se,	where, none
	Sen thou art keipar, lait and air,	keeper, late and early
20	Protector and defence of me.	
	My spreit I rander in thy handis,	spirit
	Eternal God of verity,	truth
	Quhilk hes from bailful Belial's bands[326]	which, has, company
	Redemit and deliverit me.	

Psalm 37

Noli aemulari.   [Do not emulate]

	Thou sal not follow wickit men's ways,	shall
	Have no envy thocht sinful have good days.	though
	For like the witherit hay soon sal they fade,	
	And as the grass that wallows root and blade.	withers
5	But thou in the Lord put hail thy belief	healthy
	Wirk ay his will, do not that may him grief;	grieve
	And then the fruitful land thou sal possess	
	Abundantly, thou sal have great richesse.	wealth
	Into the Lord put all thy hail delight,	
10	And he sal grant thy hartis appetite.	heart's
	Shaw furth before the Lord thy mind and will,	show
	And traist in him, he sal it weil fulfil.	trust, shall, well
	Then, as the golden morning shinis bricht,	bright
	So sal thy justice shine till every wicht,	creature
15	And, as the sun in midday shawis fair,	shows
	So sal thy virtue knawin be alquhair.	known, everywhere
	Upon the Lord have ever thine intent.	
	Before thy eyen thou have him ay present,	eyes, always
	And muse thee not at their prosperity	
20	That livis all their life richt wrangously.	right, wrongfully
	Refrain rancour and ire furth of thy thocht,	anger, forth, thought
	The evil example of wickit follow nocht.	evil, not
	For cruel men sal soon destroyit be,	
	But quha abidis the Lord richt patiently,	who, abides
25	Sal bruke the land with good possessioun	possess

---

[326] Belial is not mentioned in the original (BCP has 'I have hated them, that hold of superstitious vanities'), but 'sons of Belial' is used elsewhere in the Bible to refer to the wicked (Deuteronomy 13. 13, I Samuel 2. 12, etc.). As an abstract noun 'Belial' means something like 'worthlessness', but in English since Anglo-Saxon times it has also been the name of a demon. Paul seems to use it in the same sense in I Corinthians 6. 15.

Full peaceably without oppressioun.
Sustain a little quhile, and thou shall see — *while*
The wickit man perish before thine ee; — *eye*
Thou sal behold him and his mansioun
30 Baith he and it, brocht to confusioun. — *both, brought*
But humble men sal inherit the yeird, — *earth*
And leave in peace fra wickit mennis reird. — *speech*
The sinful man with evil will await
The innocent that can mak na debate, — *no*
35 With countenance austere sal on him girn, — *show teeth (as in rage, pain, etc.)*
His ireful heart with bale sal ever burn. — *torment*
But thou, good Lord, sal lauch him all to scorn, — *laugh*
And knawis the time that he sal be forlorn. — *knows*
The cruel men sal draw their burnished brand, — *sword*
40 And have their bow bent ready in their hand,
For till overthrow the meek and indigent, — *to*
And for to slay the just and innocent;
Their sword sal strike themself outhrou the heart, — *through*
And broken sal their bow be in all part.
45 The little of the just is more commendit,
So that it be weil win and better spendit, — *won*
Than is the great riches of wickit men,
Quhair through they do baith God and man misken. — *where, both, mistake*
The power of the wickit sal decay,
50 But God sal weil preserve the just for ay.
The times of the just, God does record,
Their heritage sal be ay with the Lord;
In great peril they sal not be oppressed,
In time of dearth their food sal be addressed.
55 But wickit men sal perish in their need,
And they that of the good Lord has na dreid; — *fear*
Like sacrifice they sal consumit be,
Quhairof but reik, thou never more sal see. — *whereof, smoke*
The wickit man will tak, and will not pay, — *take*
60 The just freely will give without delay;
Quha lufis him, and of him speakis good, — *loves*
Shall bruke the land, but quha that will delude
Or does blaspheme the kind and liberal,
Sal rootit be furth of memorial.
65 The pathis of the just God does direct,
He lufis him and will him not neglect;
Suppose he fall, by sea, or yet by land,
God raises him with his most gracious hand.

	I have been young, and comin now to age,	*come*
70	And saw I never the just left in thirlage,	*bondage*
	Nor yet have I seen his posterity	
	Begand their bread in great necessity.	*begging*
	And thocht he give and lend his goods at large,	*though*
	Till them that mister his and will him charge,	*need*
75	Yet shall his seed live into plenteousness,	*descendants*
	Abundantly possess great richesse.	
	He flees evil and followis good therefore,	
	Eternally he sal ring forevermore.	*reign*
	The Lord lufis justice and equity,[327]	
80	And leavis not his saints in misery,	
	For he on them perpetually has cure;	
	But wickit mannis seed sal not endure.	
	Just men with joy the erd sal possess,	
	And dwell for ay on it and sal incres.	*forever, increase*
85	The justis mouth, exersit with sapience,	*possessed*
	Of equity sal speak and of prudence;	
	The law of God is in his heart so hail,	
	In all his wayis, therefore, he can not fail.	
	The wickit will observe the innocent,	
90	To seek him, to slay him into judgement,	
	But God will not him leave into his need,	
	But will him save from tyrannis wickit deed.	
	They cannot him condemn quhen they accuse,	*when*
	Preservit sal he be from their abuse.	
95	Traist in the Lord and keep weel his command,	
	And he sal thee exalt in every land.	
	Possess the erd thou sal, and with thine ee,	
	The wickit men destroyit sal thou see.	
	Sometime a tyrant flourish have I seen,	
100	Like laurel tree, quhilk ever growis green;[328]	*which*
	But in short time soon was he brocht to nocht,	*naught*
	He was not found quhen he lang time wes socht.	*sought*
	Keep justice, and have ee unto the richt,	*right*
	That sal mak peace forever with God of micht;	*might*

---

[327] On equity, here and below, see note 6, p. 68.

[328] The Hebrew designates simply a native or indigenous tree. The Vulgate substitutes 'cedars of Lebanon' (*cedros Libani*), KJV and BCP a 'green bay tree'. The laurel is another name for the bay, and the green laurel was familiar in Chaucer, Gower, Langland, Skelton, and many other authors. One particular association was with the tree Daphne turned into to escape Apollo, after which he wore the laurel crown that became a symbol of poetry.

105	For wrangous men sal end mischievously,	*unjust*
	And wickit mennis fine is misery.	*end*
	The just, hail down fra the Lord descendis,	
	Their strength, that in all peril them defendis,	
	God helpis them, and sendis them supplie,	*supply*
110	And savis him fra tyrannis cruelty.	
	For cause in him thye have put their traist,	
	Glore be to the Father, Son, and Holy Gaist.	*ghost*

Psalm 64[329]

Exaudi deus orationem. [Hear, God, my prayer]

	O Lord, advert unto my voice, I cry,	*give heed*
	Now quhen I pray unto thy majesty.	*when*
	From dredour of my mortal enemy	*dread*
	Defend my life, and als deliver me.	*also*
5	Defend me from the false subtility	
	Of wickit men, and from the cruelness,	
	Of them that alwais workis unrichteousness.	*unrighteousness*

	From them that has their tongis sharp and ground	
	And sharper than ever was an edgeit sword,	
10	Like deidly dartis that givis stang and stound,	*wound, sharp pain*
	Richt sa procedis of their mouth every word,	*right*
	Quhair with to slay they think it but a bourd,	*where, jest*
	The innocent, with secreit dissemblance:	
	Without dredour of Godis vengeance.	

15	They have devisit abhominatioun,	*devised*
	Amang them selfis in thair maliciousness	
	Richt prively is thair communicatioun,	
	To set their nettis with clokit craftiness,	*cloaked*
	With sic device as it war holiness	*such*
20	That no man suld their violence espy,	*should*
	Quhilk wald revenge their fals hypocrisy.	*which, would*

	Their counsel is to sears and to inquire,	*search*
	The innocent with wrang for till accuse.	*to*
	In all this world they have no more desire,	
25	For ever in their mind of this they muse,	

---

[329] MacDonald argues that the source for this Psalm and others in the collection is Coverdale's *Ghostly Psalms* (see 7), which is evidence that this volume had greater influence than its official suppression might suggest. Coverdale's 'God be merciful unto us' is itself a translation of Luther's 'Es wollt uns Gott genädig sein'.

Quha will delayit they will mak no refuse	who
Of foe, or fule, or for suspicioun.	fool
They will bring men unto confusioun.	

But now no more their malice sal remain,	shall
30 For God sal strike without provisioun	
Of quhom they sal be plaigit with great pains	whom, plagued
And men sal hold them in derisioun,	
Their toungis sal be their awin confusioun,	own
Quhilk was so sharp in contrar innocence,	against
35 For their own selfis they sal mak no defence.	

Quhen men sal see this hasty sudden chenge	
Then sal they wonder, and clearly understand	
That it is God quhilk dois his own revenge.	
All men sal ses this work of Godis hand,	
40 And sal well know that it is his command;	
The just sal traist in God and als rejoyis,	trust, also
All trew hartis sall joy to hear this noyis.	

Psalms 114/115[330]

In exitu Israel.	[When Israel went out]
Quhen fra Egypt departit Israel,	when, from
And Jacob's house fra people barbar fell,[331]	barbarous
To Juda, Lord, thou was his Saviour,	
And to Israel baith guide and governor;	both
5 Quhilk, quhen these had seen, for fear it fled,	which
The flood Jordan yid back, it was so red.	moved
The mountains mofit and ran athwart like rammis,	moved, to and fro
The hillis dansit and lichtly lap like lambis.	lightly, leaped
O swolland sea, quhat mofit thee to flee?	turbulent, moved
10 To gang aback, Jordan, quhat ailit thee?	ailed
Quhat gart ye mountanis like rammis stert and stand,	caused, start up
And ye hillis like lambis loop and bend?	leap
It was the Lordis fear that made sic reird,	such, clamour
And Jacob's God perturbit all the eird.	earth
15 For God turnit the craig in fresh reveir.	rock, into, river
The barren bra in fountain water cleir.	steep hill
Not unto us, not unto us, O Lord,	

---

[330] United as one Psalm in the Vulgate and in the German metrical sources.

[331] As reflected in the KJV, the Hebrew means 'of strange language', but this sense is maintained here, since 'barbarous' meant originally 'not Greek', i.e. foreign speaking.

	But to thy sweet promise, and to thy word,	
	And to thy name be glore allanerly,	*exclusively*
20	Quhilk keepis thy promise faithfully.	
	Therefore let not our enemies blaspheme	
	Thy majesty, for we may not sustain	
	To hear them say: Quhair is thy great essence,	*where, divine essence*
	The godly help of thy magnificence?	
25	Our God forsooth ringis in heaven full high,	
	And quhat him listis and likis, workis he.	*desires*
	Their images of stock, stane, gilt with gold,	*wood, stone*
	Are made by men, and sine for money sold.	*afterwards*
	They have a mouth can neither say nor sing,	
30	Their ene are blind, and they can see na thing;	*eyes, no*
	They can not hear, thocht men do cry and yell,	*though*
	Their nosethirls can neither savour nor smell;	*nostrils*
	They have handis can neither feel nor grope,	
	Their fundeit feet can neither gang nor lope;	*numb, walk, leap*
35	They can pronounce na voice furth of their throatis,	*forth*
	They are overgane with mousewebs and motis.³³²	*overcome, cobwebs, dust*
	Quha makis them, or traists in their supports,	*who, trusts*
	Are like to them in all manner of sorts.	
	But thou, Israel, in God thou put thy traist,	
40	Thy protector into thy mister maist.	*distress, greatest*
	Ye house of Aaron, in God put your believe,	
	Your defender, and na man can you grieve.	
	All worshippers of God, traist in his name,	
	He is your help, and Saviour alane.	*alone*
45	The Lord has mind and mercy upon us,	
	To favour us, and bring us to his bliss,	
	To feed the house of Israel with his food,	
	And to the house of Aaron to do good.	
	Thou sal do weill to them that dredis thee,	*well, fears*
50	Baith young and old, quhat state that ever they be.	*both*
	God sal augment his people, and increase	
	Their dear sonnis and dochters mair and less.	*also, more*
	Ye are the saints ... that create heaven	
	And yeird in dayis six and nichtis seven.³³³	*earth, nights*

---

³³² A vivid addition to the Psalm, suggesting objects abandoned in an attic.

³³³ The original mentions only God's creation of heaven and earth; the number of days and nights here is technically correct, or at least defensible, since according to Genesis God rests on the seventh day, and the creation sequence counts evening and morning as one day. The seventh evening or night is thus perhaps unaccounted for.

55 The heavenis are the Lordis habitatioun,
    The yeird he gave to mannis propagatioun.
    The dead may not thee lofe amang the lave, *praise, living*
    Nor they that are descendit in their grave;
    But we that are on live sal lofe and sing *i.e. alive, praise*
60 To God forever, unto our last ending.

44. John Hall, *The Court of Virtue, Containing Many Holy or Spiritual Songs. Sonnets, Psalms, Ballads, Short Sentences As Well of Holy Scripture As Others* (1565)

[The physician John Hall had published an earlier collection of biblical paraphrases (see 26). *The Court of Virtue* was written in direct opposition to *The Court of Venus*, a collection of secular love poetry including works by Sir Thomas Wyatt. Hall's goal, like that of Sternhold and other devotional poets, was to supplant scandalous erotic songs and poems with godly ballads, including metrical Psalms. To this end, as well as metrical Psalms, Hall's *Court* contains sacred parodies of secular lyrics by Wyatt. The Wyatt family, at Allington Castle, were essentially neighbours of Hall, who lived in Maidstone, Kent. The rebellion protesting Queen Mary's proposed marriage to Philip II of Spain, led by Thomas Wyatt the younger, was supported by many local people, including some named in acrostics in poems by Hall, whom Wyatt presumably knew. 1565 also marked the publication of Hall's *A Most Excellent and Learned Work of Chirurgery*, translated from the Italian of Lanfanc of Milan, but with additions based on Hall's own professional experience. This experience also informs the medical conceits Hall adds to this Psalm paraphrase. Presumably by accident, Hall omits verse 2 of the Psalm, which he did include in earlier printed versions (see textual notes). See Rivkah Zim, 'The Maidstone Burghmote and John Hall's *Courte of Vertue* (1565)', *Notes & Queries*, 33(231).3 (1986), 320-27 and *ODNB*.]

Psalm 54

An example that God heareth all such prayers as are made with a faithful heart, out of the .liiii. Psalm.

   Every good physician,
   That doth a med'cine prove
   To take effect in curing well,
   Is stricken straight with love, *immediately*
5   Not only to give God the praise,
   For his virtue and grace:
   But doth the same in writing put,
   To comfort all his race. *people*

That all which after follow him
10 In that most godly art,
May prove the like and praise the Lord
In like case for their part.

Noble King David in such wise *manner*
Doth godly love bestow,
15 By writing med'cines for the soul,
That other men may know.

As if they doubt at any time
How he did health obtain,
He did the same declare abroad
20 In writing to remain:

That when to others' like distress
Hereafter may betide, *befall*
With clean hearts that they may prepare,
And like med'cines provide.

25 But I will never teach (quod he) *said*
In dark or doubtful way,
But such as I in practice did
By perfect proof assay:[334] *attempt*

And of my self *probatum est*,[335]
30 Such medicines I bring:
And in example to you all
In this wise will I sing.

Deus in nomine tuo. [God by thy name]

O God, I call to thee for help
In my distress and need,
35 For thy name's sake, and in thy strength,
Avenge my cause with speed.

For strangers full of tyranny
Against me rise and rave:
Such foolish folk as fear not God
40 Do seek my life to have.

---

[334] Given the persistent medical context introduced by Hall, this may suggest scientific experiment as well as general trial; *OED* notes 'proof' as a surgical probe, but the earliest date is 1611. The word seems to be used in a similar sense, however, in 1525 (Hieronymous Brunschwig, *The noble experyence of the vertuous handy warke of surgery*, sig. Mi^r).

[335] *probatum est*] Latin, 'it has been proved', a phrase traditionally attached to recipes or prescriptions.

But lo, God is my help at need,
Yea, only it is he
That doth my soul uphold and save
From their iniquity.

45   And evil shall the Lord reward
Upon mine enemies,
And in his truth destroy them all
That virtue do despise.

With off'rings of an heart most free,
50 Now will I praise thy name:
Because, O Lord, my comfort still
Consisteth in the same.

For thou, Lord, didst deliver me
From troubles manifold:
55 So that upon my foes mine eye
Doth his desire behold.

For this to give glory to God
Shall be my heart's delight,
To the Father, and to the Son,
60 And to the Holy Sprite: *Spirit*

As it from the beginning was,
And at this time is sure,
And as it shall, world without end,
Continue and endure.[336]

45. John Pits, *A Poore Man's Benevolence to the Afflicted Church* (1566)

[John Pits was also responsible for *A Prayer or Supplication Made unto God by a Young Man that He Would Be Merciful to Us* (1559), *A Prayer, and Also a Thanksgiving unto God, for his Great Mercy, in Giving, and Preserving our Noble Queen Elizabeth, To Live and Reign over Us* (1577), and, apparently, *A Marvelous Strange Deformed Swine* (1570), all of them verse broadsides. In the 1577 prayer, Pits is described as a minister, but nothing more is known about him. The afflicted Church Pits prays for is not the Church of England, but that in Scotland, France, Spain, or 'any other land', presumably, that remains Catholic. The two Psalms Pits includes in *A Poor Man's Benevolence* (67 and 100) are without music or indications of tunes to which they should be sung. The metre of Pits's Psalm 67 is different from Hopkins's (short metre, or 6.6.8.6.) in the 1562 *Whole Book*, but any tune in double common metre, such as that for Psalm 1 in the *Whole Book*, would suffice.]

[336] 57–64] See note 309, p. 211.

JOHN PITS

Psalm 67

David here in this Psalm doth teach
　　The faithful for to pray,
The Lord to show his countenance
　　That they go not astray.
5　*And that his mighty power be known,*
　　Which is of noble fame:
That all the nations on the earth,
　　May praise his holy name.

God be merciful unto us,
10　　Thus doth King David write:
In the three score and seventh Psalm
　　He doth the same recite.
And bless thou us (sayeth he) O Lord,
　　For that we stand in need:
15　The light of thy countenance show,[337]
　　Thy mercy give with speed.

That thy right was here on the earth,
　　Unto us may be known:
And thy most high and saving health,
20　　Unto all nations shown.
Let the people praise thee (O God)
　　Let all the people sing:
O let the nations on the earth,
　　Acknowledge thee their King.

25　For thou the righteous wilt defend
　　And govern everywhere:
And make the wicked in a row
　　Of thee to stand in fear.
Let the people praise thee, O God,
30　　Now let them all thee praise:
In this our most troublesome time,
　　And in these heavy days.[338]

---

[337] Pits has little control over the metre, and this line is particularly awkward. But lines 9 and 11 begin with strong stresses, while lines 13 and 15 begin with unstressed syllables. So long as he has the requisite number of syllables per line (8 and 6), Pits doesn't seem to care about their rhythm.

[338] What Pits specifically has in mind is unclear, but in 1562 French Protestants took the city of Le Havre and England sent troops to support them. The English were expelled the next year, however, and the city fell to the (Catholic) French.

Then shall the earth her increase bring,
    And thou, our God, shalt give
35 Thy only good and great blessing,
    That we with thee may live.
God shall us bless for evermore,
    And us defend from sin:
And all the ends of the whole world
40   Shall stand in awe of him.

Glory be to the Father high,
    And to the Son therefore:
And to the Holy Ghost, which spirit
    Keep us for evermore.[339]

46. Matthew Parker, *The Whole Psalter Translated into English Metre, Which Containeth a Hundred and Fifty Psalms* (1567)

[Matthew Parker (1504–1575) was born in Norwich and educated at Corpus Christi College, Cambridge, where he studied theology and was ordained a deacon and priest. He was appointed chaplain to the evangelically minded Queen Anne Boleyn in 1535. After Boleyn's fall, Parker was appointed one of the chaplains to Henry VIII. His rise through the ranks of the Church (and Cambridge University) culminated in his appointment as Archbishop of Canterbury in 1559. At Cambridge in 1549, where Parker was vice-chancellor, he came under the influence of the exiled Strasbourg reformer Martin Bucer, who became regius professor of divinity. Parker was made dean of Lincoln Cathedral in 1552, but he lost the position with the accession of Queen Mary in 1553, at which point he also resigned his mastership of Corpus Christi. Parker's whereabouts during Mary's reign are unknown, but he seems to have lived an obscure life in England rather than joining other Protestants in exile on the Continent. During this period he composed his metrical psalter, prefaced by a long poem on the 'Virtue of the Psalms', and including nine tunes by Thomas Tallis, the leading composer in England, and, remarkably, a Gentleman of the Chapel Royal from 1543 until his old age in the reign of Elizabeth I. Einar Bjorvand points out, however, that fifteen of Parker's Psalms are in metres that none of the Tallis tunes can accommodate. Parker was summoned to London on Elizabeth's accession in 1558 and, despite his protests of unworthiness, made archbishop in 1559. Parker was a scholar of broad intellectual tastes and a serious antiquarian. He bequeathed over 800 books from his library to Corpus Christi, and he was especially important in preserving a substantial number of Anglo-Saxon manuscripts. His psalter was published by John Day, probably in

---

[339] 41–44] See note 309, p. 211.

1567, the year before the Bishops' Bible, which translation Parker oversaw. The psalter was printed anonymously, but Parker's authorship is strongly suggested by an acrostic poem in fourteeners that precedes Psalm 119, as well as by contemporary documents (including his own Latin diary) that refer to the project. Parker aims at considerable metrical and formal variety, which may have influenced later Psalms translators like Philip and Mary Sidney. Parker's idiosyncratic use of colons is original, as is the format of his argument. Each Psalm is followed by a collect. Parker's psalter is also a compendium of commentary on the Psalms, including passages from the Old and New Testaments, Church Fathers like Basil, Athanasius, Chrysostom, and Augustine, a section on music, and original notes in verse and prose. On the process of composition, Parker writes, 'Verse hard in mouth: while oft I chewed, | I spied therein no waste: | Clear sent to mind: more sweetly flowed, | erst thus not felt in taste'. Parker's diligent 'chewing' is evidenced in a manuscript that survives of his first 80 Psalms, seemingly in his own hand, showing careful correction and still differing from the final versions in print. See Anne Lake Prescott, 'King David as "Right Poet": Sidney and the Psalmist', *ELR*, 19.3 (1989), 131–51; *David's Blissful Harp: A Critical Edition of the Manuscript of Matthew Parker's Metrical Psalms (1–80)*, ed. by Einar Bjorvand (Tempe: Arizona Center for Medieval and Renaissance Studies, 2015); V. J. K. Brook, *A Life of Archbishop Matthew Parker* (Oxford: Clarendon Press, 1961); David J. Crankshaw and Alexandra Gillespie, *ODNB*.]

Psalm 17

The Argument.

{ *That faith might stand* / *In upper hand* }   { *The just man pray'th full fain* }   gladly

{ *And museth in part* / *That just in heart.* }   { *Thus should be vexed in pain.* }

1. Hear thou the right: O Lord my might,
    Consider my complaint: lament
   My lips be straight: and hate deceit,   undeviating
    Give ear to my constraint.[340]   distress

5 2. Give thou assent: to mine intent,
    In hand my right to take:

---

[340] Parker's stanza is a version of the popular common metre, but with an extra internal rhyme in the first and third lines.

	Let thy good eye: my cause descry,	*discover*
	For thee my judge I make.	
	3. My heart thou tri'dst: by night thou spy'dst,	
10	Thou scorn'dst me nigh in deed:	*closely*
	Thou found'st not yet: my fault so great,	
	My thought to mouth agreed.	
	4. Men's works full nought: by them so wrought	*worthless*
	Against thy word and will:	
15	Made me to mark: their ways most dark,	
	Thy laws who do but spill.	
	5. O stay my feet: of life most meet,	*secure*
	Thy word to hold the path:	
	Lest wrong I walk: thy truth to balk,	*shun*
20	To slip in thy great wrath.	
	6. O God of all: on thee I call,	
	For thou my suit wilt hear:	*petition*
	Incline to me: thy face so free,	
	My words in hearing bear.	
25	7. Thy mercies great: extend thou yet,	
	Save them which trust in thee:	
	From such as stand: against thy hand,	
	And vain resisters be.	
	8. As ball of eye:[341] O tenderly,	
30	Keep me my Lord and King:	*guard*
	And shadow me: so close to be,	
	Hid under thy good wing.	*hidden*
	9. Defend me quite: from all the spite,	
	Of them that me molest:	*trouble*
35	My foes I see: round compass me,	*surround*
	My soul to have oppressed.	
	10. So fat and fed: they jet so red	*strut, ruddy?*
	In wealth they stand full high:	
	Proud speech to seek: even what they leek,	*like*
40	They walk disdainfully.	

---

[341] ball of eye] Parker's interpretation of the Hebrew idiom is incorrect, the literal sense 'little man of the eye' usually being interpreted as the pupil. English Bibles from Coverdale on substitute an English idiom dating back to the ninth century, 'apple of the eye', which also means pupil, though it can mean eyeball.

	11. In ways they wait: to note our gate,	
	So set on every side:	
	They bend their eyes: as crafty spies	
	On ground to cast us wide.	
45	12. Like lion sly: they privy lie,	*secretly*
	Which greedy seek'th his prey:	
	As close it were: fierce wolf or bear,	*hidden*
	Or lion's whelp they lay.	
	13. For thy renown: rise, cast him down,	
50	Destroy his sprite, O God:	*spirit*
	My soul, O save: from wicked slave.	
	Who is thy sword and rod.	
	14. From men so fond: that be thy hond,	*hand*
	O Lord, from worldly beast:[342]	
55	Who make good cheer: thou fill'st them here,	*make merry*
	They leave their babes the rest.	
	15. And I shall bold: thy face behold,	
	In righteousness so bright:	
	I shall in deed: be satisfied,	
60	Thy glory brought to light.	

Psalm 33

The Argument.

The just alway in mind bear'th this,	*always*
With heart to joy in God of his,	
To praise his name that mighty is,	
For he giveth help and heavenly bliss:	
But vain all other remedies,	
But pain all worldly policies,	
Remember this.	

Exultate justi in.   [Rejoice, you righteous, in]

	1. Rejoice in God: the Lord he is,	
	Ye righteous men and do not miss,	
	The just be bound to thank iwis.	*truly*
	Repeat ye this.[343]	

---

[342] Parker's version of these lines is particularly contorted, 'worldly beast' being simply synonymous for 'worldly men'; BCP has 'From the men of thy hand, O Lord, from the men, I say, and from the evil world'.

[343] With its three longer lines and fourth short line, set to the right, Parker's stanza seems

5	2.	Praise ye the Lord: with melodies,	
		With harp and lute, with symphonies,	
		Sing Psalms to him in psalteries.	
		Forget not this.	
	3.	Sing carols new with jubilee,[344]	
10		To God the Lord in majesty,	
		His lauds, his praise, sing heartily.	*praises*
		Well use ye this.	
	4.	His word is true most certainly,	
		His works be wrought most faithfully:	
15		Hold this in heart most constantly.	
		Abuse not this.	
	5.	He judgment loveth: and right intent,	
		The earth therewith is all besprent,	*besprinkled*
		Such grace and love he down hath sent,	
20		Well trust ye this.	
	6.	The heavens were made: by this the Lord,	
		The hosts of them: by his true word,	
		His breath of mouth: their power afford'th.	
		Distrust not this.	
25	7.	The seas on heaps: he doth them place,	
		As bottle close:[345] he them embraceth	
		The deeps he couched in secret space.	*laid*
		Denounce ye this.	
	8.	Let all the earth: the Lord yfear,[346]	*fear*
30		What man this world and mould doth bear,	*earth*
		Serve him in dread: with gentle ear.	
		Renounce not this.	

like an English version of the Sapphic, but it actually adopts the stanza of Sir Thomas Wyatt's 'Forget not yet the tried intent', especially given Wyatt's fourth line (a kind of refrain), 'Forget not yet', and in the final iteration, 'Forget not this'. Parker's ever varied refrains add considerable complexity to his version of the Psalm, almost converting it into a courtly complaint, though they match nothing in the original. In the Inner Temple MS, a note indicates that the final half line of each stanza should be repeated, though there is no indication of this in the printed text.

[344] jubilee] jubilation, exultation; though alluding also to the year of emancipation and restoration to be celebrated every fifty years, according to Leviticus 25.

[345] bottle close] A common biblical metaphor for rain clouds (the Hebrew means 'wineskin'), though Parker adds this to the Psalm.

[346] yfear] The y- prefix is archaic, used in Old or Middle English, of which Parker was an important early scholar (as also in 'iwis' in verse 1).

9. He spake the word: and done it was,
   The earth firm stood in stable case,
   What he did bide: it came to pass.
       Revolve ye this.   *consider*

10. All paynim's ways God doth reject,   *pagan's*
    Vain people's drifts by him be checked:
    Proud princes' crafts he doth detect.
        Dissolve not this.

11. God's counsels aye shall all abide,   *forever*
    His thoughts of heart shall never slide:
    From time to time on neither side.
        Respect ye this.

12. What folk hath God, Jehova, Lord,
    Elect as heir by his accord,[347]
    O blest they be by truth's record.
        Suspect not this.

13. The Lord from heaven behold'th us all,
    All kind of men both free and thrall: *enslaved*
    He seeth their rise: he seeth their fall.
        Advise ye this.

14. From his high seat: he cast'th his eyes,   *habitation*
    All men to view their tract to spy,   *course*
    Where ever they in earth do lie.
        Despise not this.

15. The hearts of all he shope no doubt,   *created*
    He know'th their thoughts within, without,
    Their works what they do go about.
        Repute ye this.

16. No king is saved by rout of host,   *mob*
    No giant strong for all his boast,
    Of strength and power though have they most
        Dispute not this.

17. Strong horse is thing: but weak again,[348]
    That man by him might safe remain,

---

[347] Israel is called God's elect (Isaiah 45. 4), and God's chosen are called elect in the New Testament (Matthew 24. 31, Romans 9. 11, 1 Peter 1), but election was a key concept for the Calvinist theology of predestination.

[348] Another verse that Parker has made cryptic; BCP has 'A horse is counted but a vain thing to save a man'.

> Both horse and man are all but vain.
>   Approve ye this.

18. Behold the Lord: hold'th eye full just,
    On fearful men which him do trust,
    With grace them guide he safely must.
        Disprove not this.

19. Their soul from death to rid them quite,
    In time of dearth to feed them right
    All painful stress he mak'th full light.
        Betroth ye this.   *pledge*

20. Our soul hath tarried quietly,
    For this our God assuredly,
    Our guide, our shield most trustily.
        Forsloth not this.   *neglect*

21. Our hearts in him will still rejoice,
    For his good name we trust the choice,
    And sing we will in joyful noice.   *noise*
        Repeat ye this.

22. Extend, O Lord, thy gentleness,
    As we in thee have trustiness,
    Thou art the Lord of righteousness.
        Forget not this.

Psalm 36[349]

The Argument.

> *Here have ye painted before your eyes twain*   *two*
> *The restless wit of the fell wicked wight,*   *savage, creature*
> *How he careth and cark'th for his lither gain,*   *worries, wicked*
> *How he flot'th aloft in high power and might,*
> *And set'th God and his hallows all in despight;*   *scorn*
> *Whose cursed steps the just mak'th his orison,*   *prayer*
> *In life not to tread to his confusion.*

Dixit injustus.   [The unjust said]

1. Musing upon the variable business,
   That this troubly world haunt'th by sea and land,[350]   *tempestuous*

---

[349] This is the second of three versions of Psalm 36 done by Parker, each in a different metre.
[350] Parker's opening resembles a courtly complaint in the mode of Wyatt or Surrey more

My heart giveth me that sin and wickedness   *shows*
Suggest'th to the wicked that he may stand
5   Without any fear, safely of God's hand,
For no fear of him is in all his sight;
Of God's law he is bereaved the shining light.[351]   *bereft of*

2. Me fell to mind that he wonted thus to go,   *was accustomed*
    To flatter aye himself in his own sight,   *always*
10   For sin, the venom, did enchant him so,
    That in it he has his whole delight,
    And think'th in heart that all is aright;
    But God will spy out his sin abominable,
    Though to the world it hath visor commendable.   *mask*

15 3. Busily in mind I gan to revolve   *began, consider*
    His words unrighteous and craftily laid,
    All truth and justice of God to dissolve,
    But mere deceit in hypocrisy weighed
    And would not be controlled of that he said;
20   To learn of any man he did disdain,
    How the very right way he might attain.

4. I noted eke so by night what he thought,   *also*
    When God's men usen: to recount their trespass,   *used*
    But his head in his bed all mischief sought,
25   Imagining all goodness to deface,   *erase*
    To banish all truth and that to disgrace;
    In no godly way set was his busy brain,
    For all wicked ways he took for his gain.

5. The wicked, thus heaping his sin on high,
30   Where by desert he might be forsake: *deservedly, forsaken*
    How marvellous, O Lord, is then thy mercy,
    That from this world thy care thou dost not take;
    High up to heaven and clouds his course doth it make,
    All men to feed, both good and eke the bad;
35   Such faithfulness ever thy promise have had.

than a biblical Psalm, but the contents are essentially the same though expanded. Lines 4 to 5 are similar in language to Wyatt's 'Stand whoso list upon the slipper top', though exactly opposite in meaning, God securing the Psalmist from the fall feared by the courtier.

[351] Parker's stanza, seven lines of iambic pentameter rhymed *ababbcc*, was used famously by Chaucer in *Troilus and Cressida* and *The Parliament of Fowls*, but also in Wyatt's 'They flee from me' and Thomas Sackville's Induction to *The Mirror for Magistrates* (1563). As a metrical Psalm stanza, it is highly unusual, though it is used later by Mary Sidney Herbert, Countess of Pembroke, for Psalms 51 and 63.

6. Thy providence, O God, most marvellous,
   To all men mortal is inscrutable;
   More stable and high than mountains hideous,
   More deep than sea bottomless, unsearchable,
40 Be thy secret judgements insuperable; — *unsurpassable*
   For not man only of thy power doth taste, — *alone*
   But brute beasts of thee also hath their repast.

7. Man might muse much, O God, this to expend,
   But what earthly man could this matter tell,
45 How thou by thy hand dost all things defend,
   In what bounty thy mercy doth excel,
   How profound eke thou art in thy counsel;
   Well Adam's children may well in thee trust,[352]
   Under thy good wings to be shadowed just.

50 8. Who will thy blessèd word trust in faith sure,
   They shall be fillèd with all plenteousness,
   For thy store house is full of all pleasure,
   For thou givest them to taste of thy Sprite's goodness, — *Spirit's*
   Whose sweet wells they shall drink by thy largess, — *generosity*
55 From whose bellies shall lively water spring, — *life-giving*
   Others to refresh to thy glorifying.

9. For with thee only be these wells of life;
   Of frail men spring but puddles of mire,
   From whom sourdeth error and crooked strife; — *arises*
60 In thee only is that we can require,
   Both light, truth, and life to fill our desire;
   For in thy light truly, light must we see,
   Or else in all darkness wrappèd shall we dee. — *die*

10. Thy gentle goodness, O Lord, impart
65 To such as faithfully thy word do keep,
   Who know thee both wise and merciful in heart,
   That from day to day they may thy face seek;
   For they to thee bear aright their hearts meek, — *rightly*
   Thy righteousness they know, and thy judgements,
70 Thy holy word and eke thy commandments.

11. Since then the meek of heart be so at ease,
    And proud be out of favour all exiled:

---

[352] The Psalm has simply 'children of men' (BCP), but Parker's insertion of Adam is justified, since 'men' in the Hebrew is actually *adam* (in Genesis, the wordplay depends upon Adam being named after what he is, *adamah* or 'earth').

Keep me, O Lord, from pride, their foul disease,
For they have both thee and thy word reviled;
75 Let not my foot be in their steps beguiled,
Keep away from my soul their violence,
That they lay no hand upon my patience.

12. Thus, deep musing with myself in a trance,
Calling to mind the ends of good and bad:
80 Though they twain here lead a life in distance,
How the bad for his mirth shall once be sad,   *i.e. bad man*
And the good for their woe shall once be glad,
How the nought shall be cast on the worse hand,[353]   *worthless*
Then deemed I in fine, that truth shall sure stand.   *in the end*

Psalm 110

The Argument.

> *Though David's reign: be somewhat meant,*
> *Yet Christ is chief: here prophesied,*[354]   *head*
> *Who was both King: in regiment,*
> *And Priest in death: then after stied,*   *ascended*
> *To heaven to sit: as Priest and King,*
> *His friends to save: his foes to wring*
> *With death the sting.*

Dixit dominus domino.   [The Lord said to [my] Lord]

1. The Lord most high: the Father thus,
Did say to Christ: my Lord his Son,
Set thou in power: most glorious,
On my right hand: above the sun,
5 Until I make: thy foes even all,
Thy low footstool: to thee to fall
    As subject's thrall.[355]   *captive*

2. The Lord shall send: from Zion place,
Of thy great power: imperial,
10 The royal rod: and princely mace,
Whence grace shall spring: original,

---

[353] Seemingly a metaphor drawn from cards.
[354] With bold square brackets to the right, Parker links the rhyming second and fourth lines of each stanza, though none of the other rhymes.
[355] Another original stanza, unusual for metrical Psalms: six tetrameter lines, rhymed *ababcc*, followed by a short dimeter with a final *c* rhyme.

>   Yea, God shall say: thou God up rise,
>   To reign amidst: thine enemies,
>   In princely wise.   *manner*
>
> 15 3. The people glad: in heart's delight,
>   Shall offer gifts: in worship free,
>   As conquest day: of thy great might,
>   In shining show of sanctity,
>   For why the dew: of thy sweet birth,   *because*
> 20   As morn new sprung: drop'th joyful mirth,
>   So seen on earth.
>
>   4. The Lord did swear: and fast decreed,
>   He will his word: no time repent:
>   Which said thou art: a priest indeed,
> 25   A kingly priest: aye, permanent,   *forever*
>   Of order named: Melchizedek,
>   Whom peace and right doth jointly deck,
>   As God's elect.[356]
>
>   5. The Lord as shield: keep'th right thy hand,
> 30   To make thy reign: invincible;
>   He shall subdue: by sea and land
>   All power adverse: most forcible;
>   He shall great kings: and caesars wound,
>   In day of wrath: all them confound   *defeat*
> 35   By fearful sound.
>
>   6. He judgement true: shall exercise,
>   As judge among: the gentile sect;[357]
>   All places he: shall full surprise,
>   With bodies dead: on earth project
> 40   Abroad he shall: in sunder smite,
>   The heads of realms: that him will spight,
>   Or scorn his might.
>
>   7. Though here exiled: he stray'th as bond,   *slave*
>   And shall in way: but water drink,
> 45   Of homely brook: as com'th to hand,
>   Pursued to death: and wished to sink.
>   Yet he for this: humility,
>   Shall lift his head: in dignity
>   Eternally.

[356] Another added reference to the Calvinist theology of predestination.
[357] In changing the 'heathen' to the 'gentile sect' Parker may be reflecting a (Christian) gentile perspective.

47. Thomas Bickley, *The Holy Bible Containing the Old Testament and the New* [The Bishops' Bible] (1568)

[The Bishops' Bible was conceived and overseen by Archbishop Matthew Parker (see 46), intended to provide a new, improved translation of the Bible for use in churches, and one that eschewed the more radical notes of the Geneva Bible. Eleven bishops and three non-clerical scholars comprised the team of translators, though in fact much of the work was done by Parker himself, working from the base text of the Great Bible. Parker also wrote introductions to many books, including the Psalms. The Bishops' Bible was the version read in most churches until it was supplanted by the King James Bible after 1611, but the Geneva Bible remained by far the most popular outside of church. The Bishops' translation has never achieved the respect of either the Geneva or the KJV, and the Hebraist Hugh Broughton (1549–1612) went so far as to say it was as full of lies as the Koran. A new edition with a revised New Testament was printed in 1572 (STC 2107), but the Old Testament remained the same; curiously, though, the Great Bible translation of the Psalms was printed alongside the Bishops' ones. Some scholars have suggested this reflected Parker's own misgivings about his translation, which seems to have been the work of his chaplain, Thomas Bickley, later Bishop of Chichester (c. 1518–1596). This may further explain why, from 1573, the BCP Psalms were substituted for the Bishops' versions of 1568, so that the latter appear in only three editions of the Bible. Bickley's initials, T. B., appear at the end of the book of Psalms. He studied at Magdalene College, Oxford, and became a royal chaplain to Edward VI, before being expelled on the accession of Queen Mary. He went into exile, studying theology in Paris and Orléans, but returned to England on the accession of Elizabeth. He had more radical leanings than Parker, but remained loyal to his superior's policies. The Psalm translations here show few substantive differences from Coverdale's BCP Psalms, occasionally changing word order or expanding without adding to the sense, almost as if the goal was to change only enough to justify calling it a new translation. See Daniell, *Bible in English*; David Norton, *The King James Bible: A Short History from Tyndale to Today* (Cambridge: Cambridge University Press, 2011); David J. Crankshaw and Alexandra Gillespie (Parker), *ODNB*.]

Psalm 23

David resembling° God to a shepherd and himself to a sheep, declareth that all commodities, plenty, quietness, and prosperity, ensueth them that be fully persuaded of God's providence: for God feedeth, nourisheth, defendeth, and governeth those that put their whole trust in him after a more ample sort than any shepherd doth his sheep.

A Psalm of David.

1. God is my shepherd,[358] therefore I can lack nothing: he will cause me to repose myself in pasture full of grass, and he will lead me unto calm waters.
2. He will convert my soul: he will bring me forth into the paths of righteousness for his name sake.
3. Yea, though I walk through the valley of the shadow of death, I will fear no evil: for thou art with me, thy rod and thy staff be the things that do comfort me.
4. Thou wilt prepare a table before me in the presence of mine adversaries: thou hast anointed my head with oil, and my cup shall be brim full.
5. Truly, felicity and mercy shall follow me all the days of my life: and I will dwell in the house of God for a long time.[359]

Psalm 59

David uttereth how he was affected at such time as wait was laid for to slay him.[360] He declareth what prayers he made against the unreasonableness of his adversaries, how greatly he trusted in God, having his mind quiet and ready to praise God his refuge and succour at all times.

To the chief° musician, destroy not, a golden Psalm of David, when Saul sent, and they did watch the house to kill him.

1. Deliver me from mine enemies, O Lord:[361] defend me from them that rise up against me.
2. Deliver me from the workers of iniquity: and save me from the bloodthirsty men.
3. For lo, they lie in wait for my soul: men of power are gathered together against me, who have committed no wickedness nor fault, O God.
4. When no fault is done, they run and set themselves in order: arise to meet me and behold.
5. And thou, O God, Lord of hosts, Lord of Israel: awake to visit all heathen, and be not merciful unto all them that offend of malice. Selah.

---

[358] As Herbert Marks points out, one sign of the inadequacy of the Bishops' translator of Psalms, whether Bickley or someone else, is that he confuses the Hebrew names of God. Both verse 1 and verse 5 have YHWH, traditionally rendered 'LORD' in English (Jews substituting 'Adonai' for the unspeakable name, when it must be spoken). 'God' is the traditional rendering of *'elohim*. *The English Bible, King James Version: The Old Testament*, ed. by Marks, vol. 1 (New York: WW Norton & Co., 2012), p. 2235.

[359] a long time] Coverdale (BCP) and the KJV have 'forever', Geneva 'a long season'. The Hebrew idiom means literally 'length of days', but since dwelling in the house of God signifies being in heaven after death, eternity is surely implied.

[360] wait was laid] someone lay in wait.

[361] See note 358. The Hebrew in this verse has *'elohim*, which should be translated 'God'.

6. They go to and fro at evening: they bark like a dog, and run about through the city.
7. Behold, they speak with their mouth, swords are in their lips: for, say they, who doth hear us?
8. But thou, O God, wilt have them in derision: thou wilt laugh all heathen to scorn.
9. I will reserve his strength for thee: for thou, O Lord, art my refuge.
10. My merciful Lord will prevent° me: the Lord will let me see my desire upon mine enemies.
11. Slay them not, lest my people forget it: but in thy stoutness° scatter them like vagabonds, and put them down, O God, our defence.[362]
12. The words of their lips be the sin of their mouth: O let them be taken in their pride, for they speak nothing but curses and lies.
13. Consume them in thy wrath, consume them that nothing of them remain: and let them know that it is the Lord that ruleth in Jacob, and unto the ends of the world. Selah.
14. And let them gad° up and down at evening: let them bark like a dog, and go about the city.
15. Let them run here and there for meat°: and go to bed if they be not satisfied.[363]
16. As for me, I will sing of thy power, and will praise thy loving kindness betimes° in the morning: for thou hast been my defence and refuge in the day of my trouble.
17. Unto thee, O my strength, will I sing Psalms: for thou, O Lord, art my refuge, and my merciful Lord.

Psalm 92

It seemeth that the prophet made this Psalm to be sung unto the people upon the Sabbath day, for to stir them up the better to know God, and to praise God in his works. He commendeth the setting forth of God's praise in musical instruments. He rejoiceth much and wondereth at God's works. But the fool understandeth not that the wicked, be they never so fortunate, shall come to a wretched end, for the wicked shall be destroyed, and the godly shall prosper. The greatest felicity that the just hath in this life, is to be planted in the house of God, there continually for to praise him.

---

[362] defence] The Hebrew here is more concrete, as reflected in the KJV, 'shield'.
[363] go to bed] The translator has mistaken the form of the verb here, which when in Qal perfect form can mean lodge or spend the night (as II Samuel 12. 16). In its Niphal imperfect form, however, it means grumble or murmur (KJV 'grudge').

A Psalm, the song for the Sabbath day.

1. It is a good thing to confess unto God:[364] and to sing Psalms unto thy name, O thou most highest.
2. To set forth in words thy loving kindness early in the morning: and thy truth in the night season.°
3. Upon an instrument of ten strings, and upon the lute: upon the harp with a solemn sound.
4. For thou, God, hast made me glad through thy works: I do rejoice in the works of thy hands.
5. O God, how glorious are thy works? thy thoughts are very deep.
6. An unwise man doth not consider this: and a fool doth not understand it.
7. Whereas the ungodly do bud up green as the grass, and whereas all workers of iniquity do flourish: that they, notwithstanding, shall be destroyed for ever and ever.
8. But thou, O God: art the most highest for evermore.
9. For lo, thine enemies, O God, lo, thine enemies shall perish: and all the workers of wickedness shall be destroyed.
10. But my horn[365] shall be exalted like the horn of an unicorn:[366] for I am anointed with excellent oil.
11. And mine eye shall see those that lie in wait for me: mine ear shall hear the malicious persons that rise up against me.
12. The righteous shall flourish like a palm tree: and shall spread abroad like a cedar in Libanus.°
13. Such as be planted in the house of God: shall flourish in the courts of our Lord.
14. They shall still bring forth fruit in their age: they shall be fat and flourishing.
15. For to set forth in words that God is upright: he is my rock, and no iniquity is in him.

Psalm 141

David humbly desireth God that his prayer may be so acceptable unto him, as if he had made a sacrifice in the temple. He prayeth God to preserve him in word and deed from all evil, that he fall into no snare of his enemies: for he had rather be reproved of the godly, then to be honoured of the wicked.

---

[364] See note 358, p. 244.
[365] horn] See note 32, p. 85.
[366] unicorn] See note 23, p. 79.

A Psalm of David.

1. O God,[367] I call upon thee, haste thee unto me: give ear unto my voice whilst I cry unto thee.
2. Let my prayer be directed before thy face as an incense: let the lifting up of mine hands be an evening sacrifice.
3. Set a watch, O God, before my mouth: and keep° the door of my lips.
4. Incline not mine heart to any evil thing, whereby I might commit any ungodly act with men that be workers of iniquity: and let me not eat of their delicates.°
5. I wish that the righteous would smite me and reprove me: for it is loving kindness.
6. But let not precious balms break mine head: for as yet even my prayer is against their wickedness.
7. Let their judges be thrust down headlong from a rock: then they will hear my words, for they be sweet.
8. Our bones lie scattered upon the grave's mouth: like as when one breaketh and heweth wood upon the earth.
9. For mine eyes look unto thee, O God, the Lord: in thee is my trust, cast not my soul out of me.
10. Keep me from the snare which they have laid forth for me: and from the traps of them that be workers of iniquity.
11. Let the ungodly fall together into their own nets: but let me in the mean season always escape them.[368]

48. Roger Edwardes, *A Book of Very Godly Psalms and Prayers, Dedicated to the Lady Lettice Viscountess of Hereford* (1570)

[Roger Edwardes (birth and death dates unknown) was Welsh, a relative of the elder William Herbert, and seems to have been a soldier as well as a spy, and his writings indicate he was also well educated. During Queen Mary's reign, Edwardes lived in exile in Paris, where he spied on the English for the French and the French for the English. Before that he had served in the household of Edward Seymour, Duke of Somerset, where he made the acquaintance of William Cecil. After Somerset's fall, Edwardes took a position with John Dudley, Duke of Northumberland. In 1569, Edwardes wrote a highly influential treatise on the succession question, '*Castra Regia*', supporting Elizabeth's right to refuse to choose an heir. Through Cecil, a presentation copy was produced and given to Queen Elizabeth, who apparently approved it highly. Though never printed, the treatise circulated widely, and was still being copied in the seventeenth and

---

[367] See note 358, p. 244.
[368] in the mean season] in the meantime.

eighteenth centuries. Edwardes fought against the Northern Rebellion under the command of Walter Devereux, Earl of Essex. This experience, along with the growing sense of Catholic conspiracy engendered by the pope's excommunication of Elizabeth (1570) and the Ridolfi Plot (1571) to replace her with Mary, Queen of Scots, led Edwardes to revise his political views both in later versions of 'Castra Regia' and in the 1576 treatise 'Cista Pacis Anglie', which still defended the royal prerogative but strongly urged the establishment of succession. This argument was held to violate the Treason Statute of 1570, and Edwardes was arrested and confined to the Tower for a year. This treatise too seems to have circulated in multiple copies. The dedicatee of Edwardes' Psalms was the wife of the Earl of Essex. Lady Lettice, Viscountess of Hereford, was, as Lettice Knollys, gentlewoman of the Privy Chamber to Elizabeth I. She married Walter Devereux, second Viscount Hereford (later the Earl of Essex) in 1560. Their children were Robert, second Earl of Essex and the favourite of the queen, and Penelope, later Lady Rich, the subject of Sir Philip Sidney's *Astrophil and Stella*. After Essex's death, the Countess of Essex married Robert Dudley, Earl of Leicester. By his own account, Edwardes, a vassal of the viscount's, composed his Psalms during a period of illness and confinement, perhaps some time during the Rebellion. Later in life, Edwardes experienced a religious turning and became preoccupied with the conversion of the Jews. His last treatise, 'Collections of the Prophets' (1580), attracted the interest of John Dee, as well as some of Elizabeth's councillors. A note in Dee's diary in 1591 is the last reference to Edwardes. Edwardes's Psalms, which are not numbered, are really collage Psalms. In the one below, which resonates powerfully with the context of the Rebellion, Edwardes begins with verse 8 of Psalm 80 and then returns to verses 1 to 7 after verse 16 (verses 17 and 18 are omitted). He then appends Psalm 69 verse 25, Psalm 79 verse 12, Psalm 83 verses 13 to 18, and Psalm 79 verse 13. See Victoria Smith, 'The Elizabethan Succession Question in Roger Edwardes's "Castra Regia" (1569) and "Cista Pacis Anglie" (1576)', *Historical Research*, 87.238 (2014), 633–54.]

Psalms

Thou broughtest a vine out of Egypt, thou threwest out the heathen, O Lord, and didst plant it in their habitations where taking root it prospered, and filled all the land.
The hills were covered with the shadow thereof, and the boughs of it were as
5   the cedar trees.
She stretched out her branches into the sea, and her sprays into the river.
Plenteous was her fruit; thy people drank of her grapes, and were refreshed.
Thou thyself tookst charge thereof, O Lord: with thine own hands didst thou fence it round about, and seemest to take high pleasure therein.
10 How is it then come to pass, that her hedges are all broken, her friths° are trodden down, her grapes be common to the spoilers°?

Yea, the wild boar doth root it up, and the wild beasts of the field devour it.

Turn thee again, O Lord God of hosts, look down and see thy vineyard, which thou thyself with thy right hand hadst planted, making the branches of it beautiful and strong for thine own pleasure, and for the plentiful commodity of thy servants.

It is cut down and burnt, the destroyers have spoiled it, and laid it waste in despite° of thee, O Lord. Behold, O God, where once thou tookest pleasure, and where thy people were refreshed, it is now mored up,[369] by the swine of the adversaries, and is become the harbour of wolves and foxes.

Hear, O thou shepherd of Israel, thou that leadest Joseph like a sheep, thou that sittest on the cherubins: stir up thy strength, O Lord, and help thy servants: destroy these men of malice.

O Lord, how long wilt thou be angry? shall thy jealousy burn like fire forever? Turn again, O God, and show us the light of thy countenance, and we shall be whole.

O remember not our sins, but have mercy upon us: and that soon, lest we fall into misery.

Help us, O Lord, for the glory of thy name: O our Saviour deliver us, be merciful to our sins for thy name's sake.

O let the sorrowful sighings of thy prisoners come before thee: according to the greatness of thy power and mercy, preserve thou those, O God, that are appointed to die.

O Lord, how long wilt thou be angry with thy servants: how long wilt thou feed them with the bread of sorrow, and give them plenteousness of tears to drink?

Thou hast made them a very strife unto their neighbours: and their enemies laugh them to scorn.

Turn thee again, O Lord God of hosts, show us the light of thy countenance, and we shall be whole.

Pour out thine indignation upon the heathen, and upon them that fear not thy name, for they have devoured thy servants, and laid waste thy dwelling place.

And for the blasphemy wherewith they have reviled thy majesty, reward thou them, O Lord, sevenfold in their bosoms.

O my God, destroy thine enemies, make them like unto a wheel, like dust before the wind, and like dry straw in the flame.

Let thy wrath be kindled against them, O Lord, like the fire that burneth up the wood, and as the flame that consumeth the mountains.

Persecute them with thy tempest, tear them asunder with thy thunderbolts, destroy them with thy storms, make them to melt in desperation, for fear of thy majesty, O God most high.

Let them be confounded° and vexed ever, more and more, let them be

---

[369] mored up] uprooted.

ashamed, and known, that thou whose name is Jehova, are th'only most high God of power and majesty over all.

55   Then we that be thy people and the sheep of thy pasture, shall rejoice and be glad, praising thy name, O Lord, with melody and thanksgiving, from generation to generation, world without end. Amen.

49. Arthur Golding, *The Psalms of David and Others. With M. John Calvin's Commentaries* (1571)

[Arthur Golding (1535/6–1606) was one of the most notable and prolific Elizabethan translators, whose prose translations, according to one estimate, amount to five and a half million words, supporting the claim of one scholar that Golding was important in shaping late sixteenth-century English prose. Golding was educated at Jesus College, Oxford. His half-sister Margery married John de Vere, sixteenth Earl of Oxford, and Golding's brother Henry became steward of the Oxford household. Golding himself eventually came to work for Oxford's son and heir after the older earl's death, when William Cecil took on the young earl as his ward. Golding's many translations include both religious and secular classical works. He is most famous today as the translator of Ovid's *Metamorphoses* (1567), his translation being one of Shakespeare's favourite books, and his translation of Caesar's *De bello Gallico* was the first (complete) in English. As a translator of religious writing, Golding was responsible for rendering many of Calvin's most important sermons into English, including those on Galatians, Ephesians, Job, and Deuteronomy, as well as the Psalms. Calvin's commentaries on the Psalms include a Latin version of the Psalms, on which Golding's original English translation seems to be based. When Calvin quotes from the Psalms within his commentary, Golding encloses his English translation within brackets to highlight the fact that they are not precisely the words Calvin quoted. Golding dedicated this translation to Edward de Vere, the seventeenth Earl of Oxford and Golding's nephew. See Louis T. Golding, *An Elizabethan Puritan* (New York: R. R. Smith, 1937); James Wortham, 'Arthur Golding and the Translation of Prose', *Huntington Library Quarterly*, 12.4 (1949), 339–67; John Considine, *ODNB*.]

Psalm 18[370]

To the chief° chanter, of David the servant of the Lord, which rehearsed° the words of this song unto the Lord, in the day that the Lord delivered him from the hand of all his enemies, and from the hand of Saul.

---

[370] Psalm 18 is virtually identical to the Psalm David sings in II Samuel 22. The only significant difference is that what Golding designates as verse 2 is missing in the version in Samuel.

2. And he said, I will love thee, O Lord, my strength
3. The Lord is my rock, my fortress, and my deliverer: my God, my strength, I will trust in him: my shield, the horn of my welfare,[371] and my refuge.
4. I will call upon the praised Lord, and I shall be saved from mine enemies.
5. The cords of death had compassed° me about, the watershots° of wickedness had made me afraid.
6. The cords of the grave had compassed me about, the snares of death had overtaken me.
7. In my distress I called upon the Lord, and I cried unto my God: and he hath heard my voice out of his temple, and my cry before him came unto his ears.
8. Then the earth moved itself and quaked, and the foundations of the mountains shook and stirred themselves, because he was wroth.°
9. There went up a smoke into his nostrils, and the fire consumed which went out of his mouth: coals were kindled at it.[372]
10. And he bowed° the heavens and came down: and there was darkness under his feet.
11. And he rode upon cherub, and flew: and was carried upon the wings of the wind.
12. He made darkness his secret place, round about him was his tent, darksomeness of water and the clouds of heaven.
13. At the brightness of his presence his clouds passed away: hailstones and coals of fire.
14. And the Lord thundered in the heavens, and the highest uttered his voice, hailstones and coals of fire.
15. And he sent out his arrows, and scattered them: and he multiplied lightnings, and astonished them.
16. The headsprings of the waters were seen, and the foundations of the round world were discovered at thy rebuking, O Lord, at the blast of the breath of thy nostrils.
17. He sent down from aloft, and took me up: he led me out of many waters.
18. He delivered me from my strong enemy, and from mine adversary: because they were too strong for me.
19. They had prevented° me in the day of my trouble: and the Lord was my stay.°

---

[371] horn] In the Bible a sign of power, based on the animal referenced in Deuteronomy 33. 17, Psalm 92. 10, etc., possibly a wild ox, though sometimes translated as a unicorn.
[372] In his commentary on this verse, Calvin notes that the Hebrew 'signifieth properly a nose or nostrils', but that some translate this 'smoke from his wrath', since 'now and then it is taken metaphorically for irefulness'. Calvin prefers the concreteness of the Hebrew, however, since 'David compareth the mists and steams, wherewithal the air is darkened, to the thick smoke which is puffed out at the nostrils of an angry man. And hereby is known the better how dreadful is the wrath of God, when he cloudeth the air with his blast'.

20. And he brought me forth at large: he delivered me because he had a favour unto me.
21. The Lord hath rewarded me after my righteousness, according to the cleanness of my hands hath he recompensed me.
22. Because I have kept the ways of the Lord, and have not wickedly shrunk from my God.
23. Because all his judgements are before me, and I have not cast his commandments from me.
24. And I have been sound° with him, and have kept myself from mine own wickedness.
25. And the Lord hath rewarded me according to my righteousness, and according to the cleanness of my hands before his eyes.
26. With the meek thou wilt deal meekly, and with the sound thou wilt deal soundly.
27. With the pure thou wilt be pure, and with the froward° thou wilt deal forwardly.
28. For thou wilt save the folk that be brought low, and cast down the eyes of the proud.
29. For thou shalt light my candle, O Lord: my God shall lighten my darkness.
30. For in thee shall I break through the wedge of a battle, and in my God shall I leap over a wall.
31. The way of God is perfect, the word of the Lord is tried° in the fire, he is a shield to all that trust in him.
32. For who is God but the Lord? And who is strong but our God?
33. It is God that hath girded° me with strength, and hath made my way perfect.
34. Making my feet like hind's feet,[373] and it is he that hath set me upon my high places.
35. Teaching my hands to fight: and mine arms shall break a bow of steel.
36. And thou hast given me the shield of safeguard, and thy right hand hath shored me up, and thy mercifulness hath increased me.
37. Thou hast enlarged my paces under me:[374] and mine ankles have not staggered.
38. I will pursue mine enemies and overtake them: and I will not return till I have consumed them.
39. I have smitten them, and they could not rise: they are fallen under my feet.
40. And thou hast girded me with strength unto battle: thou hast bowed° down mine enemies under me.
41. And thou hast given me the neck of mine enemies: and thou hast destroyed those that hate me.
42. They shall cry out, and there shall be none to save them: even unto the Lord, but he shall not answer them.

---

[373] hind's] deer's (i.e. made his feet able to be secure on the high places).
[374] BCP 'Thou shalt make room enough under me for me to go'.

43. And I shall grind them as small as the dust before the wind: as the mire in the streets shall I tread them under foot.
44. Thou shalt deliver me from the strivings of the people: thou shalt make me the head of the heathen. A people whom I have not known, shall serve me.
45. As soon as they hear, they shall obey me: the children of the strangers shall lie unto me.
46. The children of the strangers shall shrink away, and tremble in their privy° chambers.
47. Let the Lord live, and blessed be my strength, and the God of my welfare be exalted.
48. It is God that giveth me power to avenge me, and subdueth the people under me.
49. My deliverer from mine enemies, thou hast set me up even from them that have risen up against me: thou hast rid me from the cruel man.
50. Therefore will I praise thee, O Lord, among the nations, and sing unto thy name.
51. He worketh mightily the welfare of his king, and performeth mercy to David his anointed, and to his seed° forever.

Psalm 63

A song of David's, when he was in the wilderness of Judah.

2. Thou, O God, art my God, I will seek thee early: my soul hath thirsted after thee, my flesh hath hungered after thee in a barren and thirsty land without waters.
3. So have I beheld thee in thy sanctuary, to see thy strength and thy glory.
4. For thy loving kindness is better than life: my lips shall praise thee.
5. So will I praise thee in my life: in thy name will I lift up my hands.
6. My soul shall be satisfied as with marrow and fatness, and my mouth shall praise thee with lips of joyfulness.
7. Surely, I will be mindful of thee upon my bed: I will think upon thee when I lie awake.
8. For thou hast been my help, and I shall rejoice under the shadow of thy wings.
9. My soul hath raughted[375] after thee: thy right hand shall hold me up.
10. And they in seeking to destroy my soul, shall go into the lowest parts of the earth.

---

[375] raughted] reached (*OED* describes the word as rare, and two of three citations are from Golding's translations). Calvin writes: 'Forasmuch as the word [*Dabeca*] ofttimes signifieth to [raught after, or to follow after] specially when it is construed with the preposition [*Acar:*] it will agree no less to be translated thus [My soul or hie him a pace after thee.] But if the word [cleave] like any man better: yet both the ways David meaneth that his heart shall always with steady perseverance be set fast upon God' (square brackets in the original).

11. They shall cast him down upon the edge of the sword, they shall be the portion of foxes.[376]
12. But the kings shall rejoice in God: and whosoever sweareth by him shall be joyful: for the mouth of them that speak lies shall be stopped.

Psalm 78[377]

An instruction of Asaph. Hear my law, O my people, incline your ears to the words of my mouth.
2. I will open my mouth in a parable. I will utter riddles from of old time.
3. Which we have heard and known, and which our fathers have declared unto us.
4. We will not hide them from their children in the generation to come, showing forth the praises of the Lord, and his mighty power, and his wondrous work which he hath done.
5. He stablished° a covenant in Jacob, and set a law in Israel, for he hath commanded our fathers, that they should make the same known to their children.
6. That their prosperity may know it, and that the children which shall be born of them may rise up and show it unto their children.
7. That they may put their trust in God, and not forget the works of God, and that they may keep his commandments.
8. And that they be not as their fathers, a backsliding and provoking generation, a generation that hath not set their heart aright,° and whose spirit was not faithful to Godward.[378]
9. The children of Ephraim being armed and shooting in bows, turned back in the day of battle.
10. They kept not the covenant of God, and refused to walk in his law.
11. And they forgot his works, and the wonderful things that he hath showed them.
12. He wrought wonderfully in the sight of their fathers, in the land of Egypt, in the field of Zoan.
13. He cut the sea and brought them through, and made the waters to stand as a bank.
14. And he led them forth in a cloud by daytime, and all the night-time in the brightness of fire.

---

[376] foxes] or perhaps jackals. The identification of biblical animals, even the real as opposed to mythical ones, is often unclear.
[377] According to the headnote, this Psalm has 'two chief points': first, 'how God adopted himself a Church out of the seed of Abraham', and second, God's chastising of the Jews for their backsliding.
[378] to Godward] toward God.

15. He clave° the rocks in the wilderness, and made them to drink in great depths.
16. And he brought streams out of the rock, and made the waters to gush out like rivers.
17. Yet continued they still to sin against him, to provoke the most high in the wilderness.
18. And they tempted God in their heart to require meat° for their soul.
19. And they spake against God, saying: Can God prepare a table in the wilderness?
20. Behold he strake° the rock, and the waters gushed out, and the streams overflowed. Can he give bread also? Or prepare flesh for his people?
21. Therefore the Lord heard it, and was angry, and the fire was kindled in Jacob, and also wrath came upon Israel.
22. Because they believed not in God, and trusted not in his help.
23. But he had commanded the clouds above, and opened the doors of heaven.
24. And had rained down manna upon them to eat,[379] and given them of the wheat of heaven.
25. Man had eaten the bread of the mighties, he had sent them meat, even their fill.
26. He made the east wind to go forth in the heavens, and through his power he raised up the south wind.
27. And he rained flesh upon them as it had been dust, and feathered fowls as it had been the sand of the seas.
28. And made it to light in the midst of his camp, round about even into his tents.
29. And they did eat, and were thoroughly filled, and he gave them their longing.
30. They were not weaned from their desire: as yet the meat was in the mouths of them.
31. When the wrath of God came upon them, and slew the fat ones of them, and smote down the chosen of Israel.
32. For all this they sinned still and believed not his wondrous works.
33. And he consumed° their days in vanity,° and their years in haste.
34. When he slew them, they sought him: they returned and made haste unto God early.
35. And they remembered that God was their rock, and that the high God was their deliverer.
36. And they flattered him with their mouth, and dissembled with him with their tongue.
37. But their heart was not right before him, neither were they faithful in his covenant.

---

[379] manna] Miraculous food from Exodus 16.

38. And he of his mercy cleansed their iniquity, and destroyed them not: and he multiplied to turn away his anger, and did not stir up all his wrath.
39. And he remembered that they were but flesh: a spirit that passeth and cometh not again.
40. How oft did they provoke him in the desert, and grieve him in the wilderness?
41. And they went to it again, and tempted God, and set bounds about the holy one of Israel.
42. They remembered not his hand in the day that he delivered them from the oppressor.
43. When he set his signs in Egypt, and his wonders in the field of Zoan.
44. When he turned their rivers into blood, and their streams that they could not drink.
45. He sent a swarm among them, which devoured them, and the frog which destroyed them.
46. And he gave their fruits unto the caterpillar, and their labour to the grasshopper.
47. And he killed their vines with hail, and their wild fig-trees with the hailstone.
48. And he gave their cattle° to the hail, and their flocks to the thunderbolts.
49. He cast upon them the fierceness of his displeasure, even anger, wrathfulness, and vexation, and set evil angels among them.
50. He made a way to his anger: he spared not their soul from death, and he shut up[380] their cattle unto the plague.
51. And he smote all the firstborn in Egypt, the beginning[381] of strength in the tents of Cham.[382]
52. And he made his people to go out like sheep, and led them in the wilderness like a flock.
53. And he carried them forth in safety, and they were not afraid: and the sea covered their enemies.
54. And he brought them into the borders of his sanctuary, even to this hill which he hath purchased with his right hand.
55. And he drove out the heathen before them, and cast them into the lot of his inheritance: and made the children of Israel to dwell in their tents.
56. And they tempted and provoked the most high God, and kept not his testimonies.
57. And they turned back, and dealt falsely, as their fathers did: they started back like a deceitful bow.

---

[380] shut up] fenced in.
[381] beginning] The Hebrew can also mean 'chief' or 'first', but the phrase may be simply a restatement of 'firstborn'.
[382] Cham, or Ham, the cursed son of Noah, seems here to represent Egypt.

58. And they provoked him to anger with their high places: and stirred him to wrath with their graven° images.
59. God heard it and was wroth,° and abhorred Israel exceedingly.
60. And he forsook his habitation of Shiloh, the tabernacle° where he dwelt among men.
61. And he gave his strength into thraldom,° and his beauty into the hand of the adversary.
62. And he shut up his people into the sword, and was angry with his own inheritance.
63. The fire devoured his chosen, and his maidens were not praised.
64. His priests fell upon the sword, and his widows mourned not.
65. And the Lord awaked as one asleep, as a strong man that crieth out through wine.
66. And he smote his enemies behind, and put them to an endless shame.
67. And he refused the tent of Joseph, and chose not the tribe of Ephraim.
68. But he chose the tribe of Judah, the hill of Zion which he loved.
69. And he built up his sanctuary as the high places, as the earth which he hath stablished forever.
70. And he chose David his servant, and took him from the sheepfold.
71. Even from behind the ewes with young took he him to feed in Jacob his people, and in Israel his inheritance.
72. And he fed them in the singleness of his heart, and led them forth in the discretion of his hands.

Psalm 109

To the chief° chanter, a Psalm of David.

1. O God of my praise, hold not thy peace.
2. For the mouth of the wicked, and the mouth of deceit are opened upon me; they have spoken to me with the tongue of guile.
3. And they have compassed° me about with the words of hatred, and have fought against me without cause.
4. For my lovingness they have been against me: but I gave myself to prayer.
5. And they have rewarded me evil for good, and hatred for my lovingness.
6. Set thou a wicked man over him, and let the adversary stand at his right hand.
7. When he cometh in to be judged, let him go forth guilty, and let his prayer be turned into sin.
8. Let his days be few, and let another man take his charge.
9. Let his children be fatherless, and let his wife be a widow.
10. Let his children wander as vagabonds, and beg, and let them seek out their wasted places.

11. Let the extortioner entangle all that he hath: and let foreigners spoil his labour.
12. Let there be none to prolong mercy unto him: neither let there be any to pity his fatherless children.
13. Let his posterity be destroyed: and in the next generation let his very name be wiped out.
14. Let the iniquity of his father be called to remembrance before the Lord, and let not the sin of his mother be done away.
15. Let them be before the Lord alway,° and let him root out the remembrance of them from the earth.
16. Because he minded not to show mercy, but persecuted the miserable and poor man, and the sorrowful hearted, to slay him.
17. He loved cursedness, and it shall come upon him: he had no delight in blessedness, and therefore it shall be far from him.
18. And let him be clothed with cursedness as with a garment: and let it come as water into his bowels,° and as oil into his bones.
19. Let it be as a coat to cover him, and as the girdle that he always girded° himself withal.°
20. Let this be the work from God of them that be against me, and of such as speak evil against me.
21. And thou, O Lord my Lord, deal with me according to thy name: deliver me because thy mercy is good.
22. Because I am poor and needy: and my heart is wounded within me.
23. I walk forth as a shadow when it is going down: I am shaken off as a grasshopper.
24. My knees falter through fasting, and my flesh is dried up from the fatness.
25. Also I became a reproach unto them, when they see me they shake their head.
26. Help me, O Lord my God, save me according to thy mercifulness.
27. And they shall know that this is thy hand, and that thou, O Lord, hast done it.
28. They shall curse and thou shalt bless: when they rise up they shall be put to shame, but thy servant shall rejoice.
29. Mine adversaries shall be clothed with reproach, and they shall cover themselves with their own shame, as with a garment.
30. I will praise the Lord greatly with my mouth, and I will magnify him in the assembly of great men.
31. Because he standeth at the right hand of the poor, to save his life from condemnations.

Psalm 138

David's. I will praise thee with my whole heart, before the gods will I sing unto thee.

2. I will worship thee at the temple of thine holiness, and sing unto thy name because of thy mercy and truth, for thou hast magnified thy name above all things by thy word.
3. In the day that I called unto thee, then heardest thou me, and hast multiplied me[383] strength in my soul.
4. Let all kings of the earth praise thee, O Lord: for they have heard the words of thy mouth.
5. And let them sing in the ways of the Lord, because the glory of the Lord is great.
6. For the Lord is high, and yet he hath an eye to the lowly, and the most high will know them afar off.
7. If I walk in the midst of trouble, thou shalt quicken° me, thou shalt lay thine hand upon the anger of mine enemies, and thy right hand shall save me.
8. The Lord will reward upon me. Lord thy mercy endureth forever: thou wilt not forsake the works of thine hands.

50. Elizabeth Tyrwhit, *Morning and Evening Prayers, with Diverse Psalms, Hymns and Meditations* (1574)

[Elizabeth Tyrwhit (d. 1578), Lady Tyrwhit, was the daughter of Sir Goddard Oxenbridge and Anne (Fiennes), granddaughter of Richard, Lord Dacre of Herstmonceux. She married Sir Robert Tyrwhit in 1538 or 1539. Tyrwhit was a gentlewoman of the privy chamber at the court of Henry VIII and was close to Queen Katherine Parr (who was a cousin by marriage to Sir Robert Tyrwhit). Tyrwhit was zealous for reform, called by her husband 'half a Scripture woman'. Tyrwhit's *Morning and Evening Praiers* (1574) survives in a single copy, bound with the litany and Katherine Parr's *Prayers or Meditations*, in a copy which belonged to Queen Elizabeth I (to whom Tyrwhit was briefly governess). Tyrwhit's book was incorporated into Thomas Bentley's massive *Monument of Matrons*, but differently arranged and with substantially more material. Felch argues that this 1582 text may best reflect Tyrwhit's original, which was compressed and rearranged by the printers in 1574. Tyrwhit's paraphrase of Psalm 1 is the second Psalm in her 'Morning Prayer', and is actually a paraphrase of a translation of another paraphrase, based on but varying from Taverner's translation of Capito's paraphrase (see 11), converting the expository Psalm into a petitionary prayer. Tyrwhit also composed what Felch terms 'collage

---

[383] multiplied me] An example of the obsolete ethical dative, the apparently redundant pronoun emphasizing personal interest.

Psalms', which create a new 'Psalm' by rearranging verses from various biblical Psalms, as well as other books of the Bible. Felch points to Taverner-Capito's Psalm 77 and other Psalms, as well as a tiny 1555 Primer printed by Humphrey Toye as sources for Tyrwhit's 'First Psalm at Evening Prayer', but in fact much is also derived from the Psalms in the Book of Common Prayer, and Tyrwhit often adapts her sources to her needs. Only the second half of the 'Psalm' was included in 1574; the full text is from the second edition of Tyrwhit's *Morning and Evening Prayers* in Bentley. See *Elizabeth Tyrwhit's 'Morning and Evening Prayers'*, ed. by Felch; Patricia Brace, ODNB.]

Psalm 1

O Lord, suffer° me not to enter into the way of sinners with a mind to fulfil the desires and lusts of the flesh.
But whensoever through frailty of my corrupt nature I shall chance to run astray, then, O Lord, stay° me and pluck my foot back again.
5 Keep° me, that I sit not in the seat° of pestilent scorners, which cloaking their Pharisaical and devilish intents, condemn in other men thy verity° and gospel.[384]
O Lord, bring to pass that I may burn in the desire of thy law, that upon the advancement of the word, my mind may always be occupied, that I may evermore choose that which is most pleasant to thee, and hate that both in
10 myself and others, which to thee is displeasant.
Make, I pray thee, that I may be a tree planted by the sweet rivers of thy ghostly° waters, to the intent I may bring forth fruit to thy glory and to the profit of my neighbour, as often as thou shalt minister time and occasion thereunto.
Lest my leaves, which is my words and works, shall fade and fall away, but that
15 all things may prosper, whatsoever I shall do in thy name: assist me, I beseech thee.
And grant, O most merciful Father, that for Jesu Christ's sake, I may take root in the ground of life, lest with the ungodly like chaff and dust I be blown abroad with the most pernicious winds of this world, and grant that I may stand in the
20 assembly of the righteous, and that I may enter into judgement by thy mercy without punishment, and that I may escape everlasting damnation.
Glory be to the, etc.
As it was in the, etc.[385]

---

[384] This is obviously a highly Christianized paraphrase, given the anachronistic references to both the gospel and the Pharisees (and of course later Christ), since the Pharisees were founded only in the second Temple period after the Babylonian exile.
[385] 22–23] See note 309, p. 211.

The First Psalm at Evening Prayer

Bow down thine ear, O Lord, to my requests,[386] and suffer° me to exhibit my supplication up unto thee.[387] For behold, night and day I trace and hunt after thee by all means I can.[388] To thee only° early and late do I still call and cry for mercy, according as thou hast given me in commandment.[389]

For when I call to memory the time of my life evil dispent,° I quake to think upon thee, yea and my spirit faileth me, so sore am I afraid of thy judgements.[390]

Yet well pondering the process of thy grace and mercy promised me in Christ, I cease to despair, knowing that thou, O God, hast not forgotten thy gifts of grace, and that thy power to have compassion is not waxen° faint, but that both thou canst and wilt put back thy wrath most justly conceived against me for my sin.[391]

In full trust whereof, O Lord, I come unto thee, beseeching thee to hide my life with Christ within thee, and under the shadows of thy wings to defend me, that thy grace and covenant may be with me evermore.[392]

Turn not thy mercy from me, O Lord, nor bring me down to destruction as I have deserved: but show thy grace and favour unto me, that I may live, and (being exalted through thy righteousness) praise thy name most joyfully.[393]

Remember my corrupt nature, O Lord, how short my life is, and that thou madest not man for nothing. No man can deliver himself from death: no man can save his own soul from hell: thou only, O Lord, must do it, namely, to such as believe in thee.[394]

This life passeth as doth a dream, or grass in the field, which today is green, and tomorrow dry. If thou be displeased, then we be lost: if thou chafe, then we shrink for fear, for through sins we be dead unto thee; with whom a thousand years be but as one day, yea, as the least minute of an hour.[395]

---

[386] Psalm 86. 1 (BCP).
[387] Psalm 119. 170 (BCP).
[388] Virtually identical to Psalm 70. 1 in Taverner's Capito.
[389] Largely from Psalm 70. 2 in Taverner's Capito, apart from 'early and late', which was a not uncommon phrase in prayers and other works, as in the Elizabethan 'Homily on Prayer': 'Let us never faint, never slack, never give over, but let us daily and hourly, early and late, in season, and out of season, be occupied in godly meditations and prayers' (*The Second Tome of Homilies*, 1571).
[390] Largely from Psalm 70. 3 in Taverner's Capito.
[391] Based on Psalm 77. 7-10 in Taverner's Capito but considerably altered, and the reference to Christ added.
[392] Adapted from Psalm 61. 4 (BCP).
[393] No clear source, though elements are familiar from some various Psalms: 103. 4 ('Who saveth thy life from destruction'), 25. 15 ('Turn thee unto me, and have mercy upon me'), 75. 12 ('the horns of the righteous shall be exalted'), all BCP.
[394] Psalm 89. 46-47 in Taverner's Capito, only slightly altered.
[395] Psalm 90. 5-6, 4 in Taverner's Capito.

  Certès, Lord, if thou have respect to our sins, who shall continue? Show me, therefore, how many be the days of my life, that I may dispend° them wisely, to the praise of thy name, lest that I foolishly trusting upon long life, suddenly might perish and come to death.³⁹⁶

30   Come, Lord, now unto us, and comfort us. Come, O God, and hide not thy face from me, that I be not like unto those that be hurled into the pit of perdition. And after this night of calamity overpassed, let the pleasant morning of comfort luckily shine upon me, that betimes° I may hear and feel thy goodness, for in thee is all my trust.³⁹⁷

35   Deliver me this night from the snare of Satan's guard, which hunt in the dark how to pluck me from thee.

  Let me not stand in the fear of the night-evil of unbelief, and of thy strait judgement, neither let me be afraid of the fleeing arrow in the daytime.

  Let me not be in fear of that horrible pestilence, creeping in through darkness,
40 I mean, let me not be ignorant how detestable my sins be, that I dissemble them not, nor qualify them.

  Let me not dread that midday devil, which abuseth thy Church under a title and pretence of holiness; neither let Satan, though he change himself into an angel of light, strike any fear in me.

45   But both on the right side and on the left, as well in the night as in the day, that is, as well in adversity as prosperity, and as well in spiritual business, as in corporal, let thy holy angels diligently wait upon me, that I do not stumble: then shall I tread underfoot that helly° dragon.³⁹⁸

  Yea, so shall I of duty be bound alway° with courageous spirit, to praise and
50 hallow thy name: not only in the morrow,° when all things shall chance to my heart's desire, to ascribe all to thy goodness, without any deserving on my behalf: but also in the night of trouble and adversity, when I shall call unto mind thy most faithful and trusty promises, that I despair not,³⁹⁹ thus to praise thy mere and special grace, and bless thee, saying:

55   Blessed art thou, O Lord God of our fathers, for thou art praise and honour, worthy, and to be magnified forever.

---

³⁹⁶ Psalm 90. 9 in Taverner's Capito.

³⁹⁷ Adapted from Psalm 90. 13–14 in Taverner's Capito, with Psalm 143. 7–8 (BCP) blended in ('lest I be like unto them that go down into the pit. O let me hear thy loving kindness betimes in the morning, for in thee is my trust').

³⁹⁸ The preceding five verses are from Psalm 91. 3–13 in Taverner's Capito, which considerably compresses the original. The 'midday devil', perhaps a counterpart to the 'night-evil of unbelief', is seemingly a figure of hypocrisy, those who seem holy but are inwardly corrupt, but the tradition of Satan as an angel of light (II Corinthians 11. 14) is also at play. He is the dragon for Christians, based on Revelation 12. 9, and the treading of the dragon underfoot is the curse on Satan as the serpent (according to the traditional understanding) in Genesis 3. 15.

³⁹⁹ Adapted from Psalm 92. 1–4 in Taverner's Capito.

Blessed be the glory of thy holy name, for it is worthy to be praised, and above all to be magnified forever.

Blessed art thou, O Father, O Son, and O Holy Ghost, for thou art worthy to be praised, and above all to be magnified forever.

Blessed be thou in the firmament of heaven, for thou art praiseworthy forever.

O give thanks unto the Lord all his creatures, for he is kind-hearted and merciful: yea, his mercy endureth forever.

O speak good of the Lord, all ye works of his, in all places of his dominion: and let everything that hath breath praise the Lord, and give him thanks: for his mercy endureth forever.

Oh, that all men would therefore praise the Lord for his goodness, and declare the wonders that he doth for the children of men![400]

Praise thou the Lord, O my soul, and forget not all his benefits, yea, and all that is within me praise his holy name, for his loving mercy and for his truth, which endureth forever, and worlds without end,[401]

Amen.

Glory be to the Father, etc. As it was in the begin, etc.[402]

---

[400] Felch identifies the source for the preceding seven verses as the Canticle of the Three Children in the version printed in Toye's primer, but this isn't quite accurate. The primer does seem to be the source, though as so often Tyrwhit adapts liberally, but the text is not the canticle. The canticle, called in Latin the *Benedicite* and included in the BCP liturgy of Morning Prayer, as well as in Sternhold and Hopkins (in a different version), is the Song of the Three Children, one of the apocryphal additions to the Book of Daniel. This is not included in Tyrwhit's Psalm or the primer. The verses that Tyrwhit borrows from the primer seem to be an amalgamation of parts of the Prayer of Azariah, which precedes the Song of the Three Children in the apocryphal Daniel, the prayer of Tobit from that Apocryphal book, and two other Psalms. 'Blessed are thou, O Lord', 'Blessed be the glory', and 'Blessed be thou in the firmament' are verses 29, 30, and 35 of the Prayer of Azariah, but 'Blessed art thou, O Father' is not from that text, though the second half is similar to Psalm 145. 3 (BCP). Moreover, these verses are very similar to Tobit 8. 5, 'Blessed art thou, O God of our Fathers, and blessed is thine holy and glorious name forever: let the heathen bless thee, and all thy creatures' (Geneva). Tyrwhit's next verse ('O give thanks') is also from the primer, and seems to be a loose adaptation from Psalm 136, which uses the same refrain, 'his mercy endureth forever', but the call to the creatures is not in this Psalm and may come from the verse in Tobit. Psalm 150. 6 (BCP) is the source of 'let everything that hath breath', but the first half of the verse is from Psalm 103. 22 (also BCP). 'O that all men' is from Psalm 107. 8 (BCP). The anaphora in Tyrwhit (less obvious in the primer) gives the impression of an integrated composition, but these verses are really a pastiche of different texts.

[401] Psalm 103. 2, 1 (BCP).

[402] See note 309, p. 211.

51. George Gascoigne, *The Posies of George Gascoigne Esquire* (1575)

[George Gascoigne (1534/5?–1577) studied at Gray's Inn and spent his life in a series of failed attempts to achieve public and financial success. He tried farming, was elected MP, and served as a soldier in the Netherlands. Even in a litigious age, Gascoigne's history of legal disputes was remarkable, involving especially his marriage to a wealthy widow, since she may still have been married to her second husband at the time. He also sued his brother for stealing lambs, which the brother said Gascoigne had actually stolen from their mother. Though it did not bring him the success he craved, Gascoigne's greatest achievements were as a writer. In addition to his many poems, Gascoigne composed court entertainments, adapted two plays (*Supposes* from Ariosto and *Jocasta* from an Italian adaptation of Euripides's *The Phoenician Women*), and wrote diverse prose works, including *The Noble Art of Venery or Hunting* and the brilliant comic romance *The Adventures of Master F. J.* He also wrote an important treatise on poetry, *Certain Notes of Instruction*. As with so many of Gascoigne's works, the tone of his *De profundis* is difficult to pin down. The poem itself seems a serious paraphrase of Psalm 130, but the context described in the introduction is only mildly gloomy, and to present one of the most powerful of the Penitential Psalms as a response to being caught in a storm without a raincoat seems rather irreverent. Gascoigne's first collection, *A Hundred Sundry Flowers* (1573), contained only the introductory sonnet and a preceding prose description, in the (presumably fictive) voice of Gascoigne's 'editor', describing the occasion as a trip from Chelmsford to London. Gascoigne's revised collection, *The Posies* (1575), omitted the prose preface but included the Psalm itself. A further comment in the 1573 collection states that this and several other poems 'have very sweet notes adapted unto them', but no musical setting has ever been discovered. See Gillian Austen, *George Gascoigne* (Woodbridge: D. S. Brewer, 2008); Hamlin, *Psalm Culture*; G. W. Pigman III, *ODNB*.]

Psalm 130

The introduction to the Psalm of *De profundis*.	[Out of the depths]
The skies gan scowl, o'ercast with misty clouds,	began
When (as I rode alone by London way,	
Cloakless, unclad) thus did I sing and say:	unclothed
Behold, quoth I, bright *Titan* how he shrouds[403]	said, hides
5 His head aback, and yields the rain his reach,	
Till in his wrath, *Dan Jove* have soused the soil,[404]	drenched

---

[403] *Titan*] Greek god of the sun; Gascoigne's reference to classical gods is characteristically playful, though not necessarily irreverent.

[404] *Dan Jove*] Jupiter, chief of the Roman gods, the counterpart of Zeus in Greek myth; the title 'Dan', meaning 'sir' or 'master', is a deliberate pseudo-Chaucerian archaism.

And washed me, wretch, which in his travail toil.
But holla (here) doth rudeness me appeach,   *hold on!, accuse*
Since *Jove* is Lord and King of mighty power,
10 Which can command the sun to show his face,
And (when him list⁴⁰⁵) to give the rain his place.
Why do not I my weary muses frame,⁴⁰⁶
(Although I be well sousèd in this shower,)
To write some verse in honour of his name?

Gascoigne's *De profundis*.

15   From depth of dole wherein my soul doth dwell,   *grief*
From heavy heart which harbours in my breast,
From troubled sprite which seldom taketh rest,   *spirit*
From hope of heaven, from dread of darksome hell,   *gloomy*
O gracious God, to thee I cry and yell:
20 My God, my Lord, my lovely Lord alone,   *loving*
To thee I call, to thee I make my moan.
And thou (good God) vouchsafe in gree to take   *grant, goodwill*
This woeful plaint,   *lament*
Wherein I faint.
25 O hear me then, for thy great mercies' sake.⁴⁰⁷

   O bend thine ears attentively to hear,
O turn thine eyes, behold me how I wail,
O hearken, Lord, give ear for mine avail,   *aid*
O mark in mind the burdens that I bear:
30 See how I sink in sorrows everywhere.
Behold and see what dolours I endure,   *sorrows*
Give ear and mark what plaints I put in ure.   *laments, use*
Bend willing ear: and pity therewithal   *in addition*
My wailing voice,
35 Which hath no choice
But evermore upon thy name to call.

   If thou, good Lord, shouldst take thy rod in hand,
If thou regard what sins are daily done,

---

⁴⁰⁵ him list] he desires.
⁴⁰⁶ muses] Classical goddesses of artistic inspiration, typically invoked at the opening of epics.
⁴⁰⁷ The stanza of Gascoigne's Psalm involves three interlocking quatrains, the first *abba* followed by a second using the same *a* rhyme but a different rhyme for the internal couplet. The second fails to close, the expected *a* rhyme in the eight line shifting to a new *d* instead, which opens the envelope of the final couplet *deed* (lines 9 and 10 shorter than the other pentameters). The whole stanza comes to a conclusive close, though the irregular rhyme and line lengths create some uncertainty along the way.

If thou take hold where we our works begun,
40 If thou decree in judgment for to stand,
And be extreme to see our 'scuses scanned, *considered*
If thou take note of everything amiss,
And write in rolls how frail our nature is, *scrolls*
O glorious God, O King, O Prince of power,
45 What mortal wight *creature*
May then have light
To feel thy frown, if thou have list to lour? *desire, threaten*

But thou art good, and hast of mercy store, *sufficient supply*
Thou not delight'st to see a sinner fall,
50 Thou hearknest first, before we come to call.
Thine ears are set wide open evermore,
Before we knock thou comest to the door.
Thou art more pressed to hear a sinner cry, *impressed*
Then he is quick to climb to thee on high.
55 Thy mighty name be praisèd then alway, *always*
Let faith and fear
True witness bear.
How fast they stand which on thy mercy stay. *secure, wait*

I look for thee (my lovely Lord) therefore.
60 For thee I wait, for thee I tarry still,
Mine eyes do long to gaze on thee my fill.
For thee I watch, for thee I pry and pore. *spy, gaze*
My soul for thee attendeth evermore.
My soul doth thirst to take of thee a taste,
65 My soul desires with thee for to be placed.
And to thy word (which can no man deceive)
Mine only trust,
My love and lust,
In confidence continually shall cleave.[408]

70 Before the break or dawning of the day,
Before the light be seen in lofty skies,
Before the sun appear in pleasant wise, *manner*
Before the watch (before the watch, I say)
Before the ward that waits therefore alway: *guard*
75 My soul, my sense, my secret thought, my sprite,
My will, my wish, my joy, and my delight:[409]

[408] cleave] A complex word that may introduce a note of uncertainty into the Psalmist's apparently confident commitment, since it can mean both 'stick together' and 'divide'.
[409] Gascoigne delights in patterns of repetition, here linking the first five lines through

Unto the Lord that sits in heaven on high,
With hasty wing   *rush*
From me doth fling,
80   And striveth still, unto the Lord to fly.   *always*

    O Israel,[410] O household of the Lord,
O Abraham's brats,[411] O brood of blessed seed,   *children, descendants*
O chosen sheep that love the Lord indeed:
O hungry hearts, feed still upon his word,
85   And put your trust in him with one accord.
For he hath mercy evermore at hand,
His fountains flow, his springs do never stand.
And plenteously he loveth to redeem
Such sinners all,
90   As on him call,
And faithfully his mercies most esteem.

    He will redeem our deadly drowning state,
He will bring home the sheep that go astray,
He will help them that hope in him alway:
95   He will appease our discord and debate,
He will soon save, though we repent us late.
He will be ours if we continue his,
He will bring bale to joy and perfect bliss.   *misery*
He will redeem the flock of his elect
100   From all that is,
Or was amiss.
Since Abraham's heirs did first his laws reject.

               Ever or never.[412]

---

anaphora ('Before the …'), then further repeating 'before the watch', and following up with a chain of epithets for God (each prefaced by 'my'), all the denser due to the use of asyndeton (lack of conjunctions). There is also a great deal of alliteration ('light', 'lofty'; 'soul', 'sense'; 'will', 'wish') and assonance ('be seen'; 'light', 'skies'). The whole Psalm is thick with these figures.

[410] Israel] The metre requires three syllables.
[411] brats] Unlike in modern English, 'brats' does not necessarily have a negative connotation.
[412] Gascoigne's 'posie', a device or signature.

52. Robert Fills, *Godly Prayers and Meditations, Paraphrastically Made upon All the Psalms, Very Necessary for All the Godly, Translated out of French into English* (1577)

[Robert Fills (c. 1521–1578) was a clergyman and translator. His early history is obscure, but during the reign of Catholic Queen Mary he and his wife joined John Knox's congregation of exiles in Geneva. After returning to England, Fills became chaplain to Robert Dudley, Earl of Leicester. He translated a number of religious works by Continental reformers including Luther and Theodore Beza. The only surviving copy of *Godly Prayers and Meditations* has a publication date of 1577, but there may have been an earlier edition, since it was entered into the Stationers' Register in 1566/67. The earlier date would also make better sense of Fills's dedication to the Viscount Hereford, who in the 1560s was Walter Devereux, created Earl of Essex in 1572. From 1572 to 1576, the Viscount Hereford was Robert Devereux, not yet in his teens. See David J. Crankshaw, ODNB.]

Psalm 3

A prayer upon the third Psalm.

Lord, I perceive that many be furiously risen up against me and say among themselves, there is no help for him in his God: I beseech thee, therefore, receive me under thy holy protection and blessed safeguard, be my buckler, give me succour that I may walk in thy truth before thee, and rejoice with an upright
5 heart only in thee, hear me from Zion thy holy mountain, as often as I cry unto thee, drive out of me all vain fear: yea, although ten thousand men should make war against me, O Lord, all help and salvation is from thee only, thy blessing be upon thy people, rise up, then give me succour, O Lord, and bless me. So be it.

53. Anthony Gilby, *The Psalms of David, Truly Opened and Explained by Paraphrasis [...] Set Forth in Latin by That Excellent Learned Man Theodore Beza* (1580)

[Anthony Gilby (c. 1510–1585) graduated BA and MA from Christ Church, Oxford, where he was presumably ordained, and was learned in Latin, Greek, and Hebrew. An early convert to Protestantism, he wrote polemical pamphlets and biblical commentary during the reign of Edward VI and fled to the Continent on the succession of Catholic Queen Mary, first to Frankfurt and then to Geneva. Gilby was one of the translators of the Geneva Bible, a friend to Theodore Beza as well as Knox, Whittingham, and Christopher Goodman, and the only real Hebraist among the English exiles. After returning to England, Gilby continued to translate, producing editions of Cicero as well as Calvin and Beza, under the patronage of Henry Hastings, Earl of Huntingdon, a friend of

King Edward's. With his patron's support, Gilby worked for the rest of his life to more thoroughly evangelize the English Church, especially in Leicestershire. His translation of Beza's Psalm paraphrases was dedicated to Katherine Hastings, Countess of Huntingdon, sister of Robert Dudley, Earl of Leicester. Beza himself had dedicated his Psalms commentaries to Henry Hastings, whom he likely met in Geneva. Gilby must have produced his translation quickly, since Beza's *Psalmorum Davidis* was first published in 1579 and Gilby may actually have been working from the 1580 edition printed in London. Beza began the section on each Psalm with a prose 'argument' (really a compact commentary), and then had a Latin prose paraphrase and a verse-by-verse interpretation side by side. Finally, there was a verse paraphrase in a variety of classical metres. Gilby translates only the arguments and the prose paraphrase. See Edward A. Gosselin, 'David in Tempore Belli: Beza's David in the Service of the Huguenots', *The Sixteenth Century Journal*, 7.2 (1976), 31–54; G. Lloyd Jones, *The Discovery of Hebrew in England: A Third Language* (Manchester: Manchester University Press, 1983); Claire Cross, *ODNB*.]

Psalm 40

1. I have waited for the Lord's help a very long season,° but with good success: for he hath given ear unto me at the length, and hath declared indeed that he hath heard my cry.

2. For he hath drawn me forth of the most deep pit, and most tough mire, and hath set me upon an high rock, where I walk most firmly.

3. Wherefore he hath ministered unto me the matter of a new song, even to set forth the praises of our God, whereby all that look upon me, set forth as an example of his mercy, may learn to worship God, and to fear him and to trust in him.

4. Oh, blessed is that man who putting all his confidence in the Lord turneth away from men, that are puffed up with most vain and deceitful confidence.

5. O Lord, my God, how many and marvellous are thy works? Who is able to comprehend in his mind, or to declare and utter thy thoughts towards us, seeing they are innumerable?

6. Howbeit, this doth chiefly set forth the greatness of thy benefits, that all this doth proceed freely of thine unspeakable mercy. For thou hast not required of me the oblations° and sacrifices of the law, as though I could satisfy thee by them, which were a madness for any man to persuade himself: but thou hast required this one thing for all manner of oblations and offerings, that I should hear thee, the which thing also thou hast granted unto me, making me apt and ready to hear thee.

7. Wherefore, I trusting to this thy grace, have straightways again answered within myself. Lo, I am here, for in the very beginning of the book of thy law, I do hear myself thus called, when thou sayest: Hear, O Israel.

25   8. Neither dost thou command us, O my God, to hear thee for any other cause, but that we should obey thee when thou speakest. Seeing thou hast granted unto me, O Lord, this will, I have testified my will, and that thy law is settled in the secret of my heart.

9. Neither have I done this dissemblingly, for I have openly declared thy
30   righteousness, neither will I ever cease to declare it, for fear of any peril, of the which my will thou art witness, O Lord, unto me.

10. I have not kept secret, I say, thy righteousness, which I did know in my heart, but I have most plainly professed how faithful thou art in thy promise, and that all our salvation doth consist in this thine only goodness, and I have
35   testified thy mercy and truth also before all the assembly of thy people.

11. Now thou again, my God, seeing that new enemies do arise, continue as thou hast done hitherto, to have mercy upon me, and join near unto me those thy faithful keepers, even thy mercy and fidelity in keeping thy promises.

12. For innumerable troubles do again hang over my head, and so many, and
40   so great punishments due unto my sins do press° me, that I can scarcely behold them afar off with mine eyes, for they are above the number of the hairs of mine head and my very heart faileth me.

13. Let it please thee, therefore, O Lord, to deliver me, O Lord, I say, make haste to help me.

45   14. Cause them to be confounded,° ashamed and frustrate of their expectation that seek my death, and let them be turned back with shame, void of their purpose which bend themselves wholly to hurt me.

15. Let them suffer the same blot of infamy for a reward of their wickedness, wherewith they would have spotted me, which cried, ha, ha, in my misery.

50   16. But contrariwise, let all that seek thee, being confirmed and comforted by mine example, rejoice, and they that have set all their hope of salvation in thee: let them exhort one another to praise thee. I was miserable and destitute of all men's help, but the Lord provided for me and mine affairs; thou wast my helper, thou wast my deliverer: and now, O my God, I beseech thee make no delay.

Psalm 97

1. The Lord being so long enclosed, as it were within the small and narrow bounds of one people, now at the length he beginneth his kingdom over all the world: wherefore, let the earth rejoice, and all ye most great countries, even beyond the seas, be ye joyful.[413]

5   2. For he is come, although very mild and meek towards his, yet to be reverenced of his own, both for his divine majesty, and also terrible to his enemies, how fierce soever they be, even compassed° about with the black

---

[413] The Psalm simply celebrates God's kingdom, but Gilby's opening verse would have obvious appeal to a zealous supporter of international Protestantism, keen to spread the gospel 'beyond the seas', or at least across the Channel.

darkness of the clouds, and sitting upon a throne, stayed,° as it were, with two unmoveable pillars: namely, justice, which he showeth in keeping promise with his own, and defending them by his covenant: and most severe judgement, whereby he punisheth his adversaries.

3. A flaming fire shall then go before him, and shall take hold on his enemies on every side.

4. The lightnings breaking forth from his judgement seat shall fill the world with glittering light: they shall see this in the end, even against their wills, which are most blind, and they shall tremble throughout the compass of the earth.

5. The hills at the sight of the Lord, at the sight, I say, of the Lord of all the earth shall melt.

6. But unto others that are willing to be taught, and ready to obey, he will show himself so just, and mindful of his mercy promised, that the very heavens, being astonished with so great and so glorious bounty, poured out by him upon all people, as far as the heavens are extended, shall set forth this so great a benefit, as it were with a sounding voice.

7. Go to then,[414] be ye ashamed of your most filthy servitude, O ye slaves of the idols: but, O ye even the very angels, worship him as your Lord and King.[415]

8. But who will hear these things? Verily, the true Zion, who, with the residue of the cities of her dominion, as a mother with her daughters, being for this cause replenished with joy, and comforted with thy judgements, O Lord, will rejoice.

9. Go to then, O Lord, sitting upon thy most high throne, rule thou the whole earth, and exalt thyself above all that is aloft anywhere.

10. And ye that love the Lord, continue to hate that which is evil: and doubt nothing, but that he which hath freely embraced you with so great favour, will defend you also most mightily, and will deliver you from the wicked.

11. And though this light of the mercy of God doth not straightway shine unto the godly, let them remember, that like as the seeds which are sown in the earth do not forthwith spring up: nay, though they lie longer hid° in the bowels° of the earth, yet they come forth more plentifully: even so the light of righteousness is sown for them that love that light, whereby it shall wholly come to pass, that all they that lead an upright life, are replenished with incredible joy.

12. Rejoice ye therefore in the Lord, so great a King, O all ye just: and magnify the holy remembrance of him continually.

---

[414] go to then] go to work, get to it.
[415] Beza's argument emphasizes the confirmation of various prophecies in the Psalm by New Testament writers, such as Hebrews 1. 6, which states that when God brought his son into the world, he said, 'let all the angels of God worship him' (Geneva, which also notes the Psalm verse in the margin).

54. John Stubbs (MS 1580?)

[John Stubbs (c. 1541–1590) studied at Trinity College, Cambridge (BA), and Lincoln's Inn. Stubbs's first publication was a translation of Theodore Beza's life of John Calvin, and he remained a zealous, evangelical Puritan, impatient with the conservatism of the Elizabethan Church. In 1579, Stubbs published *The Discovery of a Gaping Gulf*, a critique of Queen Elizabeth's proposed marriage to the Catholic Duke of Anjou. Elizabeth was outraged and issued a proclamation condemning the book. Stubbs was arrested, charged with sedition, and had his hand chopped off in the marketplace at Westminster. Before the cleaver descended, Stubbs was said to have cried out, with grim wit, 'Pray for me now my calamity is at hand'. After this, Stubbs signed his name 'John Stubbs, scaeva' ('left-handed'). Stubbs's twenty metrical Psalms were presumably written while he was in the Tower awaiting punishment in 1580. He was released in 1581 and published *Christian Meditations upon Eight Psalms*, translated from Beza, in 1582. See *John Stubbs's 'Gaping Gulf' with Letters and Other Relevant Documents*, ed. by Lloyd E. Berry (Charlottesville: University of Virginia Press for the Folger Shakespeare Library, 1968); Natalie Mears, *ODNB*.]

Psalm 5

	1.	Bend lightening ear to this my speech,[416]	*flashing*
		O Lord, descry and know	*discover*
		Th'unlettered breath from musing heart,	
		Which through whist lips I blow.	*silent*
5	2.	Pressed by distress, if I pray forth	
		Some rude importune cry,	
		Deign yet, Lord, in time opportune	
		To hear effectually:	
		For unto thee, my King and God,	
10	3.	Lo, hear my moan bewrayed.	*divulged*
		My soonest call, good Lord, prevent	*anticipate*
		With timely ear of aid:	
		The first fruits of my morrow lips	*morning*
		A sacrifice I make;	
15		Early and late, I wait and watch,	
		The scout watch I ought wake:	
	4.	Almighty though thou be, yet Lord,	
		Thou canst not mischief brook,	*tolerate*
		Nor yet within thine heavenly tents	
20		Can ill dwell or once look:	*evil*

[416] lightening ear] Stubbs may be aiming at a synaesthetic effect here, since usually it's eyes that flash, rather than ears, but who is to say what God's ears (an anthropomorphism anyway) may do.

5. Mad-boasting sinners cannot stand
      One glance of thy sharp eye:
   Which hates and throws consuming beams
      At such as do lewdly.   *wickedly*
6. The liar self God's vengeance just
      His lying tongue oft spills;
   Murd'rer unkind and treacher false,   *traitor*
      Like cruel treason kills:
   For why? the Lord him loathes and thrusts   *why*
      From false protection,[417]
   Such as renounce to bear
      His just subjection.
7. But mine address and whole success   *ability*
      On thy large bounty stays;   *waits*
   At threshold of thy presence great,
      Prostrate thy servant prays:
8. In right paths, Lord, me set and hold:
      Thy ways make plain to me
   (Lest men profane through me blaspheme
      And good men grievèd be) or
   That men seeing my shining light
      My God may glorify:
9. For rash mouths are of unstayed speech,   *unchecked*
      Their heart thinketh neighbour's bane,   *harm*
   Their strong breathed throats are gaping graves,
      With tongues smooth filed they feign: *polished*
10. Judge them of sin, O God, make their
      Counsels fall contrary;
    O'erthrow these oft-swerving revolts,
      Yea, stark rebels to thee:
11. But thy safe shroud ay makes th'heart joy,   *always*
      Tongue shout, and body dance:
    Thou shield'st complete all those that love
      Thy glorious name t'advance:
12. For thou the righteous man dost still
      Lord bless in all throughout;
    Thy shield of kindness well ypleased[418]
      Doth fence him round about.

---

[417] protection] The metre requires four syllables ('pro-tec-ti-on'), as does 'subjection' below.
[418] A moving use of the familiar shield metaphor, since most instances emphasize military strength (Psalms 28. 7, 35. 2, 59. 11, II Samuel 22. 3, Deuteronomy 33. 29).

55. Sir Philip Sidney (MS c. 1580–1586)

[Sir Philip Sidney (1554–1586) was one of the most important English writers of the Elizabethan period, and one of the most influential. He was the eldest son of Sir Henry Sidney, courtier and Lord Deputy of Ireland, and his mother, Mary, was the daughter of John Dudley, Duke of Northumberland, and a gentlewoman of the privy chamber to Queen Elizabeth, from whom Mary caught smallpox. Sidney studied at Shrewsbury School, where he met his lifelong friend and future biographer Fulke Greville. In 1567 he was enrolled in Gray's Inn, and in 1568 in Christ Church, Oxford. In 1572, Sidney travelled to the Continent, and he was in Paris during the St Bartholomew's Day Massacre of French Protestants, hiding out in the embassy of Sir Francis Walsingham. Sidney's further travels gained him the admiration of a wide circle of European Protestant writers and intellectuals, and exposed him to the literature and art that thrived in Renaissance courts. Despite Sidney's growing European reputation, however, he never achieved success at the English court, his knighthood bestowed only so that he could stand in as proxy for the Polish prince Johann Casimir at the Garter ceremony. He died fighting the Spanish in Zutphen in 1586, when a leg wound became infected. His funeral was one of the most lavish of the age, the procession of 700 mourners recorded on an engraved funeral scroll thirty-five feet long. The poets who mourned him in verse include Nicholas Breton, Henry Constable, Samuel Daniel, Michael Drayton, Ben Jonson, Sir Walter Raleigh, and Edmund Spenser, as well as James VI of Scotland, the future James I of England. Sidney's work in several genres set the standard for subsequent English writers, and his influence was long and widespread. *Astrophil and Stella* was one of the most brilliant Renaissance sonnet sequences in the Petrarchan tradition, *The Countess of Pembroke's Arcadia* (in the original and a massive incomplete revision) was the greatest English prose Romance, and *The Defence of Poesy* the most accomplished English work of literary criticism. Most of Sidney's works were printed only after his death, and it was his sister, Mary, who was responsible, largely shaping his posthumous reputation. Sidney began translating the Psalms at his sister's house at Wilton, probably in the 1580s, completing the first forty-three before his death; Mary Sidney completed the project, which was both to cast the Psalms into the very best English verse, reflecting a sense (however little understood) of the pre-eminence of the poetry of the Hebrew Psalms, and to demonstrate the capability of poetry in English. Almost every one of the Sidney Psalms used a different metre or stanza form. They were admired by John Donne, Sir John Harington, Samuel Daniel, and many others, and manuscripts of the Psalms circulated widely. Donne, Harington, and Francis Davison hoped they might be printed, but they remained in manuscript until the nineteenth century. See Alan Stewart, *Sir Philip Sidney: A Double Life* (London: Chatto & Windus, 2000); Richard Hillyer, *Sir Philip Sidney, Cultural Icon* (New York: Palgrave MacMillan, 2010); *The Sidney Psalter: The Psalms of*

Psalm 6

Domine, ne in furore.   [Lord, do not in anger]

    Lord, let not me, a worm, by thee be shent   *disgraced*
        While thou art in the heat of thy displeasure:
    Ne let thy rage of my due punishment
                Become the measure.[419]
5 But mercy, Lord, let mercy thine descend,
        For I am weak, and in my weakness languish:
    Lord, help, for ev'n my bones their marrow spend
                With cruel anguish.
    Nay, ev'n my soul fell troubles do appal.   *dreadful*
10   Alas, how long, my God, wilt thou delay me?
    Turn thee, sweet Lord, and from this ugly fall,
                My dear God, stay me.   *secure*
    Mercy, O mercy, Lord, for mercy's sake,
        For death doth kill the witness of thy glory.
15   Can of thy praise the tongues entombèd make
                A heav'nly story?
    Lo, I am tired while still I sigh and groan;
        My moistened bed proofs of my sorrow showeth:
    My bed (while I with black night mourn alone)
20   With my tears floweth.
    Woe, like a moth, my face's beauty eats,
        And age pulled on with pains all freshness fretteth;[420]   *wears away*
    The while a swarm of foes with vexing feats
                My life besetteth.

---

[419] Even more than Parker's Psalm 33 (see 46), Sidney's stanza here strongly suggests an English adaptation of the Sapphic, with three longer pentameters followed by the shorter five-syllable adonic (to use the Greek term that Sidney surely knew, though the original was five syllables in quantitative metre). Greek Sapphics were unrhymed, but the alternating rhyme creates an interesting tension between the close of the third pentameter and the additional short line, which almost (especially when enjambed) has the effect of a hexameter. The inevitable association of the Sapphic with Sappho may also lie behind Sidney's choice of feminine rhymes (with an extra, unstressed syllable) in alternate lines. Sidney uses the same metre in poem 59 in *The Old Arcadia* ('Get hence foul grief, the canker of the mind'), the first stanza of which even uses the same rhyme: 'pleasure'/'treasure'.

[420] The image of the moth fretting a garment (though here, horribly, a face) comes from Psalm 39. 12 (see Sidney's below).

25 Get hence, you evil, who in my ill rejoice,   *evil*
    In all whose works vainness is ever reigning:
    For God hath heard the weeping, sobbing voice
        Of my complaining.   *lamentation*
    The Lord my suit did hear, and gently hear;   *petition*
30   They shall be shamed and vexed, that breed my crying:
    And turn their backs, and straight on backs appear   *immediately*
        Their shameful flying.

Psalm 13

Usquequo, Domine?   [How long, Lord?]

  How long, O Lord, shall I forgotten be?
      What? Ever?[421]
  How long wilt thou thy hidden face from me
      Dissever?   *sever*
5 How long shall I consult with careful sprite   *troubled, spirit*
      In anguish?
  How long shall I with foes' triumphant might
      Thus languish?
  Behold me, Lord, let to thy hearing creep
10   My crying.
  Nay, give me eyes and light, lest that I sleep
      In dying.
  Lest my foe brag, that in my ruin he
      Prevailèd:
15 And at my fall they joy that, troublous, me
      Assailèd.
  No, no, I trust on thee, and joy in thy
      Great pity.
  Still therefore of thy graces shall be my
20   Song's ditty.   *lyrics*

Psalm 26

Judica me, Domine.   [Judge me, Lord]

  Lord, judge me and my case,
    For I have made my race
  Within the bounds of innocence to bide:[422]

---

[421] Ringler suggests that the metre may have been inspired by the halting syntax of the prose translation in BCP: 'How long wilt thou forget me, O Lord, for ever?'
[422] race] Sidney increases the pace of the metaphor, the Psalmist saying simply 'I have walked innocently' (BCP).

And setting thee for scope
    Of all my trustful hope,
I held for sure, that I should never slide.

Prove me, O Lord most high,
    Me with thy touchstone try:⁴²³   *test, inward parts*
Yea, sound my reins, and inmost of my heart.
    For so thy loving hand
    Before my eyes did stand,
That from thy truth will not depart.⁴²⁴

I did not them frequent,
    Who be to vainness bent,
Nor kept with base dissemblers company.
    Nay, I did ev'n detest
    Of wicked wights the nest,   *creatures*
And from the haunts of such bad folks did fly.

In th'innocence of me
    My hands shall washèd be;
And with those hands, about thy altar wait,
    That I may still express
    With voice of thankfulness
The works performed by thee, most wondrous great.

Lord, I have lovèd well
    The house where thou dost dwell,
Ev'n where thou mak'st thy honour's biding place.
    Sweet Lord, write not my soul,
    Within the sinners' roll: *scroll*
Nor my life's cause, match with blood-seekers' case,

With hands of wicked shifts,   *devices*
    With right hands stained with gifts.
But while I walk in my unspotted ways
    Redeem and show me grace
    So I in public place
Set on plain ground will thee, Jehovah, praise.

---

⁴²³ touchstone] Sidney's addition, a black stone used to test the purity of gold and silver, and, figuratively, any test of genuineness. A familiar metaphor in religious contexts: 'the touchstone of God's word (*The Sermons of John Calvin Upon the Epistle of St. Paul to the Ephesians*, 1577), 'the touchstone of the Gospel' (Heinrich Bullinger, *Fifty Godly and Learned Sermons*, 1577), 'the touchstone of the Scriptures' (John Lyly, *Euphues. The Anatomy of Wit*, 1578).
⁴²⁴ An irregular line, two syllables missing from all major manuscripts (Ringler).

Psalm 30

Exaltabo te, Domine. [I will magnify thee, Lord]

O Lord, thou hast exalted me
   And saved me from my foes' laughing scorn:
   I owe thee praise, I will praise thee.[425]

For when my heart with woes was torn,
5   In cries to thee, I showed my cause:
   And was from ill, by thee upborne.

Yea, from the grave's most hungry jaws
   Thou wouldst not set me on their score,   *list*
   Whom Death his cold bosom draws.

10 Praise, praise this Lord then evermore,
   Ye saints of his, rememb'ring still
   With thanks his holiness therefore.

For quickly ends his wrathful will
   But his dear favour where it lies,
15 From age to age life joys doth fill.

Well may the evening clothe the eyes
   In clouds of tears,[426] but soon as sun
   Doth rise again, new joys shall rise.

For proof, while I my race did run
20 Full of success, fond I did say,
   That I should never be undone.

For then my hill good God did stay:[427]   *secure*
   But, ah, he straight his face did hide,   *immediately*
   And what was I but wretchèd clay?[428]

25 Then thus to thee I praying cried,
   What serves, alas, the blood of me
   When I within the pit do bide?

---

[425] Sidney here uses the interlocking terza rima, used famously by Dante in the *Divine Comedy*, but also by Wyatt in his *Penitential Psalms*.

[426] clothe … tears] Sidney's metaphorical elaboration on the Psalm's 'heaviness may endure for a night' (BCP).

[427] The note in the Geneva Bible paraphrases, 'I thought thou hadest established me in Zion most surely', Zion being a specific hill in Jerusalem that came to stand for the whole city or Israel. Sidney adds the clay (see note 428), borrowed from the 'earth' of verse 10, to play the high and low ground, hill and clay, against each other.

[428] Man is created out of the dust of the ground (Genesis 2. 7).

Shall ever earth give thanks to thee?
　　Or shall thy truth on mankind laid
30　　In deadly dust declarèd be?

Lord, hear, let mercy thine be stayed
　　On me, from me help this annoy.　　　　　　　*discomfort*
　　This much I said, this being said,

Lo, I that wailed, now dance for joy:
35　　Thou didst ungird my doleful sack,　　　　　　*sackcloth*
　　And mad'st me gladsome weeds enjoy.[429]　　*clothing*

Therefore my tongue shall never lack
　　Thy endless praise: O God, my King,
　　I will thee thanks forever sing.

Psalm 39

Dixi, custodiam.　　　　　　　　　　　　　　[I said, I will guard]

Thus did I think, I well will make my way,
　　Lest by my tongue I hap to stray.　　　　　　　*happen*
　　I muzzle will my mouth, while in the sight
　　　　I do abide of wicked wight.　　　　　　　*creature*
5　　And so I nothing said, I muët stood,　　　　*mute (disyllable)*
　　　　I silence kept, ev'n in the good.[430]

But still the more that I did hold my peace,
　　The more my sorrow did increase.
　　The more methought, my heart was hot in me,
10　　And as I mused such world to see,
　　The fire took fire and forcibly out-brake;
　　　　My tongue would needs and thus I spake:

Lord, unto me my time's just measure give,
　　Show me how long I have to live:
15　　Lo, thou a span's length, mad'st my living line.[431]
　　　　A span? Nay, nothing in thine eyne.　　　*eyes*
　　What do we seek? The greatest state I see,
　　　　At best is merely vanity.[432]

---

[429] The metaphorical change of clothes here picks up on the figure for evening earlier, both added by Sidney, though clothing metaphors are familiar from other Psalms (73. 6, 102. 26, 104. 2, etc.).
[430] Sidney uses the same stanza form that Beza does for his translation of this Psalm (Ringler).
[431] BCP 'thou hast made my days as it were a span long'. The 'living line' added by Sidney suggests the thread of life spun out by the classical Fates.
[432] Sidney creates what seems a realistic, and impassioned, voice by means of pauses,

	They are but shades, not true things where we live:	*shadows*
20	Vain shades, and vain, in vain to grieve.[433]	
	Look but on this: man still doth riches heap,	
	And knows not, who the fruit shall reap.	
	This being thus, for what, O Lord, wait I?	
	I wait on thee with hopeful eye.	
25	Oh help, oh help me; this far yet I crave,	
	From my transgressions me to save.	
	Let me not be thrown down to base shame,	
	That fools of me may make their game.	
	But I do hush, why do I say thus much,	
30	Since it is thou that mak'st one such?	
	Ah! Yet from me let thy plagues be displaced.	
	For with thy handy strokes I waste.	
	I know that man's foul sin doth cause thy wrath,	
	For when his sin thy scourging hath,	
35	Thou moth-like mak'st his beauty fading be:	
	So what is man but vanity?	*that which is worthless*
	Hear, Lord, my suits and cries; stop not thine ears	*petitions*
	At these my words all clothed in tears:	
	For I with thee on earth a stranger am,	
40	But baiting, as my fathers came.	*sojourning*
	Stay then thy wrath that I may strength receive	*halt*
	Ere I my earthly being leave.	

56. Richard Stanihurst, *The First Four Books of Virgil, his Aeneis Translated into English Heroical Verse by Richard Stanyhurst, with Other Poetical Devices Thereto Annexed* (1582)

[Richard Stanihurst (1547–1618) was born in Dublin and educated at Kilkenny, University College, Oxford, and Furnival's and Lincoln's Inns. An exceptional scholar, Stanihurst published a study of the neo-Platonic philosopher Porphyry in 1570 at the urging of the Jesuit Edmund Campion. Stanihurst contributed substantially to the history of Ireland in Holinshed's *Chronicles*. In 1582 he published his translation of the first four books of Vergil's *Aeneid* in English quantitative hexameters. Included in this volume were four metrical Psalms,

exclamations, rhetorical questions, and self-contradictions that complicate the verse line and stanza form. The technique looks forward to the lyrics of John Donne, though Wyatt was experimenting in similar ways earlier in the century.

[433] The threefold repetition of 'vain', one more than in BCP, and picking up on the 'vanity' of the previous verse, recalls the famous expression of emptiness at the beginning of Ecclesiastes: 'vanity of vanities, all is vanity' (Ecclesiastes 1. 2, Geneva).

also in quantitative metres. The metres, in order and by his own description, are iambical verse, heroical and elegiacal verse, asclepiad verse, and Sapphic verse. These translations also featured Stanihurst's innovative English spelling system (not preserved here), designed in part to facilitate the classical metre, a graphic system that depended upon the placement of consonants and vowels rather than on any 'quantities' one might actually hear. What one does hear in these Psalms is the absence of regular accentual-syllabic metre, which combined with the lack of rhyme creates a peculiar effect, not prose exactly, but not verse either, at least in sixteenth-century English terms. Stanihurst continued to publish on Irish history and geography, including a biography of St Patrick. Stanihurst lived in Dublin, then Dunkirk, and then Madrid, where his alchemical experiments were supported by Philip II. Stanihurst returned to the Spanish Netherlands and continued to work for a Catholic succession to the English and Irish thrones. He was ordained a Jesuit priest in the first decade of the seventeenth century. See Hamlin, *Psalm Culture*; Colm Lennon, *Richard Stanihurst the Dubliner, 1547–1618* (Blackrock: Irish Academic Press, 1981); Lennon, *ODNB*.]

Psalm 1

Beatus vir. [Blessed is the man]

1. That wight is happy and gracious,   *creature*
   That tracks no wicked company;
   Nor stands in ill men's seignory;   *evil, domination*
   In chair ne sits of pestilence.[434]

5 2. But in the sound law of the Lord
   His mind, or hest is resiant: *command, resident*
   And on the said law meditates,
   With hourly contemplation.[435]

   3. That man resembleth verily
10   The grass by river situate;
   Yielding abundant plentiness
   Of fruit, in harvest seasonèd.

   4. With heavenly joys still nourishèd
   His leaf by no means vanisheth;
15   What thing his heart endeavoureth,
   Is prosperously accomplishèd.

---

[434] pestilence] Following the Vulgate, *pestilentia*, rather than the 'chair of the scornful' (BCP) as it is in the Hebrew. As a Roman Catholic, Stanihurst translates from the Vulgate throughout.
[435] contemplation] The metre requires pronunciation as five syllables.

5. Not so the sinful creatures,
    Not so their acts are prosperous;
    But like the sand, or chaffy dust,
    That windy puffs from ground do blow.

6. Therefore in hour judicial,
    The ungodly shall unhanced remain;[436]   *unexalted*
    And shall be from the company
    Of holy men quite sunderèd.

7. Because the Lord precisely knows
    The godly path of ghostly men;   *spiritual*
    The fleshly trace of filthy deeds
    Shall then be clean extinguishèd.   *completely*

Psalm 2

Quare fremuerunt gentes.   [Why do the nations roar?]

1. With frantic madness why frets the multitude heathen?   *worries*
    And to vain attemptings what fury stirs the people?
2. All the worldly regents, in clustered company,   *crowded,*
    For to tread and trample Christ with his holy godhead.[437]
3. Break we their hard fetters, we that be in Christian household,
    Also from our persons pluck we their iron yokes.
4. He scorns their working, that dwells in blessèd Olympus:
    And at their brainsick trumpery folly fleereth.[438]   *trickery, mocks*
5. Then shall he speak to those in his hard implacable anger,
    And shall turmoil them, then, with his heavy fury.
6. I reign and do govern, as king, by the Lord his appointment,
    Of mount holy Zion; his will eke heavenly preaching.   *also*
7. The Father hath spoken: thou art my dearly begotten;   *conceived*
    This day thy person for my great issue breeding.
8. To me frame thy prayers, eke of ethnics the heir will I make thee, *pagans*
    Also to thy seisin wide places earthly give I.   *possession*
9. With the rod hard steeled thou shalt their villainy trample;
    Like potter's pipkin[439] naughty men easily breaking.   *wicked*

---

[436] unhanced] 'unhaunst' in the original; Wycliffe's Psalm 37. 35 has 'The unpitouse above hauncid'; Stanihurst also uses 'haunced' in *Aeneid* IV. 77.

[437] The Psalm has obviously been Christianized, although this jars with the classical references (like 'Olympus') that Stanihurst also adds. Such juxtapositions may not have troubled Renaissance readers, given the tendency to syncretize the biblical and the classical.

[438] Despite his classical experiment, eschewing English metre and rhyme, Stanihurst has an almost excessive delight in alliteration like 'persons pluck [...] yokes', or 'folly fleereth'. He was mocked for this later in the century, most notably by Thomas Nashe.

[439] potter's pipkin] A small pot or bottle.

20	10. You that are earthly regents, judges terrestrial hearken,	
	With the lore of virtue warily to be schooled.	*teachings*
	11. To God your service with fearful duty betake ye;	*entrust*
	With trembling gladness yield to that highness honour.	
	12. Learn well your lessons, lest that God ruffle in anger,	*stir with anger*
	And from the right straggling, with fury snatched, ye perish.	
25	13. When with swift posting his dangerous anger approacheth,	
	They shall be blessed which in his help be placed.	

Psalm 3

Domine, quid multiplicati sunt.   [Why, Lord, are they multiplied?]

	1. Lord, my dreary foes why do (they) multiply?[440]	
	Me for to ruinate sundry be covetous.	*ruin*
	2. Him shields not the godhead, sundry say to my soul.	
	3. Th'art, Lord most vigilant, wholly my succourer,	
5	And in the all my staying shall be still harboured:	
	Th'art my most valiant victory glorious.	
	4. To our Lord loud I cried: from holy place heard he me;	
	5. In grave new buried fast have I slumbered.	
	I rose to life again through God his holiness.[441]	
10	6. I fear not furious multitude infinite,	
	With compass labouring, my body for to catch.	
	Rise, Lord omnipotent, help me, my champion.	
	7. Lord, thy clear radiant righteous equity[442]	
	Hath squizèd all my foes, falsely me ransacking.	*squeezed*
15	8. Our Lord participates safety with happiness:	*possesses*
	With gifts, heav'nly Godhead, thy people amply bless.	

Psalm 4

Cum invocarem.   [When I called]

	1. When that I callèd, with an humble outcry,
	The God of justice, meriting my safety,
	In many dangers my weak heart upholding
	Swiftly did hear me.
5	2. Therefore all freshly, like one oft enurèd
	With thy great goodness, yet again do crave thee,

---

[440] This metre in particular seems to have forced Stanihurst into some especially contorted English syntax.

[441] The Psalmist refers only to rising after sleep, not resurrection from the dead, even if metaphorical.

[442] On equity, Stanihurst's addition, see note 6, p. 68.

	Mercy to render, with all eke to grant me	also
	Gracious hearkening.	
	3. Wherefore of mankind ye that are begotten,	conceived
10	What space and season do ye catch for hardness,	time
	Vanity loving, too too fondly searching	foolishly
	Trumpery falsehood.	trickery
	4. Know ye for certain, that our heavenly rector	ruler
	His sacred darling specially choosèd:	best-loved
15	And the Lord therefore, when I pray, will hearken	
	To my requesting.	
	5. For sin expirèd, see ye rest in anger,	
	And future trespass, with all haste, abandon:	
	When that in secret ye be fleshly tickled,	irritated
20	Run to repentance.	
	6. Righteous incense sacrifice hereafter	
	In God, our guider, your whole hope reposing.	
	Fondly do diverse say, what haughty great lord	
	Us doth enable.	
25	7. Thy star of goodness in us is reshining,	
	Sound reason granting, with all heavenly comfort:	
	With these budge presents to mine heart affording	solemn
	Gladness abundant.	
	8. Their wheat and vineyards, that are happily sprouting,	
30	And oil, in plenty to the store cell herded,	small room
	With pride, and glory to the stars enhanceth	
	Worldly men huffing.	swelling
	9. Though that I see not, with a carnal eyesight,	fleshly
	The bliss and glory, that in heaven is harboured:	
35	Yet with hope stand I, to be there reposèd,	
	And to be resting.	
	10. By reason that thou, my God heavenly, settlest	
	Me, thy poor servant, in hope, and that highly:	
	To be partaker with all heavenly dwellers	
40	Of thy bliss happy.	

57. Thomas Bentley, *The Fifth Lamp of Virginity Containing Sundry Forms of Christian Prayers and Meditations, To Be Used Only of and for All Sorts and Degrees of Women, in their Several Ages and Callings* (1582)

[Little is known about Thomas Bentley (c. 1543–1585), apart from family records, except that he was warden at St Andrew's, Holborn, and the author of *The Monument for Matrons*, an immense compilation of devotional texts of various sorts for women, including biblical excerpts, prayers and meditations, and descriptions of biblical and other eminent (pious) women. There were seven volumes printed between 1582 and 1584, each entitled a 'lamp'. In keeping with the design of the *Monument*, Bentley shifts the pronouns in this Psalm from masculine to feminine, and adds references to women, mothers, and sisters. Bentley recommends to his reader that when she is 'in long and sore labour' she should 'call earnestly upon God' and say either the Penitential Psalms or this one. The condition of being 'in labour' obviously has a second meaning particularly relevant for women readers. See Colin B. Atkinson and Jo B. Atkinson, *ODNB*.]

Psalm 22

Called the Complaint° of Christ on the Cross.[443]

My God, my God, why hast thou forsaken me? It seemeth that I shall not obtain deliverance, though I seek it with loud cries.

My God, I will cry all the day long, but thou wilt not answer; and all the night long I make piteous moan, without taking any rest.

5 The mean time, thou most holiest seem'st to sit still, not caring for the things that I suffer, which so oft hast helped me heretofore, and hast given to thy people Israel sufficient argument and matter to praise thee with songs, wherewith they have given thanks to thee for thy benefits.

Our forefathers and mothers[444] were wont° to put their trust in thee, and as 10 often as they did so, thou didst deliver them out of their distress.

As oft as they cried for help to thee, they were delivered: as oft as they committed themselves to thee, they were not confounded,° nor put to any shame.

But as for me, I seem rather to be a worm than a woman, the dunghill of 15 Adam and Eve,[445] the outcast of the vulgar people.

---

[443] Not in the Hebrew, though this was the traditional Christian reading of the Psalm, portions of which are incorporated into the gospels and remarked upon as prophecy fulfilled. Most strikingly, Christ on the cross utters the first verse of the Psalm in Aramaic in Mark and Matthew. It is not clear whether Bentley recognized that this typological interpretation complicated, in intriguing ways, the reading of the Psalm in the voice of Christ.

[444] mothers] Bentley adds to the Psalm a number of references to women and changes the gender of pronouns to appeal to his targeted readers. Interestingly, though, when he might have included in the Psalmist's self-loathing the standard patriarchal condemnation of Eve, Bentley has his Psalmist identify as the dunghill (borrowed from Job) of both Adam and Eve.

[445] dunghill] Borrowed from Job, who famously sat upon a dunghill and calls man a worm (25. 6). The dunghill is not actually in any of the English Bibles, but it is in the Vulgate (*sterquilinio*), which is based on the slightly different version in the Septuagint. Familiarity with Job on the dunghill was everywhere in literature beyond the Bible and in visual depictions of Job.

As many as have seen me laugh, have laughed me to scorn, and reviled me, and shaking their heads in derision at me, have cast me in the teeth,⁴⁴⁶ saying:

She is wont to boast and glory that she is in great favour with God, wherefore let God now deliver her, if he love her so well.

20   By thy procurement, O Lord, I came out of my mother's womb, and thou gavest me good comfort, even when I sucked my mother's breasts.

Through thy means I came into this world, and as soon as I was born, I was left to thy tuition, yea, thou wast my God, when I was yet in my mother's womb.

Wherefore go not far away from me, for danger is even now at hand, and so
25   none in earth will or can help me.

Many bulls have closed me in both strong and fat, they have compassed° me round about.

They have opened their mouth against me, like unto a lion that gapeth upon his prey, and roareth for hunger.

30   I am poured out like water, and all my limbs loosed one from another, and my heart is melted within me as it were wax.

All my strength is gone and dried up like unto a tilestone,° my tongue cleaveth to the roof of my mouth, and at the last I shall be buried in the earth, as the dead be wont.

35   For dogs have compassed me round about, and the most wicked have conspired against me, they wound even my very heart, hands, head, and feet.

I was so ungently entreated of them, that I might easily number all my bones,⁴⁴⁷ and after all the pain and torment that they did to me, with grievous countenance they stared and looked upon me.

40   They divided my clothes among them, and cast lots for my coat.

Wherefore, Lord, I beseech thee, go not far from me, but forasmuch as thou art my power and my strength, make haste to help me.

Deliver my soul from danger of the sword, and keep my life destitute of all mortal help, from the violence of the infernal dog.⁴⁴⁸

45   Save my soul from the mouth of the lion, and take me from the horns of the unicorns.⁴⁴⁹

So will I show unto my brethren and sisters the majesty of thy name, and when the people are most assembled together, I will praise and set forth thy most worthy acts and deeds.

50   All that worship the Lord, praise him; all the posterity of Jacob magnify him, all ye that be of the stock of Israel, with reverence serve and honour him.

For he hath not despised and set at naught his poor handmaid, because of

---

⁴⁴⁶ cast me in the teeth] reproached, insulted me.
⁴⁴⁷ I might easily number all my bones] She is so thin she can count her ribs.
⁴⁴⁸ infernal dog] Adding an apocalyptic dimension to the Psalm's ordinary dog (perhaps alluding to Cerberus, the guardian of classical Hades).
⁴⁴⁹ unicorns] See note 23, p. 79.

her misery, nor he hath not disdainfully turned away his face from her, but rather as soon as his poor handmaid cried unto him for help, he heard her by and by.

I will praise thee therefore with my songs openly in the multitude of people, and I will perform my vows in the sight of them that honour thee.

The poor shall eat and be satisfied, they shall praise the Lord, that study to please him, and as many of you as continue still such, your hearts shall live.

All the ends of the world shall consider these things, and be turned to the Lord, and all heathen nations shall submit themselves, and do homage unto thee my God.

For the Lord hath a power royal, and an imperial dominion over the heathen.

The most mighty and greatest of all them that dwell on the earth, have eaten, and after that they have tasted the spiritual gifts of the Lord, they have submitted themselves, and made humble suit° unto him.

Yea, and all the dead, which are buried in the earth, shall kneel and make reverence in his honour, because he hath not disdained to spend his own life for them.

They that shall come after us, shall honour and serve him. These things shall be written of the Lord, that our posterity may know and understand them.

That they also may come and show these things to the people that shall be born of them, that the Lord hath done these things, which be so marvellous.

58. William Hunnis, *Seven Sobs of a Sorrowful Soul for Sin, Comprehending Those Seven Psalms of the Princely Prophet David, Commonly Called Penitential* (1583)

[See headnote to 27. *Seven Sobs* proved to be extremely popular, being printed fifteen times up to 1636, and there may have been an additional issue even before 1583. Hunnis provided each of the Penitential Psalms with a simple unison tune, though the music was not included in all editions. The verses of the Psalm proper are set in italics, with Hunnis's massive interpolations — often drawing on many other biblical passages — in roman. In the margin beside each italicized section of the Psalm Hunnis includes the Latin Vulgate text. As Clare Costley King'oo points out, Hunnis's book contained more than just the Penitential Psalms paraphrases, and was in fact constructed much like a late medieval prayer book, with creeds, the Lord's Prayer, and other prayers for various occasions. Despite the traditional contents, however, the theology of Hunnis's *Sobs* is fiercely Calvinist, emphasizing original sin and the terrors of divine judgment. *Seven Sobs* was published by John Harington of Stepney, who had also published Wyatt's *Certain Psalms* thirty-four years earlier. It was Harington who began compiling the Arundel-Harington Manuscript, containing Wyatt's Penitential Psalms, and other Psalms by Wyatt, Surrey, John and Robert Dudley, and the Sidneys. Harington's son, Sir John Harington of Kelston, who was himself a metrical Psalmist, continued the collection after his father's death. See Clare Costley King'oo, *Miserere Mei*; King'oo, 'William Hunnis and the Success of the *Seven Sobs*', *Renaissance Studies*, 29.4 (2015), 615–31.]

Psalm 51

Miserere mei. [Have mercy on me]

The first part.

 1. O thou that mad'st the world of nought,[450]   *nothing*
   Whom God thy creatures call,
Which formedst man like to thyself,
   Yet suffer'dst him to fall:
5 2. Thou God, which by thy heavenly word
   Didst flesh of virgin take,
And so becam'st both God and man,
   For sinful flesh's sake:[451]
 3. O thou that sawest when man by sin
10   To hell was overthrown,
Didst meekly suffer death on cross,
   To have thy mercy known:
 4. Thou God, which didst the patriarchs
   And fathers old divine,
15 From time to time preserve and keep,   *guard*
   By mercy great of thine:
 5. O thou that Noah keptst from flood,
   And Abram day by day,
As he along through Egypt passed,
20   Didst guide him in the way:
 6. Thou God that Lot from Sodom's plague
   Didst safely keep also,
And Daniel from the lion's jaws,
   Thy mercy great to show:
25 7. O thou good God, that didst divide
   The sea like hills to stand,
That children thine might thorough pass   *through*
   From cruel Pharaoh's hand;

---

[450] Hunnis's 'of nought' is not part of the original, adding the theological idea of creation *ex nihilo*, which holds that God created everything out of nothing, rather than out of some pre-existing matter, or out of himself, say.

[451] One of the functions of Hunnis's interpolations is to Christianize the Psalm, making David an exceptionally prescient prophet.

>   8. So that when Pharaoh and his host,
>   Thy children did subdue,
>   Thou overthrew'st them in the sea,
>   To prove thy sayings true:⁴⁵²
>   9. O thou that Jonah in the fish
>   Three days didst keep from pain,
>   Which was a figure of thy death,
>   And rising up again:⁴⁵³
>   10. I say, thou God, which didst preserve
>   Amidst the fiery flame,
>   The three young men, which sang therein
>   The glory of thy name:⁴⁵⁴
>   11. *Thou God have mercy on my soul,*
>   *Thy goodness me restore,*
>   *And for thy mercies infinite*
>   *Think on my sin no more.*
>   12. O Lord the number of my sins   *counted*
>   Is more than can be told,
>   Wherefore I humbly do desire
>   Thy mercies manifold.
>   13. For small offense thy mercy small
>   May soon small faults suffice,
>   But I (alas) for many faults
>   For greater mercy cries.
>   14. And though the number of my sins
>   Surpass the salt sea sand,
>   And that the filth of them deserve
>   The wrath of thy just hand:
>   15. Yet do thy mercies far surmount
>   The sins of all in all,
>   Thou wilt with mercy us relieve,
>   For mercy when we call.
>   16. Right well I know, man hath not power
>   So much for to transgress,
>   As thou with mercy may'st forgive
>   Through thine almightiness.

---

⁴⁵² Exodus 14.
⁴⁵³ Jonah, as well as Jesus's typological application of the story to himself in Matthew 12. 40.
⁴⁵⁴ The story of Shadrach, Meshach, and Abednego is in Daniel 3, and the song they sang on their deliverance ('The Song of the Three Children', in Latin the 'Bendicite') was sung or recited as a canticle in the English service of Morning Prayer.

	17. I do confess my faults be more
65	Than thousands else beside,
	More noisome, and more odious,
	More fouler to be tried,
	18. Than ever was the loathsome swine,
70	Or menstrual cloth berayed:⁴⁵⁵ *defiled*
	To think thereon my woeful soul,
	(Alas) is yet afraid.
	19. Wherefore, good Lord, do not behold
	How wicked I have been,
75	*But wash me from my wickedness,*
	And cleanse me from my sin.
	20. The Israelites being defil'd⁴⁵⁶
	Durst not approach thee nigh, *closely*
	Till they their garments and themselves
80	Had washèd decently.⁴⁵⁷
	21. The priests also eke cleansèd were *also*
	Ere they thy face would see,
	Else had they perished in their sin;
	Such, Lord, was thy decree.
85	22. Alas, how much more need I then
	To crave while I am here,
	To wash my foul and spotted soul
	That it may clean appear?
	23. Polluted cloths with filth distained *stained*
90	Do many washings crave,
	Ere that the launder can obtain *launderer*
	The thing that he would have.
	24. My soul likewise (alas) doth need
	Thy many dews of grace,
95	Ere it be clean; for cankered sin *corrosive*
	So deep hath taken place.
	25. The leprosy that Naman had,
	Could not be done away,
	Till he seven times in Jordan flood
100	Had washed him day by day.⁴⁵⁸

---

⁴⁵⁵ Both these items are unclean according to Jewish law, which prohibits eating pork (Leviticus 11) and touching women until they have been purified after menstruation (Leviticus 15).
⁴⁵⁶ The metre requires an awkward stress on the second syllable of 'being'.
⁴⁵⁷ Leviticus 6, 11.
⁴⁵⁸ Naaman's story is in II Kings 5, and the ritual cleansing of leprosy is described in Leviticus 14.

26. How many waters need I then
  For to be washèd in,
Ere I be purgèd fair and clean,
  And cleansèd from my sin?
27. But, Lord, thy mercy is the soap,   *alkaline laundry fluid*
  And washing lye also,
That shall both scour and cleanse the filth
  Which in my soul do grow.
28. Why should I then (alas) despair
  Of goodness thine to me,
When that thy justice willeth me
  To put my trust in thee,
29. Thy promise, Lord, thy mouth hath passed,
  Which cannot be but true,
That thou wilt mercy have on them,
  That turn to thee anew.
30. I know, when heaven and earth shall pass,
  This promise shall stand fast: *secure*
  Wherefore into thy majesty,
  I offer now at last,
31. An heart contrite and sorrowful,
  With all humility;
For heinous sins by it conceived
  Through mine iniquity.
32. *I do acknowledge all my faults,*
  My sins stand me before;
I have them in remembrance, Lord,
  And will for evermore.
33. Because thou shouldst the same forget
  I still do think thereon,
And set it up before my face,
  Always to look upon.
34. *Against thee only have I sinned*   *alone*
  And done ill in thy sight;   *evil*
In whom it lies to punish me,
  Or to forgive me quite.
35. But sure my hope is firmly fixed,
  That thou wilt me forgive;
For with thine honour shall it stand,
  To suffer me to live: *allow*
36. *That all the world may witness thee,*
  A judge most just to be,
For that thou wilt thy promise keep,
  To all that trust in thee:

 145 37. That is, our sins thou wilt remit,
     And clean forget them all,   *completely*
    And bend thine ears unto our plaints,   *laments*
     When we upon thee call.

   The second part.

    1. O Lord consider with thyself,
 150   What mettle I possess;
   Behold in sin I was conceived,
     And born in wickedness,
    2. From Adam first this sin was drawn,[459]
     Whereby I am made prone
 155 To do the ill should thee offend,   *evil*
     And let the good alone.
    3. Yea, many a time I am so drawn
     To do I would not do,[460]
   And that I would I leave undone,
 160   For want of might thereto;
    4. Such is, O Lord, the strength and force
     Of my concupiscence: *lust*
   But yet of greater force than this,
     Is, Lord, thine indulgence.
 165 5. For thou wilt mercy show to them,
     That mercy do require;
   And wilt not turn thy face from such
     As mercy do desire.
    6. Surely of honour more is thine,
 170   Through pity men to save;
   Than by thy justice to condemn
     Such as deservèd have.
    7. Therefore, O Lord, receive me now,
     Which do myself accuse;
 175 To th'end thou should'st my sins forgive,
     And all my faults excuse.
    8. O Lord, I do not hide my sins,
     But show them unto thee;
   Because thou should'st thy mercy grant,
 180   As thou hast promised me.

---

[459] Unusually, especially in the context of Psalm 51. 5 (in BCP, 'in sin hath my mother conceived me'), Hunnis ascribes blame for original sin not to Eve but to Adam.

[460] Echoing Romans 7. 15–16, 'For that which I do I allow not: for what I would, that do I not; but what I hate, that do I. If then I do that which I would not, I consent unto the law that is good', and so forth (KJV).

9. For never yet thou hast been found
    In any word unjust,
Ne canst thou now begin at me,
    Since that in thee I trust.
10. *Thou, Lord, hast ever lovèd truth,*   *truth*
    And truth thou art most sure,
Thou art the very verity
    For ever to endure.
11. Thou promisedst to Abraham,   *descendants*
    His seed to multiply,
Even as the stars, and as the sand
    That in the sea doth lie.[461]
12. To Isaac and to Jacob eke,
    Like promise didst thou make;
And thou the same performèd hast,
    For this thy promise sake.
13. Thou promisedst to Joshua,
    To strength him with thine hand;
And so he slew the Canaanites,
    And did divide their land.[462]
14. To Gideon thou promise mad'st,
    That he should set at large
The Israelites, which were in thrall,   *captivity*
    And in their en'mies charge.[463]
15. When Hezekiah lay sore sick;
    And well nigh at death's door;
Thou promis'dst him his health again,
    To live fifteen years more.[464]
16. Thus, hast thou kept thy promises,
    To thousands else beside;
Who have reposèd trust in thee,
    Thou hast not help denied.
17. Even so, good Lord, thy promise keep
    With me that am unjust,
A scabbèd sheep, one of thy flock,[465]
    And overcharged with lust.

---

[461] Genesis 22. 17.
[462] Joshua 6. 2.
[463] Judges 6–7.
[464] II Kings 20.
[465] Hunnis may have in mind a popular saying, 'one scabbed sheep is enough to infect a whole flock' (Golding's translation of Calvin's *Sermons on Galatians* (1574), though it appears in many works).

18. Which of long time have run astray,
    The time since I was born,
Yet now returned with heavy heart,
    That's with repentance torn.
19. Thus hath thy grace now callèd me,
    With mercy of thine hand;
And what thy will and pleasure is,
    By grace I understand.
20. *Thou hast revealèd unto me*
    The things that be unknown,
The secret points of wisdom thine
    Thy grace to me hath shown.
21. The mysteries that hidden were
    Within thy sacred word,
Thou hast to us made manifest,
    By Jesus Christ our Lord.
22. I am now fed with bread of life,
    That shall my hunger slake;
And from Dame Wisdom's watersprings
    My drink I often take.[466]
23. Now Wisdom hath cast out her flood,
    The plants all watered be,
And still she seeks to lighten those
    That put their trust in thee.
24. Of this her flood Saint Paul did drink,
    And he us taught thereby,
Thy wisdom, Lord, which secret was,
    And hidden long did lie:[467]
25. As thou to him didst manifest,
    By thy free Spirit before,
Which searcheth out the very depth
    Of secrets thine and store.
26. Of this, Lord, part I tasted have,
    Through mercy showed to me,
And am now taught by them to know,
    Mine own infirmity:
27. And by it am I taught likewise
    Thy goodness for to know,
Beseeching thee this work begun,
    May never part me fro.

diminish

---

[466] Proverbs 18. 4. Wisdom and Folly (though the latter is not so named) are both personified as women in Proverbs.
[467] 1 Corinthians 10 and 12. 13.

>   28. So that the light which kindled is
>   In me by thy great grace,
>   May so increase, as darkness, Lord,
> 260   May never more take place.[468]

The third part.

> *With hyssop, Lord, besprinkle me,*
>   *And cleanse me from my sin:*[469]
> *More whiter then shall I be made*
>   *Than ever snow hath been:*
> 265 2. Thou didst command this herb with blood
>   A sprinkle for to be,
>   To sprinkle such as cleansèd were
>   From loathsome leprosy.[470]
>   3. A bundle of this herb, O Lord,
> 270   Thou didst command also
>   To dip in blood of simple sheep,
>   And therewithal to show   *in addition*
>   4. Upon the door-posts of the house,
>   The slayer might it see,
> 275 Whereby the plague might shun the place
>   And from thy people flee.
>   5. These unto us do represent
>   The blood of thy dear Son,
>   Without the which no man is clean,
> 280   Whatever can be done.[471]
>   6. And he that marks his soul therewith
>   And puts his trust therein,
>   The slayer hath no power to hurt,
>   Nor plague him for his sin.
> 285 7. If with this grace thou sprinkle me,
>   I shall be white, I know;
>   And though as blood my sins appear,
>   They shall be like the snow:
>   8. Yea, though my sins as purple were
> 290   Or as the scarlet dye,

[468] Compare Matthew 6. 22–23.
[469] Lock and Norton both use this word in their paraphrases of Psalm 51. See 36 and 40.
[470] Leviticus 14.
[471] In Exodus 12, Moses instructs the Hebrews to take hyssop and sprinkle the lintels of their doors with blood to protect them from the slaying of the Egyptian firstborn. Typologically, this prefigures and is superseded by the use of hyssop to give Jesus a sponge of vinegar on the cross, since Jesus's blood saved mankind from sin. See also Hebrews 9.

Thy grace shall make them as the wool,
    T'appear before thine eye.
9. *Then shall I hear the words of joy,*
    Of gladness so likewise,
That Nathan to King David spake,
    Whom thou didst not despise.[472]
10. That is, my sins are now put out,
    Whatever I have done,
And are forgiven me quite and clean,   *completely*
    By Jesu Christ thy Son.
11. Then shall I hear the words Christ spake,
    To him the palsy had;
My son, thy sins are thee forgiven,
    Arise, go home, be glad.[473]
12. Then shall I hear thee also speak
    By inspiration,
Whereby I shall be comforted
    In tribulation.
13. Yea, Lord, *the bones thou broken hast,*
    Shall then again rejoice
Through working of thy heavenly grace
    And sweetness of thy voice:
14. That is, the powers of my poor soul
    Whom sin so weak hath brought,
Whereby it wanted power to work
    The good it long time sought,
15. Shall then recover that was lost,
    And be reviv'd again,
And through the quick'ning of the Spirit   *enlivening*
    Sin shall no more remain.
16. Wherefore, *thy face turn from my sins,*
    And wipe my faults away,
And eke all mine iniquities;
    Most humbly I thee pray:
17. I mean, the face of justice thine,
    Wherewith thou dost behold
The sins we daily do commit,
    To punish manifold:
18. This face, good Lord, turn thou from me
    And from the faults I make,

---

[472] II Samuel 12.
[473] Matthew 9. 2.

And them forget, and me forgive,
    For thy great mercy sake.
19. But, Lord, the face of mercy thine,
    From me turn not away,
But therewithal behold me still,
    And help me day by day.
20. For what am I, if that thy grace
    Thou take away from me?
A bondman under sin and death,   *one in bondage*
    And cast away of thee.
21. And every man thy grace that wants
    Shall have an heart of stone,
As Pharaoh had, after thy grace
    Departed was and gone.[474]
22. He shall both see and hear indeed,
    Yet shall be deaf and blind;
His ears and eyes shall stoppèd be,
    The truth he shall not find.[475]
23. His heart likewise shall frozen be,
    Or as the stony wall;
He shall thy creatures like and love,
    And love not thee at all:
24. Yea, such a heart, O Lord, in me
    Long time hath taken place,
Which no way can be mollified,   *softened*
    But by thy special grace.
25. Wherefore I pray thee heartily,
    Remove this heart from me;
And, Lord, in me a new heart make,
    That flexible may be:
26. A fleshy heart, both soft and meek,   *not hard and stony*
    An heart that I may know
Thou art the Lord, without whose grace
    No goodness I can show.
27. This grace it is that must revive
    A right spirit, Lord, in me.
My spirit through sin is crooked made,
    And loathsome for to see.
28. *Make it upright therefore to be,*
    And that decline it may

---

[474] God hardens Pharaoh's heart throughout Exodus 4–14.
[475] Matthew 13. 15 and Isaiah 6. 10.

      From worldly pleasures light and vain,
          That vanish soon away.
      29. Vouchsafe, O Lord, to heavenly things   *grant*
          My spirit may still aspire,
375 And with thy grace replenished be,
          Most humbly I desire.
      30. Let neither yet adversity,
          Nor worldly wealth also,
      Pluck down my spirit, nor hinder it,
380   Where it desires to go.
      31. *Nor cast me off at any time,*
          From presence of thy face;
      Ne take from me thy Holy Spirit,
          O Lord, in any case.
385 32. My sins, good Lord, behind thee cast,
          There ever to remain:
      But cast not me from thy sweet face,
          As thou didst wicked Cain.[476]
      33. Nor from thy favour cast me so,
390   As thou didst cast King Saul,[477]
      For if that I thy presence lose,
          I cannot choose but fall.
      34. O Lord how sweet and gracious[478]
          Is this thy Spirit most pure!
395 It leadeth those that loveth thee,
          Where righteous folk endure.
      35. Grant, Lord, that this thy Holy Spirit
          May dwell within me still,
      And me confirm in righteousness,
400   According to thy will.

The fourth part.

O Lord, my God, restore to me
    Thy saving health again,
And stablish me with thy chief Spirit,   *establish, head*
    That it may still remain.
405 2. My sins, O Lord, have been the cause
          That I thy grace did want,
      And when thy grace departed was,
          I found thy Spirit but scant:

---

[476] Genesis 4. 12.
[477] 1 Samuel 15. 28.
[478] gracious] The metre requires three syllables ('gra-ci-ous').

3. The loss whereof did grieve me much,
      And by the same I found
All goodness gone, all wickedness
      Within me to abound.
4. For light and darkness may not be
      At one time in one place;
No more may sin and wickedness
      Associate be with grace.
5. Wherefore, the greatness of my loss
      Hath made my grief the more;
And where in sin I had delight,
      I now repent it sore.
6. Behold, therefore, most mighty God,
      Mine inward grief of mind;
And of thy goodness me restore
      To that I cannot find:
7. I mean, thy holy sacred Spirit,
      Which I through weakness lost,
Mine enemies were strong and fierce,
      And cruelly me tossed:
8. So that my soul too feeble was,
      Their power for to withstand;
Good Lord, in grace yet once again
      Confirm me with thy hand:
9. And let thy Spirit no more depart,
      No, Lord, not when I die,
But that it may still with my soul
      Remain continually.
10. Then shall I steadfastly instruct
      The wicked in thy way,
Whereby they may to thee return,
      That long have gone astray.
11. I will my self put forth, O Lord,
      To sinners all that be,
As an example them to cause
      For to return to thee.
12. I will not cease for to declare
      Thy justice everywhere,
And of thy judgement bring them all
      In terror and in fear.
13. And then will I again extol
      Thy mercies over all,
To pluck them from despairing, Lord,
      Lest any therein fall.

14. Thus shall I able be to do
    Being confirmed in thee,
By working of thy Holy Spirit,
    Which thou shalt put in me.
15. Thy servant Moses was afraid
    To go on message sent,
Till thou promis'dst to be with him,
    When he to Pharaoh went:
16. After which time he doubted not,
    But forth went on his way,
Accomplishing thy holy hest,   *request*
    As thou didst bid him say.[479]
17. The seventy elders of the host,
    To thee whom Moses brought,
Till part of Moses' spirit they had,
    Were able to do naught:
18. But after that, they prophesied,
    And did the people guide,
And rulèd them with righteousness
    And truth on every side.[480]
19. Lord, Peter, at a woman's voice,
    Thy sweet Son Christ denayed,   *denied*
And ready was him to forsake;
    He was so sore afraid:[481]
20. Until that thou revivedst him
    With this thy Spirit of grace:
Yea, Lord, thy son's apostles all
    Were bidden for a space
21. To bide within Jerusalem,
    In prayer and in love;
Till they were with thy Holy Spirit
    Fulfillèd from above.[482]
22. Wherefore, send down thy noble Spirit
    In me the same to be,
And from the guiltiness of blood,
    Good God deliver me.

---

[479] Exodus 3–4.
[480] Exodus 24.
[481] Matthew 26. 69–72.
[482] Acts 1. 4 to 2. 4.

The fifth part.

Thou God, that God art of my health,
490   *Deliver me, I pray,*
From sin that I committed have
        Against thee day by day.
  2. A multitude of sins there be
        From flesh and blood that grow,
495 Which I through my concupiscence   *lust*
        Have daily done, I know.
  3. And this corruption is in me
        By nature, as I find;
For what is he can make that clean,
500   That is unclean by kind?   *nature*
  4. How can a man of woman born
        Be clean? I fain would know;   *gladly*
The child that is but one day old
        Is yet unclean also.
505   5. Thus flesh and blood such works bring forth,
        As aye corrupted be,   *always*
And therefore cannot heaven enjoy,
        Ne dwell and reign with thee.
  6. Upon corrupted nature mine,
510   O Lord, pour forth thy grace;
And from these bloods deliver me,
        And all my sins deface.   *blot out*
  7. Then, Lord, shall I be purgèd clean
        From all my wickedness,
515 Which grant, good God, *So shall my tongue*
        Exalt thy righteousness:
  8. In that thou mercy show'st to me,
        Being a wicked man,
Giving me grace pensive to be,
520   My grievous sins to scan.   *consider*
  9. Making me just that am unjust,
        Wherein thou, God, art found,
In mercy, truth, and righteousness
        Most perfect, sure and sound.
525 10. But yet, O Lord, before my tongue
        Thy righteousness can raise,
My lips and mouth thou open must,
        Whereby to show thy praise.

       11. For else, unseemly praise will be,
530   Where lips be licked with sin;
       And where the mouth with wickedness
           Is stuffèd full within.
       12. Good Lord, the prophet Isaiah,
          When he thy glory saw,
535 Confessed his lips to be unclean,
          And therefore stood in awe,
       13. Until such time a seraphin
          Thou sent'st, with burning coal
       His lips to touch, and therewithal
540   He by and by was whole:[483]
       14. I mean, that his unrighteousness
          Was then forgiven him quite,
       And all his sins and wickedness
          Was clean put out of sight.   *completely*
545 15. O Lord, my God, in such a sort
          Vouchsafe my mouth to touch,
       That I thy glory may set forth
          Too little and too much.
       16. *To offer sacrifice to thee,*
550   *Or offerings burnt were vain;*
       No pleasure, Lord, hast thou in them,
          Nor ought in them remain.
       17. They were but figures of that thing,
          Which now to pass is come,
555 That is, the lively sacrifice   *life-giving*
          Of Jesus Christ thy Son.[484]
       18. To offer gold to thee, O Lord,
          Or treasure of the land,
       It needeth not; sith all the world   *since*
560   Is thine, and at thy hand.
       19. And yet I will not empty come,
          But offer unto thee
       An humble spirit, with heart contrite,
          For mine iniquity.
565 20. *This sacrifice, O Lord, I know*
          Thou wilt no time despise;
       But it behold, and look thereon
          With thy most gracious eyes:

---

[483] Isaiah 6.

[484] A compact description of biblical typology, in which matters in the Old Testament are seen as figures of Christ and the truths of the gospels.

21. And, Lord, for that there nothing should
     Be left behind in me,
Both body, soul, and all their powers
     I offer unto thee:
22. And as a lively sacrifice,
     As Hezekiah did,
Such time as he thy favour got,
     And health recoverèd.[485]
23. The same did Mary Magdalen
     Offer in humble sort:[486]
The thief also upon the cross
     To his endless comfort.[487]
24. Great numbers more unspeakable
     By this thy favour wan;   *won*
And I, through grace, now penitent,
     Although a sinful man,
25. Do claim no less of mercy thine,
     For to be showed to me:
Because thou art, as then thou wast,
     And evermore shalt be.
26. *To Sion, Lord, likewise show forth*
     Thy favour and thy grace;
That is, unto thy faithful flock
     Dispersed from place to place.
27. Such as depend on thee alone,
     And do themselves forsake,
Upon the walls of this thy fort
     Thou, Lord, must undertake
28. Watchmen to set, continually
     The same for to defend,
Lest that the en'mies unawares
     Bring all to woeful end.[488]

---

[485] II Chronicles 29.
[486] Probably a reference to the woman who anoints Jesus's feet with precious ointment in Matthew 26. Though unnamed in Matthew, and in the corresponding passages in Mark and Luke, she is identified as Mary the sister of Martha and Lazarus in John 11. 1–2. This Mary and Mary Magdalene were traditionally conflated, though without any basis.
[487] All the gospels state that two others were crucified with Jesus, described as thieves in Matthew, Mark, and Luke. In Matthew and Mark the thieves are said to mock Jesus, but Luke includes a more extended narrative in which the thieves speak, the one taunting Jesus, and the other chastising his fellow thief and praying to Jesus to remember him when he comes into his kingdom. Matthew 27, Mark 15, Luke 23, John 19.
[488] Psalm 127. 1, Isaiah 62. 6.

29. Thou know'st, O Lord, of what small force
        Mankind hath ever been,
Since first our father Adam fell,
        When he committed sin.
30. Help us, therefore, most mighty God,
        So with thy heavenly grace.
As we in building Sion here,
        By faith may see thy face:
31. So shall we then, through mercy thine
        Be squarèd stones meet found
To building of Jerusalem,
        Whose walls do still abound
32. With lively stones of thy true Church
        Here militant in earth;[489]
Where thine elect still offer shall,
        While thou shalt spare them breath,
33. Such off'rings burnt, as thou best lov'st
        Which is of thanks and praise,
We shall not spare the same to do,
        While life shall length our days.
34. *This sacrifice of justice is,*
        Which all thy creatures crave
To give the same only to thee,
        Most worthy so to have.
35. This is the bullocks of our lips,
        Whereof the prophet says,[490]
We shall with lips unto thy name
        Confess most condign praise: *deserved*
36. Which shall to thee accepted be,
        Ten thousand times much more,
Than were the bullocks great and fat,
        Offered in time before.
37. Lord grant we may in number be
        Of thine elected sort,
Which shall this sacrifice present
        Unto our soul's comfort:

---

[489] Hunnis adapts the Psalm's promise of rebuilding Jerusalem to a metaphor in which the 'lively stones' (also 'squared', meaning cut square for building as well as morally framed or regulated) are the godly elect and Jerusalem is thus a figure for the Church, not an actual city.
[490] Hosea 14. 2, 'so will we render the calves of our lips' (Geneva).

38. And that as burning incense sweet
    Thou wilt receive the same,
Upon thine altar, which is Christ,
640   Our mean for sin and blame: *Amen.*

59. William Patten, 1583. *An: Foelicissimi Regni Reginae Elizabeth: XXVI.*
['In the 26th Year of the Most Happy Reign of Queen Elizabeth']
The Psalm by the Old Translation Called Deus Judicium (1583)

[William Patten (d. c. 1598) was a minor cleric and scholar, born in London to a clothworker, though his grandfather was brother to William Waynflete (born Patten), Bishop of Winchester and founder of Magdalen College Oxford. His history of *The Expedition into Scotland of the Most Worthily Fortunate Prince Edward, Duke of Somerset* (1548), in which Patten participated, was used by Holinshed in his *Chronicles*. In 1548 he was also appointed Collector of Customs in London. He was granted a lease on the manor of Stoke Newington, became Justice of the Peace for Middlesex, and was appointed Receiver-General of revenues for Yorkshire. Patten's career crashed abruptly, however, when almost 8000 pounds was discovered missing from his accounts. A member of the Society of Antiquaries, Patten published works on ancient biblical languages (he was the first English expert in Armenian, into which the Bible had been translated in the fifth century), as well as his two metrical Psalms, both issued as broadsides. Both were also dedicated to, and adapted to praise, Queen Elizabeth, and Patten's introductory notes indicate that they were intended for her Accession Day celebrations on November 17. Both Psalms are printed down the right-hand side of the page, with the Latin translation of Johannis Campensis printed on the left, spaced to match Patten's version verse by verse. Psalm 72 is provided with a unison tune for singing. Patten's name does not appear on the broadside, but the only surviving copy has a sketch of the Patten coat of arms, probably in Patten's hand, and the format is identical to Patten's 1599 Psalm (see 72). Brian O'Kill describes Patten as 'badly infected with monarchophilia', though it might be said that the Psalmist suffers from the same condition. In his *The Calendar of Scripture* (1575), Patten includes a fifteen-page disquisition on the significance of the number seven, and Elizabeth is called 'The Seventh of My God'. Patten's Psalm 72 has seven stanzas, each of seven lines, as does his Psalm 21 (see 72). See Brian O'Kill, 'The Printed Works of William Patten', *Transactions of the Cambridge Bibliographical Society*, 7.1 (1977), 28–45; Peter Sherlock, *ODNB*.]

Psalm 72

1. O power divine of mortal eye not seen,
   That hast and dost so mercifully bless
   With gift of rightful regiment our Queen,

			The daughter of a king: with evenness	
	I			
5		2.	Justly to judge 'tween bigger and the less,	
		3.	So as is brought by mounts and hillocks small	
			Justice and peace upon her people all.[491]	
		4.	Rendering to poor aye rightful doom by law,	*always, judgment*
			Revenge for wrongs upon their children done,	
10		5.	That all of thee, O Lord, may stand in awe,	
	II		From age to age while sun and moon do run:	
		6.	Justice doth light whereas her people won,	
			Like rain that on new reapèd ground doth fall,	
			And showers on field for drought that chinks withal.	*gasps, as well*
15		7.	Justice triumphs within her lands we see,	
			In course full as the moon doth peace abound:	
		8.	By seas and floods extends her sovereignty,	
	III	9.	Her enemies crouch and lick dust from the ground,	
			Her friendship sought by kings about her round,	
20			The Dutch, the Dane, the Muscovite and Sweathen,	*Swede*
			With these the very infidel and heathen.	
		10.	Kings far, of seas and islands many one,	
			Of Saba, Moluccs, Araby, and Ind,	*the Moluccas or Spice Islands*
			By gifts of gold, of pearl and precious stone,	
25	IV	11.	What honour they her bear do show their mind:	
		12.	The poor that cry at home, her pity find,	
			How graciously their wrongs it doth redress,	
			Who else were sure to perish in distress.	
		13.	Pity she hath on them in misery,	
30			Upraising by relief the cast down wight,	*creature*
		14.	Quites him from spoils of craft and injury,	*repays*
	V		So dear her subject's blood is in her sight.	
		15.	Long shall she flourish in glory, fame, and might,	
			Presented oft with pure Arabian gold,	
35			Honoured alway with praises manifold.	*always*
		16.	On mountain tops, with her grows wheat at fill,	
			That strong of stalk, and ears well fillèd been,	
			Whistling like cedar trees on Leban hill,	*Lebanon*

---

[491] Elizabeth is portrayed here in one of her popular mythical guises, Astraea, goddess of Justice, the last immortal to leave the earth in the Iron Age, but whose return brings peace and prosperity. The wordplay (polyptoton) on 'justly', 'judge', and 'justice', however, echoes (flattery skating toward blasphemy) the similar treatment of justification in paraphrases of Psalm 51 by Wyatt, Lock, and others.

	VI	Her burghers spring as grass in meadow green,[492]
40	17.	Spread shall her name and last full bright and sheen
		As sun, that all estates must yield in heart,
		Her to be blessed, and all that take her part.

	18.	High heried be thou, Lord of England, God,	*exalted*
		That wonders work'st and blessed our Queen always	
45		With happy reign at home and fame abroad,	
	VII	And like to this will grant her many a day:	
	19.	Blessed be thy digne majesty for aye,	*worthy, forever*
		With fullness of that majesty again,	
		Let all the earth resound, Amen, Amen.	

60. George Flinton, *A Manual of Prayers Newly Gathered out of Many and Diverse Famous Authors As Well Ancient As of the Time Present* (1583)

[George Flinton (fl. 1580s) was a translator, compiler, and printer living and working in Rouen. A layman and merchant, Flinton was persuaded to establish and run the English Catholic Press by Robert Parsons. The *Manual of Prayers* proved popular and was reprinted in many editions, either on the Continent or at clandestine presses in England. The prose version of Psalm 79 (78 in the Catholic numbering) is included in the chapter 'containing necessary prayers for the prosperity of our brethren, friends, and neighbours', and is a translation based on a Latin paraphrase by Frans Titelmans, a Flemish Franciscan who was an opponent of Erasmus. His *Elucidatio in omnes psalmos iuxta veritatem vulgatae* was printed in Antwerp in 1531. See Eamon Duffy, 'Praying the Counter-Reformation', in *Early Modern English Catholicism: Identity, Memory, and Counter-Reformation*, ed. by James E. Kelly and Susan Royal (Leiden and Boston: Brill, 2017), pp. 206–25; 'Frans Titelmans', in *Contemporaries of Erasmus*, ed. by Beitenholz, III, 326–27.]

Psalm 79[493]

A prayer for the church afflicted.

O God, the gentiles, barbarous nations, and infidels, which have no faith in thee, nor knowledge of thy name, are entered into thy heritage; they have taken thy people by force of arms, and as vanquishers they occupy our cities; they have defiled with their abhominations thy temple, dedicated to thy honour and

---

[492] burghers] A curious addition, taking the literal statement of the Psalmist ('his fruit [...] shall be green in the city', BCP) and turning it into a kind of civic metaphor.
[493] Numbered 78 in the text, according to Catholic numbering.

5   service, they have polluted the vessels consecrated for the service of the temple, and used them profanely.⁴⁹⁴

We are become a reproach and laughing-stock to our neighbours, in such sort that they scorn, despise, and make a jest of us, rejoicing at our afflictions, and in their mirth they upbraid us: but thou, O Lord, upon whose will we wholly
10 depend, how long wilt thou be angry with us?

And wherefore dost thou so deliver us into the hands of our enemies, as though thou haddest shaked us off, and hereafter would have no more care over us: wherefore dost thou show the fury of thy wrath towards thy people, which are the sheep of thy holy pasture, whereof thou art the ruler, shepherd, defender,
15 and protector?

Be mindful, O Lord, of thy holy Church, and leave it not in the hands of thy enemies, but deliver it by thy strong power; behold, and consider, the league and testament made with the elect.⁴⁹⁵ Remember thy promise made unto them, that thou wouldest not forsake them that were contrite in heart,⁴⁹⁶ but wouldest
20 save them that were humble in spirit.

For in truth we are kept under, afflicted and brought to nothing, we are contemptible, abject,° and miserable, in such sort that we are a gazing-stock° and ignominy to all nations: wherefore, O Lord, dost thou not turn thy face to us thy poor servants? why dost thou turn thy face from them, and suffer° thy
25 enemies so cruelly to rage against them? why dost thou not behold the misery and affliction wherein we thy servants (destitute and desolate of all help, and having no comfort but in thee) are afflicted and tormented of our enemies?

Awake, O Lord God, dissemble no longer⁴⁹⁷ but come to succour thy people, and make haste to help thy faithful servants, and save us from the hands of our
30 enemies (we humbly beseech thee) for thy most glorious name's sake, for thine own self, and for thy infinite mercy: that we the posterity may a little taste the sweetness of thy promises, which our forefathers have so abundantly felt.

---

⁴⁹⁴ By omitting the Psalm's specific reference to Jerusalem, Flinton makes easier the identification of the Psalmist's situation with that of English Catholics.

⁴⁹⁵ elect] Appropriating for Catholicism the key Protestant notion of those predestined by God for salvation. In fact, St Paul writes of election in Romans (8–11), and predestination was not exclusive to Protestant theology, despite the popular association with Calvinism.

⁴⁹⁶ The familiar figure for true penitence, the 'contrite heart', comes from Psalm 51. 17.

⁴⁹⁷ dissemble] An odd behaviour to ascribe to God, perhaps connected to the necessity of Catholics practicing deceit in a Protestant nation. Not only Jesuits and fugitive priests, but lay Catholics, whether recusants or church-papists, were forced into dissembling of various kinds, including the infamous practice of equivocation that condoned outward deceit, so long as the truth was maintained to God in one's heart.

But we that are thy people, and the sheep of thy pasture, which worship no other God, which seek no other shepherd and governor besides thee, which put our whole trust and confidence in thee, and desire to be fed, ruled, and governed by thee only,° we will render thee most humble thanks, and set forth thy glory for ever and ever.

We will declare and show thy praises from generation to generation, for thou of thy mere° good will, hast restored us to the liberty which we have required: we therefore (in adversity as well as in prosperity, or howsoever it shall please thee to dispose of us) will serve thee with joy and gladness: we will continue still in thanksgiving, attending patiently thy aid and help. Amen.

61. King James VI of Scotland, *The Essays of a Prentice in the Divine Art of Poesy* (1584)

[James Charles Stuart (1566–1625), King James VI of Scotland, and from 1604 also James I of England, was an exceptionally well educated, scholarly, and literary monarch. Having acceded to the throne at the age of thirteen months, he did not begin ruling in his own right until the 1580s. During his minority, James was educated in the Protestant faith and tutored by George Buchanan, a learned humanist and one of the most accomplished neo-Latin dramatists and poets, though also apparently a harsh taskmaster. James may have begun his lifelong devotion to the Psalms under Buchanan's instruction, since Buchanan's translation of the Psalms into classical Latin metres was widely circulated and admired across Europe. In Scotland, James led and patronized a group of court poets known as the Castalian Band (including Alexander Montgomerie), and he himself wrote poems and prose in Scots and translated Psalms, including Psalm 104, printed along with other early poems and translations in 1584. A note after the title states that James translated from Immanuel Tremellius, a Jewish convert to Protestant Christianity whose Latin Bible (1575–1579) was popular with learned Protestants. The eight-line iambic pentameter stanza used by James is entirely unlike the popular metres of the Sternhold Hopkins tradition, and may be derived from the late medieval French stanza known as 'double croisée' (rhymed *ababbcbc*). James termed it 'ballet royal' in chapter 8 of his *Reulis and Cautelis to be Observit and Eschewit in Scottish Poesie* ('Rules and Cautions to be Observed and Eschewed in Scottish Poetry'), which immediately preceded Psalm 104 in *The Essays*. See James Doelman, *King James I and the Religious Culture of England* (Cambridge: D. S. Brewer, 2000); Jenny Wormald, *ODNB*.]

Psalm 104[498]

  O Lord, inspire my spreit and pen, to praise   *spirit*
  Thy name, whose greatness far surpassis all:
  That syne, I may thy gloir and honour blaise,   *afterwards, proclaim*
  Which cleithis thee over: about thee like a wall   *clothes*
5 The light remainis. O thou, whose charge and call   *command*
  Made heavens like curtenis for to spread abreid,   *abroad*
  Who bowed the waters so, as serve they shall   *bent*
  For crystal silv'ring over thy house to gleid.[499]   *glide*

  Who walks upon the wings of restless wind,
10 Who of the clouds his chariot made, even he,
  Who in his presence still the spreits doth find,
  Ay, ready to fulfil ilk just decree   *the same*
  Of his, whose servants fire and flammis they be.
  Who set the earth on her foundations sure,
15 So as her brangling none shall ever see: *shaking*
  Who at thy charge the deip upon her bure.   *deep, carried*

  So, as the very tops of mountains high
  Be fluidis were onis overflowed at thy command,   *floods, once*
  Ay, while thy thund'ring voice soon made them fly
20 O'er hideous hills and howes, till nought but sand   *hollows, nothing*
  Was left behind, syne with thy mighty hand
  Thou limits made unto the roaring deip.
  So shall she never droun again the land,
  But brek her wawes on rockis, her mairch to keip.   *break, border*

25 Thir are thy workis, who made the strands to breid, *these, streams, spring forth*
  Syne rinn among the hills from fountains cleir,   *run*
  Whereto wild asses oft dois rinn with speid,
  With other beasts to drink. Hard by we heir
  The chirping birds among the leaves, with beir   *clamour*
30 To sing, while all the rocks about rebound.
  A wondrous work, that thou, O Father deir,
  Maks throtts so small yield furth so great a sound!   *forth*

  O thou, who from thy palace oft lets fall
  (For to refresh the hills) thy blessèd rain:
35 Who with thy works mainteins the earth and all:

---

[498] After title, 'translated from Tremellius'.

[499] God's chambers are obviously grand enough that James would find them comfortable. Note also the 'palace' in line 33, whereas in the original God simply waters the earth 'from above' (BCP).

JAMES VI

Who maks to grow the herbs and grass to gain.
The herbs for food to man, grass dois remain   *livestock*
For food to horse, and cattle of all kind.
Thou causest them not pull at it in vain,
40 But be thair food, such is thy will and mind.

Who dois rejoice the heart of man with wine,
And who with oil his face maks cleir and bright,
And who with food his stomach strengthens syne,
Who nourishes the very treis aright.
45 The cedars even of Leban tall and wight   *Lebanon, strong*
He planted hath, where birds do big their nest.   *build*
He made the fir treis of a wondrous hight,
Where storks dois mak thair dwelling place, and rest.

Thou made the barren hills, wild goats' refuge.
50 Thou made the rocks, a residence and rest
For Alpin rats,[500] where they do live and ludge.   *Alpine, lodge*
Thou made the moon, her course, as thou thoght best.
Thou made the sun in time go to, that lest
He still should shine, then night should never come.
55 But thou in order all things hes so dressed,   *has*
Some beasts for day, for night are also some.

For lions young at night beginnis to rair,
And from their dens to crave of God some prey:
Then in the morning, gone is all their care,   *as soon as*
60 And homeward to their caves rinnis fast, fra day   *appear, frighten*
Begin to kythe, the sun dois so them fray.   *from*
Then man gois forth, fra time the sun dois rise,
And while the evening he remanis away
At leesome labour, where his living lies.   *proper*

---

[500] BCP, Geneva, and KJV all have 'conies', though the Hebrew probably designates the rock hyrax, a small mammal native to Africa and the Middle East. Alpine rats are an unusual choice, though the basis is Tremellius's *Montium mures* (mountain rats). Curiously, Huldrich Zwingli mentions the Alpine rat (*mus alpinus*) in a sermon on divine providence. *Ad illustrissimum Cattorum principem Philippum sermonis de providentia dei anamnema* <http://www.irg.uzh.ch/static/zwingli-werke/index.php?n=Werk.166> [accessed 8 August 2020]. Another Swiss writer, the naturalist Conrad Gessner, wrote about the Alpine mouse in his *Historia animalium*, partly translated in 1607 as *The History of Four-Footed Beasts*, but printed originally in Zürich from 1551 to 1558. Oddly, though, Gessner states that the Alpine mouse or marmot is not the animal called in Hebrew *saphan*, the word used in Psalm 104, which is in fact a cony.

65 How large and mighty are thy workis, O Lord!
    And with what wisdom are they wrought, but fail.[501]
    The earth's great fulness, of thy gifts record
    Dois bear: heir of the seas (which diverse scale
    Of fish contenis) dois witness bear: ilk sail
70 Of diverse ships upon the swolling wawes
    Dois testify, as dois the monstrous whale,
    Who frayis all fishes with his ravening jaws.   *frightens, bloodthirsty*

    All thir (O Lord), yea, all this wondrous heap   *these*
    Of living things, in seasoun craves their fill
75 Of food from thee. Thou giving, Lord, they reap:
    Thy open hand with gude things fills them still
    When so thou list: but contrar, when thou will   *please, on the other hand*
    Withdraw thy face, then are they troubled sair,   *sore*
    Their breath by thee received, soon dois them kill:
80 Syne they return into their ashes bair.   *naked*

    But notwithstanding, Father dear, in case
    Thou breath on them again, then they revive.
    In short, thou dois, O Lord, renew the face
    Of all the earth, and all that in it live.
85 Therefore immortal praise to him we give:
    Let him rejoice into his works he made,
    Whose look and touch, so hills and earth dois grieve,
    As earth dois tremble, mountains reikis, afraid.   *smokes*

    To Jehova I all my life shall sing,
90 To sound his name I ever still shall cair: *take care*
    It shall be sweit my thinking on that King: *sweet*
    In him I shall be glaid for evermair: *glad*
    O let the wicked be into no whair
    In earth. O let the sinful be destroyed.
95 Bless him my soul who name Jehova bear:
    O bless him now with notes that are enjoyed.
              Hallelujah.

---

[501] Presumably James does not mean that God has failed, but the implication is hard to ignore coming immediately after the statement that God has made his works with such wisdom. Perhaps, as a good Calvinist, James has in mind the effects of the Fall, which is the fault of Adam and Eve, but since humans are not mentioned here, the result is confusing. This clause is not in Tremellius.

62. King James VI of Scotland (MS late 1580s)

[See headnote to **61**. James's Scots translations of Psalms 1–7, 9–21, 29, 47, 100, 125, 128, 133, 148, and 150 survive in a manuscript with several other biblical translations, in several different hands, including James's own. Like his printed translation of Psalm 104, these are in sophisticated metres, none of them appropriate to congregational singing, at least in the tradition of Sternhold and Hopkins and the Scottish Psalter of 1564. The dating of these translations is uncertain, but presumably they were completed well before his move to England. Psalm 121 is in the stanza later named for Shakespeare's *Venus and Adonis*, but used earlier by Surrey, Sidney, and Spenser. George Gascoigne, in his *Certain Notes of Instruction Concerning the Making of Verse* (1575), describes this as one type of 'ballade' stanza. Psalm 133 is a single through-composed stanza. *The Poems of James VI. of Scotland*, ed. by James Craigie, vol. II (Edinburgh and London: William Blackwood & Sons Ltd., 1958).]

Psalm 21

	1.	The King, O Lord, rejoiceth in thy strength,	
		And of thy glorious health is wondrous glaid;	*glad*
	2.	His hairtis desire thou given him hes at length,	*heart's, has*
		And also fruitful hes his prayeris made;	
5	3.	Yea, thou with prosperous blessingis him praevenis,	*goes before*
		And crownis his head with gold that purest sheinis.[502]	
	4.	He askit life of thee, quhiche thou him gave,	*which*
		With length of days forever to endure.	
	5.	The glory is great thy health dois make him have,	
10		A majesty thou placit unto him sure;	
	6.	For thou did give him blessingis lasting aye,	*forever*
		And by thy face rejoiced him every way.	
	7.	And since the king dois firmly put his trust	
		In Jehovah quhom of such proof he found,	*whom*
15		Thairfore upon the goodness lean he must	
		Of the most high, quho rules this massive round,	*who*
		Quhairby his throne shall not be set on sand	*whereby*
		But groundit sure for aye shall stable stand.	*forever*
	8.	Thy hand thy wicked foes dois overtake,	
20		Even thy richt hand findis out thy haitteris all;	*right, haters*
	9.	Thou like a fiery furnace will thaim make,	
		How soon thy wraithful face thaim kendill shall;	*kindle*

---

[502] Few Psalms poets can have felt this Psalm so personally as James, king from the age of two, and ultimately of two different kingdoms.

>   God shall thaim swelly up unto his ire, *swallow, anger*
>   As if they wair consumed by burning fire.
> 25   Thou dois their fruit from earth destroy and tine, *ruin*
>   And from the sons of men their seed dois race, *descendants, pluck up*
>   11.   Because they hairme meant unto thee and thine,
>   And in thaire mindis to fraudful thochtis gave place, *thoughts*
>   Quhiche they for all that cannot bring about
> 30   According to their purpose to fall out.
>
>   12.   For thou dois make a mark and butt of thaime, *archery target*
>   And sine thou fittis thine arrowis for thy bow, *then*
>   And archerlike thou at their face dois aim,
> 35   And sorely shootis their wrack and overthrow. *punishment*
>   13.   Then of thy force, O Lord, rejoice on hicht; *high*
>   Let us sing praises of thy wondrous micht. *might*

Psalm 133

>   1.   How good and pleasant thing, lo, doth appear
>   Accord amongst thaim selfis of brethren dear, *harmony*
>   Quho dwellis together in a godly love; *who*
>   2.   It is most like that precious unguent clear
> 5   Poured on the head sine trickling like a tear, *and afterwards*
>   Upon the beard doun flowing from above,
>   At last doun Aaronis clothis doth softly move,
>   Quhill to his garmentis borderis lou it were *until, low*
>   And round about thaime run of his behove, *benefit*
> 10   Like crystal dew distilled on Hermon tall
>   Or balmy droppis that dois on Zion fall.[503]
>   For on those men God sendis his blessing sure,
>   The quhiche is life forever to endure. *which*

63. William Byrd, *Psalms, Sonnets, and Songs of Sadness and Piety, Made into Music of Five Parts* (1588)

[William Byrd (1539x43–1623) was one of the greatest composers of the English Renaissance. About his early life there is little certainty. He was likely born in London, son of Thomas Byrd, profession unknown. Byrd's older brothers were choirboys at St Paul's, but there is no evidence that he followed them there. Given Byrd's close lifelong relationship with Thomas Tallis, he may have been

---

[503] This version perfectly captures the triple downward movement noted by Alter of oil, beard, and dew.

a choirboy in the Chapel Royal, where Tallis was a Gentleman singer, organist, and composer from 1543. In 1563, Byrd was appointed organist and master of the choristers at Lincoln Cathedral. He married in 1568 and had several children. He became a Gentleman of the Chapel Royal in 1572 and moved to London or Westminster. Queen Elizabeth granted Byrd and Tallis a monopoly for the printing of music in 1575, though it brought them little money. Byrd was a prolific composer, writing many volumes of church music in both Latin and English. Byrd converted to Catholicism at some point before 1577, perhaps quite early (his family seems to have conformed to the national church), and he remained committed to this faith throughout his life. He was subject to fines for recusancy, yet he retained his position in the Chapel Royal until at least 1592, as well as the favour of Elizabeth, which presumably prevented his facing more serious punishment. Sometime after 1593, Byrd and his family moved to Essex, joining a Catholic community surrounding Sir John Petre of Ingatestone. Byrd's compositions in this period, including three masses and two collections of liturgical music (*Gradualia*, 1605, 1607), were for the private worship of his fellow English Catholics. The masses were printed surreptitiously, but the *Gradualia* were printed by Thomas East, the most important music printer in London (and likely also responsible for the masses). This is further testimony to Byrd's status, since the worship for which his music was obviously written and printed was illegal. Byrd also wrote a body of music intended for domestic recreation, including many works for the virginal and three volumes of sacred and secular songs, for singing in parts or with instruments. All of these contained Psalm settings. From 1563, when John Day printed *The Whole Psalms in Four Parts*, various editions of Sternhold and Hopkins were published with simple, four-part, hymn-style settings that could be sung at home or in church. Byrd's Psalm settings were more complex, contrapuntal, and often melismatic, designed to be sung by more skilled, though not necessarily professional, musicians. The 1588 *Psalms, Sonnets, and Songs* opened with nine Psalms: 55, 123, two sections of 119, 13, 15, 12, 112, and 6. As Jeremy Smith has demonstrated, the selection and organization of this set of Psalms is artful and deliberate. Some of the texts are drawn from existing translations, including two (55 and 6, which begin and conclude the set) from *The Whole Book of Psalms*. Others have been adapted or newly translated, likely by Byrd himself, specifically to lament his precarious condition as a member of England's oppressed Catholic community — in the terms of this translation of Psalm 123. 4, 'a people that despised are'. It is telling that Byrd begins this sequence with Psalm 55, chosen by so many prisoners in the Tower (see 18, 25, and 32) to express their sense of betrayal, and ends it with Psalm 6, the first of the Penitential Psalms. The volume closes with funeral songs for Sir Philip Sidney, just after a setting of 'Why do I use my paper, ink, and pen?', a lament for the martyred Jesuit Edmund Campion. *Psalms, Sonnets, and Songs* was reprinted a remarkable five times. It was dedicated to Sir Christopher Hatton, who was rumoured to be sympathetic to the Catholic faith, though he was Elizabeth's Lord Chancellor and staunchly anti-papist in policy, having been one of the commissioners that found Mary, Queen of Scots guilty of treason in 1587. See Roger Bray, 'William Byrd's English Psalms', in *Psalms in the Early Modern World*, ed. by Linda Phyllis Austern, Kari Boyd McBride, and David L. Orvis (Farnham: Ashgate, 2011), pp. 61–76; Jeremy L. Smith, *Verse & Voice in Byrd's Song Collections of 1588 and 1589* (Woodbridge: The Boydell Press, 2016); Craig Monson, ODNB.]

Psalm 123

1. Mine eyes with fervency of sprite,   *spirit*
    I do lift up on high:
 To thee, O Lord, that dwell'st in light,
    Which no man may come nigh.   *near*

2. Behold even as the servant's eyes,
    Upon their master wait:
 And as the maid her mistress' hand,
    With careful eye and straight,   *undeviating*

3. Attends:[504] So we, O Lord our God,
    Thy throne with hope and grief
 Behold, until thou mercy send,
    And give us some relief.

4. O Lord, though we deserve it not,
    Yet mercy let us find:
 A people that despisèd are,
    Thrown down in soul and mind,

5. The mighty proud men of the world,
    That seeks us to oppress:
 Have filled our souls with all contempts,
    And left us in distress.
        FINIS.

Psalm 12

1. Help, Lord, for wasted are those men,
    Which righteousness embrace:[505]

---

[504] Whatever the poetic effect of the running of this sentence across from one verse to another, it creates an impossible problem in performance, since the music ends decisively with each stanza, repeating the final line. Verse three thus begins awkwardly, after a pause, with the orphaned verb, 'Attends'. It is possible that only the first verse was intended to be sung.

[505] BCP, Geneva, and Sternhold and Hopkins all translate the adjective modifying the men

		And rarely found that faithful are,	
		But all the truth deface.	*erase*
5	2.	Each to his neighbour falsehood speaks,	
		And them seeks to beguile;	
		With flattering lips and double heart,	
		When smoothest he doth smile.	
	3.	All flattering lips, the Lord our God,	
10		In justice will confound:	*put to shame*
		And all proud tongues, that vaunt great things,	*boast*
		He will bring to the ground.	
	4.	Our tongues say they, shall lift us up,	
		By them we shall prevail:	
15		Who should us let, or stop our course,	
		That thereof we should fail.	
	5.	For the destruction of the just,	
		And such as be oppressed:	
		And for the mournings of the poor,	
20		That likewise be distressed.	
	6.	I will rise up now, saith the Lord,	
		And ease their grief and care:	
		Of those which he full craftily,	
		Hath drawn into his snare.	
25	7.	Like silver fine that trièd is,	*refined*
		Seven times by heat of fire:	
		So are thy words, Lord, pure and clean,	
		To such as them desire.	
	8.	Thou, Lord, wilt keep, and wilt defend,	*guard*
30		All such as in thee trust:	
		And from that cursèd race of men,	
		Save all such as be just.	
	9.	When evil men exalted be,	
		The wicked gad about:	*wander*
35		Far from all fear of pain, but thou,	
		O Lord, wilt root them out.	
		FINIS.	

in verse one as 'godly', which Byrd eschews, given its strong Protestant connotations, though the book was marketed to a general audience, presumably largely Protestant.

64. William Byrd, *Songs of Sundry Natures, Some of Gravity, and Others of Mirth* (1589)

[See headnote to **63**. Byrd's second secular collection of songs began with three-part settings of the Penitential Psalms and included also settings of Psalms 133 and 121 in six parts. All of the Psalm translations are original and may have been composed or adapted by Byrd himself, following the common metre of the Sternhold and Hopkins Psalms, sometimes rhyming *abcb*, sometimes *abab*. The translations of the Penitential Psalms are unremarkable, except for Psalm 38, which signals that the speaker is a woman. A female voice is featured in other songs like 'Susanna fair' and 'Penelope that longed for the sight', which suggests that Byrd was catering at least in part to a female market. In keeping with a common practice in songbooks, Byrd sets only the first verses. It is possible that subsequent verses would be sung to the same music, but Byrd does not provide the texts. Byrd sets the entirety of Psalm 133, which is only four verses long, but in two parts, one each for verses 1–2 and 3–4. Unusually for Byrd, he chooses a positive and uplifting Psalm to set, one that celebrates concord. The Psalm's emphasis on anointing oil might suggest its use in many Catholic sacraments, rejected by Protestants, but Jeremy Smith has argued that it may actually be Byrd's tribute to Queen Elizabeth and her *via media*. Like all English monarchs, she was anointed with oil at her coronation. *Songs of Sundry Natures* was dedicated to Henry Carey, Baron Hunsdon, Privy Councillor and Lord Chamberlain, and in the latter role a prominent patron of the theatre. See Smith, *Verse & Voice*.]

Psalm 38

Lord in thy wrath correct me not,
    Nor in thy fury vex;
Give tears, give grace, give penitence,
    Unto my sinful sex.
5 For that the arrows of thy wrath
    Are fixèd in my heart,
And thou hast laid thine hand on me,
    For my most just desert.   *reward*

Psalm 133

Behold how good a thing it is,
    For brethren to agree,
When men amongst them do no strife,
    But peace and concord see.
5 Full like unto the precious balm,
    From Aaron's head that fell,

And did descend upon his beard,
　　His garment skirts until.
And as the pleasant morning dew,
10　　The mountains doth relieve:[506]
So God will bless, where concord is,
　　And life eternal give.

65. Richard Robinson, *A Golden Mirror Containing Certain Pithy and Figurative Visions Prognosticating Good Fortune to England and All True English Subjects, with an Overthrow to the Enemies* (1589)

[Richard Robinson (fl. 1573–1589) was apparently a north country man who wrote two collections of anti-Catholic verse, *The Reward of Wickedness* (1574) and *A Golden Mirror*. The title page of the earlier work represents him as a servant of the Earl of Shrewsbury, George Talbot; it was written in Sheffield Castle, where Mary Queen of Scots was imprisoned under Shrewsbury's care. He seems to have been fond of acrostics. The acrostic of his Psalm 6 reads 'Thomas Leighe esquyar' (i.e. esquire); Thomas Leigh/Legh (1547–1601) was the half-brother of Ralph Egerton of Ridley, whose illegitimate older half-brother Thomas was Lord Chancellor and first Viscount Brackley, and later first Baron Ellesmere. His son was John Egerton, first Earl of Bridgewater, Lord President of Wales, his installation in this position celebrated by Milton's *Comus*. John married Frances Stanley, sister of Anne Brydges (see **119**), both daughters of Ferdinando Stanley, Lord Strange, and Alice Spencer. Drawing this family web still tighter, Thomas Egerton, after the death of his first wife, married Alice Spencer, the widow of Lord Strange, and the mother of his son's wife. Even more confusingly, Thomas Egerton's granddaughter, Mary, married Thomas Leigh, first Baron Leigh, who seems unrelated in any clear way to the Thomas Leigh of Robinson's Psalm. The paraphrase is a broad one, perhaps due to the constraints of the acrostic. See Brian Cummings, *ODNB*.]

Psalm 6

A Psalm penned upon the etymology of the name of the right worshipful Thomas Leigh of Adlington, in the county of Chester, Esquire: to the note or tune of *Dominus in furore*.

T　hy mercy Lord, my faith persuades,
　　Although my sins be red:　　　　　　　　　　　　*i.e. bloody?*
H　ow I shall be made free to thee:
　　By Christès blood that's shed.

---

[506] Compare the version by James I/William Alexander (see **62**). Byrd entirely misses the parallel downward movement of oil, beard, and dew (which Alter notes).

5 O f all my wand'ring wilful days
        And reckless rudeful toys: *frivolities*
   M y faithful hope is for to mount,
        To thee in lasting joys.
   A nd as I wickedly did sin,
10   I faithfully repent:
   S uch is thy mercy that I know,
        My tears shall thee content.
   L o hear, my tears the witness is,
        My sin doth grieve me sore:
15 E steem, O Lord, my woeful plaints,   *laments*
        I trust t'offend no more.
   I n thee my only hope remains,
        On thee is all my stay: *support*
   G ive ear unto my woeful cries,
20   When I shall pass away.
   H ave mind upon thy mercy, Lord,
        Forget thy wrath and ire,   *anger*
   E rect my spirit into thy bliss,
        I humbly thee desire.

25 E lse all my tears and grievous plaints
        Return without reward:
   S o shall I wear, and waste in woe,
        My cries shall not be heard:
   S eem not therefore to turn thy face,
30   Accept my woeful suit: *petition*
   Q uit me from Satan's nets and snares,[507]
        His traps, good Lord, confute.
   U nto thy majesty, O Lord,
        I dedicate myself:
35 Y ield I do my soul to thee,
        And leave the world my wealth.
   A ccept thereof, thou glorious God,
        Thus still on thee I cry:
   R evenge not Lord, but mercy have,
40   And never let me die.

   All glory be unto thy name:
        And to thy only son:
   And to the Holy Ghost, with whom
        To us thy kingdom come.

---

[507] Satan] Added by Robinson, the Psalmist simply praying for deliverance from death and the pit (BCP).

66. Michael Cosworth, *Psalms* (MS *c.* 1590?)

[Michael Cosworth (fl. 1576–1610) was born in London, son of John Cosworth and Dorothy Locke, and was related through his mother to Henry Lok, son of Anne Vaughan Lock. Another cousin was the Cornish antiquary and poet Richard Carew, who wrote two commendatory poems for Cosworth's Psalms collection, praising his cousin for 'calling home' the Psalms, exiled from their 'native soil [...] in soil of barbarism'. Cosworth studied at St John's, Cambridge, and was appointed to rectorships in Devon and Cornwall, eventually moving to Cornwall permanently when he became clerk to Sir John Bramston the elder. Cosworth wrote a dedicatory poem to Henry Lok's *Ecclesiastes*, and Lok reciprocated with a poem for Cosworth's Psalms in which he laments the 'modern wanton Muse' that delights in 'borrowed fabling toys' while they abuse the 'Muse of Muses'. Carew's two dedicatory poems were for the same collection, and Cosworth also included a poem to his 'best cousin' Barbara Loke, presumably a sister of Henry. See Artemis Gause, *ODNB*.]

Psalm 118

O praise the Lord for good he is,
And's mercy doth endure forever:
Let Israel's tribe to confess this
That's mercy doth endure forever.

5   Let Aaron's house confess the same,
That's mercy doth endure forever:
Let all confess that fear his name,
That's mercy doth endure forever.

When I in heaviness did lie,
10 Unto the Lord I made my moan:
And he above did hear me cry
And left me not in woes alone.

The Lord himself defendeth me,
Therefore I will not greatly fear
15 What cruel man's conspiring be
That I to death consumèd were.   *wasted away*

The Lord himself doth me defend
And is with them that succour me,
Therefore I my desire at th'end
20 Upon my wicked foes shall see.

It better is to trust the Lord
Than to have confidence in man;
It better is to trust the Lord
Than trust to that great'st princes can.

25 All nations now in compass be[508]
　　But in God's name I'll them destroy;
　　The same compass, the same compass me,   *encircle*
　　But in God's name with little joy.

　　And as a swarm of stinging bees
30 Which murmur through th'unwounded sky,[509]
　　That I might all my comfort leese,   *lose*
　　Thy swith full troops about me fly.   *extremely*

　　But as oft thorns the quenchèd fire
　　Can but with's bitter smoke annoy,
35 So shall I quench their burning ire
　　For in God's name I'll them destroy.

　　Some thou indeed at me didst thrust
　　That I down to the ground might fall,
　　But I in God repose my trust,
40 And he did send me help withal.   *as well*

　　The Lord he is the strength of me
　　And he shall be my joyful song,
　　For by him gone those grieving be,
　　Which have in thrall my soul so long.   *captivity*

45 The Lord's right hand doth mighty things,
　　With glory 'tis exalted high,
　　And down the pride of man it brings,
　　His right hand still doth valiantly.

　　I shall not die but still shall live,
50 That I of God's great works may tell,
　　And though his wrath doth me sore grieve
　　He hath not thrust me down to hell.

　　Ope wide the gates of God's own house,
　　Where his great righteousness is known,
55 That by this entering in of us
　　With promise his mercies may be shown.

　　This is the gate, here God doth dwell,
　　Here hath his church assembled been;

---

[508] in compass] all around, i.e. surrounding us.
[509] th'unwounded sky] Cosworth's addition to the Psalm's description of enemies like bees; it is peculiar, perhaps meaning that the bees harm the Psalmist as little as they do the sky through which they fly?

60 When righteous men of this here tell,
    With joyful heart they'll enter in.

    For now the stone which was refused
    Of them who greatest builders were
    Is for the cornerstone chief used,
65 And up the building best doth bear.

    This in our eyes a marvel seems,
    But this the Lord's own doing is,
    And us this day the Lord redeems,
    Let us be glad and joy in this.

70 O Lord we all thee do entreat,
    Now save us Lord, O Lord now save,
    Now prosper us and make us great,
    We for thy mercy's sake now crave.

    O blessèd he that in God's name
75 Doth with a blessing come to us;
    We have blessed you, the blessing came
    From God himself to bless you thus.[510]

    The Lord he is a mighty Lord
    And he hath given light to our eyes;
80 Then to his altars which accord
    Let's bind th'accepted sacrifice.

    Thou art my God and I'll thee praise,
    Thou art my God and I'll praise thee;
    O praise the Lord for good is he,
85 And's mercy doth endure always.

Psalm 135

    O praise the Lord, praise ye his name,
    Ye servants of the Lord it praise;
    Ye of his church, praise, praise you the same,
    And you in's court attend always.
5   For tis a good, and comely thing,
          Since God is good, his praises sing.

---

[510] An example of polyptoton, the repetition of a word in different forms, often (as here) for emphasis. Pronunciation adds to the effect, since the two instances of 'blessed' are pronounced differently.

He Jacob chose out from his own,
And Israel his chief treasure is.
I know our Lord is great alone,
10   And he hath done what so him please
            In heaven and earth and in deep seas.

He from the world's most utmost end
Brings for the dews engendered cloud;
He the bright lightnings forth doth send
15 With rains which roar aloud;
        He from his treasures forth doth bring
            The winds which down do all things fling.

With death all the first born he smote
Of Egypt, man and beast be;
20 Tokens and wonders strange he wrack,   *wrought*
O Egypt, in the midst of thee,
        King Pharaoh and his power can tell,
            And Pharaoh's servants know it well

He many nations did smite,⁵¹¹
25 Many mighty kings he slew,
As Sehon king of th'Amorite
And Og the king of Bashan's crew,
        And all the kings of Canaan
            Where streams of milk and honey ran;

30 And this their fruitful land he gave
His people for an heritage.
The Lord would Israel should have
The use of it from age to age,
        And as the Lord decreed his will
35   So they had it and have it still.

O Lord thy name's memorial
Shall live out all enduring age,
And none shall make his people thrall   *enslaved*
But he'll revenge their evil rage;
40   But though amiss his people do,
            But he'll be good and gracious too.

As for the heathen images,
They are of silver and of gold;

---

[511] nations] The metre requires a trisyllabic pronunciation. The same applies to 'Canaan' (line 28) and 'Israel' (line 32) below.

The works of man's hand hath made these
45 And forged them in a crafty mould.
    They have wide mouths yet cannot say,
    They have broad eyes, yet cannot see;

They have their ears, yet hear they not,
Nor in their mouths is any breath.
50 They that the monstrous shapes begot
Of men become like them uneath,   *almost*
    And they who trust in them do bring
    Are like unto an idol thing.

The house of Israel praise the Lord,
55 The Lord, ye house of Aaron praise;
Ye Levi's tribe his praise record,
Ye that fear him praise him always,
    Ye out of Sion praise ye him
    Who dwelleth at Jerusalem.

67. Abraham Fraunce, *The Countess of Pembroke's Emmanuel* (1591)

[Abraham Fraunce (1559?–1592/3?) was educated at Shrewsbury, St John's, Cambridge, and Gray's Inn, and became a lawyer as well as an important poet, writing under the patronage of the Sidney Circle, especially Philip Sidney, a fellow Shrewsbury student, and Mary Sidney Herbert, Countess of Pembroke. He wrote an important treatise on rhetoric and poetics, *The Arcadian Rhetoric* (1588), notable for quoting from Spenser's as-yet-unpublished *The Faerie Queene*, as well as several verse collections dedicated to the Countess of Pembroke. The first of these, *The Countess of Pembroke's Emmanuel*, contained several metrical Psalms as well as verse narratives of the Nativity and Passion of Christ. *The Countess of Pembroke's Ivychurch* (1591) included a translation of Tasso's play *Aminta*. In most of his verse, Fraunce attempted to import the classical hexameter line into English. Derek Attridge calls him 'the most prolific and the most popular of the Elizabethan quantitative poets' (p. 192). For this he was called a fool by Ben Jonson, but others, including Spenser, Gabriel Harvey, and Thomas Nashe, found his poetry worthy of praise. Attridge argues that Fraunce's success (like that of his patroness, the Countess of Pembroke) lay in combining a quantitative pattern of sufficient rigor to satisfy the classicists with a line rhythmically regular enough to be read as English verse. He is perhaps at his best when the content and tone of the Psalms he chooses match the epic style of his hexameter line and heightened diction. See Derek Attridge, *Well-Weighed Syllables: Elizabethan Verse in Classical Metres* (Cambridge: Cambridge University Press, 1974); Hamlin, *Psalm Culture*; William Barker, *ODNB*.]

Psalm 29

You kings and rulers, you lords and mighty monarchies,
Whose hands with sceptres, and heads with crowns be adornèd.
Kneel to the King of Kings, and bring your dutiful off'rings;
Lout to the living Lord; ascribe all might to the mighty,   *bow*
5 Always-mighty Monarch: and learn to be ruled by the Ruler.
Which heav'n, earth, and hell, rules, overrules in a moment.[512]
   For this is only that one, whose thund'ring voice from the clustered
Clouds breaks forth and roars, and horror brings to the whole world.
For this is only that one, whose fearful voice from the heavens
10 Cedars, tall cedars, tears, rents, and rives from the rooting,   *pulls up, digging up*
Cedars of Libanus constrains like calves to be leaping: *Lebanon*
And Cedar-bearing Libanus, with frightened Hermon
Like to a young unicorn[513] makes here and there to be skipping.
   For this is only that one, whose threat'ning voice, the devouring
15 Lightning's flakes throws down, and terror brings to the deserts,
Tears down trees and woods, makes hinds for fear to be calving,   *deer*
And that forlorn waste of Kadesh for to be trembling.
   Every voice his voice, his praise, and glory pronounceth,
His sacred temple with his honour daily resoundeth.
20 Over gulfs and deeps his royal throne he reposeth,
Overwhelming gulfs, and drowning deeps he represseth,
And still a living Lord, still a King almighty remaineth,
And yet a father still: for he leaves not, still to be sending
Strength to his own elect, and inward peace for a blessing.[514]

Psalm 50

God, the triumphant God, th'eternal great God of all Gods
Hath sent forth summons with a thund'ring voice from the heavens,
World-warning summons, commanding all in a moment,
All from th'east to the west, to be pressed, and make an appearance,   *drafted*

---

[512] Fraunce demonstrates his rhetorical facility with the parallelism of hands/sceptres: heads/crowns, the alliteration of 'mighty monarchies' and 'King of Kings' (adding a kind of visual alliteration with the silent first letter of 'Kneel'), the internal rhyme of 'Kings [...] bring [...] off'rings', and the polyptoton of 'might [...] mighty [...] Always-mighty' and 'ruled [...] ruler [...] rules [...] overrules'. The alliteration of 'clustered | Clouds' in the following two lines combines with the enjambment to convey the breaking forth of God's thundering voice.
[513] unicorn] See note 23, p. 79.
[514] Rather than 'his own people', an obvious reference to Israel, Fraunce substitutes 'his own elect', signalling instead the Calvinist sense of election, designating those predestined for salvation.

5 And perform their suit to the court, to the great, to the high court,   *petition*
   Great high Zion's court, sweet Zion: where he appeareth
   With surpassing grace, exceeding beauty abounding.
      God shall come, shall come with a voice almightily sounding;
   Greedy devouring fire shall go with glory before him,
10 And blust'ring tempests shall roar with terror about him.
   Heav'n from above shall he call, and quaking earth to be witness,
   Of this just edict and sentence rightly pronouncèd.
      Bring my saints, saith God, go bring my saints to my presence,
   Which have vowed their hearts, and sworn their souls to my service:[515]
15 And of this judgement from Judge almighty proceeding,
   Those bright-burning globes of crystal-mantled Olympus,[516]
   Shall be reporters true, and always shall be recorders.
      Hear me, my dear flock, and thou, O Israel, hear me,
   Hear me, thy God, thy Lord; and know, that I am not aggrieved,
20 Nor displeasèd a whit, for want of customed off'rings   *a bit*
   Burnt off'rings, sacrifice, and honours due to my altars.
   What do I care for a goat? or what do I care for a bullock?[517]
   Sith goats and bullocks, and beasts that range by the deserts,   *since*
   Sith cattle feeding on a thousand hills be my own goods?   *livestock*
25 Mine own proper goods be the fowls that fly to the mountains,
   Mine be the beasts that run by the fields, and watery fountains.
      If that I hunger, alas what need I to tell thee, I hunger?
   Sith that th'earth is mine, and all that on earth is abiding.
   Think not, think not, alas, that I take any joy to be eating
30 Bull's flesh: think not, alas, that I take a delight to be drinking
   Goat's blood, guiltless blood: but make acceptable off'ring
   Of thanks-giving heart, and pay thy vows to the highest.
   Call me to help, when so thou find'st thyself to be helpless,
   Cry for grace, when so thou think'st thy soul to be past grace:
35 And I will hear, and help, give grace, and strongly protect thee,

---

[515] The term 'saints' was repurposed by Protestants to designate not the Catholic intercessors and makers of miracles but the elect chosen by God through predestination. All the early modern English Bibles, even the Catholic Rheims-Douay, have 'saints' in Psalm 50. 5 (and elsewhere), but the Hebrew word means something broader like 'faithful', 'pious', or even 'kind'.

[516] Olympus] The use of the classical mountain of the gods in reference to the Christian heaven is likely related to Fraunce's choice of classical metre.

[517] Fraunce creates a more naturalistic voice for God than one usually hears in English Psalms, using techniques like sharp rhetorical questions, interjections like 'alas', and repetitions that create an effect like second thoughts ('Goat's blood, guiltless blood'). We can infer God's 'frowning look' even before Fraunce describes it. Compare Coverdale's relatively characterless, 'I will take no bullock out of thine house' (BCP).

And thou laud, and love, sing, serve, and worthily praise me.	*praise*
But with a frowning look, this God spake thus to the godless;	
With what face dar'st thou my sacred name be prophaning	
With those lying lips, and mouth with murder abounding?	
40 With what face dar'st thou with a filèd tongue be professing,⁵¹⁸	*lying*
And by defilèd life, and foulèd soul be denying?	
With what face dar'st thou for an ostentation only	
Seek to reform others, thyself so foully deformèd?	
When thou meet'st with a thief, thou seek'st by theft to bethriving,	*be profiting*
45 And walk'st side by side as a copsemate fit for adulters.⁵¹⁹	*lover, adulterers*
Thy mouth's made to beguile; and monstrous villany utt'reth,	
Thy lips let forth lies: thy tongue untruly defameth	
Thine own mother's son: these, these be thy holy proceedings,	
These be thy works; and sith that I seem'd for a while to be silent,	
50 Thou thought'st (wicked thought) my thoughts were like to thy own thoughts,⁵²⁰	
And so runn'st headlong. But I come; but plagues be approaching,	
And when I come, then I strike; when I strike, then I beat thee to powder.	
Thy bloody thoughts, lewd words, vile deeds will I open in order,	
And show all to thy face: which thou shalt see to thy sorrow,	
55 Know, and acknowledge to thy own confusion endless.	
You that forget God, think on this; lest he remember	
And forget not you; but root you out in his anger.	
Then shall no man come, your damnèd souls to deliver.	
Praise and thanksgiving is a most acceptable off'ring;	
60 And, if a man by my laws his conversation order,	
Unto the same I myself will my salvation offer.	

                  Psalm 104

Living Lord, my soul shall praise thy glory triumphant,	
Sing thy matchless might, and show thine infinite honour.	
Everlasting light thou put'st on like as a garment,	
And purple-mantled welkin thou spread'st as a curtain:	*firmament*

---

[518] Here, as elsewhere, Fraunce employs the figure of anaphora, common in the Bible, repeating the same word or phrase at the beginning of successive lines. Fraunce also expands the Psalm, describing verbal sins at particular length, with the 'lying lips' and 'filèd tongue' and even a mouth somehow abounding with 'murder', as if slander could kill. Slander was a sin particularly common, and particularly feared, at the Tudor court.

[519] copsemate] A wonderfully evocative compound word, a 'copse' being the sort of close thicket lovers might frequent. It is not recorded in the *OED* but not original to Fraunce, since William Warner uses it ('cops mate') in his 1586 *Albion's England*. Fraunce was fond of it, though, using it also in Tasso's *Aminta*.

[520] A bravura performance of polyptoton, repeating a word in different forms.

5 Thy parlour pillars on waters strangely be pitchèd,[521]
  Clouds are thy chariots, and blust'ring winds be thy coursers,   *horses*
  Immortal spirits be thy ever-dutiful heralds,
  And consuming fires, as servants daily be waiting.
    All-maintaining earth's foundation ever abideth,
10 Laid by the Lord's right-hand, with seas and deeps as a garment
  Covered; seas and deeps with threat'ning waves to the huge hills
  Climbing; but, with a beck their billows speedily backward   *command*
  All do recoil; with a check their course is changed on a sudden;
  At thy thund'ring voice they quake: And so do the mountains
15 Mount upward with a word; and so also do the valleys
  Down with a word descend, and keep their places appointed:
  Their meres are fixed, their banks are mightily barrèd,   *pools*
  Their bounds known, lest that, man-feeding earth by the rage of
  Earth-overwhelming waters might chance to be drownèd.
20   Still-springing fountains distil from the rocks to the rivers,
  And crystal rivers flow over along by the mountains:
  There will wild asses their scorchèd mouths be refreshing,
  And field-feeding beasts their thirst with water abating.
    There by the well-welling waters, by the silver-abounding
25 Brooks, fair-flying fowls on flowring banks be abiding,
  There shall sweet-becked birds their bowers in boughs be a-building,   *beaked*
  And to the waters' fall their warbling voice be a-tuning.[522]
    Yea, those sun-burnt hills, and mountains all to be scorchèd,
  Cooling clouds do refresh, and watery dew from the heavens.
30   Earth sets forth thy works, earth-dwellers all be thy wonders:
  Earth earth-dwelling beasts with flow'ring grass is a-feeding;
  Earth earth-dwelling men with pleasant herbs is a-serving.
  Earth brings heart's-joy wine, earth-dwelling men to be heart'ning,
  Earth breeds cheering oils, earth-dwelling man to be smoothing,   *i.e. his skin*
35 Earth bears life's-food bread, earth-dwelling men to be strength'ning,
    Tall trees, up-mounting cedars are cheerfully springing,
  Cedars of Libanus, where fowls their nests be preparing;   *Lebanon*
  And storks in fir-trees make their accustomed harbours.
    Wild goats, does, and roes do rove and range by the mountains,

---

[521] parlour pillars] Fraunce elaborates (and alliterates) what in BCP is simply the 'beams of his chambers'.

[522] It may not mimic birdsong, but Fraunce's language in these lines creates a remarkable aural density, with the alliteration of 'brooks' and 'banks' enclosing all the 'f' words, 'fowls' and 'flowring' also rhyming, with the 'b's of the next line even thicker than the 'f's of the previous: 'becked birds […] bowers […] boughs be […] building'. The line ends are also what in modern poetics might be called off-rhyme: 'abating', 'abounding', 'abiding', 'a-building', as if the same word were repeated with shifting internal vowel sounds.

40 And poor silly conies to the ragged rocks be repairing. *innocent, rabbits*
    Night-enlightening moon for certain times is appointed,
    And all-seeing sun knows his due time to be sitting.
    Sun once so sitting, dark night wraps all in a mantle,
    All in a black mantle:[523] then beasts creep out from the dungeons,
45 Roaring hungry lions their prey with greedy devouring
    Claws and jaws attend, but by God's only appointment:
    When sun riseth again, their dens they quickly recover,
    And there couch all day: that man may safely the day time
    His day's work apply, till day give way to the darkness.
50   O good God, wise Lord, good Lord, and only the wise God,
    Earth sets forth thy works, earth-dwellers all be thy wonders.
    So be seas also, great seas, full fraught with abundant *filled*
    Swarms of creeping things, great, small: there, ships be a-sailing,
    And there lies tumbling, that monstrous huge Leviathan.[524]
55 All these beg their food, and all these on thee be waiting;
    If that thou stretch out thine hand, they feed with abundance,
    If thou turn thy face, they all are mightily troubled;
    If that thou withdraw their breath, they die in a moment,
    And turn quickly to dust, whence they were lately derivèd,
60 If thy Spirit breathe, their breath is newly created,
    And the decayèd face of th'earth is quickly revivèd.
        O then, glory to God, to the Lord then, glory forever,
    Who in his own great works may worthily glory forever.
    This Lord looks to the earth, and steadfast earth is a-trembling,
65 This God toucheth mounts, and mountains huge be a-smoking.
    All my life will I laud this Lord; whilst breath is abiding *praise*
    In my breast, this breath his praise shall still be a-breathing.
        Hear my words, my Lord, accept this dutiful off'ring,
    That my soul in thee may evermore be rejoicing;
70 Root the malignant race, raze out their damnable offspring; *i.e. root out*
    But my soul, O Lord, shall praise thy glory triumphant,
    Sing thy matchless might, and show thine infinite honour.

---

[523] An example of anadiplosis, the repetition of a word or phrase at the end of one line and the beginning of another, though here with incremental repetition, adding the adjective 'black'.

[524] Leviathan] The giant sea-creature from Job 41, mentioned in other Psalms and Isaiah 27, possibly a whale, though more likely mythical.

68. Barnabe Barnes, *A Divine Century of Spiritual Sonnets* (1595)

[Barnabe Barnes (bap. 1571–d. 1609) was a poet and playwright, son of Richard Barnes, Bishop of Durham, and Fridismunda Gifford. He attended Brasenose College, Oxford, but did not obtain a degree. Barnes wrote two sonnet sequences, one secular, one sacred. *Parthenophil and Parthenophe* (1593) was written under the influence of Sidney's *Astrophil and Stella*, though its physical eroticism was much bolder and occasionally even scandalous. Barnes also read Italian, and used madrigals and a sestina in the sequence as well as a variety of sonnet forms. Like so many sonnet poets, including Petrarch, Barnes interweaves religious and erotic language and themes, just as he blends together two Marys: his mistress and the Virgin. *A Divine Century of Spiritual Sonnets* (1595) is a sincere Protestant devotional work, one of many collections of religious sonnets in the late Elizabethan period, a phenomenon not always recognized by literary histories. Barnes's sonnet 13 prays to Christ as 'David's son (whom thy forefathers have | In psalms and prophecies unborn foretold)', and sonnet 35, included here, is a paraphrase of the first four verses of Psalm 68, expanding the generic 'enemies' to 'sinful foes of Babel' (borrowed perhaps from Psalm 137), and adding the supping on dregs and the drinking 'with the strumpet's cup', the latter a jab at the Catholic Mass by way of Revelation's Whore of Babylon. The sestet of the sonnet jumps to singing the riding of the heavens, clouds, and thundering of verses 32 to 36. Barnes also wrote *Four Books of Offices* (1606), a moral work dedicated to James I, and an anti-papal play, *The Devil's Charter* (1607), played at court by the King's Men. He was involved in the pamphlet war between Gabriel Harvey and Thomas Nashe in the early 1590s, on Harvey's side, and was charged with attempted murder in 1598, though he escaped prison and the charge was not pursued. See Helen Hackett, 'The Art of Blasphemy? Interfusions of the Erotic and the Sacred in the Poetry of Donne, Barnstable, and Constable', *Renaissance and Reformation/Renaissance et Réforme*, 28.3 (2004), 27–54; Deirdre Serjeantson, 'The Book of Psalms and the Early Modern Sonnet', *Renaissance Studies*, 29.4 (2015), 632–49; John D. Cox, *ODNB*.]

Psalm 68

Arise, thou mighty God of heav'n, rise up,
Against thy sinful foes of Babel rise:[525]　　　　　　　　　*Babylon*
And scatter thou like dust thine enemies:
Let them dregs of thine indignation sup:

---

[525] The confusion or perhaps deliberate substitution of Babel (the name of the tower in Genesis 11. 9) for Babylon has a basis in Hebrew, which uses the same word for both. There may also be a historical basis, since the temple of Marduk in Babylon was a massive ziggurat or tower.

5 That have been drunken with the strumpet's cup:[526]
   Like smoke which vanisheth into the skies
   Discover them, and like the wax (which fries
   Before the fire) so melt, and burn them up.
   O magnify the Lord, and praises sing
10 Unto the mighty God of heav'n, who makes
   The clouds to thunder, and his bolts doth wing   *thunderbolts*
   With fire and fury: who the round world shakes:
      Before whose face kings with their armies fly,
      And at whose feet proud emperors dead lie.

69. Francis Sabie, *Adam's Complaint. The Old World's Tragedy. David and Bathsheba.* (1596)

[Francis Sabie (fl. 1586–1596) was a Lichfield schoolmaster who published several volumes of poetry, including this one featuring a biblical complaint in the mode established by Robert Southwell's *Saint Peter's Complaint*, published after Southwell's execution the previous year. Sabie may himself have been Catholic, since he dedicates his adaptation of Robert Greene's *Pandosto* to two Northamptonshire Catholic gentlemen, one of whom, Francis Tresham, was later involved in both the Essex rebellion and the Gunpowder Plot. *The Old World's Tragedy* is a brief epic and *David and Bathsheba* an epyllion, to which is appended 'David's Ode', a metrical paraphrase of Psalm 51, traditionally understood as David's repentant prayer after the Bathsheba affair, which, Sabie emphasizes in the verse epilogue, also confirms that David was forgiven. A number of metrical Psalms were written in the loose form of the English Pindaric ode, but Sabie's is one of the first of these, earlier even than the *Odes in Imitation of Seven Penitential Psalms* of the Catholic Richard Verstegan (1601). Sabie uses a stanza characteristic of later English odes by Ben Jonson, Abraham Cowley, and others, combining long and short lines in an original pattern. Sabie dedicated this volume, printed in London, to Richard Howland, Bishop of Peterborough. Howland was an opponent of Puritans but of Catholic recusants as well, even though he did preside over the funeral of Mary, Queen of Scots, in his cathedral in 1587. See Sidney Lee, rev. Eleri Larkum (Sabie), William Joseph Sheils (Howland), *ODNB*.]

---

[526] Barnes adds an apocalyptic reference to the Whore of Babylon as described in Revelation, who has a 'cup of gold in her hand, full of abominations, and filthiness of her fornications' (17. 4, Geneva). The woman relates to the reference to Babel, since although Babylon was an ancient enemy of Israel known to the Psalmist, in Revelation, the woman has on her forehead 'A Mystery, great Babylon, the mother of whoredoms, and abominations of the earth' (17. 5, Geneva).

Psalm 51

DAVID'S ODE.

    O great Creator of the starry pole,
        And heavenly things:
    O mighty Founder of the earthly mole,   *mould*
        Chief King of Kings.
5 Whose gentle pardon evermore is near,
    To them which cry unfeignedly with fear,   *without pretence*
        Distressed with sin,
        I now begin,
    To come to thee, O Lord give ear;

10 O Lord look down from thy crystallin throne,[527]
        Environed round,   *surrounded*
    With seraphins, and angels many one,
        Thy praise who sound:
    Such favour Lord on me vouchsafe to send,   *grant*
15 As on thy chosen flock thou dost extend.
        To thee alone
        I make my moan.
    Some pity Father on me send.

Remember, Lord, that it is more than need,
20   To send redress;
My sore will grow (unless thou help with speed)
        Remediless.
Therefore in mercy look down from above,
And visit me with thy heart-joying love.
25   Alas, I see
        No cause in me
Which unto pity may thee move.

With sin I only have offended thee,   *alone*
        O Lord my God,
30 And therewithal I purchased have to me   *in addition*
        Thine heavy rod:
The weight of it doth press me very sore,   *torture*
And brings me well nigh to despair his door.   *almost*
        Alas, I shame
35   To tell the same,
It is before thee evermore.

---

[527] crystallin] The metre requires a stress on the middle syllable.

And this is not first time I sinned, alas,
    By many more:
Within the womb in sin conceived I was,
40   Born was I so.
And since that day I never yet did cease,
From time to time thy highness to displeasure,
    My life hath been
    A race of sin:[528]
45 Me with thy comfort somewhat ease.

Oh, why did I offend thy glorious grace
    So heinously?
Why feared I not the presence of thy face
    Who stoodest by?
50 Because I should acknowledge thee most just,
And in mine own uprightness should not trust:
    Frail is my flesh[529]
    I must confess,
And nought is it but sin and dust.   *nothing*

55 If thou shalt me asperge with sprinkling grass,[530]
    Or hyssop green:
As crystal pure, or as the shining glass,
    I shall be clean,
And if thou wilt me wash with water clear,
60 More white then Scythan snow I shall appear[531]

---

[528] race of sin] A clever pun, since 'race' meant both a contest of speed and family (the modern sense of ethnic group originating later), so that Sabie here combines the sense of inherited sin (from his mother's womb), sin as something persistent through his life, as well as something he has striven to outrun.

[529] Hamlet cries 'Frailty thy name is woman', but frailty was a quality attributed to all flesh, all humanity in the sixteenth century, due to the corruption following the Fall. Joshua Sylvester's translation of Du Bartas's vast meditation on Genesis, *Divine Weeks and Works*, for instance, refers to 'frail flesh' four times, and the phrase (with variations) appears in many sermons and biblical commentaries.

[530] asperge] Following the Vulgate *asperges me*, which also suggests a traditional Catholic liturgical context, an instrument called the aspergillum being used to sprinkle holy water during certain services, including during Holy Week when Christ's crucifixion is commemorated; hyssop is used to give Jesus vinegar to drink on the cross. Even Protestant translators include sprinkling with water in their translations of Psalm 51, since it is in the text as well as biblical practice for healing lepers. To use the Latin verb 'asperge', however, for which the *OED* offers no citations between 1547 and 1637, strongly suggests a Catholic perspective.

[531] The coldness of Scythia and its heavy snows seem to have been commonplace from the time of Herodotus.

>   Than whitest snow
>   Which wind doth blow
> From place to place both far and near.
>
> My mind, O Lord, infectious and foul,[532]
> 65   Make clean and pure:
> Into thy hands I humbly give my soul
>   To heal and cure.
> Out of thy book all mine offences blot,[533]
> And with thy blood quite take away my spot.
> 70   So shall my heart
>   Be free from smart,   *pain*
> And mine offences quite forgot.
>
> Turn back thy face which all things doth behold
>   From heaven's vault:
> 75 Least thou espy my trespass manifold,
>   And heinous fault.
> My faults, which are in number many more
> Than little sands which are upon the shore,
>   Refrain thine ire,   *anger*
> 80   I thee desire,
> And also heal my deadly sore.
>
> Within my breast (O Lord) an humble spirit.
>   Do thou create:
> And of thy comfort do not me disherit,   *disinherit*
> 85   I thee entreat.
> Let me enjoy the sunshine of thy face,
> Take not from me the solace of thy grace,
>   The Holy Ghost:
>   My comfort most
> 90 Let me retain in any case.

---

[532] infectious] The metre requires four syllables ('in-fec-ti-ous').

[533] Coverdale (BCP) has 'put out all my misdeeds', the Geneva Bible 'put away all mine iniquities', and the Bishops', 'wipe out my wickedness', but the version of Psalm 51. 9 used as an opening sentence for Morning Prayer in the BCP is 'Turn thy face away from our sins (O Lord) and blot out all our offences'. This was picked up in the version of Psalm 51, otherwise following Coverdale's BCP translation, included among the other Penitential Psalms in the 1559 *Christian Prayers and Meditations*, known as Queen Elizabeth's Prayer Book, a copy having been presented to her by Matthew Parker. The Hebrew doesn't necessarily imply erasing from a book, but the use of blotting out in some versions of the Psalm may have suggested to Sabie the figure of God's book of life, featuring throughout the Bible from Exodus (32. 33) to Revelation (3. 5).

My tongue untie, my lips (O Lord) resolve,
    Thou art the key:
So will my tongue thy mercy great revolve,   *consider*
    From day to day
95 Then shall the wicked learn by mine example,
To keep thy statutes which be sweet and ample
      And seeing me,
        shall turn to thee,
And in the right way learn to trample.

100 Wouldst thou have been with sacrifice content,
    Much fat of rams,
Much incense sweet on thee would I have spent
    And blood of lambs:
But thou (O God) thereto hast no respect,
105 A broken heart thou never wilt reject:
    That sacrifice
    Is of most price,
That only with thee takes effect.

Be gentle, Lord, to thy Zionian town,
110   Bow down thy face,
And on thy Shalem send thy mercy down,[534]
    And loving grace:
Re-edify her bulwarks like to fall,
And up again build her decaying wall.
115   Then will I praise
    Thy name always.
And give burnt off'rings therewithal.   *in addition*

Thus did the psalmist warble out his plaints,   *laments*
    And ceaseth not from day to day to moan,
120 His heart with anguish of his sorrow faints.
    And still he kneels before his Maker's throne.
At midnight sends he many a grievous groan.
    So did his God in mercy on him look.
    And all his sins did race out of his book.[535]   *erase*

    FINIS.

---

[534] Shalem] Hebrew spelling (transliterated) of 'Salem', i.e. Jerusalem.
[535] The addition of the closing narrative frame resembles the similar though more extensive frames in Wyatt's Penitential Psalms and Gascoigne's *De Profundis*, as well as Sabie's narrative poem *David and Bathsheba*.

70. Henry Lok, *Ecclesiastes, Otherwise Called, The Preacher* (1597)

[Henry Lok (d. in or after 1608) was the son of Anne Vaughan Lock and cousin of Michael Cosworth. The religious sonnets in his *Sundry Christian Passions* (1593) were reprinted in his 1597 volume *Ecclesiastes*, which also included a metrical paraphrase of Ecclesiastes, 'Sundry Psalms of David', and sixty dedicatory sonnets to what has been described as 'a veritable who's who of late Elizabethan literary patrons' (Brennan). Lok's choice of the sonnet as the form for his devotional poems may have been influenced by his mother (though he used a different rhyme scheme), assuming that she was the author of the first sonnet sequence in English, the paraphrase of Psalm 51, *A Meditation of a Penitent Sinner* (see 36). Lok's Psalms appear to be in fourteener couplets but might better be thought of as in common metre (with unrhymed odd lines, as in Sternhold's Psalms), though printed in long lines. He was an early pioneer of the kind of devotional poetry that flourished in the next century, and he may have specifically influenced poetry collections by Barnabe Barnes and Nicholas Breton. See Michael G. Brennan, *ODNB*.]

Psalm 27[536]

1. The Lord he is my saving light, whom should I therefore feare?
2. He makes my foes to fall, whose teeth would me in sunder tear.
3. Though hosts of men besiege my soul, my heart shall never dread:
4. So that within his court and sight, my life may still be led.
5. For in his Church from trouble free, he shall me keep in hold:
6. In spite of foes, his wondrous praise, my song shall still unfold.
7. Have mercy (Lord) therefore on me, and hear me when I cry;
8. Thou bad'st me look with hope on thee, for help to thee I fly.
9. In wrath, therefore, hide not thy face, but be thou still my aid;
10. Though parents fail, thou wilt assist, thy promise so hath said.
11. Teach me thy truth, and thy right path, lest that the enemy
12. Prevail against my life, whose tongues entrap me treacherously.
13. My heart would faint for fear, unless my faith did build on thee,
14. My hope, my God, and comfort's strength, who will deliver me.

Psalm 71

1. In thee (O Lord) I trust, therefore from shame deliver me;
2. Perform thy promise, save thou me, who call for help to thee.
3. Be thou my rock of strength and shield, whose power is great and might.
4. Deliver me from wicked men, and put my foes to flight.
5. For in thee only from my youth, have I my trust reposed; *alone*

---

[536] Whether it was part of Lok's intention or not, this Psalm is formally a perfect box, with fourteen lines down, each line fourteen syllables long. The modern poet John Hollander experimented with a similar but slightly shorter form he entitled *Powers of Thirteen*.

6. Thou hast had care of me, whilst yet in womb I was enclosed.
7. Thee will I praise, who art my help, when men at me do scorn;
8. My mouth thy mercies still records, who help'st the mind forlorn.
9. In time of age forsake me not, or when my strength doth fail,
10. Lest that the counsels of my foes, against my soul prevail.
11. Who say, my God hath me forgot; they therefore me pursue:
12. But be thou Lord at hand to me, who canst my strength renew.
13. Shame and reproach let be their share, which my destruction seek;
14. But on thee always will I wait, with humble heart and meek.
15. My mouth thy mercies shall rehearse, whose measure doth excel,   *recite*
16. And in thy trust my steps shall walk, and tongue thy truth shall tell.
17. Even from my youth thou hast me taught, thy wonders well I know
18. And whilst I live (if thou assist) I will thy judgements show.
19. Thy justice, Lord, I will exalt: whose works are like to thine?
20. Who threw'st me down, and raised me up, who else in dust had leine.   *lain*
21. Thou canst man's honour soon increase, and show thy cheerful face:
22. Upon the viol will I sing thy praise,[537] O God, of grace.
23. My lips shall joy to talk of thee, who hast my safety wrought:
24. My freed soul, shall still confess, who hath my safety bought.

71. James Melville, *A Fruitful and Comfortable Exhortation Anent Death* (1597)

[James Melville (1556–1614), nephew of the famous theologian and principal of Glasgow University Andrew Melville (himself the author of accomplished neo-Latin translations of the Psalms), was educated at St Andrews, where, after hearing John Knox preach, he decided to join the ministry. Melville taught at Glasgow and St Andrews. He became a leading figure in the Church of Scotland, arguing against conformity with the Church of England, and he wrote a number of devotional works as well as ecclesiastical history, and wrote poetry, including a Greek lament for the Kirk. He was a staunch opponent of episcopacy and a thorn in the side of James VI (later VI and I), whose attempts to assert royal supremacy over the Kirk he energetically resisted. Two of the Scots metrical Psalms (23 and 121) in *A Fruitful and Comfortable Exhortation* were reprinted, without attribution, in *The Mind's Melody* (1605, see 79). The texts were somewhat anglicized and were laid out in shorter lines (the internal rhymes in lines one and three as printed here, for instance, indicate the line breaks), making it more obvious that they were intended to be sung to the quite sophisticated tune of Alexander Montgomerie's popular 'Solsequium'. See James Kirk, *ODNB*.]

---

[537] As with flora and fauna, many of the musical instruments of ancient Israel were unknown to early translators and remain mysterious. Translators substituted instruments they knew, like the viol.

JAMES MELVILLE

Psalm 23

To the tune of *Solsequium*.[538]

The Lord most high, I know will be, ane hird to me,	*a, shepherd*
I cannot long have stress, nor stand in need:	
He makes my lear, in fields sa fear, that I but cear,	*bed, fair, go my way*
Repose, and at my pleasure safely feed.	
5 He sweetly me convoys, to pleasant springs,	
Where na thing me annoys, but pleasure brings:	*no*
He gives my mind, peace in sik kind	*such, manner*
That fear of foes, nor force, cannot me reave,	*deprive*
By him I am led, in perfit tread,	*perfect, path*
10 And for his name, he will me never leave.	
Though I suld stray, even day be day, in deadly way,[539]	*should*
Yet wald I be assured, and fear none ill.	*would, evil*
For why thy grace, in every place, dois me embrace,	*because*
Thy rod and sheephird's cruik, comforts me still.	*crook*
15 In despite of my foe, my table grows,	*defiance*
Thou balms my head with joy, my cup overflows.	
Kindness and grace, mercy and peace,	
Sall follow me, for all my wretched days	*shall*
Then endless joy, sall me convoy,	
20 To heaven where I with thee sall be always.	

Psalm 121

When I behold these montaines cold, can I be bold	*mountains*
To take my journey through this wilderness,	
Wherein dois stand, on either hand, a bludy band	*company*
To cut one off, with cruel craftiness:[540]	
5 Here subtle Satan's slight dois me assail,[541]	*cunning*

---

[538] A *solsequium* ('sun' plus 'follow') is a marigold. Alexander Montgomerie's poem 'Like as the dumb solsequium' was an exceptionally popular erotic paean to King James VI, representing his courtiers as marigolds to his lifegiving sun.

[539] Melville's 'deadly way' reduces the familiar 'valley of the shadow of death' to something more within the realm of experience of a sheep. He probably did not know it, but his translation is actually truer to the original Hebrew, which meant simply 'dark shadows' or 'total darkness', but was repointed (different vowels converting *tsalmut* into *tsalmawet*) in the rabbinic period to convey the more apocalyptic 'shadow of death'. Robert Alter, on the other hand, suggests that the idea of 'shadow of death' is implicit even in *tsalmut*, at least as a pun or folk etymology.

[540] Even before he inserts Satan, Melville elaborates a much more dramatic narrative than the original, in which the Psalmist simply looks to the hills for help from the Lord.

[541] Satan is inserted into the Psalm by Melville, the adjective 'subtle' linking him to the serpent of Genesis 3. 1, 'more subtle' than any other animal (Geneva).

	There his proud warldly might thinks to prevail:	*worldly*
	In every place, with pleasant face,	
	The snares of sin besets me round about,	
	With poison sweit, to slay the spreit,	*sweet*
10	Conspirit all to take my life but doubt.	*conspired*

	Bot God is he will succour me, and let me see	
	His saving health, ay ready at command:	*always*
	Even Jehovah, that create a, both great and sma,	*all, small*
	In heaven and air, and in the sea and land.	
15	Fret not then fearful heart, my breist within,	*worry*
	This God will take thy part, thy course to rin:	*run*
	He will thee guide, thou sall not slide,	*shall*
	Thy feet sall steadfast stand in the right way;	
	He will thee keep, he will not sleep:	*guard*
20	Nor suffer foes to catch thee as a prey.	*allow*

	The Lord dois keep Israel his sheep, and will not sleep;[542]	
	Beneath his shadow thou sall safely lie,	
	Right sure and ferm; with his right arm, save thee from harm	
	He sall, and all thy fearful foes defy:	
25	The day hot sun's offence sall not thee grieve,	
	Nor cold moon's influence by night thee mieve:	*move*
	God of his grace, from his high place,	
	Sall save thee from all ill. In every way	*evil*
	Thou goes about, baith in and out,	*both*
30	He sall thee bless, and prosper now and ay.	

72. William Patten, *Anno foelicissimi regni augustae reginae nostrae Elizabeth quadragesimo primo, fauste iam incepto. psal. terseptimus: domine in virtute tua* (1598)
['In the Forty-First Year, Already Promisingly Begun, of the Most Happy Reign of Our August Queen Elizabeth. The Three-Times-Seventh Psalm: Lord, in your strength']

[See headnote to 59.]

Psalm 21

Domine in virtute tua. [Lord, in your strength]

1. O Lord, thy queen revolving in her mind
    Thy power, surmounting all other power so far,
    Herself, therewith, how joyful doth she find,

---

[542] Melville reinserts the sheep from Psalm 23 here, making his two Psalms a matching pair.

	I	1.	But at thy help so vanquishaunt in war,	*vanquishing*
5			Triumph she doth, lifts it as high as star:	
		2.	Her heart's desire thou givest her joyfully,	
			Her prayers eke thou dost not her deny.	*also*
		3.	Lord, of thy bounteous liberality,	
			That hast her set in sovereignty supreme,	
10			Blessed her with thy gifts of principality,	
	II		Made her the queen of this thy noble ream,	*realm*
			Crowned her with a monarchal diadem:	
		4.	Life hath she asked, which thou most graciously,	
			Hast granted her in perpetuity.	
15		5.	Great is the glory of her high estate,	
			But as thou hast of mere benignity,	*pure*
			Above so mighty kings her elevate,	
	III		In honour, brightness, and famous dignity,	
		6.	So shalt thou make her blessèd for to be,	
20			With happiness still in continuance,	
			And gladness of thy joyful countenance.	
		7.	Our queen trusts in God and in the great bounty	
			Of thee, most high, thou, Lord of sea and land:	
			Therefore slip can she not, but certainly	
25	IV	8.	Thy foes and hers shall feel and understand	
			The mighty power and strength of thy right hand:	
			They thereby forced (e'en maugre of their heart)	*despite*
			To be more quiet or else be made to smart.	*sting*
		9.	Heat thou them hot as furnace is by fire,	
30			In time of thy most dreadful indignation,	
			Quell them with torments of thy wrathful ire,	
	V		In vengeance, Lord, without commiseration;	
			Flames them devour and spoil in cruel fashion,	
		10.	Their plants from earth shalt root up, and again,	
35			Destroy their offspring forever among men.	
		11.	Against thee and her in damnable desire,	
			One prank (among the rest) most execrable	
			Assayed they a malice, mischief, sword and fire,	*attempted*
	VI		Which yet to achieve (alas) they were unable:	
40			What got they by that practice detestable?	
			But slaughter and flight and most infamous shame,	
			With a fretting corsie perpetual to their name.[543]	*wasting, corrosive*

[543] The Psalmist does speak of 'intended mischief' and 'a device' (BCP), but given the specific address to Queen Elizabeth as monarch of Protestant England, Patten is likely thinking of a

	12.	Tis thou that makest them run away apace,	*quickly*
		Thy bowstring is it, that in a full despight,	*disdain*
45		Terribly shall flirt them at their very face:	*flout*
	VII 13.	Advance thyself, O Lord God, in thy might,	
		So shall we sing all cheerful in delight,	
		Thy praise, thy glory, and celebrate withal,	*as well*
		Thy puissant power that reigns and ever shall.	*mighty*

73. Mary Sidney Herbert, Countess of Pembroke (MS by 1599)

[Mary Sidney Herbert, Countess of Pembroke (1561–1621), was the daughter of Sir Henry Sidney and sister of Philip and Robert Sidney. The Sidneys were one of the most remarkable and accomplished literary families in English history. Philip, Robert, and Mary were all poets and translators, as were Robert's daughter Mary, Lady Wroth, author of the Romance *The Countess of Mongomery's Urania* and the sonnet sequence *Pamphilila to Amphilanthus*, and Mary's son, William Herbert, third Earl of Pembroke. Mary was seven years younger than Philip and two years older than Robert. Barred from schooling or university as a woman, she nevertheless received a superb humanist education at home. She was invited to court by Queen Elizabeth in 1575 and attended the entertainment for the queen at Kenilworth, for which George Gascoigne had written a masque (cancelled due to weather). In 1577 her uncle, Robert Dudley, Earl of Leicester, arranged her marriage to Henry Herbert, second Earl of Pembroke. Considerably older than Mary, Herbert was one of the wealthiest men in England, which placed her in a position of considerable power. Mary was close to her older brother, who wrote many of his major works at her estate at Wilton, and she managed his reputation after his death, principally by controlling the publication of his works. She was a major patron of other writers too, including Abraham Fraunce, for instance, as well as Nicholas Breton, Thomas Moffett, Samuel Daniel, and perhaps Edmund Spenser. Henry Herbert supported a company of players, Pembroke's Men, that toured in the early 1590s and performed some of Shakespeare's plays. During the same years, the Pembrokes hosted other playing companies, including the Queen's Men, Strange's Men, Worcester's Men, and Essex's Men, at Ludlow Castle, which the earl occupied as Lord President of the Council Marches, a position he took over from his father-in-law, Henry Sidney. Mary's own literary work included a number of original poems, as well as a variety of important translations: the drama *Antonius*, from Robert Garnier's French (which influenced Shakespeare's *Antony and Cleopatra*), *A Discourse of Life and Death*, from the French of Phillippe de Mornay, and Petrarch's *Triumph of Death*. Her greatest and most

particular 'prank', the Armada sent from Spain in 1588, which was defeated and wrecked, supported by (it was believed) God's providence. 1598 was the tenth anniversary.

influential achievement was the translations of the Psalms, a project begun by Philip Sidney, perhaps in his sister's presence, and continued by Mary after his death. She completed Psalms 44 to 150, revised some of Philip's first 43, and shaped the whole into a complete psalter, adding two dedicatory poems of her own, one to her late brother, and the other to Queen Elizabeth. The Tixall manuscript of the Sidney Psalms, which contains the dedicatory poems, may have been intended as a presentation copy to the queen. Mary's technical virtuosity is if anything even more impressive than her brother's; her Psalms include sonnets, acrostics, several classical quantitative metres (including Sapphics), and a wide array of stanza forms of her own invention. Her Psalms (along with Philip's) were praised by John Donne, Samuel Daniel, Sir John Harington, and many others, and shaped not only subsequent metrical Psalms but the seventeenth-century religious lyric. George Herbert's *The Temple*, for instance, is inconceivable without the model of the Sidney Psalter. See Margaret P. Hannay, *Philip's Phoenix: Mary Sidney, Countess of Pembroke* (New York and Oxford: Oxford University Press, 1990); *The Sidney Psalter*, ed. by Hamlin, Brennan, Hannay, and Kinnamon; *The Collected Works of Mary Sidney Herbert, Countess of Pembroke*, ed. by Hannay, Kinnamon, and Brennan, 2 vols (Oxford: Clarendon Press, 1998).]

Psalm 52[544]

Quid gloriaris? [Why do you glory?]

Tyrant,[545] why swell'st thou thus,
    Of mischief vaunting?   *boasting*
Since help from God to us
    Is never wanting?

5 Lewd lies thy tongue contrives,   *wicked*
    Loud lies it soundeth:[546]
Sharper than sharpest knives
    With lies it woundeth.

---

[544] One of the most dramatic of Pembroke's Psalms, the short lines, close rhymes, and strong (trochaic) stresses in the first lines of the opening several stanzas creating the voice of a character angry, impatient, and contemptuous.

[545] Tyrant] The Hebrew suggests a mighty man, perhaps a chief, but Pembroke follows Coverdale (BCP) as well as the Geneva note in using this loaded term. Great controversy was generated by the 1579 publication *A Defense of Liberty Against Tyrants* (*Vindiciae Contra Tyrannos*), which argued that the people could resist a wicked or unjust king. The author was unnamed but has been identified as either Hubert Languet or Philippe Du Plessis Mornay, both friends of Philip Sidney.

[546] The similarity of 'lewd' and 'loud' is heighted in manuscripts by spelling the second 'lowd', underscoring the repetition of lies, intensified by the alliteration of the lapping 'l's. Like Wyatt, Pembroke also delights in polyptoton, as 'sharper'/'sharpest' and 'fearing'/'fearful' below.

Falsehood thy wit approves,
10   All truth rejected:
Thy will all vices loves,
        Virtue neglected.

Not words from cursèd thee,
        But gulfs are pourèd.
15 Gulfs wherein daily be
        Good men devourèd.

Think'st thou to bear it so?
        God shall displace thee;
God shall thee overthrow,
20   Crush thee, deface thee.   *erase*

The just shall fearing see
        These fearful chances:
And laughing shoot at thee
        With scornful glances.

25 Lo, lo, the wretched wight,   *creature*
        Who God disdaining,
His mischief made his might,
        His guard his gaining.

I as an olive tree,[547]
30   Still green shall flourish:
God's house the soil shall be
        My roots to nourish.

My trust on his true love
        Truly attending,
35 Shall never thence remove,
        Never see ending.

Thee will I honour still,
        Lord, for this justice:
There fix my hopes I will,
40   Where thy saints' trust is.

Thy saints trust in thy name,
        Therein they joy them: *rejoice*
Protected by the same
        Naught can annoy them.

---

[547] There is a marked shift in tone in verse nine as well as the first use of the first-person singular pronoun, 'I'. The olive tree metaphor recalls the blessed man 'like a tree planted by the water side' in Psalm 1 (BCP).

Psalm 55[548]

Exaudi, Deus. [Hear, O God]

My God, most glad to look, most prone to hear,
    An open ear, O let my prayer find,
        And from my plaint turn not thy face away.   *lament*
        Behold my gestures, hearken what I say,
5   While uttering moans with most tormented mind,
My body I no less torment and tear.
For lo, their fearful threat'nings wound mine ear,
    Who griefs on griefs on me still heaping lay,
        A mark to wrath and hate and wrong assigned;
10   Therefore, my heart hath all his force resigned
    To trembling pants; death's terrors on me prey;
I fear, nay shake, nay quiv'ring quake with fear.

Then say I, oh, might I but cut the wind,
    Borne on the wing the fearful dove doth bear:
15   Stay would I not, till I in rest might stay.
        Far hence, oh, far, then would I take my way.
    Unto the desert, and repose me there,
These storms of woe, these tempests left behind.
But swallow them, O Lord, in darkness blind,
20   Confound their counsels, lead their tongues astray,   *confuse*
        That what they mean by words may not appear.
        For mother Wrong within their town each where,
    And daughter Strife their ensigns so display,[549]
As if they only thither were confined.

---

[548] In addition to Surrey's version of this Psalm, Pembroke may well have known that of John Dudley, Earl of Leicester, since he was her uncle. This Psalm is a dazzling formal tour-de-force, though managed so smoothly that it is easy not to notice. Every stanza has twelve lines, arranged in mirroring pairs of the same three rhymes, though each in a different order: *abc/cba, acb/bca, bac/cab*, etc. The two groups of six lines comprising each stanza begin and end with the same rhyme: 'hear'/'tear', 'ear'/'fear', etc. Each stanza begins and ends with the same rhyme, on a larger scale following the same mirror pattern: *a/a, b/b, c/c, c/c, b/b, a/a*. An even harder mirroring to discern is in the order of the sestets (half-stanzas), the first and last of the Psalm rhyming *abc/cba*, the second and second-to-last *acb/bca*, etc. This patterning has been compared to the reversibility of a palindrome, but the rhetorical figure it mimics is chiasmus, repeating words or phrases in reverse order, and Pembroke also employs this verbal figure throughout the Psalm, as in 'fear, nay shake' and 'quake with fear', 'only he, he only', 'Whom unto me, me unto whom'. Patterning on multiples of three may allude to the Trinity, but the Trinity is also traditionally expressed by means of a chiastic phrase, 'three in one and one in three' (as in Philip Sidney's translation of Philippe Du Plessis Mornay's *Work Concerning Trueness of the Christian Religion*), which may be the germ of Pembroke's ingenious structure.

[549] The Psalmist has observed these evils in the city, but Pembroke personifies them as allegorical agents, like Homer's Strife.

25 These walk their city walls both night and day;
  Oppressions, tumults, guiles of every kind
    Are burgesses and dwell the middle near;
      About their streets his masking robes doth wear   *disguising*
    Mischief clothed in deceit, with treason lined,
30 Where only he, he only bears the sway.[550]   *alone, authority*
  But not my foe with me this prank did play,
    For then I would have borne with patient cheer   *frame of mind*
      An unkind part from whom I know unkind,
      Nor he whose forehead Envy's mark had signed,[551]
35   His trophies on my ruins sought to rear,
From whom to fly I might have made assay.   *attempt*

But this to thee, to thee impute I may,   *ascribe*
  My fellow, my companion, held most dear,
    My soul, my other self, my inward friend:
40   Whom unto me, me unto whom did bind
    Exchangèd secrets, who together were
God's temple wont to visit, there to pray.   *accustomed*
Oh, let a sudden death work their decay,
  Who speaking fair such cankered malice mind,   *corrosive*
45   Let them be buried breathing in their bier.
      But purple morn, black ev'n, and midday clear
    Shall see my praying voice to God inclined,
Rousing him up, and naught shall me dismay.

He ransomed me, he for my safety fined[552]
50   In fight where many sought my soul to slay;
    He, still himself to no succeeding heir
      Leaving his empire shall no more forbear
    But at my motion, all these atheists pay,[553]
By whom, still one, such mischiefs are designed.
55 Who but such caitiffs would have undermined,   *wretches*
  Nay, overthrown, from whom but kindness mere   *pure*
    They never found? Who would such trust betray?
      What buttered words! Yet war their hearts bewray.   *reveal*

---

[550] The drama almost seems transported to the streets of Elizabethan London.

[551] A further personification (following Mischief, earlier in the stanza), marking the envious foe in the forehead like the mark given to Cain (Genesis 4. 15). The more dangerous enemy is the false friend without any mark.

[552] fined] paid the fine, refined.

[553] atheists] A broader term in the sixteenth century, including immorality and impiety, but it could also designate those who say 'there is no God', as Psalm 14 describes the fool. Golding uses the term in the Epistle Dedicatory to his translations of Calvin's Commentaries on the Psalms.

       Their speech more sharp than sharpest sword or spear
60 Yet softer flows than balm from wounded rind.⁵⁵⁴   *bark*

But, my o'erloaden soul, thyself upcheer,
    Cast on God's shoulders what thee down doth weigh
        Long borne by thee with bearing pained and pined:
        To care for thee he shall be ever kind;
65   By him the just in safety held alway
Changeless shall enter, live, and leave the year:
But, Lord, how long shall these men tarry here?
    Fling them in pit of death where never shined
        The light of life, and while I make my stay   *support*
70   On thee, let who their thirst with blood allay
    Have their life-holding thread so weakly twined
That it, half-spun, death may in sunder shear.⁵⁵⁵

             Psalm 58⁵⁵⁶

Si vere utique.   [Do [you] indeed?]

And call ye this to utter what is just,
    You that of justice hold the sov'reign throne?⁵⁵⁷
And call ye this to yield, O sons of dust,⁵⁵⁸
        To wrongèd brethren every man his own?
5   Oh no, it is your long-malicious will
        Now to the world to make by practice known
            With whose oppression you the balance fill,
Just to yourselves, indiff'rent else to none.

But what could they, who ev'n in birth declined
10   From truth and right to lies and injuries?

---

⁵⁵⁴ The balm is thus not just figurative 'healing' but the aromatic sap that flows from certain trees, including (as Pembroke might have known) frankincense and myrrh.
⁵⁵⁵ Pembroke adds to the Psalm this classical image of life as a thread spun by the Fates.
⁵⁵⁶ Psalm 58 is the fiercest invective in the Bible, calling down truly horrendous curses on the enemy. At least one modern edition of the Book of Common Prayer omitted it entirely, and commentators and paraphrasers have often tried to soften its blows by selective omission or allegorizing. Pembroke takes the opposite approach, intensifying the curse, elaborating in particular the image of the aborted foetus. Pembroke was one of the few translators of this Psalm to have any direct experience of childbirth.
⁵⁵⁷ Pembroke boldly shifts the focus from the 'congregation' (BCP) and ordinary people to unjust monarchs.
⁵⁵⁸ sons of dust] Pembroke's substitution for 'sons of man'. Adam is made out of dust in Genesis 2. 7, and God curses Adam after the sin of eating the forbidden fruit, saying 'dust thou art, and unto dust thou shalt return' (Genesis 3. 19). The connection between humans, dust, and death is much developed in Job, and is the source of the familiar 'ashes to ashes, dust to dust' in the Burial Service.

To show the venom of their cankered mind   *corrupted*
  The adder's image scarcely can suffice.
   Nay, scarce the aspic may with them contend,   *asp*
  On whom the charmer all in vain applies
15   His skilfull'st spells: aye missing of his end,   *always*
  While she self-deaf and unaffected lies.[559]

Lord, crack their teeth; Lord, crush these lions' jaws;
  So let them sink as water in the sand:
When deadly bow their aiming fury draws,
20   Shiver the shaft ere past the shooter's hand.[560]
   So make them melt as the dishousèd snail
  Or as the embryo, whose vital band[561]
   Breaks ere it holds, and formless eyes do fail   *unformed*
  To see the sun, though brought to lightful land.

25 Oh, let their brood, a brood of springing thorns,[562]
  Be by untimely rooting overthrown   *unseasonable, digging up*
Ere bushes waxed, they push with pricking horns,   *grew, leafless branches*
  As fruits yet green are off by tempest blown:
   The good with gladness this revenge shall see,
30   And bathe his feet in blood of wicked one,
   While all shall say: the just rewarded be,
  There is a God that carves to each his own.[563]

Psalm 73[564]

Quam bonus Israel.   [How good to Israel?]

It is most true that God to Israel,
  I mean to men of undefilèd hearts,[565]
   Is only good, and naught but good imparts.

---

[559] Considerably elaborating upon the original: 'even like the deaf adder, that stoppeth her ears' (BCP). See also note 289, p. 198.
[560] shiver the shaft] shatter the arrows.
[561] vital band] power of life.
[562] Compare Ecclesiastes 7. 6, 'For as the crackling of thorns under a pot, so is the laughter of the fool'.
[563] God gives to all persons what they desire, as at a dinner table carving the roast (a disturbing image given the visceral ferocity of the Psalm).
[564] Another of Pembroke's most remarkable vocal creations, converting the Psalm into something like a Shakespearean soliloquy, conveying a sense of thought in process by means of rhetorical questions, second thoughts, self-contradiction, and hesitation.
[565] Pembroke borrows from and alludes, both playfully and seriously, to her brother's massively influential Petrarchan sequence, *Astrophil and Stella*, the fifth sonnet of which

	Most true, I see, albe I almost fell	*albeit*
5	From right conceit into a crooked mind	
	And from this truth with straying steps declined:	
	For lo, my boiling breast did chafe and swell	
	When first I saw the wicked proudly stand,	
	Prevailing still in all they took in hand.	
10	And sure no sickness dwelleth where they dwell:	
	Nay, so they guarded are with health and might,	
	It seems of them Death dares not claim his right.	

They seem as privileged from others' pain:
    The scourging plagues which on their neighbours fall,
15   Torment not them, nay, touch them not at all.
Therefore with pride, as with a gorgeous chain,
    Their swelling necks encompassèd they bear;
    All clothed in wrong, as if a robe it were:[566]
So fat become, that fatness doth constrain
20   Their eyes to swell; and if they think on aught,   *anything*
    Their thought they have, yea, have beyond their thought.
They wanton grow, and in malicious vein
    Talking of wrong, pronounce as from the skies!
    So high a pitch their proud presumption flies.

25 Nay, heav'n itself, high heav'n, escapes not free
    From their base mouths; and in the common talk
    Their tongues no less than all the earth do walk.
Wherefore ev'n godly men, when so they see
    Their horn of plenty[567] freshly flowing still,
30   Leaning to them, bend from their better will.
And thus, they reasons frame: how can it be
    That God doth understand, that he doth know,
    Who sits in heav'n, how earthly matters go?
See here the godless crew, while godly we
35   Unhappy pine, all happiness possess:
    Their riches more, our wealth still growing less.

---

begins, 'It is most true that eyes are form'd to serve | The inward light', but ends perversely, 'True, and yet true that I must Stella love'. Pembroke's Psalmist is an anti-Astrophil, and her Psalm features a speaker who, unlike Philip's alter ego, chooses the proper object of devotion, God.

[566] The clothing metaphor is original to Pembroke, though used in other Psalms. The chain and robe are signs of office familiar in Elizabethan England from local magistrates up to the Lord Chancellor.

[567] horn of plenty] cornucopia.

Nay, ev'n within myself, myself did say,
    In vain my heart I purge, my hands in vain
        In cleanness washed I keep from filthy stain,
Since thus afflictions scourge me every day:
    Since never a day from early east is sent,
        But brings my pain, my check, my chastisement.
And shall I then these thoughts in words bewray?   *expose*
    Oh, let me, Lord, give never such offense
        To children thine that rest in thy defence.
So then I turned my thoughts another way,
    Sounding if I this secret's depth might find;
        But cumbrous clouds my inward sight did blind.

Until at length nigh weary of the chase,   *nearly*
    Unto thy house I did my steps direct:
        There, lo, I learned what end did these expect,
And what? But that in high but slippery place,
    Thou didst them set, whence, when they least of all
        To fall did fear, they fell with headlong fall.[568]
For how are they in less than moment's space
    With ruin overthrown, with frightful fear
        Consumed so clean, as if they never were?   *wasted away, completely*
Right as a dream, which waking doth deface: *erase*
    So, Lord, most vain thou dost their fancies make,
        When thou dost them from careless sleep awake.

Then for what purpose was it, to what end,
    For me to fume with malcontented heart,
        Tormenting so in me each inward part?
I was a fool (I can it not defend)
    So quite deprived of understanding might,
        That as a beast I bare me in thy sight.
But as it was, yet did I still attend,
    Still follow thee, by whose upholding hand,
        When most I slide, yet still upright I stand.
Then guide me still, then still upon me spend
    The treasures of thy sure advice, until
        Thou take me hence into thy glory's hill.

---

[568] The language here strongly evokes Wyatt, whose poetic speaker (as in 'Whoso list to hunt') seems always weary of the 'chase', and who also writes of the perils of balancing on the 'slipper top' ('Stand whoso list') at the Tudor court. Here, though, it is the wicked that slip and fall, while God upholds the Psalmist.

Oh, what is he will teach me climb the skies,
        With thee, thee good, thee goodness to remain?[569]
75   No good on earth doth my desires detain.
Often my mind and oft my body tries
        Their weak defects: but thou, my God, thou art
        My endless lot and fortress of my heart.
The faithless fugitives who thee despise,
80   Shall perish all, they all shall be undone,
        Who leaving thee to whorish idols run.
But as for me, naught better in my eyes
        Than cleave to God, my hopes in him to place,
        To sing his works while breath shall give me space.

Psalm 117[570]

Laudate Dominum.   [Praise the Lord]

                                            forever

P raise him that aye
R emains the same:
A ll tongues display
I ehovah's fame.
5 S ing all that share
T his earthly ball:
H is mercies are
E xposed to all,
L ike as the word
10 O nce he doth give,
R olled in record,
D oth time outlive.

---

[569] Zim (200–01) notes the allusion to Philip Sidney's *Astrophil and Stella* 31, which begins, 'With how sad steps, O moon, thou climbst the skies'. As with other such allusion, Mary references her brother's secular verse partly in homage to the co-author of this psalter, but also to clarify the superiority of this sacred literary project, God being a far worthier object of love and desire than Philip's Stella.

[570] Psalm 117, the shortest of the Psalms, is not originally an acrostic, but the form is used in other Psalms, most notably 119, in which every section begins with a letter of the Hebrew alphabet, from Aleph to Tav.

Psalm 125[571]

Qui confidunt.   [Those who trust]

As Zion standeth very firmly steadfast,
Never once shaking: so on high Jehovah
Who his hope buildeth, very firmly steadfast
                Ever abideth.

5 As Salem braveth with her hilly bulwarks
    Roundly enforted: so the great Jehovah   *fortified*
    Closeth his servants, as a hilly bulwark
                  Ever abiding;

Though tyrant's hard yoke with a heavy pressure
10 Wring the just shoulders: but a while it holdeth,
    Lest the best minded by too hard abusing
                Bend to abuses.

As the well-workers, so the right believers,
Lord, favour, further; but a vain deceiver,
15 Whose wrièd footing not aright directed   *diverted, rightly*
                Wand'reth in error.[572]

Lord him abjected set among the number
Whose doings lawless, study bent to mischief
Mischief expecteth: but upon thy chosen
20   Peace be ever.

Psalm 134[573]

Ecce nunc.   [Behold now]

You that Jehovah's servants are,
Whose careful watch, whose watchful care,

---

[571] Pembroke translates the Gradual Psalms (120–27) into classical unrhymed quantitative metres, following the practice of her brother Philip (in his secular verse), as well as Stanihurst, Fraunce, and others. Psalm 125 uses an English version of the Sapphic stanza, with three long lines followed by a short one, spaced to the right. The Sapphic was named after Sappho of Lesbos, associated with women's love for women. While there is no evidence Pembroke was drawn to other women, the form is nevertheless especially resonant for a woman poet.

[572] There is an etymological pun here, since 'error' derives from Latin *errare*, 'to wander'.

[573] Many of the stanzas of the Sidney Psalms are original or original adaptations of traditional forms, but Psalm 134 is particularly striking, a single stanza with a highly irregular arrangement of longer and shorter lines, indented for even further irregularity. The gradual diminishment of the line from the first to 'Remain' resembles the stanza of 'Easter Wings' by George Herbert (who was deeply influenced by the Sidney Psalms), but the relationship between form and content is less clear than in Herbert.

    Within his house are spent,
    Say thus with one assent:
5   Jehovah's name be praised.
    Then let your hands be raised
        To holiest place,
        Where holiest grace
           Doth aye   *always*
10   Remain,
       And say
           Again:
    Jehovah's name be praised.
    Say last unto the company,
15   Who tarrying make
        Their leave to take,
    All blessings you accompany,
From him in plenty showerèd,
Whom Zion holds embowerèd,
20   Who heav'n and earth of naught hath raised.

Psalm 139[574]

Domine, probasti.   [Lord, you have searched]

  O Lord, in me there lieth naught,
    But to thy search revealèd lies:
        For when I sit
        Thou markest it;
5   No less thou notest when I rise:
  Yea, closest closet of my thought   *most secret, private chamber*
    Hath open windows to thine eyes.

  Thou walkest with me when I walk,
    When to my bed for rest I go,
10   I find thee there,
        And everywhere:
    Not youngest thought in me doth grow,
  No, not one word I cast in talk,
    But yet unuttered thou dost know.

---

[574] Along with Psalm 52, one of Pembroke's most anthologized Psalms. A Wisdom Psalm, 139 explores God's power and omnipresence. The original stanza form combines longer and shorter lines as well as alternating and envelope rhymes, which Pembroke handles easily and to great effect.

15 If forth I march, thou go'st before;
      If back I turn, thou com'st behind:
          So forth nor back
          Thy guard I lack,
      Nay, on me too thy hand I find.
20 Well I thy wisdom may adore,
      But never reach with earthy mind.

    To shun thy notice, leave thine eye,
      Oh wither might I take my way?
          To starry sphere?
25   Thy throne is there.
      To dead men's undelightsome stay?   *rest*
    There is thy walk, and there to lie
      Unknown, in vain I should assay.   *attempt*

    O sun, whom light nor flight can match,
30   Suppose thy lightful, flightful wings
          Thou lend to me,
          And I could flee
      As far as thee the evening brings:
    Ev'n led to west he would me catch,
35   Nor should I lurk with western things.

    Do thou thy best, O secret night,
      In sable veil to cover me:
          Thy sable veil
          Shall vainly fail.
40   With day unmasked my night shall be,
    For night is day, and darkness light,
      O Father of all lights, to thee.

    Each inmost piece of me is thine:
      While yet I in my mother dwelt,
45   All that me clad
          From thee I had.
      Thou in my frame hast strangely dealt;
    Needs in my praise thy works must shine
      So inly them my thoughts have felt.   *inwardly*

50 Thou how my back was beam-wise laid
      And raft'ring of my ribs dost know:
          Know'st every point
          Of bone and joint,
      How to this whole these parts did grow,

In brave embroid'ry fair arrayed,
    Though wrought in shop both dark and low.[575]

Nay, fashionless, ere form I took,
    Thy all and more beholding eye
        My shapeless shape[576]
        Could not escape:
    All these, with times appointed by,
Ere one had being, in the book
    Of thy foresight enrolled did lie.[577]

My God, how I these studies prize,
    That do thy hidden workings show
        Whose sum is such,
        No sum so much:
    Nay, summed as sand they sumless grow!
    I lie to sleep, from sleep I rise,
    Yet still in thought with thee I go.

My God, if thou but one wouldst kill,
    The straight would leave my further chase
        This cursèd brood
        Inured to blood:
    Whose graceless taunts at thy disgrace
Have aimèd oft, and hating still
    Would with proud lies thy truth outface.

Hate not I them, who thee do hate?
    Thine, Lord, I will the censure be.
        Detest I not
        The cankered knot,   *corrupted, company*
    Whom I against thee banded see?   *united*

---

[575] This and the preceding stanza are a brilliant expansion of verses 12–13, powerful in the original but developed by Pembroke in terms of Elizabethan crafts, both typically female (embroidery) and male (building). The alliterative beams of the back and rafters of ribs suggest the hammerbeam ceiling of a Tudor great hall. The shift in metaphor from massive oak beams to delicate embroidery is startling, though embroidery is a skill Pembroke would have known well, and that this embroidery is somehow hammered out in a 'shop both dark and low' suggests more the smithying of the Nibelung than the needlecraft of noble ladies.
[576] The paradox of a 'shapeless shape' is like Milton's Death, with a 'shape, | If shape it might be call'd that shape had none' (*Paradise Lost*, II. 666–67), except that Pembroke's is an image of nascent life, matter as yet without form (Aristotle held that it was the male seed that gave form to female matter in the womb).
[577] A Calvinist version of the biblical book of life, since this book lists not just the living but the elect.

O Lord, thou know'st in highest rate
    I hate them all as foes to me.

85 Search me, my God, and prove my heart,
        Examine me, and try my thought:
            And mark in me
                If aught there be   *anything*
        That hath with cause their anger wrought.
90 If not (as not) my life's each part,
        Lord, safely guide from danger brought.

                    Psalm 150[578]

Laudate Dominum.   [Praise the Lord]

I laud the Lord, the God of hosts commend,   *praise*
    Exalt his pow'r, advance his holiness:
        With all your might lift his almightiness;
    Your greatest praise upon his greatness spend.

5 Make trumpet's noise in shrillest notes ascend;
    Make lute and lyre his lovèd fame express:
        Him let the pipe, him let the tabret bless,   *small drum*
    Him organs' breath, that winds or waters lend.

    Let ringing timbrels so his honour sound,   *tambourine-like instrument*
10   Let sounding cymbals so his glory ring,
    That in their tunes such melody be found,
        As fits the pomp of most triumphant king.

        Conclude: by all that air or life enfold,
        Let high Jehovah highly be extolled.

74. Richard Verstegan?, *The Primer, or Office of the Blessed Virgin Mary* (1599)

[Richard Verstegan (*c.* 1548–1640) studied at Oxford under the name Rowlands, adopted by his Dutch immigrant father as more English-sounding. He resumed his ancestral name after moving to the Continent to avoid arrest as a Catholic polemicist; there he joined with leading English Catholic exiles, including William Allen and Robert Persons. He was involved in producing the Catholic

---

[578] Pembroke's final Psalm is a sonnet, a blend of English and Italian forms, with a Petrarchan octave, a third quatrain in alternating rhyme, and a final Surreyan-Shakespearean couplet. Coles notes that this is the form favoured by Philip Sidney in *Astrophil and Stella* (*Religion, Reform, and Women's Writing*). The Psalm praises God but nowhere explicitly expresses love, yet Pembroke's form itself suggests it.

martyrology *Theatrum crudelitatum haereticorum nostri temporis* (Antwerp, 1587), and wrote numerous polemical and religious tracts, poems, antiquarian studies, and news reports. He was active as an intelligence agent and kept up a large correspondence. *The Primer* of 1599, printed in Antwerp, was the first English translation of the Tridentine primer, following the Roman rather than Sarum rite. Verstegan's role as translator is signalled by the signature 'R. V.' after the address to the Christian reader. The Latin text (for the Psalms the Latin Vulgate) and English translation are printed on facing pages. Psalms 95 and 87 are part of the Office of our Blessed Lady at Matins. See J. M. Blom, *The Post-Tridentine English Primer* ([London]: Catholic Record Society, 1982); Paul Arblaster, *Antwerp & the World: Richard Verstegan and the International Culture of Catholic Reformation* (Leuven: University of Leuven Press, 2004); Arblaster, *ODNB*.]

Psalm 87[579]

The foundations thereof in the holy mountains: our Lord loveth the gates of Zion above all the tabernacles° of Jacob.
Glorious things are said of thee: O city of God.
I will be mindful of Rahab,[580] and Babylon: knowing me.
5 Behold the strangers, and Tyre, and the people of the Ethiopians: these were there.
Shall not Zion say, man, and man is born in her: and the highest himself founded her.
Our Lord will declare in Scriptures of peoples: and of those princes, which have
10 been in her,
As it were of all rejoicing: the habitation is in thee.
Glory be to the Father, and to the Son, etc.

Psalm 95

Come let us rejoice unto our Lord, let us make joy to God our Saviour: let us approach to his presence in confession, and in Psalms let us make joy unto him.
 Hail Mary, full of grace: our Lord is with thee.[581]
For God is a great Lord, and a great King above all Gods: because our Lord
5 repelleth not his people: for that in his hand are all the bounds of the earth, and he beholdeth the heights of the mountains.
 Our Lord is with thee.

---

[579] The Psalms are numbered in the text according to the Catholic tradition, 86 and 94.
[580] Rahab] A name for Egypt here, though elsewhere it refers to a sea-monster (Psalm 87. 4) and the woman in Jericho who helps the Israelites conquer the city (Joshua 2).
[581] The 'Hail Mary' or *Ave Maria*, based on Gabriel's words to Mary in Luke 1, is a traditional Catholic prayer, inserted here as a refrain to express devotion to the Virgin appropriate to the Office.

For the sea is his, and he made it: and his hands founded the dry land: come let
us adore, and fall down before God: let us weep before our Lord, that made us:
10   because he is the Lord our God: we are his people, and the sheep of his pasture.
　　　Hail Mary, full of grace: our Lord is with thee.
Today if ye shall hear his voice, harden not your hearts, as in the provocation
according to the day of temptation in the wilderness: where your fathers tempted
me: proved, and saw my works.
15   　　　　　　　　Our Lord is with thee.
Forty years was I nigh° unto this generation: and said, they always err in heart:
and they have not known my ways, to whom I sware in my wrath, if they shall
enter into my rest.
　　　Hail Mary, full of grace: our Lord is with thee.
20   Glory be to the Father, and to the Son: and to the Holy Ghost. Even as it was in
the beginning, and now, and ever: and world without end, Amen.
　　　　　　　　Our Lord is with thee.
　　　Hail Mary, full of grace: our Lord is with thee.

75. Sir John Harington (MS c. 1600)

[Sir John Harington (bap. 1560–d. 1612) was the son of John Harington of Stepney, a courtier and poet (several of whose poems were included in Tottel's 1557 *Songs and Sonnets*). Queen Elizabeth stood as his godmother, and he remained a favourite of hers throughout his life. He was educated at Eton, King's College, Cambridge, and Lincoln's Inn. He broke off his legal studies to take over the family estate when his father died in 1582. Literary history has been slow to recognize Harington's importance as a major poet and translator. He translated Ariosto's *Orlando Furioso* into English verse (1591), perhaps at the command of the queen, who according to a popular story caught him reading some of Ariosto's naughtier bits to her ladies-in-waiting. She banished him from court (so the story goes) until he had finished the whole. Harington's *The Metamorphosis of Ajax* (1596) is a peculiar yet erudite satire that is, among other things, a treatise on toilets. Perhaps most popular in his own time were Harington's 406 epigrams, modelled after Martial. Though not printed in his lifetime, they circulated widely and were read by King James I, Prince Henry (who received a presentation copy), Lucy, Countess of Bedford, and countless others. The first printed edition appeared in 1613, and many others followed. Harington was particularly interested in metrical Psalms, as his father had been. The elder Harington had begun the manuscript collection known as Arundel-Harington, which the younger continued after his father's death. Among other poems, this manuscript contains Psalms by the Dudley brothers, Sir Thomas Smith, Sir Thomas Wyatt, the Earl of Surrey, and the Sidneys. Sir John Harington completed his own metrical translation of the Psalms before his death in 1612, when he sent a copy to King James I, but the inclusion of his translation of the Penitential Psalms in the Egerton Manuscript indicates that they were probably the first stage of this project, dating from a decade earlier (Schmutzler); they are only minimally revised in the later manuscripts. See Costley King'oo, *Miserere Mei*; Steven W. May, *The Elizabethan Courtier Poets: Their Poems and Their Contexts* (Columbia and London: University of Missouri Press, 1991); Karl E. Schmutzler, 'Harington's Metrical Paraphrases of the Seven Penitential Psalms: Three Manuscript Versions', *Papers of the Bibliographical Society of America*, 53 (1959), 240–51; Jason Scott-Warren, *ODNB*.]

Psalm 38[582]

O do not, Lord, in anger me reprove,
Nor chasten me, in times of deep displeasure;
    Thy shafts so stick in me they will not move,
Thy heavy hand hath weight exceeding measure,
5   My flesh corrupts, no soundness bides therein,
    My bones want rest by reason of my sin.

    My strength doth fail such poise to undergo,   *weight*
The burden such that under it I shrink,
    So tainted is my flesh from top to toe,
10 My festering sores, corrupted, inward, stink;
    My state and staff of all my strength is broken
    And of sad griefs sad garments are a token.[583]

    Though weakness makes me mute, smart makes me roar,   *pain*
My heart is quite oppressed with inward anguish;
15   Thou seest my sighs, O Lord, that sent'st my sore,
Mine eyesight fails, my fainting limbs do languish,
    My neighbours all and friends I hold so dear
    Look on aloof, my kindred come not near.

    And yet my foes, as if all this sufficed not,
20 Do seek eftsoon to draw my vital blood;   *again*
    What plot, what practice is that they devised not?
Yet like a man both deaf and dumb I stood,
    As if that I their foul reproaches heard not,
    Or that to clear or purge myself I cared not.

[582] Harington uses the iambic pentameter stanza made especially popular by Shakespeare's *Venus and Adonis*, though he varies stanzas by the irregular introduction of feminine rhymes with an extra syllable, as in lines 2 and 4, 11 and 12, 19 and 21.

[583] Given that they are in his family manuscript collection, Harington may have Wyatt's Penitential Psalms in mind here, whose Psalm 38 not only has a 'festered' wound but emphasizes the inwardness of corruption ('secret lust', 'the worm within', 'inward contemplation').

25   For still I hoped, in midst of all this ill,
   That of this question God would make decision,
      Nor let my foes be thus insulting still,
   Nor for my plagues to have me in derision;
      I see my sores and know thy justice sent them,
30   I will confess my sins and so repent them.

      And though my foes confirm their wicked faction,
   Ungratefully for kindness rendering harm,
      And though they seek by slander and detraction
   To weaken my good name and me disarm,
35   Yet Lord, thou art my strength and succour chief,
      Make haste then, I thee pray, to my relief.

76. Richard Verstegan, *Odes in Imitation of the Seven Penitential Psalms* (1601)

[See headnote to 74. Verstegan's Psalm translations were published along with other paraphrases of devotional texts and original poems, all dedicated to 'the virtuous ladies and gentlewomen readers of these ditties'. The subtitle of the *Odes* states that they are 'To so-many several tunes of Musick'; no music is provided and none recommended, but Verstegan's metres would suit many available Psalm tunes, though such tunes were of course from Protestant psalters. The tunes corresponding to the particular Psalms translated by Verstegan, however, do not fit those same Psalms in *The Whole Book*. Paul Arblaster has argued for the shaping influence of Robert Southwell on Verstegan's religious poetry (the *Odes* volume also contains 'Saint Peter's Comfort' and 'A Complaint of St Mary Magdalene', both obviously modelled on Southwell). Verstegan's *Odes* were reprinted, without attribution and in reverse order, in Elizabeth Grymeston's *Miscellanea. Meditations. Memoratives* (1604), a devotional miscellany that was reprinted several times.]

                    Psalm 6

Domine ne in furore.   [Lord, do not in anger]

      When my misdeeds, O God,
   May thee to anger move,
   Amidst the rigour of thy rage
   Vouchsafe me not reprove.   *grant*

5   Nor when for my offence
   Thy chastisement must be,
   In thy displeasure, O dear Lord,
   Let it not light on me.

    Thy mercies, Lord, I crave,
10 Of strength I am bereft,
    O salve the soreness that my sin
    Upon my bones hath left.

    My much agrievèd soul
    In sorrows doth abound,
15 How long, O Lord, shall they endure
    Or comfort be unfound.

    O turn thy self to me
    And rid my soul of pain,
    Ev'n for thy mercies, which exceed
20 And ever do remain.

    O hasten thee, O Lord,
    To save and set me free,
    Amongst the dead (to their avail)   *aid*
    There's none can think on thee.

25 And in the depth of hell
    Where there is no redress,
    Who is it that will give the praise
    Or unto thee confess?

    My sighings for my sins
30 Have passed in painful wise,   *manner*
    And I each night will wash my bed
    With tears of wailing eyes.

    My sight is vexed with fear
    Of fury in thy rage,
35 Oh, that my sins must be my foes
    To wear me out in age.

    Away, away from me
    All ye that are unjust,
    Let him my mournful sound receive
40 In whom I put my trust.

    That I with joy may say
    How to my suits accord,   *petitions*
    Vouchsafèd hath to condescend   *deigned*
    My dear and loving Lord.

45 Let shame my foes befall
    And vexèd let them be,

Their own conversion or their shame,
Lord, let them quickly see.

    Glory, O God, to thee
50 And unto Christ thy Son,
As also to the Holy Ghost
Let endlessly be done.
    Amen.

Psalm 102[584]

Domine exaudi orationem meam.   [Lord, hear my prayer]

    O let, O Lord, thine ears inclinèd be
To hear the prayers that I make to thee:
And my heart's grief that breaketh forth in cries,
O let it have the power to pierce the skies.

5   Turn not from me thy favourable face,
What day or hour I am in heavy case:
But when I call to thee in my distress,
O hear me, Lord, and send me soon redress.

    My days and years, alas, with little gain
10 Like unto smoke how are they passed in vain:
My forces, Lord, how are they parched and dry,
Devotions lack yields moisture no supply.

    The blasted grass my image now can show,
My withered heart confirms that it is so:
15 And I forgotten have unto my grief,
To eat the bread of my soul's best relief.[585]

    And my too much regard of earthly care
Before myself for grace I could prepare,
Made reason to abandon reason quite,
20 And to affection fast itself unite.   *securely*

    But now, O Lord, since that I do begin
To see myself, and know the shame of sin,
From earthly train I will retire my mind,   *treachery*
Thee will I seek, my saving health to find.

---

[584] 101 in original.
[585] Since English Catholics were denied the Mass (as opposed to the Protestant Communion), it is possible Verstegan may be hinting at this in the elaboration of 'bread of my soul's best relief', which suggest a hunger more than physical.

25	In desert like as lives the pelican,	
	Or as the crow that doth daylight refrain,	
	Or chirping sparrow sitting all alone,	
	I shroud,[586] I watch, retired, I make my moan.	*hide*

But while, O Lord, I do endure this life,
30 Expecting peace by fleeing worldly strife,
Old friends, I find, become new noisome foes;
O love me, Lord, for loss of love of those.

My penance,[587] not restrained through scorn of theirs,
My food I take with ashes and with tears:
35 Thee more I fear, lest thou on me should'st frown,
That canst me raise, and raising cast me down.

My days decline as doth a shadow pass,
And I as hay that whilom was as grass: *formerly*
But thou from age to age shalt ever be,
40 Then evermore, O Lord, forget not me.

Vouchsafe, O Lord, in puissance to arise,   *grant, strength*
To raise thy Zion that depressèd lies:
Now is the time, the time doth now expire,
It mercy wants, and mercy doth desire.

45 This glorious work was first begun by thee,
Thy servants erst were glad the stones to see: *formerly*
And they will grieve with hearts-afflicted care,
If so the ruins thou dost not repair.[588]

But when, O Lord, thy works shall show thy fame
50 The faithless people then shall fear thy name:
And earthly kings shall bend their glory down,
At thy celestial glory and renown.

Because thy Church, thy Zion, thou didst build,
Where thou wouldst ever have thy honour hild: *sustained*
55 And hast not unregarded heard the plaint   *lament*
Of faithful folk, thrall'd in untruth's restraint.   *captive*

---

[586] shroud] A verb particularly appropriate to the condition of persecuted and often clandestine Catholics in Elizabethan England.

[587] penance] One of the Catholic sacraments, involving confession to a priest. Protestants were keen to distinguish this abolished rite from proper 'penitence', which was not only acceptable but desirable, so Verstegan's word choice is clearly motivated.

[588] ruins] Another loaded term for English Catholics, given the destruction of the monasteries by Henry VIII, their ruins still prominent across England.

      And that no time remembrance may impair,
Of thy maintainèd work, and mercy rare,
Let people now, for people to ensue,
60 Thy praise record, thy praises to renew,

      For from high heaven to this low earthly place,
From bliss to bale our Lord inclines his face: *grief*
The groans to hear, the grievèd to release,
To free from thrall, to make affliction cease.   *captivity*

65   The more may Zion now sound forth his fame,
Jerusalem his praises may proclaim:
Where in his Church his people do accord,
And whereas kings are subjects to their Lord.[589]

      Who may, O Lord, thy dateless days relate,
70 That of all ages overpass the date:
It's thou to us hast put appointed space,
O stop not me ere half I run my race.

      The world and welkin first by thee were made,   *heavens*
Thou heaven's sphere, thou earth's foundation laid,
75 Thou shalt endure, they shall consumèd be,
Thou madest time, time hath no force on thee.

      These elements by alteration strange,
Shall changèd be, and so remain in change:
But thou, O Lord, that works all at thy will,
80 Wast erst the same, the same remaining still.

      Vouchsafe, O Lord, their offspring to preserve,
That thee in fear and faith and love do serve:
And in thy ways directed to remain,
A lasting life in lasting bliss to gain.

85   Unto the Father, Son, and Holy Ghost,
All praise and glory be ascribèd most,
As herefore before the world begun
And as it now, and ever shall be done.

      Amen.

---

[589] By changing the Psalmist's 'kingdoms' (BCP) to 'kings', Verstegan makes a pointed reference to the Acts of Supremacy by which England monarchs, rejecting the pope, were declared heads of Church as well as state.

77. Henry Dod, *Certain Psalms of David, Heretofore Much Out of Use Because of Their Difficult Tunes. The Number Whereof Are Contained in the Page Following. Reduced into English Metre Better Fitting the Common Tunes* (1603)

[Henry Dod (fl. 1583?–1620) was a merchant, ridiculed as 'Dod the silkman' by George Wither, who published a collection of metrical Psalms designed 'to fit the common tunes' in 1603, followed by a complete psalter (*All the Psalms of David*) in 1620. The Geneva Bible translation was printed in the outside margins alongside Dod's metrical version in the 1603 selection. The tune printed for Psalm 111 in *The Whole Book* could be sung to Dod's version. See Jennett Humphreys, rev. Christopher Burlinson, *ODNB*.]

Psalm 111

He giveth thanks to the Lord for his merciful works to his Church. And declareth wherein true wisdom and right knowledge consisteth. Praise ye the Lord.

1. To praise the Lord with my whole heart
    I will rejoice always:
In congregations of the just,
    I will advance his praise.
2. The wondrous works of God the Lord
    In greatness do exceed:
And all men ought to seek them out,
    That love them well indeed.
3. His work is full of beauty, and
    Of glory rich in store: *sufficient supply*
His righteousness most righteously,
    Endureth evermore.
4. His wondrous works he made that we
    Should ever them remember:
Full of compassion is he[590]
    And merciful for ever.
5. A portion fair he hath bestow'd
    On them that do him dreed: *dread*
And mindful of his covenant
    He ever is indeed.
6. His powerful works to Israel
    He graciously hath showed:

---

[590] compassion] The metre requires four syllables ('com-pas-si-on').

               In that the heathen's heritage
                  He hath on them bestowed.
25   7.   His handiworks are equity,⁵⁹¹
                  And judgement: just are found
               His statutes all most plenteously
                  In truth do still abound.

       8. They are most firmly stablishèd,   *established*
30   For ever and for aye: *always*
               And eke are done in equity,   *also*
                  And in the truth alway.   *always*
       9. He sent redemption to his folk,
               His covenant shall endure
35   Forever. By divine precept   *command*
                  His name is fearful sure.

      10. His fear true wisdom doth begin,
               His laws observe do they
               That any understanding have,
40   His praise doth last for aye.

78. Simon Forman (MS 1604)

[Simon Forman (1552–1611) was a doctor, an astrologer, and a magician. He studied at Salisbury school and then attended Magdalene College, Oxford, as a poor scholar. Leaving Oxford without a degree, he continued his studies on his own in both legitimate and arcane sciences, teaching in various schools in between periods in prison. In the 1590s, Forman had a successful practice as both physician and astrologer in London, consulted even by some gentry. Though constantly in conflict with the College of Physicians, he continued to flourish, becoming prosperous and marrying the niece of Sir Edward Monnings, Anne or Joan Baker, which gave him a more established social position. Forman kept voluminous diaries, which recounted many of his medical and astrological cases as well as other aspects of his life, including many sexual adventures (the main biographical account was entitled *The Book of the Life and Generation of Simon*). Forman was also an avid theatregoer, and he records his attendance at three plays by Shakespeare: *Macbeth* (1610), *The Winter's Tale* (1611), and *Cymbeline* (no date given). Among those who consulted him professionally were Mary (Marie) Mountjoy, Shakespeare's landlady in 1604, and the poet Aemilia Lanyer. Forman was implicated in the notorious murder of Sir Thomas Overbury, who had obstructed the marriage of James I's favourite, Robert Carr, to Frances Howard, inconveniently already married to Robert Devereux, third

---

⁵⁹¹ On equity, see note 6, p. 68.

Earl of Essex. Howard seemingly asked Forman for magic love potions, but by the time of trial Forman had been dead for four years. Among Forman's writings are a number of pastiche Psalms, most semi-autobiographic or connected to his own life. Forman's Burial Psalm is unusual both in its length and in the range of Psalms he includes, thirty-two in total, as well as canticles and other Bible verses. The beginning and end of the Burial Psalm seem to be original. See Lauren Kassell, *Medicine and Magic in Elizabethan London: Simon Forman: Astrologer, Alchemist, and Physician* (Oxford: Clarendon Press, 2005); Kassell, ODNB.]

Forman 1609 Jan. 19. To be sung at his burial.

Assemble now, you people all
And mark well what I say:
The life of man is like to grass
That withereth in a day.[592]

5 For man that is of woman born
Hath but short time to live;[593]
He cometh up even as the reed
That is cut down with sith.[594]   *scythe*

He flourisheth even as a flower
10 That springeth in May-tide,[595]
And in the Autumn falls to ground
And there his head doth hide.
His glory is much like to dust
That flies with wind away.[596]
15 And like a winter's frosty night
That thaws ere it be day.[597]

And like a cloud borne in the air
Upon the fleeting wind
That carried is from place to place
20 Where none his place can find;[598]

[592] Compare Psalms 37. 2 and 90. 6, as well as Isaiah 40. 7–8.
[593] Similar to Job 14. 1 but closer to the language of the BCP Burial Service.
[594] The preceding two lines are from 'A Thanksgiving after Receiving the Lord's Supper' from the *Whole Book*.
[595] Compare Psalm 103. 15 and 1 Peter 1. 24.
[596] Close to Hopkins's Psalm 82. 13 from the *Whole Book*, though the dust recalls Psalm 22. 42, among other passages.
[597] Similar to Wisdom 16. 29.
[598] Somewhat similar to John Pullain's Psalm 148. 5 from the *Whole Book*, though compare also Job 7. 9.

    And like a bubble that doth swell
    And rise upon the water,
    That falls away when it is touched
    Or wind it soon doth scatter.[599]

25 Man's life is but a pilgrimage
    To wander for a time,
    Or like a player on a stage
    That conclude in a line;[600]
    No sooner born but to the grave
30 We straight begin to fall,
    And so the glory of each man
    Doth perish straight withal.[601]   *as well*

    And men once dead are out of mind
    And are soon clean forgot;   *completely*
35 As small effect in them is found
    As in a broken pot.[602]
    For when man dieth, all things past,
    Nothing shall he receive;
    His glory will not follow him,
40 His pomp will take her leave.[603]

    The Lord that made us knoweth our shape,
    Our mould and fashion just,
    How weak and frail our nature is,
    And how we are but dust;[604]
45 And how the time of mortal men

---

[599] The image of the bubble is striking and not biblical, though Henry Lok in his popular expanded paraphrase of Ecclesiastes writes that man will 'like a bubble vanish soon away | And in his life his vanity bewray' (*Ecclesiastes*, 1597). A similar metaphor appears among a cluster of others for vanity and mutability in *An Herbal for the Bible* (1587) by Levinus Lemnius, where he writes that in the Bible the life of man is likened 'to a Dreame, to a smoke, to a vapour, to a puffe of winde, to a shadow, to a bubble of water, to hay, to grasse, to an herb, to a flower, to a leafe, to a tale, to vanitie, to a weavers shuttle, to a winde, to dried stubble, to a post, to nothing' (p. 161).

[600] The metaphor of life as a stage is an ancient one and commonplace, but the specific language Forman uses, which is certainly not biblical, is curiously close to *Macbeth*, which Forman saw in 1610: 'Life's but a walking shadow, a poor player | That struts and frets his hour upon the stage | And then is heard no more' (v. 5. 24–26). The play is usually dated to 1606, however, so Forman could have known it before his recorded attendance.

[601] A similar observation to Job 10. 19 or Jeremiah 20. 17.

[602] Hopkins's Psalm 31. 12 from the *Whole Book*.

[603] Sternhold's Psalm 39. 17 from the *Whole Book*, slightly altered.

[604] Sternhold's Psalm 103. 14 from the *Whole Book*.

Is like the withering hay
And like the flower right fair in field
That fades full soon away.⁶⁰⁵

Whose gloze and beauty stormy wind   *false show*
50 Do utterly disgrace,
And make that after their assaults
Such blossoms have no place,⁶⁰⁶
Which in the morning shows full bright
But fadeth by and by,
55 And is cut down ere it be night
And withered dead and dry.⁶⁰⁷

Lord thou hast 'pointed out our life   *appointed*
In length much like a span;
Our age is nothing unto thee
60 So vain is every man.⁶⁰⁸
The length of all men's lives, O Lord,
And age is in thy hand;
His days are numbered in thy sight
That none can death withstand⁶⁰⁹

65 Our time is threescore years and ten
That we do live on mould;   *earth*
If any live to fourscore⁶¹⁰
They count him wondrous old.⁶¹¹
Yet of his time the strength and chief   *head*
70 The which we count upon
Is nothing else but painful grief,
And we as blasts are gone.⁶¹²

Yet presuppose we live as long
As did our fathers old,
75 Yet must we needs at length give place
And be brought to death's fold.⁶¹³
Therefore my soul with woe is filled

---

⁶⁰⁵ Sternhold's Psalm 103. 15 from the *Whole Book*.
⁶⁰⁶ Sternhold's Psalm 103. 16 from the *Whole Book*.
⁶⁰⁷ Hopkins's Psalm 90. 6 from the *Whole Book*.
⁶⁰⁸ Hopkins's Psalm 39. 6 from the *Whole Book*.
⁶⁰⁹ Hopkins's Psalm 31. 15 from the *Whole Book*.
⁶¹⁰ fourscore] The MS spelling ('fowarscore') confirms that the metre requires three syllables.
⁶¹¹ Hopkins's Psalm 90. 10 from the *Whole Book*.
⁶¹² Hopkins's Psalm 90. 11 from the *Whole Book*.
⁶¹³ Sternhold's Psalm 49. 19 from the *Whole Book*.

      And doth in trouble dwell;
      My life and breath almost doth yield
80 And draweth nigh to hell.[614]

      My sight doth fail through grief and woe;
      I call to thee, O God.
      Throughout the day my hands also
      To thee I stretch abroad.[615]
85 For through thine anger we consume,   *waste away*
      Our might is much decayed,
      And of thy fervent wrath and fume
      We are full sore afraid.[616]

      The wicked works which we have wrought
90 Thou set'st before our eyes;
      Our privy faults, yea, eke our thoughts   *hidden, also*
      Thy countenance doth espy.[617]
      For through thy wrath our days do waste,
      Thereof doth naught remain;
95 Our years consume even as a blast
      And are not called again.[618]

      The former force of man thou dost
      Abase oft in the way,
      And shorter thou dost cut their days,
100 Wherefore man oft doth stay.[619]
      My God, in midst of all my days
      Thou hast ta'en me away;
      Thy years endure eternally
      From age to age, I say.[620]

105 But we are pressed with sin to dust,
      Where dens of dragons be,
      And covered as with shade of death
      And great adversity.[621]
      Thus man to honour God hath called,
110 Yet doth he not consider,

---

[614] Hopkins's Psalm 88. 3 from the *Whole Book*.
[615] Hopkins's Psalm 88. 10 from the *Whole Book*.
[616] Hopkins's Psalm 90. 7 from the *Whole Book*.
[617] Hopkins's Psalm 90. 8 from the *Whole Book*.
[618] Hopkins's Psalm 90. 9 from the *Whole Book*.
[619] Thomas Norton's Psalm 102. 23 from the *Whole Book*, altered.
[620] Thomas Norton's Psalm 102. 24 from the *Whole Book*, slightly altered.
[621] Sternhold's Psalm 44. 19 from the *Whole Book*.

But like brute beast so doth he live,
Which turns to dust and powder.[622]

Not knowing when he is once born,
Again he must return
115 Unto the earth from whence he came,
Though he at death do spurn.[623]
Man walketh like a shade and doth
In vain himself annoy
In getting goods, and cannot tell
120 Who shall the same enjoy.[624]

Their care is to build houses high
And so determine sure
To make their fame right great in earth
Forever to endure.[625]
125 Yet shall no man always enjoy
High honour, wealth, and rest,
But shall at length taste of death's cup,
As well as the brute beast.[626]

For as for those that riches have,
130 Wherein their trust is most,
And they which of their treasures great,
Themselves do brag and boast,[627]
There is not one of them that can
His brother's death redeem,
135 Or that can give a price to God
Sufficiently for him.[628]

It is too great a price to pay,
None can thereto attain,
Or that he might his life prolong,
140 Or not in grave remain.[629]
They see wise men as well as fools
Subject unto death's hands,
And being dead, strangers possess

---

[622] Sternhold's Psalm 49. 20 from the *Whole Book*.
[623] No source found.
[624] Hopkins's Psalm 39. 7 from the *Whole Book*.
[625] Sternhold's Psalm 49. 11 from the *Whole Book*.
[626] Sternhold's Psalm 49. 12 from the *Whole Book*.
[627] Sternhold's Psalm 49. 6 from the *Whole Book*.
[628] Sternhold's Psalm 49. 7 from the *Whole Book*.
[629] Sternhold's Psalm 49. 8-9 from the *Whole Book*.

Their goods, their rents, their lands.[630]

145 For why to earth anon they fall,   *because*
     And breath doth soon depart,
     And then doth perish and decay
     The counsels of their heart.[631]

     He is afflict as dying still   *afflicted*
150 From youth this many a years;
     The terrors which do vex him still
     With troubled mind he bears.[632]
     His glory also thou dost waste;
     His throne, his joy, his mirth,
155 By thee is overthrown and cast
     Full low upon the earth.[633]

     Thou dost cut off and make full short
     His youth and lusty days,   *lively*
     and raised on him an ill report,
160 With shame and great dispraise.[634]

     And grindest man through grief and pain
     To dust or clay, and then
     In height of pride thou say'st to him,
     Return to earth again.[635]
165 What man is he that liveth here,
     That death shall never see,
     Or from the hand of hell his soul
     Can keep or once set free.[636]
     The lasting of a thousand years,
170 What is it in God's sight?
     As yesterday it doth appear,
     Or as a watch by night.[637]

     So soon as God doth scatter them,
     Then is their life and trade
175 All as a sleep, and like the grass
     Whose beauty soon doth vade.[638]   *fade*

---

[630] Sternhold's Psalm 49. 10 from the *Whole Book*.
[631] Hopkins's Psalm 146. 4 from the *Whole Book*.
[632] Hopkins's Psalm 88. 16 from the *Whole Book*, changed from first to third person.
[633] Hopkins's Psalm 89. 45 from the *Whole Book*.
[634] Hopkins's Psalm 89. 46 from the *Whole Book*.
[635] Hopkins's Psalm 90. 3 from the *Whole Book*, altered.
[636] Hopkins's Psalm 89. 49 from the *Whole Book*, altered.
[637] Hopkins's Psalm 90. 4 from the *Whole Book*, slightly altered.
[638] Hopkins's Psalm 90. 5 from the *Whole Book*.

When thou for sin dost chasten man,
He waxeth woe and wan,   *grows, sorrowful*
As doth a cloth that moths have fret   *gnawed*
180 So vain a thing is man.⁶³⁹

And yet he glorieth in his pride
Of riches, strength, and might,
And doth the poor great injury
Depriving them of right.⁶⁴⁰
185 But as sheep into fold are brought
So shall they into grave;
Death shall them eat, and in that day
The just shall lordship have.⁶⁴¹

Their image and their royal port   *bearing*
190 Shall fade and quite decay,
Whenas from house to pit they pass
With woe and wellaway.⁶⁴²   *alas*
And death shall on them hastily fall
And send them quick to hell,   *living*
195 That in despight of God do say,
On earth still will we dwell.⁶⁴³

And God shall cast them deep in pit
That thirst for blood always;
He will no guileful man permit
200 To live out half his days.⁶⁴⁴
Doubtless the just man's poor estate
Is better a great deal more
Than all these lewd and worldly men's   *wicked*
Rich pomp and heapèd store.⁶⁴⁵

205 Right dear and precious in his sight
The Lord doth still esteem
The death of all his holy ones,
Whatsoever lewd men deem.⁶⁴⁶
But sure, the wicked borroweth much
210 And never payeth again,

---

⁶³⁹ Hopkins's Psalm 39. 12 from the *Whole Book*, slightly altered.
⁶⁴⁰ No source found.
⁶⁴¹ Sternhold's Psalm 49. 14a from the *Whole Book*.
⁶⁴² Sternhold's Psalm 49. 14b from the *Whole Book*.
⁶⁴³ Hopkins's Psalm 55. 16 from the *Whole Book*, substantially altered.
⁶⁴⁴ Hopkins's Psalm 55. 25 from the *Whole Book*.
⁶⁴⁵ Whittingham's Psalm 37. 16 from the *Whole Book*.
⁶⁴⁶ Norton's Psalm 115. 16 from the *Whole Book*, altered.

Whereas the just by liberal gifts
Makes many glad and fain.[647]

For they whom God doth bless shall have
The land for heritage,
215 And they whom he doth curse likewise
Shall perish in his rage.[648]
The Lord the just man's ways doth guide
And gives him good success;
To everything he takes in hand
220 He sendeth good address.[649]

Though that he fall, yet is he sure
Not utterly to quail,
Because the Lord stretcheth out his hand
And helps and doth not fail.[650]

225 But he doth frown and bends his brows
Upon the wicked swain,   *youth*
And cut away the memory
That should of them remain.[651]
But when the just do call and cry,
230 The Lord doth hear them so
That out of pain and misery
Forthwith he lets them go.[652]

If thou wilt heaven possess, leave ill
And do some godly deed,
235 Inquire for peace and quietness
And follow it with speed.[653]
For why the eyes of God above
Upon the just are bent,
His ears likewise to hear the plaints   *laments*
240 Of the poor innocent.[654]

Refrain from ill whilst thou does live
With hearty sure intent;

---

[647] Whittingham's Psalm 37. 21 from the *Whole Book*.
[648] Whittingham's Psalm 37. 22 from the *Whole Book*.
[649] Whittingham's Psalm 37. 23 from the *Whole Book*.
[650] Whittingham's Psalm 37. 24 from the *Whole Book*.
[651] Sternhold's Psalm 34. 16 from the *Whole Book*, slightly altered.
[652] Sternhold's Psalm 34. 17 from the *Whole Book*.
[653] Sternhold's Psalm 34. 14 from the *Whole Book*, altered.
[654] Sternhold's Psalm 34. 15 from the *Whole Book*.

To judgement sin will follow thee,
Except thou do repent.[655]

245 The man is blest, therefore, O Lord,
Whose faults thou hast remitted;
And he whose sins and wretchedness
Thou hast both hid and covered;[656]
And blest is he to whom the Lord
250 Imputeth not his sin,   *attributes*
And in his heart hath hid not guile,
Nor fraud was found therein.[657]

And blest are they to whom the Lord
As God and guide is known,
255 Whom he doth choose of mere accord
To take them as his own.[658]
Blest is the man whose life is pure,
Whose works are just and straight,
Whose heart did think the very truth,
260 Whose tongue spake not deceit;[659]

Nor to his neighbour did not ill
In body, goods, or name,
Nor willingly did tell false tales
Once to impair the same,[660]
265 That in his heart regarded not
Malicious wicked men,
But those that love and feared the Lord
He made still much of them;[661]

His oath and all his promises
270 That kept most faithfully,
Although he made his covenant so
That he did lose thereby;[662]
That unto usury did not put
His money nor his coin,

---

[655] No source found.
[656] Sternhold's Psalm 32. 1 from the *Whole Book*, altered.
[657] Sternhold's Psalm 32. 2 from the *Whole Book*.
[658] Hopkins's Psalm 33. 12 from the *Whole Book*.
[659] Sternhold's Psalm 15. 2 from the *Whole Book*, altered.
[660] Sternhold's Psalm 15. 3 from the *Whole Book*, slightly altered.
[661] Sternhold's Psalm 15. 4 from the *Whole Book*, slightly altered.
[662] Sternhold's Psalm 15. 5 from the *Whole Book*.

275   Nor once to hurt the innocent
      Did bribe or else purloin;[663]

      Whose hands are harmless, and whose heart
      No spot there doth defile;
      His soul not set on vanity,
280   Whose heart hath sworn no guile.[664]
      O happy is that man, I say,
      Whom Jacob's God doth aid,
      And he whose hope doth not decay,
      But on the Lord is stayed.[665]

285   And blest is he whose hope and heart
      Doth in the Lord remain,
      That with the proud did not take part,
      Nor such as lie and fain.[666]
      And blest is he that careful is
290   The needy to consider,
      For in the season perilous
      The Lord will him deliver.[667]

      And blest is he that hath not bent
      To wicked rede his care,   *counsel*
295   Nor led his life as sinners do,
      Nor sat in scorner's chair.[668]

      Yea, blest are they that perfect are,
      And pure in mind and heart,
      Whose live and conversation[669]
300   From God's law never start.
      Yea, blest are they that give themselves
      His statutes to observe,
      Seeking the Lord with all their heart
      And never from him swerve.[670]

305   And blest is he that feareth God
      And walketh in his way,

---

[663] Sternhold's Psalm 15. 6 from the *Whole Book*, altered.
[664] Hopkins's Psalm 24. 4 from the *Whole Book*, slightly altered.
[665] Hopkins's Psalm 146. 5 from the *Whole Book*.
[666] Hopkins's Psalm 40. 5 from the *Whole Book*.
[667] Sternhold's Psalm 41. 1 from the *Whole Book*, slightly altered.
[668] Sternhold's Psalm 1. 1 from the *Whole Book*, slightly altered.
[669] conversation] The metre requires five syllables.
[670] Whittingham's Psalm 119. 1–2 from the *Whole Book*, slightly altered.

> For of thy labours thou shalt eat,
> Yea, blest art thou, I say.[671]
> O they are blessèd that may dwell
> Within God's house always,
> For they his presence shall have still
> And ever sing his praise.[672]
> From strength to strength they shall proceed,
> No faintness there shall be;
> And so the God of gods at last
> In Zion they shall see;[673]
>
> And blest is he that doth consider
> The poor when they do cry,
> And those that suffer wrong; to right
> Doth help them by and by;[674]
> Him that is such a one, the Lord
> Shall place in blissful plight,
> And God his God and Saviour[675]
> Shall place him in his sight.[676]
>
> And such a one shall still behold
> And see God's light most clear;
> His countenance shall not be dashed,
> He needs not once to fear;[677]
> Therefore the man that would live long,
> And lead a blissful life,
> Let him refrain his tongue and lips
> From all deceit and strife.[678]
>
> For all the people of the world
> That will not God remember
> From out his presence shall be cast
> Down into hell forever.[679]
> For who is he, O Lord, that shall
> Ascend into thy hill,
> Or pass into thy holy place

---

[671] Sternhold's Psalm 128. 1 from the *Whole Book*, slightly altered.
[672] Hopkins's Psalm 84. 5 from the *Whole Book*, altered.
[673] Hopkins's Psalm 84. 8 from the *Whole Book*, slightly altered.
[674] Hopkins's Psalm 146. 7 from the *Whole Book*, substantially altered.
[675] Saviour] The metre requires three syllables ('Sa-vi-our').
[676] Hopkins's Psalm 24. 5 from the *Whole Book*.
[677] Sternhold's Psalm 34. 5 from the *Whole Book*, substantially altered.
[678] Sternhold's Psalm 34. 12 from the *Whole Book*, altered.
[679] Sternhold's Psalm 9. 17 from the *Whole Book*, substantially altered.

340 There to continue still?[680]
　　Whose hands are harmless, and whose heart
　　No spot there doth defile,
　　His soul not set on vanity,
　　Who hath not sworn to guile.[681]

345 One thing of God I do require,
　　That he will not deny,
　　For which I pray and will do still
　　Till he to me apply;[682]
　　That I within his holy place
350 My life throughout may dwell,
　　To see the beauty of his face
　　And view his temple well.[683]

　　For why one day within his courts
　　Is better to abide
355 Than other where to keep or stay
　　A thousand days beside.[684]
　　For in God's house they shall be fed
　　With plenty at their will;
　　Of all delights they shall be sped,　　　　　　　　　*provided*
360 And take thereof their fill.[685]

　　For why the well of life so pure
　　Doth ever flow from thence,
　　And in that light we are full sure
　　All darkness for to quench.[686]
365 O Lord, I love thy house most dear,
　　To me it doth excel;
　　I have delight and would be now
　　Whereas thy grace doth dwell.[687]

　　What gain is in my blood, say I,
370 If death destroy my days?
　　Shall dust declare thy majesty
　　Or it thy truth shall praise?[688]

---

[680] Hopkins's Psalm 24. 3 from the *Whole Book*.
[681] Hopkins's Psalm 24. 4 from the *Whole Book*.
[682] Hopkins's Psalm 27. 4 from the *Whole Book*.
[683] Hopkins's Psalm 27. 5 from the *Whole Book*.
[684] Hopkins's Psalm 84. 11 from the *Whole Book*, altered.
[685] Hopkins's Psalm 36. 8 from the *Whole Book*, slightly altered.
[686] Hopkins's Psalm 36. 9 from the *Whole Book*, substantially altered.
[687] Hopkins's Psalm 26. 8 from the *Whole Book*, altered.
[688] Hopkins's Psalm 30. 9 from the *Whole Book*, slightly altered.

They that be dead do not with praise
Set forth, Lord, thy renown,
Nor any that into a place
Of silence do go down.[689]

And shall thy loving kindness, Lord,
Be preachèd in the grave?
Or shall with them that are destroyed
Thy truth her honour have?[690]
Shall they that lie in darkness low
Of all thy wonders wot?   *know*
Or shall they there thy justice know
When all things are forgot?[691]

Dost thou unto the dead declare
Thy wondrous work of fame?
Or shall the dead to life repair
And praise thee for the same?[692]

Lo, men once dead are out of mind,
The living thee shall praise,[693]
For unto them thy power is known,
Thou numb'rest all their days.[694]
Thou wilt not leave my soul in hell,
For, Lord, thou lovest me;
Though that my body putrify,
Mine eyes thy power shall see.[695]

And in that day when all flesh shall
To judgement just arise,
Before thy presence I shall see
Thy glory with these eyes.[696]
Wherefore, my soul, sith thou art safe,
Return unto thy rest,
For largely, lo, the Lord to thee
His bounty hath expressed.[697]

---

[689] Norton's Psalm 115. 17 from the *Whole Book*, altered.
[690] Hopkins's Psalm 88. 12 from the *Whole Book*.
[691] Hopkins's Psalm 88. 13 from the *Whole Book*, altered.
[692] Hopkins's Psalm 88. 11 from the *Whole Book*, slightly altered.
[693] Similar to Hopkins's Psalm 31. 12a from the *Whole Book*.
[694] No source found.
[695] Sternhold's Psalm 16. 9 from the *Whole Book*, substantially altered.
[696] 'The XII Articles of the Christian Faith' from the *Whole Book*, substantially altered.
[697] Norton's Psalm 116. 7 from the *Whole Book*, slightly altered.

405 For thou art now deliverèd
     From bonds of worldly thrall;⁶⁹⁸
     My soul ascend unto thy rest,
     My body to earth doth fall.⁶⁹⁹
     Into thy hands, Lord, I commit
410 My sprite which is thy due,   *spirit*
     For Lord, thou hast redeemed my soul
     And art my God most true.⁷⁰⁰

     By whom I live, in whom I trust,
     On whom I do depend
415 To have eternal joys with those
     That praise thee without end.
     When that this mortal body shall
     Immortalness put on,
     And from this earth to heaven be changed
420 When all thy power is known,

     And when before thee I shall rise
     Immortal as I live:
     Even at that day of judgement, Lord,
     My soul thy mercy give;
425 And on thy right hand, Lord, it place
     With saints that sing thy praise,
     For I have had respect unto
     Thy power and name always.

79. Alexander Montgomerie, in *The Mind's Melody, Containing Certain Psalms of the Kingly Prophet David* (1605)

[Alexander Montgomerie (early 1550s–1598) was appointed master poet to the 'Castalian Band' (modelled on the French *Pléiade*) formed by King James VI of Scotland (later also James I of England) at his court in Edinburgh. Montgomerie had considerable influence on the poetry of the young king. Because of his commitment to Catholicism, Montgomerie ran into trouble. He was eventually charged with treason and outlawed, and he died a year later. *The Mind's Melody* was published anonymously by King James's printer in Edinburgh, and its authorship is a matter of debate. The volume includes somewhat altered versions of two of Montgomerie's own metrical Psalms, one of them Psalm 1, extant in the Ker Manuscript, once in the library of William Drummond of Hawthornden

---

⁶⁹⁸ Norton's Psalm 116. 8 from the *Whole Book*, slightly altered.
⁶⁹⁹ No source found.
⁷⁰⁰ Hopkins's Psalm 31. 5 from the *Whole Book*, altered.

and the principal source of Montgomerie's poems (the manuscript also contains Montgomerie's Psalm 2, not included in *The Mind's Melody*). Montgomerie's Psalm 1 (printed here following the manuscript text) was to be sung 'to the tone of the Solsequium', that is, the tune for Montgomerie's most popular song, 'Lyk as the dum | Solsequium'. Two other Psalms in *The Mind's Melody*, Psalms 23 and 121, are by James Melville (see 71), both written to be sung to Montgomerie's 'Solsequium' tune, and both published in Melville's *Fruitful and Comfortable Exhortation Anent Death* (1597). The author of the remaining *Mind's Melody* Psalms is unknown, though arguments have been made for both Montgomerie and Melville. The printing of the Psalms in this volume takes the rhymes as marking line ends, creating long stanzas alternating long and short lines. The late medieval Scots poets apparently delighted in internal rhyme, however, which would correspond more to the compressed format in Melville's volume. See Alexander Montgomerie, *Poems*, ed. by David J. Parkinson, 2 vols (Edinburgh: The Scottish Text Society 2000); Jamie Reid Baxter, 'Montgomerie's Solsequium and *The Mindes Melodie*', in *Fresche Fontanis: Studies in the Culture of Medieval and Early Modern Scotland*, ed. by Janet Hadley Williams and J. Derrick McLure (Newcastle upon Tyne: Cambridge Scholars: 2013), pp. 361–76; R. D. S. Jack, *ODNB*.]

Psalm 1

The First Psalm to the tone of the *Solsequium*.[701]

	Weil is the man,	*virtuous*
	Yea blissèd than,	
	By grace that can	
	Eschew ill counsel and the godless gait,	*evil, way*
5	That stands not in	
	The way of sin	
	Nor does begin	
	To sit with mockers in the scornful sait;	*seat*
	Bot in Jehovahis law Delights aricht	*but, aright*
10	And studies it to knaw Both day and nicht	*know, night*
	For he sall be	*shall*
	Like to the tree	
	Quhilk plantit by the running river grovis	*which, groves*
	Quhilk fruit does beir	
15	In time of year	
	Quhais leaf sall never fade nor root sall lovis.	*whose, come loose*

[701] A *solsequium* ('sun' plus 'follow') is a marigold. Montgomerie's poem 'Like as the dumb solsequium' was an exceptionally popular erotic paean to King James VI, representing his courtiers as marigolds to his lifegiving sun.

His actionis all
  Ay prosper sall
  Quhilk sall not fall
20 To godless men bot as the chaff or sand
  Quhilk day by day
  Winds drivis away.
  Thairfore I say
The wicked in the judgment sall not stand
25 Nor sinners rise na mair Whom God disdains *no, more*
  In the assembly where The just remains.
  For why? the Lord
  Doth beir record
He knawis the richteous conversation ay, *knows, righteous, always*
30 And godless gaits
  Quhilk he so haitis
Sall doubtless perish and decay alway. *always*

80. Anon., in *The Mind's Melody, Containing Certain Psalms of the Kingly Prophet David* (1605)

[See headnote to 79.]

Psalm 19

The firmament
 And heavens out-stent, *outstretched*
 So excellent,
Thy handiwork and glorious praise proclaim
5 Each day to day,
 Succeeding ay *always*
 In their array, *arrangement*
And night to night by course do preach the same:
 No sound of breath nor speech
10   Of men have they,
 Yet everywhere they preach
  Thy praise, I say:
 Their line goeth out,
 The earth about,
15 Their voice is heard throughout the world so wide:
 There he a throne
 Set for the sun
And paylion plight, his mansion to abide. *tent, pitched*
 Who like a groom

20 Of great renoum	*renown*
Right brave doth come	
From chamber straight with comely countenance:	*narrow*
Or like a knight	
In pleasant plight,	
25 Doth haste with might	
To run the race, his honour to advance:	
His rising and his race,	
It doth appear	
Even from the out-most space	
30 Of heaven's sphere,	
Then has he ta'en	
His course again	
Through azured sky by revolution right:	
Nothing can be	
35 Hid from the eye,	*hidden*
And burning beams of that great lamp of light;	
God's word is clear,	
His law sincere,	
And most enteer,	*entire*
40 The sinful soul to him for to convert:	
His precepts pure,	*commands*
Both firm and sure,	
And can allure,	
And make rightwise the sober simple heart.	*righteous*
45 Thy ways and statutes all	
Are righteousness,	
Which glad the souls in thrall;	*captivity*
With joyfulness,	
They give clear light,	
50 To our blind sight;	
Thy fear is pure and ever permanent:	
Thou cannot rue;	*lament*
Thy judgements true,	
And righteous are, O Lord omnipotent.	
55 Much gold of price,	
Refinèd twice,	
Yea, more then thrice,	
Is not in worth with them for to be valued:	
The honey white,	
60 Pure and perfite,	*perfect*
Moving delight,	
Is not so sweet, nor so much to be craved.	

>   They make thy servants wise
>   And circumspect,
> 65   And what to enterprise
>   They him direct;
>   In keeping them
>   Great is the gain,
>   And rich reward for such laid up for ever:
> 70   But who can count
>   Sins that surmount;
>   From secret sins, good Lord, my soul deliver.
>   O Lord vouchsave,
>   I humbly crave
> 75   Me for to save,
>   And cleanse my heart from proud presumptuous sin:
>   Then shall I be.
>   From sins set free
>   That troubles me,
> 80 Preserve me, Lord, that I walk not therein:
>   And let them not prevail
>   Me to possess:
>   Then I will without fail
>   Love righteousness:
> 85   Accept my plaint,   *lament*
>   Which I present
>   Before thy sight with humble heart and voice:
>   My strength and stay,   *support*
>   Thou art for ay,
> 90 And Saviour sweet in whom I do rejoice.

Psalm 57

>   Have ruth on me   *pity*
>   Have ruth on me,
>   O Lord from high,
>   Have mercy, Lord, in thee my soul doth trust:
> 5   Until at last,
>   This stormy blast
>   Be over-past,
>   In shadow of thy wings my hope shall rest:
>   On God most high I call,
> 10   My heart's delight;
>   Who will his promise all
>   To me perfite: *perfect*

From heaven's throne
    He will send down
15 And save me from the sharp rebuke and shame
    Of cruel foes,
    That me enclose:
His mercy sure shall keep me from all blame.
    I lie beset
20   With lions' net,
    And men are met
In fiery rage my silly soul to catch: *innocent*
    Whole teeth I ween,   *suppose*
    Like arrows keen
25   Are to be seen,
Their tongues like swords some mischief for to hatch.
    Exalt thyself, therefore,
        The heavens above:
    On earth show forth thy glore,   *glory*
30   And power prove:
    A snare is made
    And grins are laid   *snares*
My steps to trap, my feet to fold withal: *likewise*
    I am oppressed,
35   A ditch is dressed
For me, but lo, my foes therein do fall.
    My heart is bent
    And permanent
    With full intent
40 To praise the Lord and to extol his name:
    My tongue alway,   *always*
    Awake I say,
    By break of day:
My harp in haste and viol do the same.
45   I will thee praise among
        The people all:
    As God and Lord most strong
        Thee praise I shall:
    Thy mercies great,
50   And truth perfite
Do reach unto the heavens and cloudy sky;
    Exalt therefore
    Thy name and glore
Above the clouds and limits of the day.

81. Sir William Temple, *A Logical Analysis of Twenty Select Psalms* (1605)

[Sir William Temple (1554/5–1627) studied at Eton and King's College, Cambridge, and eventually became provost of Trinity College, Dublin. He was a vociferous follower of the rhetorical principles of Petrus Ramus, publishing numerous works that engaged him in national and international scholarly disputes. In 1585 Temple was appointed secretary to Sir Philip Sidney, on whose *Defence of Poesie* he wrote a Ramist commentary. After Sidney's death, Temple worked for William Davison, Sir Thomas Smith, and Robert Devereux, second Earl of Essex. His connection with Essex caused his temporary ruin after Essex's failed revolt in 1601. *A Logical Analysis of Twenty Select Psalms*, dedicated to Prince Henry, Prince of Wales, may have been the means by which Temple secured a return to favour. An expanded Latin version was published in 1611, *Analysis logica triginta psalmorum*. Temple's dedication draws attention to the particular relevance of each Psalm to the young Prince Henry, seen by many as the great hope of international Protestantism. Psalm 1 'will resolve you that the person of a Prince, as he is a Prince, is not the seat of this blessedness and felicity, but so far forth as he is a person whose delight is in the law of the Lord'. In Psalm 91 the prince may 'behold as it were in a glass the singular advantages and privileges of depending on the Lord'. The Psalm translations are Temple's own. See Elizabethanne Boran, *ODNB*.]

Psalm 1

Blessed is the man that doth not walk in the council of the wicked: nor stand in the way of sinners: nor sit in the seat° of the mockers:
2. But his delight is in the law of the Lord: and in his law doth he meditate day and night.
3. For he is like a tree planted by the rivers of waters: which bringeth forth her fruit in due season: whose leaf fadeth not: so whatsoever he shall do, shall prosper.
4. The wicked are not so: but as the chaff which the wind driveth.
5. Therefore the wicked shall not stand in the judgement: nor sinners in the assembly of the righteous.
6. For the Lord knoweth the way of the righteous: and the way of the wicked shall perish.

Psalm 91

Whoso dwelleth in the covert of the most high, shall lodge under the shadow of the almighty.
2. I say: The Lord is my retreat° and fortress: he is my God on whom I trust.
3. Surely, he will deliver thee from the snare of the fowler,° and from the noisome pestilence.

4. He will protect thee with his wing, when thou shalt come under his wings. His fidelity shall be thy buckler and shield.
5. Thou shalt not be afraid of the fear of night, nor of the arrow that flieth by day:
6. Nor of the pestilence that walketh in the darkness, nor of the plague that destroyeth at noon day.
7. A thousand shall fall at thy side, and ten thousand at thy right hand: yet shall it not come near thee:
8. Only with thine eyes shalt thou behold, and see the reward of the wicked.
9. Sith° thou hast set the Lord, the God of my retrait, the most high to be thy dwelling place:
10. There shall none evil come unto thee, neither shall any plague come near thy tabernacle.°
11. For he will give his angels charge° over thee to keep° thee in all thy ways.
12. They shall bear thee with both hands, that thou hurt not thy foot against a stone.
13. Thou shalt walk upon the lion and asp: the young lion and the dragon[702] shalt thou tread under foot.
14. Because he resteth on me, I will deliver him, saith the Lord: I will exalt him, because he acknowledgeth my name:
15. When he shall call upon me, I will hear him: I will be with him in trouble: I will deliver him and glorify him:
16. With long life will I satisfy him, and cause him to see my salvation.

82. Joseph Hall, *Holy Observations. Lib. 1. Also Some Few of David's Psalms Metaphrased, for a Taste of the Rest* (1607)

[Joseph Hall (1574–1656) studied at Emanuel College, Cambridge, was ordained, appointed chaplain to the court of Prince Henry, Prince of Wales, and was later Bishop of Exeter and Bishop of Norwich. A friend of John Donne, Hall was a prolific and accomplished author of poems, satires, dystopian fiction, and Theophrastian characters, as well as religious works. His *Virgidemiarum* (1597, 1598) contained both 'Tooth-Lesse' and 'Biting' satires and was the first collection of Latin-style satires published in England. His dystopian *Mundus alter idem* (1605; translated as *A Discovery of a New World* in 1609) influenced Swift's *Gulliver's Travels*. He was a keen controversial writer, and was attacked both by Laudians, for his tolerance of Puritan beliefs, and by Puritans (and John Milton), for his defence of the episcopacy. In the dedication of his Psalms to Samuel Burton, Archdeacon of Gloucester, Hall writes that 'I were not worthy to be a Divine, if it should repent me to be a Poet with David', and confesses

---

[702] dragon] The Hebrew word designates a monster of some sort, but English translators often substitute a monster more familiar from European Romance.

that he has 'often wondered, how it could be offensive to our adversaries, that these divine ditties which the spirit of God wrote in verse, should be sung in verse; and that an Hebrew poem should be made English'. Hall translates Psalms 1 to 10, naming an existing Psalm tune by which each can be sung. The term 'metaphrase' is no more precise a term than 'paraphrase' or 'translation', though some others (notably John Dryden) have tried to suggest so. See Richard A. McCabe, *ODNB*.]

Psalm 2

In the tune of the 125 Psalm; Those that do put their conf.[703]

	Why do the gentiles tumults make,	
	And nations all conspire in vain,	
	And earthly princes counsel take	
	Against their God; against the reign	
5	Of his dear Christ?[704] let us, they sayen,	*say*
	Break all their bonds: and from us shake	
	Their thraldom's yoke, and servile chain.	*captivity's*
	Whiles thus, alas, they fondly spake,	*foolishly*
	He that aloft rides on the skies,	
10	Laughs all their lewd devise to scorn	*wicked, desire*
5.	And when his wrathful rage shall rise,	
	With plagues shall make them all forlorn,	
	And in his fury thus replies;	
6.	But I, my King with sacred horn[705]	
15	Anointing, shall in princely guise	
	His head with royal crown adorn.	
	Upon my Zion's holy mount	
	His empire's glorious seat shall be.	
	And I thus rais'd shall far recount	
20	The tenor of his true decree:	*substance*
7.	My Son thou art, said God, I thee	
	Begat this day by due account:	
	Thy scepter, do but ask of me,	
	All earthly kingdoms shall surmount.	

---

[703] Psalm 125, *Qui confident*, BCP 'They that put their trust in the Lord'.

[704] Obviously a Christianizing of the Psalm, though the Hebrew is *Messiah* ('anointed'), understood by Christians to refer to Christ. Psalm 2 also describes God acknowledging his Son in language paralleled in the gospel description of God's words spoken at Jesus's baptism by John.

[705] sacred horn] See note 32, p. 85.

25	8. All nations, to thy rightful sway,	*rule*
	I will subject; from furthest end	
	9. Of all the world: and thou shalt bray	*crush*
	Those stubborn foes that will not bend,	
	With iron mace (like potter's clay)	
30	10. In pieces small: ye kings attend;	
	And ye, whom others wont obey,	*are accustomed to*
	Learn wisdom, and at last amend.	
	11. See ye serve God, with greater dread	
	Than others you: and in your fear	
35	Rejoice the while; and (lowly spread)	
	12. Do homage to his Son so dear:[706]	
	Lest he be wroth, and do you dead[707]	*angry*
	13. Amidst your way. If kindlèd[708]	
	His wrath shall be; O blessèd those,	
40	That do on him their trust repose.	

83. Gregory Martin, *The Holy Bible Faithfully Translated into English* [Rheims-Douay Bible] (1609–1610)

[Gregory Martin (1542?–1582) was a contemporary and colleague of Edmund Campion at St John's College, Cambridge, where both were fellows and lecturers, Campion in Rhetoric and Martin in Greek. Both gave up their fellowships and went into exile on the Continent, joining the English (Catholic) College at Douay. Martin translated the Latin Vulgate into English at the request of William Allen, head of the English College, who with Richard Bristow and William Reynolds helped revise the text. The New Testament was published in 1582 at Rheims, where the college was temporarily relocated; the Old Testament, though completed at the same time, was not published until 1609–10, at Douay. The Rheims-Douay Bible has been described as a Catholic acquiescence to the fait accompli of the vernacular Bible, but the purpose of this translation was different from that of the Geneva or King James Bibles. Eventually, with substantial revisions by Bishop Richard Challoner (1749–52), the Bible became widely used by English Catholics for several centuries, but it may originally have been intended not for lay use but to aid the teaching ministry and polemical writing of English Catholic priests. The Rheims-Douay Bible has even more annotation than the Geneva, with marginal notes on the outer margin, cross-references on the inner one, more extensive notes running in between verses,

---

[706] Son] Not capitalized in standard Bible translations, but here to signal the Christian understanding that this refers to Christ.
[707] do you dead] kill you.
[708] kindlèd] The metre requires three syllables.

and still longer annotations following each Psalm. Ironically, although the Rheims-Douay Bible could not legally be printed in England and its distribution there was necessarily surreptitious, much of the New Testament was made easily available to English readers when it was reprinted in the extensive Protestant critique of the translation by William Fulke, *A Defense of the Sincere and True Translations of the Holy Scriptures into the English Tongue* (1583). See Daniell, *Bible in English*; Thomas M. McCoog (Martin), *ODNB*.]

Psalm 23

A form of thanksgiving for all spiritual benefits (described under the metaphor of temporal prosperity) even from a sinner's first conversion, to final perseverance, and eternal beatitude.

1. The Psalm of David.[709]
2. Our Lord ruleth me,[710] and nothing shall be wanting to me: in place of pasture there he hath placed me.
3. Upon the water of refection[711] he hath brought me up: he hath converted my soul.
   He hath conducted me upon the paths of justice, for his name.
4. For, although I shall walk in the midst of the shadow of death, I will not fear evils: because thou art with me. Thy rod and thy staff: they have comforted me.
5. Thou hast prepared in my sight a table against them; that trouble me. Thou hast fatted my head with oil: and my chalice inebriating[712] how goodly is it!
6. And thy mercy shall follow me all the days of my life:
   And that I may dwell in the house of our Lord, in longitude of days.

Psalm 51

King David in great sorrow for his sins of adultery and murder, most seriously prayeth God of his manifold mercies to remit and purge all his offences, and pains due for them. 12. to restore unto him the grace of the Holy Ghost, lost by his sins; 15. that he may teach others (as in deed his singular example may teach

---

[709] These four Psalms are numbered 22, 50, 107, and 139 in the text, following the Catholic numbering based on the Septuagint rather than the Hebrew, which also numbered the superscriptions.

[710] Following the Vulgate literally (*Dominus reget me*), Douai oddly begins without the Psalm's famous shepherd metaphor. The Greek *pomaino* of the Septuagint, on which the Vulgate is based, can mean both 'rule' and 'shepherd', but the Latin *regere* means simply 'rule' or 'guide'.

[711] refection] refreshment, following the Vulgate *refectionis*.

[712] inebriating] intoxicating, following the Vulgate *inebrians*.

the whole world true penance) 19. contrition of heart, worthily to offer sacrifice, for the whole Church.

1. Unto the end, a Psalm of David, when Nathan the
2. Prophet came to him, after that he had sinned with Bethsabee.
3. Have mercy on me, O God, according to thy great mercy. And according to the multitude of thy commiserations, take away mine iniquity.
4. Wash me more amply from mine iniquity: and cleanse me from my sin.
5. Because I do know mine iniquity: and my sin is before me always.
6. To thee only° have I sinned, and have done evil before thee: that thou may'st be justified in thy words, and may'st overcome when thou art judged.
7. For behold, I was conceived in iniquities: and my mother conceived me in sins.
8. For behold, thou hast loved truth: the uncertain and hidden things of thy wisdom thou hast made manifest to me.
9. Thou shalt sprinkle me with hyssop, and I shall be cleansed: thou shalt wash me, and I shall be made whiter than snow.
10. To my hearing thou shalt give joy and gladness, and the bones humbled shall rejoice.
11. Turn away thy face from my sins: and wipe away all mine iniquities.
12. Create a clean heart in me, O God: and renew a right spirit in my bowels.[713]
13. Cast me not away from thy face: and thy Holy Spirit take not from me.
14. Render unto me the joy of thy salvation: and confirm me with the principal spirit,[714]
15. I will teach the unjust thy ways: and the impious shall be converted to thee.
16. Deliver me from bloods,[715] O God, the God of my salvation: and my tongue shall exult for thy justice.
17. Lord, thou wilt open my lips: and my mouth shall show forth thy praise.
18. Because if thou wouldest have had sacrifice, I had verily given it: with holocausts° thou wilt not be delighted.
19. A sacrifice to God is an afflicted spirit: a contrite and humbled heart, O God, thou wilt not despise.
20. Deal favourably, O Lord, in thy good will with Zion: that the walls of Jerusalem may be built up.
21. Then shalt thou accept sacrifice of justice, oblations,° and holocausts: then shall they lay calves upon thine altar.

[713] bowels] See note 284, p. 194.
[714] principal spirit] From the Vulgate *spiritu principali*. When Bishop Richard Challoner revised the Rheims-Douay translation in the mid-eighteenth century, he adopted the reading of English Protestant Bibles, 'a perfect spirit'.
[715] bloods] From the Vulgate *sanguinibus*, though this is also actually closer to the Hebrew ('blood') than Coverdale's memorable coinage, 'bloodguiltiness'.

Psalm 108

The royal prophet promiseth, and rendereth praises to God, for his delivery from troubles, and advancement in the kingdom, praying God still to help man's infirmity.

1. A Canticle of Psalm, to David himself.
2. My heart is ready O God, my heart is ready: I will chant, and will sing in my glory.
3. Arise my glory, arise psalter, and harp: I will arise early.
4. I will confess to thee in peoples, O Lord: and I will sing to thee in the nations.
5. Because thy mercy is great above the heavens: and thy truth even to the clouds.
6. Be exalted above the heavens, O God, and thy glory over all the earth:
7. that thy beloved may be delivered.
Save with thy right hand, and hear me: 8. God spake in his holy:
I will rejoice, and will divide Sichem, and I will measure the vale° of tabernacles.°
9. Galaad is mine, and Manasses is mine: and Ephraim the protection of my head.
10. Judah is my king: Moab the pot of my hope.[716]
Upon Idumea I will extend my shoe: the strangers are made my friends.
11. Who will conduct me into a fenced city? Who will conduct me into Idumea?
12. Wilt not thou, O God, which hast repelled us, and wilt not thou go forth, O God, in our hosts?
13. Give us help out of tribulation: because man's salvation is vain.
14. In God we shall do strength: and he will bring our enemies to nothing.

Psalm 140

The just diversely afflicted by the wicked, pray to be defended, repose their confidence in God, who will adjudge the reprobate° to eternal punishment, and reward the good with the fruition of himself.

1. Unto the end, a Psalm of David.
2. Deliver me, O Lord, from the evil man: from the unjust man rescue me.
3. Which have devised iniquity in their heart: all the day they did appoint battles.

---

[716] In following the Vulgate for this half-verse, Martin conveys an opposite sense to the other English Bibles, which have 'Moab is my washpot', in other words, Moab is under my subjugation. Why Moab should be a pot of hope, or what such a pot is, is unclear, though in his commentary Cardinal Bellarmine explains, 'The province of Moab, now subject to me, is like a pot full of meat, abounding in riches and plenty, and giving me great hopes'.

4. They have whet° their tongues as that of a serpent: the venom of asps is under their lips.
5. Keep° me, O Lord, from the hand of the sinner: and from unjust men deliver me.
6. Who have devised to supplant my steps: the proud have hid a snare for me: And they have stretched out ropes for a snare: they have laid a stumbling block for me near the way.
7. I said to our Lord, Thou art my God: hear, O Lord, the voice of my petition.
8. O Lord, Lord, the strength of my salvation: thou hast overshadowed my head in the day of battle.
9. Yield me not, O Lord, from my desire to the sinner: they have devised against me, forsake me not, lest they perhaps be proud.
10. The head of their compass: the labour of their lips shall cover them.[717]
11. Coals shall fall upon them, thou shalt cast them down into fire: in miseries they shall not stand up.
12. A man full of tongue shall not be directed in the earth: evils shall take the unjust man into destruction.
13. I have known that our Lord will do the judgement of the needy: and the revenge of the poor.
14. But as for the just, they shall confess to thy name: and the righteous shall dwell with thy countenance.

84. William Byrd, *Psalms, Songs, and Sonnets: Some Solemn, Others Joyful, Framed to the Life of the Words* (1611)

[See headnote to 64. Like the first two, Byrd's final collection of secular songs includes a number of settings of Psalms: 149, 37, 95, 132, 81, 100, 51, 117, and 126. As with many of his earlier settings, only a few verses of each Psalm are printed with the music, and many of these settings are complex enough to suggest that only these verses would be sung, as was the practice in church motets and anthems. Furthermore, unlike his earlier Psalms, Byrd sometimes set not the opening verses but others selected from the Psalm, suggesting that, as always, his compositions and their organization were deliberate and significant. As David Fraser pointed out, the texts for many of them were taken from Richard Verstegan's English translations in the Catholic *Primer* (see 74). Several others were taken from the Book of Common Prayer, either word for word or, in the case of Psalm 51, with some variation. Notably, these translations are all in prose, unlike the Sternhold and Hopkins-style metrical Psalms texts Byrd used in his earlier settings. Byrd's musical setting of Psalm 51 is a verse

---

[717] Following the Vulgate, but nonsensical: BCP 'Let the mischief of their own lips fall upon the head of them: that compass me about'; Geneva adds two words, signalled by italics, '*As for* the chief of them, that compass me about'.

anthem, or more properly consort anthem, for solo voice and a consort of five viols, with choral sections for five and (for the close) six voices. The music is complex, through composed, and, unusually, closes with an Amen. If this piece was performed as a domestic entertainment, it would have been in a substantial household and by accomplished, even if amateur, musicians. *Psalms, Songs, and Sonnets* was dedicated to Francis Clifford, fourth Earl of Cumberland, a patron of music and drama, whose son, Henry, the fifth earl, was an accomplished metrical Psalms poet (see **119**). See David Fraser, 'Sources of Texts for Byrd's 1611 *Psalmes*', *Early Music*, 38.1 (2010), 171–72.]

Psalm 51

Have mercy upon me, O God, after thy great goodness, and according to the multitude of thy mercies, wipe away mine offences.[718]
Wash me clean from my wickedness, and purge me from my sins.[719]

85. Various Translators, *The Holy Bible Containing the Old Testament, and the New* [King James Bible] (1611)

[The King James Bible was a collaborative project, with approximately fifty scholars working on the translation from 1604 to 1608, and a smaller group working on revisions after that. The project originated in the Hampton Court Conference of 1604, when the new King James I called together the bishops and leading figures of the Church to address ecclesiastical and theological concerns, especially proposals for further reform by those called Puritans. One of these, John Reynolds, president of Corpus Christi College, Oxford, proposed a new translation of the Bible. Though Reynolds had in mind a revision of the Geneva Bible, the most popular English version but also the most scholarly, James I, who approved the plan, intended instead a revision of the Bishops' Bible that might supplant the Geneva, some of whose notes he found politically offensive. The translators did consult the Geneva Bible translation in any case, along with many others, but the result was nevertheless a relatively conservative translation, like the Bishops' Bible in spirit, if superior to it in scholarship. The translators of the new Bible were ordered not to add marginal notes; there are notes in the final text, but they are largely confined to biblical cross-references and matters of translation. The team responsible for the Psalms was the first Cambridge company: Edward Lively, Regius Professor of Hebrew; John Richardson, Regius Professor of Theology; Laurence Chaderton, Master of Emmanuel College;

---

[718] wipe away] BCP 'do away'; Byrd may have in mind the promise in Revelation that God shall 'wipe away all tears from their eyes' (Revelation 21. 4), which Robert Parsons quotes in his popular *Christian Directory* as a comfort to the afflicted.

[719] purge me] BCP 'cleanse me' better captures the Vulgate *munda me*, but 'purge me' appears in verse 7 (in BCP, Geneva, etc.).

Francis Dillingham, fellow of Christ's College; Thomas Harrison, fellow of Trinity; Roger Andrewes, fellow of Pembroke; Robert Spalding, Regius Professor of Hebrew (successor to Lively after his death in 1605); and Andrew Byng, Regius Professor of Hebrew (from 1608). See Daniell, *Bible in English*; Norton, *The King James Bible*.]

Psalm 23

David's confidence in God's grace.

A Psalm of David.

The Lord is my shepherd, I shall not want.
2. He maketh me to lie down in green pastures: he leadeth me beside the still waters.
3. He restoreth my soul: he leadeth me in the paths of righteousness, for his name's sake.
4. Yea, though I walk through the valley of the shadow of death, I will fear no evil: for thou art with me, thy rod and thy staff, they comfort me.
5. Thou preparest a table before me, in the presence of mine enemies: thou anointest my head with oil, my cup runneth over.[720]
6. Surely, goodness and mercy shall follow me all the days of my life: and I will dwell in the house of the Lord forever.

Psalm 96

An exhortation to praise God, for his greatness, for his kingdom, for his general judgement.

O sing unto the Lord a new song: sing unto the Lord all the earth.
2. Sing unto the Lord, bless his name: show forth his salvation from day to day.
3. Declare his glory among the heathen: his wonders among all people.
4. For the Lord is great, and greatly to be praised: he is to be feared above all gods.
5. For all the gods of the nations are idols: but the Lord made the heavens.
6. Honour and majesty are before him: strength and beauty are in his sanctuary.
7 Give unto the Lord (O ye kindreds of the people): give unto the Lord glory and strength.

---

[720] There is some variation among translations in the fullness of the cup. In Coverdale and Sternhold it is merely full, in the Bishops' Bible it is 'brim full', while in the Geneva and King James Bibles it overflows. Rheims-Douay, following the Vulgate, references not quantity but quality: it inebriates. The Hebrew means something like 'abundant drink'.

8. Give unto the Lord the glory due unto his name: bring an offering, and come into his courts.
9. O worship the Lord, in the beauty of holiness: fear before him all the earth.
10. Say among the heathen, that the Lord reigneth: the world also shall be established that it shall not be moved: he shall judge the people righteously.
11. Let the heavens rejoice, and let the earth be glad; let the sea roar, and the fulness thereof.[721]
12. Let the field be joyful, and all that is therein: then shall all the trees of the wood rejoice
13. Before the Lord, for he cometh, for he cometh to judge the earth: he shall judge the world with righteousness, and the people with his truth.

Psalm 114[722]

An exhortation by the example of the dumb creatures, to fear God in his Church.

When Israel went out of Egypt, the house of Jacob from a people of strange language:
2. Judah was his sanctuary: and Israel his dominion.
3. The sea saw it, and fled: Jordan was driven back.
4. The mountains skipped like rams: and the little hills like lambs.
5. What ailed thee, O thou sea, that thou fleddest? Thou Jordan, that thou wast driven back?
6. Ye mountains, that ye skipped like rams: and ye little hills like lambs?
7. Tremble, thou earth, at the presence of the Lord: at the presence of the God of Jacob:
8. Which turned the rock into a standing water: the flint into a fountain of waters.

Psalm 122

David professeth his joy for the Church, and prayeth for the peace thereof.

A song of degrees of David.[723]

I was glad when they said unto me: let us go into the house of the Lord.
2. Our feet shall stand within thy gates, O Jerusalem.
3. Jerusalem is builded as a city, that is compact together:
4. Whither the tribes go up, the tribes of the Lord, unto the testimony of Israel: to give thanks unto the name of the Lord.
5. For there are set thrones of judgement: the thrones of the house of David.

---

[721] the fullness thereof] More properly, 'what fills it'.
[722] One of the few Psalms clearly addressing a specific historical (or at least biblical) event, in this case the Exodus.
[723] Sometimes also translated 'gradual Psalm' or 'song of ascent'. See note 30, p. 84.

6. Pray for the peace of Jerusalem: they shall prosper that love thee.
7. Peace be within thy walls: and prosperity within thy palaces.
8. For my brethren and companions' sakes: I will now say, peace be within thee.
9. Because of the house of the Lord our God: I will seek thy good.

Psalm 128

The sundry blessings which follow them that fear God.

A song of degrees.

Blessed is every one that feareth the Lord: that walketh in his ways.
2. For thou shalt eat the labour of thine hands: happy shalt thou be, and it shall be well with thee.
3. Thy wife shall be as a fruitful vine by the sides of thine house, thy children like olive plants: round about thy table.
4. Behold, that thus shall the man be blessed, that feareth the Lord.
5. The Lord shall bless thee out of Zion: and thou shalt see the good of Jerusalem, all the days of thy life.
6. Yea, thou shalt see thy children's children: and peace upon Israel.

Psalm 136[724]

An exhortation to give thanks to God for particular mercies.

O give thanks unto the Lord, for he is good: for his mercy endureth forever.
2. O give thanks unto the God of gods: for his mercy endureth forever.
3. O give thanks to the Lord of lords: for his mercy endureth forever.
4. To him who alone doth great wonders: for his mercy endureth forever.
5. To him that by wisdom made the heavens: for his mercy endureth forever.
6. To him that stretched out the earth above the waters: for his mercy endureth forever.
7. To him that made great lights: for his mercy endureth forever:
8. The sun to rule by day: for his mercy endureth forever:
9. The moon and stars to rule by night: for his mercy endureth forever.
10. To him that smote Egypt in their firstborn: for his mercy endureth forever:
11. And brought out Israel from among them: for his mercy endureth forever:
12. With a strong hand and with a stretched out arm: for his mercy endureth forever.
13. To him which divided the Red Sea into parts: for his mercy endureth forever:

---

[724] Psalm 136 is unique in having a consistent refrain throughout, which suggest a liturgical call and response like the BCP Litany, in which the celebrant sings or recites the verse, and the congregation responds with the refrain.

14. And made Israel to pass through the midst of it: for his mercy endureth forever:
15. But overthrew Pharaoh and his host in the Red Sea: for his mercy endureth forever.
16. To him which led his people through the wilderness: for his mercy endureth forever.
17. To him which smote great kings: for his mercy endureth forever:
18. And slew famous kings: for his mercy endureth forever:
19. Sihon king of the Amorites: for his mercy endureth forever:
20. And Og the king of Bashan: for his mercy endureth forever:
21. And gave their land for an heritage: for his mercy endureth forever:
22. Even an heritage unto Israel his servant: for his mercy endureth forever.
23. Who remembered us in our low estate: for his mercy endureth forever:
24. And hath redeemed us from our enemies: for his mercy endureth forever.
25. Who giveth food to all flesh: for his mercy endureth forever.
26. O give thanks unto the God of heaven: for his mercy endureth forever.

Psalm 142

David showeth that in his trouble, all his comfort was in prayer unto God.

Maschil of David.[725] A prayer when he was in the cave.[726]

I cried unto the Lord with my voice: with my voice unto the Lord did I make my supplication.
2. I poured out my complaint before him: I shewed before him my trouble.
3. When my spirit was overwhelmed within me, then thou knewest my path. In the way wherein I walked have they privily laid a snare for me.
4. I looked on my right hand, and beheld, but there was no man that would know me: refuge failed me, no man cared for my soul.
5. I cried unto thee, O Lord: I said, thou art my refuge and my portion in the land of the living.
6. Attend unto my cry, for I am brought very low: deliver me from my persecutors, for they are stronger than I.
7. Bring my soul out of prison, that I may praise thy name: the righteous shall compass me about, for thou shalt deal bountifully with me.

---

[725] Maschil] or Mascil, a song or poem of contemplation.
[726] The Cave Adullam. See 1 Sam. 22.

86. Edmond Scory, *Two Psalms of David* (MS after 1611?)

[Little is known about Edmond Scory, though he may be the same man who contributed a commendatory poem to Michael Drayton's *Heroical Epistles*. 'How can he write, that broken hath his pen' appears in all editions of Drayton's work from 1597, where the author is identified only as 'E. Sc. Gent.', but in the folio collection of 1619 it is signed instead 'Edmond Scory, Knight'. Scory's two Psalms are dedicated to King James I, and the only surviving manuscript appears to be a presentation copy. He states that the 'two Psalms, the 21 and 45 in my opinion, of all the rest, are the most applicable to your Majesty'. For his translation, Scory claims to have consulted 'your Majesty's own Bible', as well as the Vulgate 'for text', and St Jerome 'for exposition'. The King James Bible translation is written in the margin alongside Scory's version, verse by verse, in a smaller script. See H. R. Woudhuysen, *Sir Philip Sidney and the Circulation of Manuscripts, 1558–1640* (Oxford: Clarendon Press, 1996).]

Psalm 21

1.
How gladsome is the King and joyed in heart;
That thou, O Lord, his strength and safety art.

2.
That thou hast given him what his heart desired;
And not denièd what his lips required.

3.
5 Preventing him with blessings manifold,   *confronting*
And crowning him with pure refinèd gold.

4.
He asked thee life; thou gav'st him length of days,
Even endless life; to give thee endless praise.

5.
His safety, through thy providence divine:
10 With honour great, and glory, makes him shine.

6.
Bliss without end thou shalt to him impart;
The sunbeams of thy face do cheer his heart.

7.
For in thy mercy, he reposeth all;
Which stays his steps, that he shall never fall.   *secures*

8.

15 But thy long hand shall reach thy foes afar,
    And find them out, when most secure they are.

9.

And them consume, when kindled is thine ire,   *anger*
As in a furnace, seven-times hot with fire.[727]

10.

Their offspring from the earth shall rooted be:
20 Their second generation none shall see:

11.

For against thee, and thine, their counsel was;
Yet had no power to bring their plot to pass:

12.

But turned their backs, and put themselves in chase;
When thou hadst bent thy bow against their face.

13.

25 Be pleased, in thine own strength, they self to raise;
    So shall we, Lord, thy power and mercy praise.

Psalm 45

1.

My heart desires to utter some good thing,
Which I have made, in honour of the king.

2.

My tongue shall be my pen, and swiftly write
What in my heart, devotion doth indite.[728]   *utter*

3.

5 Fairest of men, whose lips with grace abound,
   Whom with eternal blessing God hath crowned:

4.

Gird thy sharp sword upon thine armèd thigh,   *fasten*
And show thyself in power and majesty.

---

[727] Alter points out that a shift in pronouns in this verse, from addressing God in the second person to referring to him in the third, may be evidence that two different Psalms were at some time amalgamated into this one. Scory resolves this problem by maintaining the second person throughout.

[728] An unusual self-referential moment as the Psalmist refers to his own craft.

5.

   Pass on, with thy great honour, prosperity:
10 Reign, and triumph, and be thou mounted high:

   With faith, with justice, and with meekness, wings;[729]
   And thy right hand shall teach thee dreadful things.   *awe-inspiring*

6.

   Thine arrows keen shall make thy foes to fall:
   Which thou shalt shoot, and pierce their hearts withal.   *as well*

7.

15 Eternal is thy judgement seat (O God)
   Thy sceptre is a true-directing-rod.

8.

   Right hast thou loved, and loathed unrighteousness;
   And therefore, God, thy God, who doth thee bless,

   Hath poured on thee, O Prince of Princes best,[730]
20 More oil of gladness, than on all the rest.

9.

   The royal robes, wherewith thou art arrayed;
   Which in thine ivory wardrobes have been laid,

   Of myrrh, or aloes, and of cassia smell;
   Which odours do refresh and please thee well.

10.

25 The queen all clad in gold, at thy right hand,
   Daughters of kings, attending her, do stand.

11.

   Attend fair daughter, listen, and give ear:
   Forget thy father's house and country dear:[731]

---

[729] The wings are Scory's addition, perhaps in apposition to the other bodyparts, 'lips', 'thigh', and 'right hand', though even the fairest of men do not have wings.

[730] Scory adds this royal parallel to 'God, thy God', there being no reference to princes in the original.

[731] Queen Anne was in fact the daughter of King Christian Frederick II of Denmark, though since she had already been married to James for fourteen years when he ascended to the English throne, she had probably long since forgotten her father's house, or at least become accustomed to her husband's.

####### 12.

So shall the king take pleasure in thy beauty:
30 He is thy Lord: yield him thy love and duty.

####### 13.

The Tyrian virgins shall bring gifts to thee,
And merchants rich thy suppliants shall be.

####### 14.

The daughter of the king is rich without:
Her gown's embroidered round with gold about:
35 And yet within she is more glorious far,
The jewels of her mind more precious are.[732]

####### 15.

In finest dressing, with the needle wrought,
She, with her fellow-virgins, shall be brought:

####### 16.

They shall with joy, be brought, O king, to thee;
40 And in thy princely court, receivèd be.

####### 17.

Thou Lady, in thy father's stead, shalt gain
Sons, which, in sundry provinces, shall reign.[733]

####### 18.

Thee, Lord, shall I remember, all my days;
And all the world shall give thee endless praise.

---

[732] The Psalmist says simply that the 'King's daughter is all glorious within'; Scory's more specific reference to the 'jewels of her mind' being more precious than anything external may possibly derive from Edmund Spenser's *Amoretti* 15, which praises Spenser's beloved (his wife Elizabeth) with a blazon cataloguing eyes, lips, teeth, forehead, locks, and hands, but concludes that the fairest of her features is 'her mind adorned with virtues manifold'.

[733] To the great satisfaction of his new English subjects, when James ascended to the throne Anne had already 'gained' two sons as well as a daughter. Whatever else they thought of the new monarch, he did not present, as the childless Elizabeth had, the prospect of another succession crisis.

87. John Davies of Hereford, *The Doleful Dove: or, David's 7 Penitential Psalms, Somewhere Paraphrastically Turned into Verse*, in *The Muses Sacrifice* (1612)

[John Davies of Hereford (1564/5–1618) was a scribe, handwriting teacher (author of *Writing Schoolmaster, or, The Anatomy of Fair Writing*), and poet. His family was Welsh, and although he did not study at university, he lived in Oxford for a time teaching handwriting. By at least 1605 he was living in London. He had a wide acquaintance among the rich, powerful, and talented, including Prince Henry, Prince of Wales, John Donne, Ben Jonson, Inigo Jones, and Lord Herbert of Cherbury. Davies penned one of the most important manuscripts of the Sidney Psalter, and *The Muses Sacrifice*, a collection of his devotional poems, was dedicated to Mary Sidney Herbert, then Countess Dowager of Pembroke, as well as two other remarkable literary patronesses, Lucy, Countess of Bedford, and Elizabeth, Lady Cary. Davies was likely a Roman Catholic, self-identifying as such in 1611; none of his religious writing, however, is especially polemical. See P. J. Finkelpearl, *ODNB*.]

Psalm 32[734]

David, punished with grievous sickness for his sins, counteth them blessed, to whom God doth not impute° their transgressions. And, after that he had confessed his sins and obtained pardon, he exhorteth the wicked men to live godly; and the good to rejoice.

Most blessed are they (however cursed they be)
    Whose crimes out of God's note-book clean are crossed;[735]   *completely*
Whose sins are covered so with clemency,
    That they are hid; so, seem they to be lost.

5 And blest is he to whom the God of grace
    Imputes no sin; (for, so he shall be clear   *attributes*
Howe'er defil'd) and in whose sp'rit no base
    Deceit, shall once so much as but appear.

For, while I held my peace (that caused my war;[736]
10   For death with silence in such passion strives)
My body's props (my bones) consumèd are   *wasted away*
    While all the day I groan in sorrow's gyves.   *shackles*

---

[734] Paul quotes the opening of Psalm 32 at Romans 4. 7-8 in support of 'righteousness without works'.
[735] Davies adds the notebook metaphor, one perhaps especially appealing to a scribe and writing teacher. The parenthesis is also a stylistic addition.
[736] An internal, psychological war of the kind described in Prudentius's *Psychomachia* and often employed by poets in the tradition of Petrarchan love poems.

For, day and night thy hand (great God) doth lie
    Like lead upon my weakness: who have been
15 Converted into self-calamity,
    Whiles the thorn pricked me (or, my stinging sin);

But, lo, my faults to thee I have revealed,
    And have not cloaked my crimes, which thou dost hide:
But I confess those sins, thou hast concealed
20   Sith my misdeeds shall (so) be justified.[737]   *since*

Thus shall each pious person pray to thee
    In fitting time (your mercy's gate be sparred)   *barred up*
But when the inundations swelling be
    Of many waters, they from him are barred.

25 My 'fence (O Lord) lies only in thy hands,   *defence*
    When troubles me assail with fiercest woe:
Then, O preserve me from the impious bands   *companies*
    That me enclose, in death to close me so.   *enclose*

I will, say'st thou (dear sweet), instruct thee still,
30   And guide thee in thy way (O honeyed words)
Thine eye (thou say'st) shall me defend from ill,
    And watch to guard me from my foe-men's swords.[738]

Then be, O be not like an horse or mule,
    That are as rude as unintelligent:
35 Lord, bridle them, thy snaffle will not rule,   *light bridle*
    Till they be ruled, or else be made repent.

The plagues are great (most great) and manifold,
    That do the sinner evermore attend;
But who with hands of hope on God lays hold,
40   His boundless mercy him will comprehend.

In him therefore (ye righteous) still be glad;
    (For he in grief still glads the righteous soul)
Exult all ye, that for your sins are sad;
    And all true hearts, that stoop to his control.

---

[737] Justification, or the freeing of Christians from sin, was the focus of heated debate after the Reformation, Luther and Calvin arguing for justification by faith alone, Catholics arguing that such things as good works and sacraments are instrumental in justification.

[738] Davies's parenthetical remarks add a curious intimacy to this verse. In a different context 'honeyed words' might suggest deceit or hypocrisy, but not here, since they are God's.

45 To God the Father glory be therefore,
       And to the Son, and their coequal Spirit,
   As it was, is, and shall be evermore
       World without end: for they are infinite!

88. Francis Davison, in *Certain Selected Psalms of David* (MS c. 1612?)

[Francis Davison (1573/4–1613x19) was the son of William Davison, Secretary of State, and studied at Emmanuel College, Cambridge, and Gray's Inn. While at Gray's Inn he wrote 'The Masque of Proteus', which was performed at the Revels in 1594/95. Davison was a poet but is most famous as an anthologist, compiling *A Poetical Rhapsody* (1602), which included poems of his own and his brother, Walter, as well as those of Philip and Mary Sidney, Edmund Spenser, Thomas Campion, John Donne, and others. Davison's anthology of metrical Psalms was never printed but survives in several manuscripts, in whole and in parts, and some of his Psalms were included in Stephen Jerome's *A Serious Forewarning to Avoid the Vengeance to Come* (1613) and John Standish's *All the French Psalm Tunes* (see 111). A number of the manuscripts were penned by the scribe Ralph Crane as gifts. The anthology includes Psalms by Davison himself, his brother Christopher, and Joseph Bryan. Davison apparently also wanted to get hold of a copy of the Sidney Psalms to put them into print. The influence of the Sidney Psalms on Davison's own versions is evident in their sophisticated and diverse metres and stanzas. See Joel Swann, 'Reading the Davison Psalms in Manuscript and Print', *Renaissance Studies*, 33.5 (2019), 668–90; Amy Bowles, 'Ralph Crane and Early Modern Scribal Culture' (unpublished dissertation, Cambridge University, 2017); Woudhuysen, *Sir Philip Sidney and the Circulation of Manuscripts*; John Considine, *ODNB*.]

Psalm 23

1. God who the universe can hold
         In his fold
   Is my shepherd, kind and heedful,
   Is my shepherd, and doth keep
         Me, his sheep
5 Still supplied with all things needful.   *necessary*

2. He feeds me in fields which been
         Fresh and green
   Mottlied with Spring's flow'ry painting[739]   *mottled*

---

[739] Mottlied] Motley cloth was woven from threads of different colours, and the term was used for similarly multicoloured beds of flowers.

10   Through which creep, with murmuring crooks[740]   *curves*
                           Crystal brooks
          To refresh my spirits fainting.

    3. When my soul, from heaven's way
                           Went astray
15   With earth's vanities seducèd,
       For his name's sake, kindly he
                          Wandering me
       To his holy fold reducèd.   *restored*

    4. Yea, should I stray through death's vale   *valley*
20   Where his pale
      Shades did on each side enfold me,
      Dreadless, having thee for guide
                     Should I bide,
      For thy rod and staff uphold me.

25 5. Thou my board with messes large   *table, meals*
                     Dost surcharge,
      My bowls full of wine thou pourest,
      And before mine enemies'
                     Curious eyes
30   Balm upon my head thou showerest.

    6. Neither dures thy bounteous grace   *endures*
                     For a space,
      But it knows nor bound, nor measure: *neither*
      So my days, to my life's end
35   I shall spend
      In thy courts, with heav'nly pleasure.

---

[740] crooks] Likely punning on the shepherd's crook that substitutes in some versions of the Psalm for verse 4's 'rod and staff'.

Psalm 23 (Another)

To St Bernard's *Cur Mundus militat* etc.[741]

1. The Lord my pastor is,[742] he tends me heedfully,   *shepherd*
   He still supplies my wants, with all things needfully.

2. In fields he pastures me, clad with amenity,   *pleasantness*
   Through which a silver brook slideth with lenity.   *gentleness*

3. Through busy labyrinths roaming audaciously[743]
   Ready to lose myself, my shepherd graciously
   For his name's-glory-sake eftsoons reduced me   *soon after, brought back*
   Unto his holy fold, whence sin seduced me.[744]

4. Yea, through death's valleys a frightful obscurity
   If I should walk, I should walk in security
   If thou dost guard me; for in tribulation
   Thy rod, and sheep-hook are my consolation.

5. Before mine enemies, enviously vicious,
   Thou hast prepared my board, with meats delicious,   *table, foods*
   With sweetly-swelling balms my head thou drownèd hast
   With sweetly-tasting wine, my bowls thou crownèd hast.

---

[741] This Latin hymn was popular in the late Middle Ages and sixteenth century and many times translated into English. One such translation is the first item in *The Paradise of Dainty Devices* (1578 and further editions), in which each pair of Latin lines is followed by a paraphrase in six English hexameters. *Paradise* is a collection designed for singing, either by one voice to an instrument or in five parts, as the dedicatory epistle by the printer Henry Disle makes clear. Music was not provided, however, English music printing being at a primitive stage, and settings circulated either by ear (tunes) or in manuscript part-books. Some of these have survived, including songs from *Paradise*, but not the *Cur mundus*. That Davison's Psalm is in the same metre as the *Paradise Cur mundus* suggests that it may have been associated with and the source of the tune he recommends, and which must have been accessible to his readers in some non-printed form.

[742] Davison plays on the Latin and English meanings of 'pastor', shepherd and minister respectively.

[743] labyrinths] A feature of aristocratic gardens (as in Titania's description of 'quaint mazes in the wanton green' in *A Midsummer Night's Dream*, II. 1. 102), signalling (like the previous version's 'crystal brooks') the debt to pastoral poetry in this description of the Psalm's landscape.

[744] Davison's added clause here introduces considerable complication to both the time frame of the Psalm's narrative and the stability of the place of comfort it describes. Has the Psalmist been led in the 'paths of righteous' (KJV) before, but then strayed from them, seduced by sin? Are the pastures, streams, and paths thus distinct from the house described at the end, the former perhaps in this world, the latter in the world to come? Yet that's not clear in the original Psalm. Moreover, given the pervasive personification and metaphor (sheep and shepherd, Death in his valley), should we read 'sin' as an active agent, working against the shepherd? Or is it merely the sheep who can't help wandering off?

6. Thy love I need not doubt, and thy gratuity
   Shall me accompany to perpetuity;
   So in this house I shall (O blessed condition)
   Of heaven's endless joys, here taste fruition.

Psalm 133

1. What is so sweet, so amiable
       As brothers' love, unfeignèd?   *sincere*
   Whose hearts in bands invincible   *bonds*
       Of concord are enchainèd?

2. It's like unto that precious ointment
       Whose odour far did spread,
   Used to embalm, by God's appointment
       The high-priest Aaron's head.
   Whence, in a fragrant shower descending
       It dew'd his beard, and face,
   Then to his robes, his sweetness lending
       About his skirts did trace.[745]

3. Or to the dew wherewith grey morning
       Empearls Mount Hermon's head,
   His greens with pearlèd flowers adorning,
       Artlessly dispread   *spread out*
   From Hermon to Mount Zion, pouring
       His fertile rivulets,
   And all engreening, and enflowering
       Those pleasant mountainets.   *hills*

4. Where this love-knot remains unbroken[746]
       God, heaps of bliss doth send,
   Yea, heavenly bliss, it doth betoken
       Exempt from change, or end.

---

[745] Alter notes the parallel downward movement in the Psalm's description of the ointment, Aaron's beard, and the dew, all of which fall down. Davison's repetition of 'dew' as a verb for the ointment is a clever reflection of the parallel, as is the consonance of 'dew' and 'shower'.

[746] Davison imports an image from secular love poetry, here imaging the family bond as a 'love-knot', which matches his elaboration of the 'dew of Hermon' into a scene worthy of the Song of Solomon.

89. Christopher Davison, in *Certain Selected Psalms of David* (MS *c.* 1612?)

[Nothing is known about Christopher Davison apart from the Psalms he wrote for his brother Francis's collection. Another brother, Walter, was a contributor to the *Poetical Rhapsody*, and was later a soldier fighting in the Netherlands.]

Psalm 15

Domine, quis habitabit. [Lord, who shall dwell]

1. Lord, in thy house, who shall forever bide,
   To whom shall rest in sacred mount betide,   *befall*
2. Ev'n unto him, that leads a life unstainèd,
   Doth good, and speaks the truth from heart unfeignèd.   *sincere*
3. Who with his tongue deceit hath never used,
   Nor neighbour hurt, nor slandered, nor accused;
4. Who, loving good men, is from bad estrangèd,
   Who keeps his word (though to his loss) unchangèd.
5. To usury who hath no money lent,
   Nor taken bribes against the innocent.
   Who in this course doth constantly persevere
   In holy hill (unmov'd) shall dwell forever.

90. Joseph Bryan, in *Certain Selected Psalms of David* (MS *c.* 1612?)

[The records of Gray's Inn note the admission of 'Joseph Bryan, son of John Bryan, of Northampton, gent.' on 6 November 1607. Bryan's use of compounds like 'sole-giver', 'seed-man', 'fire-sire' is striking and original. Bryan expands Psalm 65 into a lush pastoral decorated with all the resources of poetic artifice and bustling with rural activity, reminiscent of Aemilia Lanyer's seminal country house poem, 'The Description of Cookham' (1611).]

Psalm 65

1. Praise (O God) attends thy will,
         In thy hill,
   Vows to thee shall be performèd;
2. To thee, with open ear,
         Prayers dost hear,
   Comes all flesh which thou hast formèd.
3. Wickedness hath me assailèd,
         And prevailèd
   On my soul with vil'd oppressions: *degrading*

10   But thou (O Lord) in mercy wilt
       Purge my guilt
  And our numberless transgressions.

 4.   Blessed is he (O Lord) whom thou
       Dost allow
15   In thy courts to have his dwelling:
  His large soul shall have her fill,
       Tasting still
  Joys and pleasures past all telling.

 5.   Dreadful signs (O Lord) we know   *awe-inspiring*
20   Thou wilt show
  For thy chosen's preservation:
  O thou God, of earth's whole scope
       The sole hope,
  And of the yet-unknown-nation.

25 6.   By thy power thou settest fast   *securely*
       Mountains vast,
  Heaven-affronting, cloud surmounting,
  Strength and glory thee accost,
       And the host
30   Of thy power passeth counting.

 7.   Thou the raging seas dost still,
       At thy will,
  The vast-swelling surges 'suaging;   *assuaging*
  At thy beck the headless rout   *command, mob*
35   Mad, not stout
  Straight are hushed, though ne'er so raging.   *immediately*

 8.   Dwellers beyond Thule's bands[747]   *companies*
       In far lands,
  At thy signs shall be affrighted:
40   Morn's bright gate, and ruddy west
       Be their guest,
  Are with light and heat delighted.

 9.   Thou distill'st refreshing drops,
       And the shops
45   Of the parchèd earth are closèd.
  Thou the mould dost much enrich,   *earth*

---

[747] Thule] Mythical farthest north land.

     By the which
 Large increase is still proposèd.

   Thou prepar'st us corn; for so,   *grain*
50   Long ago,
 Thou (our God) hast preordainèd:
10. Furrows else (plough'd, saw'd in vain),
      By thy rain,
 Are with blades and ears maintainèd;

55   Thou send'st rain into the dales
      And the vales,   *valleys*
 Pranking them with curious flowers;   *adorning*
 And the stiffened earth makes soft
      With thy oft
60 Sweet and soft descending showers.

   Thou dost speed the seed-man's hand[748]
      In the land,
 His dead-seeming seed reviving   *descendants*
 And the tender bud (unless
65   Thou dost bless)
 Blasts, and frosts would keep from thriving.

 11. Thou the year with plenty's horn   *cornucopia*
      Dost adorn,
 Crowning it with large increasing:
70 And the clouds, with timely drops
      Yield fat crops,
 Mel and manna never ceasing.[749]   *honey*

 12. These thy gracious showers still
      Fall, and fill
75 With thy blessing, barren places,
 And the lesser hills are seen
      Fresh and green
 Deck'd with Flora's[750] various graces.[751]

---

[748] Echoing the popular ballad written *c.* 1500, 'God speed the plow', known later as 'The Farmer's Toast' or 'The Jolly Farmer'. A play with this title was performed in London in 1593, and a pamphlet so titled defending traditional husbandry was printed in 1601.
[749] manna] Miraculous food from Exodus 16.
[750] Flora] Roman goddess of spring and flowers.
[751] Bryan is a remarkably good poet, as evidenced in this stanza by the enjambment across lines 1–2 of this stanza, setting up the fall of 'Fall', and the ringing of 'still | Fall […] fill', reinforced two lines below with the internal rhyme in 'hills'.

	13.	The fat pastures curlèd locks,	
80		With large flocks	
		Shall be poll'd, yet shall be growing:	*sheared*
		Plenteous crops the vale shall yield,	
		And the field	
		Bounteously shall pay for sowing;	
85		Thus the land enjoying peace,	
		And increase	
		In so ample manner bringing,	
		Men for very joy shall shout,	
		All about	
90		Praising thee, and to thee singing.	

Psalm 70[752]

	1.	Haste thee (O God) to rescue me, oppressed;	
		Make speed to help thy servant, sore distressed.	
	2.	Let shame and swift confusion on them light	
		That look to slay and overthrow me quite.	
5		Pervert (O Lord) and subtervert them all	*subvert*
		That joy to see a mischief me befall.	
	3.	Let them be sore abased that wish to see	
		And (seeing) frolic in my misery.	
	4.	But let them all that seek thee still rejoice,	
10		And to their joy tune their well-pleasing voice.	
		Such as delight in thy salvation (Lord)	
		Let them still praise thy name with one accord.	
	5.	As for thy servant, I am poor; O haste,	
		Haste to my succour, else my hope is past.	
15	6.	Thou art my sole-Redeemer, my sole Aid,	
		O stay not long, for I am sore dismayed.	

Psalm 114

	1.	When from Egypt's servile land	
		(From the hand	
		Of proud Pharaoh flinty-hearted)	
		Israel, old Jacob's seed	*descendants*
5		(Being freed	
		From the barbarous rout), departed.	*mob*

[752] Verses 16–21 of Psalm 40 almost exactly repeat this Psalm. Bryan's block of sixteen iambic pentameter lines is rather like a sonnet (and it may be worth noting that Shakespeare's sonnet 126, like this Psalm, is in rhyming couplets).

2. God,⁷⁵³ in Judah showed forth
                  His great worth;
  And his holiness, sure grounded,
    And in Israel, his own
                  Might was shown
  And his power and strength unbounded.

3. The sea seeing him come nigh
                  Straight did fly,   *immediately*
  As one frighted, and perplexèd;
  All his surges from earth part
                  To his heart
  Ran to succour it, so vexèd.

  Jordan with a liquid wing
                  To his spring
  Fled, as to his life's sole-giver,
  If the sea, amaz'd did flee,
                  Much more he,
  But a brook, a petty river.   *small*

4. Mountains leapt, like frolic rams
                  And like lambs,
  Frisking in some flow'ry valley,
  Mountainets did trembling trip,   *hills*
                  Dance, and skip,
  Seeming sportfully to dally.

5. Say, O sea, what ailèd thee
                  So to flee
  And thy channel to discover?
  Jordan, why had'st thou recourse
                  To thy source
  And thy wonted way gav'st over?   *accustomed*

6. Mountains, why leapt ye like rams,
                  And like lambs
  Frisking in some flow'ry valley?
  Mountainets, why did ye trip,
                  Dance, and skip,
  Seeming sportfully to dally?

7. The firm-founded earth did quake,
                  Shrink, and shake

---

⁷⁵³ Bryan names God here, though the Psalm simply refers to 'he'.

45	At the Lord's all-daunting presence,	
	At his presence, whose hand wrought	
	All of nought,[754]	*nothing*
	Jacob's God, all creatures' essence.	

8. Who the dry hard craggy rock
50   With a knock
    Makes a fountain fully flowing,
    And the fire-sire flint a pool[755]
           So to rule
    Israel, with thirst's heat glowing.

91. Henry Ainsworth, *The Book of Psalms: Englished in Both Prose and Metre with Annotations* (1612)

[Henry Ainsworth (1569–1622), born in Norfolk the son of a yeoman farmer, studied at St Johns and Gonville and Cauis Colleges, Cambridge, and became a leader among English Separatists, moving to Amsterdam in the mid-1590s. Ainsworth was a prolific writer of both religious polemic and biblical studies. An exceptional Hebrew scholar, Ainsworth's translations of the Psalms were used by both the Amsterdam Separatists and the Pilgrim Fathers who emigrated to Massachusetts. For each Psalm, Ainsworth provided both a prose version and a metrical version for singing (with tunes), side by side, followed by extensive annotations. Following the Hebrew text, but unlike most other English translators, Ainsworth includes the headnotes of the Psalms among the numbered verses, though these are omitted from the singing versions. The singing versions were later printed on their own, without the prose translations or annotations, presumably for use in worship. The hyphenation is an attempt to capture in English the verbal compounds of the Hebrew text and so has here been preserved, along with Ainsworth's idiosyncratic punctuation. See Richard A. Muller, *After Calvin: Studies in the Development of a Theological Tradition* (Oxford: Oxford University Press, 2003); Michael E. Moody, *ODNB*.]

Psalm 8

1. To the master of the music upon Gittith°; a Psalm of David.
2. Jehovah, our Lord, how wondrous-excellent is thy name in all the earth: which hast given thy glorious-majesty above the heavens.
3. Out-of the mouth of babes, and sucklings, thou hast founded strength;
5   because of thy distressers: to make cease the enemy, and self-avenger.

---

[754] See note 450, p. 288.
[755] fire-sire] father of the fire.

	4.	When I behold thy heavens, the deed of thy fingers: the moon and the stars, which thou hast stably-constituted.	
	5.	What is sorry-man that thou rememb'rest him: and the son of Adam, that thou-visitest him?	
10	6.	For thou hast made-him-lesser a little, than the Gods:[756] and crowned him with glory and comely-honour.	
	7.	Thou gavest-him-dominion, over the works of thy hands: all, thou-didst-set under his feet.	
	8.	Sheep and oxen all of them: and also, the beasts of the field.	
15	9.	The fowl of the heavens, and the fishes of the sea: that-which-passeth-through, the paths of the seas.	
	10.	Jehovah our Lord: how wondrous-excellent is thy name, in all the earth.	

	2.	O Jah, our Lord, how excellent-great is	Jehovah
		Thy name in all the earth: thou which hast given	
20		Thy glorious-majesty above the heaven.	
	3.	From mouth of babes, and sucklings, thou firmness	
		Foundedst; because of them that thee distress.	
		To make the foe, and self-avenger cease:	
	4.	When I behold thy heavens, thy fingers' deed:	
25		The moon and stars, which thou hast stablishèd.	established
	5.	What is frail-man that him thou rememb'rest?	
		And Adam's son, that him thou visitest?	
	6.	For thou a little lesser hast made him,	
		Than be the Gods: and crowned him with glory	
30		And-eke with honourable-decency.	also
	7.	Of thy hand-works, thou gavest him ruling:	
		Under his feet, thou set didst everything.	
	8.	Sheep and beeves all: and field beasts with the same.	beef cattle
	9.	Fowl of the heav'ns, fish of the sea also:	
35		That through the pathways of the seas doth go.	
	10.	O Jah, our Lord: how excellent-great-fame	
		In all the earth hath thy renownèd-name.	

---

[756] Most English translations (BCP, KJV) render this as 'angels', but the Hebrew, *'elohim*, is one of the most common names for God. It is already a plural form, but is usually translated as the singular 'God'. The Geneva Bible has 'God', with a note explaining, 'touching his first creation'. Ainsworth's choice may depend on passages like Job 1, in which the 'sons of God' (KJV; *ben 'elohim*), presumably angels, are said to present themselves before him, or Genesis 3. 22, when God says, 'Behold, the man is become as one of us' (KJV), seemingly referring to a collective of heavenly beings, perhaps God and angels.

Psalm 23

1. A Psalm of David. Jehovah feedeth me, I shall not lack.
2. In folds of budding-grass,⁷⁵⁷ he maketh me lie-down: he easily-leadeth me, by the waters of rests.
3. He returneth my soul: he leadeth me in the beaten-paths of justice, for his name sake.
4. Yea, though I should walk, in the valley of the shade of death, I will not fear, evil, for thou wilt be with me: thy rod and thy staff, they shall comfort me.
5. Thou furnishest before me, a table, in the presence of my distressers: thou makest fat my head with oil; my cup is abundant.
6. Doubtless, good and mercy shall follow me, all the days of my life: and I shall converse in the house of Jehovah,⁷⁵⁸ to length of days.

Sing this as the 8. Psalm.

1. Jehovah feedeth me, I shall not lack.
2. In grassy folds, he down doth make me lie:
He gently-leads me, quiet waters by.
3. He doth return my soul: for his name sake,
In paths of justice leads-me-quietly.
4. Yea, though I walk, in dale of deadly-shade,
I'll fear none ill; for with me thou wilt be:
Thy rod, thy staff eke, they shall comfort me.
5. 'Fore me, a table thou hast ready-made,   *also*
In their presence that my distressers be.   *before*
Thou makest fat mine head with ointing-oil;   *anointing*
6. My cup abounds. Doubtless, good and mercy
Shall all the days of my life follow me:
Also within Jehovah's house, I shall
To length of days repose-me-quietly.

Psalm 84

1. To the master of the music upon Gittith°: a Psalm to the sons of Korah.
2. How amiable are thy dwelling-places; O Jehovah of hosts!
3. My soul, longeth and also fainteth, for the courts of Jehovah: my heart and my flesh, do shout, unto the living God.
4. Yea, the sparrow, findeth an house, and the swallow, a nest for her, where she layeth her young: thine altars, Jehovah of hosts; my King, and my God.

---

⁷⁵⁷ The Hebrew means something like 'grass pastures', but the word for grass (*dese'*) implies new, young, green shoots.

⁷⁵⁸ converse] In seventeenth-century usage to live, dwell, keep company, as well as to talk.

5. O blessed are they that abide in thine house; still, they shall praise thee, Selah.
6. O blessed is the earthly-man,[759] whose strength is in thee; they in whose heart, are the high-ways.
7. They that passing through the vale° of Baca,[760] put him for a well-spring: also with blessings, the rain covereth.
8. They shall go, from power to power: he shall appear, unto God in Zion.
9. Jehovah, God of hosts, hear thou my prayer: give-ear, O God of Jacob, Selah.
10. See thou O God, our shield: and look-upon, the face of thine anointed.
11. For, better is a day in thy courts, than a thousand: I have chosen, to sit-at the-threshold, in the house of my God; rather than to remain, in the tents of wickedness.
12. For Jehovah, God, is a sun, and a shield: Jehovah will give, grace and glory: he will not withhold good, from them that walk in perfection.
13. Jehovah of hosts: O blessed is the earthly-man, that trusteth in thee.

2. O Lord of hosts, how amiable are places
Wherein thou dost dwell!
3. My soul, doth long and faint also,
Ever for the courts of Jehovah:
My heart and my flesh, shout do they,
To come the living God unto.
4. Yea the sparrow, an house findeth
And swallow nest, where she layeth
Her young ones: thine altars, O Jah   Jehovah
Of hosts; my King, and-eke my God.   also
5. They that in thine house have abode,
Are blessed: they still, praise thee, Selah.
6. Blessed is the man, whose strength thou art:
They that highways have, in their heart.
7. That passing-through the Baca vale,   valley
Do put him for a welling-stream:
With blessings eke, rain covereth them.
8. From power to power, proceed they shall:
To God in Zion, shall appear.
9. Lord, God of hosts, my prayer hear:
Give-ear, O Jacob's God, Selah.
10. O our shielding-protection,

---

[759] The Hebrew, *'adam*, means simply 'man', though it is also the name (Adam) given to the first man, but the author of Genesis plays the word for 'man' against the etymologically related word for the earth out of which he is made (*'adamah*). Ainsworth may be trying to recreate the same wordplay in his compound noun.
[760] Baca] The Hebrew means 'weeping'.

		See thou O God: and look upon,	
45		Face of thine ointed-Messiah.	*anointed*
	11.	For, better is a day within	
		Thy courts, than thousand elsewhere been:	
		I chosen have, me to depress	
		At threshold, in house of my God;	
50		Rather-than for to have abode,	
		Within the tents of wickedness.	
	12.	For Jah God, is a sun and shield:	
		Both grace and glory, Jah will yield:	
		Not any good withhold will he,	
55		From them that walk in perfectness.	
	13.	O Lord of armies: blessèd is	
		The earthly-man, that trusts in thee.	

92. Sir John Harington (MS *c.* 1612?)

[See headnote to 75.]

Psalm 4

Cum invocarem.   [When I called]

		O hear, my God, my humble cries,	
	1.	My justice weigh in grace's weights;	
		Thou mad'st me room in greatest straits,	
		Thou wilt not then my prayer despise.	
5	2.	O women's sons, O men, how long	
		Will ye my name and glory wrong	
		And place your thought's vain toys among	*trivialities*
		Still seeking lies?	
	3.	But rather know, for this is true,	
10		That when my Lord did me elect[761]	
		He did my lowly mind respect,	
		For he my soul's devotion knew.	
		My Lord will lend his loving ear,	
		When I my voice to him do rear;	
15	4.	Then learn with reverence him to fear	
		And sin eschew.	

---

[761] Harington's use of 'elect' for what the Psalmist refers to as 'chosen to himself' (BCP) is the term used by Protestants, especially Calvinists, for those predestined for salvation. Harington's own faith seems to have leant toward Catholicism, but he once referred to himself as a 'protesting Catholic Puritan', so he obviously wasn't entirely orthodox in any sense.

        Of secret thoughts take inward view,
        In silence sad your chamber close,   *private*
        And there to God your sin disclose;[762]
20 5. The sacrifice to him most due
           Is this, to do the things are just,
           To lay aside all lawless lust,   *desire*
           And in his word to put your trust
                  That still is true.

25 6. But who to us will riches show,
        Thus many murmur in their moods,
        Who goodness leave and look for goods;
        Yet better I to wish do know,
    7.   I wish to me and all my race   *posterity*
30   The fairest favour of thy face,
           Thy countenance and saving grace
                  On me bestow.

    8. Increase of oil, wine, corn, and sheep,   *grain*
        Which by thy blessings we have had,
35   Their heart yet makes not half so glad
        As, when I lay me down to sleep,
           I joy to think my slumb'ring senses
           Not charg'd with load of great offenses;
           Repose in me whose soul thy fences
40   In safety keep.

Psalm 66[763]

Jubilate Deo.   [O be joyful in God]

  1. O laud the Lord you lands, his name be glorious;   *praise*
      Say thus to God, O Lord, thy pow'r is such,
  2.   Thy wondrous work and fame is so notorious,
      Thy foes for fear are glad to fawn and crouch,[764]
5 3.   For nations far and wide resound thy fame,
      They worship thee, they sing and praise thy name.

---

[762] Harington intensifies the sense of privacy and inwardness in this verse, linking it more closely than in the original to the 'sacrifice', perhaps following Wyatt's emphasis on 'inward Zion' and the sacrifice of 'sprite contrite' (see 23).

[763] Harington uses the same stanza he did in Psalm 38 (see 75), made popular by Shakespeare's *Venus and Adonis*. He particularly favours alliteration, as 'laud [...] Lord [...] lands', 'wondrous works', and 'foes [...] fear [...] fawn'.

[764] Harington's alliteration of 'foes', 'fear', and 'fawn' may recall Wyatt's similar effect in 'Whoso list to hunt' (since Harington's manuscript included a copy), where the frustrated lover/hunter sputters, 'as she fleeth afore | fainting I follow'.

4.   Behold, you sons of men, behold with wonder,
    He turned the swelling seas and made it dry;
5.   The rivers' streams he parted so in sunder
    That men on foot might safely pass thereby.
6.   He rules the world, his eye is each where searching,
    And pulls the proud unfaithful from his perching.

7.   Then, people, all resound and sing his praise
8.   That saves our souls, nor lets our foot to slide.
    For thou, O Lord, hast prov'd us many ways,
9.   As silver pure by heat of fire is tried.   *refined*
10.   Yea, thou dost trap our footsteps by a train,   *trickery*
    In bitter bonds thou bound'st us with a chain.

11.   Men rode above our heads and on our backs
    To do us all disgrace, and as we passed,
    We felt both flames of fire and water's wracks,   *punishments*
    But yet thou didst enlarge us at the last,   *release*
12.   And brought'st to fruitful fields; and therefore now
    Unto thy house I come to pay my vow.

13.   What then my lips did vow in time of smart   *pain*
    I now will pay and offer sacrifices
    Of lambs and calves the fat and inmost part,
    With bearded goats and bulls of biggest sizes.[765]
14.   O ye that fear the Lord, come, do not shun
    To hear what God for my poor soul hath done.

15.   I called on him, my tongue his praise pronounced,
16. But if my heart some wickedness shall taint,
    I should by him eftsoon be quite renounced,   *immediately*
17. But now he hears and marketh my complaint.   *lament*
    Then will I praise his name and not be daunted,
    Since he my suit so graciously hath granted.   *petition*

Psalm 82

Deus stetit.   [God stands]

1. God stands between the prince, the peer, the judge,
    Chief Judge, and God among these demigods.
2. Why judge ye wrong for favour or for grudge?
    Where cause is ev'n, shall persons make an odds?[766]

---

[765] Harington follows Philip Sidney's translation of this Psalm, which also specifies animals 'of greater size'.
[766] i.e. shall rank or status make the difference?

5	3.	Defend the poor and orphan and the ward,	
		Whose weaker state hath oft the stronger right.	
	4.	See thou the right, and not the rich, regard,	
		Nor let the poor be 'pressed by men of might.	*oppressed*
	5.	They will not learn nor understand or mark,	
10		Corrupted is this earth on which they trod.	
		They loved not light but wilful walk in dark.	
	6.	'Tis true, I called you gods and sons of God,[767]	
	7.	But you shall fall and fail as mortal men;	
		Ev'n princes shall be punished for transgression.	
15	8.	Arise, O Lord, and come to judgement then,	
		For thou shalt take the heath'n to thy possession.	

Psalm 116[768]

Dilexi quoniam. [I love [the Lord], because]

	1.	All hearty love my Lord I bear,	
		Who me my heart's desire did give.	
	2.	He lent my suit a gracious ear,	*petition*
		I shall invoke him while I live.	
5	3.	In snares of death, in woes, in anguish,	
		My grievèd soul of late did languish.	
	4.	When thus I called upon his name,	
		O Lord, my soul some succour send,	
	5.	Eftsoon I found some succour came,	*immediately*
10		For of his mercies is not end.	
	6.	He doth the innocent set free;	
		In my distress he succoured me.	
	7.	Return to rest now free from fears;	
		My soul, thy Lord hath heard thy calling.	
15	8.	Thy life from death, thine eyes from tears,	
		The Lord hath freed, and feet from falling.	
	9.	Henceforth I shall with due thanksgiving	
		Before him walk in land of living.	

---

[767] The word Harington translates as 'gods' (as in BCP and KJV) is *'elohim* in Hebrew, a plural noun used most frequently as a name for 'God', though in a few instances as a plural, for angels (as in Job). The Hebrew rendered as 'God' in the same verse (BCP 'most Highest', KJV 'most High') is *'elyon*, which can also mean simply 'upper' or 'top', but in some instances (especially in Psalms) is used for God.

[768] In the Septuagint and the Catholic and Eastern Orthodox traditions that follow it this Psalm is divided into two.

> 10. I spake as then I had belief,
> Much troubled in my deep desires,
> And said, perplexed with fear and grief,   *perplexed*
> I find that men are all but liars.
> 11. What recompense shall God then have
> For all the gifts he to me gave?
> 12. I'll call on him and praise his name
> And drink the health of his salvation.
> 13. To pay my vows I will not shame
> In light of all the congregation;
> For he doth deem his saints so dear,
> Their death or tortures touch him near.
>
> 14. Behold, I am thy servant sworn
> And born thy slave, thy handmaid's son.
> But thou my fetters all hast torn,
> My bitter bands thou hast undone.   *bonds*
> 15. Unto thy name with prayer and praise
> I'll sacrifice in all my days.
>
> 16. To thee my vows, a debt most due,
> I'll pay in sight of all estates,
> In open courts where all may view,
> And in the midst of Salem's gates.
> And all my people shall accord
> To sing with me, O praise the Lord.

Psalm 123[769]

Ad te levavi.   [To thee I lifted]

> 1. To thee, O Lord, I lift mine eyes
> That sit'st aloft in starry skies,
> 2. As men on lords dependent
> Do wait to win their favour,
> As maids on dames attendant
> Look well to their behaviour.[770]
>
> Ev'n thus our looks on God attend
> Until he please his mercy send.
> 3. O Lord, have mercy then

---

[769] The Countess of Pembroke uses this unusual rhyme scheme in two Psalms (102, 119), but with different metres.

[770] Changing the Psalmist's 'masters' and 'mistress' (BCP) to 'lords' and 'dames' relocates the scene to the kind of Renaissance court with which Harington was highly familiar.

10   On us that are despisèd,
 4. Whose souls by scornful men
    And rich are tyrannizèd.

Psalm 131

Domine non. [O Lord I am not]

 1. O Lord, I have no vast desire,
       I do not bear a lofty look;
 2. To matters high I not aspire
       Nor bigger than my state can brook.   *tolerate*
5 3. But as a child but newly took
       From mother's teats of milk beguiled,
       Yet back unto those breasts doth look,
       So fares my soul like weanèd child.[771]
 4. O Israel, to trust persevere
10   In great Jehovah now and ever.

Psalm 132[772]

Memento Domine. [O Lord, remember]

 1. Lord, call to mind King David's trouble,
       What then he sware remember now,
 2. And how he did that oath redouble
       And bind it fast with solemn vow.   *secure*
5 3. I will, said he, myself allow
       No entry to my home or nest,
 4. Mine eyes and lids shall take no rest,
 5. Until a plot most fit I find
       Where I Jehova's house may build,
10   A house to Jacob's God assigned,
       Where men to God may worship yield.[773]
 6. At Ephrata,[774] amid the field
       And in the woods we sought and found
       This pleasant plot of holy ground.

---

[771] The infant's backward look is Harington's addition, a nice realistic touch although it complicates the Psalmist's position.
[772] Harington uses the rhyme royal rhyme scheme (*ababbcc*) but with a shorter, tetrameter line.
[773] Harington must have found this Psalm especially compelling, since he was deeply involved in the restoration of Bath Abbey from around 1595.
[774] Ephrata] i.e. Bethlehem, according to ancient tradition.

15	7.	Then enter, prostrate, all at length,	
		His tent, and at his footstool fall.	
	8.	Now raise, O Lord, thine ark, thy strength.	
	9.	Let priests most pure be clothèd all,[775]	
		And let the saints make joy not small.	
20	10.	O Lord, ev'n for thy David's sake,	
		Some care of his successors take.	
	11.	To David thou didst make this oath,	
		And what thou say'st shall sure succeed.	
	12.	I'll bless him and his issue both	
25		And fix the sceptre in his seed.	descendants
	13.	If they unto my word take heed	
		And 'gainst my laws make no transgression,	
		His seed shall have a sure succession.	
	14.	For why our Lord hath made of old	because
30		Sweet Zion hill his resting place,	
		He longs her beauties to behold.	
	15.	He there will sport an endless space,	
		His presence still shall do it grace.	
	16.	So bless her fruits, so bless her ground,	
35		Her beggars shall with bread abound	
	17.	I will endow her priests with health,	
		Her saints shall sing with great delight,	
		And David's house I'll bless with wealth,	
		And make it shine like lantern bright.	
40		His foes for shame shall fly the light,	
		But he shall grow in great renown;	
		I 'stablish shall his royal crown.	establish

93. Sir William Leighton, *The Tears or Lamentations of a Sorrowful Soul* (1613)

[William Leighton (c. 1565–1622) was a poet and composer and gentleman pensioner, one of the monarch's personal guards. His father, also William, was chief justice of the Welsh marches. Leighton likely attended Shrewsbury School, which had a strongly Calvinist curriculum, and where Philip Sidney also studied. His first book, *Virtue Triumphant, or, A Lively Description of the Four Virtues Cardinal* (1603), was dedicated to James I and may have led to his knighthood.

---

[775] Harington literalizes the Psalmist's metaphorical prayer that 'thy priests may be clothed in righteousness' (BCP). Given his Catholic sympathies, he may be concerned with the poor condition of outlawed and hunted Catholic priests, rather than their righteousness.

Tears or Lamentations of a Sorrowful Soul, dedicated to Prince Charles, was a collection of 'hymns and spiritual sonnets' designed to be sung at home as part of domestic devotions. Leighton published a second volume by the same name in 1614 containing musical settings of many of the texts published earlier, by eminent composers of the day, including William Byrd, Orlando Gibbons, John Dowland, Thomas Weelkes, Alfonso Ferrabosco, and John Milton, father of the poet, as well as Leighton himself. Anyone performing the part-songs would find it useful to have the earlier volume to hand as well, since only a single verse of text was included with each setting (the parts arranged across two pages in the part-book style designed for domestic performance). Alfonso Ferrabosco composed a setting for Leighton's Psalm 6 (printing the verse 'In depth no man remembreth thee'), and John Dowland set 'An heart that's broken and contrite', a confessional prayer that Leighton has obviously based on Psalm 51, but music is not provided for all the Psalms. Yet Leighton noted in the 1613 volume that even those 'not skilful in music' could sing the hymns or Psalms to 'the common and ordinary tunes', even though none of these tunes were provided. See Daniel Hahn, *ODNB*.]

Psalm 38

Put me not to rebuke and shame,
Nor in thine anger chasten me:
O righteous God, for thy great name,
Pardon my sins and set me free.
5 In me thine arrows fast do stick,   *securely*
Thy heavy hand doth press me down:
My flesh, my bones, and heart are sick,
When thou in wrath on me dost frown.

I have no rest in any joint,
10 By reason of my deadly sin:
With balm of mercy me anoint,
And bring me to thy heavenly inn.
My dismal deeds do plunge me sore,
Like raging billows of the main: *sea*
15 O waft me to thy blissful shore,
And be mine anchor-hold again.[776]

My festered wounds breed mine annoy,   *grief*
By reason of my foolish guise:

---

[776] The Psalmist laments that 'my wickednesses are gone over my head', which Leighton takes and elaborates as a metaphor for drowning (though it isn't in the Hebrew), as in Psalm 44: 'all thy waves and storms are gone over me' (BCP). The anchor is a traditional symbol for hope, based on Hebrews 6. 19.

>   Chasing my heart and soul from joy,
> 20 All day I mourn with woeful cries.
>   Full of diseases are my loins,
>   And limbs decay in every part:
>   Languor unto my flesh adjoins,
>   And anguishment consumes my heart.
>
> 25 Thou knowest all my heart's desires,
>   My groanings are not hid from thee: *hidden*
>   Extinguish these outrageous fires,
>   O Lord, and cure mine agony.
>   My heart doth pant, my strength doth fail,
> 30 My neighbours did their love exchange:
>   And darkness did my sight assail,
>   My very kindred waxèd strange.[777]   *grew*
>
>   Mine enemies that sought my life,
>   Laid snares for me in every place:
> 35 Plotting all day to work my strife,
>   And bring my name into disgrace.
>   But as one deaf that could not hear,
>   Their taunting scoffs I did neglect:
>   And like the dumb did speech forbear,
> 40 For thou their slanders wilt correct.
>
>   For in thee ever do I trust,
>   To right my wrongs and plead for me:
>   Against my foes, O God most just,
>   For all revenge belongs to thee.
> 45 Of thee most humbly I did crave,
>   That they in triumph should not rise:
>   If I by chance a foil might have,   *defeat*
>   They would exalt with joyful cries.
>
>   With deadly plagues I am beset,
> 50 And heavy thoughts in me do stay:
>   My horrid sins I'll ne'er forget,
>   But mourn for them both night and day.
>   My cruel foes are great in strength,
>   And they in number do exceed:
> 55 Therefore, O Lord, aid me at length,
>   And succour me in time of need.

[777] The punctuation here is unavoidably confusing, because Leighton has scrambled verses 10 and 11, the former about heart, strength, and eyes, the latter about neighbours and kindred.

Psalm 143

    To my petitions bow thine ear,
    Good Lord consider my desire:
    O comfort me in dreadful fear,
    For thy truth's sake I thee require.
5 With us in judgement enter not,
    No man is righteous in thy sight:
    O let thine anger be forgot,
    And thine anointed us acquite.   *acquit*

    The enemy hath vexed my soul,
10 And cast my life down to the ground:
    My bones in darkness he doth roll,
    That like a dead man I am found.
    Therefore my spirit is oppressed,
    My heart within me grievèd sore:
15 That I can find no quiet rest,
    But desolation evermore.

    Yet former times to mind I call,
    Musing upon thy works begun:
    And exercise my self in all
20 The wondrous acts which thou hast done.
    To thee, do I stretch out my hand,
    And unto thee my soul doth groan:
    Even as the dry and thirsty land,
    That for her moisture maketh moan.

25 Hear me O Lord, and that with speed.
    Because my spirit waxeth spare: *grows, lean*
    Hide not thy face in time of need,
    Lest that I fall into the snare.
    O let thy comfortable love
30 Betimes into my soul distil: *early*
    And let thy Spirit like a dove,
    Dwell in my heart and keep me still.   *guard*

    Upon thee only I depend,   *alone*
    Direct me in the perfect way:
35 And guide me to my journey's end,
    For thou art my support and stay.   *prop*
    Good Lord, defend me from my foes,
    For unto thee I fly for aid:
    Under thy wings hide me from those,
40 That for my soul, their snares have laid.

Teach me to do the thing aright,   *justly*
That may be pleasing to thy mind:
And amiable in thy sight,
That I, thy favour still may find,
45 Thou art my God and only guide,
Which dost protect me with thy hand:
O let thy Spirit with me abide,
And lead me to the holy land.

For thy name's sake, Lord, quicken me.   *enliven*
50 And for thy righteousness I crave:
O set my soul from troubles free,
And let it never see the grave.
And for thy goodness' sake destroy,
Mine enemies that me pursue:
55 And to my soul would work annoy,   *trouble*
O Lord, confound that damnèd crew.   *defeat*
I am thy servant, O my God,
Dear Father, guide me with thy rod.

94. Thomas Campion, *Two Books of Ayres* (1613)

[Thomas Campion (1567–1620) was born in London and was admitted to Peterhouse Cambridge as a gentleman pensioner, leaving without a degree. He was admitted to Gray's Inn in 1586, where he contributed some songs to *Gesta Grayorum*, performed at court in 1594. Early in the next century, Campion went to France and received an MD in 1605 from the University of Caen. He does seem to have practiced medicine, but he is far better known as a poet and composer. His *Observations in the Art of English Poesy* (1602) argued for the use of classical quantitative metres in English poetry, but Campion himself wrote only a single song following this system, though he did also write a considerable amount of Latin verse. Campion is best known for his lute songs, published in several volumes: *A Book of Ayres* (1601, words by Campion, music by Philip Rosseter), *Songs of Mourning: Bewailing the Untimely Death of Prince Henry* (words by Campion, music by John Coperario), *Two Books of Ayres* (1613, words and music by Campion), and *A Third and Fourth Book of Ayres* (1617 or after, words and music by Campion). He also wrote a treatise on counterpoint, and a number of important court masques, including *The Lords' Masque* for the wedding of Princess Elizabeth in 1613. Campion's collections included sacred as well as secular songs, including these two paraphrases of the biblical Psalms, as well as others that borrow from Psalms more obliquely. See *The Works of Thomas Campion*, ed. by Walter R. Davis (Garden City: Doubleday, 1967); David Lindley, *ODNB*.]

Psalm 130

1.

Out of my soul's depth to thee my cries have sounded,
Let thine ears my plaints receive on just fear grounded:[778]   *laments*
Lord should'st thou weigh our faults, who's not confounded?   *damned*

2.

But with grace thou censur'st thine when they have errèd,
Therefore shall thy blessed name be loved and fearèd,
Ev'n to thy throne my thoughts and eyes are rearèd.

3.

Thee alone my hopes attend, on thee relying;
In thy sacred word I'll trust, to thee fast flying,
Long ere the watch shall break, the morn descrying.   *discovering*

4.

In the mercies of our God who live securèd,
May of full redemption rest in him assurèd,
Their sin-sick souls by him shall be recurèd.   *restored*

Psalm 137

1.

As by the streams of Babylon,
Far from our native soil we sat,
Sweet Zion thee we thought upon,
And every thought a tear begat.

2.

Aloft the trees that spring up there
Our silent harps we pensive hung:[779]
Said they that captived us, Let's hear
Some song which you in Zion sung.

3.

Is then the song of our God fit
To be prophaned in foreign land?
O Salem, thee when I forget,
Forget his skill may my right hand!

---

[778] grounded] based, founded; but there is a musical pun here, since a 'ground' is also a repeated melody, bass line, or harmonic structure upon which variations are played out.
[779] pensive] thoughtful; but there is a complex multilingual etymological pun with the verb 'hang'. The Latin for 'hang' is *pendere*. The word 'pensive' is unrelated, but Campion's wordplay exploits the similarity in sound, imagining a shared, though false, etymology.

4.

Fast to the roof cleave may my tongue   *securely*
If mindless I of thee be found:
15 Or if when all my joys are sung
Jerusalem be not the ground.[780]

5.

Remember Lord how Edom's race   *offspring*
Cried in Jerusalem's sad day,
Hurl down her walls, her towers deface,
20 And stone by stone all level lay.

6.

Curst Babel's seed for Salem's sake,   *Babylon's, descendants*
Just ruin yet for thee remains:
Blessed shall they be thy babes that take,
And 'gainst the stones dash out their brains.

95. Sir Edwin Sandys, *Sacred Hymns: Consisting of Fifty Select Psalms of David and Others, Paraphrastically Turned into English Verse* (1615)

[Sir Edwin Sandys (1561–1629) was the son of Edwin Sandys, Archbishop of York, and brother of George Sandys, poet, adventurer, and translator of Ovid and biblical texts, including Psalms (see 121). He was educated at Merchant Taylors' School, where his classmates included Lancelot Andrewes and Edmund Spenser, and Corpus Christi College, Oxford, where he studied with Richard Hooker, whose *Laws of Ecclesiastical Polity* he later sponsored. Sandys joined the Middle Temple and was active as a Member of Parliament and became the leader and champion of the Commons. He was also named to the council of the Virginia Company. Unlike his prolific brother, Sandys published little: two books on the state of religion, and *Sacred Hymns*. Sandys's Psalms were provided with music by Robert Tailor (perhaps the same man who wrote the play *The Hog Hath Lost his Pearl*), designed to be sung in five parts with accompaniment by viol, lute, or orpharion, intended for domestic entertainment. See Theodore K. Rabb, *ODNB*.]

---

[780] ground] basis, foundation; the same musical pun as in Campion's Psalm 130 (a 'ground' being also a repeated melody, bass line, or harmonic structure upon which variations are played out), but with an additional element, in that the whole crisis of Psalm 137 is that the Israelites are on foreign ground.

Psalm 17[781]

David grounding[782] upon the innocency of his own life and conscience, appealeth to God for relief against the oppression and cruelty of his unjust enemies: who men of the world, place their happiness wholly in the corporal pleasures of this life. Whereas his felicity consisteth in enjoying God's favour in his righteous life here, and in the glorious vision of God in the life after the Resurrection. This Psalm seemeth to have been made, upon occasion of the second expedition which Saul made against David, at the first instigation of the Ziphites: at which time David flying from the Desert of Ziph to that of Maon, was in a plain there between the mountains enclosed by Saul. But by reason of a sudden message that the Philistines did invade the land, Saul left following of David; who so escaped.[783]

    High Judge of world, cast down thy righteous eyes;
Attentive hear, while right for justice humbly cries.
    Not causeless fear, nor slight of feigning lips,   *cunning*
Or needless doubts presents, or plot disguised uprips:
5   Just grief appeals; and sentence from thy face,
Of thee craves due redress: thou then just plea embrace.[784]

    Thou oft my soul, yea oft in night didst view;
When thoughts in silent rest present appearance true:
    And oft my heart with fiery storms hast seen
10 Dissolved; and trial made what dross therein hath been.
    Nought counterfeit, no palliate thing hast found: *nothing, concealed*
What secret mind doth think, that mouth doth truly sound.
    All as my words, so deeds toward men do frame:
Thy sacred word my rule: the violent wrongers blame,
15   I see, and shun. O still my feet contain   *confine*
In righteous paths; still hands from acts not just restrain.

    Thee, Lord, I call: for sure thou wilt me hear:
Ah, then receive the plaint which faithful soul doth rear.   *lament*

---

[781] Sandys chooses an unusual metre for Psalms 17 and 139, alternating lines of iambic pentameter and hexameter, rhyming in couplets. Unlike poulter's measure, which also alternates lines of different lengths (hexameter and fourteener), Sandys's shorter lines do not tend to break into the shorter lines of singing Psalm metres. The closest precedent may be classical elegiacs, which alternate the same metres but in reverse order, hexameter followed by pentameter.

[782] grounding] i.e. grounding his argument.

[783] 1 Samuel 23.

[784] Sandys the lawyer emphasizes the courtroom scene in this opening stanza. BCP has 'Hear the right, O Lord, consider my complaint' and the Psalmist begs for a 'sentence', but Sandys's Psalmist calls God 'High Judge', and pleads for 'justice', with 'just grief' and a 'just plea'.

Divide thy acts: display thy mercies free
20 (Thou Saviour of thy saints[785] from those who them and thee
　　With wicked hate attempt): as light of eye[786]
Me fencèd, under, Lord, thy shadowing wing let fly.
　　There let me rest; there safe from impious crew,
My deadly foes, protect: who circling rage renew,
25　　My strength to waste, my life to earth to bring;
Engrossed with fat; and proud, out-thund'ring threats do ring.   *swollen*

　　As lion fierce, with ireful hunger whet,   *sharpened (fig.)*
Flings out his prey to seek; which joyous having met,   *rushes*
　　Stands foaming rage: or else as lion's whelp,
30 Who coucheth close in cave,[787] his strength with sleight to help,   *cunning*
　　Nor bold, nor yet afraid: so Lord my foes,
Now round with ramping troops our ways and walks enclose,
　　Presenting death: and now with spiteful eye,
Downcast, dissembling leer, advantage to espy.
35　　Then Lord arise, and with encounter swift
Affront their savage looks: and blood since is their drift,
　　Midst wicked troops, that blood may blood repay,
To save us by thy hand, with sword mow down thy way.

　　So Lord from men, my grieving soul enfree,   *make free*
40 From men of baser world: who here we beast-like see
　　In fading life their portion all possess;
And paunches vile, their god,[788] from thy rich storehouse bless.   *bellies*
　　Like sire, like son: same course their offspring runs;
Full gorge themselves; what's left, that to their infants comes.
45　　But I, by faith, in righteous life, shall view
Thy gracious face. And when thy power shall death subdue;
　　Awakened, Lord, eternal glorious sight
Of semblance thine, me like, shall fill with pure delight.

Psalm 139[789]

David, in this divine meditation, addressed to God, acknowledgeth at large God's knowledge of all things, even before they have being; and in particular of

---

[785] Sandys substitutes 'saints', a term used by Protestants for the godly elect, in place of the Psalmist's more general 'them, which put their trust in thee' (BCP).
[786] Sandys's 'light of eye' diverges from the Hebrew. See note 341, p. 234.
[787] coucheth close] lies hidden.
[788] Sandys likely has in mind the contemporary term 'belly-god', or perhaps those mentioned in Philippians 3. 19, 'whose God is their belly, and whose glory is in their shame, who mind earthly things' (KJV).
[789] On the metre, see note 781, p. 431.

all the thoughts and ways of man: rend'reth a reason of this omniscience, from the creation of all, and particularly from the marvellous fabric of man: which ravisheth his mind into such admiration, that breaking into most affectionate praises of the manifold works and ways of God; he professeth also that his thoughts are no sooner after sleep awakened but they first are seasoned with this sweet contemplation. Contrarily falling into extreme detestation, yea, and imprecation against those wicked ones, who blasphemous toward God, vainly extol God's enemies: he concludeth with fervent prayer, that himself may be purified by the grace of God, and so conducted through the ways of this world, as to attain finally his everlasting rest.

> Eternal light; 'gainst whose all-seeing eye,
> Man's thoughts, his cares, and ways, do all transparent lie:
>   Lo, here my soul; which thou with piercing view,
> Hast searchèd, and dost know; so liv'st her witness true.
> 5   Great Judge of hearts; who secret plights unfold'st;   *misfortunes*
> Who past with future things all present ay behold'st: *always*
>   Thou know'st my course, when down I sit, when rise;
> Yea, thoughts unborn[790] far off thy foresight strange descries.   *discovers*
>   By day my walks, at night my silent rest
> 10 Thou dost environ,[791] with skill to all my paths addressed.   *surround*
>   Observ'st my tongue: no word unweighed dost leave:
> Yea, lips ere words produce, or thoughts hid speech conceive.   *hidden*
>   And grasp'st me so with thy all-guiding hand,
> Behind, before, as pressed at pleasure thine to stand.[792]   *conscripted*
> 15   Science profound; of strange transcending law!   *knowledge*
> That man nor it can sound, nor self from it withdraw.
>   For whither go, how should I bend my flight,
> Thy Spirit Lord to balk, or cloud me from thy sight?   *shun*
>   If soar toward heavens; in heaven thy throne resides:
> 20 If flag 'longst earth; lo, earth thy footstool low abides: *fly low*
>   If stoop to hell, and jaws which ghastly gape;
> Nor hell thy view, nor fiends thy thund'ring stroke escape.

[790] Sandys's description of unborn thoughts plays on the later verses about God knowing the Psalmist from the womb.
[791] environ] The metre requires pronunciation as a disyllable: 'envir'n'.
[792] Sandys's 'Behind, before' may be indebted to John Donne's Elegy 19, which includes a longer chain of prepositions: 'Before, behind, between, above, below'. The contexts are entirely different, Donne's being a strongly erotic poem, but it is suggestive that Sandys's metre is an adaptation of elegiacs, which in the classical period (as with Ovid) was the metre for erotic verse, and Donne's 'On his Mistress' is one of the period's most famous erotic elegies. Donne's poem was not yet in print, but it was likely written during his time at the Inns of Court where such verse was popular, and since Sandys was also at the Inns in the 1590s, it is possible he saw a copy in circulation among the young students.

> If eastern steeds, and morning's crimson wings
> I timely mount, which round to utmost ocean brings;
> 25   Thou East's great course, and morn's fair wings dost guide;
> Nor utmost ocean's gulfs from thine aspect can hide.
>   Perhaps might say, yet darkness me may heal;
> She with her sable robe from searching'st eye conceal.[793]
>   And canst once think, weak shade which sun dispels,
> 30 Should light of lights eclipse, who thousand suns excels?
>   Fond, base conceit! To thee, O light divine,
> Both dark and bright are like; grim night as day doth shine.
>
>   For just and right, that thou Creator high,
> Who all hast framed, thy frame shouldst naked all descry: *discover*
> 35   And who my heart, my reins in womb didst form;   *inward parts*
> With limbs support; attire with skin, with sense adorn;
>   Shouldst heart and thoughts, shouldst sense and ways possess.
> Stupendious work! which ay great architect shall bless.[794]
>   A little world; yet world of wonders great:[795]
> 40 Which well my mind conceits, and tongue of it shall treat.   *understands*
>   My bones in weak, in place obscure my sight,
> In earth beneath my mind, fair spark of heavenly light,
>   Thou didst produce: embroidering every part
> With work so rare, that use with beauty strives in art.[796]
> 45   And doubt we yet if thou thy work didst know?
> Or can our tongues forbear thy glorious praise to show?
>   Yea, tender mass,[797] while formless it remained,   *unformed*
> And day by day new shape through virtue thine agained: *gained*
>   Thine eye saw all, enrolled in book divine;
> 50 Where all thy works to come, as present, clearly shine.

[793] Not a biblical metaphor, though one familiar in secular poetry, as in Spenser's *Faerie Queene* (I. 11): 'sad succeeding night, | Who with her sable mantle gan to shade | The face of earth', or the play *The Fleire* (1607) by Edward Sharpham, whom Sandys might have known at the Middle Temple: 'tongueless night put off thy sable robe'.

[794] Sandys's description of God as architect may be inspired by the Countess of Pembroke's architectural metaphors in her translation of Psalm 139 (see 73). Despite the epithet, Sandys himself does not use figures of building.

[795] Sandys's addition, alluding to the idea of the human body as a microcosm of the world as a whole, as when James I writes (in his 1604 *Counterblast to Tobacco*) of 'the diverse parts of our microcosm or this little world within ourselves' (sig. B3r).

[796] The Hebrew verb connotes weaving or needlework, but Sandys may have found the image of embroidery in Mary Sidney's celebrated version of the Psalm (see 73).

[797] The raw female matter which, according to early modern notions derived from Aristotle and Galen, waited to be stamped with masculine form.

Be blessed, great Lord: thy wisdom's beauteous ways
How precious, dearly sweet, to thee my soul do raise?
In skill, man's wit; in count, they pass the sands:
That still my wakened mind, with thee first present stands;
55 Admiring all thy works. O righteous King;
At length then please thy world to first estate to bring.
Extermine race defil'd. Ye men of blood, *exterminate*
Whose base flagitious minds despise th'eternal good; *wicked*
Who grace his foes; of him profanely prate; *chatter*
60 Avaunt from me; yourselves, and damnèd ways I hate. *depart*
Ah, sovereign Judge, to thee my soul appeals,
My Witness true; whose Spirit man's secret'st thoughts reveals.[798]
That love of thee, 'gainst them griev'd hatred breeds,
Whose venomous hate 'gainst thee breaks out in hostile deeds.
65 Thy foes are mine: with them I league forsake:
And firm in perfect hate to vengeance just betake. *entrust*

Then thou, my Lord, to whom I stand, or fall;
Who righteous minds approv'st, yet none canst perfect call:
Review my heart, explore my thoughts again;
70 And weigh what grieving course doth in my life remain.
Refine my soul: purge out corrupted use:
And safe through worldly waves to thy sweet rest conduce. *conduct*

Psalm 146

The Psalmist vowing perpetual praises to God, adviseth not to fix our trusts or hopes on perishing princes; but upon the unchanging truth and fidelity of God, the Creator of all things: who is the protector and reliever of all that are in distress; the overthrower of the wicked with all their ways and counsels; and the King of his Church for ever.

ALLELUIA.

My soul, with joy thyself address,
The mighty Lord, thy God to praise:
My tongue his sacred name shall bless;
My heart toward him I'll alway raise. *always*
5 While life doth last, the glorious King,
Yea, whilst I am, his praise I'll sing.
No towers of hopes on princes raise.
What aid can mortal man perform?
Whose breath departs; and ended days

---

[798] Spirit] The metre requires pronunciation as a monosyllable, perhaps 'Sprite'.

10 From dust derived to dust return.
    His thoughts and projects die withal: *likewise*
    Your tow'ring hopes to ground do fall.[799]
But blessèd they who choose his name,
Whose hopes and helps with him abide,
15 Who heavens and earth and seas did frame,
And world of guests which there reside.
    His thoughts no wavering can assail:
    His words are deeds, and never fail.
Then thee, our Lord and God, we sing;
20 Thou Jacob's God still blessèd be:
Who justice to the wrong'd dost bring;
The hungry feed, the prisoner free.
    Who blind with joyous fight dost cheer;
    And curbèd limbs dost upright rear.
25 The just he loves; the stranger guards;
He widow shields, and orphan guides:
But mischief dire just wrath awards
To wretch who righteous way derides.
    The Lord eternal King shall reign;
30 And Sion's God ay so remain.   *forever*
    Alleluia.

96. Sir David Murray, *A Paraphrase of the CIV Psalm* (1615)

[Sir David Murray of Gorth (1567–1629) was a Scot, a gentleman of the bedchamber and then groom of the stool to Prince Henry, Prince of Wales, who was particularly attached to Murray. In addition to his Psalm paraphrase, Murray wrote an Italian-style tragedy, *The Tragical Death of Sophonisba* (for which Michael Drayton wrote a commendatory poem), a sonnet sequence, *Caelica*, and a pastoral, *The Complaint of the Shepherd Harpalus*. Murray's Psalm was dedicated to Prince Henry: 'none worthy David's muse and harp but he'. His choice of Psalm 104 seems likely to have been influenced by the early published version of the same Psalm by James VI of Scotland, later James I of England (see **61**), though this Psalm describing the riches of the natural world was generally popular. See S. M. Dunnigan, *ODNB*.]

---

[799] The tower metaphor is added by Sandys, perhaps suggesting a biblical project of human pride like the tower of Babel (Genesis 11) or what Spenser called the 'proud tower of Troy' (*Faerie Queene* II. 9).

Psalm 104

My soul praise thou Jehovah's holy name,
For he is great, and of exceeding might,
Who cloth'd with glory, majesty, and fame,[800]
And covered with the garments of the light,
5   The azure heaven doth like a curtain spread,
    And in the depths his chalmer beams hath laid.   *chamber (Scots)*

The clouds he makes his chariot to be,
On them he wheels the crystal skies about,
And on the wings of Aeolus,[801] doth he
10 At pleasure walk; and sends his angels out,
    Swift heralds that do execute his will;
    His words the heavens with fiery lightnings fill.

The earth's foundation he did firmly place,
And laid it so that it should never slide;
15 He made the depths her round about embrace,
And like a robe her naked shores to hide,[802]
    Whose waters would o'erflow the mountains high
    But that they back at his rebuke do fly.

At the dread voice of his consuming thunder,
20 As these retire, the mountains in the sky
Do raise their tops, like pyramids of wonder,[803]
And at their feet the pleasant valleys lie,
    And to the floods he doth prescribe a bound,
    That they earth's beauty may no more confound.   *destroy*

25 The fertile plains he doth refresh and cheer
With pleasant streams which from the mountains fall,
To which (to quench their thirst) all beasts draw near,
Even to the ass whom never yoke did thrall: *make captive*
    And on the trees by every crystal spring,
30   Heaven's quiristers do sweetly bill and sing.   *choristers, caress bill to bill*

---

[800] fame] Though the English words used to praise God in this Psalm vary, they generally do not (nor do the Hebrew terms) have to do with 'fame', a classical rather than biblical virtue, also valued in the Renaissance. The classicizing of the Psalm is also evident in the insertion of Aeolus, Phoebus, and Thetis later.

[801] Aeolus] Greek god of the winds.

[802] The Psalmist does praise God for covering the earth with the sea 'as with a garment' (BCP), but the 'naked' shores are Murray's addition, adding a curious eroticism and also representing the earth as female. The Hebrew noun is feminine, but Murray may have more in mind the classical mythologizing of the earth as the goddess Gaia.

[803] pyramids] Murray's addition.

The thirsty tops of sky-menacing hills
He from the clouds refresheth with his rain,
And with the goodness of his grace he fills
The earth, with all that doth therein remain;[804]
35   He causeth her both man and beast to feed,
   The wholesome herbs, and tender grass to breed.

The fruitful ivy strict-embracing vine,[805]
To glad man's heart he hath ordained and made,
And gives him oil to make his face to shine,
40 And to increase his strength, and courage breed;
   The mighty trees are nourished by his hand,
   The cedars tall in Lebanon that stand.

On whose wide-spreading, high and bushy tops,
The flightering birds may build their nests in peace,   *fluttering*
45 And in the fir that pitchy tears forth drops,
He hath prepared the stork a dwelling place;
   The mountains are unto the goats refuge,
   And in the rocks the porcupines do lodge.[806]

He hath appointed seasons for the moon,
50 To fade, to grow, whiles fair to look, whiles wane,   *sometimes*
And makes bright Phoebus when the day is done,
In Thetis' lap to dive his head again:[807]
   He clouds the skies, and doth in darkness pight,   *fix*
   Ov'r all the earth the curtains of the night;

55 Then all the beasts from out the forest creep,
To seek his prey the lion loudly roars,

---

[804] Murray's enjambment effectively representing the fullness of God's grace to overflowing.
[805] The ivy and vine are Murray's additions, though the vine is implied by the Psalm's reference to wine. The imagery may be a combination of classical and biblical, the ivy entwining a tree a classical symbol of love (as in Shakespeare's *A Midsummer Night's Dream*, IV. 1. 44–45: 'the female ivy so | Enrings the barky fingers of the elm'), while Christ calls himself 'the true vine' entwisting and giving fruit to the branches, his people (John 15. 1–6).
[806] The usual animal in this verse in English Bibles is the cony, which may or may not be understood to be the Middle Eastern rock hyrax. In his own version of Psalm 104, King James I, another Scot, opted for the Alpine rat. Murray's porcupine seems an original choice, but it may actually derive from the Vulgate's *ericius*, or hedgehog.
[807] Phoebus was another name for Apollo, the Greek god of the sun, but that Thetis is his wife, welcoming him home at the end of day may be Murray's invention. Many accounts have Helios (another sun god, sometimes identified with Apollo) resting in the ocean at the end of the day, and Thetis was an ocean goddess, which is perhaps the source of Murray's idea. Alternatively, he may have conflated Thetis and Thaea, the wife of Hyperion, father of Helios and another sun god in his own right.

>   The serpents hiss, the crocodile doth weep,
>   As if she would bewail them she devours;[808]
>   And when the sun returns they all retire,
> 60   And in their dens do couch themselves for fear.   *lie*
>
>   And then doth man in safety freely go,
>   To ply his work with diligence till night.
>   Thy wondrous wonders who, O Lord, can show?
>   The earth is fillèd with thy glory bright,
> 65   And thou hast stor'd the deep-wide ocean sea,   *stocked*
>   With fish, beasts, monsters, numberless that be.
>
>   There do the wingèd wooden forts forth go,[809]
>   To climb the glassy mountains with their keels,
>   There Leviathan wanders to and fro,
> 70 And through the walt'ring billows tumbling reels,   *rolling*
>   Who in that liquid labyrinth enclos'd
>   Doth play and sport as thou him hast dispos'd.
>
>   All living things, O Lord, do wait on thee
>   That in due season thou mayst give them food,   *time*
> 75 And thou unfolds thy liberal hands most free
>   And gives them every thing may do them good:
>   Thy blessings thou so plenteously distils,
>   That their abundance all things breathing fills.
>
>   But if thy face thou do withdraw in wrath,
> 80 Thy creatures all then languish, grieve, and murn,   *mourn (Scots)*
>   Or if thou angry take away their breath,
>   They perish straight and into dust return: *immediately*
>   But when thy Sprite thou sends them to renew,   *Spirit*
>   All fresh doth flourish, earth regains her hue.
>
> 85 In his most glorious works let God rejoice,
>   Who makes the earth to tremble with a look,
>   Let men admire and angels with their voice
>   Extol his name, whose touch makes mountains smooke;   *smoke*
>   To this thought-passing speech-expressless, Lord,   *surpassing*
> 90   While breath extends will I still praise afford.
>
>   He will receive my humble suit in love,   *petition*
>   And in his favour I shall ever joy;

---

[808] Murray adds the serpent (resonant given its role in Genesis) and the crocodile, whose weeping for its victims is a classical legend recorded by Plutarch.
[809] wooden forts] ships.

The wicked from the earth he will remove,
And wholly heaven-despising worms destroy.[810]
95   But whilst they buried lie in endless shame,
My soul praise thou Jehovah's holy name.

97. Henry Dod, *All the Psalms of David with Certain Songs and Canticles of Moses, Deborah, Isaiah* [etc.] (1620)

[Dod's complete psalter, including other biblical songs, was dedicated to John Brewen of Stapleford and two Dod relatives, John of Tussingham and John of Broxon, but without any other publication information. It may have been published on the Continent, since in his dedication Dod refers to 'our native country about you', as if perhaps he wasn't himself in England. Also included is an act of parliament for public thanksgiving in memory of the delivery from the Gunpowder Plot, 5 November 1605, which Dod translates into verse 'meet for song'. In the decades since his first Psalms publication, Dod seems to have developed little as a poet, rivalling the translators of the Bay Psalm Book for rhythmic and syntactic insensitivity. He claimed he had been waiting 'for the performance of this worthy work, by some godly learned, whom I hoped would have done it in manner better beseeming the same'. Wither may have been correct in saying that authorities condemned Dod's Psalms to the fire, likely because the publication violated the Stationers' monopoly. See Doelman, *King James I and the Religious Culture of England*.]

Psalm 87

The nature and glory of the Church, 4. The increase, honour, and comfort of the members thereof.

A Psalm or song for the sons of Korah.

1. Within the holy mountain is
      His strong foundation.
2. The Lord doth more than Jacob's tents
      The gates love, of Zion.
5 3. Things glorious are spoke of thee
      O city of God. Selah.
4. I will of Rahab mention make[811]
      And Babylon display:

---

[810] The worms are Murray's addition. They are metaphorical, but even in a celebration of creation like Psalm 104, worms are despised.
[811] Rahab] See note 580, p. 357.

                Unto them that do me know,
                    Behold all they of Tyre,
                Philistia with Ethiop
                    This man was born there.
           5.   And it shall be of Zion said,
                    That this and that man there
                Was born: and he the highest shall
                    Himself establish her.
           6.   Jehovah, when he writeth up
                    The people, thus shall say,
                In his account, that such a man
                    Was born in her. Selah.
           7.   As well the singers, as these men
                    That skilfull players be
                On instruments, they shall be there:
                    My springs are all in thee.

98. William Loe, *Songs of Sion Set for the Joy of God's Dear Ones, Who Sit Here by the Brooks of this World's Babel, and Weep When They Think on Jerusalem Which Is On High* (1620)

[William Loe (d. 1645) was a clergyman, preacher, and writer. He studied at St Alban Hall and Merton College, Oxford, began his career as a vicar in Churcham, Gloucestershire, and was appointed prebend of Gloucester Cathedral in 1602. He was made rector of Stoke Severn, Worcestershire, in 1611, and then, despite his resistance to Laudian high church policies, was appointed chaplain to James I. In 1618, Loe became pastor of the English company of Merchant Adventurers in Hamburg. Here he wrote *Songs of Sion*, a collection of metrical paraphrases of Scripture, most notable for Loe's decision to use only monosyllables, based on the notion that 'our English tongue in the true idiom [...] consisted altogether of monosyllables, until it came to be blended, and mingled with the commixture of exotic languages'. He also claims that since 'God's children did reckon seven times seven years before they could enjoy their year of Jubilee', he has 'made allusion in this little essay to tune forth seven times seven sobs for sin', writing everything in multiples of seven (stanzas, sections). Hunnis is also obviously an inspiration (see **58**). Loe offers what he calls a 'metaphrase' of some Psalms, as well as the Song of Solomon and Lamentations, but the former seem really collage Psalms. Admittedly, however, Loe's decision to use only single syllable words makes identifying the Psalms (or verses of Psalms) he is translating difficult, and his commitment to seven four-line stanzas may have led him to choose select verses, since most Psalms have more than seven. Loe returned to England after less than a year abroad, and again became chaplain to James, preaching and publishing until his death, whereupon he was buried in Westminster Abbey. See Steven Wright, *ODNB*.]

The First Strain

Lord, hear my suit, my plaint,   *lament*
    That my soul makes to thee.[812]
Lord, in thy truth one look of grace
    Grant in thy love to me.

5 Lord, see the moan I make,
    Look on me in thy grace;[813]
Let not my sighs come back in vain
    But show to me thy face.[814]

Lo, I was born in sin.
10   My kind, my shape, my all;[815]
My stock, my flock, my self from birth,
    O Lord, from thee did fall.[816]

And I, poor soul, am set
    In grief, in pain, in woe;
15 My sins come on, my soul doth faint,
    O quit me of my foe.[817]

My sins the hairs do pass
    That are set on my head,[818]
My heart doth fear, and faint, and fail,
20   And I am as one dead.[819]

---

[812] Perhaps based on Psalm 55. 1–2, 'Give ear to my prayer, O God; and hide not thyself from my supplication. Attend unto me, and hear me: I mourn in my complaint, and make a noise' (KJV).

[813] Similar to Psalm 119. 132, 'Look thou upon me, and be merciful unto me' (KJV).

[814] Similar to Psalm 13. 1, 'how long wilt thou hide thy face from me?' (KJV).

[815] Clearly a version of Psalm 51. 5, 'Behold, I was shapen in iniquity; and in sin did my mother conceive me' (KJV).

[816] Perhaps derived from Psalm 139. 13, 'For thou hast possessed my reins: thou hast covered me in my mother's womb' (KJV).

[817] Similar in part to Psalm 119. 81, 'My soul fainteth for thy salvation: but I hope in thy word' (KJV).

[818] Close to Psalm 40. 12, 'For innumerable evils have compassed me about: mine iniquities have taken hold upon me, so that I am not able to look up; they are more than the hairs of mine head: therefore my heart faileth me' (KJV).

[819] Similar in part to Psalm 143. 3, 'For the enemy hath persecuted my soul; he hath smitten my life down to the ground; he hath made me to dwell in darkness, as those that have been long dead' (KJV).

Thus go I grieved, and gored,
    And fret in heart and sprite;[820]   *spirit*
Thus am I faint with fear and death,
    My sins they do me fright.[821]

25 The deeds that I have done
    Are set in view of eye.
My faults, my thoughts, my sin, my shame
    Thy laws thy looks do spy.[822]

99. Thomas Carew (MS 1620s?)

[Thomas Carew (1594/5–1640) studied at Merton College, Oxford, and at Middle Temple. Though his father was a notable civil lawyer, Carew did not pursue a legal career. He was appointed gentleman of the privy chamber to Charles I in 1630, but is best known for the poems he wrote during the 1620s, including 'The Rapture' and 'To Saxham', as well as the masque *Coelum Brittanicum*, performed at the Banqueting House at Whitehall in 1634. The only Psalms-related poem that appeared in Carew's 1640 *Poems* (and later collected works) was his commendatory poem to the Psalms translations of his friend, George Sandys. His metrical Psalms remained in manuscript: one (91) was included in one of the manuscripts of Francis Davison's Psalms anthology (see 88) and printed in an elegiac collection of the poems of Abraham Holland in 1626; it and the others were later included in a number of verse miscellanies. Carew's poems were among the most widely copied in the period. His Psalm 91 was also included in a folio volume of anthems used in the Chapel Royal at Whitehall, stamped with the Royal Arms (*c.* 1635). In the poem on Sandys's Psalms, which appeared in 1636, Carew claims that his friend's poems have converted him to write only sacred poetry, but this does not mean that Carew's Psalms date from his last years. In his late nineteenth-century edition of Carew, Joseph W. Ebsworth dismissed the Psalms, writing that 'the atmosphere of Sternhold and Hopkins hangs about them like a miasma'. In fact, Carew's Psalms are not at all like Sternhold and Hopkins but instead follow the model of the Sidneys, aiming not for singing-Psalms but sophisticated poems in a variety of metres. Rhodes Dunlap suggests the Psalms may have been written

---

[820] Psalm 73. 21, 'Thus my heart was grieved, and I was pricked in my reins' (KJV).
[821] Somewhat similar to Psalm 55. 4–5, 'My heart is sore pained within me: and the terrors of death are fallen upon me. Fearfulness and trembling are come upon me, and horror hath overwhelmed me' (KJV).
[822] Somewhat similar to parts of Psalm 44. 13–15, 'Thou makest us a reproach to our neighbours, a scorn and a derision to them that are round about us. Thou makest us a byword among the heathen, a shaking of the head among the people. My confusion is continually before me, and the shame of my face hath covered me' (KJV).

during a period of disgrace after Carew was dismissed from the service of the Venetian Ambassador Dudley Carleton in 1616. John Kerrigan challenges this 'disgrace', however, noting both Carew's later employment in other positions of responsibility and Carleton's own instability. Carew's versions of Psalms 104 and 137 were published in 1655, unattributed, in *Psalms of a New Translation*, which also included Psalm 20 and parts of 66 and 111 from the translation by George Sandys. No music was included, and it may never have been composed; the intention of the little booklet was clearly political, a lament for the martyred Charles I. The title page announced that these were to be 'sung in verse and chorus of five parts, with symphonies of violins, organ, and other instruments', composed by Henry Lawes. See *The Poems of Thomas Carew with his Masque Coelum Britannicum*, ed. by Rhodes Dunlap (Oxford: Clarendon Press, 1964); John Kerrigan, 'Thomas Carew', *Proceedings of the British Academy*, 74 (1988), 311–50; Scott Nixon, *ODNB*.]

Psalm 51

1. Good God, unlock thy magazines   *stores (as of arms)*
   Of mercy, and forgive my sins.[823]

2. O, wash and purify the foul
   Pollution of my sin-stained soul.

5 3. For I confess my faults, that lie
   In horrid shapes before mine eye.

4. Against thee only and alone,
   In thy sight, was this evil done,
   That all men might thy justice see,
10   When thou art judged for judging me.

5. Even from my birth I did begin
   With mother's milk to suck in sin.

6. But thou lovest truth, and shalt impart
   Thy secret wisdom to my heart.

15 7. Thou shalt with hyssop purge me so
   Shall I seem white as mountain snow.

8. Thou shalt send joyful news, and then
   My broken bones grow strong again.

---

[823] Carew may be either borrowing from or alluding to Mary Sidney's Psalm 51, verse 15 of which begins, 'Unlock my lips, shut up with sinful shame'.

	9.	Let not thine eyes my sins survey;	
20		But cast those cancelled debts away.[824]	
	10.	O, make my cleansed heart a pure cell,	*small room*
		Where a renewèd spirit may dwell.[825]	
	11.	Cast me not from thy sight, not chase	
		Away from me thy Spirit of grace.	
25	12.	Send me thy saving health again,	
		And with thy Spirit those joys maintain.	
	13.	Then will I preach thy ways, and draw	
		Converted sinners to thy law.	
	14.	O God, my God of health, unseal	
30	15.	My blood-shut lips,[826] and I'll reveal	
		What mercies in thy justice dwell,	
		And with loud voice thy praises tell.	
	16.	Could sacrifice have purged my vice,	
	17.	Lord, I had brought thee sacrifice;	
35		But though burnt offerings are refused,	
		Thou shalt accept the heart that's bruised:[827]	
		The humble soul, the spirit oppress'd,	
		Lord, such oblations please thee best.	*offerings*
	18.	Bless Zion, Lord! Repair with pity	
40		The ruins of thy holy city.	
	19.	Then will we holy dower present thee,	*dowry*
		And peace offerings that content thee;	
		And then thine altars shall be pressed	
		With many a sacrificèd beast.	

---

[824] cancelled debts] BCP 'misdeed'; Carew's 'cancelled debts' seem especially appropriate for a fashionable Caroline courtier.

[825] spirit] Here, and in the next two verses, pronounced as a monosyllable.

[826] A strikingly original image, extended beyond the Psalm's simple 'lips'. Are the lips tainted with blood (from the 'bloodguiltiness', Coverdale's term, of v. 14?), or is this a reference to slander, always a danger at court?

[827] bruised] Possibly a bilingual pun, since 'contrite' (the adjective typically modifying 'heart' in English translations) derives from Latin, *contritus*, 'bruised'.

Psalm 91[828]

1,2,3.	Make the great God thy fort, and dwell	
	In him by faith, and do not care	
	(So shaded) for the fires of hell,	
	Or for the cunning fowler's snare,	*bird-catcher*
	Or poison of th'infernal air.	

4,5.   His plumes shall make a downy bed
        Where thou shalt rest: he shall display
        His wings of truth over thy head,
            Which (like a shield) shall drive away
            The fears of night, the darts of day.

6,7.   The wingèd plague, that flies by night,
        The murdering sword, that kills by day,
        Shall not thy quiet peace affright,
            Though on the right-, and left-hand they
            A thousand, and ten-thousand slay.

8,9,10.   Only thine eyes shall see the fall
        Of sinners: but, because thy heart
        Dwells with the Lord, not one of all
            These ills, nor yet the plaguey dart
            Shall dare approach near where thou art.

11,12,13.   His angels shall direct thy legs,
        And guard them in the stony streets:
        On lions' whelps and adders' eggs
            Thy steps shall march: and if they meet
            With dragons,[829] they shall kiss thy feet.

14,15,16.   When thou art troubled, he will hear
        And help thee, for thy love embraced
        And knew his name; therefore he'll rear
            Thy honours high, and, when thou hast
            Enjoyed them long, save thee at last.

---

[828] Both Psalms 91 and 137 use a tetrameter stanza rhymed *ababb*, but the rhythmic treatment of their lines is quite different. Carew's 91 is generally iambic, though he sometimes (as in line 1) begins with a strong stress, and the frequent enjambment, combined with caesurae at different points, works to break the integrity of the line (punctuated by rhyme) in favour of the structure of the syntax. The effect is something closer to ordinary speech than the more regular metre of Psalm 137, in which the integrity of the line is generally maintained.

[829] dragons] See note 702, p. 387.

Psalm 137[830]

1. Sitting by the streams that glide
    Down by Babel's tow'ring wall,[831]   *Babylon's*
  With our tears we filled the tide
    Whilst our mindful thoughts recall
5   Thee, O Zion, and thy fall.

2. Our neglected harps unstrung,
    Not acquainted with the hand
  Of the skilful tuner, hung
    On the willow trees that stand
10   Planted in the neighbour land.

3. Yet the spiteful foe commands
    Songs of mirth, and bids us lay
  To dumb harps, our captive hands,
    And (to scoff our sorrows) say
15   Sing us some sweet Hebrew lay.   *song*

4. But, say we, our holy strain   *melody*
    Is too pure for heathen land,
  Nor may we God's hymns profane,
    Or move either voice or hand
20   To delight a savage band.   *company*

5. Holy Salem, if thy love
    Fall from my forgetful heart,
  May the skill by which I move
    Strings of music tuned with art
25   From my withered hand depart![832]

6. May my speechless tongue give sound
    To no accents, but remain

---

[830] Carew uses the same stanza as in Psalm 91, but in this case consistently beginning on a stressed syllable, the metre technically a tailless (missing a final unstressed syllable) trochaic tetrameter. Trochaic metres are relatively uncommon in English poetry, though they are among the many used in the Sidney Psalms (38, 42, 43, 71, 85, 93, 119, 129, 149).

[831] Carew's use of enjambment is especially skilful, enacting the gliding in this stanza, the hanging harps in the next, and the possibility of falling love in stanza five.

[832] Carew's addition of the heart (the Psalmist prays simply, 'if I forget thee') may be due to the familiar Latin pun on heart (*cor*) and strings (*chorda*), here only implicit for the knowledgeable reader. The rhyme of 'heart' and 'art' may also be a perfect one, depending upon whether Carew (like so many English of the period) dropped the letter h. A similar argument has been suggested, for instance, in the last line of the first poem in *Astrophil and Stella*, where the Muse tells the poet, 'look in thy heart and write'.

>   To my prison roof fast bound,
>   If my sad soul entertain
> 30   Mirth, till thou rejoice again!
>
> 7. In that day, remember, Lord,
>   Edom's brood, that in our groans
>   They triumph; with fire and sword
>   Burn their city, heap their bones
> 35   And make all one heap of stones.
>
> 8. Cruel Babel, thou shalt feel
>   The revenger of our groans,
>   When the happy victor's steel
>   As thine, ours, shall hew thy bones,
> 40   And make thee one heap of stones.
>
> 9. Men shall bless the hand that tears
>   From the mother's soft embraces
>   Sucking infants, and besmears
>   With their brains, the rugged faces
> 45   Of the rocks and stony places.

100. John Milton, *Poems of Mr. John Milton, Both English and Latin* (1645, composed 1623)

[John Milton (1608–1674) is generally acknowledged as one of the greatest poets in the English language, author of *Paradise Lost*, *Paradise Regained*, *Samson Agonistes*, *Lycidas*, and other shorter poems. He also wrote a considerable amount of controversial prose, both in English and Latin, especially during the 1650s and 1660s when he was active in politics during the Civil War and Interregnum. From 1649 to 1660 Milton was Secretary for Foreign Tongues for the Puritan Commonwealth. He was born in London to John Milton, Sr, a scrivener by profession and an active composer, and Sara Jeffrey. He had private tutors at home, but attended St Paul's School from perhaps 1620 and then was admitted to Christ's College, Cambridge, in 1625, where he graduated both BA and MA, demonstrating his considerable ability in Latin and Greek. Milton was preoccupied with the Psalms all his life. His father composed several settings for Thomas Ravenscroft's *The Whole Book of Psalms* (1621), a popular edition of the Sternhold and Hopkins psalter with musical settings for domestic singing. It is reasonable to think that the Psalms may have been sung in the Milton home in Bread Street during the poet's early childhood. Milton's Psalms 114 and 136 may be his earliest exercises in poetry. They were printed in his first published collection in 1645, but identified as having been written when the author was fifteen years old. Milton's 1673 *Poems* included two further sets of metrical

Psalms, one (Psalms 80–88) in the Sternhold-Hopkins style, dated 1648, and the other (Psalms 1–8) in the Sidneian mode, dated 1653. Even *Paradise Lost* has been argued to be suffused with the Psalms. The iambic pentameter couplets of Milton's Psalm 114 distinguish it from any of the metres popular for singing Psalms, and the references to Terah and 'Pharian fields' show off his precocious learning. An even greater bravura performance is his translation of this same Psalm 114 into Homeric Greek, not published during his lifetime but sent to his friend Alexander Gill in 1634. Milton's Psalm 136 became popular as a church hymn and continues to be sung in churches to various tunes, including *Monkland* by John Antes (1790), harmonized by John Bernard Wilkes. See Ernest Brenneke, *John Milton the Elder and his Music* (New York: Columbia University Press, 1938); Mary Ann Radzinowicz, *Milton's Epics and the Book of Psalms* (Princeton: Princeton University Press, 1989); Gordon Campbell, ODNB.]

Psalm 114

A Paraphrase on Psalm 114

This and the following Psalm were done by the author at fifteen years old.

When the blest seed of Terah's faithful son,[833]	*descendants*
After long toil their liberty had won,	
And past from Pharian fields to Canaan Land,[834]	
Led by the strength of the Almighty's hand,	
5 Jehovah's wonders were in Israel shown,	
His praise and glory was in Israel known.	
That saw the troubl'd sea, and shivering fled,	
And sought to hide his froth-becurlèd head	
Low in the earth, Jordan's clear streams recoil,	
10 As a faint host that hath received the foil.	*defeat*
The high, huge-bellied mountains skip like rams	
Amongst their ewes, the little hills like lambs.	
Why fled the ocean? And why skipped the mountains?	
Why turnèd Jordan toward his crystal fountains?	
15 Shake earth, and at the presence be aghast	
Of him that ever was, and aye shall last,	*forever*
That glassy floods from rugged rocks can crush,	
And make soft rills from the fiery flintstones gush.	*brooks*

---

[833] Terah's faithful son] i.e. Abraham. See Genesis 11.
[834] Pharian fields] i.e. Egypt. Pharos, not mentioned in the Bible, is an island off Alexandria where the famous lighthouse stood, one of the wonders of the ancient world. The youthful Milton is showing off his learning.

Psalm 136

Let us with a gladsome mind
Praise the Lord, for he is kind,
   For his mercies aye endure,   *always*
   Ever faithful, ever sure.

5 Let us blaze his name abroad,
For of gods he is the God;
   For, &c.

O let us his praises tell,
That doth the wrathful tyrants quell.
10   For, &c.

That with his miracles doth make
Amazèd heav'n and earth to shake.
   For, &c.

That by his wisdom did create
15 The painted heav'ns so full of state.
   For his, &c.

That did the solid earth ordain
To rise above the wat'ry plain.
   For his, &c.

20 That by his all-commanding might,
Did fill the new-made world with light.
   For his, &c.

And caus'd the golden-tressèd sun,
All the day long his course to run.
25   For his, &c.

The hornèd moon to shine by night,
Amongst her spangled sisters bright.
   For his, &c.

He with his thunder-clasping hand,
30 Smote the first-born of Egypt Land.
   For his, &c.

And in despite of Pharaoh fell,   *defiance*
He brought from thence his Israel.
   For, &c.

35 The ruddy waves he cleft in twain,	*two*
Of the Erythræan main.[835]	*Red Sea*
For, &c.	

    The floods stood still like walls of glass,
    While the Hebrew bands did pass.   *companies*
40   For, &c.

    But full soon they did devour
    The tawny king with all his power.
        For, &c.

    His chosen people he did bless
45   In the wasteful wilderness.   *desolate*
        For, &c.

    In bloody battle he brought down
    Kings of prowess and renown.
        For, &c.

50   He foiled bold Seon and his host,
    That ruled the Amorrean coast.
        For, &c.

    And large-limbed Og he did subdue,
    With all his over hardy crew.
55   For, &c.

    And to his servant Israel,
    He gave their land therein to dwell.
        For, &c.

    He hath with a piteous eye
60   Beheld us in our misery.
        For, &c.

    And freed us from the slavery
    Of the invading enemy.
        For, &c.

65   All living creatures he doth feed,
    And with full hand supplies their need.
        For, &c.

    Let us therefore warble forth
    His mighty majesty and worth.
70   For, &c.

---

[835] Erythræan] Ancient name for the Red Sea, after a legendary King Erythras.

That his mansion hath on high
Above the reach of mortal eye.
   For his mercies ay endure,
   Ever faithful, ever sure.

101. Sir John Davies, *The Psalms Translated into Verse* (MS 1624)

[Sir John Davies (bap. 1569–d. 1626) was educated at Winchester, Queen's College, Oxford, and Middle Temple. In 1598, Davies entered Middle Temple Hall with two swordsmen and beat Richard Martin, who had insulted him. For this, he was expelled, disgraced, and briefly imprisoned. After several years, and at the urging of Sir Thomas Egerton, Lord Keeper, the Temple readmitted Davies, and he prospered due to the support of other powerful patrons, most notably Queen Elizabeth, of whom Davies was a favourite. James I admired Davies too, and appointed him solicitor-general for Ireland. He was elected speaker of the Irish Parliament and was later elected MP in England. Davies was appointed chief justice of the king's bench by Charles I in 1626. He was also a respected poet, author of the influential *Nosce Teipsum* (c. 1594), about the immortality of the soul, *Hymns of Astrea*, dedicated to Elizabeth I, and *Orchestra, or, A Poem of Dancing* (1596), as well as other shorter works. A serious antiquary, Davies worked with Sir Robert Cotton and others in the early seventeenth century to re-establish the Society of Antiquaries. He married Eleanor Touchet, a prolific author and self-styled prophetess. Madness, or at least unorthodox behaviour, ran in the Touchet family: Eleanor's brother, Mervyn, the second Earl of Castlehaven, was executed for rape and sodomy after one of the most scandalous trials of the period. Davies wrote 56 metrical Psalms, including 1–50 as well as 67, 91, 95, 100, 103, and 150. The Psalms survive in a single manuscript that belonged to Davies's daughter Lucy, presumably copied from his own papers. Lucy Davies married Ferdinando Hastings, sixth Earl of Huntingdon, at the age of eleven. See Robert Krueger and Ruby Nemser, 'Introduction', to *The Poems of Sir John Davies*, ed. by Krueger (Oxford: Clarendon Press, 1975); Sean Kelsey, *ODNB*.]

Psalm 10[836]

Why standest thou, O Lord, so far away,
And hid'st thy face when troubles me dismay?
The wicked for his lust the poor man spoils;   *passions*
Lord, take him in the trap of his own wiles: *deceits*
5 He makes his boasts of his profane desires,

---

[836] In the Septuagint, and the Catholic and Eastern Orthodox traditions deriving from it, this Psalm is combined with Psalm 9. In the Hebrew, the two are linked formally by an alphabetical acrostic.

Condemning God while he himself admires;
He is so proud that God he sets at nought; *nothing*
Nay, rather God comes never in his thought.
Thy judgements, Lord, are far above his sight;
10 This makes him to esteem his foes so light,
And in his heart to say, I cannot fall,
Nor can misfortune light on me at all.
His mouth is full of execrations vile;
Under his tongue doth sit ungodly guile.
15 Close in the corners of the ways he lies, *secret*
And lurks and waits, the simple to surprise.
Even as a lion lurking in his den
T' assault and murder innocent poor men;
'Gainst whom his eyes maliciously are set,
20 To catch them when they fall into his net.
Himself he humbles, bows, and crouching stands,
Till poor men fall into his powerful hands;
Then in his heart he saith God hath forgot,
He turns away his face and sees it not.
25 Arise, O Lord, and lift thy hand on high!
The poor forget not, which oppressèd lie.
For why should wicked men blaspheme thee thus:
Tush, God is careless, and regards not us.
Surely thou seest the wrong which they have done,
30 And all oppressions underneath the sun;
To thee alone the poor his cause commends
As th' only friend of him that wanteth friends.
Lord, break the power of malicious mind,
Take ill away, and thou no ill shall find. *evil*
35 The Lord is King and doth forever reign;
Nor miscreants shall within his land remain.
He hearkeneth to the poor, but first prepareth
Their hearts to pray, then their petition heareth;
That he poor orphans may both help and save,
40 That worldly men on them no power may have.

Psalm 28

Hear (Lord my strength) the cries I make to thee;
I am but dead if thou seem deaf to me.
Hear, when with humble prayer I thee entreat,
With lifted hands before thy mercy seat,
5 But rank me not with those which wicked are,

    Whose lips speak peace, whose hearts are full of war.
    According to their actions, let them speed,
    And as their merit is, so make their meed.   *recompense*
    For that they see thy works, and yet neglect them,
10 Thou shalt destroy and never more erect them.
    The Lord be praised, who hath vouchsafed to hear,   *deigned*
    And lend unto my prayer a gracious ear.
    His shield protects, his strength doth me advance;
    My tongue shall sing his praise, my heart shall dance.
15 He to his servants force and virtue gives,
    Through him, in safety, his anointed lives.
    Save thy peculiar people, Lord, and bless them,   *chosen*
    And lift their heads above them that oppress them.

Psalm 35

    Plead thou my cause, O Lord my advocate![837]
    Against all those with whom I have debate;
    Fight against them that do against me fight,
    Take up thy shield, and help me with thy might;
5 Lift up thy lance, stop them which me pursue,
    Say to my soul, I am thy Saviour true;[838]
    Let shame on them which seek my ruin light,
    And with confusion turn them all to flight.
    Let them be like the dust before the wind,
10 With God's fierce angel following them behind;
    Set them in slippery ways, and dark withal,   *as well*
    And let God's angel smite them as they fall;
    For they have spread a net and digged a pit,
    Even without cause to catch my soul in it:
15 But in that pit let them fall unawares,
    And be entangled in their proper snares;   *own*
    But thou my soul, who God thus guides from ill,
    Rejoice in him, and his salvation still;
    My bones shall say, Lord who is like to thee?
20 Who poor weak men from their strong foe dost free:
    False witnesses arose with oaths untrue,
    And chargèd me with things I never knew;
    They to my grief did ill for good requite,   *evil*

---

[837] By calling God his advocate and describing the conflict as a debate, Davies takes the Psalmist's opening 'Plead my cause' (BCP) fully into the courtroom with which he was so familiar.

[838] An obvious Christianizing. KJV has simply 'thy salvation'.

	And recompensed my kindness with despite;	*contempt*
25	Yet in their sickness I did sackcloth wear,	
	And fast and pray with many a secret tear;	
	I could not more for friend or brother mourn,	
	Or if my other to her grave were borne:	
	But in my woe they made great mirth and glee,	
30	The very abjects mocked and mowed at me;	*wretched, grimaced*
	Base flatterers and jesters came withal,	*likewise*
	And gnashed their teeth to show their bitter gall.	*bile*
	How long shall this be Lord? My soul withdraw	
	From these men's wrongs, and from the lion's jaw:	
35	So in thy church[839] shall I my thanks proclaim,	
	And in our great assembly praise thy name;	
	Let not my foes triumph on me again,	
	Nor with their mocking eyes show their disdain;	
	They meet and part, but peace they do not seek	
40	But to supplant the peaceable and meek;	
	They gape and draw their mouths in scornful wise	*manner*
	And cry, fie, fie, we saw it with our eyes.	
	But thou their deed (O Lord!) dost also see;	
	Then be not silent so, nor far from me.	
45	Awake, stand up, O God and Lord of might,	
	Avenge my quarrel, judge my cause aright;	*justly*
	To thy doom rather let me fall or stand	*judgment*
	Than subject be to their insulting hand;	
	Then they should say, so, so, these things go right,	
50	We have our will, and have devour'd him quite.	
	Shame be to them that joy in my mischance,	
	And which to cast me down themselves advance;	
	Let them be glad that my wellwishers be	
	And bless the Lord that hath so blessèd me.	
55	As for my tongue it shall set forth thy praise,	
	And celebrate thy justice all my days.	

---

[839] church] The Hebrew (*qahel*) designates merely an assembly. Other translations have 'congregation' (BCP, Geneva, KJV), but Davies's choice has the Psalmist proclaiming in a specifically Christian institution like the Church of England. Tyndale and Sir Thomas More argued about a similar translation issue involving the Greek *ekklesia*, whether it should be rendered 'congregation' (Tyndale) or 'church' (More), the latter designating the institution and the former perhaps just a gathering.

Psalm 42

As for the streams the hunted hart doth bray,   *cry*
So for God's grace my heart doth pant and pray.
My soul doth thirst (O God of life!) for thee;
When shall I come thy blessèd face to see?
5 My tears are all my food both night and day,
While, where is now thy God? the wicked say.
I pourèd out my heart, while thus I thought
And to God's house the multitude I brought:
With songs of praise and thankfulness withal,   *as well*
10 To celebrate the Lord's great festival:
Then why art thou my soul so full of woe,
Unquiet in thyself and vexèd so?
O put thy trust in God and thankful be,
For his sweet help his presence yields to thee.
15 My soul is griev'd remembering all the ill
I felt in Jordan's vale and Hermon hill.   *valley*
One depth of sorrow doth to another call,
Thy waves, O God, have overgone me all:
I prais'd at night God's bounty of the day,
20 And unto him that gives me life did pray.
God of my strength, why hast thou left me so,
With heavy heart oppressèd by my foe?
My foe doth cut my bones as with a sword,
While he in scorn repeats this bitter word,
25 Where is thy God? his speech to me is such:
Where is thy God, of which thou talk's so much?[840]
But why art thou my soul dejected so?
Why art thou troubled and so full of woe?
Trust thou in God, and give him thankful praise
30 Who is thy present help in all thy ways.

Psalm 44

Lord! of thy works, our fathers have us told,
Some in their days, and former times of old;[841]
How thou hast rooted out the pagan race,
And thy choice people planted in their place:
5 Who did not with their own sword win the land,

---

[840] The rhetorical repetition is added by Davies.
[841] As the plural pronoun signals, this Psalm is a collective complaint, contrasting past and present conditions in the way of many other Psalms.

JOHN DAVIES

    Nor make the conquest with their proper hand;   *own*
    But by thine arm, thy favour and thy grace,
    Thy countenance and brightness of thy face;
    Thou art my King, O God, and royal guide,
10 And thou for Jacob's safety dost provide.
    We, through thine aid, our foes do boldly meet,
    And by thy virtue cast them at our feet;
    Therefore, my trust I place not in my bow,
    Nor in my sword, to save me from my foe.
15 Thou only sav'st us from our enemies,   *alone*
    Confounding them that do against us rise.   *defeating*
    We boast and glory in our strength, therefore,
    And to thy name sing praises evermore;
    But now thou standest off and leav'st us quite,
20 And dost not lead our armies out to fight;
    Thou mak'st us fly before our foes with fear,
    While they from us rich spoils away do bear;
    Like sheep, to feed them thy poor flock is given,
    Or scattered into several nations driven.
25 Thine own dear people thou dost sell for naught,
    And sets on them no price when they are bought;
    Thou hast us made unto our neighbours all,
    An object of reproach and scorn withal: *as well*
    To nations which do worship idols dumb,[842]
30 We are a byword of contempt become;
    All the day long my shame is in my sight,
    Which makes me hide my face and shun the light,
    Not able to endure the blasphemies
    And scorns of my revengeful enemies.
35 For all these ills we do not thee forget,
    Thy blessèd covenant we renounce not yet.
    Our hearts recede not from the law divine,
    Nor do our footsteps from thy paths decline;
    Though we in dens of dragons have been placed,
40 And with death's fearful shadows overcast.
    If we the name of our true God forget,
    And idols false we in his place do set,[843]

---

[842] The idolatry is Davies's addition, perhaps thinking of Continental Catholic nations that scorn Protestant England.
[843] Davies renders what the KJV translates as 'a strange god' as false idols, and he inserts them earlier in the Psalm too, elaborating 'heathen' (BCP, KJV) as 'nations which do worship idols dumb'. There is frequent condemnation of idol worship in the Old Testament, but

Shall not he search it out, whose eye doth see
The heart of man, whose thoughts most troubled be?
45 But for thy cause, Lord, we are martyred still,
Like sheep which slaughter-men cull out to kill.
Up Lord! why dost thou seem to slumber thus?
Awake, and be not always far from us:
Why hidest thou from us thy blessèd face,
50 Forgetting our distress and wretched case?
Our souls even to the dust are humbled low,
Our prostrate bodies to the ground do grow.
Arise and help us, Lord! defend us still,
And save us for thy mercy's sake from ill.   *evil*

102. Sir Robert Ker, *Psalms in English Verses, to the Measures of the French and the Dutch* (MS 1624)

[Sir Robert Ker (1578–1654), eventually first Earl of Ancram, was groom of the bedchamber to Prince Henry and Princess Elizabeth, and became a member of James's privy chamber and captain of the king's guard in Scotland. After the death of Prince Henry, Ker became a gentleman of the bedchamber to Prince Charles. Some of Ker's Psalms, including two chosen here, are English versions of the Latin paraphrases of George Buchanan. Buchanan (1506–1582), renowned Scottish humanist scholar, political theorist and historian, tutor of Mary Queen of Scots and her son James the VI (the future James I) and teacher (at a school in France) of Montaigne, was one of the greatest Renaissance neo-Latin poets. In addition to a large body of poems in various genres, he wrote Latin verse tragedies on biblical topics, and his Latin Psalms were read and admired across Europe. According to Buchanan's autobiography, most of his Psalms were written from 1550 to 1552 while he was in confinement in Portugal. Ker's English Psalm 37 was written in Spain, where he had gone to join Prince Charles and the Duke of Buckingham in their controversial (and unsuccessful) mission to woo the Spanish infanta, Maria Anna. Ker's career prospered during the reign of Charles I, but after the king's defeat and execution his fortunes turned and he went into exile in the Netherlands, where he died in debt. Ker wrote little himself but had connections with a number of major poets, including John Donne, William Drummond of Hawthornden, and Samuel Daniel. His Psalm translations were inspired by hearing Psalms sung in French and Dutch. He lamented that 'the Reformed Church' was fractured, separated by language through 'the curse which [God] inflicted on mankind at Babel', and he hoped

---

Davies may have in mind the idolatry of contemporary Catholicism. As solicitor-general for Ireland, for instance, he advocated the expulsion of Catholic priests and complained that even the Irish Protestant clergy were 'meer idols and cyphers'.

[they might worship God 'with one heart and voice [...] howsoever they differed in speech'. Ker dedicates the manuscript to his son William, first Earl of Lothian, for whom it was obviously prepared. See David Stevenson, *ODNB*.]

Psalm 37[844]

This he turned when he was in Spain, with the Prince, 1623.   *fashioned*

Vex not thy heart to see the wicked thrive,
Nor envy their unsatisfying wealth;
In those vain worldly things there is no health,
They cannot keep men happy nor alive;
5   Their false felicity doth soon decay,
    Like grass cut down soon withered into hay.

Trust thou in God, to do well give thy mind,
And thou shalt have the land for to possess,
And that which best is for thee more or less;
10 Delight thyself in him, and thou shalt find
    That he will give thee thy full heart's desire,
    And greater blessings than thou canst require.

Thy honour, life, affairs to him commit,
And do not doubt but he will do the best,
15 And will thy virtue also manifest;
And what thou hast done well, the least of it
    He will make evident in all men's sight;
    The sun at noonday shall not shine more bright.

Leave all to God, and do not fret nor fume,   *worry*
20 Nor grudge at all for their prosperity,   *grumble*
Who do all evil with such dexterity,
That on the success thereof they presume,
    Lest thou be tempted to commit the like,
    And so with them be whipped when God doth strike.

25 For sure God's judgments shall on evil men fall,[845]
To cut them off, when they are most secure;
When good men shall have peace, which shall endure,
And shall possess the land in sight of all;
    But godless men shall so be overthrown,
30   That where they dwelt the place shall scarce be known.

---

[844] In the Hebrew, this Psalm is an alphabetical acrostic.
[845] evil] The metre requires pronunciation as a monosyllable, a relatively common occurrence in English poetry (as later in this Psalm). Readers might have rendered it something like 'ill'.

>   And yet they practice still against the just,
>   And in their foolish spite they gnash their teeth;
>   But God doth laugh at them, for well he seeth
>   Their day at hand in which they answer must,
> 35   Though they had drawn their sword, their bow had bent
>   For to destroy the poor and innocent.
>
>   Their sword shall enter in their own proud heart;
>   The bow wherein they trust shall broken be.
>   This good they reap of such vain things we see.
> 40   The godly therefore have the better part;
>   For better is their little well-got store   *sufficient supply*
>   Than all the wicked's wealth, though far much more.
>
>   For of the wicked man the arm and strength
>   Shall be enfeebled; but the Lord of might
> 45   Hath his own children always in his sight,
>   And will them free from all their fears at length,
>   And from all perils will them sure deliver,
>   And their inheritance shall last forever.
>
>   When evil days come they shall not fear nor blush,
> 50   And in the sorest famine shall he be fed,
>   When wicked men shall starve for lack of bread,
>   And all his enemies the Lord will crush;
>   For as the fate of lambs they shall decay,
>   And like to smoke so shall they pass away.[846]
>
> 55   The wicked borrows, but he never pays;
>   But godly men do always mercy show,
>   Lending to poor men, paying what they owe;
>   And in such blessèd actions spend their days.
>   So in the land all see that they endure;
> 60   But they whom God doth hate have no thing sure.
>
>   A good man's steps are ordered from above,
>   For God almighty doth direct his way,
>   And sets him right if he do chance to stray;
>   And so delights in him whom he doth love,
> 65   That if he slide he holds him by the arm,
>   And though he fall he can receive no harm.

---

[846] Ker somewhat obscures the connection between these last two lines, the smoke being caused by the burning 'fat of lambs' (KJV), not their 'fate' (clearly the word in his manuscript), except in a more general sense.

I have been young, and now am very old,[847]
Yet never saw the just man's seed so poor
That they did beg their bread from door to door;
70 Nor in my life I never heard it told.
    As they are merciful and freely lend,
    So God provides enough for them to spend.

Depart from evil and do the good ye can,
And ye shall dwell forever in the land;
75 For God, that hath all power in his hand,
Never forsakes the just and upright man.
    But they that wicked be in word and deed
    Shall surely be cut off, they and their seed.   *descendants*

But sure the righteous shall possess the land,
80 And their posterity shall still enjoy it;
God will provide that nothing shall destroy it;
They are defended by his mighty hand;
    Their heart is wise, their mouth the same declares,
    They speak of judgement and of great affairs.

85 The law of God is in a good man's heart,
And all his steps are measured by his will;
The wicked watcheth how he may him kill,
But he is safe, for God doth take his part,
    Who will not leave him in his cruel hand,
90   But brings him off if he in judgement stand.

Wait on the Lord, and strictly keep his way,
And he shall honour thee and all thy race,[848]   *posterity*
And thou shalt have a lasting dwelling-place,
When wicked men shall utterly decay;
95   For certainly God will destroy them all,
    And with thine eyes thou shalt behold their fall.

An ill man I have seen exceeding great,   *evil*
Glorious and spread like to a fair bay tree,
Yet all could not avail, for all did see   *help*
100 That God his might and pride did so defate,   *defeat*
    And root him out from off the earth so clean,   *completely*
    That not a sign remain'd where he had been.

---

[847] A self-description highly unusual in the Psalms, more familiar from Ecclesiastes, where the character of the preacher-narrator is more fully developed. Ker, as he was writing, was 45, hardly old, but then not young by seventeenth-century standards.

[848] race] Ker's addition, which did not have its modern meaning (which developed in the eighteenth century) but more commonly meant family or nation.

    Then mark them that are perfect in their ways,
    In whatsoever trouble they do fall,
105 The Lord in end doth free them from them all,
    So that in peace and rest they end their days;
        And though the wicked lived in wealth and joy,
        Yet at the last the Lord doth them destroy.

    But the salvation of the upright man
110 Is of the Lord, he is his strength and stay;   *support*
    So no adversity can him dismay,
    Not proud men's practices, do what they can.
        Who put their trust in God omnipotent,
        Against all dangers may be confident.

Psalm 62

Out of Buchanan, to the measure of the French tune.[849]

    My soul on God doth wholly rest,
    In all my straits he is my hope;
    How can I fear to be oppressed,
    That am sustained by such a prop?[850]
5   Yet why are wicked men so bent
        To overthrow the innocent?

    Whilst their own ruin is at hand,
    Even at the very point to fall,
    And certainly they cannot stand
10 More than a rotting tottering wall;
        Yet all their might they do employ
        How they the righteous may destroy.

    When in their hearts they would devour,
    With their false tongues they soothe and praise;
15 But thou, my soul, never give o'er
    To cleave to God in all thy ways;
        Trusting to him thou canst not fail
        When force or fraud doth thee assail.

    My hope of life on him depends;
20 He is my glory, strength, and health;[851]

---

[849] Buchanan's Latin version is in iambic strophes, formally nothing like Ker's English stanzas.
[850] prop] 'rock' in KJV; Buchanan has *munimine*, 'fortress' or 'defense'.
[851] Verses 5–6 of the Psalm virtually repeat verses 1–2, in KJV as in Buchanan's Latin, though not in Ker.

To him I do commit my ends,
My house, my children, and my wealth.
    O man, whatever come to thee,
    Do thus, if thou would happy be.

25 All grief and sadness of thy mind
Bring unto God, for to be eased;
Nor let contentment make thee blind,
But thank him still when thou art pleased;
    And whatsoe'er thou goest about,
30   Think he dost guide thee in and out.

Trust not the frothy might of kings,   *unsubstantial*
Who are but sons of mortal men;
Princes are frail as frailest things,
They die, they know not how, nor when;
35   They weigh their fame with vanity,   *emptiness*
    And it is full as light we see.[852]   *frivolous*

On goods ill got, nor foolish strength,
Do not rely; wealth melts away,
And all thy body's force at length
40 Sickness or age will make decay.
    Though wealth well got flow ne'er so fast,
    Yet thou must leave it at the last.

But mark what God himself doth say,
Yea, more than once so seriously,
45 That he alone all things doth sway,   *govern*
Even as he will imperiously.
    Unto the good a friend most kind,
    Foe to the bad and ill inclined.

---

[852] A remarkable stanza for Ker to have written, neither kings nor princes being part of the original Psalm, which has simply 'children of men' (BCP; the KJV has 'men of low degree' and 'men of high degree', but there is no such distinction in the Hebrew). Even if this was not written (like Psalm 37) in Spain, with Prince Charles alongside him, Ker's status at court and in society depended entirely on King James and later King Charles. Furthermore, Ker gained his position largely through the influence of his cousin, also Robert (Kerr or Carr), James's favourite and perhaps lover. It is perhaps no wonder Ker's Psalms remained in manuscript. Ker follows Buchanan's version, 'The boasted power of kings and princes is vainer than vanity', no doubt reflecting his bitterness in being imprisoned by King João III. (Translation by Dana Sutton, *The Philological Museum*, posted 2007, revised 2017 <http://www.philological.bham.ac.uk/buchpsalms/> [accessed 24 May 2022].)

Psalm 145

Out of Buchanan, to the measure of the French tune; or to the tune of the 49 Psalm, or the 104.[853]

So long I will thee praise, my Lord and King,
As sun and moon be in the firmament;
And unto thee, my God, alone I'll sing,
Each day, each night, each hour, shall hear me vent
5   Thy lauds, who art the health of everything;   *praises*
  Wise, just, and merciful, omnipotent,
     All ages will thy glorious works rehearse,   *recite*
     Thy praise shall be the anthem of my verse.

Our long-lived fathers, and their short-lived breed,
10 With one accord thy attributes will show;
This man will call thee great, that just and good,
To pardon easy, and to anger slow;
Thy righteousness they all will sing aloud,
Old, young, rich, poor, strong, feeble, high, and low.[854]
15   But most of thy great clemency will tell
     For merciful doth all thy names excel.

Heav'ns starry frame,[855] and all that it contains,
Thy wisdom and thy strength do clearly preach;
And they whose life no foul corruption stains,
20 Thy saints shall bless thee, and all mankind teach
How large thy empire is,[856] whose mighty reins   *power (fig.)*
To east and west, and south and north, do reach;
     Thy sceptre from all laws of time is free,
     Thy kingdom lasts to all eternity.

25 When wrong or weakness makes us slip or fall,
Thou keep'st us firm, or takes us up again.

---

[853] As in the previous Psalm, Ker does not attempt to imitate Buchanan's form, a three-line stanza consisting of a dactylic hexameter, a dactylic dimeter, and an iambic dimeter.

[854] The line shows a flair beyond much of Ker's writing. The sequence of adjectives without conjunctions (the figure is asyndeton) save for the last is similar to Milton's famous line in *Paradise Lost* describing rebel angels travelling through hell, over 'Rocks, caves, lakes, fens, bogs, dens, and shades of death' (II. 621). Ker plays with a similar technique in the penultimate stanza.

[855] Buchanan, *stellantis machina caeli*, 'the frame of the starry heaven' (Sutton). KJV has simply 'All thy works'.

[856] The expansion of 'kingdom' (KJV) to empire is Buchanan's (*imperium*). It may be worth noting that James I had strongly imperial ambitions; king of both England and Scotland, he proclaimed himself King of Great Britain in 1604.

All things that fly or swim, or walk or crawl,
In th'air, or water, wood, or hill, or plain,
Their eyes do wait on thee, thou fill'st them all,
30 And in due season dost their life maintain; *time*
    Such is thy care of those that in thee trust,
    Thy works all holy are, thy ways are just.

How readily thou lends a gracious ear
To all that humbly call upon thy name;
35 And those that worship thee in truth and fear
Thou certainly dost save, and so wilt blame
The wicked sort, whose roots thou wilt up-tear,
Defeat their purposes, turn them to shame;
    And therefore all the world doth ring of thee.
40   My mouth shall sing thy praise where'er I be.

103. Sir Francis Bacon, *The Translation of Certain Psalms into English Verse* (1625)

[Francis Bacon (1561–1626), one of the most famous men of Renaissance England, was the son of Sir Nicholas Bacon, counsellor to Elizabeth I. Educated at Trinity College, Cambridge, Bacon became a lawyer and, at the age of 20, an MP. His remarkable political career led to positions as Solicitor-General, Attorney-General, Lord Keeper, and finally Lord Chancellor. For his services he was made Baron Verulam and Viscount St Albans. His career ended in disgrace, however, in 1621: in debt and charged with corruption, Bacon was fined, briefly committed to the Tower, and barred from future office. Bacon was an important figure in the development of empirical science, author of, among other works, the *Novum Organum* (1620), part of a vast projected work, the *Instauratio Magna*, proposing a reformation of all knowledge, and the *Historia Naturalis et Experimentalis* (1622). Bacon was prolific in many fields, writing the influential educational treatise *The Advancement of Learning* (1605), the utopian *The New Atlantis* (1627), as well as religious meditations, and works of history, politics, and law. Perhaps most famously, in his *Essays*, published in numerous editions (1597, 1612, 1625), Bacon imported this genre, recently invented in French by Michel de Montaigne, into English. Bacon's metrical Psalms, written apparently after a period of serious illness, were dedicated to his 'very good friend' George Herbert, who at that time was a public orator and Member of Parliament, having not yet entered the diaconate, let alone the priesthood. That Bacon translates seven Psalms, after regaining his health, suggests that he conceived these on the model of the Penitential Psalms, even if the specific Psalms he chose were not the traditional seven. See Markku Peltonen, *ODNB*.]

Psalm 12

    Help, Lord, for godly men have took their flight,
    And left the earth to be the wicked's den:[857]
    Not one that standeth fast to truth and right,   *secure*
    But fears, or seeks to please, the eyes of men.
5 When one with other falls in talk apart,
    Their meaning goeth not with their words, in proof;[858]   *experience*
    But fair they flatter, with a cloven heart,[859]
    By pleasing words, to work their own behoof.   *benefit*

    But God cut off the lips, that are all set
10 To trap the harmless soul, that peace hath vowed;
    And pierce the tongues, that seek to counterfeit
    The confidence of truth, by lying loud:
    Yet so they think to reign, and work their will,
    By subtle speech, which enters everywhere:
15 And say, our tongues are ours, to help us still,
    What need we any higher power to fear?

    Now for the bitter sighing of the poor,
    The Lord hath said, I will no more forbear
    The wicked's kingdom to invade and scour,
20 And set at large the men restrained in fear.
    And sure, the word of God is pure, and fine,
    And in the trial never loseth weight;   *test*
    Like noble gold, which since it left the mine,
    Hath seven times passèd through the fiery strait.

25 And now thou wilt not first thy word forsake,
    Nor yet the righteous man, that leans thereto;
    But wilt his safe protection undertake,
    In spite of all their force and wiles can do.   *deceits*
    And time it is, O Lord, thou didst draw nigh,   *near*
30 The wicked daily do enlarge their bands;   *companies*

---

[857] Perhaps evoking the myth of Astraea, goddess of Justice, last immortal to leave the earth at the wicked Iron Age. The Psalmist says simply that the godly man 'ceaseth' (KJV).

[858] in proof] Bacon's addition, especially interesting (as also 'trial' below) given his commitment to scientific study, empirical research, and arguments based on experience.

[859] cloven heart] Bacon's adaptation of the Psalm's 'double heart', perhaps an inversion of the 'cloven tongues' of fire that descend upon the disciples in Acts 3, giving them the ability to preach the Word, whereas those of a cloven heart are hypocrites whose word cannot be trusted. The Devil also traditionally has a cloven foot, or 'hoof,' which may be subtly implied by the surrounding rhymes, 'proof' and 'behoof', the latter actually containing the implied word.

And that, which makes them follow ill a vie,   *evil, life*
Rule is betaken to unworthy hands.⁸⁶⁰   *entrusted*

Psalm 126

When God returned us graciously
   Unto our native land,
We seemed as in a dream to be
   And in a maze to stand.

5 The heathen likewise, they could say,
   The God, that these men serve,
Hath done great things for them this day,
   Their nation to preserve.

Tis true, God hath poured out his grace
10   On us abundantly,
For which we yield him Psalms, and praise,
   And thanks, with jubilee.   *rejoicing*

O Lord, turn our captivity,
   As winds that blow at south,
15 Do pour the tides with violence
   Back to the river's mouth.

Who sows in tears, shall reap in joy,
   The Lord doth so ordain:
So that his seed be pure and good,
20   His harvest shall be gain.

104. Anon., *One and Forty Divine Odes Englished, Set to King David's Harp by S.P.L.* (1627)

[The identity of 'S.P.L.' remains unknown. STC and EEBO identify him, without supporting evidence, as Sir James Sempill (1566?–1626), a courtier close to King James VI and I, both in Scotland (where Sempill was born) and later in England. Sempill assisted James in preparing *Basilikon Doron* (1599), and James presented him with a jewel formerly belonging to Mary, Queen of Scots, of whom both Sempill's parents were favourites. Sempill was educated by George Buchanan together with the young King James, which may be significant for the attribution of the *Divine Odes*. The volume has a second title page, *An Assay, or Buchanan his Paraphrase on the First Twenty Psalms of David Translated* (also

---

⁸⁶⁰ Bacon's addition of 'rule' makes it hard not to think of the monarch (the Psalmist says more generally that 'the vile are exalted', in the KJV), though Bacon still had King James's favour in 1615 and was raised to the peerage a few years later.

1627, though naming a different printer). Sempill wrote polemical prose works but also poetry, translating from the Dutch an anti-Catholic poem, *The Pack-Mans Pater Noster* (1624), which proved popular. An 'S.P.L.' is mentioned several times, not further identified, by Daniel Featley as a go-between carrying letters to and from him and the Jesuit Priest Thomas Everard, with whom Featley had debated matters of faith. See Featley, *The Grand Sacrilege of the Church of Rome* (London, 1630); Stephen Wright, ODNB.]

Psalm 9[861]

Of thee I sing, great guardian of all things,
To thee my heart her duties tribute pays;
Thy wonders to our seed that after springs   *descendants*
I will declare, and thence thy glory raise.

5 Safe guided by thy hand I'll nothing fear,
But cheerful notes will sing with cheerful mind,
And will thee praise, who supreme rule dost bear,
Chief Justice of the heav'ns, and heav'nly kind.

   3. My prouder foe, who, without counsel led,
10 Conceiv'd vain hopes, hath turn'd, and took his flight,
And thy right-hand pursuing whilst he fled,
With more than human force hath foil'd him quite.

   4. My greedy foes wide yawning for my blood,
Thy wreakful rage confounds, and rends their jaws;   *vengeful, defeats*
15 Thine aid reliev'd while guilty-like I stood,
And from thy throne thy doom did end my cause.   *judgment*

   5. Thou tam'st the fury of the savage rout,   *mob*
Thy matchless might did so my foes dispel,
As in the rolls of fame they were left out,
20 That none their names in after-age should tell.

   6. Lo, to what end come all these swelling threats?
Lo, him that towns would level, and lay plain,
That where in former times stood stately seats,
No memory should of their state remain.

---

[861] In the Septuagint and the Catholic and Eastern Orthodox traditions deriving from it, this Psalm is joined with Psalm 10 in a single Psalm. In the Hebrew, both together constitute an alphabetical acrostic.

    7. But he that sways eternally this ball,[862]
       By justice fixed his everlasting throne,
    8. To distribute the laws by righting all,
       And ruling men that each may have his own.

    9. When force doth sit to hatch high-swelling pride,
       Thy gate of grace stands open for the poor;
       Thy castle of safe refuge thou set'st wide,
       That all distressed may enter at the door.

    10. And therefore well may they in thee alone,
       Who know thy wide-spread name, their trust repose,
       When all the world hath by experience known,
       Thou leav'st not thine to th' mercy of their foes.

    11. Then sing due praise unto the Lord, whose hand
       And watchful eye keeps his lov'd Zion sure,   *guards*
       Spread wide his wise decrees in ev'ry land,
       Them let no bounds less than the world immure.   *enclose*

    12. For guiltless blood he takes a strict account,
       Revenging it with plagues, and inward fears,
       And suffers not pride unreveng'd to mount
       And press the poor, whose cries soon pierce his ears.   *oppress*

    13. But thou, dear God, look nearer to my cause,
       Whom armèd force pursues with deadly spite,
       And take me from the fell and direful jaws   *wicked*
       Of death, whose hue is black as pitchy night.[863]

    14. That all so high as Zion lifts her head,
       And sets her towers so far, so wide to view,
       I may thy name with vows and praises spread,
       And daily thanks for hourly help renew.

    15. Perfidious wights in waves of self-bred wrong   *creatures*
       Tossed, and turmoiled, have worthily been drown'd,
       And in the nets, which they were knitting long
       For others laid, themselves were helpless bound.

---

[862] S.P.L.'s rendering of what the KJV and BCP designate as 'world' (accurately reflecting the Hebrew). Ancient Greeks knew that the Earth was a sphere, though this knowledge may not have been shared by the Psalmist.

[863] The Psalmist's prayer to be delivered from 'the gates of death' (KJV) is elaborated into a vision like the medieval hell mouth, the entrance to hell represented as a monstrous beast.

16. Who but admires heav'n's equal ballanc'd right?
Who weav'd the web of fraud himself was caught,
A thing so oft perform'd in all men's sight
60 Should be enrolled and kept in inward thought?

17. But so it is. Time not foreseen arrests[864]
The godless men, who have not heav'n in mind,
Then sudden death wounds their rebellious breasts,
And hides them in his pit where no sun shin'd.

65 18. But modest minds which breathe but air divine,
Hopeless of help, but what from heaven descends,
God in his heart doth them a place assign,
Where causeless grief at last finds large amends.

19. Up, up, Creator of all things, arise,
70 And let not man, not many spans in length,[865]
Mount to a monster of deformèd size
To crush the poor; curb thou men's lawless strength.[866]

20. Thou with the boundless weight of endless might,
Strike horror deep into their fiercer minds,
75 That man may know his feeble state aright,
Whose weaker parts no lasting cement binds.

Psalm 41

Blest is the man commiserates the poor,
And brings him help when hope begins to die,
And when he finds him trampled on the floor,
Scowls not at him with a disdainful eye.
5   Whom men would think to be in pieces rent,
   Him God will rear, and cheer him wholly spent.

2. With faithful care God will him fence about,
And set him free from harms, that safe and sound
Amongst the living here enjoy he mought   *might*
10 A blessèd life where all contents abound,
   3. When on his couch grief lays his aching head,
   He helps him then, and makes his easeful bed.

---

[864] The caesura after the first short sentence is effective rhetorically, but it is not in the original and would be impossible to preserve in singing to any standard tune.

[865] spans] Short spaces of time, especially the short duration of a human life (perhaps from Psalm 39. 6 in BCP, 'thou hast made my days as it were a span long').

[866] The giant oppressing the poor is a curious addition, perhaps a metaphor for swollen pride, or massive wealth and power. It is the inverse of Spenser's egalitarian giant in book v of *The Faerie Queene*.

And all his grief that pain'd him so before,
    4. He turns to sweet repose. So when decayed
15 With bitter grief vexèd full sore,
Of thee, O God, I crav'd relief, and said,
      My wounded soul of that foul sore recure,   *recourse*
      Which sin hath made so loathsome to endure.

    5. My foe with direful imprecations sends
20 Me to the pit of hell, and in my loss
He triumph makes. And thus he saith, when ends
That loathèd life of his? When shall that dross
      Of his impurer carcass in one night,
      Together with his name be put out quite.

25 6. And if by chance one of this crew espy
Me drooping go in body or in mind,
He fains as if he mourn'd in passing by,
And sighs, forsooth, after a sporting kind.   *playful nature (?)*
      When going on, and that his back's but turn'd,
30   He spits his gall, that in his bosom burn'd.   *bile*

    7. The wicked crew conspiring against me,
Whisper in one another's ear their spite,
And closely plot their mischiefs, and agree
To join in one, and over-bear me quite:
35   8. And boast that heaven sent this dire plague to grieve
      And bound me with his bonds, nor will relieve.

He lies, say they, dejected in his bed,
Breathing his last breath in his latter night.
    9. But he, in house, at board, who dwelt, and fed,   *table*
40 My mate with whom my life I thought I might
      And livelihood have left in surest guard,[867]
      Even he, as fierce and fell as who most dar'd,   *wicked*

He taking part with my proud foes, did spurn
    10. And kick at me. But thou whose hand doth give
45 Me help and health, and all base spite didst turn
Unto my good, that I might sweetly live,
      Thine eye of grace, and hand of help, Lord, tender,
      That to my foes I like for like may render.

    11. This of thy grace the surest pledge shall be,
50 And of thy constant purpose in mine aid,

---

[867] The same complaint about betrayal by a 'familiar friend' (BCP, KJV) that is made in Psalm 55, translated by so many imprisoned courtiers.

When as my foe, shall not triumph o'er me,
And though he storm his courage shall be laid.
    12.   My body now his former strength retains,
My innocence still in my mind remains.

55 And all proceeds from this, that thou thy hand
Extend'st to me, who took'st me to thy charge,
That I might safe by thy protection stand,
And always fenc'd. Now set by thee at large,
    13.   Thee let the world acknowledge and adore
60 (Whom Isaac's race doth serve, and no gods more),   *posterity*
And let them sing thy praise while day and night
Betwixt them share the darkness and the light.[868]

105. Alexander Top, *The Book of Praises, Called the Psalms. The Keys and Holy Things of David* (1629)

[Alexander Top was active as a writer between 1597, when he published *Saint Peter's Rock*, and 1629, the date of *The Book of Praises*. In between, Top published a study of language, *The Olive Leaf* (1603), described as an 'integration of Humanist, Neoplatonic, and cabalistic interest in orthography and alphabetical symbolism' (Elsky, p. 251). The dedication of his first book to William Lyon ('Lions' as Top has it), Bishop of Cork, Ross, and Cloyne, suggests that Top may have been born in Ireland, though he writes from London, and the condemnation of Peter in *Saint Peter's Rock* confirms he was not Catholic. Top's Psalms are printed without verse numbers, direct speech indicated by italics (preserved here). *The Olive Leaf* contains a dedicatory poem by Henoch Clapham, separatist preacher, controversialist, and author of biblical paraphrase. Curiously, the gist of Clapham's poem is that he had done his best to tidy up a mess of a manuscript before it went to press. *The Book of Praises* was dedicated to King Charles I but printed in Amsterdam, perhaps, like Wither, because publication in London was blocked by the Stationers (see 114). Top's address to the reader states that the 'psalms do carry a fair outward style, but their treasure is within them', a treasure partly accessible through mystical numerology of the sort explored in *The Olive Leaf*. With Top's Psalms translations, the margins (left of verso, right of recto) included three columns in which Top provides copious cross-references to other Psalms, to the Law and 'first Prophets', and to 'last Prophets' and New Testament. Top's arguments follow

---

[868] The coda about darkness and light, adding an extra two lines to the final stanza, is original, though metaphors of light and dark abound in the Bible (as 1 John 1. 5, 'God is light, and in him is no darkness at all', KJV). The line about Isaac's race is also original, perhaps thinking of Paul's redefinition of God's chosen from the Israelites to Christianity: 'Now we, brethren, as Isaac was, are children of promise' (Galatians 4. 28, KJV).

the psalter, each consisting of a relatively straightforward exposition as well as more arcane notes on 'construction' and 'genesis' (or grammar), the former for Psalm 16 stating that 'the two letters pointing at Jehovah, show abstaining from all strange gods', while the latter for that Psalms observes, 'the kinds of quiescents [silent letters or diacritics] are many, as wealth, and pleasure, and delight, and joys, and counsel and instruction from God'. See Martin Elsky, 'George Herbert's Pattern Poems and the Materiality of Language: A New Approach to Renaissance Hieroglyphics', *ELH*, 50.2 (1983), 245–60.]

Psalm 16

A Mictam,[869] or Illustration of David.

Keep° me, O thou Mighty One,[870] for I rely upon thee. O my wealth, say thou to the Eternal, *I am not for thee; I am for the famous saints of the earth, which are my whole delight*: Great be their sorrows that run to any other. I will offer none of their bloody offerings, nor take their names once in my lips.

5   The Eternal maintain my lot, *he is my portion, my part, and my cup. My measures light in pleasant places, and a goodly heritage is fallen to me*. I thank the Eternal: he counselleth me, and my reins° teach me by night, I set the Eternal always by me at my right hand that I slip not.

Therefore my heart is glad, my body rejoiceth, and my flesh dwelleth assured:
10 that thou wilt not leave me at hell; nor let thy sacred one see the pit below; but wilt show me the path of life, the fullness of joys that are before thee, and pleasures at thy right hand for ever.

Psalm 89

A Mascil,[871] of Ethan the Ezrachite.

I will ever sing the kindnesses of the Eternal, and to all generations make known thy faithfulness with my mouth. To wit, *The kindness that the world was built by*,[872] *and thy faithfulness which thou hast confirmed in the heavens*, I have made a covenant and sworn to my servant David: I will establish thy seed° for ever,
5 and build up thy throne for all generations surely. *And let the heaven confess thy wonderfulness, O Eternal, yea thy faithfulness in the congregation of the holy*

---

[869] Mictam] or Michtam, a technical term appearing in Psalms, meaning unknown.
[870] mighty one] A literal translation of the Hebrew *El*, usually rendered in English Psalms as 'God'. Top generally relies on the Hebrew more closely than other English translators. Thus, 'the eternal' is a more specific translation of YHWH than the usual 'God'. Neither 'O my wealth' nor 'O my soul' (BCP, KJV), however, has any basis in the Hebrew.
[871] Mascil] or Maschil, a song or poem of contemplation.
[872] kindness] The Hebrew denotes rather 'firmness' or 'steadiness' (KJV 'faithfulness').

ones;⁸⁷³ For who among the children of the gods in the cloudy skies, equalleth or may compare with the Eternal? a terrible God in the council of the holy ones, and dreadful over all that be about him? O Eternal, God of war, who is so mighty a God as thou art, and thy faithfulness about thee? *Thou rulest over the pride of the sea,*⁸⁷⁴ *and allayest the waves thereof, when they rise, the main ocean thou beatest down like a slain man,*⁸⁷⁵ *and with thy strong arm scatterest thine enemies. the heavens are thine, yea the earth is thine, the whole world, and all the implements thereof, for thou foundedst them; the north and the south, thou hast created them, Tabor and Hermon to resound out thy name. Thou hast a conquering arm, and thy right hand doth highly prevail, the firm base of thy throne is justice and judgement, and kindness and faithfulness stand before thy face.* Happy are the people that know triumphing, and walk, O Eternal: in the light of thy countenance, and are daily merry with thy name, and exalted with thy justice.

Because thou art the ornament of their strength, and by thy good will is our horn exalted.⁸⁷⁶ For our defender is the Eternal's, and our King the holy ones of Israel, when as thou spakest in a vision to thy gracious one and sayedst; I have levied and raised an aid, and a chosen one out of the people above a worthy. I have found my servant David and anointed him with my holy oil, with whom my hand shall firmly be, and mine arm shall strengthen him. No enemy or injurious child shall intercept him, or oppress him. I will beat down his foes, and them that hate him, flat before him, and my faithfulness and lovingkindness shall be with him, and in my name shall his horn be exalted, and upon the sea and upon the rivers will I make his right hand to be. He shall call me, O my Father, my God and rock of my salvation, and I will make him my eldest son, and the sovereign of all the kings of the earth, I will make his seed, and his throne to be for everlasting like the days of heaven, and if his children forsake my law, and walk not in my judgements, if they violate my prescriptions, and keep not my commandments: I will visit their transgressions with rods, and their iniquity with scourges; but my lovingkindness will I not break off from him, neither deal falsely in my faithfulness. I will not violate my covenant, nor change the thing that is gone out of my lips.

I have once sworn in my holiness, and shall I lie unto David? His seed shall be forever and his throne as the sun before me, he shall be established as firm as

---

⁸⁷³ holy ones] Here and throughout, Top avoids the traditional rendering 'saints', which is misleading in the context of early modern Protestant usage as equivalent to the elect, opting for a more neutral translation.

⁸⁷⁴ pride of the sea] Closer to the Hebrew (which can also denote a swelling or rising, as of sea or smoke) than the KJV's 'raging'.

⁸⁷⁵ main ocean] In this instance Top opts for dynamic rather than formal equivalence. The Hebrew has *Rahab* (rendered as is in KJV), the name of an ancient sea monster.

⁸⁷⁶ horn] See note 32, p. 85.

the moon,[877] a faithful witness in the sky for ever surely. And thou loathest and drawest back, and art angry with thine anointed. Thou avoidest the covenant of thy servant, and defilest his garland on the ground;[878] thou hast broken down all his walls, and made a ruin of all his fortifications, all travellers by the way
45 trample on him, he is a reproach unto his neighbours. Thou holdest up the right hand of his foes, and makest all his enemies glad, yea thou turnest the edge of his sword, and makest it not to stand in the battle, thou makest it rest from his brightness, and hast pulled down his throne to the ground. Thou hast shortened the days of his youth, and covered him over with bashfulness surely. How long
50 wilt thou continue hid; and shall thy hot anger burn like fire? O remember thou of what continuance I am, wherefore in vain hast thou created all human men? What strong man is there that shall not see death, or his life shall escape from the hand of hell, surely? Where are thy first kindnesses, O Lord, which thou swearest to David, in thy faithfulness?
55 Remember, O Lord, the enemies' reproach of thy servants, which I put up in my bosom, of all the great ones of the nations where with thine enemies have reproached, O Eternal, where with thine enemies have reproached the steps of thine anointed. Blessed be the Eternal for ever. Again and Again.

106. Francis Quarles (MS 1620s–1630s?)

[Francis Quarles (1592–1644) was born in Romford, Essex, at his family's manor, granted to his father for service to Queen Elizabeth. He graduated from Christ's College, Cambridge, and then studied law at Lincoln's Inn. In 1613, Quarles likely participated in the *Masque of Middle Temple and Lincoln's Inn* celebrating the marriage of Princess Elizabeth and Frederick, the Elector Palatine, which also involved a progress to Heidelberg. In 1627 he bought a house in London near St Paul's and the next year married Ursula Woodgate, with whom he had eighteen children, including John, also a poet. Quarles was secretary to James Ussher, Bishop of Armagh, and moved with him to Ireland from 1626 to 1630. From 1632 to 1638 he and his family lived in Essex, where he gained the friendship and patronage of Edward Benlowes, who also patronized Phineas Fletcher. Quarles published a number of verse paraphrases of biblical books in the 1620s, including *A Feast for Worms* (Jonah, 1620), *Job Militant* (1624), *Sion's Elegies* (Lamentations, 1624), *Sion's Sonnets* (The Song of Solomon, 1624), and *The History of Samson* (1631). But it was as an emblem poet that Quarles found his greatest gifts. His *Emblems* (1634) was followed by *Hieroglyphics of the Life of Man* (1638), and both proved immensely popular, continuing to be reprinted well into the nineteenth century. Quarles continued

---

[877] The moon simile is original but a peculiar one, since the waxing and waning moon is traditionally a symbol for mutability and fickleness.
[878] garland] Top's rather classical version of the Psalm's 'crown' (as in KJV and BCP).

to publish a variety of poetic, historical, and moral works, but, although he was appointed official Chronologer of London, he fell into poverty and died a pauper in 1644. Some of Quarles's difficulties may have been political, in trying to maintain a position as a moderate Protestant (anti-Catholic and anti-Arminian) and royalist in the midst of increasing sectarian hostility. The sole manuscript of Quarles's eight metrical Psalms was discovered in 1992 among papers of the Duke of Portland, and its earlier provenance is unknown. The hand, not Quarles's own, seems to date from the 1620s or 30s, so the Psalms were likely composed during the time of Quarles's other biblical paraphrases. Each psalm is followed by a 'pause' or meditation, a format Quarles used in his paraphrase of Job and other works. Though no other Psalms by Quarles survive, there is evidence for more. His wife, Ursula, asked London stationers for the return of several of her husband's manuscripts, including 'the Psalms of David put and composed into English verses'. There is also an account by John Josselyn, an Essex gentleman, of his trip to Boston in 1638, in which he claims to have delivered to John Cotton 'from Mr. Francis Quarles the poet, the Translation of the 16, 25, 51, 88, 113, and 137 Psalms into English Meeter, for his approbation'. Some scholars have argued on this basis that Quarles must have contributed to the Bay Psalm Book of 1640, but the text of these Psalms bears no resemblance to any of Quarles's poetry, including the eight metrical Psalms. Six of the eight are in metres compatible with church singing, but the third is in rhyming tetrameter couplets and the seventeenth in rhyming pentameter couplets, and the 'pauses' also suggest these are Psalms for reading and meditation, not singing. See Karl Josef Höltgen, 'New Verse by Francis Quarles: The Portland Manuscripts, Metrical Psalms, and the Bay Psalm Book (with text)', *English Literary Renaissance*, 28.1 (1998), 118–41; Höltgen, *ODNB*.]

Psalm 7

1. In thee, my God, Jehovah, I repose,
   Save and deliver me from all my foes.
2. Lest like a lion he my soul should tear,
   And rend in pieces while no help is near.
3. My God, Jehovah, if I have done this,
   Or if my wrongful hands have done amiss,
4. Against my friend if ever I transgressed
   (Nay more, my causeless foes I have released),
5. Then let my foe surprise my soul, and thrust
   My life to earth, and glory in the dust.
6. Lord, rise in wrath, for my distressers, rage,
   Hasten that help thy promise did engage;
7. And troops of saints before thy throne shall lie,
   And for whose sakes exalt thyself on high.

15	8.	The Lord will judge the world: Lord, judge thou me,	
		As the uprightness of my cause shall be.	
	9.	Consume the wicked's way, confirm th'upright,	
		For hearts and reins, just God, are in thy sight.	*inward parts*
	10.	In God, my shield, is placèd all my fear,	
20		The Saviour of the heart that is sincere;[879]	
	11.	God is a Judge most just in all his way,	
		His anger threats the wicked every day.	*threatens*
	12.	If he return not, he will whet his blade,	*sharpen*
		His bow is bended, and his mark is made.	
25	13.	At him the tools of death his hands address,	
		And shafts for those that furiously oppress.	
	14.	Lo, he shall travail in iniquity,	
		For he conceives in pain, brings forth a lie.	
	15.	His hand hath digged a ditch, and delvèd it,	
30		And fell into his own destroying pit.[880]	
	16.	Upon his head his evil shall revert,	
		And on himself his violent wrongs shall dart.[881]	
	17.	I'll praise the Lord, for he is just, and I	
		Will sing my songs unto the Lord most high.	

                       Pause: 7

35 Just Judge of earth in whom I trust,
     Make sharp thy sword and bend thy bow,
     Consume the wicked, save the just.
     For thou the reins and heart dost know.   *inward parts*
     Then shall my tongue sing forth thy praise,
40   And praise thy justice all my days.[882]

107. John Vicars, *England's Hallelujah. Or, Great Britain's Grateful Retribution, for God's Gratious Benediction* [...] *Together with Diverse of David's Psalms, According to the French Metre and Measures* (1631)

[John Vicars (1580–1652) was born in London, orphaned young, and raised and educated at Christ's Hospital. He studied briefly at Queen's College, Oxford, but returned to Christ's Hospital where he served as an usher for most of his life. He must have gained knowledge of languages at Oxford, since in 1632,

---

[879] KJV's 'which saveth the upright in heart' is more accurate, Quarles's version inserting a Christian perspective.

[880] **Marg.** 'Heb: shachath (or *sahat*, a pit).' Why Quarles should feel the need to provide the Hebrew of this word and the one below, among so many, is unclear.

[881] **Marg.** 'Heb: Chamas (or *hamas*, wrongs or violence).'

[882] The final stanza is Quarles's addition, reiterating verses 12, 9, and 17.

shortly after his Psalms translations, he published a translation of Virgil's *Aeneid*. In the 1640s, Vicars published four books chronicling the English Civil Wars, favouring the parliamentarian side. In 1617, Vicars translated into English stanzas a Latin poem in hexameters on the Gunpowder Plot (*Pietas Pontificas*) by the physician and poet Francis Herring, under the title *Mischief's Misery*. The number of commendatory verses, by authors including the translator of Du Bartas, Joshua Sylvester, testifies to the interest in the publication. In 1641 Vicars published a different translation of Herring's poem, this time into pentameter couplets, and the number of commendations swelled, including one by the Puritan leader William Prynne. Vicars continued publishing polemical works until his death, and several appeared in print posthumously. *England's Hallelujah* was dedicated to two of the governors of Christ's Hospital, Sir Hugh Hammersley and Sir Robert Parkhurst, Alderman and later Lord Mayor. Vicars is a sophisticated poet writing in the Sidneian mode, casting his Psalms in various complex metres and stanzas, including a version of English Sapphics (101), the short lines of which he handles especially adeptly. He handles the alternation of longer and shorter lines effectively, and plays with alliteration and compound nouns. See Julia Gasper, ODNB.]

Psalm 53[883]

1.

The faithless fool in heart his God denies,
    Their facts are full of foul abhomination;   *deeds*
    Ill, is the end of all their consultation,
    None of them will good actions exercise,
5   All are unwise.

2.

On man below, God looked from heaven's high throne,
    To see, if any wisely him affected;
    But, all were nought, all had the Lord neglected,   *worthless*
    Goodness was gone, good men (alas) were none,
10   O no, not one.

3.

The wicked workers of iniquity
    Know not, that they, like cannibals detested,
    As bread, my people's flesh, have eat, digested,[884]   *eaten*

---

[883] Psalm 53 is virtually identical to Psalm 14, with some small variations. The most significant difference is the use of '*elohim* for God's name instead of *YHWH*, which may indicate an origin in the Northern Kingdom rather than the Southern.

[884] The Psalmist protests that enemies are 'eating up my people as it were bread', which is

Not minding me: and, when no cause was nigh, *near*
15   Fear made them fly.

4.

The Lord hath broke thy bold besiegers' bones,
    And them destroyed which never God rely on;
    But, thy salvation, out of sacred Zion,
    Give, to thine Isr'el mitigate their moans,
20   Their sighs and groans.

5.

When God in goodness, and his own free choice,
    His people captived, captains makes, victorious,
    And with firm freedom makes them glad and glorious;
    Then, Jacob's Heart and Isr'el's shall rejoice,
25   With cheerful voice.

Psalm 101

1.

Of mercy and of judgement, I am writing;[885]
    Thy most due praise, my lays are now inditing;
    For unto thee (O Lord) alone belongs
            Such Psalms, such song.

2.

5 In perfect ways my feet shall walk precisely,
    And I, at home, my works will order wisely,
    Until my soul sincere approach thy sight,
            All-blest, all-bright.

3.

By me, bad works shall not be imitated,
10   By me, back-sliders' actions, ever hated;
    These, all of these, my heart shall quite disdain,
            Refuse, refrain.

---

easy to read figuratively, but Vicars's cannibals are less ambiguous. Montaigne's essay on new world cannibals was available in English from 1603, but stories of cannibalism due to hunger were part of accounts of the Roman siege of Jerusalem, and there were similar reports of the ravages of the French countryside during the religious wars of the sixteenth century.

[885] KJV has 'I will sing' which more accurately reflects the Hebrew.

4.

My upright soul shall never be acquainted
    With wicked men, whose works with sin are tainted;
15   From me, a peevish and a perverse heart
        Shall pack, shall part.

5.

Back-biters' tongues that wickedly have wounded
    Neighbours' good name, by me shall be confounded;   *defeated*
I never could a supercilious look,
20   Once bare, once brook.

6.

Mine eyes of love shall ever be reflected
    On faithful men, to be by me protected;
With me the man that lives religiously[886]
        Shall live and die.

7.

25 A fellow fraught with sly dissimulation,   *filled*
    Shall never have, with me, cohabitation;
A liar, from my presence, presently,
        Shall fall, shall fly.

8.

I will destroy (and that, with expedition)
30   All wicked-wilful-workers of transgression;
Not one of these, in God's most holy land
        Shall stay, shall stand.

---

[886] Vicars elaborates the description of slander, the use of 'back-biters' and 'wounded' together implying an almost physical injury, the effect heightened by alliteration. Vicars's syntax, especially in the final short line, is sophisticated and effective, though not biblical.

Psalm 124

Paraphrased by way of thanksgiving for our great deliverance from the Papists' Powder Plot.[887]

> King David against the Philistines;
> King James against the Antichristians.

1.

Now may England
Confess and say surely;
   If that the Lord,
   Had not our cause maintained,
5 If that the Lord,
   Had not our state sustained;
     When Antichrist,[888]
     Against us furiously,
   Made his proud brags,
10 And said, we should all die.[889]

2.

Not long ago,
They had devoured us all;
   And swallowed quick,   *alive*
   For ought that we could deem:
15 Such was their rage,
   As we might well esteem:
     And as proud floods,   *vigorous*
     With mighty force do fall;
   So their mad rage,
20 Our lives had brought to thrall.   *captivity*

---

[887] In 1605, a group of Catholic conspirators planned to blow up the House of Lords, killing not only the members, but King James and other members of the royal family, the Privy Council, and the leaders of the Church (all bishops being members of the House of Lords). Kegs of dynamite were in place in the basement, but the plot was discovered and the conspirators caught and executed. The date of the plot, 5 November, became a national day of thanksgiving.

[888] Antichrist] Not mentioned in the Psalm, and indeed the term is only used in I and II John. It was a term used by Protestants for the pope, however, which is probably the relevant context for this Psalm of deliverance from Catholic conspiracy.

[889] Vicars again writes in a distinctly Sidneian mode, though the stanza for this Psalm is original, not found in the Sidney Psalter.

3.

Our King and Queen,
The Prince and princely race;
   Their council grave,
   And chief nobility;   *head*
25 The judges wise,
And prime tribe of Levi;
   With all the prudent,
   Statesmen of the land,
By powder fierce,
30 Had perished out of hand.

4.

The raging streams
Of Rome with roaring noise,
   Had with great woe,
   O'er-whelmed us in the deep:
35 O blessèd Lord,
Thou didst us safely keep,   *guard*
   From bloody teeth,
   And their devouring jaws;
Which as a prey,
40 Had gripped us in their claws.

5.

But, as a bird,
Out of the fowler's gin,   *bird-catcher's, snare*
   Escapes away:
   Right so it fared with us;
45 Broke were their nets,
And we have scapèd, thus,   *escaped*
God that made heaven
   And earth was our help
   His mercy saved us (then)
50 From these wicked men.

6.

O let us therefore,
With all thanks and praise,
   Sing, joyfully,
   To Christ our heavenly King;
55 Whose wisdom high,

This fact to light did bring:
    Grant then, O Lord,
    We do thee humbly pray,
We may accord,
60 And praise thy name alway.　　　　　　　　　　　　　　*always*
    Amen.

108. William Slatyer, *Psalms, or Songs of Sion Turned into the Language, and Set to the Tunes of a Strange Land. By W. S. Intended for Christmas Carols* (1631)

[William Slatyer (*c.* 1587–1647) was a clergyman and writer, educated at St Mary's Hall and Brasenose College, Oxford. Slatyer's clerical career was on the rise, with an appointment as treasurer of St David's cathedral (1616), rectorship of Newchurch, Romney, Kent (1617), and a chaplaincy to Queen Anne. Learned in languages, Slatyer published a set of elegies and epitaphs to the queen in Hebrew, Greek, Latin, and English after her death in 1619, and in 1621 a massive Latin and English poem on the history of Great Britain, supplemented by an appendix in 1630 tracing the descent of James I from Adam. In the same year, his *Psalms, or Songs of Sion*, caused a scandal, perhaps because of a list of popular tunes to which the Psalms might be sung, though this was common practice. In any case, the book was ordered to be burned, and Slatyer was censured by Archbishop Laud for wearing riding clothes instead of clerical garb. His career never recovered. In 1643, Slatyer published the remarkable *Psalms of David in 4 Languages and 4 Parts*, which printed in four columns, across facing pages left to right, the Psalms in Greek, Latin, English, and Hebrew, along with music in four parts by (principally) Thomas Ravenscroft. The metre of Slatyer's Psalm 42 is almost like Skeltonics, with an irregular alternation of longer and shorter lines (generally two- and three-stress), the syllable count varying. The unusual rhyme scheme begins with four couplets and then shifts to *abacccb*, which is repeated. The whole pattern is then repeated. Slatyer gives the tune as 'The Borders of Scotland'. His Psalm 124 is in iambic pentameter, again a rough version of it, with occasional extra syllables and awkward stresses. The tune for this is 'Fair Angel of England, or Sweet Robin', presumably the popular 'Bonny Sweet Robin' set by many composers and sung by Shakespeare's Ophelia in her madness. See E. I. Carlyle, rev. Vivienne Larminie, *ODNB*.]

Psalm 42

Like th' hart that strays,
Breathes, pants, and brays,　　　　　　　　　　　　　　　　*cries*
To the rivers fair to gain,
Even so my poor heart right fain.　　　　　　　　　　　　*glad*

5 My soul, I cry,
   Thirsts; O when nigh   *closely*
   To the living God of might
   Shall I come to appear in his sight?
   All times my tears
10 Are my repast and food,
   And more my fears,
   When wicked men deride,
   Where now is God thy guide?
   Stood I at the tide
15 In sad and heavy mood.
   My soul ev'n faints,
   Void of her best delight,
   Since now she wants
   What freedom once she had,
20 When to the Temple glad,
   As her train, she led
   Music and songs, she might.
   Why art thou so
   Surcharged with woe,
25 O my soul, and robbed of rest?
   Hope and help is in God most blest:
   Trust in his name,
   And praise the same.
   O my God, my soul is sad,
30 Yet thee I remember, glad:
   For Jordan's land,
   And little Hermon hill,
   Whiles great deeps, and
   Griefs, one another call,
35 Ills, like to waterfalls,
   Storms, whose noise appals;
   Thy floods o'erwhelm me still.
   In God by day
   Mercy and grace I find,
40 By night alway   *always*
   I unto him will sing;
   And as oft prayer bring,
   As my heavenly King,
   God of my life I mind.
45 To God, I say, my strength and stay,   *support*
   Why hast thou forgotten me,
   Though I mourn and oppressed be?
   Or why else so

    Do I troubled go,
50 As heavy and ill apaid,   *contented*
    Whiles enemies me upbraid?
    My bones as 'twere
    Smit with a sword asunder,   *smitten*
    Whiles those I fear,
55 My foes that me upbraid,
    Where now is God thine aid?
    To me daily said,
    Making at me a wonder.
    Why art thou so
60 Vexed, O my soul, and sore
    Perplexed with woe?
    O trust in God most high,
    For on his help rely,
    Praise him ay will I,   *forever*
65 My God and hope evermore.

Psalm 124

    If the Lord himself had not been on our side,
        May Israel now say, but he is our guide:
    If the Lord had not been on our side, when men
        Rose so furious against us, they had swallowed us then.
5 They had swallowed us up quick in wrathful displeasure,[890]   *alive*
        Their anger was kindled so hot above measure.
    The waters had drowned us then without control,
        The deep stream had gone even over our soul.
    The fierce swelling waters of envy and pride,
10   Had gone over soul with such a strong tide:[891]
    But praised be the Lord, that hath not given us o'er
        For a prey to their teeth, that our souls would have tore.
    Our soul is escapèd like a bird with good speed,
        From the snare of the fowler, that broken, we freed.   *bird-catcher*
15 Our help's in the name of the Lord always,
        That hath made heaven and earth, to his name be the praise.

---

[890] An example of the figure of anadiplosis, Slatyer repeating the clause from the end of one line at the beginning of the next. The Psalm itself is full of repetition, as in the first two verse halves (Slatyer's lines 1 and 3).
[891] There is a process of increasing figurativeness between the Hebrew, standard English versions, and Slatyer. The Hebrew has 'proud waters', as does the KJV, the BCP has 'deep waters of the proud', which implies the waters are a metaphor for proud enemies. Slatyer goes further and allegorizes the waters as 'envy and pride' themselves.

109. Sir John Glanville, The Younger, *A Paraphrase upon the Psalms of David* (MS 1615–1631)

[Sir John Glanville (1585/6–1661), son of the judge John Glanville, studied at Lincoln's Inn and was called to the bar. He was elected MP in 1614 and again, following the death of James I, in 1625 and thereafter. Appointed king's serjeant in 1640, Glanville surrendered to parliament in 1644, was imprisoned in the Tower, and impeached. He was required to pay a substantial fine, but he retained his property. With the Restoration in 1660, Glanville was reappointed king's serjeant and designated prime serjeant. Glanville states in his manuscript, addressed to his wife, Winifred, that he began his metrical paraphrase of the Psalms in 1608 at his birthplace in Tavistock, Devonshire, and completed it in the Tower from 1643 to 1645. The Psalm included here appears to date from a middle period, from the late teens to the 1620s. See Stuart Handley, *ODNB*.]

Psalm 22

To the chief musician upon aijeleth shahar,[892] a Psalm of David.   *head*

      My God! my God! why hast thou thus forsaken
      My troubled sense with utmost sorrows shaken?[893]
      Why art thou so far off from helping me?
      And from my words, which rather roarings be?
5 2. Lord! in the daytime unto thee I cry,
      And in the night I do not silent lie,
      While thou (as if thou didst my woes despise)
      Nor hear'st my morning nor mine evening cries.
    3. Yet art thou just, O thou which here dost dwell!
10   Thou, subject of the songs of Israel!
    4. Our fathers erst did put their trust in thee,   *at first*
      And from their troubles thou didst set them free;
    5. They cried unto thee, and had powerful aid:
      They trusted in thee, and were not dismayed.
15 6. But I, a worm am and no man: one born
      To be the shame of men, and the world's scorn:
    7. One whom all they that see me do deride
      With shaken heads and lips distorted wide,
    8. Saying, he trusted erst that you would save him
20   And let him do so now if he will have him.

---

[892] aijeleth shahar] A transliteration of the Hebrew, perhaps designating the tune to which the Psalm should be sung ('the hind of the dawn').
[893] The first verse of this Psalm was recited by Christ on the cross, in Aramaic, in the accounts of Mark and Matthew. Many other features of the Psalm (the mocking, piercing of hands and feet, casting lots for clothing) are incorporated into the gospel accounts of the Crucifixion as fulfilments of prophecy, the Psalm foretelling Christ's sacrifice.

9. However, thou art he that didst me take
   Out of the womb at first, and then didst make
   My hopeful soul on thee alone to rest,
   While yet I hung upon my mother's breast:
10. Yea, I no sooner erst was born to see
    This wretched world, but I was cast on thee.
    And ever since I left that strait abode *narrow*
    My mother's belly, thou hast been my God.
11. O be not then far off! for grief draws on,
    Yea, hard at hand: and helper there is none.
12. My foes (fierce bulls) about me do abound:
    Strong bulls of Basan have beset me round.
13. And on my person the confusèd crowd
    Gapes, like a ravenous lion roaring loud.[894]
14. I am like thinnest water all at once
    Poured forth, and out of joint are all my bones.
    Also my heart such burning pains hath felt,
    It doth like wax within my bowels melt. *inner organs*
15. My strength (dried like a potsherd) is quite past:
    And my faint tongue unto my jaws sticks fast. *secure*
    Yea, thou by death hast me to dust applied:
16. For dogs have hemmed me in on every side.
    Th'unjust assembly did enclose me round,
    And doth my hands and feet with piercing wound.
17. I may tell all my bones, they are so bare *count*
    Of flesh; yet on me still they gaze and stare.
18. Amongst them then my garments they divide
    And whose my coat should be by lots is tried.
19. But be not thou far off: O Lord, my strength
    Hast to mine aid! 20. And free my soul at length,
    My solitary soul, both from the power
    Of sword and dog; which would the same devour!
21. O save me from the horrid lion's paws!
    And rescue me from his wide yawning jaws!
    Thou, which hast heard me from amongst the horns
    Of swift assailing dangerous unicorns![895]
22. So will I show my brethren thy great name,
    And in the congregation sing thy fame.

---

[894] Glanville's enjambment is effective, emphasizing the verb 'gapes' and perhaps conveying a sense of a crowd swelling across the line break. Similarly sharp enjambments work across lines 45-46, 51-52, 55-56, 71-72, and 77-78. They are always within rather than between couplets.

[895] unicorns] See note 23, p. 79.

23. O ye that fear Jehovah! praise his deed:
60 O glorify him all ye Jacob's seed!   *descendants*
    And O, with reverent fear before him dwell,
    Ye blessed issues of old Israel!
24. For he nor scorned the state, nor stood addicted   *bound*
    To loathe th'affliction of the most afflicted:
65 Nor from his troubles did he turn his face:
    But when he cried, both heard and helped his case.
25. Wherefore, I vow with public acclamation
    To sound thy praise, in the great congregation:
    And in the sight of those that reverence thee
70 Shall my just vows herein performèd be.
26. The meek shall eat, and be replenished: those
    That seek the Lord his praises shall disclose:
    Also their hearts eternal life shall find.
27. And all earth's ends shall call themselves to mind,
75 Turning to God: yea, falling low before thee,
    All kingdoms and all nations shall adore thee.
28. For lo, the kingdom is the Lord: and he
    Amongst all nations still must ruler be.
29. The fat on earth shall yet be more replete;
80 And worship him the author of their meat.   *provider (and creator), food*
    Yea, all those which must needs go down to dust
    Shall bow before him in a holy trust.
    For none whose life is in his nostrils' breath
    Can of himself keep his own soul from death.
85 30. A seed shall serve him once with acceptation   *descendant*
    E'en to be call'd the Lord's own generation.
31. For they shall then assemble and express
    The truth of his accomplished righteousness
    To those which that blest age to life shall bring;
90 Namely that thou alone hast done this thing.

110. King James I and William Alexander, Earl of Stirling, *The Psalms of King David Translated by King James, Cum Privilegio Regiae Maiestatis* (1631)

[King James's name appeared on the title page, and the king himself was represented full-length, he (right) and David (left) receiving into their hands the Book of Psalms from heaven (a hand descending out of a cloud, surmounted by the radiant tetragrammaton). A complete new psalter would be the culmination of James's lifelong interest in the Psalms, providing, as Doelman puts it, 'a unifying element in all the British churches' by a poet-king modelled after David himself ('The Reception of King James's Psalter', p. 456). Indeed, James's plan for this psalter was instrumental (along with the jealous monopoly of the Stationers' Company) in preventing any other replacement of Sternhold and Hopkins from being printed. This was certainly a frustration for George Wither (see 114), and others whose Psalms may have been prevented from wide publication, including Henry Dod, Joseph Hall, and perhaps even Francis Davison. William Alexander (1577–1640) worked on the Psalms with the king and probably did the greater share of work, amending and revising the Psalms even after James's death. Alexander was a courtier, made gentleman of the privy chamber to Prince Henry in 1607, and then gentleman usher to Prince Charles in 1612, after Henry's death. He continued his political rise, becoming master of requests for Scotland, gaining a grant to establish the colony of New Scotland (eventually Nova Scotia and New Brunswick, though Alexander's plans failed), and finally being appointed secretary of state for Scotland in 1626. In 1633 he was made Earl of Stirling and Viscount of Canada. Alexander was a prolific writer, author of a sonnet sequence, *Aurora* (1604), a collection of Senecan closet dramas, *The Monarchic Tragedies* (1604), *An Elegy on the Death of Prince Henry* (1612), and *Doomes-Day, or, The Great Day of the Lord's Judgement* (Edinburgh 1614, London 1620), and a supplement to Sir Philip Sidney's revised but unfinished *Arcadia* that is included in editions to this day. He was a close friend of William Drummond of Hawthornden. Alexander obtained from Charles I exclusive rights to sell metrical Psalms in Scotland, but the James I-Alexander *Psalms* was rejected by the Scottish Kirk as part of Charles's ecclesiastical policy for Scotland. Charles included a note in the 1631 volume expressing his approval of his father's psalter and authorizing it to be used in 'all the Churches of our Dominions'. It was printed in only one more edition, in 1636, with the text revised (presumably by Alexander), and in two formats: an octavo with the prose of the King James Bible in the margin, without music, and a folio without the prose text but with tunes provided. Not surprisingly, the translation stays quite close to that in the King James Bible, though the metre is Sternhold's, without the additional rhyme added by Hopkins (*abcb* rather than *abab*). See Doelman, *King James I and the Religious Culture of England*; Doelman, 'The Reception of King James's Psalter', in *Royal Subjects: Essays on the Writing of James VI and I*, ed. by Daniel Fischlin and Mark Fortier (Detroit: Wayne State University Press, 2002), pp. 454–75; David Reid in *ODNB*.]

Psalm 93

    The Lord doth reign, with majesty
        He clothèd is throughout,
    He clothèd is with strength, wherewith
        He girds himself about.   *equips*

2. The world likewise it 'stablished is,   *established*
        And firm in every part:
     Thy throne is fixed of old, and thou
        From everlasting art.

 3. The raging floods behold, O Lord,
        All lifted up, do sound:
     Impetuous floods tumultuously
        Make all about rebound.

 4. Even many waters joining sounds,[896]
        Whose height with terror swells:
     And the large sea, with all her waves,
        The Lord for power excels.

 5. Thy testimonies, grounded well,
        Exceedingly are sure:
     And holiness becomes thy house,
        Forever to endure.

Psalm 105[897]

  O praise the Lord, upon his name
     Do call with grateful hearts:
  And make his actions known among
     The people, in all parts.
 2. Sing unto him with cheerful minds,
     Sing Psalms to him with joy:
  And liberally of his great works
     To talk your tongues employ.

 3. To glory in his holy name,
        With due respect accord:
     And let that heart delighted be
        Which seeks unto the Lord.

 4. Seek ye the Lord and his great strength,
        To which all things give place:
     And seek, inflamed with sacred zeal,
        Continually his face.

 5. His works with admiration breed,
        With reverence call to mind:
     And all the judgements of his mouth,

---

[896] The preceding quatrain nicely mirrors the rebounding sounds in the fluid assonance of 'Impetuous floods tumultuously'.

[897] This long Psalm rehearses the history of Israel told in Genesis and Exodus.

		With wonders oft designed.	
20	6.	O you, his servant Abraham's seed,	*descendants*
		That should obey his voice:	
		And you that Jacob's children are,	
		Of whom he did make choice.	
25	7.	He is the everlasting God,	
		That still our God hath been:	*always*
		His judgements, more than eminent,	
		Through all the earth are seen.	
	8.	That sacred covenant of his	
30		He hath remembered still:	
		And to a thousand of descents	
		The word that showed his will.	

The second part.

	9.	A covenant with Abraham,	
		which first contracted stood:	
35		And unto Isaac by an oath	
		Was solemnly made good.	
	10.	Which for a law, to be observed,	
		He unto Jacob gave:	
		And unto Israel for a league,	
40		That never end should have.	
	11.	And said, Canaan's fertile land[898]	
		I unto you will give:	
		The lot of your inheritance	
		Where you may safely live.	
45	12.	When they of men were but a few,	
		Against their foes to stand:	
		Yea, at the first but very few,	
		And strangers in the land.	
	13.	From nation unto nation long,	
50		When they so oft removed:	
		And from one kingdom parting straight,	*immediately*
		Another people proved.	
	14.	He suffering none to do them wrong:	
		From danger them redeemed:	
55		And did reprove kings for their cause,	
		As whom he more esteemed.	

---

[898] Canaan's] The metre requires a trisyllabic pronunciation ('Ca-na-an').

15. Do not (said he) touch them at all,
        Whom I anointed have:
    And let my prophets by your means
        No kind of harm receive.
16. He, moreover, for a famine called
        Upon the land in wrath:
    And straight did break the staff of bread,[899]
        By threatening dearth and death.

The third part.

17. He sent a man most excellent
        Before them, to provide:
    Who unto bondage was betrayed,
        Even Joseph, for their guide.
18. Whose feet were laid in fetters base,
        To be tormented so:
    Yea, he a heavy weight of iron,
        Was forced to undergo.
19. Until his word accomplished was,
        In the appointed time:
    The Lord his word him strictly tried,
        Though guilty of no crime.
20. Then sent the king, and did command
        That he enlarged should be: *released*
    He that the people's ruler was,
        Did send to set him free.
21. A Lord to rule his family,
        He raised him, as most fit:
    To him of all that he possessed,
        He did the charge commit.
22. That he, according as he pleased,
        His princes might command:
    And teach his ancients, what was fit
        For them to understand.
23. Then Israel did to Egypt come,
        Which him when weak revived:
    And Jacob, in the land of Ham,[900]

---

[899] break the staff of bread] cut off the food supply (biblical idiom). Some scholars posit that ringed bread was threaded on poles (Alter).
[900] land of Ham] i.e. Egypt, after the cursed son of Noah, traditionally thought to have settled in Africa.

   A straying stranger lived.
 24. His people then exceedingly
   He did increase so long:
95   That even then those who them oppressed
   They did become more strong.

The fourth part.

 25. He turned their hearts, that they to hate
   His people did arise:
  And with his servants subtilly   *subtly*
100   To deal they did devise.
 26. Mild Moses, that his servant was,
   He in embassage sent: *mission*
  And Aaron whom he did elect,
   With him together went.
105 27. They all his threatening signs to them,
   Most manifestly cleared:
  And all the monstrous prodigies
   That in Ham's land appeared.
 28. He darkness sent and clouded them,
110   As if wrapped up in hell:[901]
  And they against his sacred word
   In no sort did rebel.

 29. Their waters, that should have refreshed,
   He did transform to blood:
115   The fishes straight empoisoned thus   *immediately*
   Lay dead in every flood.
 30. Their land abundantly bred frogs
   From which no part was free:
  Which searched the chambers of their kings,
120   Where they did use to be.

 31. And when he spoke, incontinent   *immediately*
   To execute his will,
  Huge swarms of vermin, lice and flies,
   Their coasts each where did fill.
125 32. The rain, that them should have refreshed,
   He unto hail did turn:
  And in their country ominous flames
   Like fatal fires did burn.

---

[901] This line's reference to hell is added by James-Alexander.

The fifth part.

      33. He smote their fig-trees, and their vines,
130   And trees of all their coasts:
      34. Sent caterpillars, grasshoppers,
          Innumerable hosts.
      35. The growing grass in every field
          They quickly did confound: *destroy*
135   And did devour the needful fruits
          That beautified the ground.

      36. He did so smite the land's firstborn
          His steps by blood were traced:
      Even the beginning of their strength,
140   In whom their hopes were placed.
      37. He brought them forth, enrichèd all
          with silver and with gold:
      And of their tribes there was not one,
          Whom weakness did withhold.

145   38. All Egypt was extremely glad
          Whenas they did depart:
      The fear of them so long before,
          Had seized on every heart.
      39. He with a cloud did cover them,
150   Yet not excluding light:
      And still a fire did clear their way,
          So long as it was night.

      40. He brought unto the people quails,
          When they for them did call:
155   And with a bread rained down from heaven,   *i.e. manna*
          Did satisfy them all.
      41. He opened wide the solid rock,
          And waters forth did flow:
      Which, having quenched the thirsty parts,
160   Did like a river grow.

      42 Because his holy promises
          He then did call to mind:
      Which with his servant Abraham
          A covenant did bind.
165   43 He led his people forth with joy
          Through many sundry grounds:
      And them whom he elected had,
          With loud triumphing sounds.

	44	And gave to them the heathen's lands
170		Whom they were to destroy:
		That which the people's labours gained,
		He gave them to enjoy.
	45	That they his statutes might observe,
		According to his word:
175		And that they still might keep his laws,
		Give praise unto the Lord.

Psalm 144

	1.	Blessed be the Lord, who is my strength,	
		And rules my actions right:	
		He doth my hands teach how to war,	
		My fingers how to fight.	
5	2.	My goodness, fortress, and my tower,	
		My Saviour, and my shield,	
		In whom I trust: and who to me	
		Doth make my people yield.[902]	
	3.	Lord, what is man, that thou of him	
10		Should'st any knowledge take?[903]	
		Or yet man's son, that thou of him	
		So great account should'st make?	
	4.	Man (lo) resembling vanity,	
		Uncertain here doth stray:	
15		His days (like shadows) dark and swift,	
		Do vanish straight away.[904]	*immediately*
	5.	Bow down thy heavens, and (Lord) come down,	*bend*
		I humbly thee invoke:	
		Do thou but once the mountains touch,	
20		And they (all moved) shall smoke.[905]	
	6.	Cast glancing flames of lightning forth,	
		And make them scatter soon:	
		Shoot out thine arrows, to destroy,	
		Till they be quite undone.[906]	

[902] This Psalm is partly a pastiche of earlier Psalms, perhaps providing a precedent for early modern collage Psalms. The opening attribution of 'my strength to God' is similar to the opening of Psalm 18, which also refers to God 'my fortress' and 'my buckler' (KJV).
[903] Compare Psalm 8. 4, 'What is man, that thou art mindful of him? And the son of man, that thou visitest him' (KJV).
[904] Compare Psalm 102. 11, 'My days are like a shadow that declineth' (KJV).
[905] Compare Psalm 104. 32, 'he toucheth the hills and they smoke' (KJV).
[906] Compare Psalm 18. 14, 'Yea, he sent out his arrows, and scattered them; and he shot out lightnings, and discomfited them' (KJV).

25	7.	Send from above thine hand, me rid,	
		Me from great waters free:⁹⁰⁷	

<pre>
25   7. Send from above thine hand, me rid,
             Me from great waters free:⁹⁰⁷
         And from the hand of children strange,
             That would take hold of me.
     8. Whose mouth speaks nought but vanity,   nothing, that which is worthless
30   Which fondly they conceive:⁹⁰⁸   foolishly
         And their right hand, a right hand is
             Of falsehood, to deceive.⁹⁰⁹
     9. I (Lord) will sing a song to thee,
             That I of new have found:
35   On instruments that have ten strings,
             Thy praises I will sound.⁹¹⁰
     10. Lo, he it is, who only gives   alone
             Salvation unto kings:
         His servant David from the sword
40   Who still in safety brings.
     11. Rid me, and from strange children's hand,
             Who vainly speak, me save:
         For their right hand, a right hand is
             Of falsehood to deceive.
45   12. That like to plants our sons may be,
             In youth grown up that are:⁹¹¹
         Our daughters as the cornerstones,
             To grace a palace rare.
     13. That in our garners, of all sorts,   storehouse for grain
50   All may with plenty meet:
         That thousands may our sheep bring forth,
             Ten thousands in our streets.
     14. That for the labour, always strong,
             Our oxen do not faint:
55   That none break in, nor yet go out,
             In all the streets no plaint.   lament
</pre>

⁹⁰⁷ Compare Psalm 32. 6, 'surely in the floods of great waters they shall not come nigh unto him' (KJV).
⁹⁰⁸ Compare Psalm 10. 7, 'His mouth is full of cursing and deceit and fraud: under his tongue is mischief and vanity' (KJV).
⁹⁰⁹ Compare Psalm 26. 10, 'In whose hands is mischief, and their right hand is full of bribes' (KJV).
⁹¹⁰ Compare Psalm 33. 2–3, 'sing unto him with the psaltery and an instrument of ten strings. Sing unto him a new song' (KJV).
⁹¹¹ Compare Psalm 128. 3, 'thy children like olive plants round about thy table' (KJV).

15. The people happy is, that is
       With such-like blessings stored: *stocked*
    Yea, happy is that people still
60   Who hath for God the Lord.

111. John Standish, in *All the French Psalm Tunes with English Words, Being a Collection of Psalms According to the Verses and Tunes Generally Used in the Reformed Churches of France and Germany* (1632)

[John Standish assembled a collection of metrical Psalms by himself and other translators, most never before printed, in a complete psalter that he presumably intended to be sung in churches, since he provided unison tunes. Nothing more is known of him, though there was a clergyman of the same name who died in 1570, chaplain to Edward VI and Archdeacon of Colchester, and another who preached before James II at Whitehall in 1675. Standish labelled each Psalm in terms of genre or mode, including prayer, consolation, doctrine, thanksgiving, 'prayer and prophecy', 'doctrine of politic government', and 'of praise public'. Standish also included a 'pause', or several, in the middle of many longer Psalms, the function of which is not specified. Standish's use of French and German tunes accommodates a greater variety of metres and stanza forms than is usual in English singing Psalms. The authors of the various translations are not indicated in the volume, but were identified by William Drummond of Hawthornden in a manuscript commonplace book, presumably on the basis of Psalms he had seen in manuscript circulation. James Doelman, 'A Seventeenth-Century Publication of Three of Sir Philip Sidney's Psalms', *Notes and Queries*, 38 (1991), 162–63.]

Psalm 61

Prayer

Lord my God, hear thou my crying,
To thee flying,
Give ear to my prayer and moan.
2. From earth's end, when griefs oppress me
5   And distress me,
I will cry to thee alone.

To the rock, than I far higher,
I aspire;
By thy aid, O lead thou me,
10 3. For thou art my safe strong tower,
Thy great power
Saves me from my enemy.

4. In thy sacred house before thee
   To adore thee,
15 Evermore will I remain
   Under thy wings' shade, protection
   And refection
   Confident I shall obtain. Selah.

   5. For thou, Lord my God, hast deignèd,
20 When I plainèd,   *lamented*
   To my plaints thy gracious ear,   *laments*
   And hast giv'n me by thy Spirit,
   To inherit
   With them who thy name do fear.

25 6. To the royal king elected,
   High erected,
   Length of days thou added hast;
   Many years to thy anointed,
   Hast appointed,
30 Which from age to age shall last.

   7. In God's presence him safe guiding,
   He abiding
   Shall remain eternally:
   Make thou for his preservation
35 Preparation
   Of thy grace and verity.   *truth*

   8. So shall I with thanks abounding,
   Psalms resounding,[912]
   Sing praise to thy name for aye,   *forever*
40 That I with my best endeavour
   May persever
   Daily all my vows to pay.

112. Joshua Sylvester, in *All the French Psalm Tunes with English Words* (1632) (see 111)

[Joshua Sylvester (1562/3–1618) was a poet and translator, educated at Southampton grammar school, whose headmaster, Adrian Saravia, was later one of the translators of the King James Bible. Leaving school early, Sylvester apprenticed as a merchant but soon turned to translation from French, which

---

[912] Standish adds the specific self-reference to Psalms, the original having simply 'So will I sing praise' (as KJV renders it).

he had learned at Southampton. His major work was translating the religious work of Guillaume de Salluste Du Bartas, especially *La Semaine*, a hexameral epic recounting the story of Creation in Genesis, and *La Seconde Semaine*, a history of the world. Sylvester published several parts leading up to the complete *Bartas his Divine Weeks and Works* in 1605, with commendatory verses by Ben Jonson and Samuel Daniel, and dedicated to James I, though it was his son, Prince Henry, who rewarded Sylvester with a pension. James had been enthusiastic about Du Bartas since childhood, being given a copy of *La Semaine* by his nurse. He himself translated Bartas's *L'Uranie* into Scots, and he commissioned his courtier Henry Hudson to translate the poet's *Judith* (printed 1584), both from an earlier collection, *La muse chrestienne*. Du Bartas was already popular in England as well as Scotland, and Sylvester's translation made it even more so, attracting a wide readership and influencing poets from Spenser to Milton. Sylvester's metrical Psalms were printed, along with those of several other poet-translators, by John Standish in a complete psalter presumably intended for singing in churches. Of all the Psalms included, only those of John Vicars had previously been printed. The authors of the various translations are not indicated in the volume, but were identified by William Drummond of Hawthornden in a manuscript commonplace book, presumably on the basis of Psalms he had seen in manuscript circulation. Doelman ('A Seventeenth-Century Publication') and Swann ('Davison Psalms') point out that Standish makes changes to Psalms by the Sidneys and Davison in order to accommodate the tune he gives them for singing. There is no way of telling, since no other copies are extant, but it is conceivable that Standish may have tinkered similarly with other Psalms he included. See Doelman, 'A Seventeenth-Century Publication'; Doelman, 'The Accession of King James I and English Religious Poetry', *SEL*, 34.1 (1994), 19–40; Susan Snyder, *ODNB*.]

Psalm 5

Prayer

Unto the words of my complaining, *lamentation*
O Lord, incline thy gracious ear,
Vouchsafe to understand and hear, *deign*
O thou that in the heav'ns art reigning,
5 My cause of plaining. *lamenting*

2. Hear thou, and that with expedition,
My crying voice, my God, my King,
For only unto thee I bring
And offer up with all submission
10 This my petition.

3. Lord, in the morn my prayer ascending,
If it may please thee, thou shalt hear:
My voice when morning doth appear
Will I to thee address, attending
15 Thy grace descending.

4. Thou art a God, all gods excelling,
Who art not pleased with wickedness,
Nor winkest at ungodliness:
Ill doers have not any dealing
20 With thee, nor dwelling.

5. The foolish, rash, the proud dare never
Thy dreadful presence come before:
For thou abhorrest evermore
The wicked all, that still persever
25 In bad endeavour.

6. The smooth deceiver, and the liar,
That make good evil, evil good:
The murderer, the man of blood
Thou wilt in fine confound in fire,   *in the end, defeat utterly*
30 In thy fierce ire.   *anger*

7. But I for mercy will implore thee:
Thy mercies great and many be,
In reverence and fear to thee,
Toward thy sacred house before thee
35 I will adore thee.

8. Guide me, my God, and safe protect me,
According to thy righteous guise,
From ambush of my enemies,
And in thy way made plain direct me,
40 Upright erect me.

        Pause.

9. For in their mouth, no truth remaineth,
Their heart is double wickeder,
Their throat an open sepulchre,
Their tongue by smoothing, soothing, gaineth,
45 And always feigneth.

10. Lord let them ever quite be quellèd,
Confound them in their own device,
Disperse them for their heinous vice:

For they against thee have rebellèd,
50 And proudly swellèd.

11. But let all those whose expectation
Is fixed on thee, in thee rejoice:
And joy they aye in heart and voice   *always*
That have thy name in admiration
55 For their salvation.

12. For Lord, the just thou aye dost tender,
And them thou cover'st with thy grace,
As with a shield in every place:
Thou free from danger them dost render,
60 As their defender.

Psalm 127

Doctrine

Unless the Lord the house doth build,
The builders cost and care is vain,
Their charge is lost, and all their pain,
Though stuff be strong, and men be skilled;   *building materials*
5 Unless the Lord the city guard,
In vain men watch, in vain they ward.   *guard*

2. In vain so early up ye are,
In vain ye go so late to bed,
In vain ye pain both hand and head:
10 In vain so homely hard ye fare,[913]
Unless God bless wake they or sleep;
Whom he doth love, he safe will keep.

3. Lo, also when a man is blessed
With hopeful issue of his own,
15 His heirs to what he hath possessed,
It is the gift of God alone:
God only of his goodness gives   *alone*
The womb due fruit,[914] that after lives.

---

[913] The figure of anaphora, repeating a word or phrase at the beginning of lines or clauses, is common in biblical rhetoric, though not in this Psalm. Sylvester uses it to underscore the theme of vanity and to link this stanza with the previous one.

[914] In seventeenth-century English, the 'fruit' of the womb was more than a metaphor, since the word actually meant 'fetus'.

4. And when the children men become
20 Of body strong, and stout of mind,
So apt and active in their kind,   *disposition*
That arrows to the head drawn home,
With strongest arm and nimblest flight,
Seem not more terrible in sight.

25 5. He happy is, who hath fulfilled
His quiver with such shafts as these,
For in the trial of their pleas
They shall not be abashed nor ill'd: *maligned*
Nay, they shall make their foes ashamed
30 Before the Judge and justly blamed.

113. Thomas Salisbury, in *All the French Psalm Tunes with English Words* (1632) (see 111)

[Thomas Salisbury (1566/7–1622) was a printer and member of the Stationers' Company. Born in Clocaenog, Denbighshire, Salisbury was also a champion of the Welsh language (which he calls 'British'), publishing, with Simon Stafford, a translation of the Psalms into a variety of Welsh metres by William Midelton. Midelton completed his *Psalmae y brenhinol brophwyd Dafydh* ('Psalms of the Royal Prophet David') in Panama, anchored at an island in the Mosquito Gulf, where he had sailed with the expedition of Francis Drake and John Hawkins. Midelton died in 1596 just before his returning ship reached London. His cousin, the merchant Thomas Myddelton, supported the posthumous publication by Salisbury and Stafford (1603). In his address to the reader, Salisbury claims also to have begun printing another version of the Psalms 'in the like kind of metre in British as they are usually sung in the Church of England', but it is not clear what became of this project. His *ODNB* biographers claim that they were printed by Stafford in 1603 for Salisbury, as *Rhann o Psalmae Dafydd Prophwyd* ('Part of the Psalms of the Prophet David'), the Psalms actually translated by Salisbury, Edward Kyffin providing an introduction to the selection. However, Kyffin's biographer states that he wrote the Psalms, as Salisbury made clear in a letter to Sir John Wynn of Gwydir. Salisbury's interest in Welsh Psalms persisted, since he apparently made reference in 1610 to Edmund Prys promising to produce a complete Welsh metrical psalter. Prys's Psalms were not printed until 1621, but they then dominated Welsh church singing in the way Sternhold and Hopkins did in English. Salisbury's English metrical Psalm must have circulated in manuscript and found its way into the hands of John Standish, who included it in *All the French Psalm Tunes*. Its authorship was identified by William Drummond. Doelman ('A Seventeenth-Century Publication') and Swann ('Davison Psalms') point out that Standish makes changes to Psalms by the Sidneys and Davison in order to accommodate the tune he gives them for singing. There is no way of telling, since no other copies are extant, but it is conceivable that Standish may have tinkered similarly with other Psalms he included. See Gruffydd Aled Williams (Midleton and Prys), and D. L. Thomas, rev. Anita McConnell (Salisbury) in *ODNB*.]

Psalm 104

Praise.

    Bless thou the Lord my soul, O Lord my God,
    Thy greatness far exceedeth all abroad:
    Thou majesty most glorious daily wearest,
    With honour thou most beautiful appearest.
5 2. With light most bright, resplendent every morn,
    As with a robe, thyself thou dost adorn:
    The firmament bedecked with stars extending,
    Like curtains drawn forth by thy power transcending.
    3. Thou layest fast thy lofty chamber beams   *securely*
10 Upon the seas' and waters' gushing streams:
    Thou on the clouds which in the air are biding,
    Triumphant com'st, as on a chariot riding.
    And when to walk it is thy sacred mind,
    Thou marchest on the wings of every wind.
15 4. Thy angels all are spirits of thy own framing,[915]
    Thy ministers are like a fire flaming.

    5. Foundations of the earth so vastly round,
    On bases thou didst set, so fastly found: *securely*
    That thou hast made it ever firm and stable,
20 No power but thine to move it shall be able.
    6. And this same earth thou underneath the deep,
    As underneath a mantle close dost keep: *secret*
    Whilst thou great God didst cause the wat'ry fountains
    To rise and flow, and stand above the mountains.
25 7. But then as soon as thy rebuke they heard,
    They passed away, and fled as all afeared:
    And at the voice of thy most dreadful thunder,
    They haste away, each one their way asunder.
    8. Up by the hills they high ascend amain,   *at full speed*
30 Down by the dales they low descend again:

---

[915] spirits] The metre requires pronunciation as a monosyllable, perhaps 'sprites'.

    Until in their own place they be surrounded
    Which at the first for them thy wisdom founded.
        Pause.

    9. Beyond the bounds which for them thou hast set,
    The surging waves restrained, can never get:
35 Lest if they should at any time pass over,
    The surface of the earth they would recover.
    10. Into the vales below thou deign'st to bring   *valleys*
    The wholesome sweet clear water of the spring,
    Which midst the hills a pleasant murmur keepeth,
40 Whilst through the vales the silent current creepeth.

    11. The rivers' store of water, drink doth yield,   *stock*
    To every beast that rangeth in the field:
    And the smooth brook, which here and there still passes,
    Doth quench the thirst of wild and savage asses.
45 12. By these the fowls of heav'n do take delight,
    To make their nests, abiding day and night:
    By thee each bird melodious notes advances,
    Amidst the trees' young tender slender branches.

    13. From chambers high among the clouds he fills
50 With showers of rain, enriched the fertile hills,
    Yea, the whole world with his works fruits aboundeth,
    And satisfied therewith, his praise resoundeth.
    14. He maketh grass out of the earth to grow,
    The brutish beasts he doth provide for so:
55 And for man's use, the useful herbs he planteth,
    That they may till the ground, which labour wanteth.

    15. He maketh wine which hath a secret art,
    To cure the sad, and to make glad man's heart.
    He maketh oil, which makes men's faces shining,
60 And bread that breeds heart's strength, the powers combining.
    16. Of the great Lord, the trees are very great,
    In sap, in growth, either for show or meat: *food*
    The cedars high on Libanus that groweth,   *Lebanon*
    God's plants, not man's, than man's more goodly showeth.

65 17. In them the birds do make their downy nest
    By native skill, and take therein their rest:
    As for the stork, while other liketh others,
    Amidst the firs her and her young she smothers.   *conceals*
    18. For the wild goats upon the highest hills,

70 Their refuge they do make, and sport their fills:
   On th'other side among the rocks so stony,
   Thou placest safe the wild and fearful cony.   *rabbit*

          Pause.

   19. The changing moon he sets upon her change,
   From west to east in seasons fit to range:
75 He makes the sun know his fixed course near slowing,
   In th' east his rise, i'th west his downward going:
   20. He darkness makes, and takes away the light,
   The glorious day is turned to obscure night:
   Within their dens, the forest beasts all sleeping,
80 Out of their dens then boldly all come creeping.

   21. The lion's young that lurk beside the way,
   Do rage and roar incessant for their prey:
   These seek their food by mere instinct with crying,
   From the strong God, their want of food supplying.
85 22. Yet in the morn at rising of the sun,
   They gather them in one, and homeward run:
   There in their dens, close couching they repose them   *hidden, lying*
   Till night, so that no eye can there disclose them.

   23. With break of day man breaks his rest and goes
90 To labour, where the field him profit shows.
   In husbandry, whose painful toil near endeth,
   Till towards even, the shadow longer tendeth.
   24. O holy Lord, what register can hold
   Thy wondrous works, they are so manifold:
95 From wisdom of thy providence proceeding,
   The earth is full of riches, thine exceeding.

   25. So likewise is the deep and spacious sea,
   Stretching its arms to every creek and key:
   Where swim and creep creatures innumerable,
100 Both small and great, to name them who is able?
   26. The goodly ships therein do ride and sail,
   And therein thou hast made the mighty whale:
   There swims the huge Leviathan, in straying,
   Thy greatness shows, and in his sportive playing:

          Pause.

105 27. All these, all else, beasts, fishes, flying fowls,
   Await on thee, for to refresh their souls:

That thou should'st give them meat in meetest season,
Which else should want their food, as they want reason.
28. What thou dost please, in goodness them to give,
They gladly take, and thereby they do live:
When once thy hand of bounty is extended,
All good to thy good creatures is expended.

29. But when thou hid'st thy face, the place of joy,
No comfort then, all trouble and annoy: *grief*
When thou withdraw'st their breath life is adjourned,[916]
And to dead dust, is living dust returned.
30. Thou sendest forth thy Spirit, Lord, and then
In forms and seeds they are remade again,
And when they fail, with force from thee endued
The surface of the old earth is renewed.

31. The glorious praise of our good gracious Lord,
From age to age all ages shall record.
And in his works which he in wisdom framed,
He shall rejoice so oft as they are named.
32. If against earth he bend his angry brow,
Thereof the strength and pillars trembling bow:
If but to touch the hills, him wrath provoketh,
For very fear, the hills with terror smoketh.

33. So long as God that I shall live shall please,
Unto that God to sing I will not cease:
Yea, while I shall in being be protected,
Unto my God, my Psalms shall be directed.[917]
34. All my discourse of him, and thoughts of heart,
Shall sweetness to him, to myself impart:
No sorrow shall from him my solace sever,
My joying in the Lord shall be forever.

35. Men that are given to sin, be all consumed,
None wicked be on earth, except entombed
Up, up, my soul to God in thanks be raisèd,
The world's great God, of all the world be praisèd.

---

[916] breath] *ruah* in Hebrew, meaning literally 'breath' but by extension 'spirit', 'life'.
[917] Salisbury adds the specific self-reference to 'Psalms', the original having simply 'I will sing praise' (as in KJV).

114. George Wither, *The Psalms of David Translated in Lyric-Verse, According to the Scope of the Original* (1632)

[George Wither (1588–1667) was one of the most prolific authors of the English Renaissance, and one of the most preoccupied with the Psalms. He was born into a large and prosperous Hampshire family, and studied at Magdalen College, Oxford, and Middle Temple. Wither published in a very wide range of genres, including elegy, epigrams, satire, pastoral, emblems, political polemic, prophecy, and newspaper journalism. Wither's *A Preparation to the Psalter* (1619) was an important study of the Psalms, including the nature of Hebrew poetry. Wither got no further than his contemporaries in understanding Hebrew poetics, but he gathered together much earlier scholarship on the subject. The next year, Wither published *Exercises upon the First Psalm* (1620), which offered a metrical version and a prose paraphrase of the Psalm, as well as a gathering of commentary, an exposition by Wither, and meditations and prayers. Wither published *The Songs of the Old Testament Translated into English Measures* (which did not include Psalms) in 1621, and *The Hymns and Songs of the Church* in 1623. Wither was granted a patent by James I to have his *Hymns and Songs* bound with all English psalters; it was reprinted several times, but the patent was generally neither obeyed nor enforced. Finally, in 1632, Wither produced his metrical psalter, *Psalms of David*. Like so many other metrical Psalmists, Wither intended to replace Sternhold and Hopkins with a church psalter of superior quality, but somewhere his project went astray, perhaps due to opposition from the Company of Stationers. Wither's *Psalms* was printed only once, in the Netherlands, in a tiny volume, then quickly sank from sight. Wither made no attempt at an original translation, let alone from the original languages; he professed to be staying as close as possible to 'our English translation' (presumably the King James Bible). A manuscript of Wither's Psalms survives, seemingly reflecting an early draft of his translations, though it is a clean copy in a scribal hand, signed by Wither, and in the address to the reader, he states that after much labour this work is now finished. The substantial changes between the manuscript and the printed text reveal how much care Wither took with his Psalms, a greater care (Pritchard suggests) than with any of his many other works. No tunes were provided in Wither's *Psalms*, since the metres were designed to be sung to those already in use. See Doelman, *King James I and the Religious Culture of England*; Hamlin, *Psalm Culture*; Allan Pritchard, 'A Manuscript of Wither's "Psalms"', *Huntington Library Quarterly*, 27.1 (1963), 73–77; Michelle O'Callaghan, *ODNB*.]

Psalm 69

To the chief° musician Shosannim a Psalm of David.[918]
It personates Christ taking upon him our sins and infirmities; humbling himself before his Father; declaring the condition of his adversaries; showing the bitterness of his passion; signifying the judgements prepared for sinners; and praying for his elect etc. Christ's members may use it to those purposes.

      Help, Lord, for floods enclose my soul,
      In groundless depths I am bemired,   *bottomless*
      Above my head, great waters roll,
      My parchèd throat, with cries is tired.
5   Mine eyes are dimmed in seeking thee,
      More than my hairs, my foes are grown,
      My spoilers are too strong for me;   *despoilers*
         And take as theirs, what is mine own.
  2. Thou knowest how I am to blame;
10   But, for my sake, let none of those
      (Lord God of Isr'el) suffer blame,
      Who do in thee their trust repose.
      For I sustain reproachful scorn.
      And am disgracèd for thy sake.
15   My brethren, of my mother born,
         Of me, likewise, a stranger make.
  3. Zeal to thy house, hath worn me out,
      Thy scorners, my reproachers be;
      My fastings, and my tears they flout,
20   And, when I mourn, they laugh at me.
      Of me, the rulers, evil spake;
      The drunkards, made of me their songs:
      But, Lord, my moan I timely make,
         In mercy, mark therefore my wrongs.
25 4. Me, by thy truth's protection keep,
      That miry-depths, nor spiteful-foes,
      Devouring-floods, nor whirlpools deep,
      Nor dungeon's mouth my soul enclose.
      But, Lord, of thy abounding grace,
30   (For thy love-sake) return, and hear;
      To me, thy servant, show thy face,
         And, in my need, incline thine ear.

---

[918] Shosannim] Hebrew *shuwshan* (lilies), perhaps referring to the tune to which this Psalm is to be sung.

5. Draw nigh, and save, and set thou free   *near*
   My soul, from those who bear me spite;
   For all my wrongs are known to thee,
   And all my foes are in thy sight.
   Rebukes and scorns, my heart nigh broke,
   With griefs oppressed, I made my moan;
   But, where I did for pity look,
       They would (alas) afford me none.

6. They, for my meat, did gall prepare,   *food, bitter substance*
   Sharp vinegar to quench my thirst;
   Their board, therefore, shall them ensnare,   *table*
   And blessings be to them accursed.
   Their eye shall be deprived of sight:
   A cureless grief their back shall shake:
   God's heavy wrath shall on them light,
       His vengeance them shall overtake.

7. None shall in their abiding-place,
   Or in their tent, be dwelling found:
   For whom thou smot'st, those they did chase,
   And grievèd him whom thou didst wound.
   More sinful still they shall become,
   And in God's justice have no share,
   Nor in that book of life have room,
       Wherein the just enrollèd are.

8. But I, that poor and scornèd am,
   Shall by thine aid, O Lord, be raised;
   For which, I'll magnify thy name,
   And in my songs thou shalt be praised.
   And that, O Lord, more pleases thee,
   Than horned and hoofèd ox to give;
   Which, when the meek (thee seeking) see,
       It shall with joy, their heart revive.

9. God's praise, ye heav'ns and earth, declare
   Him praise, thou sea, and all in thee:
   For to the poor he lends his ear.
   And he doth set the prisoner free.
   He, Zion saves in time of need,
   And Judah's towns he will erect,
   To be for those, and for their seed,   *descendants*
       Who serving him, his name affect.

Psalm 85

To the chief musician a Psalm for the sons of Korah. The Church acknowledgeth God's benefits; desires their continuance, and the forbearance of his wrath, etc. We may sing it to praise God for his bounty to his Church and kingdom, and to desire the continuation of our happiness, by still vouchsafing mercy with his justice.

  Thou hast, O God, thy kingdom graced
    And Jacob's thrall repealed;   *captivity*
  Thy people's faults, thou pardoned hast,
    And all their sins concealed. Selah.
5 Thine anger, thou hast quite appeased,
    And thy just wrath forborne;
  O Lord of hosts, now thou art pleased
    Let us to thee return.
 2. For why should'st thou still wroth remain?   *angry*
10   And vexèd rather be,
  Than cheer thy people's hearts again,
    That they may joy in thee?
  To save us, Lord, thy favour show,
    And, let us hear (in peace)
15 Thy word among us preachèd so,
    That we from sin may cease.
 3. Then, shall thy saving-health abide,
    Near those who fear thy name;
  And in our land shall still reside,
20   Thy glories and thy fame.
  Then truth and love shall meet and kiss,
    And justice, peace embrace;[919]
  Yea, truth on earth and righteousness
    From heav'n shall show her face.
25 4. The Lord, with every needful store,   *necessary, supply*
    Shall make our kingdom flow;
  And send his righteousness before,
    That we his way may know.

---

[919] The key terms in this often-quoted verse are usually translated as 'mercy' and 'truth', and 'righteousness' and 'peace', respectively, as in both Coverdale (BCP) and the KJV. Hopkins's translation in *The Whole Book of Psalms* has 'truth' and 'mercy', 'peace' and 'justice'. Wither's choices are within the semantic range of the Hebrew nouns, however.

115. Richard Crashaw, *Steps to the Temple: Sacred Poems, with Other Delights of the Muses* (1646, composed 1633?)

[Richard Crashaw (1612/3–1648) was born in London, son of the clergyman and author William Crashaw. He was educated at Charterhouse and Pembroke College, Cambridge, where he excelled as a poet and a Latinist. At Cambridge, Crashaw embraced the high church Anglicanism associated with William Laud. He was elected to a fellowship at Peterhouse in 1635, and at this time he also became a frequent visitor at Nicholas Ferrar's Anglican community at Little Gidding (which had been frequented earlier by George Herbert). Crashaw's early *Epigrammatum sacrorum liber* (1634) was followed by *Steps to the Temple: Sacred Poems, with Other Delights of the Muses* (1646), its title an homage to George Herbert's *Temple*. This was one of the most important seventeenth-century lyric collections, and it was many times reprinted. During the Civil War, Crashaw went into exile and converted to Roman Catholicism. *Steps to the Temple* was published after Crashaw's departure, perhaps without his involvement. Crashaw moved to Rome, where he lived in the English College. He struggled to find employment, and, though he was eventually taken on by Cardinal Palotto, he achieved little success. He died at the pilgrimage site of Loreto. *Carmen deo nostro* was published posthumously in 1652. Crashaw's two metrical Psalms were included in the 1646 *Steps to the Temple* but were written much earlier. Most of Crashaw's English poetry seems to have been written during his years at Cambridge. A translation by Crashaw of Psalm 1 into Latin also survives in at least two manuscripts. See *The English Poems of Richard Crashaw*, ed. by Richard Rambuss (Minneapolis and London: University of Minnesota Press, 2013); Thomas Healy, *ODNB*.]

Psalm 23

Happy me! O happy sheep!
Whom my God vouchsafes to keep;   *deigns, guard*
Even my God, even he it is
That points me to these ways of bliss;
5 On whose pastures cheerful spring,
All the year doth sit and sing,
And, rejoicing, smiles to see
Their green backs wear his livery.   *uniform*
Pleasure sings my soul to rest,
10 Plenty wears me at her breast,
Whose sweet temper teaches me
Nor wanton, nor in want to be.[920]

---

[920] A nice bit of wordplay, adding to the Psalm's 'I shall not want' (KJV) the relief from 'wantonness', a temptation for young Cambridge men if not, generally, for sheep.

> At my feet the blubb'ring mountain,
> Weeping, melts into a fountain,[921]
> 15 Whose soft silver-sweating streams
> Make high noon forget his beams:[922]
> When my wayward breath is flying,
> He calls home my soul from dying,
> Strokes and tames my rabid grief,
> 20 And does woo me into life:
> When my simple weakness strays,
> (Tangled in forbidden ways)[923]
> He (my shepherd) is my guide,
> He's before me, on my side,
> 25 And, behind me, he beguiles
> Craft in all her knotty wiles: *deceits*
> He expounds the giddy wonder
> Of my weary steps, and under
> Spreads a path clear as the day,
> 30 Where no churlish rub says nay[924]   *obstacle*
> To my joy-conducted feet,
> Whilst they gladly go to meet
> Grace and peace, to meet new lays   *songs*
> Tuned to my great shepherd's praise.
> 35 Come now, all ye terrors, sally,
> Muster forth into the valley,
> Where triumphant darkness hovers
> With a sable wing, that covers
> Brooding horror. Come, thou death,
> 40 Let the damps of thy dull breath
> Overshadow ev'n the shade,
> And make darkness' self afraid;[925]

---

[921] Crashaw is the great poet of bodily fluids, tears especially, but there was a general aesthetic and theology of tears in the seventeenth century. See Marjorie E. Lange, *Telling Tears in the Renaissance* (Leiden and New York: E. J. Brill, 1996).

[922] Crashaw converts the simple landscape of the Psalm into one more familiar from Renaissance pastoral, including the green 'livery' of the pastures (converting the Psalmist into a country lord) and the streams that sweat silver.

[923] The elaboration of the allegorical landscape seems to have taken Crashaw beyond the Psalm, since there is nothing in it suggesting forbidden ways. Even the valley is not forbidden, just dangerous. Or perhaps these ways are the implied alternative to the 'paths of righteousness' along which God leads the Psalmist.

[924] rub] A term originally from the game of bowls, appropriate among the country pleasures of Crashaw's aristocratic rural scene. A churl (the root of 'churlish') is a base country peasant.

[925] Crashaw's valley seems almost gothic.

    There my feet, even there shall find
    Way for a resolvèd mind.
45 Still my shepherd, still my God
    Thou art with me, still thy rod,
    And thy staff, whose influence
    Gives direction, gives defence.
    At the whisper of thy word[926]
50 Crowned abundance spreads my board: *table*
    While I feast, my foes do feed
    Their rank malice not their need,
    So that with the self-same bread
    They are starved, and I am fed.
55 How my head in ointment swims!
    How my cup o'erlooks her brims!   *overflows*
    So, even so, still may I move
    By the line of thy dear love;[927]
    Still may thy sweet mercy spread
60 A shady arm above my head,
    About my paths, so shall I find
    The fair centre of my mind,
    Thy temple,[928] and those lovely walls
    Bright ever with a beam that falls
65 Fresh from the pure glance of thine eye,
    Lighting to eternity.
    There I'll dwell for ever, there
    Will I find a purer air
    To feed my life with, there I'll sup
70 Balm and nectar in my cup,
    And thence my ripe soul will I breathe,
    Warm, into the arms of death.[929]

[926] In a Psalm, we might expect 'word' to have some sense of the Word, or Christ, but Crashaw conveys more the *sotto voce* order of a Lord to his wait staff. In most printed versions, 'Word' is capitalized, but then so is 'Board' and most other nouns, and in the 1648 edition these are lower case.

[927] line] Meaning unclear, perhaps 'rule' or 'mark'.

[928] Crashaw very cleverly plays the biblical sense of 'temple' (for the Psalm's 'house of the Lord') against the anatomical, following so close on the 'centre of my mind'. The latter is also a curiously intellectual rather than spiritual place for the Psalmist-sheep to end up.

[929] Some versions of Psalm 23 take the final verse to be about eternity in heaven, others about living a godly life on earth. Crashaw is unique in ending his version in the embrace of death's (not God's) welcoming arms, a figure used in secular poems by Michael Drayton, William Drummond, and William Browne, but never in Bible translations.

Psalm 137

On the proud banks of great Euphrates' flood,[930]   *vigorous*
    There we sat, and there we wept:
Our harps that now no music understood,[931]
    Nodding on the willows, slept,
5   While, unhappy, captived, we,
      Lovely Zion, thought on thee.

They, they that snatched us from our country's breast
    Would have a song carved to their ears   *served*
In Hebrew numbers, then (O cruel jest!)   *metres*
10   When harps and hearts were drowned in tears:
      Come, they cried, come sing and play
      One of Zion's songs today.

Sing? play? to whom (ah) shall we sing or play,
    If not, Jerusalem, to thee?
15 Ah, thee, Jerusalem! Ah, sooner may
    This hand forget the mastery
      Of music's dainty touch, than I
      The music of thy memory.[932]

Which when I lose, O may at once my tongue
20   Lose this same busy speaking art,
Unperched, her vocal arteries unstrung,[933]   *displaced*
    No more acquainted with my heart,
      On my dry palate's roof to rest
      A withered leaf, an idle guest.

25 No, no, thy good, Zion, alone must crown
    The head of all my hope-nursed joys.
But Edom, cruel thou! thou criedst down, down
    Sink Sion, down and never rise;
      Her falling thou didst urge and thrust,
30   And haste to dash her into dust.

---

[930] The geographical detail is added by Crashaw, the Euphrates being the river along which Babylon was built, where the Jews were taken into exile and captivity.

[931] A very clever pun, playing the sense of 'understood' as 'comprehended' against its root sense of standing under, which the Israelites presumably are, since they have hung their harps upon trees.

[932] The abrupt, halting questions, parenthetical sigh, and stuttering repetition convey a strong sense of passion, though the style is more baroque than biblical.

[933] arteries] Crashaw has in mind the Latin etymology, *arteria*, meaning 'trachia' or 'windpipe'.

> Dost laugh? proud Babel's daughter! do, laugh on,   *Babylon's*
>   Till thy ruin teach thee tears,
> Even such as these; laugh, till a venging throng   *avenging*
>   Of woes, too late do rouse thy fears.
> 35   Laugh, till thy children's bleeding bones
>   Weep precious tears upon the stones.[934]

116. Phineas Fletcher, *The Purple Island, or The Isle of Man, Together with Piscatory Eclogues and Other Poeticall Miscellanies* (1633)

[Phineas Fletcher (1582–1640) came from a family of writers: his father, Giles, was a poet of some note as well as a politician; his younger brother, Giles, was also a poet, author of *Christ's Victory and Triumph in Heaven and Earth, over and after Death* (1610); and his cousin, John, was one of the most famous playwrights of the seventeenth century, frequently collaborating with Francis Beaumont as well as William Shakespeare. Phineas was educated at Eton and King's College, Cambridge, where he was ordained. He spent most of his life at the parish of Hilgay in Norfolk. Fletcher's poetry, heavily influenced by Edmund Spenser, was largely written during his Cambridge years, though much of it was published later. *The Locusts, or, Apollyonists*, an apocalyptic response to the 1605 Gunpowder Plot, was printed in 1627. Fletcher's greatest work was *The Purple Island, or, The Isle of Man* (1633), an allegorical poem elaborating the conceit of man's body as an island. Fletcher's metrical Psalms were appended to *The Purple Island*, along with a set of piscatory (fishing) eclogues and several other shorter poems. Many of the Psalms were prefaced by notes suggesting they be sung to a certain tune. Since these (mostly secular) tunes were not provided, and do not survive elsewhere, it is uncertain whether Fletcher seriously intended the Psalms to be sung. In 1632, Fletcher had published *The Way to Blessedness, A Treatise or Commentary on the First Psalm*, in which he writes of the Psalms, 'we here behold lively drawn, by God's own finger, not only the face, and hands (the outward profession, and actions) but the very heart of that man, who was according to God's own heart'. See Hamlin, *Psalm Culture*; Joan Grundy, *The Spenserian Poets* (London: Edward Arnold, 1969); P. G. Stanwood, *ODNB*.]

---

[934] Crashaw does not quite skirt the violence of the Psalm's conclusion, but rather than an angry vengeful mob he substitutes an allegorical 'throng of woes', and the dashing of the children against the stones is omitted, even if it is implied in the weeping of blood from their bones.

Psalm 42

Psalm 42. which agrees with the tune of 'Like the Hermit Poor'.[935]

Look as[936] an hart with sweat and blood imbrued,   *stained*
Chased and embossed, thirsts in the soil to be;   *concealed in a thicket*
So my poor soul with eager foes pursued,
Looks, longs, O Lord, pines, pants, and faints for thee:
5   When, O my God, when shall I come in place
    To see thy light, and view thy glorious face?

I dine and sup with sighs, with groans and tears,
While all thy foes mine ears with taunting load;
Who now thy cries, who now thy prayer hears?
10 Where is, say they, where is thy boasted God?
    My molten heart deep plunged in sad despairs
    Runs forth to thee in streams of tears and prayers.[937]

With grief I think on those sweet now-past days,
When to thy house my troops with joy I led:
15 We sang, we danced, we chanted sacred lays;   *songs*
No men so haste to wine, no bride to bed.[938]
    Why droop'st, my soul? why faint'st thou in my breast?
    Wait still with praise; his presence is thy rest.

My famished soul driv'n from thy sweetest word,
20 (From Hermon hill, and Jordan's swelling brook)
To thee laments, sighs deep to thee, O Lord,
To thee sends back her hungry longing look:
    Floods of thy wrath breed floods of grief and fears;
    And floods of grief breed floods of plaints and tears.[939]   *laments*

25 His early light with morn these clouds shall clear,
These dreary clouds, and storms of sad despairs:

---

[935] The poem 'Like hermit poor in pensive place obscure', attributed to Sir Walter Raleigh, was set to music by Alfonso Ferrabosco the Younger in his *Ayres* (1609), though it is not certain that this is the tune Fletcher has in mind.

[936] Look as] Possibly 'see how'?

[937] Fletcher participates in what has been called the seventeenth-century poetry of tears, a cross-denominational taste for excessive bodily fluids of all sorts, melting, streaming, flowing, pouring in an expression of devotional passion. See Lange, *Telling Tears in the Renaissance*.

[938] Fletcher's Psalm is a decade too early, but in spirit and descriptive detail it anticipates the royalist cavalier poets of the 1640s.

[939] This seems an example of the pathetic fallacy, attributing to nature a sympathy with human emotions, yet since it is God who is experiencing these emotions, perhaps this is an exceptional case where nature might actually respond.

    Sure am I in the night his songs to hear,
    Sweet songs of joy, as well as he my prayers.
        I'll say, my God, why slight'st thou my distress,
30   While all my foes my weary soul oppress?

    My cruel foes both thee and me upbraid;
    They cut my heart, they vaunt that bitter word,   *boast*
    Where is thy trust? where is thy hope? they said;
    Where is thy God? where is thy boasted Lord?
35   Why droop'st, my soul? why faint'st thou in my breast?
        Wait still with praise; his presence is thy rest.[940]

Psalm 63

Psalm 63. which may be sung, as 'The Widow, *or* Mock-widow'.[941]

      O Lord, before the morning
        Gives heav'n warning
      To let out the day,
      My wakeful eyes
5   Look for thy rise,
    And wait to let in thy joyful ray.
Lank hunger here peoples the desert cells,   *lean*
    Here thirst fills up the empty wells:
How longs my flesh for that bread without leaven![942]
10   How thirsts my soul for that wine of heaven!
Such (oh!) to taste thy ravishing grace!
Such in thy house to view thy glorious face![943]

      Thy love, thy light, thy faces
        Bright-shining graces,
15   (Whose unchangèd ray

---

[940] Fletcher greatly multiplies the number of taunting questions.

[941] A ballad published sometime in the first half of the seventeenth century, entitled 'Fond Love why dost thou dally, or, The Passionate Lover's Ditty', was to be sung to the tune of 'The Mock Widow'.

[942] The Psalmist is only thirsty in the original, but Fletcher makes him hungry as well, and the unleavened bread that he longs for is a Christianizing reference to the Eucharist. Jews eat unleavened bread at the Passover (Exodus 12), but Paul writes of Jews and Christians using a metaphor of bread, calling for the latter to purge the 'old leaven' and become a 'new lump, as ye are unleavened' (1 Corinthians 5. 7). The 'wine of heaven' in the next line adds the second element of the Eucharist.

[943] Fletcher substantially expands the 'barren and dry' landscape of the Psalm, adding hermits, wells, and the biblical unleavened bread (Exodus 12; 1 Corinthians 5. 8) and the 'wine of heaven' (Matthew 26. 29; John 15. 1).

    Knows nor morn's dawn,
     Nor evening's wane)
   How far surmount they life's winter day!
My heart to thy glory tunes all his strings;⁹⁴⁴
20 My tongue thy praises cheerly sings:
And till I slumber, and death shall undress me,⁹⁴⁵
   Thus will I sing, thus will I bless thee.
Fill me with love, O fill me with praise;
So shall I vent due thanks in joyful lays.   *songs*

25 When night all eyes hath quenchèd,
    And thoughts lie drenchèd
    In silence and rest;
    Then will I all
    Thy ways recall,
30 And look on thy light in darkness best.
When my poor soul wounded had lost the field,
 Thou wast my fort, thou wast my shield.⁹⁴⁶
Safe in thy trenches I boldly will vaunt me,   *boast*
 There will I sing, there will I chaunt thee;
35 There I'll triumph in thy banner of grace,
My conqu'ring arms shall be thy arms' embrace.

   My foes from deeps ascending,
    In rage transcending,
    Assaulting me sore,
40   Into their hell
    Are headlong fell;
  There shall they lie, there howl, and roar:
There let deserved torments their spirits tear;
 Feel they worst ills, and worse yet fear.
45 But with his spouse thine anointed in pleasure
  Shall reign, and joy past time or measure:
There new delights, new pleasures still spring:
Haste there, O haste, my soul, to dance and sing.

---

⁹⁴⁴ The familiar implicit Latin pun on heartstrings. See note 123, p. 122.
⁹⁴⁵ An even more erotic image of death than the embracing arms at the end of Crashaw's Psalm 23 (see **115**), the 'clothing' being put off presumably the body, playing on the flesh-spirit dichotomy running through the New Testament (e.g. Romans 8).
⁹⁴⁶ Borrowing the fort metaphor from Psalms 18, 35, 71, 91, 144, and the shield from many others (as well as Paul's 'shield of faith' from Ephesians 6. 16), also adding the 'trenches', a detail from actual contemporary warfare.

Psalm 127

To the tune of that Psalm.[947]

If God build not the house, and lay
The ground-work sure; who ever build,
It cannot stand one stormy day:
If God be not the city's shield,
5   If he be not their bars and wall;
    In vain is watch-tower, men, and all.[948]

Though then thou wak'st when others rest,   *act before*
Though rising thou prevent'st the sun;
Though with lean care thou daily feast,
10 Thy labour's lost, and thou undone:
    But God his child will feed and keep,
    And draw the curtains to his sleep.

Though th'hast a wife fit, young, and fair,
An heritage heirs to advance;
15 Yet canst thou not command an heir;
For heirs are God's inheritance:
    He gives the seed, the bud, the bloom;
    He gives the harvest to the womb.[949]

And look as arrows, by strong arm,
20 In a strong bow drawn to the head,
Where they are meant, will surely harm,
And if they hit, wound deep and dead;
    Children of youth are even so;
    As harmful, deadly, to a foe.

25 That man shall live in bliss and peace,
Who fills his quiver with such shot:
Whose garners swell with such increase,   *storehouses*
Terror and shame assail him not;
    And though his foes deep hatred bear,
30   Thus arm'd, he shall not need to fear.

---

[947] In the *Whole Book* the tune for 'The Lord's Prayer' is recommended for singing to Psalm 127, and this tune works for the Fletcher version as well, with the occasional extra syllable.
[948] Fletcher adds architectural detail.
[949] Anaphora is the prevailing figure of this Psalm of Fletcher's, in the conditionals ('If') of stanza one, and the repeated 'Though' of stanza two and 'He gives' of stanza three.

Psalm 137

To be sung as, 'See the building'.[950]

 Where Perah's flowers[951]   *Euphrates'*
 Perfume proud Babel's bowers,   *Babylon's*
  And paint her wall;
 There we laid a-steeping
5 Our eyes in endless weeping,
  For Zion's fall.
 Our feasts and songs we laid aside;
  On forlorn willows
  (By Perah's billows)
10 We hung our harps, and mirth and joy defied,
 That Zion's ruins should build foul Babel's pride.

 Our conqu'rors vaunting
 With bitter scoffs and taunting,
  Thus proudly jest;
15 Take down your harps, and string them,
 Recall your songs, and sing them,
  For Zion's feast.
 Were our harps well-tuned in every string,
  Our heart-strings broken,[952]
20   Throats drowned, and soaken
 With tears and sighs, how can we praise and sing
 The King of heav'n under an heathen king?[953]

 In all my mourning,
 Jerusalem, thy burning
25   If I forget;

---

[950] A ballad published about 1625, 'Sweet-heart, I love thee', was to be sung to the tune of 'See the building', a popular melody that survives in multiple versions.

[951] In the Geneva (though not the KJV), Genesis 2. 14, one of the four rivers flowing out of Eden is called Perah, with a note in the margin identifying this as the Euphrates. The Hebrew is 'Perath'. If Fletcher knew any Hebrew, he might also be playing on the similarity between 'Perath' and 'perach', meaning 'flower'.

[952] The linking of heart-strings and harp strings is based on a pun available in Latin on *cor* ('heart') and *chorda* (string), though Fletcher also has in mind the principle of sympathetic vibration, whereby the plucking of one string can set another vibrating if it has a harmonic relation to it.

[953] This line is a clever example of chiasmus verging on antimetabole, the former a repetition of ideas in reversed order, the second a repetition in reversed order of identical words: here, 'king ... heav'n' and 'heathen king'. The words 'heave'n' and 'heathen' sound identical at beginning and end, and the middle-voiced consonants are close.

>   Forget thy running,
>   My hand, and all thy cunning   *knowledge*
>   To th' harp to set:
>   Let thy mouth, my tongue, be still thy grave;
> 30   Lie there asleeping,
>   For Zion weeping:
>   O let mine eyes in tears thy office have;
>   Nor rise, nor set, but in their briny wave.
>
>   Proud Edom's raging,
> 35   Their hate with blood assuaging,
>   And vengeful sword,
>   Their cursèd joying
>   In Zion's walls destroying
>   Remember, Lord:
> 40 Forget not, Lord, their spiteful cry,
>   Fire and deface it,   *erase*
>   Destroy and raze it;   *demolish*
>   O let the name of Zion ever die:
>   Thus did they roar, and us and thee defy.
>
> 45   So shall thy towers
>   And all thy princely bowers,
>   Proud Babel, fall:[954]
>   Him ever blessed,
>   Who th' oppressor hath oppressed,
> 50   Shall all men call:
>   Thrice blessed, that turns thy mirth to groans;
>   That burns to ashes
>   Thy towers, and dashes
>   Thy brats 'gainst rocks, to wash thy bloody stones   *children*
> 55 With thine own blood, and pave thee with thy bones.

117. John Donne, *Poems* (1633)

[John Donne (1572–1631) was one of the greatest poets of the late sixteenth and early seventeenth centuries, though during his lifetime he was more renowned as a preacher. Donne was born into a Catholic family, and Donne's relationship to Catholicism has been the subject of considerable debate. He attended Hart Hall, Oxford, but left without taking a degree, perhaps because his faith prevented him from taking the necessary oath. Donne attended Thavie's Inn

---

[954] Fletcher's delaying of the verb across two lines, the first enjambed, almost creates a syntactical, typographical version of the fall he is describing.

and Lincoln's Inn, where he composed a number of poems, including satires, elegies, verse epistles, and epithalamions, and some of what later became known as *Songs and Sonnets*. After working as secretary for Sir Thomas Egerton, Lord Keeper of the Great Seal, Donne surreptitiously married Egerton's niece, Anne More, and fell into disgrace. After a period of rusticated semi-exile in Mitcham (though with frequent trips to London), he began writing polemical religious prose: *Pseudo-Martyr* (1610), arguing for Roman Catholics to take the oath of allegiance, and *Ignatius his Conclave* (1610), a virulent anti-Jesuit satire. Donne wrote two long verse elegies (1611 and 1612) for Elizabeth Drury, a girl who had died at 14, and Donne was invited by her father, Robert, to travel with the family on the Continent. On his return, Donne continued to write religious works, both poetry and prose, and he was ordained in 1615 and was made royal chaplain the same year. He was appointed reader in divinity at Lincoln's Inn and began his illustrious career as a preacher with sermons at court, Paul's Cross, and elsewhere. Psalm 137 appeared in Donne's posthumously published collected *Poems* in 1633, but it was rejected by Herbert J. C. Grierson, who relegated it to a section of misattributed poems in his seminal edition of 1912. Grierson noted that Donne's Psalm 137 was included in the manuscript of metrical Psalms by Francis Davison and others, there attributed to Davison. A strong counter-argument has more recently been made by Lara Crowley, who suggests that the misattribution is in the Davison collection (or rather in Ralph Crane's copies, since other manuscripts attributed the Psalm to Donne), and that Davison may have acquired Donne's Psalm along with others he hoped to publish. The Psalm survives in a number of manuscripts beyond the Davison collection, including a single part-book with a musical setting attributed to Martin Pierson, master of the choristers at St Paul's while Donne was Dean. See R. C. Bald, *John Donne: A Life* (New York: Oxford University Press, 1970); Lara M. Crowley, 'Donne, not Davison: Reconsidering the Authorship of "Psalme 137"', *Modern Philology*, 105.4 (2008), 603–36; David Colclough, ODNB.]

Psalm 137

I.

By Euphrates' flow'ry side[955]
    We did bide,
From dear Judah far absented,[956]

---

[955] Like Fletcher (see 116), Donne may be playing on the similarity in Hebrew between 'Perah' (the Euphrates) and 'perach' ('flower').

[956] Judah] The Southern Kingdom of Israel. The Northern Kingdom, called 'Israel' proper, was conquered and destroyed by the Assyrians in the eighth century. The Babylonians conquered the Southern Kingdom and took Jews into captivity in Babylon, from whence this Psalm purports to be written.

       Tearing the air with our cries,
5   And our eyes,
       With their streams his stream augmented.

II.

   When poor Zion's doleful state,
              Desolate;[957]
   Sackèd, burnèd, and enthrallèd,
10 And the temple spoiled, which we
              Ne'er should see,
   To our mirthless minds we callèd.

III.

   Our mute harps, untuned, unstrung,
              Up we hung
15 On green willows near beside us,[958]
   Where, we sitting all forlorn,
              Thus, in scorn,
   Our proud spoilers 'gan deride us.   *despoilers, began to*

IV.

   Come, sad captives, leave your moans,
20   And your groans
   Under Sion's ruins bury;
   Tune your harps, and sing us lays   *songs*
              In the praise
   Of your God, and let's be merry,

V.

25 Can, ah, can we leave our moans?
              And our groans
   Under Zion's ruins bury?
   Can we in this land sing lays
              In the praise
30 Of our God, and here be merry?

---

[957] The isolation of 'desolate' in its line reinforces its meaning. The word 'desolate' has an especially powerful resonance in the English Bible (and in the Vulgate its equivalent, *desolata*), as in Lamentations 1. 4 ('all her gates are desolate'), Jeremiah 12. 11 ('the whole land is made desolate'), Job 16. 7 ('thou hast made desolate all my company'), Zephaniah 3. 6 ('their towers are desolate, I made their cities waste'), and elsewhere. Etymologically, 'desolate' means to make solitary or alone, though the Hebrew (*samem*) means astonished or put to silence.

[958] A nice example of enjambment, almost a convention for paraphrases of this Psalm, since Campion (see **94**) and Carew (see **99**) use it too.

VI.

No; dear Zion, if I yet
        Do forget
Thine affliction miserable,
Let my nimble joints become
35   Stiff and numb,
To touch warbling harp unable.

VII.

Let my tongue lose singing skill,
        Let it still
To my parchèd roof be glued,
40 If in either harp or voice
        I rejoice,
Till thy joys shall be renewed

VIII.

Lord, curse Edom's traitorous kind,
        Bear in mind
45 In our ruins how they revelled,
Sack, kill, burn, they cried out still,
        Sack, burn, kill,
Down with all, let all be levelled.

IX.

And thou, Babel, when the tide   *Babylon*
50   Of thy pride
Now a-flowing, grows to turning;[959]
Victor now, shall then be thrall,   *captive*
        And shall fall[960]
To as low an ebb of mourning.

X.

55 Happy he who shall thee waste,
        As thou hast
Us, without all mercy, wasted,

---

[959] One of the most common uses of enjambment is to reinforce a sense of flowing or overflowing, as the tide of pride here, though even more common is its use for falling, as later in the stanza.

[960] Like 'hung' above, a conventional use of enjambment (used also in Carew's Psalm 137) but none the less effective for being so.

And shall make thee taste and see
        What poor we
60 By thy means have seen and tasted.

          XI.

Happy, who thy tender barns   *children*
        From the arms
Of their wailing mothers tearing,
'Gainst the walls shall dash their bones,
65   Ruthless stones
With their brains and blood besmearing.[961]

118. George Herbert, *The Temple* (1633)

[George Herbert (1593–1633) was the greatest devotional poet of the seventeenth century and influenced all those who came after him, including Richard Crashaw, Henry Vaughan, and Edward Taylor. Herbert's mother, Magdalene, was a friend and dedicatee of John Donne, and his older brother, Edward, who became first Baron of Cherbury, was also a poet. Herbert studied at Westminster School and Trinity College, Cambridge, where he stood out as one of the best scholars of his generation. He was made university orator in 1620 and gave a speech in 1623 before James I, who (according to Isaak Walton) recognized him as 'the Jewel of that University'. Herbert served as MP in 1624 and may have had ambitions in politics or at court, but he applied to be ordained deacon that same year and embarked on a career in the church. Herbert was married in 1629 and was given a rectorship of the little church of St Andrew's in Fugglestone with Bemerton which he held until his death. He was ordained priest at Salisbury Cathedral in 1630. That Herbert took his priestly duties seriously is evident from his *The Country Parson his Character and Rule of Holy Life*, written during his Bemerton years. He had begun writing poetry, in both English and Latin, at Cambridge, contributing two Latin poems, for instance, to a collection of elegies on the death of Prince Henry. None of the poems on which Herbert's fame rests, however, were published during his lifetime. Herbert left his poems with his friend, Nicholas Ferrar, leader of the religious community at nearby Little Gidding, instructing him to publish them if he thought they might be spiritually useful, but otherwise to burn them. Ferrar gave the collection its title, *The Temple*, and it was published in 1633 and in five more editions in the next decade. Though steeped in biblical language, Herbert's poems were not translations, with the exception of a single Psalm. Nevertheless,

---

[961] Donne hardly avoids the violence of the Psalm, but he deflects the agency of the violence by attaching the adjective 'ruthless' to the stones rather than to those who dashed the children on them.

as a number of scholars have demonstrated, Herbert's principal model for his devotional collection was the psalter, and the Sidney Psalter in particular, with its rich array of verse forms. Like those of the Sidneys, Herbert's poems are formally experimental, yet his one Psalm translation chooses the simple common metre popularized by Sternhold and Hopkins. Laura Sterrett has suggested that Herbert's Psalm is not as simple as it appears, however, arguing that it is subtly crafted as an answer poem to Christopher Marlowe's pastoral invitation poem, 'The Passionate Shepherd to His Love'. See Chana Bloch, *Spelling the Word: George Herbert and the Bible* (Berkeley: University of California Press, 1985); Coburn Freer, *Music for a King: George Herbert's Style and the Metrical Psalms* (Baltimore: Johns Hopkins University Press, 1972); Laura Sterrett, 'Refiguring Pastoral Love in George Herbert's "The 23 Psalme"', *George Herbert Journal*, 42.1–2 (2018/2019), 53–80; Helen Wilcox, *ODNB*.]

Psalm 23

The God of love my shepherd is,
    And he that doth me feed:
While he is mine, and I am his,
    What can I want or need?

5 He leads me to the tender grass,
    Where I both feed and rest;
Then to the streams that gently pass:
    In both I have the best.

Or if I stray, he doth convert
10   And bring my mind in frame:
And all this not for my desert,   *reward*
    But for his holy name.

Yea, in death's shady black abode
    Well may I walk, not fear:
15 For thou art with me; and thy rod
    To guide, thy staff to bear.

Nay, thou dost make me sit and dine,
    Ev'n in my enemies' sight:
My head with oil, my cup with wine
20   Runs over day and night.

Surely thy sweet and wondrous love
    Shall measure all my days;
And as it never shall remove,
    So neither shall my praise.

119. Lady Anne Blount[962] (MS c. 1620s?)

[This version of Psalm 25 was included in the commonplace book of Lady Anne Southwell (née Harris, bap. 1574–d. 1636), who began keeping a commonplace book when she married her second husband, Captain Henry Sibthorpe, in 1626, though the contents are diverse and have a complicated provenance, some written by Southwell, some by scribes, at different times and points in the manuscript (i.e. not necessarily in order), and some tipped into the folio volume she was given by her husband. The materials include poems by Sir Walter Raleigh, Henry King, and Southwell herself. A note in the manuscript, not entirely legible due to cropping, states that the Psalm was 'written by the Lady A[mie?] B[lount?] [daughter?] to the first Earl of Castlehaven'. The illegibility adds to the uncertainty of authorship and context. If the author was Anne Blount, this was indeed the daughter of George Touchet, first Earl of Castlehaven, who married Edward Blount of Harleston, Derbyshire. The note might also indicate, however, that the Psalm was written 'to' (i.e. for) Touchet. Castlehaven, Touchet's earldom, was in the county of Cork, in Ireland, and the Sibthorpes were in Cork from 1626 to 1627, which may be how Lady Anne acquired the manuscript. There was a second 'Anne B.' in this family, however, and if the author was Anne Brydges (1580–1647), this was Ferdinando Stanley, Lord Strange's daughter, who first married Grey Brydges, fifth Baron Chandos, and then, after Brydges's death in 1621, Mervyn Touchet, second Earl of Castlehaven, eldest son of George the first earl. Mervyn Touchet was convicted by his peers of having his wife and daughter raped and sodomizing a servant in one of the most scandalous events of the century. He was beheaded on Tower Hill in 1631, along with two of his servants who had been accomplices. After Touchet's execution, his wife resumed her first husband's name and title, so she might have been named as Brydges even in Southwell's manuscript. The connection with the second earl might be supported by a satirical strain in Southwell's own writing, condemning adultery as well as more specifically a 'double damning vile Hermaphrodite', seemingly a practitioner of sodomy like Touchet. Southwell's interest in the Psalm translation might then have been more for its association with a wicked husband and father than because it is a Psalm. When the Sibthorpes were in Cork, the Castelhaven estate was actually in the possession of the second earl, who inherited in 1617, although he and his family lived at Fonthill Gifford in Wiltshire. See *The Southwell-Sibthorpe Commonplace Book, Folger MS. V.b.198*, ed. by Jean Klene (Tempe: Medieval and Renaissance Texts and Studies, 1997); Cynthia B. Herrup (Mervyn Touchet), *ODNB*.]

---

[962] The first name in the manuscript, despite being partly cropped, is fairly clearly 'Amie', but since it was Anne Blount who was daughter to the first Earl of Castlehaven and Anne Brydges who was married to the second, this would seem to be an error.

Psalm 25

David's confidence in prayer; he prayeth for remission of sin and for help in affliction.

To thee my soul I raise,
My God, I trust in thee;
Let not my life with shame be stained,
Nor foes triumph on me.
5   Let none that on thee wait
Be of their hope ashamed;
Let those that causelessly transgress
Be rightfully infamed.[963]   *made infamous*
Jehovah, show thy ways,
10 Me teach thy paths most straight;   *undeviating*
Lead me in truth, my saving God,
On thee I daily wait.
Thy loving kindness, Lord,
Thy mercies manifold
15 Recall to mind, which thou didst pour
On me in times of old.
Forget my sins of youth,
Of faults no notice take,
But Lord in mercy think on me,
20 Even for thy goodness sake.
Upright and good is God,
He sinners will instruct
In ways of life, and all the meek
In judgement will conduct.
25 The footsteps of the Lord
Are truth and mercy still
To those that do his cov'nant keep
And witness of his will.
Now for thy holy name,
30 Jehovah, I entreat,
Vouchsafe me pardon for my sin,   *grant*
For I confess it great.
Who so doth fear the Lord

---

[963] The Psalmist prays 'let me not be ashamed' but rather 'let them be ashamed which transgress without a cause' (KJV), but this translation intensifies the focus on shame with addition of staining and infamy. If Anne Brydges did write this Psalm, she may have chosen it because it contains more references to shame ('ashamed' four times) than any other except the massive Psalm 119.

Shall learn to choose his way;
35 His soul in goodness shall be lodged,⁹⁶⁴   *descendants*
His seed on earth shall stay.
To those that fear the Lord
His mysteries are shown;
His gracious cov'nant unto them
40 He maketh clearly known.
Mine eyes are humbly bent
The Lord still to behold,
For he shall pluck my tangled feet
From nets that them enfold.
45 With mercy turn to me
For I am desolate;
The troubles of my heart increase,
Redress my woeful state.
O Lord, behold my pain,
50 Afflictions and distress;
Forgive my sins, consider well
The hate my foes express.
For great their number is,
They hate with violence;
55 Discharge my soul, prevent my shame,
I trust in thy defence.
Integrity and truth,
Let them preserve me still;
I wait on thee, O God, redeem
60 Thine Israel from hell.⁹⁶⁵

120. Henry Clifford, Fifth Earl of Cumberland, *Poetical Translations of Some Psalms and the Song of Solomon with Other Divine Poems* (MS early 1630s?)

[Henry Clifford, fifth Earl of Cumberland (1592–1643), was born at Londesborough in Yorkshire, son of Francis Clifford the fourth earl. George Clifford, the third earl and Henry's uncle, was a major figure in the Elizabethan Accession Day tournaments and wrote poetry, including 'My heavy sprite

---

⁹⁶⁴ An original personification, the original being more literal (KJV, 'His soul shall dwell at ease').

⁹⁶⁵ The last word is the one major alteration made to the Psalm, since hell (a Germanic word) is a concept alien to ancient Israel. The Hebrew word most often translated as 'hell', *sheol* (translated by the Greek *Hades* in the Septuagint), designates some sort of dark underworld but nothing like the Christian hell. The Psalmist prays simply for deliverance from troubles (KJV; Hebrew *sara*).

oppressed with sorrow's might', set to music as the first song in Robert Dowland's *Musical Banquet* (1610). Lady Anne Clifford, the influential patron of the arts known for her diary and correspondence, was a cousin, and she complained that Clifford and his father had detained lands from her that she ought to have inherited. He took a BA at Christ Church, Oxford, and went on to Gray's Inn. In 1610 he married Lady Frances Cecil, daughter of Robert Cecil, Earl of Salisbury, lord treasurer, secretary of state, and master of the wards. Clifford served twice in Parliament as an MP for Westmorland and was appointed to the House of Lords in 1628. He played a significant military role on the Royalist side in the Bishops' Wars, though he worked to keep peace in Yorkshire. A broadly accomplished man, Clifford was an athlete, a scholar, especially of mathematics and architecture, a poet, and a musician. He patronized musicians, poets, and painters, planned a masque to entertain James I when he visited Francis Clifford at Brougham Castle in 1617, and he was responsible for the performance of a masque at Skipton Castle in 1637. (Despite being entitled 'Comus', it seems not to have been Milton's *Masque Presented at Ludlow Castle, 1634*.) Clifford's only poems to survive are in a single manuscript written shortly after his death, including a number of metrical Psalms (1, 8, 35, 38, 51, 65, 73, 93, 103, 104, 107, 113, 114, 121 (two versions), 125, 127, 130, 131), a metrical translation of the Song of Solomon, and other religious poems, including 'An Historical Meditation, Upon the Birth, Life, Passion, Resurrection, and Ascension of Christ' and verse meditations upon saints' days, which may indicate Catholic sympathies. The second version of Psalm 121 in the manuscript includes a note that it was 'turned into verse for my daughter Dungarvon now with child'. Clifford's only daughter, Elizabeth, married Richard Boyle (brother of Robert the scientist) in 1635. Boyle eventually became first Earl of Burlington and second Earl of Cork, but from 1620, when his father was first ennobled, he became Viscount Dungarvon. The translation of Psalm 121 must date from at least 1639, when the Boyles' first son was born, but it appears in a second group of Psalms in the manuscript, so the first group (the majority) may have been written earlier. The Psalms are in a variety of metres following the practice of the Sidney Psalter and are among the most accomplished Psalms in this literary mode. See May, *Elizabethan Courtier Poets*; David Norbrook, *Poetry and Politics in the English Renaissance*, rev. ed. (Oxford: Oxford University Press, 2002); Toby Barnard (Boyle), Richard T. Spence (Clifford), *ODNB*.]

Psalm 1

1. Happy, thrice happy man, whose constant heart
    No wicked art
  Hath turned aside, nor spent his looser days
    In sinners' ways,

5	2.	Nor sits in scorner's chairs, but his delight	
		Is day and night	
		To search th'Almighty's law, and overlook	
		His sacred book.	
	3.	He's like the tree set by the water's side,	
10		Whose beauteous pride	
	4.	Nor summer heat nor winter's angry stour	*storm*
		Can once deflower;	
		But his increase and timely fruitfulness	
		doth daily bless	
15		The master's longing hopes, his good endeavour	
		shall prosper ever.	
	5.	Not so the wicked, 'tis not so with them,	
		Which God condemn;	
		But as the chaff which from the earth below	
20		The whirlwind blow	
		In the wide empty air, till out of sight	
		It vanish quite.	
	6.	Wherefore, when God to judge the world shall come	
		With righteous doom,	*judgement*
25		The wicked shall not their pale face uprear	
		For guilty fear,	
		Nor rangèd in the godly's cheerful band	*company*
		In judgement stand.	
	7.	For God his just men's actions doth respect	
30		And ways direct,	
		But the rebellious, whom he hath not known,	
		Shall be o'erthrown.	

Psalm 73

	1	How surely God loves wondrous well	
		Even all the sons of Israel	
		(All those I mean	
		whose hearts are clean).	
5	2.	I hardly could my footsteps stay,	*halt*
		They were so apt to slide away.	
	3.	I'll tell you why,	
		I did envy	
		The wicked and ungodly fry,[966]	
10		That swam in such prosperity.	

---

[966] fry] small fish or human offspring.

		Freed from mischance,

4.   Freed from mischance,
              They sing, they dance;
5.   No sad misfortune falls on them,
     Nor are they plagued as other men.
6.   This makes them fly
              With pride so high,
     And that doth break out instantly
     In greedy acts of cruelty.
7.   Their eyes are fed
              To keep their head,
     Do wander all abroad with lust,   *desire*
     And what they love, that must be just.
8.   All men they teach,
              Within their reach,
     Blasphemous words and oaths to swear,
9.   As if from heaven they God would tear;
              Through earth doth fly
              This blasphemy.
10. Good people fear to hear them curse,
     And think no devil can do worse.[967]
11.   Tush, tush, they say,[968]
              Can God survey
     Or can his knowledge hold a light
     To make him see the works of night?
12.   Must only those
              Live at their ease,
     And all good people beg their food
     From this devouring wicked brood?
13.   In vain, said I,
              I wail and cry;
     My heart, alas, in vain I cleanse
     And wash my hands in innocence;
14.   Who from daylight
              Am whipped till night.
15. But here I stayed; they go too far,
     That with their Maker's counsel war,

---

[967] The devil is Clifford's addition.
[968] The exclamation 'tush' is used in Coverdale's BCP version of this Psalm, but it may ultimately derive from Tyndale's translation of Genesis 3. 4, where it is the expression used by the serpent to counter Eve's statement about the forbidden fruit. Clifford's introduction of a devil in the previous line may suggest an awareness of the earlier context of the exclamation.

               For he loves best
               The poor distressed.
16. All day I laboured in this doubt,
    By human reach to find it out.
          Oft on my bed
          I rubbed my head,
17. But all in vain; till God all good
18. Did show me how these idols stood
          On slippery ice,[969]
          Down in a trice,[970]
19. And at his word are broken small
    As glasses dashed against a wall,
          So suddenly
          They break, they die.[971]
20. Oh, how in haste their glory spends,
    And drowns them in their fearful ends,[972]
          As dreams forsake
          Us when we wake,
    But mocking fancies: so, once down,
    These shadows fade in court and town.[973]
21.   Thus fretting pains   *gnawing*
           Ran through my reins.   *inner parts*
22. They grieved my heart; a beast, a fool,
    Not then well entered in thy school.
23.   But now I stand,
          Raised by thy hand,
24. And thou hast made thy law my guide
    To bring me to thee, glorified.
25.   What gracious God
          In heaven's abode,
    What other friend have I but thee?
    And earth bears none so dear to me.
26.   My flesh decayed
          And heart dismayed
    Thou, God, so lov'st, and lest I fall
    Thou mak'st thyself my rampire wall.   *rampart*

---

[969] Clifford makes the Psalmist's 'slippery places' more specific and concrete.
[970] in a trice] in an instant.
[971] A very effective combination of enjambment and a medial caesura, emphasizing the sudden 'break'.
[972] Breaking through the slippery ice?
[973] The haunts of an English earl more than an ancient Israelite ('court' is added by Cumberland).

27.	But these that fly	
	From thee shall die,	
	They shall in endless torments die	
	For their profane idolatry.	
28.	But 'tis my best	
	On God to rest,	
	So good to me, as to my last	
	By faith I'll hang upon him fast;	*secure*
	His works relate	
	In Zion's gate.	

Psalm 121

1.	Unto the mountains high, from whence	
	Comes my defence,	
	I lookèd up, and aid waited;[974]	
2.	The glorious Lord	
	Doth helps afford,	
	That heaven, and earth, and sea created.	
3.	Thy sliding footsteps in his ways	
	He shall up raise,	
	And will remove who thee encumber,	
4.	For he ne'er sleeps	
	That Israel keeps;	*guards*
	His watchful eyelids never slumber.	
5.	The Lord thy great defence shall stand	
	At thy right hand,	
6.	And th'angry planets fiery charm,	
	The sun by light,	
	The moon by night,	
	Shall work thee no infectious harm.	
7.	Thy fainting soul he shall preserve,	
	That it ne'er swerve	
	From his divinest ordinances,	*commands*
8.	And shall persever	
	Both now and ever	
	To bless thy ways from all mischances.	

---

[974] The line seems to lack a syllable, but it is possible 'aid' could be pronounced as a disyllable.

121. George Sandys (MS *c.* 1633?)

[George Sandys (1578–1644) was a poet, translator, and traveller. He came from a family of biblical translators. His father Edwin, Archbishop of York, was one of the translators of the Bishops' Bible, and his older brother, the MP Sir Edwin, was author of the metrical Psalms published as *Sacred Hymns* in 1615 (see **95**). One of Sandys's godfathers was George Clifford, third Earl of Cumberland, uncle of the Psalms-translating fifth earl, Henry (see **120**). Sandys was educated at St Mary Hall, Oxford, and Middle Temple. In 1610 he travelled to Europe and the Middle East, including Constantinople, Alexandria, Cairo, and Jerusalem, adventures recounted in his widely read *A Relation of a Journey Begun an. Dom. 1610* (1615). Sir Edwin Sandys was a leading member of the Virginia Company, and with his help George Sandys became the colony's treasurer and a member of its council of state. He travelled to Virginia in 1621, where he had been granted land. Before his departure, Sandys had begun a translation of Ovid's *Metamorphoses*, which he continued on the voyage and completed in the colony. An elaborate edition was printed in 1632 with dedications to Charles I and Queen Henrietta Maria. Returning to England, Sandys became a gentleman of the privy chamber to the king and joined the intellectual circle around Lucius Cary, second Viscount Falkland, at Great Tew. Sandys published *A Paraphrase upon the Psalms* in 1636, with a long dedicatory poem by Falkland. In 1638 another edition appeared in *A Paraphrase upon the Divine Poems*, along with paraphrases of Job, Ecclesiastes, and Lamentations, along with further dedicatory poems by Henry King, Thomas Carew, and Edmund Waller, as well as tunes for the Psalms by Henry Lawes. A translation of Hugo Grotius's Latin play *Christus patiens* was published in 1640. Sandys's Song of Solomon, completed earlier with the other *Divine Poems*, though not included with them, was published in 1641. Sandys continued to be involved with the Virginia colony, though he never returned to it, dying in England in 1644. Sandys was encouraged in his translation of the Psalms by King Charles, who kept a copy of them with him while imprisoned years later on the Isle of Wight, this said to be one of the works in which he particularly delighted. Marginal annotations in 1636 (omitted in 1638) indicated a variety of sources behind Sandys's paraphrases: the Latin Bibles of Immanuel Tremellius and Franciscus Junius, and Sebastian Castellio, and paraphrases and commentaries by Theodore Beza, Joannes Lorinus, Johann Piscator, and others. That the Latin metrical Psalms of George Buchanan were of particular importance to Sandys is evident in a hitherto unnoticed early manuscript that brings some of Sandys's Psalms within the chronological scope of this volume. This undated manuscript includes six of Sandys's Psalms, unattributed, written on facing pages with Buchanan's originals, and includes a prefatory note stating that these were composed 'to Command'. The command presumably came from King Charles, and this suggests that these are the first Psalms Sandys paraphrased, before he conceived the project of completing the entire psalter. Examples of Sandys's own hand are scarce, which makes comparison difficult, but since this was a presentation manuscript Sandys likely employed a professional scribe. Sandys became gentleman of Charles's privy chamber between 1626 and 1628; his *Metamorphoses* was by this time finished, and he could easily have been encouraged to move toward biblical translations. See Karl E. Schmutzler, *George Sandys' Paraphrases on the Psalms and the Tradition of Metrical Psalmody: An Annotated Edition of Fifty Selected Psalms, with Critical and Biographical Introduction*, unpublished dissertation (The Ohio State University, 1957); James Ellison, *George Sandys: Travel, Colonialism, and Tolerance in the Seventeenth Century* (Cambridge: D. S. Brewer, 2002); James Ellison, *ODNB*.]

Psalm 80

Thou shepherd of thy Israel,
That, flock-like, leadest Joseph's race: *posterity*
Who twixt the cherubims dost dwell,
O hear! show thy enlightening face.
5 Exalt thy saving power before
Manasseh, Ephraim, Benjamin:
O, from captivity restore,
And let thy beams upon us shine.
Great God of battle, wilt thou still
10 Be angry, and our prayers despise?
Bread, steeped in tears, our stomachs fill;
We drink the rivers of our eyes.[975]
Our scoffing neighbours fall at strife
Among themselves, to share our right:
15 Great God, restore the dead to life;[976]
And comfort by thy quick'ning light.   *enlivening*
This vine, from Egypt brought (the foe
Expelled) was planted by thy hand:
Thou gav'st it room and strength to grow,
20 Until her branches filled the land.

---

[975] Sandys's additional metaphor for tears, perhaps thinking of the rivers by which the exiled Psalmist sits in Psalm 137, picking up on the Psalm's 'bread of tears', which hovers between the literal and metaphorical. The bread might be interpreted metaphorically, like the 'rivers' Sandys's Psalmist 'drinks', or as bread tainted by grief, or even causing tears; instead, Sandys has the bread 'steeped in tears', which seems literal, though there may still be some lingering figurative sense (a lot of tears being required to soak bread).

[976] Sandys's addition, perhaps hinting toward a Christological reading of the Psalm, since the reference to the vine brought from Egypt also prefigures (for Christians) Jesus's self-description as 'the true vine' (John 15. 1).

The mountains took a shade from these,
Which like a grove of cedars stood:
Extending to the Tyrian seas,
And to Euphrates' rolling flood.
25 O, why hast thou her fences razed?   *demolished*
Whilst every straggler pulls her fruit:
The browsing herd her branches waste;
And savage boars plough-up her root.[977]
Great God, return; this trampled vine
30 From heaven behold with mild aspect:
Once planted by that hand of thine;
The branches of thy own elect.[978]
Which now cut down, wild flames devour;
Through thy fierce wrath to ruin brought:
35 Protect thy people by thy power;
And perfect what thyself hath wrought.
Revived, we shall thy name adore;
Nor ever from thy pleasure swerve.
O from captivity restore,
40 And by thy powerful grace preserve!

Psalm 104

As the 72.[979]

My ravished soul, great God, thy praises sings;
Whom glory circles with her radiant wings,
And majesty invests: than day more bright;
Clothed with the beams of new-created light.
5 He, like an all-infolding canopy,
Framed the vast concave of the spangled sky:
And in the air-embracèd waters set
The basis of his hanging cabinet.[980]
Who on the clouds, as on a chariot, rides;

---

[977] boars] Given the original, this is the appropriate word in this verse, but Sandys's original spelling, 'boors', allows for a pun on the word meaning 'peasant', 'rustic', or 'lout', which might point to the growing class tensions that led to the Civil War. Charles I dismissed parliament and began his period of 'personal rule' in 1629.

[978] elect] The notion of election, of particular interest to Protestants, is added by Sandys.

[979] Indicating the tune to which the Psalm should be sung. Sandys included Psalm 72 in the early manuscript, and it was in the same metre, but no tunes were provided there, nor were they in the complete printed edition of 1636. Only in the 1638 edition of *Divine Poems* were the tunes printed, composed and harmonized by Henry Lawes.

[980] cabinet] private chamber; treasure chest.

10 And with a rein the flying tempest guides.⁹⁸¹
   Bright angels his attendant spirits made;
   By flame-dispersing seraphims obeyed.
   The ever-fixèd earth clothed with the flood;
   In whose calm bosom unseen mountains stood;
15 At his rebuke it shrunk with sudden dread,
   And from his voice's thunder swiftly fled.
   Then hills their late concealèd heads extend,
   And sinking valleys to their feet descend.
   The trembling waters through their bottoms wind,
20 Till they the sea, their nurse and mother, find.
   He to the swelling waves prescribes a bound;
   Lest earth again should by their rage be drowned.⁹⁸²
   Springs through the pleasant meadows pour their drills,   *rivulets*
   Which snake-like glide between the bord'ring hills;
25 Till they to rivers grow; where beasts of prey
   Their thirst assuage, and such as man obey.
   In neighbouring groves the air's musicians sing,⁹⁸³
   And with their music entertain the spring.
   He from celestial casements showers distils,
30 And with renewed increase his creatures fills.
   He makes the food-full earth her fruit produce;
   For cattle grass, and herbs for human use.   *livestock*
   The spreading vine long purple clusters bears,
   Whose juice the hearts of pensive mortals chears:
35 Fat olives smooth our brows with suppling oil;
   And strength'ning corn rewards the reapers' toil.   *grain*
   His fruit-affording trees with sap abound.
   The Lord hath Lebanon with cedars crowned:
   They to the warbling birds a shelter yield,
40 And wand'ring storks in lofty fir-trees build.
   Wild goats to craggy cliffs for refuge fly;
   And conies in the rocks' dark entrails lie.   *rabbits*
   He guides the changing moons alternate face:
   The sun's diurnal and his annual race.   *daily*

---

⁹⁸¹ rein] Modern spelling removes a possible pun, since Sandys spells the word 'reign', which might also designate God's rule.

⁹⁸² Sandys's addition, alluding to God's promise never again to destroy the earth by flood (Genesis 9. 15).

⁹⁸³ air's] Likely punning on 'ayre' or 'song', the birds thus singing the kind of music popular at the Caroline court (the songs of Henry Lawes, for instance, who wrote the music for Sandys's Psalms).

45 'Twas he that made the all-informing light;
And with dark shadows clothes the agèd night.
Then beasts of prey break from their mountain caves;
The roaring lion pinched with hunger craves
Food from his hand. But when heaven's greatest fire[984]
50 Obscures the stars, they to their dens retire.
Men with the morning rise, to labour pressed;[985] *conscripted*
Toil all the day, at night return to rest.
Great God! how manifold, how infinite
Are all thy works! with what a clear foresight
55 Didst thou create and multiply their birth!
Thy riches fill the far extended earth.
The ample sea; in whose unfathomed deep
Innumerable sorts of creatures creep:
Bright-scalèd fishes in her entrails glide,
60 And high-built ships upon her bosom ride:
About whose sides the crooked dolphin plays, *curved*
And monstrous whales huge spouts of water raise.[986]
All on the land, or in the ocean bred,
On thee depend; in their due season fed. *time*
65 They gather what thy bounteous hands bestow,
And in the summer of thy favour grow.
When thou contract'st thy clouded brows, they mourn;[987]
And dying, to their former dust return.
Again created by thy quick'ning breath, *enlivening*
70 To resupply the massacres of death.
No tract of time his glory shall destroy:
He in th'obedience of his works shall joy:
But when their wild revolts his wrath provoke,
Earth trembles, and the airy mountains smoke.
75 I all my life will my Creator praise;
And to his service dedicate my days.
May he accept the music of my voice,
While I with sacred harmony rejoice.

---

[984] heaven's greatest fire] i.e. the sun.
[985] According to Genesis 3. 19, God curses Adam and his male descendants with earning their bread by hard agricultural labour.
[986] Sandys naturalizes the Leviathan of the original. See note 524.
[987] Figures like the 'summer of thy favour' and 'clouded brows' are normally metaphors (as when Shakespeare's Richard III speaks of 'the winter of our discontent'), but since all things were created by and even in some sense are God, he is the one person of whom these might be said literally.

Hence, you profane, who in your sins delight;
80 God shall extirp, and cast you from his sight.   *extirpate*
My soul, bless thou this all-commanding King:
You saints and angels, Hallelujah sing.

Psalm 148

You, who dwell above the skies,
Free from human miseries;
You, whom highest heaven embowers,
Praise the Lord with all your powers.
5 Angels, your clear voices raise,
Him you heavenly angels praise.
Sun and moon with borrowed light,
All you sparkling eyes of night,
Waters hanging in the air,
10 Heaven of heavens his praise declare.
His deservèd praise record,
His, who made you by his Word,[988]
Made you evermore to last,
Set you bounds not to be passed.
15 Let the earth his praise resound;
Monstrous whales and seas profound,[989]
Vapours, lightning, hail, and snow,
Storms which, when he bids them, blow,
Flow'ry hills and mountains high,
20 Cedars, neighbours to the sky,
Trees that fruit in season yields,
All the cattle of the fields,   *livestock*
Savage beasts, all creeping things,
All that cut the air with wings,
25 You who awful sceptre's sway,
You inurèd to obey,
Princes, judges of the earth,
All of high and humble birth,
Youths and virgins flourishing,
30 In the beauty of your spring,
You who bow with age's weight,

---

[988] God does speak Creation into existence in Genesis, as the Psalm states, but the capital letter added by Sandys Christianizes the reference, which then invokes the 'Word' (Christ as *logos*) of John 1. 1.

[989] Sandys normalizes the 'dragons' of other English translations into whales, which he likely saw on his many travels.

You who were but born of late,
Praise his name with one consent.
Oh how great! How excellent!
35 Than the earth profounder far,
Higher than the highest star.
He will his to honour raise.
You his saints resound his praise,
You who are of Jacob's race,   *offspring*
40 And united to his grace.
      Hallelujah.

122. Sir Henry Wotton, *Reliquiae Wottonianae, or, A Collection of Lives, Letters, Poems, with Characters of Sundry Personages and Other Incomparable Pieces of Language and Art* (1651; composed post-1627)

[Sir Henry Wotton (1568–1639) was educated at Winchester and New College, Oxford, moving to Hart Hall (later Hertford College) and then Queen's where he finally graduated BA. At Hart Hall he met John Donne, who became a lifelong friend and correspondent. Francis Bacon was also a close friend, and a distant relative. In 1589, Wotton left for the Continent where he travelled for six years, studying law at Heidelberg and Vienna, then journeying to Italy. He spent a year living with the renowned scholar Isaac Casaubon in Geneva, and returned to England in 1594 where he became a secretary to the Earl of Essex. Wotton and Donne both sailed with Essex on his expedition to the Azores, and Wotton accompanied the Earl to Ireland in 1599. Wotton left Essex's household before the earl's disastrous fall, and he began a second tour of Europe. After the death of Queen Elizabeth, Wotton wrote to Robert Cecil, who remained Secretary of State under James I, offering his loyalty and service. James knighted Wotton and made him ambassador to Venice in 1604, a post he retained until his resignation in 1610. In the spring of 1612, Cecil sent Wotton to Savoy as ambassador-extraordinary. Wotton failed to secure an alliance with England through marriage with Prince Henry, and he briefly lost King James's favour. Through a combination of strategic publication and strong support for the king's interests in parliament, Wotton regained James's confidence, and in 1614 he was again appointed to an ambassadorship, this time to the Dutch Republic. Wotton worked in the Hague until 1615, and then had two further embassies to Venice, 1616–1619 and 1621–1623. In between these appointments, in 1620 Wotton was sent as ambassador-extraordinary to the German princes James hoped would support his son-in-law Prince Frederick, Elector Palatine, who had declared himself King of Bohemia. Frederick's forces were defeated by the army of Emperor Ferdinand II at White Mountain before Wotton could reach Vienna to appeal to the emperor. Wotton's last position was in England, as Provost of Eton College. Wotton was a skilled diplomat and a learned and cultured man, immersing himself in the cultures of the many countries in which he lived. He published a book on architecture in 1624, adapted from the work of Vitruvius, and was an accomplished poet, his most famous poems being the very widely circulated 'The Character of a Happy Life' and 'On his Mistress, the Queen of Bohemia', set to music by Michael East. Wotton and Donne exchanged verse epistles. In 1627, Wotton was ordained a deacon in the Church of England, writing to Charles I, 'if I can produce nothing else for the use of the Church and State, yet it shall be comfort enough to the little remnant of my life, to compose some Hymns unto his endless glory, who hath called me'. The metrical paraphrase of Psalm 104 seems to have been one of these works. In his 1811 anthology *Select Psalms in Verse*, Walter Aston, ninth Lord Aston of Forfar, called Wotton's Psalm 104 'the finest specimen I have met of sacred poetry among our earlier authors, [it] will be highly acceptable, I doubt not, to every reader of taste'. See A. J. Loomie, ODNB.]

Psalm 104

My soul, exalt the Lord with hymns of praise:
    O Lord, my God, how boundless is thy might?
Whose throne of state[990] is clothed with glorious rays
    And round about hast robed thyself with light;
5   Who like a curtain hast the heavens displayed,
      And in the wat'ry roofs thy chambers laid;

Whose chariots are the thickened clouds above;
    Who walk'st upon the wingèd winds below;
At whose command the airy spirits move,
10   And fiery meteors their obedience show;
      Who on his base the earth didst firmly found,
      And mad'st the deep to circumvest it round.   *enwrap as with a garment*

The waves that rise would drown the highest hill,
    But at thy check they fly, and when they hear
15 Thy thundering voice, they post to do thy will,
    And bound their furies in their proper sphere;   *own*
      Where surging floods and 'vailing ebbs can tell,   *i.e. prevailing*
      That none beyond thy marks must sink or swell.

Who hath disposed, but thou, the winding way
20   Where springs down from the steepy crags do beat,
At which both fostered beasts their thirsts allay,   *domestic*
    And the wild asses come to quench their heat?

---

[990] The 'throne of state' is not part of the Psalm's description of God's court, but it was a feature of the English royal court, which Wotton knew well.

>   Where birds resort, and, in their kinds, thy praise
>   Among the branches chant in warbling lays?   *songs*
> 25 The mounts are watered from thy dwelling place;
>   The meads and barns are filled for man and beast;
>   Wine glads the hearts, and oil adorns the face,
>   And bread the staff whereon our strength doth rest;[991]
>   Nor shrubs alone feel thy sufficing hand,
> 30   But even the cedars that so proudly stand.
>
>   So have the fowls their sundry seats to breed,[992]   *residence*
>   The ranging stork in stately beeches dwells,[993]
>   The climbing goats on hills securely feed,
>   The mining coneys shroud in rocky cells;   *rabbits, hide*
> 35   Nor can the heavenly lights their course forget,
>   The moon her turns, or sun his times to set.
>
>   Thou mak'st the night to over-veil the day: *shroud*
>   Then savage beasts creep from the silent wood,
>   Then lions' whelps lie roaring for their prey,
> 40   And at thy powerful hands demand their food;
>   Who, when at morn they all recouch again,   *return to sleep*
>   Then toiling man till eve pursues his pain.
>
>   O Lord, when on thy various works we look,
>   How richly furnished is the earth we tread!
> 45 Where, in the fair contents of nature's book,[994]
>   We may the wonders of thy wisdom read;
>   Nor earth alone, but lo, the sea so wide,
>   Where, great and small, a world of creatures glide.
>
>   There go the ships that furrow out their way;
> 50   Yea, there of whales enormous sights we see,[995]
>   Which yet have scope among the rest to play,
>   And all do wait for their support on thee;

---

[991] Isaiah refers to 'the stay and staff, the whole stay of bread' (3. 1, KJV).

[992] Wotton may be playing on the 'country seat', the rural estate of landed gentry or the wealthy, the subject of country house poems like by Ben Jonson's 'To Penshurst' and Thomas Carew's 'To Saxham'.

[993] Wotton converts the Psalm's fir-trees (in the BCP version; perhaps originally cypresses) into beeches, familiar from the Kentish woods near where he grew up.

[994] Wotton adds and elaborates the familiar image of the book of nature, traditionally one of the two books of divine revelation, the other being the Bible.

[995] whales] 'Leviathan' in the original, a mythical sea beast of enormous size, sometimes naturalized as either the whale or crocodile.

>   Who hast assigned each thing his proper food,
>   And in due season dost dispense thy good. *time*
>
> 55 They gather when thy gifts thou dost divide;
>   Their stores abound, if thou thy hand enlarge;
>   Confused they are, when thou thy beams dost hide;
>   In dust resolved, if thou their breath discharge;
>   Again, when thou of life renew'st the seeds,
> 60   The withered fields revest their cheerful weeds. *dress again, clothing*
>
>   Be ever gloried here thy sovereign name,
>   That thou may'st smile on all which thou hast made,
>   Whose frown alone can shake this earthly frame,
>   And at whose touch the hills in smoke shall vade. *fade*
> 65   For me, may (while I breathe) both harp and voice
>   In sweet indictment of thy hymns rejoice!
>
>   Let sinners fail, let all profaneness cease;
>   His praise (my soul), his praise shall be thy peace.

GLOSSARY

a	all
abidis	abides
abject	wretched
abreid	abroad
accord	harmony
acquite	acquit
addict	bound
address	1. guidance; 2. ability
adhortatory	strongly encouraging
adrad	dreadful
advert	give heed
affect	intention, disposition
affiance	faith, trust
afflict	afflicted
afford	put forth
affray	frighten
again	gain
against	in front of
ailit	ailed
air	early
albe	albeit
algate	continually
allane	alone
allanerly	exclusively
alone	only
Alpin	Alpine
alquhair	everywhere
als	also
alture	high altitude
alway	always
amain	at full speed
amenity	pleasantness
ane	a, one
annoy	discomfort, annoyance, grief, trouble
anon	1. at once; 2. again
apace	quickly
apaid	contented
appair	weaken

appeach	accuse
aricht	aright
aright	justly, rightly
array	arrangement
ascence	ascent
aspic	asp
assay [noun]	attempt
assay [verb]	1. attempt; 2. prove, test
assemble	assembly
assoil	absolve
astone	astonish, strike mute
astonied	rendered powerless
athwart	to and fro
atween	between
aught	anything
author	provider
avail	aid, help
avaunt	depart
avoid	1. go away, depart; 2. make void
awin	own
ay(e)	forever, always
Babel	Babylon
bain [noun]	bath
bain [verb]	bathe
bair	naked
bait [noun]	temptation
bait [verb]	sojourn
baith	both
bale	misery, torment, grief
Baliallis	Belial's
balk	shun
band	1. bond; 2. company
banded	united
bane	1. death; 2. harm, ruin
bar	defence, bulwark
barbar	barbarous
barns	children
Barsabe	Bathsheba
beck	command
becked	beaked
beeves	beef cattle
begand	begging

begotten	conceived
behight [noun]	promise
behight [verb]	promise
behoof/behove	benefit
beir	clamour
beknow	acknowledge, confess, know
believe	belief
bening	gracious, benign
berayed	defiled, befouled
bereaved	bereft of
besprent	besprinkled
betake	1. take its way; 2. entrust
bethink	consider
bethriving	be profiting
betide	befall
betimes	early, in good time
betroth	pledge, engage
bewray	divulge, expose, reveal
big	build
bill	caress bill to bill (as birds)
blaise	proclaim
bloodwite	fine for murder
board	table
bolt	thunderbolt
bond	slave
bondman	one in bondage
boon	request, prayer
bootless	helpless
borrow	deliverer
bot	but
boun	bound
bow [noun]	bough
bow [verb]	bend down
bowed	bent
bowels	1. inner organs; 2. interior; 3. seat of sympathetic emotions
bra	steep hill
brace	bind
brand	sword
brangling	shaking
brats	children (not necessarily negative connotation)
brawl	confusion
bray	1. loudly cry; 2. crush, pound

bread	1. breadth; 2. manna
breid	spring forth
brek	break
bricht	bright
brocht	brought
broil	quarrel
brook	tolerate
bruit	1. noise; 2. report; 3. renown
bruke	possess, enjoy
buckled	girded
budge	solemn
bure	carried, bore
butt	archery target
cabinet	1. private chamber; 2. treasure chest
cair	take care
caitiff	wretch, captive
cankered	corrupted, corrosive
careful	troubled
cark	worry (3 sg. 'cark'th')
carnal	fleshly, worldly
carve	serve
cast	determine
cattle	livestock
cear	go my way
cell	small room
certes	certainly
chalmer	chamber
charge	command
charm	magic power
cheer	1. spirits, demeanour, mood, frame of mind; 2. countenance
chief	head
childer	children
chink	gasp
chord	string
circumvest	clothe
clave	cleaved, split
clean	entirely, completely
cleap	call
cleithis	clothes
clokit	cloaked, disguised
close [adj.]	1. secret, hidden, private; 2. enclosed, shut

close [verb]	enclose
closet	private chamber
compace	compass
compass (about)	surround, encircle
complaining	lamentation
complaint	lament
complish	accomplish
conceit	conceive, understand
concupiscence	lust, desire
condign	deserved, fitting
conduce	conduct, lead
con(e)y	rabbit
confedered	confederate
confound	1. put to shame; 2. defeat utterly; 3. destroy
confounded	shamed, confused, utterly ruined, damned
congregation	assembly (not necessarily implying a religious gathering)
conjured	conspiring
conspirit	conspired
constraint	1. distress; 2. compulsion
consume (away)	waste away, wear away
consumed	eaten away
contain	confine
contrar	1. against; 2. on the other hand
contrite	contrition
convent	convene
copsemate	companion, lover
corn	grain
corsie	corrosive
couch	lie
coursers	horses
craft	strength
craig	rock
croce	cross
crook	curve
crooked	curved
cruik	crook
cumbered	overwhelmed
cunning	knowledge, skill
darkly	secretly
darksome	gloomy
darling	best-loved

dee	die
deface	blot out, erase
defate	defeat
deid	death
deip	deep
delicates	delicacies
denayed	denied
deprecation	intercessory prayer
descry	discover, catch sight of
desert [adj.]	deserving (also 'by desert' for 'deservedly')
desert [noun]	reward, recompense
despite/despight	scorn, defiance
devise	1. desire; 2. resolve
devisit	device
digne	worthy
discuss	set free
disease	distress
disherit	disinherit
dispartedly	dividedly
dispend	spend, consume
dispread	spread out
dissever	sever
distained	stained
ditty	lyrics, poem
diurnal	daily
dole	grief
dolour	pain, sorrow
doom	judgement
dower	dowry, offering
down	featherbed
dreadful	awe-inspiring
dreadis	fears
dredour	dread, terror
dreed, dreid	dread, fear
drench	drown
drill	rivulet, stream
dung	fertilize
dure	endure
e	eye
ear	stalk of grain
echone	each one
eftsoon(e)(s)	1. again; 2. soon after, immediately

egall	equal
eird	earth
eiris	ears
eke	also
embassage	mission
embossed	concealed in a thicket
enforted	fortified
engine	device
engrossed	swollen
enlarge	release
ensample	example
enteer	entire
environ	surround
erst	formerly, at first
eterne	eternal
ethnics	pagans
extermine	exterminate
extirp	extirpate, root out
eyen/eyne	eyes
fa	foe
fact	deed
fain [adj.]	glad
fain [adv.]	gladly
fast [adj.]	secure
fast(ly) [adv.]	secure(ly)
fault	hidden sin
fear	fair
fell	1. savage; 2. dreadful
'fence	defence
fere	comrade
figured	patterned
filed	1. polished, smooth; 2. lying
(in) fine [noun]	(in the) end
fine [verb]	1. pay the fine; 2. refine
flag	fly low
flagitious	wicked
fleer	mock, smirk (3 sg. 'fleereth')
fleering	grinning
fleshy	not hard and stony
flightering	fluttering
fling	rush
flirt	flout

fluidis	floods
foil	defeat
fondly	foolishly
fordulled	clouded
'fore	before
forecast	foresight
foredamned	damned beforehand
forespeak	prophesy
formless	unformed
forsloth	neglect
fostered	domestic
fowler	bird-catcher
fra [adv.]	as soon as
fra [prep.]	from
fraughted	1. fraught, laden; 2. filled
fraughtful	burdened
fray	frighten (3 sg. 'frayis')
fret	1. gnaw; 2. wear away; 3. worry
fretting	wasting, gnawing
friths	copses, undergrowth
fromward	away from
frothy	unsubstantial
froward	perverse, wicked
fry	1. small fish; 2. human offspring
fundyit	numb
furth	forth
gad	wander
gait	way, road
gall	bile, bitter substance
gan	began
gang	walk
garland	crown
garner	storehouse for grain
gart	caused
gazing-stock	one on whom others gaze
ghost	spirit
ghostly	spiritual
ginneth	begins
gird	1. fasten; 2. equip, dress
girn	to show teeth (as in rage, pain, etc.)
gittith	a stringed instrument
give	show (3 sg. 'giveth')
glaid	glad

gleid	glide
glore	glory
glosing	flattering
gloze	pretence, false show
gratis	freely
grave	engrave
gree	goodwill
gren, grin	snare
grief	grieve
gripes	clutches
grit	great
groundless	bottomless
grovis	groves
grudge	grumble, complain
gyrne	trap
gyves	shackles
hail	1. perfect; 2. healthy, safe
hairtis	heart's
haitteris	haters
hale	drag down
hap [noun]	fortune
hap [verb]	happen
helly	hellish
heried	exalted
herns	hiding places
hes	has
hest	1. command; 2. behest, request
hicht	high
hid	hidden
hild	sustained, held
hind	female deer
hird	shepherd
hoar	grey
holden	held
holla	hold on!
holocaust	burnt offering
hond	hand
horn	1. leafless branch; 2. cornucopia, when paired with 'plenty'
host	sacrifice
howes	hollows
huffing	swelling

ilk	the same
ill [adj.]	evil
ill [noun]	evil
ill [verb]	malign
imbrue	stain
immure	enclose
impute	ascribe, attribute
in	into
incontinent	immediately
indite	utter
indured	hardened
indwellers	inhabitants
infame	make infamous
inly	inwardly
insuperable	unsurpassable
ire	anger
iwis(s)	certainly, truly
Jah	Jehovah
jet	strut
joy	rejoice
jubilee	rejoicing
keep	guard
keipar	keeper
kendill	kindle
kind	disposition, nature
knap	snap, break (3 sg. 'knappeth')
knaw	know
knawin	known
knot	company
knowledge	acknowledge
kythe	appear
lade	load
lait	late
lank	lean
lap	leaped
largess	generosity
lauch	laugh
laud [noun]	praise
laud [verb]	praise
launder	launderer
lave	living

lay	song, poem
lear	bed
learn	teach
Leban	Lebanon
leech	physician
leek	like
lees	sediments
leese	lose
leesome	proper
leine	lain
lenity	gentleness
lewd	wicked
lewdly	wickedly
Libanus	Lebanon
lichtly	lightly
light	frivolous, of little weight
lightening	1. comforting; 2. flashing
like	please
liquor	liquid
list	1. please; 2. desire
listis	desires
lither	wicked
(on) live	alive, living
lively	life-giving
livery	garb, uniform
lofe	praise
(')long	belong
lope	leap
lore	teachings
lou	low
lour	threaten
lout	bow
love [noun]	praise
love [verb]	praise, extol
lovely	loving, loveable
lovis	come loose
ludge	lodge
lust [noun]	desire
lust [verb]	desire, delight
lustiness	vigour, lustfulness, delight
lusty	lively, cheerful
luvis	loves
lye	alkaline laundry fluid

magazine	store (as of arms)
main	sea
mair	more
mairch	border
maist	greatest
make	spouse, mate
marketstead	marketplace
masking	disguising
maugre	despite
may'st	may (negate with 'ne')
meat	food
meed	recompense
mel	honey
mennis	men's
mere [adj.]	pure
mere [noun]	pool
messes	meals, courses
micht	might
mids	middle
mieve	move
mining	undermining
misken	mistake
mister	need, distress
moe	more
mofit	moved
mole	mould, frame
molest	disturb, trouble
mollified	softened
Moluccs	the Moluccas or Spice Islands
montaines	mountains
morrow	morning
motis	dust
mottlied	mottled, variegated
mought	might
mould	earth
mountainets	hills, small mountains
mousewebs	cobwebs
moving	causing motion or action
mow	grimace
murn	mourn
na	no
nane	none
naughty	wicked

needful	necessary
nicht	night
nigh	near(ly), close(ly)
nilt	do not will
nocht	not, naught
noice	noise
(for the) nonce/nones	1. for once; 2. for the purpose
nor	neither
not-availing	ineffectual
nought [adj.]	worthless (esp. with intensifier 'full')
nought [noun]	nothing
numbers	metres, verse
oblations	offerings
ocht	anything
o'erlook	overflow
ointed	anointed
ointing	anointing
onis	once
only	alone
opprobry	shame
ordinance	command
orison	prayer
out-stent	outstretched
overgane	overcome
overhand	upper hand
over-veil	shroud
paise	ponder
pall	rich robe; altar cloth; cloth spread over coffin
palliate	concealed
participate	possess
passing	surpassing
pastor	shepherd
patching	deceitful
pate	head
paunch	belly
paylion	tent, pavilion
paynim	pagan
peculiar	chosen
Perah	Euphrates
perfit(e) [adj.]	perfect
perfite [verb]	perfect
petty	small

pight [adj.]	resolved
pight [verb]	fix, set up
pipkin	small pot or bottle
plain	complain, lament
plaint	lament
plaintful	sorrowful
pleasance	pleasure
plight [noun]	misfortune, sin
plight [verb]	pledge, pitch, fold
'pointed	appointed
poise	weight
poll	shear
pore	gaze
port	bearing
praevenis	goes before
pranking	adorning
prate	chatter
precept	command
press	torture, oppress
pressed	1. impressed, conscripted, drafted; 2. oppressed
pretence	claim, usually false
prevent	1. anticipate, act before; 2. frustrate in advance; 3. confront; 4. welcome
prick	drive
pricking	piercing
privy [adj.]	private, hidden
privy [adv.]	secretly
proof	experience
proper	own
proud	vigorous
pry	spy
puissance	strength
puissant	mighty
quha, quho	who
quhair	where
quhairby	whereby
quhairof	whereof
quhais	whose
quhen	when
quhiche	which
quhile	while
quhilk	which

quhill	until
quhom(e)	whom
quick	living, alive
quicken	enliven, restore
quickening	enlivening
quiristers	choristers
quite	repay, requite
quod/quoth	said
race [noun]	1. posterity, offspring; 2. people, kindred
race [verb]	1. pluck up; 2. erase
rampire	rampart
rankle	fester
ravening	bloodthirsty
ravin	predatory greed
raze (up)	demolish
ream	realm
reave	deprive
rebate	reduce
record	witness
recouch	return to sleep
rector	ruler
recure [noun]	recourse
recure [verb]	restore
red	1. ruddy; 2. bloody
rede	counsel
redound	contribute
reduce	restore, bring back
reft	taken away
rehearse	recite
reik [noun]	smoke
reik [verb]	smoke
reins	1. inward parts, seat of affections and passions; 2. power (fig.)
reird	1. speech, utterance; 2. clamour
renoum	renown
repair	abode
reprobate	unredeemable
resembling	comparing
resiant	resident
resoune	resound
respectless	impartial (similarly, 'without respect' for 'indiscriminately')

retrait	refuge
reveir	river
revest	dress again
revolve	consider, meditate
richesse	wealth
richt	right
richteous	righteous
rightwise	righteous
rill	brook
rind	bark
ring	reign
rin(n)	run (3 pl. 'rinnis')
rive	pull up
roll	scroll
rooting	digging up
rought	reached
rout	mob
rub	obstacle
rue	regret, lament
ruffle	stir with anger
ruinate	ruin
ruth	pity
ruthful	compassionate, merciful
sack	sackcloth
sair	sore
sait	seat
salbe	shall be
sall	shall
sayen	say
scan	consider, perceive
scape	escape
scathe	harm
science	knowledge
score	account, tally, list
season	time
seat	residence, habitation
seed	descendants, generation
seignory	domination
seisin	possession
selah	Hebrew word relating to recitation or singing, precise meaning unknown
self	same

sembly	assembly
sen	since
senior	elder
shades	shadows
shamefastness	ashamedness
shawis, shewes	shows
shent	disgraced, ruined
shift	device
shope	created
shore	threaten
shroud	hide, shelter
sic, sik	such
silly	helpless, innocent
sine	then, afterwards
sith [conj.]	since
sith [noun]	scythe
slake	diminish
sl(e)ight	cunning
slipper	slippery
sma	small
smart [noun]	pain
smart [verb]	sting
smit	smitten
smoking	steaming
smooke	smoke
smother	conceal
snaffle	light bridle
solein	solitary
sonour	sonorous
sooth	truth
sound [noun]	healthy, robust
sound [verb]	test, investigate
sourd	arise (3 sg. 'sourdeth')
souse	drench
spare	lean
sparpled	scattered
sparred	barred up, closed
sped	provided
splat	cut up
spoilers	despoilers
sprent	sprinkled
sprite	spirit
squize	squeeze

stablish	establish
stacker	stagger
stane	stone
stang	wound
stay [noun]	1. support, prop; 2. rest
stay [verb]	1. wait; 2. secure; 3. halt
stert	start up
still	always
stint	stop
stintless	endless
stock	wood
stond	last
store [noun]	sufficient supply
store [verb]	stock
stound	sharp pain
stour	storm, tumult
stout	resolute
stoutly	proudly
stoutness	firmness, courage
straight [adj.]	1. narrow; 2. undeviating, direct
straight [adv.]	immediately
strain [noun]	melody
strain [verb]	sing
strake	struck
strand	stream
stripe	a stroke or lash with a whip or scourge
sty	ascend
(')suage	assuage
subtervert	subvert
subtilly	subtly
suffer	allow
suit	petition
suld	should
supernal	divine, lofty, heavenly
supple	soften, anoint
supplie	aid
sured	assured
sway [noun]	authority (e.g. 'bear the sway over' is 'have authority over'), rule
sway [verb]	govern
Sweathen	Swede
sweit	sweet, pleasant
swelland	turbulent

swelly	swallow
swith	extremely (*archaic intensifier*)
syne	afterwards
tabernacle	hut, tent, booth
tabret	small tabor or drum
tell	count
tenor	substance
therewithal	in addition, with all that
thir	these
thirlage	bondage
thocht [conj.]	though
thocht [noun]	thought (pl. 'thochtis')
thorough, thorow	through
thrall [noun]	bondage, captivity
thrall [verb]	make captive
thral(l)dom	captivity
thralled	enslaved, captive
threat	threaten
threpe	scold
tickled	irritated, vexed
tilestone	brick or tile
till	to
timbrel	tambourine-like instrument
tine	ruin
tofore	before
toys	trivialities, frivolities
tract	course
train	trickery, treachery
traist	trust
trance	swoon
travail	labour, childbirth
treacher	traitor
tread	path
trial	test, experiment
tried	refined
trip	mis-step
troubly	tempestuous
trump	trumpet
trumpery	trickery
turn	fashion
turtle	turtle-dove
twain	two, both

unclad	unclothed
uncouth	desolate
undermindeth	undermine
uneath	almost (*rare*)
unfeigned	sincere
unfeignedly	without pretence
unhanced	unexalted
unlose	unloose
unmete	unsuitable
unperched	displaced, unsettled
unstayed	unchecked
untimely	unseasonable
upholden	upheld
ure	use, practice
Urie	Uriah
usen	used
vade	fade, go away
vain	empty
vainglory	unwarranted pride
vale	valley
vanity	1. that which is worthless, futile; 2. pride
vanquishaunt	vanquishing, victorious
vaunt	boast
venging	avenging
verity	truth
vie	life, way
vil'd	degrading
visor	mask
vivifit	came alive
vouchsafe	grant, deign
wail	bewail
waker	watchful
wald	would
wallow	wither
walt'ring	rolling, tumbling
wan	won
wanish	wan, pale
ward	guard
wark	work
warldly	worldly
wasteful	1. unused; 2. destructive; 3. desolate
watershot	flood

wax	grow
way	away; also in phrases, e.g. 'do way' for 'do away with'
weanling	child newly weaned
weed(s)	clothing
weel	well
ween	suppose
weil	virtuous, well
welkin	firmament, sky, heavens
wellaway	alas
whelmed	overwhelmed
whet [adj.]	sharpened (lit. and fig.)
whet [verb]	sharpen
whiles	sometimes
whilom	formerly
whist	silent
whit	a bit
(for) why	because
wight [adj.]	strong
wight, wicht [noun]	creature
wiles	deceits
wise	manner (e.g. 'in this wise')
withal	1. likewise, as well, moreover; 2. with the rest; 3. nevertheless
withouten	without
withstand	resisted, withstood
wode	insane, ferocious
woe	sorrowful
wont(ed) [adj.]	accustomed
wont [noun]	custom
wont [verb]	to be accustomed
wot	know
wrack [noun]	punishment
wrack [verb]	wrought
wrangous	unjust
wrangously	wrongfully
wreakful	vengeful
wried	diverted
wroth	angry
yede	proceed, move (pa. t: 'yeid')
yfear	fear
yielden	surrendered
yshorn	shorn

TEXTUAL NOTES

As with all volumes in the MHRA Tudor & Stuart Translations, texts have been modernized in spelling and punctuation, except in cases where the metre requires a pronunciation indicated by the old spelling. My practice has been somewhat idiosyncratic, however, and I hope appropriately so, given the enormous variety of these texts and the special peculiarities of some of them that seemed worth preserving. I have also occasionally preserved the original virgules (/), where these help clarify the metre. The Psalms in Scots present special problems. I have generally followed the precedent set by Gordon Kendal's excellent edition of Gavin Douglas's *Aeneid*. My own practice has been guided by the competing principles of modernizing for clarity and maintaining some sense of the distinctiveness of the Scots. The collations here are intentionally inconsistent. In many cases, only a single text survives. In some, like the major Bible translations, so many different editions exist that a full collation would be both daunting and beyond any usefulness for this volume. In some cases, too, when thorough collations already exist in standard scholarly editions I have simply referred to the reader to those. Otherwise, I have attempted to provide a useful collation of available early texts. Incipits (the first words in Latin) have generally been preserved where they were included, as have some headnotes where they were of reasonable length.

Publication information is taken from STC unless otherwise indicated. The collation includes editions available on EEBO to provide ease of electronic access, and the editions consulted are representative rather than exhaustive. Place of publication is London unless otherwise indicated. In the case of Psalms for which substantial modern editorial work has been done, this edition relies on the most recent standard editions. These editions, and other important modern editions, are listed in the notes.

1. 1530 George Joye, *The Psalter of David in English*

Copy-text

The Psalter of David in Englishe purely a[n]d faithfully tra[n]slated aftir the texte of Feline (Argentine [i.e. Antwerp]: Francis Foxe [i.e. Martin de Keyser], 1530) STC 2370

Other early editions

STC 2371 (Thomas Godfray, [1534?])
STC 2374 (Edward Whitchurch, [1544?])

2. 1530 George Joye, *Ortulus animae*

Copy-text

Ortulus anime the garden of the soule (Argentine [i.e. Antwerp]: Francis Foxe [i.e. Martin de Keyser], 1530) STC 13828.4

There are no further early editions.

3. 1534 George Joye, *David's Psalter*

Copy-text

Davids Psalter, diligently and faithfully tra[n]slated by George Joye (Antwerp: [Martin Emperor], 1534) STC 2372

There are no further early editions.

Psalm 19
10 pursue] peruse 2372

4. 1534 George Joye, *A Primer in English*

Copy-text

A prymer in Englyshe with certeyn prayers [et] godly meditations, very necessary for all people that understonde not the Latyne tongue. Cum priuilegio regali (John Byddell for William Marshall, [1534]) STC 15986

Other early editions

STC 15988 (John Biddell for William Marshall, 1535 [newly corrected and expanded])

Psalm 119
5 instructed] instructe 15986; instructed 15988
72 instructed] instruct 15986; instructed 15988
111 perform it] perform in 15986, 15988
121 let me not, shamed, be disappointed] let me not shamed disappointed 15986; let me not, shamed, be disappointed 15988
130 mercifully] merciably 15986; mercifully 15988

5. 1534 Miles Coverdale, *A Paraphrasis upon All the Psalms*

Copy-text

A paraphrasis upon all the Psalmes of David, made by Johannes Campensis, reader of the Hebrue lecture in the universite of Lovane, and translated out of Latine into Englysshe (Thomas Gibson, 1539) STC 2372.6

There are no further early editions.

6. 1535 Miles Coverdale, *Biblia. The Bible* (The Coverdale Bible)

Copy-text

Biblia. The Bible, that is, the holy Scripture of the Olde and New Testament, faithfully and truly translated out of Douche and Latyn into Englishe ([Cologne?: Printed by E. Cervicornus and J. Soter?], 1535) STC 2063

Other early editions

STC 2064 (Southwark: James Nicolson, 1537)
STC 2065 (Southwark: James Nicolson, 1537)
STC 2080 (Zurich: Christopher Froschover for Andrew Hester, 1550)

Psalm 23
Numbered 22 in 2063, 2065, 2080; 23 in 2064
4 I fear] fear I 2065

Psalm 43
3 shut] shot 2063; shut 2064, 2065, 2080
5 in to] into 2063; unto 2064, 2065, 2080

7. 1535 Miles Coverdale, *Ghostly Psalms*

Copy-text

Goostly psalmes and spirituall songes drawen out of the holy Scripture, for the co[m]forte and consolacyon of soch as love to rejoyse in God and his Worde (John Rastell for] John Gough, [1535?]) STC 5892

There are no further early editions.

8. 1536 Anon., *Stories and Prophesies out of the Holy Scripture*

Copy-text

Storys and prophesis out of the Holy Scripture, garnyschede with faire ymages, and with devoute praeirs and thanckgevings unto God. With grete diligence (Antwerp: Simon Cock, 1536) STC 3014

There are no further early editions.

9. 1537 John Rogers, *The Bible* (The Matthew Bible)

Copy-text

The Byble, which is all the holy Scripture: In which are contained the Olde and Newe Testament truly and purely translated into Englysh by Thomas Matthew ([Antwerp?]: Richard Grafton and Edward Whitchurch, 1537) STC 2066

TEXTUAL NOTES

Other early editions

STC 2077 (John Day and William Seres, 1549 [rev. notes, etc. by Edmund Becke])
STC 2078 (Thomas Raynalde and William Hill, 1549)
STC 2086 (William Bonham, 1551)

Psalm 23
5 no] 2066, 2078, 2086; not 2077

Psalm 60
19 cast us out] 2066, 2078, 2086; cast out 2077

10. 1539 Miles Coverdale, *The Bible in English* (The Great Bible)

Copy-text

The Byble in Englyshe that is to saye the content of al the holy scrypture, both of ye olde and newe testament, truly translated after the veryte of the Hebrue and Greke textes, by the dylygent studye of diverse excellent learned men, expert in the forsayde tonges ([Paris: Francis Regnault; London] Richard Grafton and Edward Whitchurch, 1539) STC 2068

Other early editions

STC 2069 (Thomas Petit and Robert Redman for Thomas Berthelet, 1540)
STC 2070 (Edward Whitchurch, 1540)
STC 2071 (Richard Grafton, 1540)
STC 2072 (Richard Grafton, 1541)
STC 2074 (Edward Whitchurch, 1541)
STC 2075 (Edward Whitchurch, 1541)
[etc.]

The bibliographic history of the 'Great' Bible has been in need of correction for well over a century, since Nicholas Pocock pointed out the significant variation among different early editions. Pocock's observations seem to have been ignored by every history of the English Bible since. One key point for this volume is that the Coverdale Psalms later typically bound with or included in the BCP were those of STC 2075 (November 1541). There are sometimes considerable variations among earlier editions, which have yet to be tracked and explained. See Pocock, '"The Great Bible", A.D. 1539', *Book-Lore*, 7 (1885), 1–5, and 'Cranmer's Bible', *Book-Lore*, 13 (1885), 22.

Psalm 2
1 grudge] 2068, 2069; so furiouslye rage 2070, 2071, 2072, 2074, 2075
11 warned] 2068, 2070; lerned 2069, 2071, 2072, 2074, 2075

Psalm 22
9 the head] the heade, sayenge: 2071, 2072, 2074, 2075
9 let him deliver him] that he wolde delyver hym 2071, 2072, 2074, 2075
14 here] there 2071, 2072, 2074, 2075
15 Great] Many 2069, 2070, 2071, 2072, 2074, 2075
15 fat] greate 2069, 2070, 2071
32 abhorred] abhorreth 2071
41 and live so hardly] omitted in 2071, 2072, 2074, 2075
41 before him] before him, and my soule shall lyve to serve him and 2069, 2070; before him, and no man hath quickened his awne soule 2071, 2072, 2074, 2075

Psalm 23
5 staff comfort] staff they comfort 2069, 2070

Psalm 46
1-2 will we not] wyll not we 2072, 2074, 2075

Psalm 81
[leaves missing from 2069 on EEBO]
4 for Israel] of Israel 2072, 2075
9 upon thee] upon me 2074
10 O Israel] of Israell 2070, 2071

Psalm 90
1 to] unto 2072, 2074, 2075
4 turnest man to destruction] causest man to return unto contrycion 2069, 2070
4 ye children] chyldren 2072, 2074, 2075
5 is past] in past 2072 [obvious typo]
17 feareth] fareth 2072, 2075
23 the glorious] thy glorious 2075

Psalm 95
4 strength] heightes 2069, 2070
6 prepared] fourmed 2069, 2070

Psalm 107
[Equivalent of lines 47-56 missing since leaf missing in 2069 on EEBO.]
3 lands] all lands 2071
18 therefore praise] prayse therefore 2071
37 delivereth] delivered 2069, 2070
39 bringeth] bringeht 2074 [obvious typo]
49 blessed] blesseth 2071, 2074, 2075

Psalm 121
[leaves missing from 2069 on EEBO]

11. 1539 Richard Taverner, *The Most Sacred Bible* (The Taverner Bible)

Copy-text

The most sacred Bible, whiche is the Holy Scripture conteyning the Old and New Testament / translated into English, and newly recognised with great diligence after most faythful exemplars, by Rychard Taverner (John Byddell for Thomas Berthelet, 1539) STC 2067

Other early editions

STC 2082 (*The thyrde parte of the Byble*, John Day and William Seres, 1550 [rev. Edmund Becke])
STC 2088 (John Day, 1551 [rev. Becke])

Psalm 23
[numbered 22 in 2067, 23 in 2082, 2088]
5 no] not 2082, 2088

Psalm 77
[numbered 76 in 2067, 77 in 2082, 2088]
10 spirit] sprite 2067; spirit 2082, 2088
16 in displeasure] in displeasure. Selah. 2082, 2088
34 footsteps] fetesteppes 2067; fotesteppes 2082; footesteppes 2088

12. 1539 Richard Taverner, *An Epitome of the Psalms*

Copy-text

An epitome of the Psalmes, or briefe meditacions upon the same, with diverse other moste christian prayers, translated by Richard Taverner ([Richard Bankes? for Anthony Clerke?], 1539) STC 2748

Other early editions

STC 2747.5 (John Byddell, 1539)

Psalm 47
3 renown] renouns 2748

13. 1540 Miles Coverdale, *The Psalter or Book of Psalms*

Copy-text

The Psalter or boke of Psalmes both in Latyn and Englyshe. wyth a kalender, & a table the more eassyer and lyghtlyer to fynde the psalmes contayned therin (Richard Grafton, [1540]) STC 2368

There are no further early editions.

14. 1540s John Croke, *A Book of Certain Chosen Psalms*

Copy-text

British Library Add. MS 30981 *A boke of certen chosen psalmes translated into ynglysh meter by John Croke esquyer my father when he was one of the six clerkes of the Chauncery*

There are no further early texts.

Psalm 32
55 be] been MS

15. 1544 Anon., *Prayers of Holy Fathers*

Copy-text

Praiers of holi fathers, patryarches, prophetes, judges, kynges, and renowmed men and wemen of eyther testament ([London: Richard Grafton for William Tilotson, 1544?]) STC 20200

There are no further early editions.

Psalm 37
16 ungodly] godly 20200

16. 1544 Katherine Parr, *Psalms or Prayers Taken out of Holy Scripture*

Copy-text

Psalmes or prayers taken out of holye scripture (London: Thomas Berthelet, 1544) STC 3002

Other early editions

STC 3002.7 (Thomas Berthelet, 1545)
STC 3003 (Thomas Bertholet, 1545)
STC 3004 (Thomas Bertholet, 1545) no copy on EEBO
STC 3005 (Thomas Bertholet, 1548)
STC 3006 (Thomas Bertholet, 1553–1558)
STC 3007 (William Copland for John Waley and William Seres, 1559)

The Thirteenth Psalm
39 go] be 3006
46 made] make

Psalm 22
[numbered 21 in 3002, 3003, 3005, 3006]
16 have] thei 3006
22 thy] my 3007

39 lots] lottes 3007; lot 3002, 3003, 3005, 3006; lotte 3002.7
54 a] the 3007
69–70 missing in 3006 (next page blank, though the appropriate catchword, 'That', at bottom of page)

17. 1546 Anne Askew, *The First Examination*

Copy-text

The first examinacyon of Anne Askewe lately martyred in Smythfelde, by the Romysh popes upholders, with the elucydacyon of Johan Bale (Marburg [i.e. Wesel: Printed by Derik van der Straten], 1546) STC 848

Other early editions

STC 850 ([Wesel: Dirik van der Straten], 1547) Psalm 54 not included
STC 851 ([Nicholas Hill?], 1547)
STC 852 (W. Hill, 1548) Psalm 54 not included
STC 852.5 ([William Copland?], c. 1550) no copy on EEBO
STC 853 (s.n., c. 1560) Psalm 54 not included
STC 849 (Robert Waldegrave, 1585?) Psalm 54 not included

18. c. 1546–1547? Henry Howard, Earl of Surrey

Copy-text

Harington MS Temp. Eliz. (Arundel-Harington, mid-late sixteenth century, compiled by John Harington of Stepney and Sir John Harington of Kelston) 'A'

Other early texts

British Library Add MS 36529 (folio verse miscellany mid-late sixteenth century compiled by John Harington of Stepney and Sir John Harington of Kelston) includes Psalms 88, 73 (with prologue), 55
Certayne Chapters of the proverbes of Salomon drawen into metre by Thomas Sterneholde, late grome of the kynges Magesties robes (London: John Case for Willyam Seres, [1549–1550]) STC 2760 [includes Psalm 88, without prologue]
Text based on Hughey's published transcription; collation with 36529 hers, with 2760 this editor's.

Psalm 8 A No further early texts.
Psalm 55 A, 36529
Psalm 73 A, 36529
Psalm 88 A, 36529, 2760

Modern editions

The Poems of Henry Howard, Earl of Surrey, ed. by Frederick M. Padelford (Seattle: University of Washington Press, 1920)
Poems, ed. by Emrys Jones (Oxford: Clarendon Press, 1964)
Selected Poems, ed. by Dennis Keene (Manchester: Carcanet Press, 1985)

Psalm 55
5   spirit] sprite 36529
30 moves] moveth 36529
39 half] hafte 36529
43 coats] Coales A; cootes 36529
47 the other] the thother 36529
48 *Iacta curam ... enutriet. id est*] *Iacta curam ... enutriet.* 36529
49 final line omitted in 36529

Psalm 73
19 appair] appere 36529
34 with] lyke 36529
42 effects] affects 36529
47 when] as 36529
54 powers] power 36529
55 dreams] dream 36529
63 spirits] sprits 36529
71 others' succours] other succor 36529

Psalm 88
Parts of lines 12 and 13 obscure in EEBO copy
15 thy] thine 2760
17 me cast / headlong] cast me hedling 36529
22 have] hath 2760
25 do] did 36529, 2760
26 thine] thy 36529
29 so be] be so 2760
30 thy] thine 2760
32 praise] faith 36529, 2760
34 nor] as 36529
35 blazed] blasted 36529, 2760
35 mouths] mouthe 2760
36 shut] shitt 36529
37 thy word] thys worlde 2760
38 Must] Nor 2760
40 limbs] bones 2760
44 not appear, O Lord] thou lorde appease 2760
44 should'st] sholdest 36529; shoulde 2760

46 Of one, from youth] Cast not from the 2760
50 swallow] follow 2760
52 to] for 36529, to 2760

19. 1547? Thomas Sternhold, *Certain Psalms*

Copy-text

Certayne psalmes chose[n] out of the Psalter of David, and drawe[n] into Englishe metre by Thomas Sternhold grome of ye kynges Majesties roobes ([Nicholas Hill for] Edward Whitchurch, [1547?]) STC 2419

There are no further early editions.

20. 1548 John Bale, *A Godly Meditation*

Copy-text

A godly medytacyon of the christen sowle, concerninge a love towardes God and hys Christe, compyled in frenche by lady Margarete quene of Naverre, and aptely translated into Englysh by the ryght vertuouse lady Elyzabeth doughter to our late soverayne Kynge Henri the. Viij ([Wesel]: [Derik van der Straten], 1548) STC 17320

Other early editions

STC 17320.5 (Henry Denham, 1568?)

Psalm 14
6 To] The 17320
16 flock] folcke 1548

21. 1549 John Bale, *A Dialogue or Communication*

Copy-text

A dialoge or communycacyon to be had at a table betwene two chyldren, gathered out of the holy scriptures, by Johan Bale, for his .ij. yonge sonnes Johan and Paule ([Stephen Mierdman] for Richard Foster, 1549) STC 1290

Other early editions

STC 1294 (*An Expostulation or complaynte agaynste the blasphemyes of a franticke papyst of Hamshyre*) (1552) [Psalm 130 appended to this different publication]

Psalm 130
7 health] helpe 1294

22. 1549 John Hopkins, *All Such Psalms*

Copy-text

Al such psalmes of David as Thomas Sternehold late grome of [the] kinges Majesties Robes, didde in his life time draw into English Metre (Edward Whitchurch, 1549) STC 2420

Other early editions

STC 2422 (Edward Whitchurch, 1551?)
STC 2423 (Thomas Berthelet, 1551?)
STC 2424.6 (Edward Whitchurch, 1553?)
STC 2424.8 (Edward Whitchurch, 1553?) EEBO copy incomplete (missing Hopkins's Psalms)

Psalm 30
1 that] the 2424.6
26 chance] chaunge 2424.6
37 did I] I 2424.6
47 this simple] thus my 2424.6

23. 1549 Sir Thomas Wyatt, *Certain Psalms*

Copy-text

British Library Egerton MS 2711 (Folio collection mostly of Wyatt's verse, some in his own hand *c.* 1530s) 'E'

Other early texts

STC 2726 *Certayne psalmes chosen out of the psalter of Dauid, commonlye called the .vii. penytentiall psalmes, drawen into englyshe meter by Sir Thomas Wyat knyght, wherunto is added a prolage of [the] auctore before euery psalme, very pleasau[n]t [and] profetable to the godly reader* (Thomas Raynald and [i.e. for] John Harington, 1549)
Harrington MS Temp. Eliz. (Arundel-Harington, mid- to late sixteenth century) 'A'
British Library Royal MS 17a (mid-sixteenth-century copy of Penitential Psalms) 'R'

Modern editions

Collected Poems of Sir Thomas Wyatt, ed. by Kenneth Muir and Patricia Thomson (Liverpool: Liverpool University Press, 1969)
The Complete Poems of Sir Thomas Wyatt, ed. by R. A. Rebholz (Harmondsworth: Penguin, 1978)

Following (as Muir/Thomson and Rebholz) Egerton, though E missing some lines. A the text for these. Text crossed out in E (which is considerable) not

TEXTUAL NOTES

included here, due to limitations of space. For what will surely be the authoritative text and editorial analysis, see Jason Powell's forthcoming Oxford edition. Punctuation kept minimal, though Wyatt's own generally included (/ represented by a comma). Asterisks inserted between Psalms and narrative links.

1 subject] subiectes 2726, A
3 himself] hymselfes 2726
4 David's] David E; Davides 2726, A
5 dazed] David A
7 Touch] Toucht R
7 senses] sinews 2726
7 overruns] over ranne A
8 sparpled] spark led 2726, A; sparcled R
10 moist] noisome 2726
10 heart he] heart A
11 the] his A
12 this] his R
12 brawl] braule E; brawle 2726, A
16 thing] a thing 2726, A
17 forgot] he forgot 2726
18 these] this A
18 doth] do A, R
22 idol's] Jeweles 2726
24 die] be 2726
31 this] his A
32 things] thinge E, A
32 naught] nothing 2726
34 rueful] ruthfull A
34 sets] set A
38 show'th him] show'th 2726; sheweth R
40 amazed this aged woeful] amsed was, thys woful aged 2726
41 meets] meateth 2726; mete A
42 limbs] lymyttes 2726
43 droopeth] droppeth 2726, R
45 heat] health R
45 and] his 2726
45 fear] fyre 2726
47 pall] pauler 2726
47 lets] letteth 2726
49 The] Then 2726
49 of state and] and statelie R
50 rebates] rebate 2726, R

51 Thinner] Th'inner A
51 clotheth] clothed 2726
53 of] with R
54 hair] hears A
55 selfsame] same 2726
57 taketh] takes A
57 in hand] in his hand R
58 his plaints] playnts 2726
59 distils] dystylleth 2726
60 him] him selfe 2726
60 dark] darke depe A
61 ground] grownds A
61 wherein] wher 2726; whenne R
62 Fleeing] Flyinge 2726; fflyeng A
65 But he] But 2726
66 Of that] Rof that E
66 that] whyche 2726
67 say] said R
68 fraughted] yfraughted A
69 his cheer coloured like clay] depe draughts of hys decaye 2726; and touchinge of the stringes R
70 Dressed] dressing R
71 song] songes 2726

Psalm 6

1 since in] since 2726, R
2 call] to call 2726
3 my harp hope taken] my harp, he taken 2726
6 Only comfort of] Of onely comfort to 2726
8 By thy goodness, of thee this thing require] By the goodnes of thee, this thynge require 2726; By thy goodness R
13 Thee, thee to dread] Thee too dreade 2726; thee for to dread A
15 not in] in A
17 furor] furie R
17 my] myne 2726, R
24 stray'th] strays R
25 I sick without] and seke without 2726; I seeke without A; I seke without R
28–81 leaf missing from E, these lines based on A
30 Threateth] Tretith R
33 worldly] Worlds R
33 vanity] vanities 2726
34 the weak] the 2726
37 use] pleasure 2726

TEXTUAL NOTES

38 shadow] shade 2726, R
44 O Lord I thee beseech] I beseche thee O Lorde 2726
45 thine] thine 2726 (adopted); thy A
46 Reduce, revive my soul; be thou the leech] Reduce, revive, my soule be thou the leche R
48 ta'en] had 2726
53 His great offence] his offence R
53 turns] turneth 2726; turnith R
59 For that in death] line missing in A
66 nilt] wilt 2726
67 thy] thee 2726
67 mercy for] mercy 2726
69 In moment] In a moment 2726
73 down] denne 2726; done A; down Rebholz
74 itself] hym selfe 2726
75 suffers now] suffreth none 2726; sufferth newe R
76 nightly] myghtye 2726; mightye A
79 stir] stere 2726
82 beset] besettes A
84 to my weeping eyes, lo] to me, my weeping eyes 2726; to my weping eyes R
85 The cheer, the manner] The chere, manere R
85 and] or 2726
88 Those] These 2726
89 my] myne R
90 my] myne R
91 show the] show 2726
93 these] the 2726
94 mine] my 2726, A
95 com'th] comes A
96 heart] harpe 2726
96 these] those A
97 I dare] Dare 2726
103 the rule] thee rule 2726; therefore A
104 the] that thee 2726
104 glosing] glawncynge A
106 lie] do lye 2726
109 confusion's stroke] confusion as stroke 2726, A
114 with the hot] with the heate 2726; with the heat A, Rebholz; with heat R
114 or] or with A
115 fervour] furour A; fevour 2726
118 the] his 2726
118 eyes] eyen 2726
119 adown] downe 2726

123 error] terrour 2726; terror Rebholz
125 willed] wyll 2726
126 beknowing] by knowing A
127 to] for to A, 2726
128 Eased] And 2726
128 feeleth] filleth A
129 Seemeth horrible] Nowe semeth feareful 2726
131 or] of 2726
132 doth] dyd 2726
133 had] hathe A
133 kneel] kneeling 2726
133 the] a A
137 looketh] loked 2726
138 bethought] besought A
140 unto] into 2726
140 rought] caught A
144 crieth] cryed 2726

Psalm 32
4 none] not 2726, R
7 cover'th] covert 2726
13 other's fault] other faultes 2726
18 But] And 2726
19 new] and new A
21 hid] had A
24 feels his health to be hindered] fyndeth, hys healthe hindered 2726; feleth his helth to be hindred
26 leech's] Leathis A
29 Thy] The 2726
33 hath] have 2726
33 green] grain Rebholz
37 hide from thee my] hide from my R
38 quod] quoth 2726
45 harm him miss] harm 2726
49 joy] loys 2726
49 scapes] scapeth 2726
50 bonds] bandes 2726
50 in his] in 2726
51 Such joy, my joy] Such is my joye 2726
53 light] sight 2726, R
53 port] light 2726, R
55 look] boke 2726; booke R
58 address] redresse A

TEXTUAL NOTES

59 Mine] My 2726
59 eye] eyes A
60 alone] onelye 2726
61 mule] moyle A
61 man doth] men do 2726
62 doth not] doth 2726, R
63 the good thou dost him, must be tied] thee good, thou muste hym betide 2726, A
64 guide] maister R
65 are the] there are 2726
66 in] and 2726
67 in] and 2726
70 to] so A
70 bind] blynde 2726; blynd A
73 Joy and rejoice, I say, ye that] Joyce, and rejoyce, I say: you that 2726; Joye and rejoyce saye ye that A
76 All ye that be of] All you that be, of 2726; All that be of an A
77 stint] skant R
78 about he] he about 2726
79 cave] the Cave A
79 withouten] withoute 2726
81 this peace] hys harpe 2726
82 cry] call 2726
83 mercy's plentiful] mercy full hand ['plentifull' inserted above] E; plentyfull mercies 2726, R; plentifull mercyes A; mercy's plentiful Rebholz
84 where] whi R
85 servant that] servant 2726
86 Finding] ffynding the A
89 David, that seemed in that] David, semed in thee 2726; david did seme as in that R
90 A marble image] Marble image A; Marble ymage R
91 in the rock] in Rock A
91 hands] hande 2726
92 as] is 2726
93 This] The A
93 sends] sendeth 2726
94 was] theare was A, R
94 cloud] sonne 2726
95 on the] on his A
95 descends] descendethe 2726
96 chords] world 2726
97 lustre] glister A
97 the] his A

97 extends] extendethe 2726
99 start] stette 2726
101 then] more 2726
104 And just] Just 2726
104 the t'other] the other 2726
105 his] thee 2726
106 Sure] For 2726
106 and] hys 2726
107 sought] eke sought ['eke' inserted above] A
108 voice] looke A

Psalm 38
1 thee have] have thee 2726
2 no] none R
8 of famine] a famin R
8 and] of 2726, A
10 plunged up, as] plucked up, as 2726; plonged up like R
12 thy] thine R
18 weight] weightes 2726
19 stop] stoupe 2726, R; shrinck A
19 to] to the 2726
23 rankled] ranked 2726
26 with his] with 2726
27 worm] wounde R
29 mine] mye A
30 the] my 2726, R
30 that hath] that 2726
33 it hath] it 2726
34 the inward] thinwarde 2726; inward R
39 mine] my 2726
40 mine] my A
42 did] did me A
43 stand] stode A
47 wits] wit 2726
50 One] Not one 2726
50 thy] thyne 2726
51 and thou, O Lord] and thou lorde 2726; and thow Lord A; thou, Lord Rebholz
51 supply] replye 2726
52 thee] that 2726
55 showed] shew A
56 And] That 2726
58 that] and A

61 safe] styll 2726
62 provokers] provokes A
62 do] do moche A
65 pursuit] presente 2726
67 My Lord, I am] My Lord (I am) A
67 know'st well] knowest 2726
73 of] of the 2726
74 wearied] wery 2726
77 t'one] one A
78 t'other] other 2726, A
78 to mercy] still to marcye A
79 sonour] foure 2726; Sower A
79 extends] pretendes 2726
81 from] of 2726
81 storm] streame 2726, A
83 bain] vayne 2726
84 to that that] so that A
85 sigh] sight E; syghe 2726, sighe A
86 heaven's] heaven 2726
87 who] who so A
87 had] hathe 2726
87 cave's] cave 2726
88 he] hym 2726
91 so close the cave was and] the Cave close was and eke A
94 The woeful plaint and of their king the tears] Of theyr kygne the wofull playnts and teares 2726
95 some] sonne 2726
96 affrays] affayres 2726
97 seemeth] seemed 2726
99 violence] vyolente 2726
100 fear dismays] dispayre dismayde 2726
101 voice] herte 2726; hert R
101 his heart] the same R
102 cries] cryeth 2726

Psalm 51
1 Lord] good lorde R
3 the world] thy worde 2726
8 those mercies] hys mercie 2726
9 way] a way 2726
9 sins] synne 2726
9 that so] that 2726
10 Again] Ofte tymes agayne 2726; Ofte tymes A; Oft times

11 sin] sinnes 2726
11 mak'th] makes, 2726, A
12 ay] ever 2726
13 no number] now, none 2726
14 remission of offence] remyssyon of synne 2726
15 hearts] harte 2726
15 hath] hast R
16 fault, my] faulte and my 2726
17 sin] synnes 2726
18 Thereof] Thearfore A
19 alone] above 2726
20 measure] cure 2726
24 mind] sight 2726
28 justly able] justiciable 2726
33 this] these 2726
33 my] myne 2726, A
33 alas] ah alas 2726
34 necessity] necessitie inward 2726
35 loves] lovest 2726, R; lov'ste A
35 inward] the 2726
36 my] mooste 2726
37 frailty] frayle 2726; fraile R
38 led] leade 2726
42 yet] as yet A, R
49 shall] shalte 2726
50 afore] before 2726
53 midst] middell 2726
54 voided] voide A
54 filthy] all fithie ['all' inserted above] A
55 thine] thye 2726
56 thy] thee 2726
57 rest] heste 2726
58 with] wyth the 2726
59 goodly] godlye 2726, A
60 ways] waie R
61 They] Theise A
63 praises] prayse 2726
68 first] at furst A
72 delights] delytest 2726; delyghtest A
78 ghost] hoste 2726
79 the] thy 2726
80 these] the 2726
81 As] Of a 2726

82 line missing in 2726
83 here] ther 2726
85 and] eke, and A
86 The greatness did so astone himself a space] Thy goodnesse dyd so, astony hym apace 2726
88 alas] ah alas 2726
91 but not] but 2726
92 paiseth] poiseth Rebholz
93 that erst] that 2726
93 forth afford] foorde abrode 2726
94 points] pointeth 2726
94 wonders] wondreth 2726
95 hides] hydethe 2726
96 complisheth] accomplysheth 2726
98 graces] grace 2726
100 mercies] mercye 2726
100 fault] fautes 2726
101 sinners] Synnes 2726, A
101 infinite] Infinytye 2726
101 treasure] mercie R
102 termless] celestyall 2726
103 dure] endure 2726
104 'gainst] gaine E; agayne 2726; gaynste A
104 no] none R
106 heaven's] heaven E, 2726, A
107 hath] had 2726
109 From] For 2726
110 finds] fyndeth 2726
110 much] so much A
110 therewith] therewith al A
111 dare importune] importeth on 2726
112 to] that to 2726
113 parentheses follow Rebholz

Psalm 102
2 Unto the Lord] Unto the, lord 2726; Unto thee, Lord Rebholz
3–4 Do not from me ...] Do not from me, tourne thy merciful face | Unto my selfe, leavynge my government 2726
6 to] unto 2726
7 my] myne 2726
8–9 Readily grant ...] Redely graunte, theffecte of my desire | Boldely too please thy Majestye 2726
11 as smoke] a synke 2726

11 been] are 2726
12 as] as a 2726
14 Because] by cawse E; But 2726
16 plaintful sighs and my] painful sighs and very 2726; playntfull sighes and for my dread A; plaintful sighes and eke my R
18 Sprite] spirite 2726
19 As] I, as A
20 I me] I am 2726
20 solein] soden 2726; solemne A
21 fleeth] flyeth 2726, A; flieth R
23 ruin life] ruyne lyfe
32 mine eyes] mye eyes downe A
32 do] dyd 2726
33 Because] by cawse E
37 know] knew A
38 dry] crye 2726
39 crown] dorwne 2726
44 thy] the 2726
46 that doth thy] that thy 2726
46 servants] servannt R
48 sin's] his R
50 lower] lore 2726
53 this] thi R
55 The] Hee A
56 he him] him 2726
61 height] high 2726
62 in] on 2726
64 foul] soche 2726
66 gracious] glorious 2726
67 his] this R
71 The Lord that above] The Lord that is above 2726; The Lorde above A, Rebholz
72 But to this sembly] But to this samble E; But these feble 2726; But to this Sample A; But this semble R
74 they may not dure] they are not sure 2726
75 term] tyme 2726
76 hearty] hart 2726
77 take me not, Lord, away] take me not awaye 2726; lord take me not awaye A
78 In mids] In the middes 2726
81 alway] ay R
82 age] aye 2726
85 the] thy 2726
85 well] hole 2726
86 wast] was 2726

86 shalt] shal R
90 the world] thie worde A
93 Sprite] spyryte 2726
93 returned] retourne 2726
95 Sprite] spyryte 2726
97 music's art] musycke arte 2726
98 this] that, I wys 2726
99 Sprite] spirite 2726
102 have] hathe 2726
107 ginneth] begynneth 2726
109 damn'th] dampnethe this A
110 whit] what 2726
114 contrite] contrite hart 2726
117 void] owne 2726; worde A

Psalm 130
1 from a] from 2726
1 deep] dirk R
11 ear thereto] eare sette therto 2726
12 thou do observe] thou observe R
12 offend] doo offende 2726
13 put thy native] put native A
14 demand] demaund a A
16 Dread, and not reverence] dede, and no reverence 2726
17 reign large] runne at large 2726
18 mercy's] mercye A
19 move] eke move A
27 By the] by thy 2726; By this his A
27 thrust] thurst A
29 are] arn E, R, Rebnholz; are 2726, A
37 sword] worde 2726
37 humble ear] humilitie 2726
39 Eternal life] Eternallye 2726
44 The glint] The glute 2726; The glutt A, R; Than glint Rebholz
44 in the] in A
45 redeemed] redeemeth 2726
47 David] To David 2726
54 his] thys 1549
57 And he delights] And delights R
60 sin] synnes 2726
61 pursuit] suyte 2726
62 sured] sure 2726
63 begins] begynne 2726; begynnethe A

Psalm 143
2 answer] supply thou 2726, R
3 by] for my 2726
6 the] that 2726
7 not of] of 2726
8 thy] thee 2726
12 spurs] sours A
13 risen] rysyng A
14 my] myne 2726
14 en'my] enemyes 2726
15 foiled] soyled 2726
16 For that in herns] For that in heins E; fforreyne Realmes 2726, A; For in hernes R
17 forced] first A
20 to] two R
23 those] these 2726
26 barren] bare 2726
28 sure] ever 2726
28 sprite] spiryte 2726
30 headlong] hedlyng E; headlinge 2726; hedling R
33 hand] hands 2726
36 them] those A; that R
37 be] me R
41 upright sprite] spirite upryght 2726, R
42 In land of] In laude of 2726; In lawde of A; In laude and R
43 name, Lord] name 2726
43 sprite] spiryte 2726
46 their] the 1549
47 Thou shalt also] also A
49 ay most] moste 2726

24. 1549 Robert Crowley, *The Psalter of David*

Copy-text

The Psalter of David newly translated into Englysh metre in such sort that it maye the more decently, and wyth more delyte of the mynde, be reade and songe of al men. Wherunto is added a note of four partes, wyth other thynges, as shall appeare in the epistle to the readar ([Richard Grafton and Stephen Mierdman for] Robert Crowley, 1549) STC 2725

There are no further early editions.

25. 1549 Sir Thomas Smith, *Certain Psalms or Songs of David*

Copy-text

British Library MS Royal 17A xvii (prison writings of Sir Thomas Smith 1549–1550)

There are no further early texts.

Psalm 86
14 laud] lade MS

Modern edition

Acta Universitatis Stockholmiensis: Stockholm Studies in English XII: Sir Thomas Smith: Literary and Linguistic Works (1542. 1549. 1568) Part I: Certaigne psalmes or songues of David: translated into Englishe meter by Sir Thomas Smith, Knight, then Prisoner in the Tower of London, with other prayers and songues by him made to pas the tyme there. 1549, ed. by Bror Danielson (Göteborg, Stockholm: Almqvist & Wiksell, 1963)

26. 1550 John Hall, *Certain Chapters Taken out of the Proverbs*

Copy-text

Certayne chapters take[n] out of the Prouerbes of Salomon, wythe other chapters of the holye scrypture, and certayne psalmes of Dauid (Thomas Raynald, 1550?) STC 12631

Other early texts

STC 12631.3 (Thomas Raynald, 1550?) [Psalm 25 omitted]
STC 12631.5 (Thomas Raynald, 1550?) [Psalm 25 omitted]
STC 12634 (Thomas Raynald, c. 1550?)
STC 12632 [*The Court of Virtue*] (Thomas Marshe, 1565)

Psalm 25
Psalm 25] misnumbered in 12631
1–4 12632 omits the quatrain headnote and substitutes a longer introduction
5 To thee I lift my soul, O Lord] To thee oh lorde I lyfte my soule 1632
9–12 For all they that ... confounded of thee] Ne yet let such as in thee truste, | Rebuke or shame susteyne: | But rather confounde scornefull men, | That spitefully dysdeyne 12632
13 My King, my God, I pray to thee] To the I praye my jyng and god 12632
14 Show me now] O shewe to me 12632
15 O Lord, and teach thy paths] And teach thy pathes O lord 12632
16 And I will give thee the] Thy name that I may 12632

17 Lead me, Lord, thy truth to speak] O lorde leade me to speake thy truthe 12632
19 Thou art my God and my Saviour eke] Myne only god and sauying health 12632
21 O call to thy remembrance] Forget not lorde but call to minde 12632
23 And eke thy loving kindness, Lord] Let not thy louying kyndes slacke 12632
25 Remember not my sins, O God] Forget my sinnes, remember not 12632
26 And frailty] The fraylnes 12632
27 mercy's sake] mercy lorde 12632
28 Think on me, Lord] Thynke vpon me 12632
29–30 How friendly and ... Lord of might] O righteous lorde with frenlynes, | Wytsafe to shewe thy myght 12632
31 Therefore, he will] Whereby thou shalt 12632
32 the] thy 12632
33 he doeth leade aright] thou doest teache & guyde 12632
34–36 And keepeth them ... right in his way] Thy perfect ways to knowe, | And thou doste suche instructe aright | As humble be and lowe 12632
37 The ways of God] Thy ways O lorde 12632
38 And faithfulness is plight] Thy faithfulness is bent 12632
39 his testament] thy couenant 12632
40 covenant aright] faythfull testament 12632
41 O living Lord] therfore O lorde 12632
43 for they be] that are so 12632
45 What so ever he be] Who so therfore doth feare the lorde 12632
46 That feareth the Lord] He wyll hym shewe 12632
47 He shall to him show his] His hyghe and his diuine 12632
48 And eke his] His pure and 12632
49 dwell] be 12632
50 Thereof I you insure] His wayes shal prosper well 12632
51 seed] sede also 12632
51 possess the land] possesse 12632
52 Forever to endure] The lande, therin to dwell 12632
53 The secrets of the Lord are known] The lorde his secretes dothe shew forth 12632
54 them that] such as 12632
55 He showeth to them] Declaring them 12632
57 Mine eyes are looking to the Lord] O lorde my god to the therfore 12632
58 On whom my trust is set] I wyll myne eyes directe 12632
59 For by his might, he shall pluck out] And praye to thee tyll thou haste losde 12632
61 Turn] O turne 12632
61 O God] therfore 12632

63 Have mercy, Lord, on me] Consider lorde my mysery 12632
64 For] Howe 12632
65 be] are 12632
66 Full sore it doth] Ryght sore they doe 12632
67 O bring me out of troubles, Lord] O ryd me from these troubles all 12632
68 In thee I do] For in thee I 12632
69 Look upon my misery] O loke on myne aduersitie 12632
70 mine adversity] my great mystery 12632
71 O Lord] also 12632
72 I have] Where I 12632
74 Be many, much and great] Are many and peruearte 12632
75 And bear an heart malicious] That towardes me maliciously 12632
76 For they would me defeat] Are bent with hatefull hearte 12632
77 O keep thou my soul, O God] Oh, preserue thou my soule therfore 12632
78 And eke deliver me] Within thy kepyng iust 12632
79 Let me not be confounded, Lord] And let me not confounded be 12632
80 I put my trust in thee] For in thee doe I truste 12632
81 Righteous dealing and innocency] Let iust dealyng and innocent 12632
82 Now with me let them] O god styll wih me 12632
83 out of his] from all vyle 12632

Psalm 34
1–4 12632 omits the quatrain headnote and substitutes a longer introduction
3 to] of 12632
11 The poor oppressed shall hear thereof] The poore opprest that heare therof 12631.3; That poore oppressed men may here 12632;
12 and gladly shall] The same, them to 12632
13–16 I do you now … name to magnify] Together let vs nowe | In honor doe our partes, | His name to prayse and magnifie, | With meke and humble hartes 12632
17 For I myself besought the Lord] For I besought the lorde 12631.3; For when I him besought 12632
18–20 He heard me … did deliver me] He heard my prayer so, | That he did streyght delvuer me, | From all my care and wo 12632
21 O come and be you lightened] O then recyue the light 12631.3, 12631.5; Receaue therefore the light 12632
23 then withouten] so without all 12632
25 This poor man cried unto the Lord] This poore man cryed to god 12631.3, 12631.5; For I poore man made once 12632
26–28 And he did hear … him full fair] To him my playnte and mone: | He heard me crye, and dyd me ryd, | From troubles euery one 12632
29–32 The angel of … safe and sound] His angell pytched hath | His tente about his shepe, | I meane all suche as feare the lorde, | In saftie them to kepe 12632

33-34 How friendly ... see, who lust] His friendshyp proue and see, | And take therof a taste 12632
35 And blessed is that man] And blessed is that man therefore 12631.3, 12631.5; For they that truste in hym are sure 12632
36 That in him putteth his trust] Most happy at the laste 12632
37 his holiness] hys sayntes 12631.3, 12631.5; all ye 12632
38-40 See that ye do ... shall have ease] Is saynctes of him electe: | For such as feare him lacke nothing, | He doth them well protecte 12632
41 The rich shall suffer hunger great] The rych shall hunger moch 12631.3, 12631.5; The lyons ofte doe lacke 12632
42 want that living] hunger for their 12632
43 that seek the Lord shall lack] which seke the lord, shal wante 12632
44 that which] the which 12632
45 Come hither, O you children] Come hether o you babes 12631.3, 12631.5; Ye children all I saye 12632
46 And] Come 12632
47 shall you teach the fear of God] wyll you teache to feare the lorde 12632
48 therein] in him 12632
49 Whoso lusteth for to live] Wo so lusteth to liue 12631.3, 12631.5; If thou to lyue in ioye 12632
50 To see good days is] and se good days is 12632.3, 12631.5; And see good dayes be 12632
51 Let him his tongue and lippes keep] Thy lippes & tongue from guile & wrōg 12632
52 All evil to] See that thou doe 12632
53 All evil things let them eschew] Let them eschewe al yll 12631.3, 12631.5; Se that thou doe none ill 12632
54 Do good, and] In goodnes 12632
55 And let him seek and eke ensue] But se thou seke and folowe faste 12632
56 To live in rest] On quietnes 12632
57 For why the eyes of God are set] The eyes of god are set 12631.3, 12631.5; The lorde does fixe his eyes 12632
58-60 Upon the righteous ... provideth for them] On iust men louingly, | And to their prayers openly | He doth his eares applye 12632
61 The face of God is also bent] The face of god also 12631.3, 12631,5; Contrariwyse the Lord 12632
62-64 Thy wicked men to ... all their memory] the wicked men doth ... al the memorye 12631.3, 12631.5; Doth bende his countenance, | Of from the earth ill men to moue | And their remembrance 12632
65-68 When righteous men ... them help anon] But to the iuste the lorde | Doth so inclyne his eare, | That when they praye he wyll them ryd | From all trouble and feare 12632
69 near unto all them] nere to them 12631.3, 12631.5; nyghe to suche 12632

70 That] As 12632
71 help] saue 12632
73 The troubles of the righteous] The troubles of good men 12631.3, 12631.5; Though iust mens troubles be 12632
74–76 Although that they … will them entreat] both manifolde and great, | The lord from care wyl make them free, | When they doe him intreate 12632
77–80 He keepeth all … stripe or wound] Their bones he wyll defende, | And kepe so free from cryme: | That not so muche as one of them | Shall breake at any tyme 12632
81 But yet misfortune great] But yet mysfortune greate 12631.3, 12631.5; Misfortune or ill happe 12632
83 they that hate the righteous] such as doe the iust men hate 12632
84 be accused of] peryshe in their 12632
85 the soul save] saue the soules 12632
86 them that doth] all that doe 12632
88 That they shall never] Shall not in peryll 12632

27. 1550 William Hunnis, *Certain Psalms*

Copy-text

Certayne psalmes chosen out of the psalter of Dauid, and drawen furth into Englysh meter by William Hunnis seruant to the ryght honorable syr Wyllyam Harberde knight newly collected [*and*] *imprinted* (Katherine Herford for John Harington, 1550) STC 2727

There are no further early editions.

28. 1551 William Forrest, *Certain Psalms*

Copy-text

British Library Royal MS 17 A. XXI *To the moste worthie prince/ Edwarde Duke of Somerset/ Uncle unto our moste dredde soveraigne Lorde/ Kinge Edwarde the, vi; bee favoure in god/ with honour & peace/ in prosperous estate longe to continue/ so wischethe is humble orator/ W, fforreste.*

There are no further early texts.

29. 1553 Francis Seagar, *Certain Psalms*

Copy-text

Certayne Psalmes select out of the Psalter of Dauid, and drawen into Englyshe metre, wyth notes to euery Psalme in iiij. parts to synge, by F.S. ([Nicholas Hill for] William Seres, 1553) STC 2728

There are no further early editions.

30. 1553 Thomas Bownell, *A Godly Psalm of Mary Queen*

Copy-text

A godly psalme of Marye Queene which brought us comfort al, through God, whom wee of dewtye prayse, that gives her foes a fal. By Rychard Beeard. Anno domini. 1553 ([John Kingston for] William Griffith, [1553]) STC 1655

There are no further early editions.

31. 1554 Thomas Becon, *A Comfortable Epistle*

Copy-text

A comfortable epistle, too Goddes faythfull people in Englande wherein is declared the cause of takynge awaye the true Christen religion from them, and howe it maye be recovered and obtayned agayne, newly made by Thomas Becon (Strasbourg [i.e. Wesel?: By Joos Lambrecht?], 1554) STC 1716

There are no further early editions.

Psalm 103
15 He, of mere grace and] He of mere, 'grace', and 1716

32. 1554 John Dudley

Copy-text

Harrington MS Temp. Eliz. (Arundel-Harington, mid-late sixteenth century)

There are no further early texts.

33. 1554 Robert Dudley

Copy-text

Harrington MS Temp. Eliz. (Arundel-Harington, mid-late sixteenth century)

There are no further early texts.

34. 1558 William Kethe, in *The Appelation of John Knox*

Copy-text

The appellation of John Knoxe from the cruell and most injust sentence pronounced against him by the false bishoppes and clergie of Scotland, with his supplication and exhortation to the nobilitie, estates, and co[m]munaltie of the same realme (Geneva: [J. Pullain and A. Rebul?], 1558) STC 15063

There are no further early editions.

35. 1560 *The Bible and Holy Scriptures* (The Geneva Bible)

Copy-text

The Bible and Holy Scriptures conteyned in the Olde and Newe Testament. Translated according to the Ebrue and Greke, and conferred with the best translations in divers languges. With moste profitable annotations upon all the hard places, and other things of great importance as may appeare in the epistle to the reader (Geneva: Rowland Hall, 1560) STC 2093

Other early editions

STC 2095 (Geneva: s.n., 1561)
STC 2106 (Geneva: John Crispin, 1570)
STC 2117 (Christopher Barker, 1576)
STC 2118 (Christopher Barker, 1576)
STC 2119 (Christopher Barker, 1579)
[etc.]

Psalm 23
4 name's sake] name's 2095 [omission of 'sake' an obvious error]

Psalm 48
[missing from 2093 on EEBO; consulted in Hendrickson facsimile]

Psalm 98
9 praise] praises 2117

Psalm 106
16 them] 2093, 2106, 2117, 2118, 2119; him 2095
33 stood] stand 2093, 2106, 2117, 2118, 2119

36. 1560 Anne Vaughan Lock?, in *Sermons of John Calvin*

Copy-text

Sermons of John Calvin, upon the songe that Ezechias made after he had bene sicke and afflicted by the hand of God, conteyned in the 38. chapter of Esay. Translated out of Frenche into Englishe. 1560 (John Day, 1560) STC 4450

Other early editions

1574 (destroyed)

Modern editions

The Collected Works of Anne Vaughan Lock, ed. by Susan M. Felch (Tempe: Arizona Center for Medieval and Renaissance Studies, 1999)

A meditation of a penitent sinner: Anne Locke's sonnet sequence with Locke's epistle, ed. with introduction by Kel Morin-Parsons (Waterloo: North Waterloo Academic Press, 1997)

18 others] other 4450
51 my] by 4450 [typo suggestion by Felch]

37. 1561 William Kethe, in *Four Score and Seven Psalms*

Copy-text

Foure score and seven Psalmes of Dauid in English mitre by Thomas Sterneholde and others: conferred with the Hebrewe, and in certeine places corrected, as the sense of the prophet requireth. Whereunto are added the Songe of Simeon, the ten Commandments and the Lords Prayer ([John Day], 1561) STC 2428

There are no further early editions.

38. 1562 William Whittingham, in *The Whole Book of Psalms*

Copy-text

The whole booke of Psalmes collected into Englysh metre by T. Starnhold, I. Hopkins, and others, conferred with the Ebrue, with apt notes to synge the[m] withal; faithfully perused and allowed according to thordre appointed in the Quenes Majesties injunctions; very mete to be used of all sortes of people privately for their solace and comfort, laying apart all ungodly songes and ballades, which tende only to the norishing of vyce, and corrupting of youth (John Day, 1562) STC 2430

Hundreds of subsequent editions. The most complete collation is in Quitslund and Temperley.

Psalm 51
39 Sprite] spirite 2430 [metre requires a monosyllable]
43 Sprite] spirite 2430 [metre requires a monosyllable]
47 Sprite] spirite 2430 [metre requires a monosyllable]

39. 1562 John Hopkins, in *The Whole Book of Psalms*

See 38.

40. 1562 Thomas Norton, in *The Whole Book of Psalms*

See 38.

TEXTUAL NOTES 597

41. 1564 John Craig, in *The Form of Prayers*

Copy-text

The forme of prayers and ministration of the sacraments etc. used in the English church at Geneva, approved and received by the Churche of Scotland. Whereunto besydes that was in the former bokes, are also added sondrie other prayers, with the whole psalmes of Dauid in English meter (Edinburgh: Robert Lekprevik, 1564) STC 16577

Other early editions

STC 16577a (Edinburgh: Robert Lekprevik, 1565)
STC 16579 (Geneva: s.n., 1571)
STC 16579.3 (Geneva: s.n., 1571) [incomplete]
STC 16579.5 (Edinburgh: John Ros, 1575)

Also included in *The CL Psalms of David in English Metre* (Edinburgh: Thomas Bassandine, 1575) STC 16580, and *The Psalms of David in Metre* (Edinburgh: Andro Hart, 1611) STC 16591, both with many further editions

Psalm 56
2 me] men 16577a, 16579, 16579.5, 16580

42. 1564 Robert Pont, in *The Form of Prayers*

See 41.

Psalm 76
11 bound] 16591; boune 16577, 16577a, 16579, 16580; bowne 16579.5

Psalm 83
32 band] badn 16577, 16577a [an obvious error]
52 foremost] formest 16577, 16577a, 16579, 16579.5, 16580, 16591
64 Jabin] Iasin 16577, 16577a, 16579, 16579.5, 16580, 16591
101 o'er] ouer 16577, 16577a, 16579, 16579.5, 16580, 16591 [contraction required by metre]

43. 1565 John Wedderburn?, *Godly and Spiritual Songs*

Copy-text

Ane Compendeous Buke, of Godlye Psalmes and Spirituall sangis Newly translatit out of Latine into Inglis, gadderit out of mony and divers Scripturis, with mony plesande Ballatis, and cheangit. Out of vaine sangis in Godlie sangis for tyll avode Syn and harlatrye ([Edinburgh: John Scot] for Thomas Bassandyne, 1565) STC 2996.3

This exceptionally rare first edition, the only copy of which was discovered recently in Göttingen, has been meticulously edited by Alasdair MacDonald and fully collated with later editions. The 1565 text is taken from this edition.

Other early editions

STC 2996.5 *Hier follouis...* ([Edinburgh: John Scot] for Thomas Bassandyne, c. 1567)

STC Ø ([John Scot for Thomas Bassandyne, c. 1570])

STC 2996.7 *Ane compendious buik...* (Edinburgh: John Ross for Henry Charteris, 1578) [earliest on EEBO]

Modern edition

The Gude and Godlie Ballatis, ed. by Alasdair A. MacDonald (Woodbridge: The Scottish Text Society, 2015)

Psalm 31
18 They] Thy 2996.3 (MacDonald, based on the Latin)

Psalms 114–15
53] Ye are the saints ...] two syllables seem to have been lost in 2996.3 and the other early texts (MacDonald)

44. 1565 John Hall, *The Court of Virtue*

Copy-text

[*The courte of vertue.*] ([London: Thomas Marshe, 1565]) STC 12632

An earlier version of Hall's Psalm 54 was included in the following:

STC 12631 *Certain Chapters Taken Out of the Proverbs* (Thomas Raynalde, 1550?)

STC 12631.3 (Thomas Raynalde, 1550?) [Psalm 25 omitted]

STC 12631.5 (Thomas Raynalde, 1550?) [Psalm 25 omitted]

STC 12634 (Thomas Raynalde, c. 1550?)

Since the text is identical across *Certain Chapters*, only 12631 is collated.

There are no further early editions.

Modern critical edition

John Hall, *The Court of Virtue, 1565*, ed. by Russell A. Fraser (New Brunswick: Rutgers University Press, 1961)

Psalm 54
All earlier texts have an introductory quatrain rather than the longer introduction in 12632:

How that the ryghteous man
   for helpe to god doeth call
And how that he incontynente
   had his desyres all
33 O God, I call to thee for help] For helpe I call to the o god 12631
34 In my distress and] because that I haue 12631
36 Avenge my] delyuer me 12631
[12632 omits, presumably by accident, verse 2:
Heare my prayer my god my kinge
   whan I to the shall praye
Consyder wel the wordes of me
   that I to the wyll saye]
37 For strangers full of tyranny] The straungers & the mighteones 12631
38 rise and rave] doth surreckt 12631
39 Such foolish folk as fear not God] Whyche haue not god before theyr eyes 12631
40 Do seek my life to have] my soule they wold in feckt 12631
43 my soul uphold and save] uphold my soule in dede 12631
46 Upon] unto 12631
47 his truth destroy them all] thy truth thou shalt destroy 12631
48 That virtue do] them that do thee 12631
49 With off'rings of an heart most free] I wyl offer to the o lorde 12631
50 Now will I praise thy name] and geue thy name the prayse 12631
51 Because, O Lord, my comfort still] O lord because thou comfortest me 12631
52 Consisteth in the same] and helpest me alwayes 12631
53 didst] haste 12631
54 troubles manifold] al myne agonye 12631
55 upon my foes mine eye] mine eyes seyth hys desire 12631
56 Doth his desire behold] upon myne enemyes 12631
57–64 the doxology is not included in earlier versions

45. 1566 John Pits, *A Poor Man's Benevolence*

Copy-text

A poore mannes beneuolence to the afflicted Church (Alexander Lacy, 1566)
   STC 19969

There are no further early editions.

46. 1567 Matthew Parker, *The Whole Psalter*

Copy-text

The whole Psalter translated into English metre, which contayneth an hundreth and fifty Psalmes. The first quinquagene (John Day, [1567?]) STC 2729

Other early texts

Inner Temple Library, Miscellaneous MSS No. 36 (MS) [Psalms 1–80]

For a more detailed transcript of the manuscript as well as a transcript of further corrections in two different hands, one of them Parker's, to the copy of STC 2729 in the Parker Library, Corpus Christi College, Cambridge, see *David's Blissful Harp: A Critical Edition of the Manuscript of Matthew Parker's Metrical Psalms (1–80)*, ed. by Einar Bjorvand (Tempe: Arizona Center for Medieval and Renaissance Studies, 2015).

Psalm 17
Argument 1 might] shuld MS
3 and hate deceit] voyde of deceyt MS
5 thou assent] iugëment MS
Verse 3 original (deleted)
    Thou hast both tried & visited
      my hart and thought by night
    No wyked deede: haust in me thou spyed
      To hart my mouth is right
10 nigh] ful MS
12 thought] thoughtes MS
Verse 4 original (deleted)
    Mens works so euyl against thi wyl
      so wrought in cursed skyl
    haue made me wayt: ther ways so strayt
      thi lamb who do but spyl
19 Lest] Lesse MS
20 in thy] in to thi MS
26 which] that MS
Verse 8 original (deleted)
    As ball of eye that tendrelye
      So kepe me o Lord my king
    And vnder hyde me bi thi syde
      In shadowe of thi wynge
32 Hid] close MS
38 full] so MS
45 they] that MS
46 Which] and MS

47 close] as MS
50 Destroy his spite] prevent his face MS
51 My soul, O save: from wicked slave] And ryd me fro this wiked so MS
Verse 14 original (deleted)
>   of childer store thei haue the moe
>   for them thei suete & swynk
>   and what remain of al their gayn
>   thei leaue ther babys to drynk

Verse 15 original (deleted)
>   But as for me: iust that I se
>   thi rightwise presence aye.
>   my trust is fre, to wake lyke the
>   In wye with the to staye

Psalm 33
Argument 1 alway in mind] in mind MS
9 carols] carol MS
17 He judgement loveth: and right intent] He loveth both right & iugement MS
22 by his true] iust bi his MS
31 gentle] redy MS
34 firm] so MS
43 neither] euery MS
46 as heir by his] his heyre bi godes MS
62 giant strong for] strong man sure with MS
69 hold'th] seth MS
86 have] set MS

Psalm 36
Argument 4 high power] power MS
Argument 5 all in] in MS
Argument 7 life] hart MS
1 variable] restles MS
18 weighed] layd
27 set was] was MS
31 then thy] thy MS
35 ever thy promise have] thi promyse that euer MS
41 of thy power doth taste] doth thi powr preserue MS
42 of thee also hath their repast] therto his comfort do serue MS
45 things] thing MS
49 good wings] winges MS
55 water] waters MS
63 dee] be MS
64 Thy gentle goodness, O Lord, impart] But thig ret goodnes o lord prolonge MS

66 wise and merciful in heart] merciful wise & strong MS
67 That from day to day they may] that thei maye from daye to daye MS
69 judgements] iugement MS
70 commandments] commandemente MS
71 Since then] When MS
73 foul] sore MS
81 the bad for his mirth shall once] onys the bad for his myrth shal MS
82 woe shall once] trouble shal MS
84 shall sure] shal MS

47. 1568 Thomas Bickley, in *The Holy Bible* (The Bishops' Bible)

Copy-text

The. holie. Bible. conteynyng the olde Testament and the newe (Richard Jugge, 1568) STC 2099

Other early editions

STC 2105 (Richard Jugge, 1569)
STC 2107 (Richard Jugge, 1572)

[Latin incipits added in 2105, 2107; BCP Psalms printed alongside in 2107]

Psalm 59
6 nor] or 2107
13 Behold, they speak with their mouth] Beholde wordes passe a pace from their mouthes 2105

Psalm 92
1 confess] make a confession 2105
19 see] see the destruction of 2105
19 hear the] hear the ruin of 2105

Psalm 141
11 But let not precious balms] But I would not that baulmes should 2105
11 for as yet] for continually 2105
13 Let their judges be] O that their judges were 2105
13 will] would 2105
21–22 their own nets: but let me in the mean season] his nettes: but with al I pray thee that I may 2105

48. 1570 Roger Edwardes, *A Book of Very Godly Psalms*

Copy-text

A boke of very Godly psalmes and prayers dedicated to the Lady Letice Vicountesse of Hereforde (William Griffith, 1570) STC 7510

There are no further early editions.

49. 1571 Arthur Golding, *The Psalms of David and Others*

Copy-text

The Psalmes of David and others. With M. John Calvins commentaries (Thomas East and Henry Middleton for Lucas Harrison and George Bishop, 1571) STC 4395

There are no further early editions.

50. 1574 Elizabeth Tyrwhit, *Morning and Evening Prayers*

Copy-text

Morning and evening prayers, with divers psalms himnes and meditations (1574) STC 24477.5

Other early editions

In Thomas Bentley, *The monument of matrones conteining seven severall lamps of virginitie, or distinct treatises; whereof the first five concerne praier and meditation: the other two last, precepts and examples, as the woorthie works partlie of men, partlie of women; compiled for the necessarie use of both sexes out of the sacred Scriptures, and other approved authors* (London: H. Denham, 1582) STC 1892

Modern editions

Elizabeth Tyrwhit's Morning and Evening Prayers, ed. by Susan M. Felch (London: Routledge, 2008)

Psalm 1 is based on STC 24477.5, the 'First Psalm' on both this and the expanded version in Bentley. For a full description and collation of the texts, see Felch.

51. 1575 George Gascoigne, *The Posies*

Copy-text

The poesies of George Gascoigne Esquire (London: Henry Binneman for Richard Smith, 1575) STC 11636

Other early editions

A Hundreth Sundrie Flowres bounde up in one small poesie ([Henry Binneman and Henry Middleton] for Richard Smith, 1573) STC 11635

Modern editions

George Gascoigne's *A hundreth sundrie flowres*, ed. by C. T. Prouty (Columbia: University of Missouri Press, 1942)

George Gascoigne, *A hundreth sundrie flowres*, ed. by G. W. Pigman III (Oxford: Clarendon Press, 2000)

52. 1577 Robert Fills, *Godly Prayers and Meditations*

Copy-text

Godly prayers and meditations, paraphrasticallye made upon all the Psalmes very necessary for al the godly, translated out of Frenche into Englishe (William Seres, 1572) STC 10867

There are no further early editions.

53. 1580 Anthony Gilby, *The Psalms of David*

Copy-text

The Psalmes of David truely opened and explaned by paraphrasis, according to the right sense of every Psalme. With large and ample arguments before every psalme, declaring the true use therof. To the which is added a briefe table, shewing whereunto every Psalme is particularly to be applied, according to the direction of M. Beza and Tremelius. Set foorth in Latine by that excellent learned man Theodore Beza. And faithfully translated into English, by Anthonie Gilbie (John Harrison and Henry Middleton, 1580) STC 2033

There are no further early editions.

54. 1580? John Stubbs

Copy-text

British Library Harleian MS 3230, fols 80ʳ–82ᵛ

I am indebted to Christopher Burlinson for allowing me to use his careful transcription of Stubbs's manuscript, which I have modernized. Words revised or crossed out have been omitted, the text following Stubbs's latest corrections.

There are no further early texts.

55. *c.* 1580–1586 Sir Philip Sidney

Copy-text

Penshurst MS (A)

This text follows Noel Kinnamon's edited text for the Oxford World's Classics edition (*The Sidney Psalter: The Psalms of Sir Philip and Mary Sidney* (Oxford: Oxford University Press, 2009)), which takes as its copy-text the Penshurst MS (A), a late sixteenth-century copy of the autograph MS of Mary Sidney Herbert. For the most complete descriptions and collations of existing manuscripts, see the standard editions by Ringler and Hannay et al.

Other early texts

Tixall MS 'J'
Bodleian, MS Rawlinson poet. 25 'B'
(fifteen other early MSS)

Important modern editions

The Poems of Sir Philip Sidney, ed. by William A. Ringler, Jr (Oxford: Clarendon Press, 1962)

56. 1582 Richard Stanihurst, *The First Four Books of Virgil*

Copy-text

Thee first foure bookes of Virgil his Aeneis translated intoo English heroical verse by Richard Stanyhurst, wyth oother poëtical divises theretoo annexed (Leiden: John Pates, 1582) STC 24806

Other early editions

STC 24807 (Henry Bynneman, 1583)

57. 1582 Thomas Bentley, *The Fifth Lamp of Virginity*

Copy-text

The fift lampe of virginitie conteining sundrie forms of christian praiers and meditations, to bee used onlie of and for all sorts and degrees of women, in their severall ages and callings [...] *A treatise verie needful for this time, and profitable to the Church: now newlie compiled to the glorie of God, & comfort of al godlie women, by the said T. B. Gentleman* (Henry Denham for William Seres, 1582) STC 1893

There are no further early editions.

58. 1583 William Hunnis, *Seven Sobs of a Sorrowful Soul*

Copy-text

Seven sobs of a sorrowfull soule for sinne: comprehending those seven Psalmes of the princelie prophet David, commonlie called Poenitentiall; / framed into a forme of familiar praiers, and reduced into meeter by William Hunnis [...] *Whereunto are also annexed his Handfull of honisuckles; the Poore widowes mite; a Dialog betweene Christ and a sinner; divers godlie and pithie ditties, with a Chrisian confession of and to the Trinitie* (Henry Denham, 1583) STC 13975

Other early texts

STC 13975.5 (Henry Denham, 1585)
STC 13976 (Henry Denham, 1587)
STC 13977 (Henry Denham, 1589)
STC 13977.5 (Richard Yardley and Peter Short, 1592)
[etc.]

18 Abram] Abraham 13975.5
30 subdue] pursue 13975.5, 13976, 13977, 13977.5
61 not] no 13975.5, 13976, 13977, 13977.5
81 also eke cleansed] eke clensed also 13976, 13977, 13977.5
123 sins] sin 13977.5
242 us] was 13976, 13977
291 Thy] The 13977
323 iniquities] iniquitie 13975.5, 13976, 13977, 13977.5
374 may still] may 13976, 13977, 13977.5
383 Ne] Nor 13976, 13977, 13977.5
394 thy] my 13977, 13977.5
444 return to] remember 13976, 13977, 13977.5
470 the] thy 13975.5, 13976, 13977, 13977.5
485 noble] holie 13975.5, 13976, 13977, 13977.5

488 God] Lord 13977, 13977.5
515 God] Lord 13977, 13977.5
542 forgiven him] forgiven 13976, 13977, 13977.5
571 their] hir 13975.5, 13976, 13977, 13977.5
610 stones] stone 13976, 13977, 13977.5

59. 1583 William Patten, *1583. An: Foelicissimi Regni*

Copy-text

1583. An: Foelicissimi regni Reginae Elizabeth: XXVI. The Sallmby the olld Translation called Deus Judicium, David made for soothsay and wish of many blessings unto hiz son in hiz Rein (Abel Jeffes, [1583]) STC 2368.3

No text available on EEBO. Sole surviving copy at University of Essex Library, formerly in the Harsnett Library at Colchester.

There are no further early editions.

60. 1583 George Flinton, *A Manual of Prayers*

Copy-text

A manual of prayers newly gathered out of many and divers famous authours aswell auncient as of the tyme present ([Rouen: Father Parson's Press], 1583) STC 17263

Other early texts

STC 17264 ([Rouen: George L'Oyselet], 1589)
STC 17264.5 ([Father Garnet's First Press, 1593?])
STC 17265 ([English Secret Press, 1595])
STC 17278.6 ([English Secret Press, *c.* 1596]) no copy on EEBO
STC 17278.7 ([English Secret Press, *c.* 1596]) no copy on EEBO

Not identified as Psalm 79 (78) in STC 17264.5. In STC 17265 a woodcut of Christ showing his wounds is featured at the beginning of the Psalm.

Psalm 79
9 wholly] only 17264.5
14–15 defender, and protector] protector and defendor 17264.5
18 unto] to 17264.5
30 most glorious] glorious 17264.5
30 name's] name 17265, 17266
31 mercy] mercies 17264.5

61. 1584 King James VI of Scotland, *The Essays of a Prentice*

Copy-text

The essayes of a prentise, in the divine art of poesie (Edinburgh: Thomas Vautroullier, 1584) STC 14373

Other early editions

STC 14374 (Edinburgh: Thomas Vautroullier, 1585)

Psalm 104
8 silv'ring] syilring 14373, 14374

62. Late 1580s James VI of Scotland

Copy-text

British Library Royal MS 19.B.xvi

There are no further early texts.

63. 1588 William Byrd, *Psalms, Sonnets, and Songs*

Copy-text

Psalmes, sonets, and songs of sadnes and pietie, made into musicke of five parts (Thomas East, 1588) STC 4253.3

Other early editions

STC 4253 (Thomas East, 1588) no copy on EEBO
STC 4253.7 (Thomas East, 1588)
STC 4254 (Thomas East, 1599?)

64. 1589 William Byrd, *Songs of Sundry Natures*

Copy-text

Songs of sundrie natures some of gravitie, and others of myrth, fit for all companies and voyces (Thomas East, 1589) STC 4256 (1589)

Other early texts

STC 4256.5 (Thomas East, 1589 [i.e. 1595?])
STC 4258 (Lucretia East, 1610)

65. 1589 Richard Robinson, *A Golden Mirror*

Copy-text

A golden mirrour conteining certaine pithie and figurative visions prognosticating good fortune to England and all true English subjectes, with an overthrowe to the enemies: whereto be adjoyned certaine pretie poemes written on the names of sundrie both noble and worshipfull (Roger Ward for John Proctor, 1589) STC 21121.5

There are no further early editions.

66. c. 1590? Michael Cosworth

Copy-text

British Library Harley MS 6906

Psalm 135
20 wrack] wrafke (?) MS; the previous line is missing a syllable, suggesting perhaps that this stanza was left unfinished.

There are no further early texts.

67. 1591 Abraham Fraunce, *The Countess of Pembroke's Emmanuel*

Copy-text

The Countesse of Pembrokes Emanuel Conteining the nativity, passion, buriall, and resurrection of Christ: togeather with certaine Psalmes of David (Thomas Orwyn for William Ponsonby, 1591) STC 11338.5

Other early texts

STC 11339 ([Thomas Orwyn] for William Ponsonby, 1591)

68. 1595 Barnabe Barnes, *A Divine Century*

Copy-text

A Divine Centurie of Spirituall Sonnets (John Windet, 1595) STC 1467

There are no further early editions.

69. 1596 Francis Sabie, *Adam's Complaint*

Copy-text

Adams complaint. The olde worldes tragedie. David and Bathsheba (Richard Jones, 1596) STC 21534

There are no further early editions.

70. 1597 Henry Lok, *Ecclesiastes*

Copy-text

Ecclesiastes, otherwise called The preacher Containing Salomons sermons or commentaries (as it may probably be collected) upon the 49. Psalme of David his father (Richard Field, 1597) STC 16696

There are no further early editions.

71. 1597 James Melville, *Ane Fruitful and Comfortable Exhortation*

Copy-text

Ane fruitful and comfortable exhortatioun anent death (Robert Waldegrave, 1597) STC 17815.5

There are no further early editions.

72. 1598 William Patten, *Anno foelicissimi regni*

Copy-text

Anno fœlicissimi regni augustæ reginæ nostræ Elizabeth quadragesimo primo (Thomas Purfoot, 1598) STC 2368.5

There are no further early editions.

73. By 1599 Mary Sidney Herbert, Countess of Pembroke

Copy-text

Penshurst MS

This text follows the text edited by Noel Kinnamon et al. for the Oxford World's Classics edition (*The Sidney Psalter: The Psalms of Sir Philip and Mary Sidney* (Oxford: Oxford University Press, 2009)), which takes as its copy-text the Penshurst MS (A), a late sixteenth-century copy of the autograph MS of Mary Sidney Herbert. For the most complete descriptions and collations of existing manuscripts, see the standard edition by Hannay et al.

TEXTUAL NOTES   611

Other early texts

Tixall MS (J)
Bodleian, MS Rawlinson poet. 25 (B)
(fifteen other early MSS)

74. 1599 Richard Verstegan?, *The Primer*

Copy-text

The primer, or, Office of the Blessed Virgin Marie in Latin and English, according to the reformed Latin (Antwerp: Arnold Conings [Arnout Conincx], 1599) STC 16094

Other early texts

STC 16095 (Antwerp: Arnold Conings [Arnout Conincx], 1604)
STC 16101.4 ([Rouen: John Le Cousturier, 1633])

75. *c.* 1600 Sir John Harington

Copy-text

Egerton MS 2711, fols 104–07 (E)

Other early texts

Bodleian MS Douce 361 (D)
Ohio State University SPEC.RARE.MS.ENG.0016 (JH)

Psalm 38
2 times] tyme D, JH
5 bides] is D, JH
6 want] lacke D, JH
7 such poise] this waight D, JH
13 makes … makes] make … makes D, JH
15 my] the D, JH
16 Mine] my D, JH
21 is] that D, JH
24 or] and JH

76. 1601 Richard Verstegan, *Odes in Imitation*

Copy-text

Odes In imitation of the seaven penitential psalmes, with sundry other poemes and ditties tending to devotion and pietie (Antwerp: Arnout Coninx, 1601) STC 16094

There are no further early editions.

77. 1603 Henry Dod, *Certain Psalms of David*

Copy-text

Certaine Psalmes of David, heretofore much out of use because of their difficult tunes (Robert Waldegrave, 1603) STC 2730

There are no further early editions.

78. 1604 Simon Forman

Copy-text

Bodleian MS Ashmole 802

There are no further early texts.

33 men] mens MS
37 dieth/diedst MS [the MS has been corrected, but the detail is unclear]
100 oft] originally 'ought' in MS, deleted
102 Thou] initial word in MS unclear, written over
309 blessèd] originally 'bleste' but corrected for metre; dwell] 'dadwell' MS
335 presence] presents
393 hell] [MS: word scratched out, 'hell' added (thou wilt not leave)]
399 presence] presents (and another time?)

79. 1605 Alexander Montgomery, in *The Mind's Melody*

Copy-text

Alexander Montgomerie, *Poems*, ed. by David J. Parkinson (Edinburgh: The Scottish Text Society, 2000).

Parkinson's meticulous edition is based on the authoritative Ker Manuscript at Edinburgh University Library (Drummond De.3.70), originally in the possession of William Drummond of Hawthornden. The manuscript was composed by one Margaret Ker, presumably a member of this prominent Scottish family, between 1595 and 1627. The younger Mark Ker (whose father was abbot of Newbattle Abbey), who may have been Margaret's father, was Master of Requests to James VI and created first Earl of Lothian in 1606.

Other early texts

The mindes melodie Contayning certayne psalmes of the kinglie prophete David (Robert Charteris, 1605) STC 18051

STC 18051.3 (Robert Charteris, 1606)

Psalm 1
[The lineation is different in the printed versions, each of the half-lines (as in 9–10) on a separate line.]
1 Weil] blest 18051, 18051.3
2 blissed] happie 18051, 18051.3
4 gait] gates 18051, 18051.3
5 That stands] And walkes 18051, 18051.3
7 does] doth 18051, 18051.3
8 sait] sates 18051, 18051.3
11 For he] That man 18051, 18051.3
13 Quhilk] Fast 18051, 18051.3
14 Quhilk] That 18051, 18051.3
16 Quhais … sall lovis] Whose … unlouse 18051, 18051.3
19 Quhilk] Which 18051, 18051.3
20 To … chaff] The … calfe 18051, 18051.3
21 Quhilk] That 18051, 18051.3
22 Winds] winde 18051, 18051.3
29 He knawis] Doth know 18051, 18051.3
31 Quhilk] Which 18051, 18051.3
32 Sall doubtless … alway] Shall quite die, perish, and doubtless decay 18051, 18051.3

80. 1605 Anon., in *The Minds Melody*

Copy-text

The mindes melodie Contayning certayne psalmes of the kinglie prophete David (Robert Charteris, 1605) STC 18051

Other early texts

STC 18051.3 (Robert Charteris, 1606)

81. 1605 Sir William Temple, *A Logical Analysis*

Copy-text

A logicall analysis of twentie select Psalmes (Felix Kingston for Thomas Man, 1605) STC 23870

There are no further early editions.

82. 1607 Joseph Hall, *Holy Observations*

Copy-text

Holy observations. Lib. 1. Also some fewe of Davids Psalmes metaphrased, for a taste of the rest (H. L[ownes] for Samuel Macham, 1607) STC 12671

Other early editions

STC 12672 (Thomas Purfoot for Samuel Macham, 1609)

Psalm 2
7 thraldom's] thraldome 12672

83. 1609–1610 Gregory Martin, *The Holy Bible* (Rheims-Douay Bible)

Copy-text

The holie Bible faithfully translated into English, out of the authentical Latin. (Douay: Laurence Kellam, 1609–10) STC 2207

Other early editions

STC 2321 Douay: John Cousturier, 1635

Psalm 51
9 words] word 2321

Psalm 140
10 [verse 7 begins at 'they have laid a stumbling block' 2321]
16 they] thy 2321 [obvious error]

84. 1611 William Byrd, *Psalms, Songs, and Sonnets*

Copy-text

Psalmes, songs and sonnets some solemne, others joyfull, framed to the life of the words (Thomas Snodham, 1611) STC 4255

There are no further early texts.

85. 1611 Various Translators, *The Holy Bible* (King James Bible)

Copy-text

The Holy Bible conteyning the Old Testament, and the New: newly translated out of the originall tongues (Robert Barker, 1611) STC 2216

Other early editions

For a complete collation and study, see David Norton, *A Textual History of the King James Bible* (Cambridge and New York: Cambridge University Press, 2005).

86. After 1611? Edmond Scory, *Two Psalms of David*

Copy-text

British Library Royal MS 17. D. X.

There are no further early texts.

87. 1612 John Davies of Hereford, *The Muses' Sacrifice*

Copy-text

The Muses Sacrifice (T. S. for George Norton, 1612) STC 6338

There are no further early editions.

88. *c.* 1612? Francis Davison, in *Certain Selected Psalms of David*

Copy-text

BL Harley MS 6930 (Crane)

Other early texts

Bodl. Rawl. Poet. 61 (*P*) (Crane)
BL Harl. 3357 (Crane)
BL MS Add. 34752
Bodl. MS Rawl. D. 301
Bodl. MS Rawl. D. 316 (*D*) [1, 6, 13, 15, 23 (3 versions)]
Chetham's Library MS A.4.15 (*M*) [6, 13, 15, a version of 23, 30, 79, 86]
Bodl. Rawl. Poet. 117 (*O*) [23 ('God who all the world'), 130, 133]
Duke of Sutherland MS 8187b (another Crane MS discovered recently by Amy Bowles)
Stephen Jerome, *A serious fore-warning to auoide the vengeance to come* [etc.] (G. Eld for R. Jackson, 1613) STC 14516 [15, 130, 142, 86]

As Swann notes, only the three (now four) Crane manuscripts contain the complete set of Davison Psalms. Collation with Chetham based on the transcription in *The Dr. Farmer Chetham MS.*, ed. by Alexander S. Grosart, 2 vols (Manchester: The Chetham Society, 1873), II, p. 216. For the transcription of Davison's Psalm 23 in *D*, I am grateful to Dr Amy Bowles, whose unpublished Cambridge dissertation, 'Ralph Crane and Early Modern Scribal Culture', is the most complete study of these manuscripts to date. The collation here (as of Christopher Davison's and Joseph Bryan's Psalms, **89** and **90**) takes account of *O*, *M*, and *D*, but a complete collation of the Davison Psalms collection remains to be done.

Psalm 23 (1)
1 the universe can] all the world doth *O*
2 his] a *O*
3 kind and] find I *O*
4 and doth keep] and I doth keepe *D*
9 Mottlied with] Hotleid wch *D*
9 painting] paintings *O*
10 Through which creep] Throng with sneakes *O*
17 Wandering] Erringe *O*
18 holy fold] righteous pathes *O*
19 Yea, should I stray] Should I wander *O*
22 having] yet with *O*
28 mine] thy *O*
29 Curious] Envious *O*
33 nor bound] noe end *O*

89. *c.* 1612? Christopher Davison, in *Certain Selected Psalms of David*

See 88.

Psalm 15
2 in] a *M*
4 and] or 14516
6 accused] abusèd *M*
11 this] his *M*
12 dwell] live 14516

90. *c.* 1612? Joseph Bryan, in *Certain Selected Psalms of David*

See 88.

91. 1612 Henry Ainsworth, *The Book of Psalms*

Copy-text

The booke of Psalmes: Englished both in prose and metre with annotations, opening the words and sentences, by conference with other Scriptures (Amsterdam: Giles Thorpe, 1612) STC 2407

Other early texts

STC 2734.5 ([Amsterdam: Richt Right Press], 1632) singing versions only (prose omitted)
Wing B2405 (Amsterdam: Thomas Stafford, 1644)

Psalm 23
5 name] names 2734.5

Psalm 84
12 blessings] blessing B2405
37 him] them 2734.5
43 O our] Our B2405

92. 1612? Sir John Harington

Copy-text

Bodleian, MS Douce 361 (D)

Other early texts

Ohio State University, SPEC.RARE.MS.ENG.0016 (JH)

Psalm 66
11 is each where] each where is JH
15 many] manies JH

Psalm 82
9 understand] JH; underst D

Psalm 123
10 despisèd] despisd D and JH (here and below the metre requires the extra syllable, despite the MS spelling)
12 tyrannizèd] tyrannizd D and JH

93. 1613 Sir William Leighton, *The Tears or Lamentations*

Copy-text

The teares or lamentations of a sorrowfull soule (Ralph Blower, 1613) STC 15433

Other early editions

STC 15434 (William Stansby, 1614) [see note in text to 93]

Psalm 143] misnumbered 144 15433

94. 1613 Thomas Campion, *Two Books of Ayres*

Copy-text

Two bookes of ayres The first contayning divine and morall songs: the second, light conceites of lovers (Thomas Snodham for Mathew Lownes, 1613) STC 4547

No further early editions.

95. 1615 Sir Edwin Sandys, *Sacred Hymns*

Copy-text

Sacred hymns Consisting of fifti select psalms of David and others, paraphrastically turned into English verse (Thomas Snodham, 1615) STC 21723

No further early editions.

96. 1615 Sir David Murray, *A Paraphrase of the CIV Psalm*

Copy-text

A paraphrase of the CIV. Psalme (Edinburgh: Andro Hart, 1615) STC 18294

No further early editions.

97. 1620 Henry Dod, *All the Psalms of David*

Copy-text

Al the Psalmes of David with certeine songes and canticles of Moses, Debora, Isaiah, Hezekiah and others, not formerly exta[n]t for song: and manie of the said Psalmes, dayly omitted, and not sung at all, because of their defficult tunes ([Edinburgh]: s.n., 1620) STC

No further early editions.

Psalm 87
3 Jacob's] Iacods

98. 1620 William Loe, *Songs of Sion*

Copy-text

Songs of Sion Set for the joy of gods deere ones, who sitt here by the brookes of this worlds Babel, and weepe when they thinke on Hierusalem which is on highe (Hamburg: s.n., 1620) STC 16690

No further early editions.

99. 1620s? Thomas Carew

Copy-text

Psalms 51 and 137 Bodleian MS Ashmole 38 (large folio verse miscellany c. 1638) [Psalms 51, 91, 137] (Ash38)
Psalm 91 Bodleian MS Rawlinson poet. 61 [Psalm 91, in the collection by Francis Davison] (R6) [This text of Psalm 91 is followed here, since, as Dunlap notes, it seems to be the earliest of the manuscripts in which it appears, dating from c. 1625.]

Other early texts

Hollandi posthumana. A funerall elegie of King James [etc.] ([B. Alsop and T. Fawcett] for Henry Holland, 1626) (91) STC 13579
Bodleian MS English poet. c.50 [91]
Bodleian MS Rawlinson poet. 160 [91]
Bodleian MS Rawlinson poet. 23 [91]
British Library Harleian MS 6346 [91, in a collection of words for anthems used at the Chapel Royal, Whitehall]
British Library Add. MS 18220 [Psalm 137, misattributed to Lord Digby, Earl of Bristol]
British Library Add. MS 31434 [Psalm 137, set in five parts by Henry Lawes]
Nottinghamshire Archives MS. DD/Hu 1 (quarto verse miscellany mid-seventeenth century) [Psalms 51, 91]
Henry Lawes, *Select Psalmes of a New Translation, To be sung in Verse and Chorus of five parts* ([London: s.n., 1655]) Wing B2462 [Psalm 137]
Bodleian MS Don.b.9 (large folio miscellany c. 1667–1682) [Psalms 51, 91]

Modern edition

The Poems of Thomas Carew, ed. by Rhodes Dunlap (Oxford: Clarendon Press, 1957)

Psalm 91
3 (So shaded)] So shaded Ash 38, R
3 fires] power Ash 38
4 Or] Nor 13579
5 Or] Nor 13579
9 (like a shield)] like a shield Ash 38; as a Shield 13579
9 drive] chase 13579
10 fears] Dreads 13579
13 quiet peace] peacefull sleepes Ash 38, 13579
14 the] thy Ash38, 13579
16 Only thine eyes shall see] Yet shall thine eyes behold Ash 38
17 thy] thine Ash 38
19 These] those Ash 38, 13579
21–25 stanza 5 (verses 11–13) missing in 13579
24 they] thou Ash 38
26 will] shall 13579
28 therefore] wherefore 13579

Psalm 137
18 God's] our B2462
19 move] tune B2462
24 with] by B2462

27 accents] Accent B2462
33 triumph] triumph'd B2462
34 heap] hew B2462

For a more complete collation, see Dunlap's edition. A fully complete collation remains to be done.

100. 1645, composed 1623 John Milton, *Poems of Mr. John Milton*

Copy-text

Poems of Mr. John Milton, both English and Latin, compos'd at several times. Printed by his true copies (Ruth Raworth for Humphrey Moseley, 1645) Wing M2160

No further early editions.

101. 1624 Sir John Davies, *The Psalms*

Copy-text

University of Edinburgh Library, MS La. III. 444 (1624) *The Psalmes translated into verse*

No further early texts.

Modern edition

The Poems of Sir John Davies, ed. by Robert Krueger (Oxford: Clarendon Press, 1975. See this edition for a full collation.

102. 1624 Sir Robert Ker, *Psalms in English Verses*

Copy-text

National Library of Scotland MS 2065 fols 50–75

No further early texts.

Psalm 37
sign] sing MS

103. 1625 Sir Francis Bacon, *Certain Psalms*

Copy-text

The translation of certaine Psalmes into English verse ([John Havilland] for Hanna Barret and Richard Whittaker, 1625) STC 1174

TEXTUAL NOTES 621

Other early editions

STC 1174.5 ([John Havilland] for Hanna Barret and Richard Whittaker 1625)

104. 1627 Anon., *One and Forty Divine Odes Englished*

Copy-text

One and forty divine odes Englished set to King Davids princely harpe by S.P.L. (M[iles] F[lesher] and R[obert] Y[oung] for Richard Moore, 1627) STC 15110

No further early editions.

Psalm 9
25 verse number added, not in original
36 to th'] to'h 15110

Psalm 41
12 helps] helpe 15110
51 o'er] o're 15110
60 Isaac's] Isa'chs 15110

105. 1629 Alexander Top, *The Book of Praises*

Copy-text

The Book of Prayses, Called the Psalmes. The Keyes and Holly Things of David. Translated out of the Hebrew, According to the Letter, and the Mystery of them (Amsterdam: Ian Fredericksz Stam, 1629) STC 2415

Other early editions

STC 2415.2 (Amsterdam: Ian Fredericksz Stam, 1629)

Psalm 89
24 raised an aid] raysed and Ayde 2415, 2415.2

106. 1620s–1630s? Francis Quarles

Copy-text

Nottingham University Library Portland MS Pw V 358
Text based on the facsimile and transcription in Höltgen.

No further early texts.

Modern edition

Karl Josef Höltgen, 'New Verse by Francis Quarles: The Portland Manuscripts, Metrical Psalms, and the *Bay Psalm Book* (with text)', *English Literary Renaissance*, 28.1 (1998), 118–41

4 rend] rent MS
8 causeless] cauless MS
27 travail] travel MS (KJV has 'travail', and early modern spelling conventions made the two words interchangeable)

107. 1631 John Vicars, *England's Hallelujah*

Copy-text

Englands Hallelu-jah. Or, Great Brittaines Grateful Retribution, for Gods Gratious Benediction In our many and most famous Deliverances, since Halcyon-Dayes of ever-blessed Queene Elizabeth, to the present Times. Together, with divers of Davids Psalmes, according to the French Metre and Measures (Thomas Purfoot for Henry Sale, 1631) STC 24697

No further early editions.

Psalm 53
19 Isr'el] Jr'ell
24 Isr'el's] Isre'ls
stanza 5 unnumbered in 24697

Psalm 101
17 that] have

Psalm 124 numbered 123 in 24697
35 O] conjectural, word missing from EEBO copy
60 And praise] conjectural, first word and first three letters of second missing from EEBO copy

108. 1631 William Slatyer, *Psalms, or Songs of Sion*

Copy-text

Psalmes, or Songs of Sion: Turned into the language, and set forth to the tunes of a strange Land. Intended for Christmas Carols (Robert Young, 1631) STC 22635

Other early editions

Wing S3985 (Robert Young, 1642)

109. 1615–1631 Sir John Glanville, The Younger, *A Paraphrase upon the Psalms of David*

Copy-text

British Library Egerton MS 2590

No further early texts.

110. 1631 King James I and William Alexander, *The Psalms of King David*

Copy-text

The Psalmes of King David Translated by King James (Oxford: William Turner, 1631) STC 2732

Other early editions

STC 2736 (Thomas Harper, 1636)
STC 2736a (Thomas Harper, 1637)
STC 2736.5 (Thomas Harper, 1637)

Psalm 93
3 wherewith] with which 2736, 2736a, 2736.5
5 it] well 2736, 2736a, 2736.5
9 The raging floods behold] The flouds have lifted up 2736, 2736a, 2736.5
10 All lifted up, do sound] the raging floods, their voyce 2736, 2736a, 2736.5
11 Impetuous floods tumultuously] have lifted up, the flouds lift up 2736, 2736a, 2736.5
12 Make all about rebound] their waves that make a noyse 2736, 2736a, 2736.5
16 for power] on high 2736, 2736a, 2736.5
19 becomes thy house] forever, Lord 2736, 2736a, 2736.5
20 Forever to endure] becomes thy house most pure 2736, 2736a, 2736.5

Psalm 105
1 O praise the Lord, upon his name] O give due thanks unto the Lord 2736, 2736a, 2736.5
2 Do call with grateful hearts] and call upon his name 2736, 2736a, 2736.5
3 And make his actions known among] among'st the people all his deeds 2736, 2736a, 2736.5
4 The people, in all parts] to make them known proclaime 2736, 2736a, 2736.5
7 And liberally of his great works] of all his works that wondrous are 2736, 2736a, 2736.5
11 that heart delighted be] the heart of them rejoice 2736, 2736a, 2736.5
12 Which seeks] that seeke 2736, 2736a, 2736.5
13 Seek ye the Lord] The mighty Lord 2736, 2736a, 2736.5
14 To which all things give] seeke ye in every 2736, 2736a, 2736.5
15 inflamed with sacred zeal] as your chiefe happinesse 2736, 2736a, 2736.5
17 His works with admiration breed] Thinke on the works that he hath done 2736, 2736a, 2736.5
18 With reverence call to mind] which admiration breed 2736, 2736a, 2736.5
19 And all the judgements of his mouth] his wonders, and the judgements all 2736, 2736a, 2736.5
20 With wonders oft designed] which from his mouth proceed 2736, 2736a, 2736.5

21 you, his servant Abraham's seed] ye that are of Abrahams race 2736, 2736a, 2736.5
22 That should] who did 2736, 2736a, 2736.5
25 God] Lord 2736, 2736a, 2736.5
29 That sacred covenant of his] His Cov'nant he remembered hath 2736, 2736a, 2736.5
30 He hath remembered still] that it may ever stand 2736, 2736a, 2736.5
32 that showed his will] he did command 2736, 2736a, 2736.5
35 by an oath] afterward, 2736, 2736a, 2736.5
36 Was solemnly] his oath that was 2736, 2736a, 2736.5
39 And unto Israel for a league] To Israel for a Covenant 2736, 2736a, 2736.5
42 unto you will give] will bestow on thee 2736, 2736a, 2736.5
43 of your inheritance] which afterwards by you 2736, 2736a, 2736.5
44 Where you may safely live] inherited shall be 2736, 2736a, 2736.5
45 of men were but a few] in number were at first 2736, 2736a, 2736.5
46 Against their foes to stand] a few neglected men 2736, 2736a, 2736.5
47 at the first but very few] but a very few, and these 2376, 2736a, 2736.5
48 And strangers in the land] but strangers in it then 2736, 2736a, 2736.5
49 long] still 2736, 2736a, 2736.5
53 suffering none to do them wrong] did not suffer any man 2736, 2736a, 2736.5
54 From danger them redeemed] to doe unto them wrong 2736, 2736a, 2736.5
55 And did reprove kings for their cause] yea, for their sakes he did reprove 2736, 2736a, 2736.5
56 As whom he more esteemed] the Kings that were most strong 2736, 2736a, 2736.5
61 He, moreover, for a famine called] And moreover for a famine, he 2736, 2736a, 2736.5
62 in wrath] did call 2736, 2736a, 2736.5
63 And straight did break the staff of] yea, he the staff of strengthening 2736, 2736a, 2736.5
64 By threatening dearth and death] did wholly breake o're all 2736, 2736a, 2736.5
69 were laid in fetters base] with fetters charged were 2736, 2736a, 2736.5
70 To be tormented so] in iron they made him lye 2736, 2736a, 2736.5
71-72 [no equivalent, verse 18 compressed]
73 Until his word accomplished was] Till that th' appointed time did come 2736; Until the time that his word came 2736a, 2736.5
74 In the appointed time] the Lords word did him try 2736, 2736a, 2736.5
75-76 [no equivalent, verse 19 compressed]
85 according as he pleased] might binde his Princes all 2736, 2736a, 2736.5
86 His princes might command] as seem'd best in his sight 2736, 2736a, 2736.5

TEXTUAL NOTES 625

87 And teach his ancients, what was fit] and even unto his Senatours 2736, 2736a, 2736.5
88 For them to understand] that wisedome teach he might 2736, 2736a, 2736.5
89 Then Israel did to Egypt come] And aged Israel likewise then 2736, 2736a, 2736.5
90 Which him when weak revived] to Egypts kingdome came 2736, 2736a, 2736.5
91 in the land of Ham] was a sojourner 2736, 2736a, 2736.5
92 A straying stranger lived] into the land of Ham 2736, 2736a, 2736.5
95 That even those who them oppressed] That even then these that were their foes 2736; Till them, then all their foes about 2736a, 2736.5
96 They did] he made 2736a, 2736.5
98 did arise] so were mov'd 2736, 2736a, 2736.5
99 with his servants subtilly] even most subtilly to use 2736, 2736a, 2736.5
100 To deal they did devise] his servants whom he lov'd 2736, 2736a, 2736.5
101 [The fourth part begins at verse 26 in 2736.5]
103 did elect] chosen had 2736, 2736a, 2736.5
105 They all his threatening signs to them] His threatning signes among them, they 2736, 2736a, 2736.5
106 Most manifestly cleared] his wonders made them know 2736, 2736a, 2736.5
107 all the monstrous prodigies] in the land of cursed Ham 2736, 2736a, 2736.5
108 That in Ham's land appeared] his wonders made them know 2736, 2736a, 2736.5
109 He darkness sent and clouded them] He did a fearfull darknesse send 2736, 2736a, 2736.5
110 As if wrapped up in hell] and made it darke to be 2736, 2736a, 2736.5
112 In no sort did rebel] rebell'd in no degree 2736, 2736a, 2736.5
113 that should have refreshed] all that earst were pure 2736, 2736a, 2736.5
117 Their land abundantly bred frogs] The land in great abundance then 2736, 2736a, 2736.5
118 From which no part was free] most loathsome frogs brought out 2736, 2736a, 2736.5
119 Which searched] even in 2736, 2736a, 2736.5
120 Where they did use to be] which swarming crawl'd about 2736, 2736a, 2736.5
121 And when he spoke] He spoke, and then 2736, 2736a, 2736.5
127 country ominous flames] land most terribly 2736, 2736a, 2736.5
128 Like fatal fires] the flaming fire 2736, 2736a, 2736.5
130 And] brake 2736a, 2736.5
131 Sent caterpillars, grasshoppers] He spake, and Caterpillars came 2736, 2736a, 2736.5
132 Innumerable] with Locusts in great 2736, 2736a, 2736.5
133 [The fifth part begins at verse 35 in 2736.5]

133 The growing grass in every field] The hearbs that in their land did grow 2736, 2736a, 2736.5
134 They quickly did] they eating did 2736, 2736a, 2736.5
136 the] their 2736, 2736a, 2736.5
137 He did so smite the land's firstborn] He also smote their first borne all 2736, 2736a, 2736.5
138 His steps by blood were traced] by which their land was grac'd 2736, 2736a, 2736.5
139 Even the beginning of their strength] yea, even the very chiefe of all 2736, 2736a, 2736.5
140 hopes] strength 2736, 2736a, 2736.5
145 extremely] exceeding 2736, 2736a, 2736.5
149 He with a cloud did cover them] He for a covering spread a cloud 2736, 2736a, 2736.5
150 Yet not excluding] yea, and to give them 2736, 2736a, 2736.5
151 And still a fire did] He made a fire to 2736, 2736a, 2736.5
165 He led his people forth with joy] And with exceeding joy he did 2736, 2736a, 2736.5
166 Through many sundry grounds] his people all bring out 2736, 2736a, 2736.5
167 And them whom he elected had] with gladnesse, these which he for his 2736, 2736a, 2736.5
168 With loud triumphing sounds] had chus'd from all about 2736, 2736a, 2736.5
169 And gave to them the heathen's] And freely gave to them the 2736, 2736a, 2736.5
170 Whom they were to destroy] that earst the heathens were 2736, 2736a, 2736.5
171 That which the people's labours] and what the peoples toyles had 2736, 2736a, 2736.5
172 He gave them to enjoy] they did inherit there 2736, 2736a, 2736.5

Psalm 144
1 Blessed is the Lord, who is] Blest be the Lord, for all 2736; The Lord who onely is 2736a, 2736.5
2 And rules my actions right] is onely from his might 2736; for ever blessed be 2736a, 2736.5
3 He doth my hands teach how to war] My hands to war, my fingers how 2736a, 2736.5
4 My fingers how to fight] to fight, well teach doth he 2736a, 2736.5
5 and my] my high 2736, 2736a, 2736.5
13 Man (lo) resembling] Uncertaine man, mere 2736a, 2736.5
14 Uncertain here doth stray] resembleth every way 2736a, 2736.5

TEXTUAL NOTES 627

15 (like shadows) dark and swift] even as a shadow are 2736a, 2736.5
16 Do vanish straight] that passeth soone 2736a, 2736.5
17 down thy heavens, and (Lord) come down] thou thy heavens, O mighty Lord 2736a, 2736.5
18 I humbly thee invoke] and down with glory come 2736a, 2736.5
19 Do thou but once the mountains touch] Touch but the mountains, and they shall 2736a,
20 and they (all moved) shall smoke] and all of them shall smoke 2736; a cloud of smoke become 2736a, 2736.5
22 make] so 2736, 2736a, 2736.5
25 from above thine hand, me rid] then in mercy from above 2736, 2736a, 2736.5
26 Me from great waters free] thy mighty hand, rid me 2736, 2736a, 2736.5
27 And from the hand of children strange] from waters great, and from the hand 2736, 2736a, 2736.5
28 That would take hold of me] of children strange me free 2736, 2736a, 2736.5
29 speaks nought but vanity] doth utter words, which doe 2736, 2736a, 2736.5
30 Which fondly they conceive] with vanity abound 2736, 2736a, 2736.5
32 to deceive] onely found 2736, 2736a, 2736.5
33 I (Lord) will sing a song to thee] I'le sing a new song, O my God 2736, 2736a, 2736.5
34 That I of new have found] upon a Psaltery 2736, 2736a, 2736.5
35 instruments that have] instrument that hath 2736, 2736a, 2736.5
36 I will sound] sing will I 2736, 2736a, 2736.5
37 only] wholy 2736, 2736a, 2736.5
41 hand] hands 2736, 2736a, 2736.5
43 For] and 2736, 2736a, 2736.5
50 All] we 2736, 2736a, 2736.5
52 streets] street 2736, 2736a, 2736.5
53 for their labour, always strong] all our Oxen strong may prove 2736, 2736a, 2736.5
54 Our oxen do not faint] that there no breaking be 2736, 2736a, 2736.5
55 That none break in, nor yet go out] nor in, nor out, that from complaints 2736, 2736a, 2736.5
56 In all the streets no plaint] our streets may still be free 2736, 2736a, 2736.5
59 still] who 2736, 2736a, 2736.5
60 Who hath for] have for their 2736, 2736a, 2736.5

111. 1632 John Standish, in *All the French Psalm Tunes with English Words*

Copy-text

All the French Psalm Tunes with English Words, Being a Collection of Psalms Accorded to the verses and tunes generally used in the Reformed Churches of France and Germany (Thomas Harper, 1632) STC 2734

Other early editions

Wing A942A (Thomas Harper, 1650)

112. 1632 Joshua Sylvester, in *All the French Psalm Tunes with English Words*

See 111.

Psalm 5
20 nor] not A942A

113. 1632 Thomas Salisbury, in *All the French Psalm Tunes with English Words*

See 111.

114. 1632 George Wither, *The Psalms of David*

Copy-text

The Psalmes of David translated into lyrick-verse, according to the scope, of the original (Amsterdam: Cornelis Gerritis van Breughel, 1632) STC 2735

Other early texts

British Library Edgerton MS 2404 *Psalmes of King David / paraphras'd for our English Lire*

Seemingly an earlier draft, so different as to warrant printing these versions here in full. See Allan Pritchard, 'A Manuscript of Wither's "Psalms"', *Huntington Library Quarterly*, 27.1 (1963), 73–77.

Psalm 69

    Lord, saue me, for, the floudes my soule enclose;
    In depth of groundles bogges, I fastened lie,
    The tide of mightie waters, me o'reflowes,
    My roaringes tyre me; and my throate is drie:
Myne eye sight failed, whilst for God I longed,
More then my hayres, are those who me have wronged.

TEXTUAL NOTES 629

2   Strong, are my causeles foes that seeke my fall,
    And made me paie, what I did never take.
    Oh! God, thou know'st my sinnes, and follies all;
    Lord, let not thine be shamed for, for my sake.
Oh! God of Israell, lett not them be blamed
Because for thee I haue bin scorn'd, and shamed.

3   My brethren, strangers, now, are growne to bee,
    My mothers children I am banisht from;
    Thy house, hath with her zeale devoured men,
    Thy scorners, my reproachers are become.
My teares, and fastinges, to my shame they tourned:
Their Iest I was when I in sackclothe mourned.

4   They that in Iudgement sate, against me spake,
    Of me, the carrolls of the drunkards were,
    But, LORD, since timelie mone to thee I make,
    Me of thy grace, with helpe assured, heare:
That in the myre I sincke not, succor lend mee,
And from my ffoes, and waters deepe, defend mee.

5   Lest me the raginge floud should overflowe,
    Or lest, the pitt should close hir mouth on mee,
    LORD, heare me; for thy loue is sweet I know,
    In thy great mercy heeded let me bee.
I am thy servantt; with thy personne cheare mee.
I sore am troubled; oh! make speed to heare me.

6   Lord, come thou my soule, and helpe the same:
    Saue yt, because of those that beare yt spight.
    Thou knowest my reproach, my scorne, my shame,
    And all my foes are ever in thy sight.
I bruiz'd in hart, with shame and sorrow pained,
Sought ease and pittie; but haue none obtained.

7   When I was hungrie; they did gall prepare,
    And vinegar to drinke, when I was drie:
    Their table, therefore, make to them a snare,
    And for their guerdon, ruine them thereby.
That light thy see not; let their eyes be blinded;
And make them stoupe, with backs, foreuer, bended.

8   Seaze them in wrath; thine anger on them cast;
    Let in their tent or palace, none be found:
    ffor, him they chased, whome thou smitten hast
    And, they haue vexed him whome thou didst wound,

ffrom sinne to sinne, they therefore, shall persever;
And, turne to thee, by true repentance never.

9   Thou raze them shalt out out of the booke of life:
    And, to enroule them, with the iust, denie:
    But, as for me, that am in want and greife,
    Defend me, Lord, and sett me up on high.
Soe to thy name (oh Lord, foreuer livinge)
Ile sing a song of thanks, and praises giuinge.

10 ffor, that, to thee oh LORD, more pleasing is,
    Then horn'd or hoofed oxe, or steer, to giue.
    Yee meeke of hart, with gladnes, marke you this,
    And seeke the Lord that so your soules maie liue.
ffor, GOD enclines an eare to him that needeth,
And he the praier of the pris'ner, heedeth.

11 Lett heau'n, and earth, and sea, and all therein
    Sing praise to God for he will Syon saue.
    He Jacobs towres will build, which raz'd haue bin.
    That men may, there againe possessions have.
His servants, for an heritage, shall take it:
And those who love his name, their dwelling make it.

Psalm 85

Thou hast, oh LORD, thy kingdome grac't;
    And Jacob brought from thrall.
Thy peoples faults thou pardoned hast,
    Their sinnes remittinge all.
Thou quite allayed hast thine yre,
    And all thy rage forbore.
To us, oh God, oh helpe, retire;
    And chide vs now, no more.
2   ffor wilt thou angry still remayne?
        And wrath forever be?
Or wilt thou rather turne againe,
    Thy folke may ioy in thee?
Have mercy LORD, and safe vs make,
    For, we GOD's voyce will heare.
Peace, to thy Saints and people, speake,
    They may their sinnes forbeare.
3   ffor sure thy saving health doth stande,
        Nere such as honor thee;
That so, thy glory in our Lande
    Inhabitinge may be.

Now, truth and mercy, do embrace,
    And peace, and iustice, kisse:
Truth from the earth, and righteousnes,
    ffrom heav'n appearing is.
4 Yea, God the LORD, shall bounty showe:
    Our Land shall fruitful be:
Uprightnes shall before him goe:
    And walke her ways, will hee.

115. 1646 (composed 1633?) Richard Crashaw, *Steps to the Temple*

Copy-text

Steps to the Temple. Sacred poems, with other delights of the muses (T. W. for Humphrey Moseley, 1646) Wing C6836

Other early texts

British Library Add. MS 33219 (octavo verse miscellany *c.* 1630s)
British Library Add. MS 2218 (octavo verse miscellany *c.* 1630s)
Bodleian MS Tanner 465 (quarto verse miscellany, compiled by William Sancroft, Archbishop of Canterbury, *c.* 1640s and after)
Bodleian MS Tanner 466 (composite quarto verse miscellany, compiled by William Sancroft, Archbishop of Canterbury, mid-seventeenth c.)

Wing C6837 (Humphrey Moseley, 1648)
Wing C6839A (Cambridge: John Hayes, 1670)
Wing C6839 (T. N. for Henry Herringman, 1670)
Wing C6838 (T. N. for Henry Herringman, 1670)
Wing C6840 (Richard Bently, Jacob Tonson, Francis Saunders, and Thomas Bennet, 1690)

Modern editions

The Poems of Richard Crashaw: English, Latin, and Greek, 2nd edition, ed. by L. C. Martin (Oxford: Clarendon Press, 1957)
The English Poems of Richard Crashaw, ed. by Richard Rambuss (Minneapolis and London: University of Minnesota Press, 2013)

There are no variants among the early printed texts. For a collation of the manuscripts, see Martin.

116. 1633 Phineas Fletcher, *The Purple Island*

Copy-text

The purple island, or The Isle of Man together with piscatorie eclogs and other poeticall miscellanies (Cambridge: [Thomas Buck and Roger Daniel], 1633) STC 11082

Other early texts

STC 11082.5 (Cambridge: by the Printers to the University, 1633)

117. 1633 John Donne, *Poems*

Copy-text

Poems by J. D. with Elegies on the Authors Death (M. F. for John Marriott, 1633) STC 7045

STC 7046 (M. F. for John Marriott, 1635)
STC 7047 (M. F. for John Marriott, 1639)
Wing D1868 (M. F. for John Marriott, 1649)
[etc.]

British Library MS Add. 27407
British Library MS Add. 29427
British Library MS Harley 3357
British Library MS Harley 6930
Cambridge University Library MS Add. 29
Bodleian MS Eng. misc. e. 13 (Oe13)
Bodleian MS Rawl. Poet. 61
Bodleian MS Rawl. Poet. 117
Bodleian MS Tanner 466 (O44)

For a complete collation see *The Variorum Edition of the Poetry of John Donne*, vol. 7, part 2, *The Divine Poems*, ed. by Jeffrey S. Johnson et al. (Bloomington: Indiana University Press, 2020).

118. 1633 George Herbert, *The Temple*

Copy-text

The Temple: Sacred poems and private ejaculations (Cambridge: Thomas Buck and Roger Daniel, 1633) STC 13183

Other early texts

Bodleian MS Tanner 307 (the complete *Temple*, prepared by the women of Little Gidding, the community founded by Nicholas Ferrar, to whom the dying

Herbert entrusted the autograph MS of his poems)

STC 13184 (Thomas Buck and Roger Daniel for Francis Green, 1633)
STC 13184.5 (Thomas Buck and Roger Daniel for Francis Green, 1633)
STC 13185 (Thomas Buck and Roger Daniel for Francis Green, 1633)
STC 13186 (Thomas Buck and Roger Daniel for Francis Green, 1634)
[etc.]

Modern editions

The Works of George Herbert, ed. by F. E. Hutchinson (Oxford: Clarendon Press, 1967)

The English Poems of George Herbert, ed. by Helen Wilcox (Cambridge: Cambridge University Press, 2017)

For a complete collation, see Wilcox.

119. 1620s? Lady Anne Blount

Copy-text

Folger MS V.b.198

No other early texts.

Modern edition

The Southwell-Sibthorpe Commonplace Book, Folger MS. V.b.198, ed. by Jean Klene (Tempe: Medieval and Renaissance Texts and Studies, 1997)

120. Early 1630s? Henry Clifford, Earl of Cumberland, *Poetical Translations*

Copy-text

Bodleian MS Rawl. poet. 55 *Poeticall Translations of some Psalmes, and The Song of Solomon, with other Divine Poems*

No further early texts.

121. c. 1633? George Sandys

Copy-text

British Library Royal MS 18A viii

Other early texts

STC 21724 *A paraphrase upon the Psalmes of David* (London: Andrew Hebb, 1636)
STC 21725 *A paraphrase upon the divine poems* (London: [John Legatt], 1638)

Wing S673 *A paraphrase upon the divine poems* (s.n., 1648)
Wing B2380B (s.n., 1648) no copy on EEBO
Wing B2380C *A paraphrase upon the divine poems* (Printed for O. D., 1648)
Wing B2521 *A paraphrase upon the Psalmes of David* (William Godbid for George Sawbridge, 1676)
Wing B2380D *A paraphrase upon the divine poems* (J. M. for Abel Roper, 1676)
Wing B2521A *A paraphrase upon the Psalmes of David* (William Godbid for Abel Roper, 1676)
Wing B2380E (J. M. for George Sawbridge, 1676) no copy on EEBO

Psalm 80

16 thy] the 21725, Wing S673, Wing B2380C, Wing B2521, Wing B2380D, Wing B2521A
37 shall] will 21724, 21725, Wing S673, Wing B2380C, Wing B2521, Wing B2380D, Wing B2521A

Psalm 104

5 all-infolding] all unfolding 21724, Wing S673, Wing B2380C, Wing B2521, Wing B2380D, Wing B2521A
21 prescribes] prescribe 21724
29 casements] casement Wing B2521, Wing B2380D, Wing B2521A
30 creatures] creature 21724

Psalm 148

[21725, Wing S673, Wing S2380C, Wing B2521, Wing B2380D, Wing B2521A begin with an additional line, 'Hallelujah']
6 angels] armies 21724, 21725, Wing S673, Wing S2380C, Wing B2521, Wing B2380D, Wing B2521A
14 you] your Wing B2521
21 yields] yield 21725, Wing S673, Wing S2380C, Wing B2521, Wing B2380D, Wing B2521A
22 fields] field 21725, Wing S673, Wing S2380C, Wing B2521, Wing B2380D, Wing B2521A

122. After 1627 Sir Henry Wotton, *Reliquae Wottonianae*

Copy-text

Landesbibliothek Kassel, 20 MS poet. et roman. 4, pp. 44–47 (*c.* late 1640s)

Other early texts

Reliquiae Wottonianae (Thomas Maxley for R. Marriot, G. Bedel, and T. Garthwait, 1651) Wing W3648
Reliquiae Wottonianae (Thomas Maxley for R. Marriot, G. Bedel, and T. Garthwait, 1654) Wing W3649
Reliquiae Wottonianae (T. Roycroft for R. Marriott, F. Tyton, T. Collins, and J. Ford, 1672) Wing W3650
Reliquiae Wottonianae (for B. Tooke and T. Sawbridge, 1685) Wing W3651
Bodleian, MS Tanner 466, fols 16^{r-v} (mid-seventeenth century)

Psalm 104
11 his] this Wing W3650, Wing W3651
23 kinds] kind Wing W3648
26 meads and barns] Barns and Meads Wing W3648
27 hearts] heart Wing W3648
40 hands] Hand Wing W3648

PSALMS BY TRANSLATOR

Ainsworth, Henry	8, 23, 84
Alexander, William, Earl of Stirling	93, 105, 144
Anon.	19, 51, 57
Askew, Anne	54
Bacon, Sir Francis	12, 126
Bale, John	14, 130
Barnes, Barnabe	68
Becon, Thomas	103
Bentley, Thomas	22
Bibles Bishops'	23, 59, 92, 141
Coverdale	23, 43
Geneva	7, 23, 24, 48, 98, 106
Great	2, 22, 23, 46, 81, 90, 95, 107, 121, 148
King James	23, 96, 114, 122, 128, 136, 142
Matthew	23, 60
Rheims-Douay	23, 51, 108, 140
Taverner	23, 79
Bickling, Thomas (Bishops' Bible)	23, 59, 92, 141
Blount, Lady Anne (or Anne Brydges?)	25
Bownell, Thomas	146 (sels), 147 (sels), 148 (sels)
Bryan, Joseph	65, 70, 114
Campion, Thomas	130, 137
Carew, Thomas	51, 91, 137
Clifford, Henry	1, 73, 121
Cosworth, Michael	118, 135
Coverdale, Miles	2, 22, 23 (3), 43, 46 (2), 72, 81, 90, 95, 107, 121, 129, 148
Craig, John	56, 145
Crashaw, Richard	23, 137
Croke, John	6, 32
Crowley, Robert	23, 49, 74
Davies, John, of Hereford	32
Davies, Sir John	10, 28, 35, 42, 44
Davison, Christopher	15
Davison, Francis	23 (2), 133
Dod, Henry	87, 111

Donne, John	137
Dudley, John, Earl of Warwick	55
Dudley, Robert, Earl of Leicester	94
Edwardes, Roger	80
Fills, Robert	3
Fletcher, Phineas	42, 63, 127, 137
Flinton, George	79
Forrest, William	6, 11
Fraunce, Abraham	29, 50, 104
Gascoigne, George	130
Gilby, Anthony	40, 97
Glanville, Sir John	22
Golding, Arthur	18, 63, 78, 109, 138
Hall, John	25, 34, 54
Hall, Joseph	2
Harington, Sir John	4, 38, 66, 82, 116, 123, 131, 132
Herbert, George	23
Herbert, Mary Sidney, Countess of Pembroke	52, 55, 58, 73, 117, 125, 134, 139, 150
Hopkins, John	30, 61, 99
Howard, Henry, Earl of Surrey	8, 55, 73, 88
Hunnis, William	51, 113
James I, King of England (James VI of Scotland)	21, (93), 104, (105), 133, (144)
Joye, George	1, 19, 119, 131
Ker, Sir Robert	37, 62, 145
Kethe, William	58, 94, 100
Leighton, Sir William	38, 143
Lock, Anne Vaughan (?)	51
Lok, Henry	27, 71
Melville, James	33, 121
Milton, John	114, 136
Montgomerie, Alexander	1
Murray, Sir David	104
Norton, Thomas	51, 75
Parker, Matthew, Archbishop of Canterbury	17, 33, 36, 110
Parr, Queen Katherine (John Fisher)	22

Patten, William	72
Pits, John	67
Pont, Robert	76, 83
Quarles, Francis	7
Robinson, Richard	6
Sabie, Francis	51
Salisbury, Thomas	104
Sandys, Sir Edwin	17, 139, 146
Sandys, George	80, 104, 148
Scory, Edmund	21, 45
Seagar, Francis	112, 149
Sempill, James ?	9, 41
Sidney, Sir Philip	6, 13, 26, 30, 39
Slatyer, William	42, 124
Smith, Sir Thomas	55, 86
Standish, John	61
Stanihurst, Richard	1, 2, 3, 4
Sternhold, Thomas	1, 120
Stubbs, John	5
Sylvester, Joshua	5, 127
Taverner, Richard	4, 23, 47, 77
Temple, William	1, 99
Top, Alexander	16, 89
Tyrwhit, Elizabeth	1
Verstegan, Richard	6, 95, 102
Vicars, John	53, 101, 124
Wedderburn, John	31, 37, 64, 114, 115
Whittingham, William	51, 124
Wither, George	69, 85
Wotton, Sir Henry	104
Wyatt, Sir Thomas	6, 32, 38, 51, 102, 130, 143

PSALMS IN NUMERICAL ORDER

The number in parentheses refers to the page number of this edition.

1 George Joye (62); Thomas Sternhold (112); Elizabeth Tyrwhit (260); Richard Stanihurst (281); Alexander Montgomerie (381); William Temple (386); Henry Clifford, Earl of Cumberland (530)
2 Great Bible (78); Richard Stanihurst (282); Joseph Hall (388)
3 Robert Fills (268); Richard Stanihurst (283)
4 Richard Taverner (87); Richard Stanihurst (283); Sir John Harington (418)
5 John Stubbs (272); Joshua Sylvester (499)
6 John Croke (89); Sir Thomas Wyatt (122); William Forrest (161); Sir Philip Sidney (275); Richard Robinson (319); Richard Verstegan (360)
7 Geneva Bible (180); Francis Quarles (476)
8 Henry Howard, Earl of Surrey (104); Henry Ainsworth (414)
9 James Sempill/S.P.L. (468)
10 Sir John Davies (452)
11 William Forrest (162)
12 William Byrd (316); Sir Francis Bacon (466)
13 Sir Philip Sidney (276)
14 John Bale (114)
15 Christopher Davison (409)
16 Alexander Top (473)
17 Matthew Parker (233); Sir Edwin Sandys (431)
18 Arthur Golding (250)
19 George Joye (63); Anon. (382)
20 Anon. (93)
21 King James VI of Scotland (313); William Patten (340); Edmond Scory (399)
22 Great Bible (78); Queen Katherine Parr (99); Thomas Bentley (285); Sir John Glanville (486)
23 Coverdale Bible (72); Matthew Bible (76); Great Bible (80); Taverner Bible (85); Miles Coverdale (88); Robert Crowley (145); Geneva Bible (181); Bishops' Bible (243); Francis Davison (405, 407); James Melville (339); Rheims-Douay Bible (390); King James Bible (395); Henry Ainsworth (416); Richard Crashaw (511); George Herbert (526)
24 Geneva Bible (181)
25 John Hall (154); Lady Anne Blount (528)
26 Sir Philip Sidney (276)

27 Henry Lok (337)
28 Sir John Davies (453)
29 Abraham Fraunce (326)
30 John Hopkins (117); Sir Philip Sidney (278)
31 John Wedderburn (221)
32 John Croke (90); Sir Thomas Wyatt (126); John Davies of Hereford (403)
33 Matthew Parker (235)
34 John Hall (157)
35 Sir John Davies (454)
36 Matthew Parker (238)
37 Anon. (93); John Wedderburn (222); Sir Robert Ker (459)
38 Sir Thomas Wyatt (130); William Byrd (318); Sir John Harington (359); Sir William Leighton (425)
39 Sir Philip Sidney (279)
40 Anthony Gilby (269)
41 James Sempill/S.P.L. (470)
42 Sir John Davies (456); William Slatyer (483); Phineas Fletcher (516)
43 Coverdale Bible (72)
44 Sir John Davies (456)
45 Edmond Scory (400)
46 Miles Coverdale (73); Great Bible (80)
47 Richard Taverner (87)
48 Geneva Bible (182)
49 Robert Crowley (146)
50 Abraham Fraunce (326)
51 Anon. (74); Sir Thomas Wyatt (133); Anne Vaughan Lock (186); William Whittingham (201); Thomas Norton (208); William Hunnis (288); Francis Sabie (333); Rheims-Douay Bible (390); William Byrd (394); Thomas Carew (444)
52 Mary Sidney Herbert, Countess of Pembroke (343)
53 John Vicars (478)
54 Anne Askew (102); John Hall (228)
55 Henry Howard, Earl of Surrey (105); Sir Thomas Smith (149); John Dudley, Earl of Warwick (172); Mary Sidney Herbert, Countess of Pembroke (345)
56 John Craig (212)
57 Anon. (384)
58 William Kethe (198); Mary Sidney Herbert, Countess of Pembroke (347)
59 Bishops' Bible (244)
60 Matthew Bible (76)
61 John Hopkins (205); John Standish (497)

PSALMS IN NUMERICAL ORDER

62   Sir Robert Ker (462)
63   Arthur Golding (253); Phineas Fletcher (517)
64   John Wedderburn (225)
65   Joseph Bryan (409)
66   Sir John Harington (419)
67   John Pits (231)
68   Barnabe Barnes (331)
69   George Wither (508)
70   Joseph Bryan (412)
71   Henry Lok (337)
72   Miles Coverdale (70); William Patten (305)
73   Henry Howard, Earl of Surrey (106); Mary Sidney Herbert, Countess of Pembroke (348); Henry Clifford, Earl of Cumberland (531)
74   Robert Crowley (147)
75   Thomas Norton (210)
76   Robert Pont (216)
77   Taverner Bible (86)
78   Arthur Golding (254)
79   George Flinton (307)
80   Roger Edwardes (sels, 248); George Sandys (536)
81   Great Bible (81)
82   Sir John Harington (420)
83   Robert Pont (217)
84   Henry Ainsworth (416)
85   George Wither (510)
86   Sir Thomas Smith (153)
87   Richard Verstegan (357); Henry Dod (440)
88   Henry Howard, Earl of Surrey (109)
89   Alexander Top (473)
90   Great Bible (81)
91   William Temple (386); Thomas Carew (446)
92   Bishops' Bible (245)
93   King James I/William Alexander (489)
94   Robert Dudley, Earl of Leicester (174); William Kethe (176)
95   Great Bible (82); Richard Verstegan (357)
96   King James Bible (395)
97   Anthony Gilby (270)
98   Geneva Bible (182)
99   John Hopkins (206)
100 William Kethe (199)
101 John Vicars (479)
102 Sir Thomas Wyatt (137); Richard Verstegan (362)
103 Thomas Becon (168)

PSALMS IN NUMERICAL ORDER

104 King James VI of Scotland (310); Abraham Fraunce (328); Sir David Murray (437); Thomas Salisbury (503); George Sandys (537); Sir Henry Wotton (542)
105 King James I/William Alexander (490)
106 Geneva Bible (183)
107 Great Bible (83)
108 Rheims-Douay Bible (392)
109 Arthur Golding (257)
110 Matthew Parker (241)
111 Henry Dod (365)
112 Francis Seager (164)
113 William Hunnis (159)
114 John Wedderburn (226); King James Bible (396); Joseph Bryan (412); John Milton (449)
115 John Wedderburn (226)
116 Sir John Harington (421)
117 Mary Sidney Herbert, Countess of Pembroke (351)
118 Michael Cosworth (321)
119 George Joye (64)
120 Thomas Sternhold (113)
121 Great Bible (84); James Melville (339); Henry Clifford, Earl of Cumberland (534)
122 King James Bible (396)
123 William Byrd (316); Sir John Harington (422)
124 William Whittingham (203); John Vicars (481); William Slatyer (485)
125 Mary Sidney Herbert, Countess of Pembroke (352)
126 Sir Francis Bacon (467)
127 Joshua Sylvester (501); Phineas Fletcher (519)
128 King James Bible (397)
129 Miles Coverdale (88)
130 John Bale (116); Sir Thomas Wyatt (141); George Gascoigne (264); Thomas Campion (429)
131 George Joye (63); Sir John Harington (423)
132 Sir John Harington (423)
133 King James VI of Scotland (314); William Byrd (64); Francis Davison (408)
134 Mary Sidney Herbert, Countess of Pembroke (352)
135 Michael Cosworth (323)
136 King James Bible (397); John Milton (450)
137 Thomas Campion (429); Thomas Carew (447); Richard Crashaw (514); Phineas Fletcher (520); John Donne (522)
138 Arthur Golding (259)

139 Mary Sidney Herbert, Countess of Pembroke (353); Sir Edwin Sandys (432)
140 Rheims-Douay Bible (392)
141 Bishops' Bible (246)
142 King James Bible (398)
143 Sir Thomas Wyatt (143); Sir William Leighton (427)
144 King James I/William Alexander (495)
145 John Craig (213); Sir Robert Ker (464)
146 Thomas Bownell (sels, 167); Sir Edwin Sandys (435)
147 Thomas Bownell (sels, 167)
148 Great Bible (84); Thomas Bownell (sels, 167); George Sandys (540)
149 Francis Seager (165)
150 Mary Sidney Herbert, Countess of Pembroke (356)

INDEX OF TRANSLATORS AND TRANSLATIONS

Ainsworth, Henry		29, 52, **414–18**
Alamanni, Luigi		36, 119
Alexander, William, Earl of Stirling		**488–89**
Anon.		52, **74–75**, **92–95**, **382–85**, **467–72**
Aretino, Pietro		36, 119
Askew, Anne		42, 52, **101–02**
Bacon, Sir Francis		52, **465–67**, 541
Bale, John		42, 52, 101, **114–15**, **115–16**
Barnes, Barnabe		**331–32**, 337
Battiferri, Laura		36
Becke, Edmund		85
Becon, Thomas		**168–71**
Bentley, Thomas		52, **284–87**
Beza, Theodore		6, 18, 19, 20, 23, 28, 34, 36, **268–71**, **272–73**, 535
Bibles	Bishops'	6, 7, 8, 9, 10, 177, 233, **243–47**
	Coverdale	6, **71–72**, 75
	Geneva	6, 7, 8, 9, 10, 11, 12, 20, 52, 53, 70, 175, **179–85**, 216, 268, 389
	Great	6, 7, 8, 10, 12, 16, 23, 69, 71, 76, **77–85**, 207, 243,
	King James	7, 8, 11, 12, 13, 14, 15, 16, 389, **394–99**, 399, 489, 498
	Matthew	6, 71, **75–77**, 77, 85
	Rheims-Douay	7, 13, 16, **389–93**
	Taverner	6, 71, **75–77**, 77, 85
	Vulgate (*see also* Jerome)	3, 4, 9, 10, 12, 13, 15, 21, 22, 23, 42, 88, 89, 95, 103, 119, 287, 389, 399
Bickling, Thomas (*see also* Bishops' Bible)		52, **243–47**
Blount, Lady Anne (or Anne Brydges?)		52, **527–29**
Book of Common Prayer (*see also* Coverdale, Miles)		8, 28, 41, 44, 45, 49, 69, 78, 198, 243, 260, 393
Bownell, Thomas		52, 54, **166–68**
Brunfels, Otto		92–93

Brydges, Anne, *see also* Blount, Lady Anne	319
Bryan, Joseph	52, 405, **409–14**
Bucer, Martin	23, 61, 62, 64
Buchanan, George	23, 309, 358, 467, 535
Byrd, William	29, 32, 52, **314–17**, **318–19**, **393–94**, 425
Cajetan, Cardinal Tommaso de Vio Gaetani	119
Camões, Luís de	36
Campensis, Joannes	23, 69, 103, 119, 305
Capito, Wolfgang	87, 259
Campion, Thomas	29, 31, 32, 405, **428–30**
Carew, Thomas	36, 47, 52, **443–48**, 535
Castellio, Sebastian	535
Clifford, Henry, Earl of Cumberland	29, 52, 394, **529–34**, 535
Cosworth, Michael	51, **321–25**, 337
Coverdale, Miles	7, 8, 12, 13, 26, 28, 29, 41, 42, 44, 51, 52, 54, 55, **69–71**, **71–72**, **72–74**, 75, **77–85**, 85, **88–89**, 119, 179, 243
Craig, John	**211–15**
Crashaw, Richard	36, 49, 52, **511–15**, 525
Croke, John	**89–92**
Crowley, Robert	28, 29, **145–48**
Davies, John, of Hereford	**403–05**
Davies, Sir John	**452–58**
Davison, Christopher	405, **409**
Davison, Francis	274, **405–09**, 443, 489, 499, 503, 522
Davy, Jacques du Perron	36
Denham, Sir John	36
Desportes, Philippe	36
Dod, Henry	29, 33, 34, 52, **365–66**, **440–41**, 489
Donne, John	28, 29, 34, 35, 36, 44, 45, 52, 274, 387, 403, 405, 458, **521–25**, 525, 541
Dowland, John	29
Dudley, John, Earl of Warwick	52, 149, **171–73**, 358
Dudley, Robert, Earl of Leicester	52, **173–75**, 342, 358
Edwardes, Roger	51, **247–50**
Fills, Robert	52, **268**
Fisher, John	**95–96**, 119
Fletcher, Phineas	29, 36, 52, 475, **515–21**

Flinton, George — 52, 96, **307–09**
Forman, Simon — 52, 54, **366–80**
Forrest, William — 52, **160–63**
Fraunce, Abraham — 29, 47, **325–30**, 342

Gascoigne, George — 28, 29, 36, **264–67**, 342
Gilby, Anthony — 20, 28, 29, 52, 53, 179, **268–71**
Glanville, Sir John — 52, **486–88**
Golding, Arthur — 28, 29, 52, **250–59**

Hall, John — 35, **154–59**, **228–30**
Hall, Joseph — 52, **387–89**, 489
Harington, Sir John — 52, 119, 274, 287, 343, **358–60**, **418–24**
Herbert, George — 28, 29, 35, 36, 49, 52, 343, 465, 511, **525–26**
Herbert, Mary Sidney, Countess of Pembroke — 28, 29, 31, 33, 34, 35, 36, 44, 45, 46, 47, 49, 52, 53, 233, 274, 325, **342–56**, 358, 403, 499, 503
Hopkins, John — 28, 34, 44, 111, **116–18**, 198, **204–07**, 230, 489
Howard, Henry, Earl of Surrey — 28, 29, 36, 47, 58, **102–11**, 148, 164, 168, 172, 173, 358
Hunnis, William — 29, 42, 53, **159–60**, **287–305**, 441

James I, King of England (James VI of Scotland) — 29, 52, **309–12**, **131–14**, 338, 358, 366, 380, 394, 399, 436, 445, 452, 458, 467, 483, 486, **488–97**, 499, 507, 525, 531, 541

Jerome, St (*see also* Vulgate Bible) — 4, 10, 21, 22, 24, 25, 26
Joye, George — 28, **61–62**, **62–63**, **63–64**, **64–69**, 119
Jud, Leo — 71, 145
Junius, Franciscus — 6, 9, 535

Ker, Sir Robert — **458–65**
Kethe, William — 30, 44, 52, **175–78**, **197–200**
Kiffin, Edward — 502
Kochanowski, Jan — 36

Lefèvre d'Étaples, Jacques — 51
Léon, Luis de — 36
Leighton, Sir William — **424–28**
Lock, Anne Vaughan — 42, 52, **185–97**, 207, 321
Lok, Henry — 185, 321, **337–38**
Luther, Martin — 5, 31, 71, 72, 119, 221

Marot, Clément	36, 34, 36
Martin, Gregory (*see also* Rheims-Douay Bible)	7, 13, 52
Melville, Andrew	338
Melville, James	**338–40**, 381
Midelton, William	502
Milton, John	27, 35, 36, 49, 52, 387, **448–52**, 499
Molnár, Albert Szenczi	36
Montemayor, Jorge de	36
Montgomerie, Alexander	36, 52, 309, 338, **380–82**
Münster, Sebastian	23
Murray, Sir David	47, **436–40**
Norton, Thomas	42, 44, 52, 186, 200, **207–11**
Oldham, Sir John	36
Opitz, Martin	36
Pagninus, Xanthus	71, 85
Parker, Matthew, Archbishop of Canterbury	6–7, 10, 11, 29, 47, 52, **232–42**, 243
Parr, Queen Katherine	28, 52, 54, **95–101**, 259
Patten, William	52, **305–07**, **340–42**
Philips, John	51
Pits, John	52, **230–32**
Pizan, Christine de	36
Polotskii, Simeon	36
Pont, Robert	212, **215–16**
Prys, Edmund	502
Quarles, Francis	**475–77**
Robinson, Richard	**319–20**
Rogers, John	5, 6, 7, 32, 75, 77
Sabie, Francis	42, **332–36**
Salisbury, Thomas	51, **502–06**
Sandys, Sir Edwin	52, **430–36**, 535
Sandys, George	36, 52, 430, 443, **535–41**
Scory, Edmund	52, **399–402**
Scottish Psalter (1564)	211, 215, 313
Seagar, Francis	103, **164–66**
Sempill, James ?	**467–72**
Sidney, Sir Philip (*see also* Sidney Psalter)	28, 29, 31, 33, 34, 35, 36, 44, 45, 46, 47, 49, 53, 233, **274–80**, 325, 331, 342–43, 358, 386, 424, 489, 499, 503

Sidney Psalter (or Sidney Psalms)	29, 33, 34, 35, 44, 46, 403, 405, 443, 449, 478, 526, 531
Slatyer, William	483–85
Smith, Sir Thomas	52, **148**–**53**, 172, 173, 358, 386
Spenser, Edmund	36
Standish, John	497–98, 499, 502–03
Stanihurst, Richard	29, 47, 51, 52, **280**–**84**
Sternhold, Thomas (*see also* Sternhold and Hopkins)	28, 34, 35, 44, 103, **111**–**13**, 116, 154, 160, 164, 172, 173, 204, 238, 489
Sternhold and Hopkins, or *The Whole Book of Psalms*	8, 21, 29, 30, 31, 33, 36, 41, 44, 45, 52, 111, 116, 145, 168, 186, 197–98, 200, 204, 207, 211–12, 230, 313, 315, 318, 393, 443, 448, 489, 507
Strejc, Jiří	36
Stubbs, John	52, 272–73
Sylvester, Joshua	52, **498**–**502**
Taverner, Richard	85–87, 87, 259
Temple, William	386–87
Titelmans, Frans	307
Top, Alexander	472–75
Tremellius, Immanuel	9, 309, 535
Tyndale, William	4, 5, 6, 7, 13, 14, 21, 61, 69, 71, 75, 77, 179, 185
Tyrwhit, Elizabeth	52, 54, 62, 87, **259**–**63**
Utenhove, Jan	36
Vair, Guillaume du	36
Vaughan, Henry	36
Verstegan, Richard	52, 332, **356**–**58**, **360**–**64**, 393
Vicars, John	477–83, 499
Wedderburn, John	220–28
Whittingham, William	41, 52, 116, 179, **200**–**04**, 207, 268
Wither, George	29, 52, 365, 440, 472, 489, **507**–**10**
Wotton, Sir Henry	541–44
Wyatt, Sir Thomas	28, 29, 35, 36, 41, 47, **118**–**44**, 148, 168, 287, 358
Wycliffe, John	4, 5, 171
Zwingli, Huldrych	61, 63, 71

BIBLIOGRAPHY

ALTER, ROBERT, *The Art of Biblical Poetry* (New York: W. W. Norton, 1985)
—— trans. and commentary, *The Book of Psalms* (New York: W. W. Norton, 2009)
ARBLASTER, PAUL, *Antwerp & the World: Richard Verstegan and the Intellectual Culture of Catholic Reformation* (Leuven: Leuven University Press, 2004)
ARTHUR, JAKE, 'Anne Lock or Thomas Norton? A Response to the Reattribution of the First Sonnet Sequence in English', *Early Modern Women: An Interdisciplinary Journal*, 16.2 (2022), 213–36
ASTON, WALTER H., ed., *Select Psalms in Verse, with Critical Remarks* (London: J. Hatchard, 1811)
ATTRIDGE, DEREK, *Well-Weighed Syllables: Elizabethan Verse in Classical Metres* (Cambridge: Cambridge University Press, 1974)
AUSTEN, GILLIAN, *George Gascoigne* (Woodbridge: D. S. Brewer, 2008)
AUSTERN, LINDA PHYLLIS, '"For Musicke is the Handmaid of the Lord": Women, Psalms, and Domestic Music-Making in Early Modern England', in *Psalms in the Early Modern World*, ed. by Linda Phyllis Austern, Kari Boyd McBride, and David Orvis (Farnham: Ashgate, 2011), pp. 77–114
BACH, INKE, and HELMUT GALLE, *Deutsche Psalmendichtung vom 16. bis zum 20. Jahrhundert* (Berlin and New York: Walter de Gruyter, 1989)
BALD, R. C., *John Donne: A Life* (New York: Oxford University Press, 1970)
BAROWAY, ISRAEL, 'The Accentual Theory of Hebrew Prosody', *ELH*, 17 (1950), 115–35
—— 'The Bible as Poetry in the English Renaissance: An Introduction', *Journal of English and Germanic Philology*, 32 (1933), 447–80
—— 'The Hebrew Hexameter: A Study in Renaissance Sources and Interpretation', *ELH*, 2 (1935), 66–91
—— '"The Lyre of David": A Further Study in Renaissance Interpretation of Biblical Form', *ELH*, 8 (1941), 119–42
—— 'Tremellius, Sidney, and Biblical Verse', *Modern Language Notes*, 49 (1934), 146–47
BAXTER, JAMIE REID, 'Montgomerie's Solsequium and *The Mindes Melodie*', in *Fresche Fontanis: Studies in the Culture of Medieval and Early Modern Scotland*, ed. by Janet Hadley Williams (Newcastle upon Tyne: Cambridge Scholars Publishing, 2013), pp. 361–75
BEILIN, ELAINE V., ed., *The Examinations of Anne Askew* (New York: Oxford University Press, 1996)
BEITENHOLZ, PETER G., ed., Thomas B. Deutscher, assoc. ed., *Contemporaries of Erasmus: A Biographical Register of the Renaissance and Reformation*, 3 vols (Toronto: University of Toronto Press, 1985)
BENNETT, LYN, *Women Writing of Divinest Things: Rhetoric and the Poetry of Pembroke, Wroth and Lanyer* (Pittsburgh: Duquesne University Press, 2004)
BERLIN, ADELE, *The Dynamics of Biblical Parallelism* (Bloomington: Indiana University Press, 1985)

BERRY, LLOYD E., ed., *John Stubbs's 'Gaping Gulf' with Letters and Other Relevant Documents* (Charlottesville: University of Virginia Press for the Folger Shakespeare Library, 1968)

BETTERIDGE, MAURICE S., 'The Bitter Notes: The Geneva Bible and its Annotations', *The Sixteenth Century Journal*, 14.1 (1983), 41–62

BJORVAND, EINAR, 'Religious Self-Fashioning and The Book of Psalms', in *Self-Fashioning and Metamorphosis in Early Modern English Literature*, ed. by Olav Lausund and Stein Haugom Oslen (Oslo: Novus Forlag, 2003), pp. 34–44

BLOCH, CHANA, *Spelling the Word: George Herbert and the Bible* (Berkeley, Los Angeles, and London: University of California Press, 1985)

BOUWSMA, WILLIAM, J., *John Calvin: A Sixteenth Century Portrait* (New York and Oxford: Oxford University Press, 1988)

BOWLES, AMY, 'Ralph Crane and Early Modern Scribal Culture' (unpublished doctoral dissertation, Cambridge University, 2017)

—— 'Scribal Verse Manuscripts: The Poems Copied by Ralph Crane', *Études anglaises*, 73.3 (2020), 287–312

BRAY, ROGER, 'William Byrd's English Psalms', in *Psalms in the Early Modern World*, ed. by Linda Phyllis Austern, Kari Boyd McBride, and David Orvis (Farnham: Ashgate, 2011), pp. 61–76

BRENNAN, MICHAEL, 'The Queen's Proposed Visit to Wilton House in 1599 and the "Sidney Psalms"', *Sidney Journal*, 20.1 (2002), 27–53

BRENNEKE, ERNEST, *John Milton the Elder and his Music* (New York: Columbia University Press, 1938)

BRIGDEN, SUSAN, 'Henry Howard, Earl of Surrey, and the "Conjured League"', *The Historical Journal*, 37 (1994), 507–37

—— *Sir Thomas Wyatt: The Heart's Forest* (London: Faber, 2012)

BROOK, V. J. K., *A Life of Archbishop Parker* (Oxford: Clarendon Press, 1962)

BROWER, REUBEN, ed., *On Translation* (Cambridge: Harvard University Press, 1959)

BROWN, WILLIAM, ed., *The Oxford Handbook of The Psalms* (Oxford: Oxford University Press, 2014)

BUTTERWORTH, CHARLES C., *The Literary Lineage of the King James Bible* (Philadelphia: University of Pennsylvania Press, 1941)

—— *The English Primers (1529–1545)* (Philadelphia: University of Pennsylvania Press, 1953)

BUTTERWORTH, CHARLES C., and ALLAN G. CHESTER, *George Joye, 1493?–1533: A Chapter in the History of the English Bible and the English Reformation* (Philadelphia: University of Pennsylvania Press, 1962)

CAMBERS, ANDREW, 'Demonic Possession, Literacy, and "Superstition" in Early Modern England', *Past & Present*, 202 (2009), 3–35

CAMERON, EUAN, ed., *The New Cambridge History of the Bible, vol. 3, From 1450 to 1750* (Cambridge: Cambridge University Press, 2016)

CAMPBELL, GORDON, *Bible: The Story of the King James Version, 1611–2011* (Oxford and New York: Oxford University Press, 2010)

CAMPBELL, LILY B., *Divine Poetry and Drama in Sixteenth Century England* (Cambridge: Cambridge University Press, 1959)

CAVE, TERENCE, *Devotional Poetry in France c.1570–1613* (London: Cambridge University Press, 1969)

CHRISTIE-MILLER, IAN, 'Henry VIII and British Library, Royal MS. 2 A. XVI: Marginalia in King Henry's Psalter', *Electronic British Library Journal*, 8 (2015), 1–19

CLARKE, DANIELLE, '"Lover's Songs Shall Turne to Holy Psalmes": Mary Sidney and the Transformation of Petrarch', *Modern Language Review*, 92.2 (1997), 282–94

COLES, KIMBERLY ANNE, *Religion, Reform, and Women's Writing in Early Modern England* (New York: Cambridge University Press, 2008)

COLIE, ROSALIE L., *The Resources of Kind: Genre-Theory in the Renaissance*, ed. by Barbara K. Lewalski (Berkeley: University of California Press, 1973)

COLLINSON, PATRICK, *The Religion of Protestants: The Church in English Society 1559–1625* (Oxford: Oxford University Press, 1982)

CRAIG, JOHN, 'Psalms, Groans and Dogwhippers: The Soundscape of Worship in the English Parish Church, c.1547–1635', in *Sacred Space in Early Modern Europe*, ed. by Will Coster and Andrew Spicer (Cambridge and New York: Cambridge University Press, 2005), pp. 104–23

CROWLEY, LARA, 'Donne, not Davison: Reconsidering the Authorship of "Psalme 137"', *Modern Philology*, 105.4 (2008), 603–36

CUMMINGS, BRIAN, ed., *The Book of Common Prayer: The Texts of 1549, 1559, and 1662* (Oxford: Oxford University Press, 2011)

—— *The Literary Culture of the Reformation: Grammar and Grace* (Oxford: Oxford University Press, 2002)

CURTIUS, E. R., *European Literature and the Latin Middle Ages*, trans. by Willard R. Trask (Princeton: Princeton University Press, 1973)

DAHOOD, MITCHELL, ed., *Psalms I, II, and III*, The Anchor Bible, 3 vols (Garden City, NY: Doubleday, 1965, 1968, and 1970)

DANIELL, DAVID, *The Bible in English: Its History and Influence* (New Haven and London: Yale University Press, 2003)

—— *William Tyndale: A Biography* (New Haven: Yale University Press, 1994)

DAVIS, RICHARD BEALE, *George Sandys: Poet-Adventurer* (London: The Bodley Head; New York: Columbia University Press, 1955)

DAVIS, WALTER R., ed., *The Works of Thomas Campion* (Garden City: Doubleday, 1967)

DAWSON, JANE, *John Knox* (New Haven and London: Yale University Press, 2015)

DECLAISSÉ-WALFORD, NANCY L., ROLF A. JACOBSEN, and BETH LANEEL TANNER, *The Book of Psalms* (Grand Rapids and Cambridge: William B. Eerdmans, 2014)

DEMERS, PATRICIA, '"Warpe" and "Webb" in the Sidney Psalms: The "Coupled Worke" of the Countess of Pembroke and Sir Philip Sidney', in *Literary Couplings: Writing Couples, Collaborators, and the Construction of Authorship*, ed. by Marjorie Stone and Judith Thompson (Madison: University of Wisconsin Press, 2006), pp. 41–58

DEWAR, MARY, *Sir Thomas Smith: A Tudor Intellectual in Office* (London: Athlone Press, 1964)

DICKENS, A. G., *The English Reformation*, 2nd edn (University Park: Penn State University Press, 1991)

DOBBS-ALLSOPP, F. W., *On Biblical Poetry* (Oxford: Oxford University Press, 2015)

DOELMAN, JAMES, 'The Accession of King James I and English Religious Poetry', *SEL*, 34.1 (1994), 19–40

—— 'George Wither, the Stationers Company and the English Psalter', *Studies in Philology*, 90.1 (1993), 74–82

—— *King James I and the Religious Culture of England* (Cambridge: Cambridge University Press, 2000)

—— 'The Reception of King James's Psalter', in *Royal Subjects: Essays on the Writing of James VI and I*, ed. by Daniel Fischlin and Mark Fortier (Detroit: Wayne State University Press, 2002), pp. 454–75

—— 'A Seventeenth-Century Publication of Three of Sir Philip Sidney's Psalms', *Notes and Queries*, 38 (1991), 162–63

DUBROW, HEATHER, *The Challenges of Orpheus: Lyric Poetry and Early Modern England* (Baltimore: Johns Hopkins University Press, 2008)

DUFFY, EAMON, 'Praying the Counter-Reformation', in *Early Modern English Catholicism: Identity, Memory, and Counter-Reformation*, ed. by James E. Kelly and Susan Royal (Leiden and Boston: Brill, 2017), pp. 206–25

—— *The Stripping of the Altars: Traditional Religion in England c.1400–1580* (New Haven and London: Yale University Press, 1992)

DUGUID, TIMOTHY, *Metrical Psalmody in Print and Practice: English 'Singing Psalms' and Scottish 'Psalm Buiks', c. 1547–1640* (Farnham: Ashgate, 2014)

DUROCHER, RICHARD J., 'Tradition and the Budding Individual Talent: Milton's Paraphrase of Psalm 114', *Cithara: Essays in the Judaeo-Christian Tradition*, 49.1 (2009), 35–44

ECO, UMBERTO, *Experiences in Translation*, trans. by Alastair McEwan (Toronto: University of Toronto Press, 2001)

EINBODEN, JEFFREY, 'The Homeric Psalm: Milton's Translation of Psalm 114 and the Problems of "Hellenic Scripture"', *Literature and Theology: An International Journal of Religion, Theory, and Culture*, 17.3 (2003), 314–23

ELLISON, JAMES, *George Sandys: Travel, Colonialism, and Tolerance in the Seventeenth Century* (Cambridge: D. S. Brewer, 2002)

ELSKY, MARTIN, 'George Herbert's Pattern Poems and the Materiality of Language: A New Approach to Renaissance Hieroglyphics', *ELH*, 50.2 (1983), 245–60

ERICKSEN, ROY T., 'George Gascoigne's and Mary Sidney's Versions of Psalm 130', *Cahier-élisabéthains*, 36 (1989), 1–9

—— 'Typological Form in "Gascoignes De Profundis"', *English Studies*, 66.4 (1985), 300–09

EVETTS-SECKER, J., 'An Elizabethan Experiment in Psalmody: Ralph Buckland's Seaven Sparkes of the Enkindled Soule', *The Sixteenth Century Journal*, 15.3 (1984), 311–26

FAINI, MARCO, 'Pietro Aretino, St. John the Baptist and the Rewriting of the Psalms', in *Renaissance Rewritings*, ed. by Helmut Pfeiffer, Irene Fantappiè, and Tobias Roth (Berlin: Walter de Gruyter, 2017), pp. 225–52

FELCH, SUSAN M., ed., *Elizabeth Tyrwhit's 'Morning and Evening Prayers'* (London: Routledge, 2008)

—— '"Halff a Scrypture Woman": Heteroglossia and Female Authorial Agency in Prayers by Lady Elizabeth Tyrwhit, Anne Lock, and Anne Wheathill', in *English Women, Religion, and Textual Production, 1500–1625*, ed. by Micheline White (Aldershot: Ashgate, 2011), pp. 147–66

FISKEN, BETH WYNNE, '"The Art of Sacred Parody" in Mary Sidney's *Psalmes*', *Tulsa Studies in Women's Literature*, 8.2 (1989), 223–39

FRASER, DAVID, 'Sources of Texts for Byrd's 1611 *Psalmes*', *Early Music*, 38.1 (2010), 171–72

FRASER, RUSSELL A., ed., *The Court of Virtue, 1565, by John Hall* (New Brunswick: Rutgers University Press, 1961)

FREER, COBURN, *Music for a King: George Herbert's Style and the Metrical Psalms* (Baltimore and London: Johns Hopkins University Press, 1972)

—— 'The Style of Sidney's Psalms', *Language and Style*, 2.1 (1969), 63–78

FRIEDMAN, DONALD M., 'The "Thing" in Wyatt's Mind', *Essays in Criticism*, 16 (1966), 375–81

FROST, MAURICE, ed., *English & Scottish Psalm & Hymn Tunes c.1543–1677* (London: S.P.C.K. and Oxford University Press, 1953)

FULTON, THOMAS, *The Book of Books: Biblical Interpretation, Literary Culture, and the Political Imagination from Erasmus to Milton* (Philadelphia: University of Pennsylvania Press, 2021)

—— 'Toward a New Cultural History of the Geneva Bible', *Journal of Medieval and Early Modern Studies*, 47.3 (2017), 487–516

GARRETT, C. H., *The Marian Exiles: A Study in the Origins of Elizabethan Puritanism* (Cambridge: The University Press, 1938)

GLASS, HENRY A., *The Story of the Psalters* (London: K. Paul, Trench and Co., 1888; repr. 1972)

GOLDING, LOUIS T., *An Elizabethan Puritan* (New York: R. R. Smith, 1937)

GOODBLATT, CHANITA, '"High Holy Muse": Christian Hebraism and Jewish Exegesis in the Sidneian Psalms', in *Tradition, Heterodoxy and Religious Culture: Judaism and Christianity in the Early Modern Period*, ed. by Chanita Goodblatt and Howard Kreisel (Beersheba: New York University Press; Ben-Gurion University of the Negev Press, 2006), pp. 287–309

GOSSELIN, EDWARD A., 'David in Tempore Belli: Beza's David in the Service of the Huguenots', *The Sixteenth Century Journal*, 7.2 (1976), 31–54

GRAHAM, KENNETH J. E., *Disciplinary Measures from the Metrical Psalms to Milton* (London: Routledge, Taylor & Francs Group, 2016)

GRAVES, M. A. R., *Thomas Norton: the Parliament Man* (Oxford and Cambridge, MA: Blackwell's, 1994)

GREENBLATT, STEPHEN, *Renaissance Self-Fashioning* (Chicago: University of Chicago Press, 1980)

GREENE, ROLAND, 'Anne Lock's *Meditation*: Invention Versus Dilation and the Founding of Puritan Poetics', in *Form and Reform in Renaissance England: Essays in Honor of Barbara Kiefer Lewalski*, ed. by Amy Boesky and Mary Thomas Crane (Newark: University of Delaware Press; London: Associated University Presses, 2000), pp. 153–70

—— 'Sir Philip Sidney's Psalms, the Sixteenth Century Psalter, and the Nature of Lyric', *Studies in English Literature*, 30.1 (1990), 19–40

GREENE, THOMAS M., *The Light in Troy: Imitation and Discovery in Renaissance Poetry* (New Haven and London: Yale University Press, 1993)

GRUNDY, JOAN, *The Spenserian Poets* (London: Edward Arnold, 1969)

GUNKEL, HERMANN, *The Psalms: A Form-Critical Introduction*, trans. by T. M. Horner (Philadelphia: Fortress Press, 1967)

HACKETT, HELEN, 'The Art of Blasphemy? Interfusions of the Erotic and the Sacred in the Poetry of Donne, Barnstable, and Constable', *Renaissance and Reformation/Renaissance et Réforme*, 28.3 (2004), 27–54

HALASZ, ALEXANDRA, 'Wyatt's David', *Texas Studies in Literature and Language*, 30.3 (1988), 320–44

HAMLIN, HANNIBAL, '"The Highest Matter in the Noblest Form": The Influence of the Sidney Psalms', *Sidney Journal*, 23 (2005), 133–57

—— '"My tongue shall speak": The Voices of the Psalms', *Renaissance Studies*, 29.4 (2015), 509–30

—— *Psalm Culture and Early Modern English Literature* (Cambridge: Cambridge University Press, 2004)

—— 'Sobs for Sorrowful Souls: Versions of the Penitential Psalms for Domestic Devotion', in *Private and Domestic Devotion in Early Modern Britain*, ed. by Jessica Martin and Alec Ryrie (Farnham: Ashgate, 2012), pp. 211–35

HAMLIN, HANNIBAL, MICHAEL G. BRENNAN, MARGARET P. HANNAY, and NOEL J. KINNAMON, eds, *The Sidney Psalter: The Psalms of Sir Philip and Mary Sidney* (Oxford: Oxford University Press, 2009)

HAMMOND, GERALD, *The Making of the English Bible* (Manchester: Carcanet New Press, 1982)

HANNAY, MARGARET P., '"House-Confinéd Maids": The Presentation of Woman's Role in the *Psalmes* of the Countess of Pembroke', *English Literary Renaissance*, 24 (1994), 44–71

—— 'Joining the Conversation: David, Astrophil, and the Countess of Pembroke', in *Textual Conversations in the Renaissance: Ethics, Authors, Technologies*, ed. by Zachary Lesser and Benedict Robinson (Aldershot and Burlington: Ashgate, 2006), pp. 113–29

—— *Philip's Phoenix: Mary Sidney, Countess of Pembroke* (New York and Oxford, 1990)

—— '"Princes You as Men Must Dy": Genevan Advice to Monarchs in the *Psalmes* of Mary Sidney', *English Literary Renaissance*, 19 (1989), 22–41

—— 'Re-revealing the Psalms: Mary Sidney, Countess of Pembroke, and Her Early Modern Readers', in *Psalms in the Early Modern World*, ed. by Linda Phyllis Austern, Kari Boyd McBride, and David Orvis (Farnham: Ashgate, 2011), pp. 219–34

—— '"So May I With the *Psalmist* Truly Say": Early Modern English Women's Psalm Discourse', in *Write or Be Written: Early Modern Women Poets and Cultural Constraints*, ed. by Barbara Smith and Ursula Appelt (Aldershot and Burlington: Routledge, 2001), pp. 105–34

HAPPÉ, PETER, *John Bale* (New York: Twayne Publishers, 1996)

HARPER, JOHN, *The Forms and Orders of Western Liturgy from the Tenth to the Eighteenth Century* (Oxford: Clarendon Press, 1991)

HARRIER, RICHARD, *The Canon of Sir Thomas Wyatt's Poetry* (Cambridge, MA: Harvard University Press, 1975)

HEALE, ELIZABETH, 'Lute and Harp in Wyatt's Poetry', in *Sacred and Profane: Secular and Devotional Interplay in Early Modern British Literature*, ed. by Helen Wilcox, Richard Todd, and Alasdair MacDonald (Amsterdam: V. U. University Press, 1996), pp. 3–16

—— *Wyatt, Surrey, and Early Tudor Poetry* (London: Longman, 1998)

HENSLEY, CHARLES S., *The Later Career of George Wither* (The Hague and Paris: Mouton, 1969)

HILLYER, RICHARD, *Sir Philip Sidney, Cultural Icon* (New York: Palgrave MacMillan, 2010)

HINELY, JAN LAWSON, '"Freedom through Bondage": Wyatt's Appropriation of the Penitential Psalms of David', in *The Work of Dissimilitude: Essays from the Sixth Citadel Conference on Medieval and Renaissance Literature*, ed. by David G. Allen and Robert A. White (Newark: University of Delaware Press; London: Associated University Presses, 1992), pp. 148–65

HOBBS, GERALD R., '*Hebraica Veritas* and *Traditio Apostolica*: Saint Paul and the Interpretation of the Psalms in the Sixteenth Century', in *The Bible and the Sixteenth Century*, ed. by David C. Steinmetz (Durham, NC, and London: Duke University Press, 1990), pp. 83–99

—— 'Martin Bucer and the Englishing of the Psalms: Pseudonymity in the Service of Early English Protestant Piety', in *Martin Bucer: Reforming Church and Community*, ed. by D. F. Wright (Cambridge and New York: Cambridge University Press, 1994)

HOLLANDER, JOHN, *The Work of Poetry* (New York: Columbia University Press, 1997)

HÖLTGEN, KARL JOSEF, 'New Verse by Francis Quarles: The Portland Manuscripts, Metrical Psalms, and the Bay Psalm Book (with text)', *English Literary Renaissance*, 28.1 (1998), 118–41

HOUGHTON, H. A. G., *The Latin New Testament: A Guide to Its Early History, Texts, and Manuscripts* (Oxford: Oxford University Press, 2016)

HRUSHOVSKI, BENJAMIN, 'Prosody (Hebrew)', *Encyclopedia Judaica*, ed. by Cecil Roth and Geoffrey Wigoder, 16 vols (Jerusalem: Keter, 1972), XIII, 1195–1240.

HUGHES, FELICITY A., 'Gascoigne's Poses', *Studies in English Literature*, 37 (1997), 1–19

LE HURAY, PETER, *Music and the Reformation in England, 1549–1660* (Cambridge and New York: Cambridge University Press, 1978)

HUTTAR, CHARLES, 'Poems by Surrey and Others in a Printed Miscellany Circa 1550', *English Miscellany*, 16 (1965), 9–18

JACK, R. D. S., *Alexander Montgomerie* (Edinburgh: Scottish Academic, 1985)

JAMES, SUSAN E., *Kateryn Parr: The Making of a Queen* (Aldershot: Ashgate, 1999)

JASPER, DAVID, "The Twenty-Third Psalm in English Literature", *Religion & Literature*, 30.1 (1993), 1–11

JEANNERET, M., *Poésie et tradition biblique au XVIe siècle: Recherches stylistiques sur les paraphrases des psaulmes de Marot à Malherbe* (Paris: J. Corti, 1969)

JOHNSON, RONALD C., *George Gascoigne* (New York: Twayne Publishers, 1972)

JONES, ELISABETH R., 'From Chamber to Church: The Remarkable Emergence of Thomas Sternhold as Psalmist for the Church of England', *Reformation & Renaissance Review*, 11.1 (2009), 29–56

JONES, G. LLOYD, *The Discovery of Hebrew in Tudor England: A Third Language* (Manchester: Manchester University Press, 1983)

JULIAN, JOHN, ed., *A Dictionary of Hymnology*, revised repr. in 2 vols (New York: Dover Publications, 1957)

KASKE, CAROL V., 'The Curse-Psalms in Their Patristic, Renaissance, and Modern Reception', *Genre: Forms of Discourse and Culture*, 40.3–4 (2007), 129–42

KASSELL, LAUREN, *Medicine and Magic in Elizabethan London: Simon Forman: Astrologer, Alchemist, and Physician* (Oxford: Clarendon Press, 2005)

KASTAN, DAVID SCOTT, 'An Early English Metrical Psalm: Elizabeth's or John Bale's?', *Notes and Queries*, (1974), 404–05

—— '"The Noyse of the New Bible": Reform and Reaction in Henrician England', in *Religion and Culture in Renaissance England*, ed. by Claire McEachern and Debora Shuger (Cambridge: Cambridge University Press, 1997), pp. 46–68

KASTOR, FRANK S., *Giles and Phineas Fletcher* (Boston: Twayne Publishers, 1978)

KERRIGAN, JOHN, 'Thomas Carew', *Proceedings of the British Academy*, 74 (1988), 311–50

KILGORE, ROBERT, 'The Politics of King David in Early Modern Verse', *Studies in Philology*, 111.3 (2013), 411–41

KING, JOHN N., *English Reformation Literature: The Tudor Origins of the Protestant Tradition* (Princeton: Princeton University Press, 1982)

—— 'Henry VIII as David: The King's Image and Reformation Politics', in *Henry VIII and His Afterlives: Literature, Politics, and Art*, ed. by Mark Rankin, Christopher Highley, and John N. King (Cambridge: Cambridge University Press, 2009), pp. 34–52

KING'OO, CLARE COSTLEY, 'Authenticity and Excess in *The Examinations of Anne Askew*', *Reformation*, 19.1 (2014), 21–39

—— *Miserere Mei: The Penitential Psalms in Late Medieval and Early Modern Literature* (Notre Dame: University of Notre Dame Press, 2012)

—— 'Rightful Penitence and the Publication of Wyatt's *Certayne Psalmes*', in *Psalms in the Early Modern World*, ed. by Linda Phyllis Austern, Kari Boyd McBride, and David Orvis (Farnham: Ashgate, 2011), pp. 155–74

—— 'William Hunnis and the Success of the *Seven Sobs*', *Renaissance Studies*, 29.4 (2015), 615–31

KLENE, JEAN, ed., *The Southwell-Sibthorpe Commonplace Book, Folger MS. V.b.198* (Tempe: Medieval and Renaissance Texts and Studies, 1997)

KRUEGER, ROBERT, and RUBY NEMSER, 'Introduction', in *The Poems of Sir John Davies*, ed. by Robert Krueger (Oxford: Clarendon Press, 1975)

KUCHAR, GARY, 'Introduction: Distraction and the Ethics of Poetic Form in *The Temple*', *Christianity & Literature*, 66.1 (2016), 4–23

KUCZYNSKI, MICHAEL P., *Prophetic Song: The Psalms as Moral Discourse in Later Medieval England* (Philadelphia: University of Pennsylvania Press, 1995)

KUGEL, JAMES, *The Idea of Biblical Poetry: Parallelism and its History* (New Haven and London: Yale University Press, 1981)

LAMB, MARY ELLEN, 'The Countess of Pembroke's Patronage', *English Literary Renaissance*, 12 (1982), 162–79

—— *Gender and Authorship in the Sidney Circle* (Madison: University of Wisconsin Press, 1990)

—— 'The Myth of the Countess of Pembroke', *Yearbook of English Studies*, 11 (1981), 194–202

LANGE, MARJORIE E., *Telling Tears in the Renaissance* (Leiden and New York: E. J. Brill, 1996)

LARSON, KATHERINE, *The Matter of Song in Early Modern England* (Oxford: Oxford University Press, 2019)

LEAVER, ROBIN, *Goostly Psalmes and Spirituall Songes: English and Dutch Metrical*

Psalms from Coverdale to Utenhove 1535–1566 (Oxford: Clarendon Press, 1991)
—— 'John Bale: Author and Revisor of Sixteenth-Century Metrical Psalms', *Jahrbuch für Liturgik und Hymnologie*, 34 (1992/1993), 98–106
LENNON, COLM, *Richard Stanihurst the Dubliner 1547–1618* (Blackrock: Irish Academic Press, 1981)
LEWALSKI, BARBARA KIEFER, *Protestant Poetics and the Seventeenth-Century Religious Lyric* (Princeton: Princeton University Press, 1979)
LEWIS, C. S., *Reflections on the Psalms* (San Francisco: HarperCollins, 2017; orig. Harcourt Brace, 1958)
MACCULLOCH, DIARMAID, *Thomas Cranmer: A Life* (New Haven: Yale University Press, 1996)
MACDONALD, ALASDAIR A., ed., *The Gude and Godlie Ballatis* (Woodbridge: Boydell Press for The Scottish Text Society, 2015)
—— 'Writing Which, and Whose Identity? The Challenges of the *Gude and Godlie Ballatis*', *Medievalia et Humanistica: Studies in Medieval and Renaissance Culture*, 41 (2016), 157–67
MAROTTI, ARTHUR F., *Manuscript, Print, and the Renaissance Lyric* (Ithaca and London: Cornell University Press, 1995)
MARSDEN, RICHARD, and E. ANN MATTER, eds, *The New Cambridge History of the Bible, vol. 2, From 600 to 1450* (Cambridge: Cambridge University Press, 2012)
MARSH, CHRISTOPHER, *Music and Society in Early Modern England* (Cambridge and New York: Cambridge University Press, 2013)
MARTÍNEZ VALDIVIA, LUCÍA, 'Psalms and Early Modern English Poetry', in *Gathering Force: Early Modern British Literature in Transition, 1557–1623*, vol. I, ed. by Kirsten Poole and Lauren Shoehet (Cambridge: Cambridge University Press, 2019), pp. 287–305
MASON, H. A., *Humanism and Poetry in the Early Tudor Period* (London: Routledge and Paul, 1959)
MATTHIESSEN, F. O., *Translation: An Elizabethan Art* (Cambridge, MA: Harvard University Press, 1931)
MAY, STEVEN W., 'Anne Lock and Thomas Norton's *Meditation of a Penitent Sinner*', *Modern Philology*, 114.4 (2017), 793–819
—— *The Elizabethan Courtier Poets: The Poems and Their Contexts* (Columbia: University of Missouri Press, 1991)
MILSOM, JOHN, 'Tallis, the Parker Psalter, and Some Unknowns', *Early Music*, 44.2 (2016), 1–13
MITCHELL, A. F., ed., *A Compendious Book of Godly and Spiritual Songs, Commonly Known as 'The Gude and Godlie Ballatis', Reprinted from the Edition of 1567*, 2 vols (Edinburgh and London: W. Blackwood and Sons for The Scottish Text Society, 1897)
MOLEKAMP, FEMKE, 'Genevan Legacies: The Making of the English Geneva Bible', in *The Oxford Handbook of the Bible in Early Modern England, c.1530–1700*, ed. by Kevin Killeen, Helen Smith, and Rachel Willie (Oxford: Oxford University Press, 2015), pp. 38–53
MONTA, SUSANNAH BRIETZ, 'The King's Psalms — or the Pope's? Katherine Parr's *Psalms or Prayers*, Scriptural Collage, and English Catholic Devotion', *Reformation*, 26.1 (2021), 8–22

MOTTRAM, STEWART, 'Translation, Paraphrase, and Wyatt's *Penitential Psalms*: Englishing Scripture in Late Henrician England', in *Vernacularity in England and Wales, c. 1300–1550*, ed. by Elisabeth Salter and Helen Wicker (Turnhout: Brepols, 2011), pp. 147–67

MOWINCKEL, SIGMUND, *The Psalms in Israel's Worship*, trans. by D. R. Ap-Thomas (Oxford: Blackwell, 1962)

MUELLER, JANEL, ed., *Katherine Parr: Complete Works and Correspondence* (Chicago: University of Chicago Press, 2011)

MULLER, RICHARD A., *After Calvin: Studies in the Development of a Theological Tradition* (Oxford: Oxford University Press, 2003)

NIDA, EUGENE A., and CHARLES R. TABOR, *The Theory and Practice of Translation, With Special Reference to Bible Translating* (Leiden: Brill, 1969)

NIEFER, JANINA, *Inspiration and Utmost Art: The Poetics of Early Modern English Psalm Translations* (Zurich: Lit Verlag, 2016)

NORBROOK, DAVID, *Poetry and Politics in the English Renaissance*, rev. edn (Oxford: Oxford University Press, 2002)

NORTON, DAVID, *A History of the English Bible as Literature*, 2 vols (Cambridge: Cambridge University Press, 1993; rev. and repr. in one vol., 2000)

—— *The King James Bible: A Short History from Tyndale to Today* (Cambridge: Cambridge University Press, 2011)

—— *A Textual History of the King James Bible* (Cambridge: Cambridge University Press, 2005)

NUGENT, TERESA LANPHER, 'Anne Lock's Poetics of Spiritual Abjection', *English Literary Renaissance*, 39.1 (2009), 3–23

O'KILL, BRIAN, 'The Printed Works of William Patten', *Transactions of the Cambridge Bibliographical Society*, 7.1 (1977), 28–45

OSHEROW, MICHELE, 'Mary Sidney's Embroidered Psalms', *Renaissance Studies*, 29.4 (2015), 650–70

PAGET, JAMES CARLETON, and JOACHIM SCHAPER, eds, *The New Cambridge History of the Bible, vol. 1, From the Beginnings to 600* (Cambridge: Cambridge University Press, 2013)

PATRICK, MILLAR, *Four Centuries of Scottish Psalmody* (London, Glasgow, and New York: Oxford University Press, 1949)

PÉREZ FERNÁNDEZ, JOSÉ MARÍA, 'Translation and Metrical Experimentation in Sixteenth-Century English Poetry: The Case of Surrey's Biblical Paraphrases', *Cahiers Élisabéthains: A Biannual Journal of English Renaissance Studies*, 71 (2007), 1–13

PIDOUX, PIERRE, ed., *Le Psaultier huguenot du xvie siècle, Mélodies et documents*, 2 vols (Basel: Editions Bärenreiter, 1962)

PITKIN, BARBARA, 'Imitation of David: David as a Paradigm for Faith in Calvin's Exegesis of the *Psalms*', *The Sixteenth Century Journal*, 24.4 (1993), 843–63

POCOCK, NICHOLAS, 'Cranmer's Bible', *Book-Lore*, 13 (1885), 22

—— '"The Great Bible", A.D. 1539', *Book-Lore*, 7 (1885), 1–5

POWELL, JASON, 'Editing Wyatts: Reassessing the Textual State of Sir Thomas Wyatt's Poetry', *Poetica*, 71 (2009), 93–104

—— 'Marginalia, Authorship, and Editing the Manuscripts of Thomas Wyatt's Verse', in *Tudor Manuscripts 1485–1603*, ed. by A. S. G. Edwards (London: British Library, 2009), pp. 1–40

—— 'Thomas Wyatt's Poetry in Embassy: Egerton 2711 and the Production of Literary Manuscripts Abroad', *Huntington Library Quarterly*, 67 (2004), 261–82

PRATT, AARON, 'The Trouble with Translation: Paratexts and England's Bestselling New Testament', in *The Bible on the Shakespearean Stage: Cultures of Interpretation in Reformation England*, ed. by Thomas Fulton and Kristen Poole (Cambridge: Cambridge University Press, 2018), pp. 33–48

PRESCOTT, ANNE LAKE, 'Divine Poetry as a Career Move: The Complexities and Consolations of Following David', in *European Literary Careers: The Author from Antiquity to the Renaissance*, ed. by Patrick Cheney and Frederick A. De Armas (Toronto: University of Toronto Press, 2002), pp. 206–30

—— *French Poets and the English Renaissance* (New Haven and London: Yale University Press, 1978)

—— 'King David as a "Right Poet": Sidney and the Psalmist', *English Literary Renaissance*, 19.3 (1989), 131–51

PRINS, YOPIE, 'Voice Inverse', *Victorian Poetry*, 42.1 (2004), 43–59

PRITCHARD, ALLAN, 'A Manuscript of Wither's "Psalms"', *Huntington Library Quarterly*, 27.1 (1963), 73–77

PROTHERO, ROWLAND E., *The Psalms in Human Life* (London: J. Murray, 1904)

PROUTY, C. T., *George Gascoigne: Elizabethan Courtier, Soldier, and Poet* (New York: Columbia University Press, 1942)

QUITSLUND, BETH, *The Reformation in Rhyme: Sternhold, Hopkins and the English Metrical Psalter, 1547–1603* (Aldershot and Burlington: Ashgate, 1991)

—— 'Teaching Us How to Sing?: The Peculiarity of the Sidney Psalter', *Sidney Journal*, 23.1–2 (2005), 83–110

RADZINOWICZ, MARY ANN, *Milton's Epics and the Book of Psalms* (Princeton: Princeton University Press, 1989)

RAMBUSS, RICHARD, ed., *The English Poems of Richard Crashaw* (Minneapolis and London: University of Minnesota Press, 2013)

REID-BAXTER, JAMIE, 'Metrical Psalmody and the Bannatyne Manuscript: Robert Pont's Psalm 83', *Renaissance and Reformation/Renaissance et Réforme*, 30.4 (2006–2007), 41–62

RIENSTRA, DEBRA, '"Disorder Best Fit": Henry Lok and Holy Disorder in Devotional Lyric', *Spenser Studies*, 27 (2012), 249–87

ROHR-SAUER, P. VON, *English Metrical Psalms from 1600 to 1660: A Study in the Religious and Aesthetic Tendencies of that Period* (Freiburg: Universitätsdruckerei Poppen & Ortmann, 1938)

ROPE, H. E. G., 'John Davies of Hereford, Catholic and Rhymer', *Anglo-Welsh Review*, 11.28 (1961), 20–36

ROSSITER, WILLIAM T., 'Transgression *in potentia*: *Translatio* and *Imitatio* in Sir Thomas Wyatt's Poetry', in *Transmission and Transgression: Cultural Challenges in Early Modern England*, ed. by Sophie Chiari and Hélène Palma (Provence: Presses Universitaires de Provence, 2014), pp. 101–17

—— 'What Wyatt Really Did to Aretino's *Sette Salmi*', *Renaissance Studies*, 29.4 (2015), 595–614

RUSH, REBECCA M., 'Authority and Attribution in the Sternhold and Hopkins Psalter', *Renaissance and Reformation/Renaissance et Réforme*, 38.1 (2015), 57–82

SAENGER, PAUL, *Space Between Words: The Origins of Silent Reading* (Stanford: Stanford University Press, 1997)

SCHMUTZLER, KARL E., *George Sandys' Paraphrases on the Psalms and the Tradition of Metrical Psalmody: An Annotated Edition of Fifty Selected Psalms, with Critical and Biographical Introduction* (unpublished dissertation, The Ohio State University, 1957)

—— 'Harington's Metrical Paraphrases of the Seven Penitential Psalms: Three Manuscript Versions', *Papers of the Bibliographical Society of America*, 53.3 (1959), 240–51

SCHULTE, RAINER, and JOHN BIGUENET, eds, *Theories of Translation: An Anthology of Essays from Dryden to Derrida* (Chicago and London: University of Chicago Press, 1992)

SCOTT-WARREN, JASON, *Sir John Harington and the Book as Gift* (Oxford and New York: Oxford University Press, 2001)

SELDERHUIS, HERMAN J., and PETER NISSEN, 'The Sixteenth Century', in *Handbook of Dutch Church History*, ed. by Herman J. Selderhuis (Gottingen: Vandenhoeck & Ruprecht, 2015), pp. 157–258

SERJEANTSON, DEIRDRE, 'Anne Lock's Anonymous Friend: A Meditation of a Penitent Sinner and the Problem of Ascription', in *Enigma and Revelation in Renaissance English Literature: Essays Presented to Eiléan Ní Chuilleanáin*, ed. by Helen Cooney and Mark S. Sweetnam (Dublin: Four Courts, 2012), pp. 51–68

—— 'The Book of Psalms and the Early Modern Sonnet', *Renaissance Studies*, 29.4 (2015), 632–49

SESSIONS, W. A., *Henry Howard the Poet Earl of Surrey: A Life* (Oxford: Oxford University Press, 1999)

—— 'Surrey's Psalms in the Tower', in *Sacred and Profane: Secular and Devotional Interplay in Early Modern British Literature*, ed. by Helen Wilcox, Richard Todd, and Alasdair MacDonald (Amsterdam: V. U. University Press, 1996), pp. 17–32

SHELL, MARC, *Talking the Talk & Walking the Walk* (New York: Fordham University Press, 2015)

SIMPSON, JAMES, 'Martyrdom in the Literal Sense: Surrey's *Psalm Paraphrases*', *Medieval and Early Modern English Studies*, 12.1 (2004), 133–65

—— 'The Psalms and Threat in Sixteenth-Century English Court Culture', *Renaissance Studies*, 29.4 (2015), 576–94

SIMPSON-YOUNGER, NANCY L., '"Still in Thought with Thee I Go": Epistemology and Consciousness in the Sidney Psalms', in *Forming Sleep: Representing Consciousness in the English Renaissance*, ed. by Nancy L. Simpson-Younger, Margaret Simon, and Garrett A Sullivan, Jr (University Park: Pennsylvania State University Press, 2020), pp. 69–86

SLIGHTS, WILLIAM, 'The Edifying Margins of Renaissance English Books', *Renaissance Quarterly*, 42.4 (1989), 682–716

SMITH, DAVID NOWELL, *On Voice in Poetry: The Work of Animation* (Houndmills and New York: Palgrave Macmillan, 2015)

SMITH, HALLETT, 'English Metrical Psalms in the Sixteenth Century and their Literary Significance', *Huntington Library Quarterly*, 9 (1946), 249–71

SMITH, JEREMY L., *Verse & Voice in Byrd's Song Collections of 1588 and 1589* (Woodbridge: The Boydell Press, 2016)

SMITH, VICTORIA, 'The Elizabethan Succession Question in Roger Edwardes's "Castra Regia" (1569) and "Cista Pacis Anglie" (1576)', *Historical Research*, 87.238 (2014), 633–54

SPECLAND, JEREMY, 'Competing Prose Psalters and Their Elizabethan Readers', *Renaissance Quarterly*, 74.3 (2021), 829–75

STALEY, LYNN, 'The Penitential Psalms: Conversion and the Limits of Lordship', *The Journal of Medieval and Early Modern Studies*, 37.2 (2007), 221–69

STALLYBRASS, PETER, 'Books and Scrolls: Navigating the Bible', in *Books and Readers in Early Modern England: Material Studies*, ed. by Jennifer Andersen and Elizabeth Sauer (Philadelphia: University of Pennsylvania Press, 2002), pp. 42–79

STAMATAKIS, CHRIS, *Sir Thomas Wyatt and the Rhetoric of Rewriting: 'Turning the Word'* (Oxford: Oxford University Press, 2012)

STEINBERG, THEODORE L., 'The Sidneys and the Psalms', *Studies in Philology*, 92.1 (1995), 1–17

STEINER, GEORGE, *After Babel: Aspects of Language and Translation* (London and New York: Oxford University Press, 1975)

STERRETT, LAURA, 'Refiguring Pastoral Love in George Herbert's "The 23 Psalme"', *George Herbert Journal*, 42.1–2 (2018/2019), 53–80

STEVENS, JOHN, *Music & Poetry in the Early Tudor Court* (Cambridge: Cambridge University Press, 1961)

STEWART, ALAN, *Sir Philip Sidney: A Double Life* (London: Chatto & Windus, 2000)

SWANN, JOEL, 'Reading the Davison Psalms in Manuscript and Print', *Renaissance Studies*, 33.5 (2019), 668–90

TADMOR, NAOMI, 'The Social and Cultural Translation of the Hebrew Bible in Early Modern England: Reflections, Working Principles, and Examples', in *Early Modern Cultures of Translation*, ed. by Karen Newman and Jane Tylus (Philadelphia: University of Pennsylvania Press, 2015), pp. 175–88

TARGOFF, RAMIE, *Common Prayer: The Language of Devotion in Early Modern England* (Chicago: University of Chicago Press, 2001)

TEMPERLEY, NICHOLAS, '"All skillful praises sing": How Congregations Sang the Psalms in Early Modern England', *Renaissance Studies*, 29.4 (2015), 531–53

—— *Music of the English Parish Church*, 2 vols (Cambridge: Cambridge University Press, 1979)

TODD, RICHARD, 'Humanist Prosodic Theory, Dutch Synods, and the Poetics of the Sidney-Pembroke Psalter', *Huntington Library Quarterly*, 52.2 (1989), 273–93

—— '"So Well Attyr'd Abroad": A Background to the Sidney-Pembroke Psalter and Its Implications for the Seventeenth-Century Religious Lyric', *Texas Studies in Literature and Language*, 29 (1987), 74–93

TRILL, SUZANNE, 'Sixteenth-Century Women's Writing: Mary Sidney's *Psalmes* and the "Femininity" of Translation', in *Writing and the English Renaissance*, ed. by William Zunder and Suzanne Trill (London and New York: Longman, 1996), pp. 140–58

—— '"We Thy Sydnean Psalmes Shall Celebrate": Collaborative Authorship, Sidney's Sister and the English Devotional Lyric', in *Early Modern Women and the Poem*, ed. by Susan Wiseman, Patricia Pender, and Rosalind Smith (Manchester: University of Manchester, 2013), pp. 97–116

TRUDELL, SCOTT A., '"Unto the World's Ear": Wyatt's Psalms Beyond the Court', *Studies in Philology*, 110.2 (2013), 266–90
—— *Unwritten Poetry: Song, Performance, and Media in Early Modern England* (Oxford: Oxford University Press, 2019)
TWOMBLY, ROBERT G., 'Thomas Wyatt's Paraphrase of the Penitential Psalms of David', *Texas Studies of Literature and Language*, 13.3 (1970), 345–80
VAN DEUSEN, NANCY, ed., *The Place of the Psalms in the Intellectual Culture of the Middle Ages* (Albany: State University of New York Press, 1999)
VENUTI, LAWRENCE, *The Translator's Invisibility: A History of Translation*, 2nd edn (London and New York: Routledge, 2008)
WALKER, GREG, *Writing Under Tyranny: English Literature and the Henrician Reformation* (Oxford: Oxford University Press, 2005)
WALSHAM, ALEXANDRA, '"Domme Preachers": Post-Reformation English Catholicism and the Culture of Print', *Past & Present*, 168 (2000), 72–123
WATSON, J. R., *The English Hymn: A Critical and Historical Study* (Oxford: Clarendon Press, 1997)
WEINER, SETH, 'Sidney and the Rabbis: A Note on the Psalms of David and Renaissance Hebraica', in *Sir Philip Sidney's Achievements*, ed. by M. J. B. Allen (New York: AMS Press, 1990), pp. 157–62
WESTBROOK, VIVIENNE, *Long Travails and Great Paynes: A Politics of Reformation Revision* (Dordrecht: Kluwer Academic Publishers, 2001)
WESTERMANN, CLAUS, *Praise and Lament in the Psalms*, trans. by Keith R. Crim and Richard N. Soulen (Atlanta: John Knox Press, 1981)
WHITE, HELEN, *The Tudor Books of Private Devotion* (Madison: University of Wisconsin Press, 1951)
WHITE, MICHELINE, 'Protestant Women's Writing and Congregational Psalm Singing: From the Song of the Exiled "Handmaid" (1555) to the Countess of Pembroke's Psalmes (1599)', *Sidney Journal*, 23.1–2 (2005), 61–82
—— 'The Psalms, War and Royal Iconography: Katherine Parr's *Psalms or Prayers* (1544) and Henry VIII as David', *Renaissance Studies*, 29.4 (2015), 554–75
WORT, OLIVER, 'A Cuckoo in the Nest? William Forrest, the Duke of Somerset, and the *Certaigne Psalmes of Dauyd*', *Reformation*, 21.1 (2016), 25–46
—— *John Bale and Religious Conversion in Reformation England* (London: Pickering & Chatto, 2013)
WORTHAM, JAMES, 'Arthur Golding and the Translation of Prose', *Huntington Library Quarterly*, 12.4 (1949), 339–67
WOUDHUYSEN, H. R., *Sir Philip Sidney and the Circulation of Manuscripts, 1558–1640* (Oxford: Clarendon Press, 1996)
ZIM, RIVKA, *English Metrical Psalms: Poetry as Praise and Prayer, 1535–1601* (Cambridge: Cambridge University Press, 1987)
—— 'The Maidstone Burghmote and John Hall's *Courte of Vertue* (1565)', *Notes & Queries*, 33(231).3 (1986), 320–27

MODERN HUMANITIES RESEARCH ASSOCIATION
TUDOR AND STUART TRANSLATIONS

A SELECTION OF RECENTLY PUBLISHED TITLES

The First English 'Pastor Fido' (1602)
Edited by Massimiliano Morini

Anne Cooke's Englishing of Bernardino Ochino
Edited by Patricia Demers

Erasmus in English 1523–1584
Volume I: *'The Manual of the Christian Soldier' and Other Writings*
Edited by Alex Davis, Gordon Kendal and Neil Rhodes

Erasmus in English 1523–1584
Volume II: *'The Praise of Folly' and Other Writings*
Edited by Alex Davis, Gordon Kendal and Neil Rhodes

Plutarch in English, 1528–1603
Volume I: *Essays*
Edited by Fred Schurink

Plutarch in English, 1528–1603
Volume II: *Lives*
Edited by Fred Schurink

Petrarch's 'Triumphi' in English
Edited by Alessandra Petrina

Thomas May: Lucan's 'Pharsalia' (1627)
Edited by Emma Buckley and Edward Paleit

www.tudor.mhra.org.uk
To sign up to the series mailing list, email tst@mhra.org.uk

www.ingramcontent.com/pod-product-compliance
Lightning Source LLC
Chambersburg PA
CBHW071352300426
44114CB00016B/2029